Urban Violence

Urban Violence

Security, Imaginary, Atmosphere

Andrea Pavoni and Simone Tulumello

LEXINGTON BOOKS
Lanham • Boulder • New York • London

Published by Lexington Books
An imprint of The Rowman & Littlefield Publishing Group, Inc.
4501 Forbes Boulevard, Suite 200, Lanham, Maryland 20706
www.rowman.com

86-90 Paul Street, London EC2A 4NE

British Library Cataloguing in Publication Information Available

Library of Congress Cataloging-in-Publication Data

Names: Pavoni, Andrea, author. | Tulumello, Simone, author.
Title: Urban violence : security, imaginary, atmosphere / Andrea Pavoni and
    Simone Tulumello.
Description: Lanham, Maryland : Lexington Books, [2023] | Includes
    bibliographical references and index.
Identifiers: LCCN 2023023811 (print) | LCCN 2023023812 (ebook) |
    ISBN 9781793637307 (cloth) | ISBN 9781793637321 (paperback) |
    ISBN 9781793637314 (ebook)
Subjects: LCSH: Urban violence.
Classification: LCC HM886 .P33 2023 (print) | LCC HM886 (ebook) | DDC
    303.6—dc23/eng/20230724
LC record available at https://lccn.loc.gov/2023023811
LC ebook record available at https://lccn.loc.gov/2023023812

♾️™ The paper used in this publication meets the minimum requirements of
American National Standard for Information Sciences—Permanence of Paper
for Printed Library Materials, ANSI/NISO Z39.48-1992.

~

Contents

Acknowledgements

Countless people, spaces and forces deserve to be acknowledged, and thanked, for providing us with inspiration, support or much deserved humbling. It would take quite some room and effort to acknowledge them all and, we are afraid, some would unavoidably remain out, as the path that led to this book was long and tortuous at times, as it often is, especially when four hands are involved. For this reason, we have decided to keep this section minimal, only referring to those people and spaces that were fundamental for our writing together.

The long process that led to this book was materially sparked, sometime in 2016, by an invitation by Sebastian Saborio to write together on urban violence. Though, for purely practical reasons, our endeavours separated, the discussions we had at that time were crucial in formulating some questions, for instance about the 'visibility' of urban violence, that prompted us to write an article (published in *Progress in Human Geography*) and then this book. We are grateful to Sebastian for that.

We developed some of the arguments of this book, and particularly those on the imaginary (of urbanisation, of security), in the context of the preparation of the bid for, and then in the early stages of development of, project 'Urbanoscenes—Post-colonial imaginaries of urbanisation'. We are grateful to the project team, and especially Lavínia Pereira, Olivia Bina, João Felipe Brito, Tomás Donadio and Pedro Neto. During the last few years, we have discussed the urban, urbanisation and much more at the Urban Transitions Hub (UTH), an informal group loosely based at the Institute of Social

Sciences of the University of Lisbon (ICS-ULisboa), and its reading group—including a series of sessions on (urban) imaginaries. We owe the UTH for the creation of a space of collegiality, comradeship and intellectual stimulus.

We discussed different versions of chapter 1 at the conference (Im)materialities of Violence (25–27 November 2021, University of Birmingham) and with the informal group on border, security and control at ICS-ULisboa—we are particularly grateful to the organisers of the conference (Katharina Karcher and Evelien Geerts), as well as to Nina Amelung, Irene Peano and João Baptista. We are also grateful to those who participated at the issue no. 59 of journal *lo Squaderno—Explorations in Space and Society*, titled 'Beyond Urban Violence', which we edited in 2021 and provided another useful laboratory for testing and expanding our reflections. Andrea is particularly grateful to Andrea Mubi Brighenti and Caterina Nirta, Simone to Fabio Iapaolo and Fabio Bertoni, since the discussions and collaborations with them have been instrumental to developing many ideas of this book.

The cover image is an original artwork by Tanta Espanta Studio, specially produced for this book: we are grateful for that.

This book is the result of research carried out amid several projects during the last decade, and, in particular, we acknowledge funding by Fundação para a Ciência e Tecnologia for our individual grants (Simone Tulumello: grant 2020.00443.CEECIND; Andrea Pavoni: grant CEECINST/00066/2018 /CP1496/CT0001) and project "Urbanoscenes—Post-colonial imaginaries of urbanisation: A future-oriented investigation from Portugal and Angola" (grant PTDC/GES-URB/1053/2021).

Besides thematic considerations, the selection of epigraphs, along with their English translations when possible, was constrained by their availability in the public domain or under re-use licenses. We are grateful to Taylor & Francis for having granted the authorisation to republish the epigraph to the introduction for free.

~

Introduction

Writing an essay on urban violence is a Utopian if not impossible
task. There is no consistent definition of violence: the term has multiple meanings and the tools which are used for analysis derive from
disciplines which constrain their use in different ways. Moreover, the
terms violence, riots, disorders, rebellion, unrest and many more are
indistinctively used by journalists, politicians and researchers. As noted by
Wittgenstein, language has the power to make all things look alike. Com-
mentators do not seem aware that by simply using terms such as urban
violence, they include in one category phenomena that are quite distinct.[1]

Almost thirty years have passed since Sophie Body-Gendrot thus penned
the trouble of writing about urban violence. And yet, the issues the French
scholar mentioned then—the absence of a consistent definition, the lack
of a clearly delimited 'object' of study, the conflation of distinct matters
and, we add, at the same time the frequent failure to encompass crucial aspects—seem to still characterise much discourse, be it academic, essayistic,
journalistic or political, about urban violence. Granted, the last few decades have seen a proliferation of research, studies and publications, many
of which have critically inquired the fundamental problems of and with
urban violence. This can hardly be surprising: after all, we live in an age of
fast urbanisation—some call it an 'urban age'; and an age when violence,
security and fears of various sorts seem to have a somehow unprecedented
centrality for global society. One may argue that we live an urban age of
violence—and scholarship has engaged with it profusely.

1

Our starting point, however, is the perception that, for all the research, studies and publications that are available, urban violence still has a peculiar standing within social and urban research—in part precisely because of the excessive attention to the specificity of the present 'security moment' (Goldstein 2010) to detriment of the inquiry of its historical lineages. We submit—and will argue throughout the book—that the apparently simple question of 'what *is* urban violence?' has not been provided with satisfactory answers. Indeed, it is from this very definitional problem, itself just a component of the broader conceptual one, that we started to dig into urban violence a few years ago (Pavoni and Tulumello 2020). Before moving to discuss how we frame this problem, however, we should notice that, quite obviously, we (or Sophie Body-Gendrot, for that matter) are not the only ones to feel discomfort with the way urban violence is framed in academic discussions and beyond. Among critical urban scholars, there seems to be an overarching, if often silent, perception that the spatial and temporal dimensions of violence in general, and 'urban violence' in particular, are significantly under-theorised and conceptualised—a perception that has been only at times expressed explicitly (e.g., Muggah 2012; Springer and Le Billon 2016; Saborio 2019). The first argument of this book is that urban violence is under-theorised because long-term theoretical problems with both of its elements ('urban' and 'violence'), despite having been addressed at length by critical scholarship (see above all chapters 1 and 2), remain alive and kicking when the two concepts come together under the 'urban violence' label. This also depends on the fact, we argue, that a third term that is crucial to keep the concept in place—that is, security—is often kept out of the picture, or only indirectly addressed.

A contribution to unpacking the link between urban, violence and security implies answering at least three questions. First, how can violence be conceptualised in a way that opens to an understanding of the specificity of urban violence? Second, what is the urban in urban violence? Or, in other words, what makes urban violence 'urban' in the first place? And, third, how can 'urban' and 'violence' be articulated in a way that makes urban violence a category with both analytical and strategic power? Or, in other words, how can we make urban violence a concept that allows us to capture the peculiar nature of a specific—if broad—set of processes and, at the same time, a lens through which different articulations, ontologies and futures can be imagined?

The second argument of this book is that, to answer these questions, urban violence must be explored by focusing, at the same time, on questions of ontology and epistemology (and ethics). Assuming ontology and epistemology to be separated is not only a 'reverberation of a metaphysics that assumes an inherent difference between human and nonhuman, subject and object, mind and body, matter and discourse', society and nature, and so on (Barad 2003, 829). More specifically for our argument, these dichotomies have been central to those reductionist approaches to violence that have framed it as belonging merely to nature, culture or morality (see below, and chapter 1). Instead, cutting through these dichotomies, we will contend that violence is neither natural nor social, it is both: its meaning emerges out of material-discursive, power-structured relations, whose potential indeterminacy is only resolved locally and historically, and requires engaging simultaneously with violence's epistemological and ontological intersection with space (Springer 2011) and time—and therefore, for what particularly concerns us, with the urban and urbanisation.

As the last sentence implies, this effort requires a genealogical sensibility. This is why we will problematise urban violence, and its implicit relation with the present security moment, vis-à-vis a broader history and geography. The former is made up of, at least, the peculiar polity of the modern (liberal) state, and, importantly, its political and juridical theorisation of security; the global formations of capitalism; and the unfolding of colonialism. The geographic dimension is made up of the manifold ways this history comes to be actualised, frictionally so (cf. Tsing 2005), in and through the socio-material fabric of the urban, itself understood through the materialist epistemology and relational ontology we are about to introduce. A complementary effort will be that of exploring, epistemologically and ontologically, the aesthetic forms, discursive frames and concrete practices through which violence has been made visible and understood in the contemporary city, especially with respect to what we will refer to as the socio-technical imaginary *of* urbanisation (cf. Jasanoff 2015) and the political imaginary of absolute security (cf. Tulumello 2021a).

In more conventional epistemological terms, we will develop our genealogical lens at the intersection of two approaches: political economy, to expose structural and relational aspects; and a vital materialism that merges the ontological, ethical and (bio)political insights drawn from the works of Spinoza, Nietzsche, Foucault, Deleuze, Esposito, Fanon, Berlant and Haraway, among others, with recent conceptual and critical directions usually labelled as affect studies, critical infrastructure studies, post-humanism, non-representational theory and 'new materialism'. While political economy and vital materialism have barely dialogued—indeed, they have increasingly been constituted as opposite fields (e.g., Gamble et al. 2019)—we will instead pursue their articulation (cf. Laclau and Mouffe 1985).

The third, and central, argument of this book is that, through a genealogy that articulates political economic and vital materialism, urban violence can ultimately be framed as a precise category shaped by three interlocking trajectories (see Pavoni 2018a): the *process* of (capitalist) urbanisation, which ontologically structures the realm in which urban violence emerges; the spatio-political *project* of the urban, which—through the imaginaries of urbanisation and absolute security—constitutes the epistemological realm against which urban violence is rendered visible; and the concrete urban *atmospheres* in and through which the process and the project materialise, often violently, in the urban.

This argument has some corollary dimensions that are worth spelling out at this stage. To begin with, while we fully acknowledge the complex and variegated nature of the global geography of urban violence, it is important to remember that such a geography has been powerfully moulded by (colonial and post-colonial) historical relations. The way urban violence came to be conceptualised in the 'metropoles' is dependent on the imaginaries, possibilities and policies that surfaced in the colonies, especially around the question of security vis-à-vis the colonial other. The most evident component of this trajectory, which we will discuss at length, is the way concepts of civility and wilderness that emerged in the colony, and came to violently shape its juridical, spatial and affective relations, have 'boomeranged' (cf. Césaire 2000[1950]) on the metropoles, shaping the (violent) ways in which marginalised urban inhabitants have been framed, managed and oppressed.

At the intersection of these three trajectories, another concept plays a paramount role, that of police, 'the art of providing to all the inhabitants of the earth a comfortable and quiet life', per Denis Diderot and Jean Le Rond d'Alembert's famous definition[2]—and we will see the extent to which notions of comfort, tranquillity and peace are far from unproblematic (see chapter 7). Understood in its historical, broader meaning, the notion of police encompasses all the actions that the state performs in order to fabricate and maintain order, understood in its wider sense, and especially at the urban level (see Dubber 2005; Neocleous 2021[2000]). As we show especially in chapter 4, there is a profound relation between the notions of police, civilisation and urbanisation, which at times have been employed as veritable synonyms (Foucault 2007[2004]; Cavalletti 2005). This is not surprising, since all these concepts—which refer to that quintessential category of (Western) political theory, that is, security—have been significantly shaped by a notion of urban violence that they at the same time contributed to constitute, as we shall see. It is for this reason that exploring the constitutive relation between police, security and the urban is crucial, for us, to develop an understanding of urban violence able to address the urban itself according to the three interlocking trajectories above mentioned.

Finally, the way security and violence are inherently associated has profound implications for the *pars construens* of our discussion, where ontology and epistemology explicitly intersect an ethics that is understood as inseparable from them, and which we briefly introduce below. This brings us to the fourth and final argument of this book: insofar as urban violence is a concept fundamentally constructed in relation and opposition to security, only through a reformulation of security—one capable of breaking free from the (absolute) security/violence dichotomy, and from the peculiar relation this entails vis-à-vis notions of responsibility, freedom and care—can we build a strategically useful concept of urban violence.

In the remainder of this introduction, we start by tracing the main coordinates of what we consider to be the 'definitional' problem with urban violence—which is foundational for the formulation of our first argument. Then, we move to sketch the way we intend to move forward, by articulating political economy and 'vital materialism' to build the genealogical method that fits our second argument; and by introducing what we mean by vital materialism in the first place—in so doing clarifying the relevance and original contribution of our ontological and epistemological (and ethical) endeavour. Finally, we present the plan of the book and, in doing so, we present the main coordinates of the third and fourth arguments, summarising the way we build them throughout the next nine chapters and the Researching Urban Violence sections dedicated to the epistemological and methodological challenges thereof.

The Problem

What is urban violence, then? Following the steps of Robert Muggah (2012) and Sebastian Saborio (2014/2015; 2019), we began by systematically considering whether a shared, agreed upon definition—a necessary first step toward a conceptualisation—exists.[3] In broad agreement with Muggah and Saborio, we came to the conclusion that it does not.

Let us start by briefly considering the type of definitions that are commonly given to urban violence—and the unspoken assumptions thereof. According to Nelson Lourenço, writing a decade ago, urban violence is usually framed in two ways:

> One [reading], more sociological, fundamentally centred on actors and their relations with society, which is opposed, in an apparent contradiction because of their complementarity, to the anthropological perspective, [which

is] grounded on a cultural definition of violence and on the acceptance of the existence of a street culture, with its codes, rituals and its own languages,[4] where violence emerges as an identifying trait. (2012, 153; our translation)

The consequence, Lourenço continues, is that resulting definitions are always either purely descriptive or fundamentally reductionists vis-à-vis the object being defined—urban violence. Lourenço moves forward by listing a number of points to which commonly used definitions converge in describing actions associated with urban violence:

Their actors are young, though the definition of what being young implies, and particularly what is the upper limit therein, is not clear; they refer to scarcely organised actions; they define, as common object of aggression, physical or symbolical public spaces; the arbitrary character of actions, which can take different forms, from vandalism to disorders; the fact of having vast collateral effects and, often, of not being aimed at someone in particular. (idem, ibidem; our translation)

This list is relevant precisely insofar as it defines, albeit in negative terms, the field of urban violence with respect to visible, tangible *actions* that are perpetrated by a specific category of (young) subjects, explicitly or implicitly labelled as *criminals*—and, as we will see throughout the book, most often explicitly or implicitly racialised. Indeed, when urban violence is explicitly defined, this is usually done by referring to its physical, criminal dimensions. More generally, legalistic, reductionist conceptualisations of urban violence are at the core of the, enormous, body of research inspired by positivist ideas. Here, urban violence is taken for granted as an anomaly in the social body, one that can be unproblematically individuated—it corresponds to the simple sum of its visible expressions (above all, murder)—and therefore as much unproblematically 'measured', with the goal of progressively reducing and, possibly, abolishing it.[5] This set of normative and aesthetical assumptions, despite having been powerfully contested and problematised by critical thought, still shapes very much of the public, political and legal debate on (urban) violence—as we will see, for instance, in our discussion of what we refer to as violence reductionism, in chapter 1.

For our purposes, more relevant is the growing (but way smaller) body of critical research—be it inspired by Marxist, Foucauldian, post-colonial, anti-racist, queer, new materialist or other perspectives—that has problematised violence, especially with regard to its less evident or visible structural and cultural dimensions. In terms of explicit definitional efforts, the most significant endeavour has been that made by Michel Misse (2008; 2011; Misse and

Grillo 2014), Luiz Machado da Silva (2004; 2008; 2010; 2011) and Sebastian Saborio (2014/2015; 2019), who have argued that the category of urban violence emerges at the intersection of violent crime and its mainstream representations. Urban violence, Saborio maintains, can be understood as the way a given city is framed as 'violent'. It is, in other words, a category that signals the way an urban imaginary has taken a violent hue. This leads Saborio (2019, 69) to suggest that the concept should be abandoned once and for all. We will come back several times to the importance of understanding urban violence (also) in terms of its in/visibility in everyday urban life, as well as in its constitutive relation with a given urban imaginary. At the same time, we will argue for a definition that encompasses forms of violence beyond 'crime'. For the time being, what matters is noticing how the definitional effort made by Misse, Silva and Saborio is part of a broader work of expansion of the conceptualisation of urban violence. In other words, the explicit and implicit definition of urban violence has recently gone much beyond the points of convergence listed by Lourenço, coming to include violence's non-visible determinants, processes and forces. And yet, as we will discuss, there remains three main problems with the (often implicit) forms urban violence is defined within critical scholarship.

First, the (important) endeavour to broaden urban violence beyond legally defined, 'measurable' violent crimes also tends to deepen the difficulty of precisely delimiting the field urban violence encompasses by adding further—and hardly 'measurable' or even identifiable—dimensions. This is somehow an unescapable problem, especially with regard to a concept, like violence, that is 'polysemic and multidimensional', and 'attempts to account for very distinct aspects of objective reality, across many different registers, both for academics and common social actors' (Werneck et al. 2020, 288). A concept, moreover, that can have literally opposite meanings on different sites of structural and epistemological fractures—fractures that may themselves generate violence (see Feltran 2020). Incidentally, because of the global nature of urban violence, this problem is at times also one of translation. Consider, for instance, the way Body-Gendrot herself (1995) uses 'urban violence' and 'disorders' as equivalent terms—a strange move for the Anglophone reader. As Claske Dijkema explains,

> In France, urban violence is associated with juvenile violence that concerns certain marginalised spaces of the city and certain, specifically racialised, inhabitants. In comparison to British and American contexts, the term is used mostly to address anti-institutional violence: what is called *violences urbaines* in France corresponds to 'race riots' on the other side of the Atlantic. The term

'urban' violence [in France] is problematic for three reasons. First, it is used as a euphemism for a racialised representation of juvenile violence. Second, the seemingly neutral term 'urban' underplays the political significance of these forms of violence. Third, the term renders other forms of violence invisible, by symbolically confining violence to certain spaces. (2021, 17)

In short, through and beyond matters of translation,[6] we will see that a productive definition, and therefore conceptualisation, of urban violence cannot emerge from the specification of the type of actions that it encompasses.

Second, urban violence has broadly remained a category associated with specific geographies: it is studied above all in the Global South and is commonly implicitly associated with southern large—and fast growing—metropolises. It seems to us that urban violence is implicitly defined as being fundamentally a category of the Global South—as the proliferation of monographs and edited collections on violence 'in the Global South' and fundamental absence of similar works 'on the Global North' indirectly suggests. The most recent example is an edited collection (Glass et al. 2022) and, in particular, the theoretical chapter by Phil Williams (2022), which sets some of the theoretical foundations of the book by explicitly problematising the relation between global urbanisation and urban violence. Granted, as we will debate at length, we concur with Williams's argument that global patterns of neoliberal urbanisation alone cannot explain urban violence,[7] that the visible expressions and human costs of urban violence are unevenly distributed, and, therefore, that it is important to explore the regional, national and local actualisations and materialisations of urban violence. However, it seems to us that the building up of an entire scholarship on violence in the Global South has at least three problematic consequences: it effaces the importance of the global relations, (post-)colonial history and variegated geographies that have historically shaped and still shape urban violence; it naturalises what Global South is not, that is, the Global North, as a place that is immune from urban violence—while, as we will see, it is everything but, and, in certain senses, urban violence problematises the neat distinction between a Global North and South; and it misses the fact that the very concept of urban violence has historically emerged in and through the circulation of ideas between North and South. In short, a productive definition of urban violence cannot emerge from a geographical delimitation of its scope—be it to the Global South, to its metropolises or whatever else.

By arguing that urban violence cannot be conceptualised through a specific set of actions or specific geographies, we are suggesting that what matters is the underlying definition of the urban. This brings us to the third problem, which somehow encompasses and goes beyond the previous ones: to put it bluntly, much of the writing on urban violence simply glosses over what is peculiarly *urban* in urban violence. Almost universally, implicitly and therefore self-evidently, the urban is employed as a secondary adjective that simply refers to a given, bounded and static place in which urban violence occurs—that is, the city—rather than as a historical and spatial process imbricated in the very (re-)production of urban violence in the first place. As a result, 'urban violence' ends up being reduced to a simple (and redundant) shorthand for 'violence in the city'—a reduction that at the same time crystallises the urban itself into an a-historical condition, in turn considered to be *naturally* conducive to violence. This equation is a conceptual locus of urban studies since their inception, one that was most notably epitomised by the by the influential work of University of Chicago's School of Sociology (i.e., a set of scholars and ideas often referred to simply as the Chicago School, see chapter 2), and that seems to be still surreptitiously at work, more or less implicitly, also in otherwise significant explorations of urban violence.

Moving Forward

If much of the problem concerns the way the urban is conceptualised in urban violence, it follows that critical urban theory is the first place to search for novel coordinates to a deeper consideration of urban violence. In particular, we will take advantage of the debates—prompted by the intersection between the rise of southern urban critique and Neil Brenner and Christian Schmid's theses on urbanisation—on the global, planetary scale of the processes of urbanisation. From this debate we draw, in general terms, the importance of overcoming an understanding of the urban as either the place where violence takes place or the causal determinant of violence (old ideas about the urban environment as being conducive to violence). Rather, we move toward an understanding of the relations between the process of urbanisation and the geography of urban violence—something that has also been suggested, if at times implicitly, by an emerging literature that has explored the structural violence produced by the process of urbanisation (see chapter 5).

Beyond systematising this endeavour, we intend to put it in dialogue with works inspired by recent 'turns' (affect, material, post-human, nonhuman, non-representational, infrastructural, etc.) in social sciences and humanities, which had the merit to point social, geographical and urban theory towards the dense material ecology of structures, representations and bodies that constitute the urban (for a discussion on the relevant works, see Pavoni

2018a, ch. 2). Inspired by these insights, and by the key Deleuzoguattarian question of consistency—namely: 'what holds things together?' (Deleuze and Guattari 2004[1980], 327)—we sought to understand violence in infra-structural terms, albeit in a slightly different way from existent theorisations on 'infrastructural violence'. With terms that will be further qualified in the following chapter, we conceptualise violence as a tensional force that is constitutive of, and immanent to, the socio-material fabric of the urban, weaving it together and threatening to disrupt it at the same time. Violence, as critical thought elucidated, can be simultaneously understood as a force of creation, destruction or maintenance vis-à-vis socio-material relations at large. The main implication of this understanding is that violence does pro-duce effects whose consequences cannot be assessed or judged in advance, but must be explored by attending to the material and relational specificities of a given situation. Violence, we will defend, cannot be captured, in its complexity, as an abstract, moral and normative question seen through the lenses of a pre-defined judgement—that is, through a given set of principles in respect to which violence would constitute a violation. Rather, it must be understood as an ontological, epistemological and ethical question *at once*, one that necessitates to be explored *each time* with respect to the modes of life that constitute a given situation and its socio-material configuration.[8] From these premises, which we are to unpack in chapter 1, we propose to explore urban violence vis-à-vis the toxic, life-debilitating effects that the infrastruc-tural tension holding together the urban, and its specific configurations, may or may not have on the bodies that are tied to them. In broader terms, as anticipated, we will do so through a bifocal lens, pointed simultaneously at the planetary dimension of the violent process of urbanisation and its socio-economic structures; and at the material, affective relations in and through which these are concretely actualised on the urban space.

Many have recently contributed to a political economy of (urban) violence and security. Starting from, and moving beyond, pioneering concepts like structural and symbolic violence (Galtung 1969; Bourdieu 1991[1982/1983]), an extremely rich literature has dissected the ways func-tionalist-economic and symbolic-cultural dimensions participate in the pro-duction and reproduction of violence (see chapter 1). A political economic lens, in short, is necessary to overcome the first two definitional problems: to go beyond an understanding of urban violence as any specific set of *ac-tions*, and to encompass actors and actants beyond *criminals*, thereby looking at how instances of direct, physical violence are linked to and determined by broader socio-economic, cultural and political processes—the fact, that is, that violence can and does exist even in absence of visible expressions of the use of force. A political economic lens is particularly adequate to comprehend how the abstract logics and structuring process of capitalism—and, in our case, those linked to the process of urbanisation—do produce and are implicated in urban violence. In more mundane and operational terms, a political economy of urban violence serves, for instance, to expose the urban violence produced by the state in the name of fighting criminal violence, as well as the contradictions and paradoxes of the apparatus of security. Many have shown, for instance, how juridical and policing instruments and tactics (e.g., zero tolerance, predictive policing) that are officially deployed in the name of reducing violence, all too often end up being conducive to, and reproductive of, urban violence in the first place (see chapters 7 and 8). A political economy of urban violence is also necessary to deconstruct the reliance on quantitative approaches to measure criminal violence and, more generally, the statistical reductionism to which urban violence tends to be subjected. We will see, for example, why statistical data about crime tend to obscure more than clarify, and how this obfuscation is structural to the reproduction of forms of (state) violence. Granted, exposing paradoxes and contradictions, deconstructing rhetoric and ideology of urban violence has been the bread and butter of much critical scholarship. The problem, we will show, is that this is not enough: in analytical terms, structuralist (functionalist-economic and symbolic-cultural) interpretations have often produced yet another reductionism, ultimately abstracting (urban) violence (see chapter 1); in strategic terms, a political economy of (urban) violence can become debilitating, especially when it reaches the point of rejecting security altogether (see chapter 3).

To overcome these limits, we resort to the articulation of political economy with a materialist epistemology and a relational ontology. By emphasising the *ontological* dimension of this endeavour, we intend to move further with respect to valuable, and yet still too conservative, attempts at articulating radical approaches to affect, relation and materiality with political economy. For instance, in a compelling article focusing on the possibility to integrate insights from so-called 'assemblage urbanism' (e.g., Anderson and McFarlane 2011; McFarlane 2011)[9] within a political economy lens, Neil Brenner and colleagues (2011) individuate three main levels in which this may occur: the *empirical*, according to which the notion of assemblage is employed as a research object to be explored via the political-economic framework;[10] the *methodological*, according to which the notion of assemblage is employed to expand urban political economy into new realms of inquiry by providing a finer methodological sensibility vis-à-vis the socio-material relations and configurations composing the urban;[11] and the *ontological*, according to which the notion of assemblage becomes a prism to unfold a relational, emergent, heterogenous and more-than-human ontology of the urban. Brenner and colleagues take on board the first two levels, while rejecting the third. As argued elsewhere (Pavoni 2018a, 46–48), we believe that for a radically materialist approach to fully unfold its potential—that is, for being more than simply a magnifying tool employed within a pre-existent and unquestioned theoretical framework—its consequences must be carried out simultaneously at the empirical, methodological and ontological level.

This is what we mean by *articulating* political economy and vital materialism, using the notion of articulation in the sense implied—albeit in a rather different context—by Ernesto Laclau and Chantal Mouffe's definition, namely 'as any practice establishing a relation among elements such that their identity is modified' (1985, 105). Therefore, we argue that an ontological 'reassembling' is an unavoidable move if we wish to really unfold the conceptual and strategic potential of a radically materialist perspective, one able to 'depurate' political economy approaches from their anthropocentric, deterministic and excessively structuralistic tendencies. At the same time, vice versa, we remain convinced that vital materialism must be integrated with a political economy approach if we are to counter its tendency to depoliticise the urban into a flat and homogeneous, 'vital matter'. To see what we mean by that, it is time to qualify what we talk about when we talk about 'vital materialism'.

Vital Materialism[12]

Not only did late turns in social sciences and humanities move a further blow to the ontological assumptions of Western modernity and the nature/society fracture that grounds them. But the Anthropocene (Bonneuil and Fressoz 2013)—as well known through a vast array of alternative, ever-proliferating definitions (see Chwałczyk 2020)—also prompted a 'real deconstruction', to use Jacques Derrida's expression (2009[2008]), of said fracture, making it dramatically evident, both to scientific research and everyday experience, what many non-Western cosmogonies had always known (e.g., Castro 2014[2009]; Descola 2013[2005]; Kopenawa and Albert 2023[2013]). Namely, that society and history have always already been 'natural', and vice versa. It is not surprising that it is at this conjuncture that so-called 'new materialism' (e.g., Bennett 2010; Coole and Frost 2010; Dolphin and van der Tuin 2012; Gamble et al. 2019) has surfaced, drawing the consequences—or, at times, simply restating the conclusions—of at least a century of materialist, relational and processual thinking, in this way providing a renewed stress on the ecological materiality of coexistence, and the epistemological and ethical injunctions that come with thinking, and attending to, the agentic vitality of matter.

Our vital materialist approach emerges out of this variegated array of inspirations, intersects them with a political economy perspective, and draws the consequences this move implies.[13] If we were to sum them up, a simple formula, taken in its double meaning, could suffice: *everything does matter* (see Pavoni 2018a, 36–37). On the one hand, this entails the ethical and political decentring of anthropocentrism: *every entity* 'matters', although in unavoidably different ways and depending on the historically situated configurations in which it is each time taken. On the other, this emphasises an ontological nuance, insofar as meaning that every entity is in the process of *mattering* by means of entering in affective relations with other bodies. Didier Fassin (2011, 193) offers an inspiring way to capture the question this understanding of materiality points to:

> not simply, in the Marxian sense, that of the structural conditions which effectively largely determine the conditions of life of the members of a given society; it is also, in Canguilhem's sense, that of the very substance of existence, its materiality, its longevity and the inequalities that society imposes on it. To accept this materialistic orientation is not a merely theoretical issue. It is also an ethical one. It recognizes that the matter of life does matter.

It is almost too obvious to note the extent to which a movement such as Black Lives Matter literally embodies this understanding, on the one hand carrying a piercing critique of the violent structures of racialisation (and the policing of racial boundaries) while, on the other, mobilising the materiality of Blackness (e.g., Sharpe 2016) by challenging the socio-biological asphyxia of everyday life in the USA and beyond, under the appropriate cry: *I cannot breathe*. In chapter 6 we will expand more deeply on the relation between life, matter and breathing by introducing the notion of atmospheric violence. If a process such as planetary urbanisation, as we anticipated, always materialises, through frictions, in the contingency of concrete, socio-material relations, with the concept of atmospheric violence we intend to explore the toxic by-product of these frictions, and the way they unequally affect urban bodies as they are forced to flexibly cope with, and adapt, to this everyday turbulence. Prior to deal with this concept, however, a deeper, critical reflection on notions of violence, urbanisation and materiality will be required. At this stage, we limit ourselves to preliminarily, and briefly, unpack the ontology and ethics of relation, affect and life this approach implies.

Once bodies, rather than being understood as separate beings, are considered as always entangled in a relational field, the problem of establishing what a body *is* disappears, leaving the place to the quintessentially Spinozist question of exploring what a body *can*—including the consequent ethical and political question of exploring the way a given social organisation prevents or allows this potential to unfold (cf. Spinoza 2002[1677b]). The notion of affect responds to this *problématique*. In times of widespread use and abuse of this concept, it is useful to briefly come back to Spinoza's classic definition, as was provided in the *Ethics* (2002[1677a], p. III, def. 3): 'by affect I understand affections of the body by which the body's power of acting is increased or diminished, aided or restrained, and at the same time, the ideas of these affections'. Let us unpack this sentence. Bodies, in Spinoza's sense, are not pre-formed, separate entities but rather *modes* of a unique substance, which he refers to as God, or Nature. First, this means, as Gilles Deleuze observes, that 'a body can be anything' (1988[1970], 127): a stone, a human being, an image, a virus, a season, a gust of wind. Second, this modal ontology is a necessarily relational one: a body understood as a mode is not a substance but a set of relations, that is, *affections*. Bodies constantly affect each other, as they are taken in affective concatenations. Affection, in other words, means a relation of a body affecting another: my body affected by the warmth of the sun, the virus of influenza, the idea of free will, the fear of a dark alleyway. A body is constituted by the affections it undergoes and thus by the *passage* between different affections and their differential rhythm. In the temporal sense, then, a body is a *duration*, an oscillation between a 'more' and a 'less', the increase or decrease of power that result from these affections: me becoming more or less fearful, more or less cold, more or less strong. Life itself understood as an affective variation (Deleuze 1993).

If affection is a relation, *affect* is this oscillation, that is, it indicates the variation this produces in a body's 'power to act', that is, its ability to affect and be affected: in other words, my ability to move, think, imagine, feel and live. Affection in space (as relation), affect in time (as duration). A body's power to act has not to do, in this sense, with the kind of actions that a pre-constituted body can and does perform but rather with the constant becoming of that very body. A body unfolds dynamically in variation, oscillating between relations that increase and relations that decrease one's power to act—what Spinoza respectively refers to as 'joy' and 'sadness'. Joy is the empowering of my ability to enter novel relations and thus to think, feel and live, according to my own nature and constitution. Sadness is the disempowering of such ability and, more precisely, what separates myself from my powers, in this way debilitating me (Spinoza 2002[1677a], p. III; see also chapter 9). In Brian Massumi's terms, 'a power to affect and be affected governs a transition, where a body passes from one state of capacitation to a diminished or augmented state of capacitation' (interviewed in McKim 2009; see also Massumi 2015).

There is, therefore, a double nature to affects, simultaneously virtual and actual: a virtual potential (a power to affect and be affected) that is independent from the affections and is rather specific to a given body—a human, a virus or a tree will have different powers according to their nature—and the actual relations, or affections, through which such powers are actualised, or thwarted. Each body oscillates between two tendencies: on the one hand a movement of composition, as an opening into the spatiality of common relations; on the other, a movement of closure.[14] Reality is thus understood as a dynamic and processual ensemble of affective relations—or, as we will contend, atmospheres (see chapter 6)—within which bodies are always part of concatenations that may be flourishing, capacitating and *joyous*, or toxic, debilitating and *sad*. We can therefore understand why for Spinoza the question of power (*potentia*) is central. As the crux of the matter is not what a body *is* but what a body *can*, then bodies are not substances but relational powers to affect and be affected, an understanding that will also ground Spinoza's original understanding of the right of nature as power (*jus sive potentia*) (see chapter 9). At its most essential, this 'ontology of *power*' grounds Spinoza's famous understanding of *conatus*, that is, the desire that each thing has, being it human or not, to persevere in its own being by keeping the above-mentioned 'oscillation' alive, and therefore in a spiralling ascent, that is, by seeking to increase its own power to affect and be affected by means of entering in joyful, 'good' or 'healthy' relations (2002[1677a], p. III, pr. 9, scholium).[15] Existence, accordingly, unfolds in the form of a rhythmical vibration, each body oscillating according to the rhythm produced by the resonance of relations (affections) and the consequent oscillation between increase and decrease of power (affect) (Deleuze 1988[1970]).

Crucially for our understanding of violence, this is a necessarily relational effort. What the conatus entails is a double strategy, as per Laurent Bove's suggestion: on the one hand, resistance against what is toxic, poisonous and destructive; on the other, alliance with that which is healthy, empowering, and that 'agrees' with us (1996). It is with respect to the rhythmical oscillation of urban life in collective atmospheres, and the way these are shaped and acted upon by law, security, planning and other dimensions of urban politics, that the question of urban violence can be promisingly addressed.

Along this book, we will unpack the relational, material and affective premises of this ontology, with a careful attention not to assume their self-sufficient explanatory power. All too often, works stemming from above-mentioned 'turns' do just that. Fed by an understandable, if at times overenthusiastic, urge to reorient thinking and acting towards matter, they assume iconoclastic positions that, while uncritically celebrating the agency and vitality of said matter, ultimately leave it unanalysed and unexplained, with the risk of unfolding a dangerously apolitical and ahistorical understanding of life (for a critique, see Bowden 2015; Choat 2018; Gamble et al. 2019). Clive Barnett's (2011, 252) brisk words of caution are a good reminder in this context: 'just telling stories about spatially extensive networks of connection and entanglement' or praising the wondrous vitality of nonhuman matter, is not enough. While we point elsewhere for an extended critique on (this) matter (Pavoni 2018a; 2020), let us therefore stress that the critique we will move in chapter 1 to the excessive rigidity and deterministic tendencies of structuralist approaches to violence does not wish in any way to fall into the naivety of certain anti-structuralist 'flat' positions, nor into the metaphysical privileging of the value of life *per se*. If an attention to materiality necessarily implies to rethink notions of agency and causation, 'scaling down' the centrality of either the 'human' or the 'structure' by thrusting them within a complex and distributed field of material processes, this does not mean having done with notions of scale, structure or causation altogether. We do not believe scaling down should mean scaleless, that is. It should rather be a way to open up reality to the complexity of a spatially and temporally multiscalar field, where synchronisation, scale-bending, re-scaling and other more or less (dis)organising political and logistical processes unfold, by generating multiple frictions in and through the nonscalable, material singularity of life (e.g., Brenner 2004; Tsing 2012). It is precisely to explore this turbulent complexity that we resorted, as mentioned, to the articulation between the materialist and the political economic lens.

This articulation is crucial to differentiate our approach from certain uses of so-called 'flat ontologies', an approach brought forwards by Actor-Network Theory (ANT), recently revamped by the (short-lived) enthusiasm triggered by so-called Object-Oriented Ontologies (OOOs), and whose troubles vis-à-vis geography are epitomised in the words of Ignacio Farías: 'space, scale and time [are] multiply enacted and assembled at concrete local sites, where concrete actors shape time-space dynamics in various ways, producing thereby different geographies of associations', rather than being produced by 'capital relations' or 'state strategies' (2010, 6). While we deny any direct, linear causality smoothly relating 'capital relations' and 'state strategies' to the production of the social writ large (in this sense agreeing with the problematic that ANT and OOO raise), we believe that, in many uses of these theories, the urge to flatten everything has left 'unaddressed important explanatory questions regarding the broader (global, national and regional) structural contexts within which actants are situated and operate' (Brenner et al. 2011, 233).

Whereas we also caution against packing many different authors within a single critique—we are aware that labels such as ANT or OOO all too often gather authors whose specificity would deserve better critiques—we are afraid that mainstream uses of 'flat ontologies' have often gone all the way to removing politics from the picture, by reducing it to a mere question of enrolling ever-widening lists of nonhuman entities into a hybrid parliament of *things*, while the socio-political structures, power relations and asymmetrical forces that order and shape such relations are left unaccounted for (see Spencer 2011). Nowhere is this more evident than in the remarkable silence of Bruno Latour, and some of his followers, vis-à-vis questions of politics, ideology and institutional power, summarised in his notorious claim: 'like God, Capitalism does not exist' (1993[1991], 173). Unfortunately, it does. Yet, while we are willing to avoid his problematic consequences, as we are to show in the following chapter, we do share Latour's uneasiness about structuralist thinking (e.g., 2005), one that Martin Arboleda spells quite effectively:

> Considering global capitalism to be a faceless, 'structural' force that exists in a separate plane of reality to that of the mundane workings of states and firms is politically paralyzing and analytically obfuscating. (2020, 22)

Not only overlooking states and firms is of concern here, but more generally the risk of overlooking the concrete reality of structures, that is, the historically-situated, socio-material relations *in* and *through* which they are actualised and reproduced in the urban (see Toscano 2004; Cunningham 2005)—what Laurent Berlant, with a notion we will unpack in the following chapter, refers to as 'the living mediation of what organizes life: the lifeworld of structure' (Berlant 2016, 393).

Especially in chapters 6 and 7, we will investigate this dimension by exploring the relation between life, affect and urban violence—through the notion of atmospheric violence, as already anticipated. In the remainder of this section, instead, we believe it is useful to spend a few more introductory words to qualify more precisely our use of such notions as life, vitality and vitalism along this book. This is all the more important, since these are rather controversial and tricky concepts, which have dangerously hovered between the naively romantic and the reactionary/fundamentalist spectrums of the theoretical and political fields. As we will see, a variation on these terms has also recently become a sort of *terminus technicus*, employed to compare cities

around the world via so-called 'urban liveability' charts, where a narrow statistical definition of violence, unsurprisingly, is among the key indexes that
calculate whether a given city is to be assumed as more or less 'liveable'—an
adjective that today plays a very similar role to the one 'civilised' played in
older, less politically correct times (see chapter 7).

Rather than a call for the uncritical celebration of life,[16] and following
the proposition of Andrea Mubi Brighenti and Matthias Kärrholm, our vi-
talistic approach is to be understood as a 'resistance' to the perils of (social,
economic, technological, etc.) reductionism, determinism and mechanicism.
The purpose, in turn, is that of rescuing a non-totalising attitude to the
observation of socio-natural phenomena, able to attend to their 'dynamic
livingness' (Brighenti and Kärrholm 2020, 17)—in our terms, their structurally excessive quality. Life, accordingly, is not assumed as a substance, absolute value or a special essence 'contained' within the living, one that would
therefore be 'superior' to some kind of non-life. This dichotomy does not
have much sense, or is superficial at best, if we take into account the radical
line of 'vitalist' thinking from which we draw inspiration, one that ideally
connect otherwise different thinkers such as of Spinoza, Darwin, Nietzsche,
Bergson, Whitehead, Simondon, Canguilhem, Foucault, Deleuze, as well as
Viveiros de Castro, Grosz, Ingold, Barad, Stengers, Bennett, and so forth.
Accordingly, we understand 'dynamic livingness' as what *exceeds* the living,
that is, the dynamic, relational and creative—indeed 'vital'—tendency of life
itself. Deleuze refers to it as *vitality*, of which François Zourabichvili provides
a useful conceptualisation: 'it is by refusing to circumscribe life within the
limits of living forms (thereby defining life as organization), that the creative
or progressive tendency traversing the living can be thought, beyond the
unsatisfying alternatives of mechanism and formalism' (2012[2003], 187).
This does not mean that life is 'unorganised'; rather that there is always an
excessive quality to life, a *vital* dimension of life, so to speak (see Thacker
2017). Yet, and contrary to what Gamble and colleagues (2019, 120) suggest,
this perspective does not necessarily imply the acritical, ultimately moralistic
'privileging' of life. Attributing an excessive vitality to life is not a way to
remove the 'political' from the equation. Rather, it is a way to emphasise that
this excess, and its governance, has become a key locus of (urban) politics
(Pavoni 2018a). Likewise, while we agree that such an approach 'risks "flattening" the multiplicity of material practices into a vague flat ontology of
force *in general*' (Gamble et al. 2019, 120; emphasis in original), we do not
believe this must *necessarily* be the case. True, as argued elsewhere, 'much
caution is needed, it seems, if we are to avoid falling from the necessary
unfolding of a materialist ontology into its moralistic fetishisation' (Pavoni

2018a, 51). Indeed, as already stressed, it is exactly to prevent this outcome that we chose to strategically integrate vital materialism with a political economy perspective.

Let us also reassert that our approach to vitalism has nothing to do with the substantialist idea of life as a value, as reproposed in contemporary 'pro-life' rhetoric. Certainly, there *is* a 'value' to life, but to understand what that means requires re-thinking the relation between value and vitality in the first place. From Spinoza's conatus to Nietzsche's will to power, from Charles Darwin's 'inherent tendency to vary' of the living (1868) to Georges Canguilhem's understanding of life as a differential power to produce norms, many are the instances in which we find similar references to something excessive akin to what Massumi (2018) has referred to the incommensurable 'surplus-value of life': namely 'life's qualitatively-in-the-making', that is, the processual overflowing of life itself *as it becomes.*[17] As we are to see, what urban violence suffocates, and at the same time the primary target of contemporary security politics, is exactly the excessive overflowing characteristic of urban life.

Evidently, this understanding is at odds with a static notion of life as quantitative value to be captured into liveability indexes. At the same time, this prefigures a relation between life and normativity that is alien to the simplistic position that assumes an opposition between them—or that supposes an uncritical superiority of life over the norm. Vitality is neither an abstract normative value, nor a value that is beyond any norm: more precisely, it is to be understood as a value- and norm-producing force that unfolds in response to the 'vital problems' of the existence (cf. Deleuze 2004[1968])—and in chapter 1 we will further reflect on this force of both 'evaluation' and 'violation' with respect to violence. In other words, it is out of life's overflowing desire that values are produced, as Spinoza and then Nietzsche well understood. Value is not absolute, abstract and transcendent, but is produced out of the coming together of bodies, by their immanent *modes* of existence, and it is with respect to these socio-material relations, and their capacitating or debilitating effects on the bodies that constitute them, that the question of violence will have to be explored.[18]

This requires, and crucially so, for the *pars costruens* of our argument, rescuing the concept of norm from its legalistic and negative understanding, by underlining a norm-creative power of life that is 'intrinsic and immanent', while at the same time exceeding, the living (Esposito 2011[2002]). If the health of a body springs from the creative and differentiating power of life, then 'illness' corresponds to the progressive atrophy of life's creative capacity to variate by creating new alliances, co-evolving with other organisms (Canguilhem 1966). This is also the import of epidemiologist Geoffrey Rose's classic study of aetiology, where he distinguished between an individual-centred approach, in which the question is whether or not an individual *has* a given illness, with the consequence of defining a clear difference between healthy and sick, and a relative definition of 'common normality';[19] and a population-centred approach in which the question is no longer that of drawing a line between the 'sick' and the 'healthy', but that of establishing the degree of illness each one has and, therefore, of questioning at the same time a static and atomistic notion of illness, with the notion of normality that implies (Rose 1985, see chapters 1 and 6). The extent to which an individual-centred model has also marred social science is evident to everyone that is accustomed with this field. Accordingly, individuals have been framed as being 'illiberal', 'evil', or 'violent', as if they *had* some kind of disease.[20] Yet, both in sociology and epidemiology, it is never simply a case of separating the sick from the healthy, since what becomes 'sick' is not a preformed individual, but an emergent and situated relation, which in turn produces given processes of subjectivation. There are no 'essentially' or 'naturally' violent individuals, but rather violent atmospheres, as we are to see more in depth later on (see chapter 6). Even a virus only makes us ill when we are no longer able to ally with it, as biologist Luis Villarreal (2004) explained: it is our relation with the virus that becomes ill. Resistance and alliance, this is the strategic unfolding of life (cf. Bove 1996, above). It follows that, to be truly 'dangerous' for life is not the 'intrusion' of external agents, the breaching of a pre-existence carapace or identity. It is rather the weakening of the capacity for integration and transformation (Esposito 2011[2002]), and therefore the atrophy of life's capacity to enter into ever novel relations, to affect and be affected. In other words, illness here refers to the weakening, exhaustion or debilitation of life's norm- and value-creating force, that is, life's capacity for variation.

Let us qualify that we are perfectly aware of the danger that medical metaphors carry, with their tendency towards naturalisation, depoliticisation and outright discrimination (e.g., Mongoven 2006; Bell 2012). Incidentally, in chapter 1 (section Researching Urban Violence) we will show a remarkable example of the problem that a medicalising approach to urban violence might lead to, by focusing on Gary Slutkin's controversial Cure Violence approach. However, our use of concepts such as illness or poison is, following the likes of Spinoza and Deleuze, strictly non-metaphorical and non-medicalising, and cannot be understood without taking into account the ontology of relation, power (*potentia*) and in/capacitation that grounds it. It is only through this lens that the political and strategic value of this approach becomes apparent, including its potential to challenge violence (see Austin 2023). We believe that the vital materialism we have thus elaborated is able to provide an original ontological, epistemological and ethical conceptualisation of urban violence, one that emerges at the encounter between 'classic' works on biopolitics (e.g., Foucault, Agamben, Butler, Esposito), more recent reflections on the affective dimension of life (e.g., Anderson, Massumi, Bennett, Barad), and an invaluable number of works that helped us framing the slowly debilitating, attritional and suffocating effect violence may have on life itself (e.g., Fanon, Berlant, Puar, Nixon, Povinelli). It is this 'weakening' that the notion of atmospheric violence will try to capture.

We do not deny, to conclude, that there is an ambiguity to such a vital materialism. We stress that to emphasise such an ambiguity is not an argument against this approach, as often implied, but rather a testament to its strategical realism. Life's vital excess is not 'positive' as such, nor desirable in itself. Life's excessive exuberance, proliferation and variation can be dangerous, metastasising or lethal. Dealing with this excess, without suffocating its potential for capacitating the life of a collective, therefore, cannot entail the naïve and ultimately moralistic celebration of life's wondrous potential, or that of matter's vital force. This is an important question, where the ontological needs to intersect the political, if it is to avoid falling into a passive and uncritical aestheticisation. A politically valuable vital materialist stance is not one that is content with simply affirming this excess potential, but rather one that *cares for* it, by means of *securing* it against its own dangers (see chapter 9). In the words of Bruce Braun, 'demonstrating contingency can never be the goal in and of itself; it is rather just the beginning. What matters is that contingency be seized as opportunity', and how can it be translated into political necessity (2011, 391).[21] This is the biopolitical question we must face, with respect to a notion of urban violence that, we are to see, directly impinges upon, and debilitates, the vitality of urban life.

Plan of the Book

Three are the core concepts that we need to dig into in order to set the ground for our conceptualisation of urban violence: violence, urban and—as we began to suggest—security. To them are dedicated the three chapters of Part I, which lays the *foundations* of the book. Chapter 1 starts by discussing, and challenging, five forms of reductionisms that the notion of *violence* routinely undergoes in the social sciences, the humanities, and, indirectly, in the political and public discourse: first, the naturalisation of violence, that is, the understanding of violence as an endogenous anomaly to the social; second, the fetishisation of violence, that is, the acknowledgement of violence only in its direct, physical manifestations; third, the moral condemnation of violence, the labelling of violence as being a merely destructive phenomenon; fourth, the reduction of violence to culture, that is, its framing as a merely socio-cultural phenomenon; and fifth, the abstraction of violence, that is, the process of explaining violence away through its structural and symbolic processes. We move, then, to apply our approach, based on the articulation of the political economic and vital materialism, with respect to violence. Besides overcoming moralistic understandings of violence stemming from pre-defined values, we propose an ontological understanding of violence as a tensional force concerning the immanent 'consistency' of the social—that is, its 'holding-together'. In other words, we understand violence as a force that can be either/or/both conservative (that which prevents any challenge to existing configurations) and disruptive (vis-à-vis existing configurations). A force, that is, that both weaves together and threatens to disrupt the social. By taking steps from, and moving beyond, recent works on infrastructure and infrastructural violence, we thus develop the concept of infra-structural violence, as a way to rework symbolic/economic notions of structural violence away from their tendency towards deterministic causality and abstraction; and towards an onto-epistemological, dynamic conceptualisation of violence attuned to the latter's disrupting, constructive and preserving quality.

Chapter 2 moves on to discuss the problems of the conceptualisation of the *urban* and its equalisation to 'the city' as a place, characterised by peculiar phenomena and thus naturalised as an a-historical process—the natural coming together of human beings and the forms of life that result from that. In particular, we refer this problem throughout the history of urban sociology and urban studies, paying special attention to the Chicago School—which has defined some of the key ideas through which urban violence is still commonly conceptualised and dealt with. We then develop our relational and materialist approach to the urban, first by taking steps from the work of Idelfons Cerdá, who coined the very concept of 'urbanisation'. By exploring the way Cerdá framed the nineteenth-century city as a problem, and the solution he proposed, we are able to retrace the surfacing of urban modernity as a threefold trajectory: the emergence of the urban as a *project*, a problem of governance for the liberal state and capitalist system; second, the actually-existing *process* of (global, planetary) urbanisation with its historical, spatial and socio-economic characters; and, third, the *atmosphere*, that is, the onto-logical condition and phenomenological experience that the modern urban condition discloses.

By starting to discuss the relation between urbanisation and policing, chapter 2 also opens up to the need to reflect on the history of *security*, and particularly its consolidation at the centre of the project of the (European) liberal state, to set the grounds for our understanding of urban violence—this is the scope of chapter 3. This chapter is grounded on the idea that any discussion on security needs to be historically situated, in our case within the inextricable link between the political theories about security and the spatio-political project of urbanisation. To flesh out this link, we start by engaging, and make our divergences explicit, with the main critical approaches to security. In short, while endorsing the critique of security for the way it deconstructs the security-freedom balance at the core of liberal ideas on security (see Neocleous 2007), we also argue against the tendency to equalise security with the capitalist project and, therefore, to reject it altogether. We argue that it is not 'security' *per se*, but rather a specific political theory of security that is quintessential to liberalism. The core of the chapter is thus a genealogy of this political theory, which we articulate through three understandings that are often considered opposite, but we consider as coexisting facets of the same conceptual bundle. We discuss these understandings by making reference to three key thinkers: the Hobbesian projection of a society without violence; the individualistic understanding of the security/freedom link developed within the liberal tradition of John Locke; and the mechanisms, technologies and savoirs that Michel Foucault has described as governmentality.

Thus laid the foundations, it is through the *intersections* among urban, violence and security that in Part II we develop our theoretical arguments: the imaginary of urban violence that feeds the project of security; the violent process of planetary urbanisation; and the atmospheric violence that fills the urban as a result. Chapter 4 thus begins with the *imaginary*, starting with a brief reconnaissance of relevant theoretical reflections on the social imaginary. Our argument on the centrality of the imaginary of security vis-à-vis urban violence is centred on the acknowledgement and reconstruction of a foundational binary opposition at the centre of the (Western) urban imaginary, namely, the concept of domesticity, and its relation with the conceptual and ecological space of the wild. We show how the wild constitutes a fundamental problem for Western political theory, and the hidden operator around which the spatio-political project of urbanisation and police is articulated. We then move to show how the conceptualisation of the wild, and with it the very imaginary of urban modernity, has crucially developed through and within violent encounters with colonial space and the colonial other, fleshing out the implications for the way in which the nineteenth-century city appeared to bourgeois planners, legislators and police. This chapter, in short, argues that it is out of this context that the contemporary notion of urban violence emerges.

It is at this point that we can move more specifically to 'urbanising' violence. Chapter 5 begins this endeavour by developing our wide-angle lens, pointed at the global, planetary scale of the *violence of urbanisation*. We start by returning to the 'problem of the urban' in urban violence and the specific shortcomings of literature that takes the urban for granted. In particular, we argue that this problem is linked to the way urban violence is captured as a consequence of the 'urban age'. Though this is in line with long-held ideas about urban life (which we anticipated in chapter 2), in this chapter we can more precisely identify the consequences of this understanding for the dominance of (problematic) quantitative understandings of urban violence, as well as for the broad lack of engagement with the theory of the urban in most literature on urban violence. By mobilising the lenses of political economy and political theory we argue, as a way forward, for the co-constitutiveness of urbanisation and violence: we show the promising steps taken by the literature that has discussed the (direct and indirect) forms of violence of capitalist urbanisation; and highlight the limits therein, adding that a politico-economical approach to the dialectical relation between urban space and the planetary process of neoliberal urbanisation needs to be further integrated by an affective sensibility.

To this integration, and to zoom to the scale of the urban, is dedicated chapter 6, which finally articulates the violence of capitalist urbanisation, the imaginary thereof and the affective infra-structure of everyday urban life. To do so, we introduce the concept of *urban atmospheric violence*, which allows us to explore the gaseous consistency urban violence takes in the contemporary city in the form of an asphyxiating force that debilitates urban bodies and their capacity to think, sense, act, move and live. We start by framing atmospheres for their ontological qualities—their focus on how the urban 'holds together'—showing how this notion is particularly attuned to an infra-structural understanding of violence. We then move to theorise atmospheric violence, and unpack its strategic value by elaborating a materialist, not metaphorical understanding of breathing. This allows us to discuss the toxic atmospheres of urban violence, which allow to expand structural and cultural understandings of violence in space and time to encompass forms of violence where notions of causality, intentionality and agency are hardly obvious.

We can then move to Part III of the book, *extensions*, which brings together, and 'materialises', our discussion, by zooming onto the ontologies and epistemologies of the atmosphere of urban violence. We begin, in chapter 7, by complementing the discussion on urban atmospheres through a genealogical gaze. While, throughout the previous chapters we have shown how the nineteenth-century 'urban crisis'—including its very framing as crisis—was crucial in shaping both the project and the process of contemporary urbanisation, we can at this point show how the surfacing of the aesthetic and affective infrastructure of the contemporary urban atmosphere can be traced to this fateful turning point. We develop this argument by mobilising and unpacking the idea of the society of comfort; and by specifically looking at a precise juridical and aesthetic dispositif recently introduced in the Italian context, *decoro urbano* (urban decorum). In doing so, we read the genealogies of the current unfolding of urban security, the notion of urban violence that it is implicitly constructed therein and the atmospheric violence that stems.

Chapter 8, in turn, discusses a recent security policy, predictive policing, placing it within the genealogies of the attempts at managing and controlling the urban and their imaginary, one that has recently assumed the shape and lingo of the 'smart city'. We argue that this imaginary of the smart city—with the potentialities of cybernetics and the promises of algorithmic governance—fundamentally offers a new epistemological field for security, whereby the Hobbesian dream of absolute security seems capable of materialising, reframing once again, and in a further disempowering way, the normative window through which urban violence is conceptualised. The quintessential instrument through which it does so is predictive policing, the ultimate version of a long history of technological solutionism through techniques of crime mapping. We explore predictive policing through our ontological and epistemological lenses, articulating the political economy critique (of its failures and harms) and the material dimensions of its unfolding. The problem with algorithmic governance, we conclude, cannot be just analysed at the level of how it fails to realise its promises—an argument that can be captured to argue for *more and more* technological solutionism—but also at the level of the specific forms of violence that it produces, which we conceptualise, building on the work of Rocco Bellanova and his colleagues (2021), as algorithmic violence.

Chapter 9, in conclusion, comes back to security—following up our argument on the necessity to not discard the concept with its dominant imaginaries and logics. To re-think security implies precisely questioning what security is desired and by whom: what is meant to be secured. Granted, we start by distancing ourselves from the reactionary degeneration of left-wing security politics of the last decades—the point is not to capture the concept, but to give it a new ontology. Sketching the lineaments of a different understanding of security implies rethinking the plane of immanence out of which the concept is constructed. We provide some coordinates to do so via three moves meant to reconstitute many of the relations structuring the mainstream understanding of security: the relations between security and responsibility (beyond delegation), security and freedom (beyond balance), security and care (beyond *sine-cura*)—advocating for a 'security as care' (*cum cura*).

This final chapter, we believe, is not just yet another glimpse of hope attached to yet another work of critique. Rather, its contribution is precisely (re-)asserting the centrality of the ontological dimension to our endeavour. As recently argued by AbdouMaliq Simone and Vanessa Broto, 'raising ontological questions is a strategy to develop new solidarities in a world where urban inequities appear as insurmountable, where individuals adapt their coping strategies to a heightened sense of suspicion' (2022, 3). In this sense, this final chapter also makes evident our attempt, throughout the book, to build an analytical lens that is at the same time a strategic one. While critical scholarship has already raised many of the analytical points that we make vis-à-vis urban violence and security, our approach intends to reassemble critique through an ontology that has to offer a strategic way out to the traditional 'so what?' impasse. An endeavour, we are aware, that is fraught with contradictions and paradoxes as any attempt at putting critique to work (cf. Burgess 2019; Tulumello 2021a)—and yet one that, we hope this book will show, is worth pursuing nonetheless.

Epistemology: Researching Urban Violence

We have dedicated a good amount of this introduction to the ontological dimension, since we believe that rethinking the ontology of the urban is a necessary step in order to rethink the notion of urban violence. At the same time, however, we stressed that this endeavour is crucially also an epistemological one. As we will see throughout the book (see, above all, chapters 1, 2 and 5), the public, political and, if less often, academic discourses about urban violence are plagued by any number of simplifications and reductionisms—reductionisms which have very material effects in the way they provide justification to deeply violent security policies. By and beyond challenging these reductionisms, another goal of this book is that of offering some insights to those that wish to engage with urban violence critically and strategically. With this goal in mind, chapters from 1 to 8 will be concluded with a small section—somehow pedagogically titled 'researching urban violence'—dedicated to mobilising the theoretical arguments. By discussing some of the ideas and practices unfolding at the intersection between violence, security and the urban, we intend to put them concretely in context and link them to broader discussions in the social sciences and humanities.

In chapter 1, we will discuss a particularly sophisticated form of reductionism, that is, the framing of urban violence as a contagious disease, a conceptualisation that has been pushed, among others, by the World Health Organization. In chapter 2, we will focus on quantitative reductionism, by specifically engaging on the problems of relying on dramatically problematic data such as those of crime known to the police and the judiciary. In chapter 3, we exemplify the coexistence of, and clashes among, the three security paradigms—Hobbes's absolutism, Locke's liberalism and Foucault's governmentality, in brief—during the first stages of the Covid-19 pandemic, by looking at the health measures put in place, in Italy and beyond. In chapter 4, we reflect on the peculiar nature of terrorism, and on the urbanisation of terrorism, for its capacity to reframe security politics and imaginaries. In chapter 5, we discuss Broken Windows theory and the policing strategies inspired by it, as paradigmatic examples of the violence of urbanisation. Chapter 6 provides materiality to our discussion on violent (urban) atmospheres through Fanon's description of the colonial city and a discussion of racism. In chapter 7, we complement the discussion on comfort and decorum by discussing an underlying idea, that of liveability, and how it materialises in recent liveability indexes. Finally, in chapter 8, we consider the least common—and least inquired—form of predictive policing, based on individual risk assessment, to uncover its implicitly spatialised nature, which resonates with the ideas of the Chicago School and the medicalisation of violence; in doing so closing the circle that links violence reductionism with urban reductionism.

§

Before moving forward, let us close this introduction with a few words on our different standpoints, useful above all to provide a glimpse of the way we came to develop the approach sketched here. As the references to our previous works will make evident, the two poles of our approach are by and large grounded on the epistemological perspectives of each of the two of us. This is to say, the articulation of these two lenses is also, and possibly above all, the articulation of our different contributions to this book—which means that, reminding the words of Laclau and Mouffe referred above, in coming together our epistemological lenses had to undergo a process of transformation. This, however, has not implied reaching a synthesis. We explicitly decided to not subsume our voices under a unique one, since that would

have meant imposing violence over the heterogeneous and proliferating process of becoming-together this very book expresses in a minor form. As we
advanced in its writing, an assemblage has emerged, where our perspectives,
epistemologies and writing styles, while maintaining their heterogeneity,
somehow found a way to 'hold together' in a consistent, albeit hardly comfortable way. We believe that the relative frictions that at times the reader
may encounter are therefore not to be read as contradictions, but rather the
sign that articulation is a never-ending process, a 'work in progress' that is
meant to remain open.

Notes

1. Sophie Body-Gendrot. 1995. "Urban violence: A quest for meaning", Reprinted by permission of Informa UK Limited, trading as Taylor & Francis Group,
www.tandfonline.com.

2. Our translation. From L'Encyclopédie, first ed., 1751 (tome 12, pp. 904–913),
available at: https://fr.wikisource.org/wiki/L%E2%80%99Encyclop%C3%A9die/1re
_%C3%A9dition/POLICE.

3. We point the reader to a previous article (Pavoni and Tulumello 2020,
52–56 and Appendixes) for the methodological details. Suffice here to say that we
performed a systematic literature review, based on and expanding those made by
Muggah (2012) and Saborio (2014/2015, 15–27), which allowed us to collect more
than 300 texts, which we analysed through scientometric instruments, and a shorter
collection of 86 texts, which we analysed qualitatively, seeking for definitions of
urban violence.

4. Elijah Anderson's Code of the Street (1999) is probably the most iconic
ethnography of the 'culture' of (street) violence—see Wacquant (2002) for a systematic critique.

5. Here and below, 'measurable' is put amid inverted commas because the measur-
ability of crime is a large problem in and of itself (see chapter 2, section Researching
Urban Violence).

6. It is important to point out, here, that this is hardly a peculiar issue of post-colonial France. Rather, the association of race with violences urbaines is explicit where
that with urban violence is implicit in the Anglophone world—think, for instance,
to associations between urban violence and concepts, like 'inner-city violence' or
'Black on Black crime', that are deeply racialised when not bluntly racist. We do
not include this among the definitional problems of urban violence because critical
literature has long exposed these racialised assumptions—however, we will come
back time and again to the centrality of race and racialisation in the emergence and
definition of the field of urban violence.

7. An argument that Williams attribute to us, so we take this occasion to clarify
this point. Indeed, when we wrote that 'put simply, "urban violence" thus appears

as a precise historical category *emerging out* of the process of capitalist urbanisation' (Pavoni and Tulumello 2020, 64; our emphasis), we did not mean to reduce urban violence to a direct effect of urbanisation—indeed, we criticised then and will criticise in this book the common tendency to associate urban violence to urban growth or to any inherent character of 'the urban'. What we meant then and mean now is that the specific form of violence that is urban violence—a specificity that was and still is to be theoretically grasped—does emerge from the historical and global process of urbanisation; though its actualisations are as different as regional, national and urban contexts are—thence the need to articulate a political economic with a materialist lens. Indeed, much of the misunderstanding may well be that, in line with recent discussions in urban theory, we do not define urbanisation as urban growth, as we will discuss at length (chapters 2 and 5).

8. On this understanding of the difference between an 'abstract' morality articulated around normative notions of Good and Evil and a 'concrete' ethics articulated around 'chemical' notions of Good and Bad, we follow Gilles Deleuze's interpretation of Spinoza (1968). As it will also become apparent in chapter 1, our intersection of ethics, ontology and epistemology is also inspired by the concept of ethico-onto-epistemology that Karen Barad proposes in the context of scientific knowledge production and practice (2007). See also below.

9. Assemblage urbanism is one of the many, short-lived sub-labels that sought to capture the intersection between relational thinking—in this case, mostly drawing from Bruno Latour's Actor-Network Theory—and Deleuze and Guattari's notion of assemblage (*agencement*), two notions that are hardly compatible and whose coexistence is often rather problematic (see Pavoni 2018a).

10. Often, the reduction of the assemblage to a research object is premised on a further epistemological reduction, which reifies it as a noun (assemblage) whilst omitting its verbal quality (assembling), that is, the processual and emerging aspects its original term (*agencement*) connotes. The notion of *agencement* is developed to indicate the coming-together of heterogeneous parts that have at least three qualities: *emergence*, that is, the assemblage acquire novel properties that emerge from the interaction between its parts and were not pre-existent to them; *engineering*, that is, the assemblage is always immanently organised, asymmetrically so, and this asymmetry does depend on relations of power, matter and force—the assemblage is never simply innocent and 'flat'; and *excess*, that is, the assemblage, while being concrete and historical, is always exceeded by its own immanent becoming, possessing all sort of virtual tendencies and capacities which are real, albeit latent, since inscribed in its own dispositions (Deleuze and Guattari 2004[1980]; Bonta and Protevi 2004; DeLanda 2016). In chapter 6 we will develop a similar tripartite description of the notion of atmosphere.

11. In the words of Ben Anderson and Colin McFarlane, the assemblage in this way becomes a tool to zoom in into urban aspects, relations and bodies hitherto overlooked, and to cultivate 'a certain ethos of engagement with the world, one that

experiments with methodological and presentational practices in order to attend to a lively world of differences' (2011, 126).

12. We are aware that this section may result theoretically dense, especially to the reader that has less familiarity with the philosophy of Spinoza and Deleuze, as well as with recent 'new materialist' literature. While the hurried reader may be tempted to simply jump the next few pages, however, we believe that they will find the conceptual coordinates here traced to be progressively unpacked, in their sociological, geographical, methodological and analytical dimensions, across the book—thereby progressively making the strategic role for our arguments evident.

13. With 'vital materialism' we do not simply refer to the work of Jane Bennett, who appears to have coined the term in her enormously successful *Vibrant Matter* (2010), but more generally to a tradition of thinkers, mentioned below, who have differently thought the relation between life, matter and affect, at least since William James and Alfred North Whitehead, all the way to contemporary 'new materialism', within which Bennett's work is itself usually included.

14. See Pavoni (2018a, 32–35). Of course, this paragraph already moved beyond Spinoza and towards Deleuze, who provides such an elaboration of the distinction between actual and virtual, through Henri Bergson. While there is no room to discuss these terms here, it is important to stress that the concept of virtual should not be confused with that of the 'possible'. It is exactly to challenge the classical opposition between 'possible' and 'real' that the concept of virtual was created. Differently from the possible, which is by definition not real, the virtual *is* real, although non-actual. It is real since it has real effects on the actual. In this sense it is *material*: though being non-actual, it continuously 'haunts', that is, acts and insists upon the actual. In the words of one of us, 'actual and virtual are "the two sides of the Real", only formally but not ontologically distinct: neither dualism, nor univocity, but rather a *double structure*' (Pavoni 2018a, 28; emphasis in original; see especially Deleuze 2004[1968] and 1991[1966]).

15. Needless to say, rarely do we actually know what *really* make us flourish or debilitates us, what is truly joyful or sad. In this social chemistry, relations between bodies are in turn influenced by the individual and social ideas about them, which may be 'adequate' or 'inadequate': I may be in love for someone that is poisonous for me, that decreases my power to act, and yet I may delude myself in thinking otherwise (incidentally, the notion of 'adequate' and 'inadequate' ideas is key to the ethical theory of Spinoza since his early *Treatise on the Emendation of the Intellect*, where the task of his philosophy, developing adequate ideas with respect to our nature and, eventually, God, is presented. There is no room here to provide an even brief account that would be *adequate* to the complex theory of knowledge that subtends this notion). At the social level, such delusions may generate various sorts of monsters, such as the essentialised understanding of property, nation or family, the heteronormative patterning of reality, the politics of fear fostering discourses of security, and other crystallisations of power-structured configurations of force and value whose rigidity conceals their conflictual process of emergence. Likewise, the

techno-normative forms of mediation through which our daily lives unfold may be inherently debilitating (Stiegler 2016[2015]). Given that, notwithstanding more than a century of deconstruction, we still cling onto the separation between (the ideas of the) mind and (the affects of the) body, misunderstandings about the debilitating quality of relations abound in society, a blindness for the chemistry of social atmospheres, which, as we are to see, is perfectly epitomised by the way pernicious and suffocating forms of violence are routinely overlooked, and therefore keep functioning, deeply sedimented and crystallised in barely perceptible habits, structures and institutions. The relation between knowledge and affect, mind and body, ideas and matter, therefore, remains crucial, well beyond 'flat ontological' simplifications which would simply collapse their distinction. Incidentally, this is something a whole strand of contemporary materialism that often claim Spinoza among its principal inspirations has tragically forgotten: while Spinoza radically overcomes the ontological separation between mind and body that grounds the Cartesian dualism, he did not simply assume mind and body, ideas and matter, as the same thing. There remains a crucial difference between ideas and bodies, as he explains since the second definition opening his work, when observing that bodies are limited by other bodies, thoughts by other thoughts, and yet 'a body is not limited by a thought nor a thought by a body' (2002[1677a], p. I, def. 2). As Massumi notes, 'a power to affect and be affected governs a transition, where a body passes from one state of capacitation to a diminished or augmented state of capacitation. This comes with the corollary that the transition is felt. A distinction is asserted between two levels, one of which is feeling and the other capacitation or activation. But the distinction comes in the form of a connection. This separation-connection between feeling and activation situates the account between what we would normally think of as the self on the one hand and the body on the other, in the unrolling of an event that's a becoming of the two together' (2015, 48). We may trace the value of this notion of idea as an ordering principle immanent to the assemblage of bodies in two authors which have both been differently in love with Spinoza. Karl Marx and his theory of real abstraction, and Gilles Deleuze and his notion (with Felix Guattari) of diagram or abstract machine. These concepts, with all due qualifications and differences, responds exactly to the necessity to develop a materialism which would not be satisfied with assuming that everything *does* matter, but that also stresses that this does not entail ontological flatness (see Pavoni 2018a).

16. Although, we must say, it is difficult to find, in contemporary works that are usually indicated as belonging to a vital materialist perspective, the amount of naivety that critiques to this perspective often seem to imply (see Gamble 2019).

17. Thus Massumi writes: 'what is a quality of life, construed as a value? The answer is simple: a qualitative life value is something that is *lived for its own sake; something that is a value in and of itself, in the unexchangeable "currency" of experience*' (2018, T28; emphasis in original).

18. 'We neither strive for, nor will, neither want, nor desire anything because we judge it to be good; on the contrary we judge something to be good because we strive

for it, will it, want it, and desire it' (Spinoza 2002[1677a], p. III, pr. 9, scholium). It follows that there is no Good or Evil with respect to which violence would have to be defined and evaluated, but only good and bad relations, where *good* is what increases our capabilities, whereas *bad* is what poisons and debilitates us. Incidentally, this stress on capability resonates with the important work developed on this matter by the likes of Martha Nussbaum and Amartya Sen, although of course our ontological premises are radically different.

19. "'Why did *this* patient get this disease at this time?"' . . . the whole basis of the case-control is to discover how sick and healthy individuals differ' (Rose 1985, 427).

20. A classic example is the famous 1954 essay by Paul F. Lazarsfeld and Robert K. Merton on friendship on a Philadelphia mixed-race housing project.

21. See on the critical question of the role politics play vis-à-vis vital material-ism, the interesting forum (Braun et al. 2011) dedicated to Jane Bennett's *Vibrant Matter*, with reviews from Bruce Braun, Ben Anderson, Steve Hinchliffe, Christian Abrahamsson and Nicky Gregson, plus the response from the author which, argu-ably, does not manage to dissolve some of the doubts about the depoliticising poten-tial of her nonetheless intriguing approach.

PART I

~

FOUNDATIONS

CHAPTER ONE

~

Violence

> For WARRE, consisteth not in Battell lonely, or the act of fighting; but in a tract of time, wherein the Will to contend by Battell is sufficiently known: and therefore the notion of Time, is to be considered in the nature of Warre; as it is in the nature of Weather.[1]

Countless have been the analyses, speculations and conceptualisations around the notion of violence, and we do not intend to propose any comprehensive literature review here—many existing works, collections and readers are more than sufficient for this purpose (e.g., Aijmer and Abbink 2000; Schmid and Schroder 2001; Scheper-Hughes and Bourgois 2004b; Lawrence and Karim 2007b; Rae and Ingala 2019). Our objective is to set the stage for the following discussion on *urban violence*, by, first, challenging the reductionisms that the notion of violence often features in the fields of philosophy, sociology, political economy and anthropology; and, then, moving beyond them by exploring political economic and affective/material articulations vis-à-vis violence. Finally, third, we develop the concept of infra-structural violence (hyphenated because it is inspired by, but takes some steps beyond, recent works on infrastructural violence) as the main instrument we adopt to overcome said reductionism.

Before moving forward, let us remark that we are more than aware of the variety of valuable perspectives that have emerged in social research, leading critical thinking beyond many misunderstandings, stereotypes and limitations—we will resort to those perspectives throughout the entire book. Those misunderstandings, however, are still alive and kicking, framing, explicitly or implicitly, the way most of us think, imagine, feel and *see* violence; and this is particularly the case when it comes to urban violence. This will be particularly evident in the next chapters, where we show how they often orient official and everyday discussions on the relation between violence and the city, including those emerging from the fields of urban studies and geography. In a heuristic way, for the purposes of this chapter, let us indicate five main reductionist tendencies, which often intersect and overlap in thinking about (urban) violence: first, placing violence outside the social, i.e., the *naturalisation* of violence; second, recognising violence only when it manifests itself *qua* (direct) violence, i.e., the *fetishisation* of violence; third, judging violence as a merely destructive phenomenon, i.e., the *moral condemnation* of violence; fourth, framing violence as a merely socio-cultural phenomenon, i.e., reduction of violence to *culture*; fifth, explaining violence away by referring it to only deeper structural processes, i.e., the *abstraction* of violence.

Violence Reductionism

What is violence? This is a tempting question, which carries the seeds of its own contradictions, already foreclosing the problematic field that the *question* of violence promises to open. Enclosing violence in a substantial definition would equate to positioning it outside of history, geography, society: outside the dense relationality that constitutes it. To be sure, sociobiological arguments about the inherent violence of human nature are untenable as they rest on a false dichotomy, that of society *versus* nature, whose preposterousness even Western thinking is finally confronting. Further, *naturalising* violence is an equally dangerous trick: one may say, the founding stone of the conceptual matrix of political sovereignty that has oriented Western political thinking since its modern instantiation. Its most notorious locus, needless to say, can be found in Thomas Hobbes's double move: positioning violence within the brutal war of all against all that characterises the beastly state of nature; and monopolising violence into the hands of the as much beastly sovereign state (cf. Derrida 2009[2008]).

The naturalisation of violence is often accompanied by two other strategies. First, its *fetishisation* into a given form that delimits the aesthetic field of appearance of violence *qua* violence. Usually, within a positive law perspective, this is complemented by a juridical tautology, according to which the appearance of violence is determined by the legal definition of violence itself. In other words, the positioning of violence as a quintessentially non-social, or even anti-social, requires essentialising violence as a given thing, or event, which may be delimited, individuated and therefore excluded—whereas, of course, it is simultaneously, if surreptitiously, reincluded in the form of the legitimate use of force by the sovereign. Normally this has occurred by equating violence with so-called 'direct' violence, a term indicating forms of psycho-physical harm with a clearly identifiable chain of causality, between agent, intent and victim. Thus the World Health Organization defines violence as 'the intentional use of physical force or power, threatened or actual, against oneself, another person, or against a group or community, that either results in or has a high likelihood of resulting in injury, death, psychological harm, maldevelopment, or deprivation'[2]—a definition that still informs much (mainstream) scholarship on (urban) violence (Pavoni and Tulumello 2020).

Any self-evident or trivial understanding of violence unavoidably overlooks the fact that experience is always mediated by relations of power and knowledge.[3] 'A cause becomes violent in the precise sense of the word, when it enters into moral relations', wrote Walter Benjamin (1996[1921], 236), echoing the more general point made by Fredrich Nietzsche (2001[1882–87], 114) almost four decades before: 'there are no experiences other than moral ones, not even in the realm of sense perception'. Such an understanding of violence paves the way for a legalistic and statistical definition which is blind to unintentional, impersonal, systemic, institutional forms of violence, or simply those that are invisibilised by contingent socio-historical filters, as was historically (and often still is) the case for mobbing, gendered and domestic violence, racism and so on. As notable genealogies showed, the aesthetics of violence has been shaped by a process of invisibilisation that drew its normative power from the notion of civilisation, in turn shaped by the enormously violent process of colonisation (Elias 2000[1939]; Foucault 2003[1977]; Springer 2009b; Balibar 2015[2010]; Thiranagama et al. 2018).

While philosophy has long focused on ancient Greece in order to locate the inherently violent origins of Western metaphysics (Heidegger 2006[1938–39]), colonialism and the transatlantic slave trade are not just a stage in this history but also a bloody laboratory by which the perverse relation of modern political sovereignty with violence was crucially informed in conceptual, legal and aesthetic terms (e.g., Harney and Moten 2013). In the colony, the question of suppressing beastly violence through (sanctioned) beastly violence unfolded in its most explicit form, that is, as a violence against the quintessentially non-social: the uncivilised and savage other (see chapter 4). It is from the colony, moreover, that the apparatus of practices, discourses and laws constituting the 'colonial matrix of power' (Mignolo 2017) and violence boomerang back to the metropoles (cf. Césaire 2000[1950]; Arendt 1958), as we discuss further in subsequent chapters.

The problem with a trivial understanding of violence is also that of ending up with a simplistic and contradictory *moral condemnation* of violence as such: *biaphobia* (from the Greek word for violence, βία), that is, the assumption of violence as merely negative and destructive (Schinkel 2010). Violence, how-ever, can only be defined as destructive by framing it negatively with respect to some *a priori*, be it a God, the self, the community or life.[4] The definition of such an *a priori* is far from uncontroversial. In the same cul-de-sac ends up a positivistic understanding of violence, which defines it with reference to a law whose relation with violence remains unexplained. As many critical thinkers have shown, any society's condemnation of violence, whether moral or legal, is never clear-cut, but rather part of a field of negotiation around the definition, and il/legitimate use, of violence—different, and more complex, is the case of theories of nonviolence, to which we will come back below.

In a sense, the naturalisation, fetishisation and condemnation of violence constitute a violent process in itself, defining thresholds of acceptability, legitimacy and legality, which are never absolute or innocent, but in turn re-quire a (violent) process of installation. This is the core of the critical philo-sophical reflection around violence that has traversed Western thinking. Otherwise different political theories, such as Rousseau's, Hobbes's, Locke's or Bentham's, are equally grounded on the idea of a civilising process that, by means of some form of institutional monopoly of force (be it a Leviathan, general will or law), is meant to gradually expunge (direct, physical) violence from the *socius*. From Solon to Pindar, from Pascal to Weber, from Benja-min to Fanon, from Derrida to Agamben, from Butler to Esposito, Western thinking has been grappling with these contradictions for millennia. From these reflections there emerged an awareness of the violent state of exception that grounds the political paradigm of sovereignty, that is, the foundational presupposition of an 'outside', which plays the role of a negative, dialectical counterpoint that sustains the installation of authority, the legitimacy of its power and the legality of its deployment of violence. The malicious ambigu-ity of this mechanism is effectively expressed by the complex polysemy of the German word *Gewalt*—standing simultaneously for power, authority and violence—captured by Roberto Esposito's circular definition: 'in the final analysis, this is what law is: violence against violence in order to control violence' (2011[2002], 29). As Benjamin (1996[1921]) understood, the quintessential purpose of law is nothing but self-preservation (see a parallel argument on security in chapter 3).

For all the efforts to clearly define it, and thus confine it into a set of acts, behaviours, places or races, therefore, violence is rather an undefinable, mag-matic force. No attempt to instantiate an order can avoid coming to terms—

and become complicit—with violence: the result will never be an elimination of violence but rather its crystallisation in certain forms and apparatuses,
as well as its proliferation and overflowing into others. There seems to be an
excessive and overflowing quality to violence, whose consistency is akin to
that of a diffuse vapour that is part of the air we breathe: it can never be simply eliminated, but rather requires some sort of containment, a process that
is always complex, ambiguous and dangerous. As we are to see more in depth
in chapter 6, that violence is 'in the air' is neither a commonplace nor just
a metaphor for indicating its invisible normalisation but, more precisely, an
indication of its materiality. This is the key import of René Girard's (1972)
reflection on violence as a pervasive and contagious force that is constitutive
of the social, and is at the same time productive and disruptive, insofar as fu-
elling the common desire that holds the social together and, simultaneously,
threatens its collapse.[5] Violence is equivocal, ambiguous, disseminated,
as Etienne Balibar (2015) explains; like the Foucauldian power, violence
does not belong to individuals or acts but emerges from relations that are
never clearly defined once and for all—violence is mobile, metamorphic,
fluid. Elaborating on this *pharmakon*-like (i.e., simultaneously *remedy* and
poison) quality of violence, Esposito (2011[2002]) argues that the (Western)
juridical-political paradigm can be understood as an immunitary logic tasked
with neutralising the immanent tendency of social relations to overflow individual boundaries—their inherent violence—by keeping, as much violently,
the normative separation between individuals in place.

We locate our understanding with philosophical approaches to violence
as co-substantial with the very surfacing of social formations, rationality and
politico-legal institutions; and we examine it with critical theory's historical
and spatial lenses, revealing the (colonial, racialised, gendered, class, etc.)
dynamics through which violence has been crystallised in said formations
and institutions. Further, we believe it is necessary to integrate our understanding with the way anthropology has shown that violence is not simply
destructive and dis-ordering, but also a generative and creative force, feeding
processes of ordering that are not necessarily institutional, let alone oppressive. What is relevant for our argument is how this suggestion points toward
a tripartite understanding of violence. First, violence is a diffuse *continuum*
(cf. Scheper-Hughes and Bourgois 2004a), which does not 'sit' in places,
species, classes or races, but overflows these boundaries while simultaneously
contributing to their maintenance (Springer 2011).[6] Second, violence is not
exogenous but rather *endogenous* to the social, that is, articulated through
social-historical (cultural, moral, political, economic, etc.) relations, while
at the same time excessive to said relations, and therefore never fully ex-

plainable through them, nor reducible to functionalist-economic structures or ideologies. 'Violence can never be seen outside its own structure, which operates at multiple levels—historical, rhetorical, and practical', write Bruce Lawrence and Anisha Karim, adding that 'violence is always and everywhere process. As process, violence is cumulative and boundless. It always spills over' (2007a, 8–10). In this sense, our concept resonates with Jonathan Luke Austin's suggestion to understand violence as an asubjective, viscous plasma which is all pervasive, non-deterministic and felt differentially by bodies (2023; see chapter 6).[7] Third, violence is also an ontologically *productive* process, not only disordering but also ordering, not only disruptive of existent relations, but also generative of new ones (see Wall 2020; Handel 2021). We conceptualise violence, to sum up, as a diffuse, endogenous, excessive and creative process. The rest of this chapter is dedicated to unpacking this understanding, in the direction of an infra-structural conception of violence able to provide the tools for a critical diagnostics of (urban) violence that does not presuppose it—and thus explain it away—as anomalous, exogenous and non-social.

It goes without saying, this approach has no intention to either moralise or romanticise violence. Following Neil Whitehead (2007b, 41):

> The problem now is not how to end violence but to understand why it occurs in the ways it does. This involves recognition that violence is as much a part of meaningful and constructive human living as it is an imagination of the absence and destruction of all cultural and social order.

Beyond Reductionism

The notion of violence carries with itself 'the departure-from-order, the un-order, the dis-order, the out-of-order' (Rapport 2000, 41), as its etymological relation with the notion of *violation* suggests. Indeed, some, like Christopher Courtheyn (2018), suggest that violence should be understood only *as* violation. Other instances such as self-defence, though possibly harming, he argues, should not be categorised as violence, since they do not imply violation but rather a resistance against violation. How do we define, however, the self that is 'defended' against violations (cf. Butler 2020)? As for other notions such as ontological security (cf. Giddens 1991), taking for granted the ontological *a priori* that violence would supposedly *violate* exposes the reasoning to the risk of infinite regress. Elaborating on Raymond Williams's observation, that the interaction between violence and violation lies in 'the breaking of some custom or some dignity' (2007, 181), Courtheyn qualifies that with violence he refers to the 'violation of dignity'. In turn, he reformulates the concept as 'ecological dignity', namely a relation 'in which human and non-human life flourishes across networked community struggles' (2018, 743). In a similar vein, Judith Butler recently sought to think violence as an 'attack on "bonds"', that is, a violation of the interconnected relations of inter-dependency between 'human lives' as well as 'other sensate creatures, environments, and infrastructures' on which we depend and that 'depend on us, in turn, to sustain a livable world' (2020, 16). Nonviolence, in this sense, is not simple abstention from harming. It rather unfolds from acknowledging the constitutive relation of co-implication and co-dependency that constitute the common world: it is a *force* fed by 'the normative aspirations that follow from that prior social relatedness' (ibidem, idem).[8] While appreciating these attempts to rethink peace and nonviolence within an 'energetic' rather than moral conception of peace (see Dietrich 2012; chapter 9), we are wary of the contradiction that lies in developing a theory of (non)violence from the normative presupposition of an ontological *a priori* (e.g. 'social relatedness', 'ecological dignity') that is assumed as somehow free from violence.[9]

A similar contradiction emerges in those strategies that acknowledge the creative quality of violence but still seek to frame it within a normative account. This is the case of Nigel Rapport (2000), who bridges between philosophy and anthropology to provide a compelling account of the creative quality of violence. While Butler (1990) had elsewhere distinguished between 'normative violence'—i.e., the violent crystallisation of a worldview that characterises the process of socio-cultural normalisation—and a nonviolence that interrupts and destabilises the former, Rapport argues that violence cannot be expunged from the latter dimension either. If creativity is assumed as transformative vis-à-vis existing socio-cultural relations, his argument goes, then it necessarily entails violation: 'doing violence to current norms is fundamental to individual creativity' (Rapport 2000, 51). Yet, Rapport as well resorts to a normative compass to pre-emptively define what is acceptable and inacceptable violence. He thus distinguishes between 'democratic violence', which 'enables individual creativity to live beneath an ambiguous surface of social-structural calm and within a form of behavioural norms which individuals continue to share' and 'nihilistic violence', which 'breaches the surface of civil exchange, breaks the shared forms of behaviour'; a violence, therefore, 'to which others cannot adapt, behaviour which others cannot expect or predict and find meaningful in some way; only nihilistic violence makes mutual expectation and diversity impossible'. In this way, he concludes, it could be possible to 'reach a point of accommodation between the violence of universal and ubiquitous individual creativity on the one hand and the civility of social structure on the other' (idem, ibidem).

What if the 'civility of social structure' is not a given, however? Is a violence that compromises 'mutual expectations' such as the 1791 slave revolution of Haiti necessarily nihilistic? For Jacques Rancière (2001), for instance, politics cannot be positively judged upon in advance, since it entails the breaking down of the parameters on which such a judgment would have been premised. Politics, in other words, surfaces when mutual expectability and civility breaks down, in this way showing their historically contingent fabric. Again, we see the perils of any attempt that seeks to deal with violence by normatively and dialectically delimiting, a priori, its field of acceptability.

A controversial, non-normative approach was famously put forward by Pierres Clastres in his *Archaeology of Violence* (2010[1980]). By drawing on his research on so-called 'primitive society', Clastres brilliantly twisted the Hobbesian theory of violence, embracing its ontological pessimism, while dismissing its reactionary deductions. 'What is primitive society?', asks Clastres, and thus answers:

> It is a multiplicity of undivided communities which all obey the same centrifugal logic. What institution at once expresses and guarantees the permanence of this logic? It is war, as the truth of relations between communities, as the principal sociological means of promoting the centrifugal force of dispersion against the centripetal force of unification. (idem, 276–277)

Hobbes was right, Clastres argues, to emphasise the contradictory relation between violence and the State, and the extent to which the latter is constituted by an exclusionary relation to the former—that is, an exceptional logic of inclusive exclusion (cf. chapter 3). Since he was 'incapable of thinking of the primitive world as a non-natural world', however, Hobbes did commit an 'enormous error': he 'believed that the society which persists in war of each against each is not truly a society; that the Savage world is not a social world' (idem, ibidem). As Esposito sums up, for Hobbes, 'if the relation between men is in itself destructive, the only route of escape from this unbearable state of affairs is the destruction of the relation itself' (2009[1998], 27). What Clastres's interpretation suggests, instead, is that this relation is neither necessarily destructive nor natural, it is instead fully social—and violence is inherently part of it. The social is an ontological 'civil war', yet one that is rather different from the Hobbesian 'war of every man against every man'. Hobbes presupposes an ontology whose building blocks are fully-formed entities, that is, individuals. The 'multiplicity' that Clastres refers to, influenced by the thought of Gilles Deleuze, is instead a relational ontology in which 'war' does neither concern the relation with the other (as if the other would be an already constituted individual), nor a relation *between* individuals, but rather the relation itself, the relation *out of which* individuals, social formations, communities and so on emerge (see Ronchi and Stiegler 2019). 'We should ask: How can the "war of each against each" have begun before each person had been produced as each. And then we will see how the modern State presupposes the state of things that it produces' (Tiqqun 2010[2009], 95). In the Deleuzian jargon, this entails a shift from a 'molar' to a 'molecular' understanding of violence or, in the Foucauldian jargon, a shift from a macro to a microphysics of power.

In the 1975–1976 course at the College de France published as *Society Must Be Defended*, delivered in the same years in which Clastres was working on his *Archaeology*, Michel Foucault (2003[1977]) observed that power is neither to be understood as a mere mechanism of repression, nor merely within a cumbersome functionalist-economic logic—i.e., as the reproduction of relations of production. Instead, it should be understood 'first and foremost in terms of conflict, confrontation, and war' (idem, 15). Famously overturning von Clausewitz's motto, Foucault stated that 'power is war, the continuation of war by other means' and thus:

> politics is the continuation of war by other means . . . Power relations, as they function in a society like ours, are essentially anchored in a certain relationship of force that was established in and through war at a given historical moment . . . The role of political power is perpetually to use a silent war to reinscribe that relationship of force, and to reinscribe it in institutions, economic inequalities, language, and even the bodies of individuals. (idem, 15–16)

One can hardly find a more lucid description of the 'silent violence' (cf. Watts 1983) of the political order and its inscription into socio-economical, juridico-political and ideological structures. What is particularly relevant for us is the ontological premise of this reflection, presenting the social as an immanent and contingent process of emergence of social formations, heterogeneous agglomerations of forces and mutually-affecting bodies. This ontological understanding, we believe, is necessary if we are to attend to the radical materiality of violence, as the next section begins to do.

Affects, Power, Value

From the microlevel of particles, viruses and bacteria to the macrolevel of societies and ecosystems, bodies are immersed in complex relational entanglements by which are oriented and shaped prior of them becoming conscious, in ways that far surpass their awareness. I eat an apple, Annemarie Mol writes (2008), and yet my 'I' is overflown by a complex assemblage of bodies, processes and transformations occurring all the way from bacteria within my bowels to the socio-economical structure. This is why, as per Deleuze's Spinozist formula, *we do not know what a body can do*, since we only have a limited consciousness, not to mention knowledge, of the affective relations that compose us, and the powers they harbour (Deleuze 1988[1970], 18–19). We do not know, and yet we necessarily strive to persevere on our own (see introduction). This perspective, which foregrounds our argument, implies an ethics of encounter and a politics of entanglements, or atmospheres, that need be fleshed out (see chapter 6). If we understand (human and non-human) beings as always enmeshed within affective relations, then the either beneficial or toxic nature of these relations is what counts as crucial, consistent with the social chemistry we began to sketch in the introduction.

It is important to underline the double quality of affects thus understood. While affects are always mediated through power-structured relations and imaginaries, they are not exhausted into them. There is an affective structure to fear or hope, that is, a becoming-fearful, a becoming-hopeful, which can neither be explained with sole reference to a specific socio-historical context, nor independently from it (Ahmed 2004; Protevi 2009; Massumi 2015). Approaches that occupy one side or another of the structure/agency dichotomy are unable to account for the circulation of affects (which is always transversal and never secondary to the supposed free will of a self-sufficient subject) and for its excess (which overflows structuralist closures rather than expressing a simple opposition—and therefore dialectic confirmation—to the structure itself). We believe this dichotomy needs to be overcome altogether. However, this cannot be done by simply having done with structures. What is required instead is a finer understanding of the way structures materialise in and through socio-material relations, through a distributed notion of agency and a processual understanding of structur(ation). This is where Spinoza's geometry of affects, via Nietzsche's genealogical method, meets the Foucauldian micro-physics of power.

Power, according to Foucault, is a relation of forces that is immanent and productive to the social field at the 'molecular' level (hence a microphysics). Power, in other words, is the ontological premise to the surfacing of such 'molar', and indeed moral, stratifications such as subjects, families, states. This does not imply, however, that power be a pure dimension ontologically separated from the stratifications. Never pure, innocent or neutral, power is always taken into apparatuses and processes of integration, stratification and stabilisation, which are always historically situated. The social is never homogeneous and undifferentiated, but rather always synched, or 'tuned' (Pavoni 2018a), by processes of ordering, which emerge socio-historically and gain solidity through time, crystallising around stable distributions of ideas, feelings, opinions, practices, habits, norms and institutions. Each epoch is characterised by regimes, regularities, normativities and subjectivations, which emerge out of molecular intra-actions (cf. Barad 2003, see below) filtered by given apparatuses, a concept indicating, according to Foucault (1980[1977], 194),

> a thoroughly heterogeneous ensemble consisting of discourses, institutions, architectural forms, regulatory decisions, laws, administrative measures, scientific statements, philosophical, moral and philanthropic propositions—in short, the said as much as the unsaid. The apparatus itself is the system of relations that can be established between these elements.

The Nietzschean premises of the ontology we are adopting imply that there are no prior ontological forms, absolute orders or systems of values that may be assumed as given and from which transhistorical normative orientation may be provided. Obviously, this does not mean falling into chaos. The key to the genealogical method is not that of denying significance or existence to moral parameters of evaluation, but that of analysing the historical apparatuses into which power is organised, and thus the related logics of structuration, integration, stabilisation, on the premise that power is not *held* by such apparatuses but only exercised through them. Once we remove the absolute ground to morality, in other words, we do not fall into relativism, we rather open up the conditions for a strategic approach that explores the relation of power and force that make a given system of values emerge and crystallise in a given epoch.[10] What role does violence play here?

We could argue that the notion of violence as a diffuse, excessive and creative process we presented above is not so different from the understanding of power we just encountered. This is a good thing according to Lawrence and Karim (2007a, 13), since understanding violence as 'equivalent to power and endemic to the human condition' may help calibrating attention 'to ways that one can respond to its outcomes'. Others, like Johanna Oksala (2012), think instead that such a broad definition of violence ends up conceptually inhibiting and politically damaging, insofar as it risks de-legitimising protest and other forms of political contestation. This is a valuable observation, which opens up serious strategic conundrums. How to distinguish between, say, fascist and anti-fascist violence, if they remain ontologically indistinguishable?[11] Looking for a way out from this impasse, Jacob Maze (2018) seeks help from another key thinker of violence, Hannah Arendt, and proposes to understand power as what *allows*—and violence what *prevents*—the possibility to act *otherwise*, that is, the possibility to be different. Violence, in other words, would be akin to what Foucault refers to as 'domination', namely 'when an individual or social group succeeds in blocking a field of power relations' (1997[1984], 283).

Yet, is not violence, as we argued above, also a possibility to unblock a congealed relation by *violating* it and in this way releasing the possibility for *being* otherwise? In other words, is not the disruptive quality of violence as violation exactly what holds its creative potential to *unblock* a field of power relations? We believe so. While inseparable from (that is, always coexistent with) it, violence does not coincide with power. While power is a relation of forces, violence 'consists in a destruction of form, in a decomposition of relation' (Zourabichvili 2012[1994], 69). By assuming so, however, are we not falling back into the merely negative condemnation of violence we were criticising above? To avoid this contradictory conclusion requires shifting from the macro/molar to the micro/molecular level. It is at this *intensive* level where forces, value and power belong, that violence takes place as a 'destruction' since, exactly *by means of* destructing, it does open the space for the possibility of creation to emerge.[12] At this intensive level, therefore, violence is to be understood as both the force that prevents (i.e., disrupts) the unfolding of 'new relations of forces' that may threaten the stability of a given configuration, *as well as* the unblocking of a given configuration, what *makes possible* the unfolding of 'the new relation of forces that subtends it [violence] and of which it [violence] is the concomitant' (Zourabichvili 2012[1994], 69). Violence, in this sense, appears as a tensional force concerning the immanent 'consistency' of the social—that is, its 'holding-together'—in terms of creative construction, integrating conservation or destruction. As also its etymology suggests,[13] violence both weaves together and threatens to disrupt the fabric of the social. This is the entanglement we are interested to analytically and critically explore.

Anthropology, as already hinted, has provided vast supporting material for attending to the inextricable relation between violence and morality, the fact that violence works as part of any cultural order (Whitehead 2007b). This is not to say that violence is simply a matter of cultural relativism, however.

There are no 'cultures of violence'—as the rhetoric of 'violent Orientalism' (Springer 2009a, 308) goes—but there is always culture *through* violence. Violence is not simply an element to be assessed according to a given system of values, it is rather a culture-producing force, which is simultaneously creative and disruptive vis-à-vis the system of values that make a culture. The etymological root that all these terms share suggests this possibility. Violence has to do simultaneously with the disruptive process of *violation* as with the creative process of *evaluation,* and valorisation. Violence always violates *and* evaluates (i.e., creates, as well as destroys, value) at the same time. As a consequence, it cannot be statically analysed vis-à-vis a given value (e.g. dignity, security, civility), but must be dynamically analysed as regards the problematics of *evaluation* it contributes to shape. Likewise, and consistent with the discussion so far developed, we do not understand evaluation as the static and abstract interpretation that a given subject *has* of a given object; rather, as a dynamic and concrete relation of valorisation through which subjectivation unfolds—a process of individuation which is individual and collective (cf. Simondon 1992[1964]).

This is, Martin Heidegger (1979[1961]) suggested, a key sense of Nietzsche's enigmatic notion of the transvaluation of all values. Not simply the substitution of a system of values with another, but the fact that beings and values are not separated, that beings *are* values or, more precisely, processes of evaluation. Thus understood, the question of value is rescued from the abstract dogmatism of morality and rather framed with respect to the embodied ethics our notion of vital materialism points to. Properly unpacking this understanding is crucial if we are to attend to the ontological genesis—the genealogy—of violence without falling into the perils of cultural relativism, wherein nature is assumed to be a passive surface on which cultural performances are inscribed—hence the 'culture of violence' rhetorics and the various impasses of multiculturalism. On the contrary—and in opposition to the 'naturalist' biological understanding of values as innate—'perspectivism' (the assumption that there are not interpretations elaborated by abstract subjects but perspectives produced by materially-situated bodies) asserts the contingency of values and thus sets out to explore the historical surfacing, and crystallisation, of systems of values.[14] Perspectivism, in other words, is a way to revoke at once the separation between ontology, epistemology and ethics, by asserting the inextricable entanglement of matter, discourse and value. Reality is multiple and truth is always dependent on a particular *regime*, as Foucault showed, produced by an apparatus that is material, discursive and strategic at the same time.[15]

In Karen Barad's (2007) materialist interpretation, an apparatus performs a 'cut' in the multiplicity of the world, producing a particular intelligibility, visibility and truth from the perspective of another part. Knowledge claims accordingly emerge out of material-discourse relations, they are perspectival and, in this sense, 'naturalistic' (Rouse 2009). In other words, they are not merely a matter of the more or less relativistic quality of idealistic projections: they are indeed *matter*, namely a material emergence, which produces a causality that is *dependent* on specific relational arrangements (there is objective causality, therefore, and yet this is partial, that is, it only exists within the relation between two 'parts' of the world that has been produced by the *cut*). As Barad writes, 'what we need is something like an *ethico-onto-epistem-ology*—an appreciation of the intertwining of ethics, knowing, and being—since each intra-action matters' (2007, 185; emphasis in original). 'The world', it follows, 'is not an epistemically homogeneous space of reasons and normative authority' (Rouse 2009, 201), as instead presupposed by those approaches that assume knowledge of, and access to, the world take place between pre-constituted rational agents that share a common frame of reference, and that 'objective accountability of knowledge' be conflated 'with procedural or aperspectival standards of justification' (idem, 202).

We may find this tendency working implicitly also in otherwise compelling accounts of urban violence such as the well-known works of Teresa Caldeira (2000) or James Holston (2007), which, as Gabriel Feltran (2020, 12) observes, still rely on a certain 'naturalised set of assumptions; that is to say, that of the state, which, explicitly or implicitly, presupposes democracy, citizenship and the public sphere as universals to be reached'—we will further expand on this aspect in relation to security (chapter 3) and its imaginary (chapter 4). As Barad would suggest, perspectivism focuses on intra-actions, rather than interactions. Differently from *interaction*, 'which presumes the prior existence of independent entities/relata', *intra-action* allows for thinking subjects and objects as emerging out of the relations and apparatuses in which these are organised (2003, 815). Therefore, knowledge can be said to emerge out of perceptual and affective intra-action, with specific material-discursive regimes that are unavoidably shaped by power relations.[16] In other words, power is the immanent ordering of the normative shape of knowledge, justification, judgments and thus relations at large, rather than simply the oppressive force imposed by some upon others.

Violence, we posit, does neither belong to nature nor to culture, it belongs to both: not simply socio-cultural, violence is socio-natural (or socio-material) and should be therefore explored *beyond* these foundational dichotomies, including those between matter and discourse, words and worlds. The mainstream understanding of violence, instead, is still organised around a major 'cut', what Alfred North Whitehead called the 'bifurcation of nature', that is, the separation between mind and matter, which surreptitiously articulates the binary thinking about violence—most importantly, violence *versus* society—we have been criticising so far. As we are to see, this cut is also at work in the way in which violence is discussed, between a supposedly 'real' and objective violence (direct, physical) and a 'cultural' form of violence that is assumed as relativistic. The phenomenon of violence, in this sense, is assumed to be a fact rather than the aesthetic result of a given material-discursive arrangement fed by that fundamental distinction between society and violence (needless to say, key distinctions such as order/ disorder or normal/abnormal, but also epistemology/ontology, are articulated around this very cut). As we are to see more in detail over the next chapters, from the society/violence cut that articulates the dominant understanding of urban violence, there emerges an apparatus—a security apparatus—made of laws (the relation between crime and violence and, most importantly, between non-crime and non-violence), institutions (the legitimation and monopoly of state violence) and *savoirs* (the use of statistics to assess the degree of violence), through which urban violence is made visible and invisible at the same time.

Discourse, meaning, language, representations and evaluations always emerge out of world's ongoing mattering, as the result of historical conditions, or apparatuses, which establish given constrains and thus articulate the domains of what can be said (the domain of the sayable, cf. Foucault 1994[1966]), seen (the distribution of the sensible, cf. Rancière 2004[2000]) or thought (the image of thought, cf. Deleuze 1968). In Barad's words:

> discursive practices produce, rather than merely describe, the 'subjects' and 'objects' of knowledge practices. On Foucault's account these 'conditions' are immanent and historical rather than transcendental or phenomenological. That is, they are not conditions in the sense of transcendental, ahistorical, cross-cultural, abstract laws defining the possibilities of experience (Kant), but rather they are actual historically situated social conditions. (2007, 147)[17]

This theoretical toolbox allows for complexifying otherwise punctual observations such as Sophie Body-Gendrot's (1995, 525), according to whom urban violence must be explored at 'the interplay between representations and the reality that people experience in certain urban environments'; or Scheper-Hughes's and Bourgois's (2004, 318), who remark that the 'social and cultural dimensions of violence are what give it its force and meaning'.

We second these suggestions, provided they are interpreted to their radical extent, removing the ontological distinction between representation and the reality, epistemology and ontology, things and words (e.g., Doel 1999). If the meaning of violence is always historically and materially contingent, it is not simply inscribed by socio-cultural discourses onto inert bodies, but rather emerges from their affective, material-discursive and more-than-human co-mingling. This perspective pushes beyond so-called 'standpoint theories' and their emphasis on the 'position' of given knower/observer. As Joseph Rouse explains, the attention is here moved from the 'observers' to the 'phenom-ena', and to the apparatus of observation through which the latter surfaces: 'meaningful differences in knowledge and understanding are not features of knowers or their epistemic location, but patterns in the world that show themselves differently in different contexts' (2009, 205). Epistemology and ontology are inextricable.

Likewise, we can interpret in radical sense Simon Springer's observation that 'violence as a mere fact is largely meaningless. It takes on and gathers meaning because of its affective and cultural content, where violence is felt as meaningful' (2011, 92). There is always a 'sense' (in its multiple dimensions of sensoriality, meaning and affective expression) to the event of violence, and this 'taking on and gathering meanings' is a process of emergence that unfolds in the coming together of discourses, power-structured relations *and* mutually affecting bodies as they organise or 'pattern' around a given 'cut' and the relative apparatus.[18] The meaning of violence, in other words, emerges out of material-affective-discursive entanglement, whose potential indeterminacy is only resolved locally, and historically, as a result of power-structured material-discursive intra-actions.[19] This requires engaging simultaneously with violence's epistemological, ontological and ethical intersection with space (idem): as anticipated, an ethico-onto-epistem-ology of violence.

Let us unpack this further. A punch or a gunshot cannot be said to be 'violent' *per se*, even though they may surely be harmful, or even lethal. And yet, the emergent materiality of the relational situation in which something like a punch or a gunshot *becomes* violent cannot be *only* explained by making reference to economic or ideological structures: as if they were to mould a neutral matter *as* violent. Informed by Deleuze and Guattari (2004[1980], 408), a properly materialist approach to violence should refrain from 'imposing a form upon a matter', since 'what one addresses is less a matter submitted to laws than a materiality possessing a *nomos*'. What does it mean? In the same way as the carpenter working the wood does not have before herself a homogenous matter but rather a singular complexity of fissures and cracks, porosities and knots that she must follow, the 'meaning' of violence is a material-discursive emergence that requires exploration through the historically-situated fissures and cracks, porosities and knots, of its unfolding. In Barad's (2007, 152) helpful synthesis: 'the point is not merely that there are important material factors in addition to discursive ones; rather, the issue is the conjoined material-discursive nature of constraints, conditions, and practices'. One may say that guns in the USA do play a role, as agential matter that cannot be simply reduced to the socio-economic violence of American society or the representation of gun violence in its imaginary. Just in the same way, the 'stray bullets' of Rio de Janeiro, Ben Penglase (2011, 414) argues, rupture the internal dynamics of the urban economy of violence, introducing an element which is wildly aleatory and transversal to social classes, in this way contributing 'to the reification of violence as an out of control "thing", and the essentialization of Rio as a "violent city"' (see also Larkins 2015, 13). This occurs, in other words, not simply as result of the meaning of socio-economic relations that are inscribed on stray bullets, but also as result of the 'meaning' that their material existence does produce in the frictional encounter with these very structures and processes. The meaning of violence is produced by situated (urban) intra-actions, which shape—and are shaped by—material-discursive arrangements whose normative force affects the way a social field is visibilised and invisibilised, sensibilised and anaesthetised.

This means that, while we agree with Scheper-Hughes and Bourgois (2004a, 2) that violence is not *sui generis*, this does not depend on it being 'in the eye of the beholder', as they put it, but more precisely on the fact that violence is in the *bodies* of the holders and in the concatenations in which they are taken.[20] Violence, in other words, is in the bodies and their tensional holding-together—it is a question of *consistency* (Deleuze and Guattari 2004[1980], 327). It follows that it is imprecise to say that violence is 'used' by given agents. Rather, given agents *become* through the violence engrained in the specific, material-discursive arrangement to which they belong. The meaning of violence is not projected by a subject onto matter: it is a feature of the world and its aesthetic, affective, discursive and, further, technological patterning.[21] Paraphrasing Barad then, the meaning of violence we will adopt in this book is not that of an ideational or immaterial process, but rather a specific, material infra-structuration of the world, whose potential indeterminacy is resolved locally, and thus historically. Following this argument, as we are to see in the following chapters, it is evident that the *urban* of urban violence is a rather more significant dimension than simply an indication of the location where violence occurs: it rather indicates the specific, aesthetic, affective, discursive and material infra-structuration of the world out of which urban violence surfaces, and that we will explore with respect to its imaginary (chapter 4), process (chapter 5) and atmosphere (chapter 6).

In conclusion, let us qualify that understanding the genetic role that violence as violation/evaluation plays vis-à-vis systems of values—and therefore vis-à-vis social order—does not mean to say that violence is everything and everywhere, that is, to assume violence as a kind of ultimate ontological principle. This would simply make violence a useless concept. More precisely, it is about showing that any process of ordering unavoidably entails a degree of violence.[22] It is with respect to these processes of ordering that we wish to understand violence, not simply as a 'notion' which is culturally and morally framed within the power relations and discourses of a given context, but as a tensional, a rupturing force of generation, a preserving force of maintenance and a potential force of disruption of the infra-structural consistency of the world.

Critique of Violence

The attentive reader might have noticed in the last sentence more than a hint to the tripartite typology of violence that Benjamin proposed in his *Critique of Violence*. The argument of this seminal and at times enigmatic text unfolds from the assumption that violence, in itself, has never been subjected to a proper critique. What has been criticised, instead, is its field of application, assumed to be legitimate or not depending on the *way* in which, or the *ends* for which, violence was deployed. This conceptual frame—this dogmatic image of violence—is shared by the two principal traditions of legal philosophy, notwithstanding their apparent irreconcilability:

> if *natural law* can judge all existing law only in criticizing its ends, so *positive law* can judge all existing law only in criticizing its means. If justice is the criterion of ends, legality is that of means. Notwithstanding this antithesis, however, both schools meet in their common basic dogma: just ends can be attained by justified means, justified means used for just ends. Natural law attempts, by the justness of the ends, to 'justify' the means, positive law to 'guarantee' the justness of the ends through the justification of the means. (Benjamin, 1996[1921], 278; our emphases)

Benjamin's point therefore is that violence has always been addressed within the same epistemological field, namely the circle of the means-end argument, whose pernicious functioning we find at work today in the ethical deadlock of the liberal rhetoric of balance (between violence and peace, freedom and security, etc.; see chapter 3). In this way, within liberal regimes, violence is turned into a mere instrument that is functional to the preservation of the system: it is the given order, its stability and cohesion, that becomes the end in itself.[23] A proper *critique* of violence, instead, should be directed to violence itself: this is the core of Benjamin's intention to define violence *internally*, which is not to be understood as an attempt to find its essence but, more precisely, to explore violence in its *doing* (see Agamben 1998[1995]; 2005[2003]).

On the one hand, through this reflection Benjamin provides the foundational theory of the legal state of exception, showing how the historical dialectic of (state) violence is grounded on the violent imposition of an order (what he terms 'law-making' or 'law-positing' violence) which is gradually invisibilised into a legitimate monopoly of violence—that is, the structural violence aimed to preserve the order itself (what he terms 'law-preserving' violence).[24] Étienne Balibar (2015), likewise, argued that the political itself is in this sense postulated as the realm of the negation of violence. In this way, violence is lumped together, flattening its heterogeneity into a single category, which is then distributed according to different degrees of tolerability (a conceptual move that is supported by statistical reductionism, as we are to see more precisely vis-à-vis urban violence, see chapters 2 and 5). Political action, accordingly, comes to be grounded on a double negation of violence, a negation of its conditions (an attempt to make it impossible) and a negation of its material dissemination (a struggle against its perpetrators). In the system of law, the tension between the goal to eliminate violence and the need to employ (counter)violence against the perpetrators is solved via delegation/concentration of the monopoly of violence to an allegedly impartial authority and supposedly neat distinctions between peace/war, law/ transgression and so on.

On the other hand, inspired by George Sorel's *Reflections on Violence*, Benjamin introduces the obscure notion of 'divine' violence, which should neither be understood as a law-positing nor a law-preserving violence, but rather as a 'law-destroying' violence that *de-poses* the given order and, by (un)doing so, opens up the field of possibility for novel orderings to emerge. This tripartite typology of violence should be thought in the following sequence: the law-destroying violence, which de-poses the given order opening up a space of possibility; the law-positing violence, which prompts the surfacing of the stratification and stabilisation of an order out of this space of possibility; the law-preserving violence, the instrumental violence deployed to keep a given order in place, a violence that aims to preserve and *secure* the order by neutralising, that is, preventing, the potentials to be otherwise.

Benjamin's notion of pure or divine violence has been criticised for either its politically useless mysticism, or its danger to become an indirect apology of violence (e.g., Žižek 2008; Han 2018). However, Benjamin's theorisation can be co-opted to justify violence *per se* only at the price of deeply misunderstanding its conceptual force. What is peculiar to this concept is the radical refusal to enter the reproductive relation that keeps a given order in place, as well as the avoidance of any normative claim: pure violence does not *pose* or *presuppose* anything, as it does refuse any instrumental deployment of violence *against* a given order. In this sense it is radically different from the still normative theories of nonviolence we briefly touched upon, since it more precisely appears as a violence that de-poses the existent relations of power, thus opening the space of possibility for the surfacing of a different formation whose desirability, however, cannot be normatively established in advance.[25] Giorgio Agamben will subsequently elaborate this insight into his concept of 'destituent power', that is, a power that 'deactivates something and renders it inoperative . . . without simply destroying it but by liberating the potentials that have remained inactive in it in order to allow a different use of them' (2016[2014], 273; see also Boano 2021). While we second this interpretation, which simplifies and mobilises strategically Benjamin's intuition, we suggest that this notion of 'divine' or 'pure' violence could also be understood as what Clastres referred to as 'the centrifugal force of dispersion', which co-exists within every order and exceeds its 'centripetal force of unification' (2010[1980], 276–277)—in other words, with the creative and ambiguous social force of dispersion that gradually atrophies as result of the liberal instrumentalisation of violence as a mere tool to *secure* the given order.

As the attentive reader surely realised, there is more than a resonance between this creative and ambiguous force and the concept of vitality we introduced in the last chapter, namely as a differential, value- and norm-producing force that exceeds the socio-historical forms into which life itself is each time actualised. This convergence should not surprise. Violence is always potentially contained within the vital excess of life, and this goes to show both the ineliminability of violence—since eliminating violence does equate to eliminate life, by condemning it to atrophy—and the 'ambiguity' of a vital materialism that, as noted, does not lead to an uncritical celebration of life but rather prompts the ethical question of how to *care for*, and therefore *secure*, the 'surplus-value' of life (see introduction and chapter 9). The ethico-political consequence of this reasoning is crucial: the 'problem' of violence is neither that of eliminating violence *per se*, nor that of finding better ways to *use* violence, not even that of finding a *right balance* in such use; rather, it is that of addressing and reshaping the socio-historical configurations in and through which violence is each time organised, by releasing its *vital* generative force, while seeking to prevent overly destructive outcomes (we will make a parallel argument vis-à-vis security in chapters 3 and 9). In the next chapters we will develop an understanding of urban violence that attends to the frictional threshold where this ambiguous excess unfolds and to the debilitating effects that the suffocation of such excess may have on urban life at large. Prior to doing that, however, we still need to provide the conceptual basis for the relation between the urban and violence, that is, we need to engage with the economic, political and symbolic structures and discourses through which violence is always historically articulated. This is where we move next.

Structural/Symbolic Violence

Critical scholarship has provided historical, socio-economic and geographical lenses to complement the conceptual critique of the co-constitutive relation between violence and order (its making, preserving and destroying quality), by concretely exploring the apparatuses of power and knowledge that configure it, around dynamics of race, gender, class and so forth. This has complemented the philosophical de-essentialisation of violence with historical insights, linking the 'direct', physical and visible event of violence, to the cultural and linguistic background that shapes its very manifestation *qua* violence and thus naturalises it as such; and to the silent, invisible and systemic violence of economic, financial, legal and political structures. The two concepts which have played the most important role in shaping this understanding are those of *symbolic violence*, introduced by Pierre Bourdieu (e.g. 1991[1982/1983]), and *structural violence*, introduced by Johan Galtung (1969) and then elaborated in the field of anthropology by the likes of Paul Farmer, Nancy Scheper-Hughes and Philippe Bourgois, and so on. We will employ these two notions as category-umbrellas to encompass a panoply of notions which, while certainly not coincident with them, may be said to stem from the same fields of problematisation. These fields tend to converge in a structuralist understanding of violence that accounts for functionalist-economic and symbolic-cultural dimensions, and more precisely the way these dimensions function by reinforcing each other. Structural violence can be variously translated as 'abstract' (Tyner and Inwood 2014), 'normalised' (Bourgois 2001), 'colonial' (Fanon 1963[1961]), 'objective' (Zizek 2008), 'banal' (Yusoff 2012), 'silent' (Watts 1983), 'administrative' (Spade 2015) or 'infrastructural' (Rodgers and O'Neill 2012; Li 2018). Symbolic violence can be variously translated as 'epistemic' (Spivak 1988), 'epistemological' (Shiva 1988), 'cultural' (Galtung 1990), 'normative' (Butler 2004a; 2004b) or 'gendered' (Pain 2014). Of course, these distinctions are fuzzy, the intersections between these two groups abound and they cannot be explained in isolation.

Structural violence, in Galtung's account, is 'the violence [that] is built into the structure and shows up as unequal power and consequently unequal life chances' (1969, 170–171). It is unintentional and impersonal, since its intentions cannot be located within specific subjects, and its agency is distributed and systemic. Simply put, it is the invisible violence produced by structural inequalities. In Farmer's words, 'the concept of structural violence is intended to inform the study of the social machinery of oppression' (2004, 307).

Symbolic violence, on the other hand, has to do with the power-structured dialectic of recognition and misrecognition that keeps violence in place by translating, and thus invisibilising, its hierarchical asymmetries onto the backstage: 'a symbolic power is a power which presupposes recognition, that is, misrecognition of the violence that is exercised through it' (Bourdieu 1991[1982/1983], 209). Resonating with Antonio Gramsci's concept of hegemony, Bourdieu argues:

> symbolic power—as a power of constituting the given through utterances, of making people see and believe, of confirming or transforming the vision of the world and, thereby, action on the world and thus the world itself, an almost magical power which enables one to obtain the equivalent of what is obtained through force (whether physical or economic), by virtue of the specific effect of mobilization—is a power that can be exercised only if it is *recognized*, that is, misrecognized as arbitrary. (idem, 170; emphasis in translation)

While structural violence has to do with the reproduction of structural inequalities, symbolic violence supposedly smooths over such inequalities, usually pointing to the violence of ideology—this is particularly evident with the cognate concept of epistemic violence (Spivak 1988). Yet, whereas his dialectical stress on mis/recognition is quite close to the Marxian idea of ideology as false consciousness (cf. Schwartz 1997), Bourdieu developed this concept exactly as a way to overcome the 'intellectualism' of ideology theory, too reliant on notions of consciousness and representation. Merged with his well-known notion of habitus, symbolic violence is thus framed with respect to a veritable materialism of bodily dispositions, that is, by referring to the way ideological, discursive violence is 'converted into motor schemes and body automatisms' (Bourdieu 1990[1980], 69), in the form of a 'political mythology realized, *em-bodied*, turned into a permanent disposition, a durable way of standing, speaking, walking, and thereby of feeling and thinking' (idem, 69–70).[26]

For his part, in the same way as he did vis-à-vis structural violence, Galtung reframed the concept of symbolic violence, making it simpler and catchier, introducing the notion of 'cultural violence' to refer to 'those aspects of culture . . . that can be used to justify or legitimize direct or structural violence' (Galtung 1990, 291). With a tectonic metaphor, Galtung proposes to understand cultural violence as the relatively *invariant* fault line; structural violence as the rhythm of movement of tectonic plates, that is, the *process* through which 'patterns of exploitation are building up, wearing out, or torn down'; and direct violence as the manifest *event* of the actual earthquake unfolding at the surface (idem, 294). This image would suggest that cultural violence be 'a substratum from which the other two can derive their nutrients', as that 'a causal flow from cultural via structural to direct violence can be identified' (idem, 295). While conceding this is generally the case, Galtung was not fully convinced of his overtly rigid causal linearity, and therefore proposed to amend his own metaphor with another image meant to better express the interplay between these forms of violence: the 'vicious triangle of violence' (idem), composed by the three types of violence, at its vertexes, and by a causal flow of violence which may potentially occur in six different directions (two between each vertex), depending on the specific socio-spatial situation and historical sedimentation.

While this suggestion opens up to a more complex understanding, the way structural and symbolic violence have been for the most part processed by critical thinking has resonated more closely with the tectonic than with the geometric image, with symbolic and structural violence having been made to converge into forming the two sides (the ideological and the functionalist-economic, so to speak) of an often cumbersome structuralist understanding: on the one hand, the political economy of violence, which stratifies and gradually sediments into systemic, asymmetric and oppressive socio-economical formations; on the other, the ideology through which such strata are normalised into moral, aesthetic and legal frames that organise the division between legitimate and illegitimate violence, and indeed the very appearance of violence *qua* violence in a given society. This tendency is well represented by Slavoj Zizek (2008, 2) who proposes to distinguish between a 'subjective violence', *viz.* the direct and physical violence that 'is seen as a perturbation of the "normal", peaceful state of things'; and an 'objective violence', *viz.* the structural and cultural violence which is 'inherent to this "normal" state of things'. 'Objective violence is invisible since it sustains the zero-level standard against which we perceive something as subjectively violent' (idem, ibidem), the normative background with respect to which direct, subjective and physical violence is perceived as such, and given meaning and significance accordingly. If Galtung's triangle was a partial attempt to avoid a causal dichotomy, Zizek's interpretation perfectly reproduces it, in line with the most popular (rigidly) Marxist interpretation of structural violence.

Let us pause for a moment and clarify our position vis-à-vis structural violence. Not only do we believe this is a necessary concept for the value it has had, and still has, in the endeavour to de-essentialise and de-fetishise violence, in this way challenging the pernicious tendency to flatten the analysis of violence to its directly visible manifestation. But, moreover, a structurally-informed perspective is fundamental to understanding the political economic dimensions of the nexus between (global) urbanisation and violence (see chapter 5). As we discussed in the last chapter, it is with tools from political economy and vital materialism that we develop our conceptualisation of urban violence. However, this very articulation prompts us to identify, and move beyond, those approaches that rely on an excessively causal, dichotomous and deterministic understanding of the structural violence. The paths of these approaches lead towards problematic simplifications, 'collaps[ing] forms of violence that need to be differentiated, such as physical, economic, political, and symbolic variants or those wielded by state, market, and other social entities' (Wacquant 2004, 322). Within an overtly rigid Marxist lens, this occurs by conflating such forms as different projections of an overarching (violent) substratum, namely, the 'reality' of economic relations. This reductionism is quite evident in James Tyner and Joshua Inwood's (2014, 776) theorisation, according to whom '"real concrete" violence is neither transhistorical nor transgeographical, but the "appearance" of different social relations vis-à-vis access to the means of production'. While we strongly agree with their intention to de-naturalise violence by firmly positioning it within history and geography—it would be foolish, naïve or indeed dangerous to overlook the role played by such relations in shaping violence in its various forms—we believe that framing violence within such an overly functionalist-economic understanding be an over-simplification.

We are interested in exploring the relation between violence and the social also for its more ambiguous dimensions, which a utilitarian approach can hardly account for. From the archaic deployment of surplus of violence far beyond the 'limit of the useful', as explored by George Bataille (2000[1976]), to the ambiguous and coessential relation between violence, desire, communication and community theorised by René Girard (1972), to Pierre Clastres's *Archaeology of Violence* (2010[1980]), philosophy, social theory and anthropology have provided abundant challenges to this reductionism. As Clastres sarcastically asked, how do we account for the centrality of violence in the 'primitive societies' he was studying, wherein there are no logics of production and accumulation, and in which the 'ownership of the means of production' is a useless explicatory lens (2010[1980], 249; see above)? While we cannot surely fall into the conceptual deadlock of naturalising violence as intrinsic to the psycho-biological essence of the human, this suggests that the functionalist-economic lens is in need of sophistication, for several reasons.[27]

To begin with, if one of the main values of a notion like structural violence is that of challenging the acritical assumption that 'violence sits in places' (cf. Springer 2011) with its corollary stigmatisation of neighbourhoods, cities or indeed whole cultures as violent (Springer 2009a; 2009b), handling violence with linear determinism paradoxically ends up reproducing this very logic. It is again worth quoting Wacquant (2004, 322):

> a notion [of structural violence] threatens to stop inquiry just where it should begin, that is, with distinguishing various species of violence and different structures of domination so as to trace the changing links between violence and difference rather than merging them into one catchall category liable to generate more moral heat than analytical light.

The problematic strategic corollary is self-evident: reducing the question of violence to the invisible, structural oppression of symbolic/economic structures may lead to assume that once such hegemonic structures be removed and the equality between the material conditions restored, then violence will disappear from the picture. The belief in a classless society naturally free of violence is not only the symptom of a theological ontology but, as we are to see, it springs from the same utopian imaginary of the 'city without violence' that plays a paramount role in feeding contemporary (violent) politics of urban security (see chapter 4). Paradoxically, an overtly rigid, uniform and deterministic category of structural violence is vulnerable to become a measuring standard for reproposing those very evolutionary charts that the concept sought to dismantle in the first place. For instance, while the notion of structural violence, as we are to show, is usefully deployed against statistical simplification that assess cities as more or less violent according to the occurrence of crime, most notably homicide (see chapter 5); structural violence itself may become a homogenising category, positioning cities on yet another evolutionary chart that goes from the least to the most structurally violent, with the latter positions occupied by cities of the Global South, routinely framed as 'disorderly', 'feral', 'violent' and, therefore, as lagging behind in the civilising process (see chapter 4). Focusing on Farmer's own elaboration of the term, Moses Lino e Silva (2014, 316–319) for instance notes that, by positing a 'clear link between "violence", "poverty" and "slums"', structural violence ends up reproducing 'the same sort of grand schemes that divides the world into those that are assumed to be "good" and those that still need to catch up with a certain ideal of "goodness"'. In this way, the very concept of structural violence turns out to be violent, then, inasmuch as depriving the 'poor' of both agency and experience vis-à-vis violence itself.

Good intentions notwithstanding, when carelessly handled, the concept of structural violence may ultimately allow 'one to do without representation, or scripting, and to scorn the poor actors overwhelmed by their environment' (Latour and Hermant 1998, 90). While, as we showed already, we are not willing to have done with structures altogether, we cannot overlook the good deal of epistemological arrogance the notion of structural violence often implicitly betrays. Namely, the presupposition that the action of social members is guided by hidden structures of power and exploitation—i.e., the backstage of 'concrete' relations of production (the concrete, base infrastructure) where the levers and screws of the 'machinery' of oppression' is located—of which they are not aware, since under the influence of the ideological superstructure, but that the social scientist is nevertheless able to reveal, thus enlightening them (cf. Latour 2005, 250). For Moses Lino e Silva (2014) this operation ends up constituting a form of violence imposed over the very contexts investigated through the lens of structural violence.

If we are serious in understanding 'violence as operating along a continuum from direct physical assault to symbolic violence and routinized everyday violence, including the chronic, historically embedded structural violence' (Bourgois and Scheper-Hughes 2004b, 318), then it is important to get rid of a determinist causality that systematically robs of both experience and agency the very subjects who are supposed to undergo, endure, re-produce and *live* violence. 'Violence flows like a viscous plasma around us all', writes Austin (2023, 121), and this 'us' refers to a relational and dynamic ontology of bodies that are not preformed vis-à-vis violence but are rather immersed in it, at different degrees:

> While 'bounded space and enclosed communities' may exist, human beings (and other actors) are always 'in motion' between such spaces and create entanglements across them that constantly modify conditions of possibility for action. This point is important as it removes any deterministic reading of the plasma of violence. Instead, its effects are differentially felt by each and every person and in each and every situation that person may find themselves. (idem, 12)

Likewise, if we are willing to account for 'how violence itself constitutes the social and cultural order', then 'we also need to consider modes of killing and violence as important forms of cultural expression in their own right, not just as epiphenomena of "deeper" structural processes' (Whitehead 2004a, 70–71). The welcome move to deconstruct the innocence of violence's appearance *qua* violence by referring it to the symbolic-cultural and functionalist-economic structures that shape it, therefore, should not lead to explain away the materiality of violence into the abstract causality of a process in which social relations are functionally subsumed, and whose real nature is cloaked behind an ideological veneer. While providing crucial tools for understanding the 'macro', so to speak, forms of violence that stem from both security politics (see chapter 3) and urbanisation (see chapter 5), if they are used to explain deterministically the emergence of violence at the 'micro' level—e.g., by attributing all forms of physical violence as the direct result of the anomie produced by the forces of (re)production of the capitalist system—both notions of structural and symbolic violence risk abstracting violence. For this to be avoided, and to work towards a conceptualisation capable of articulating the macro and the micro, the economy and materiality of violence need to be rethought.

Infrastructure

We have argued that the trajectory of the concepts of symbolic and structural violence as an attempt to remove violence from nature risks ending up into the opposite cul-de-sac, that is, reducing violence to social and cultural structures. This is the risk one often encounters when dialectical synthesis is used to overcome, rather than unravel, conceptual dichotomies (society and nature, form and matter, discourse and reality, structure and agency). As observed, violence does neither belong to nature nor to culture: it is socio-natural. If violence 'can never be seen outside its own structure', write Lawrence and Karim, such structure 'operates at multiple levels—historical, rhetorical, and practical' (2007a, 8), and it is the interplay among these dimensions that (re)produces violence. Our goal is to find a way to account for this ongoing reproduction that does not jettison the value of structural thinking, while at the same time overcoming its deterministic and abstract understanding of causation, agency and ontology. Infrastructures hold the 'promise' to do so (Anand et al. 2018), expressing the tensional relations through which the encounter between structures and experience, abstraction and concreteness, materialises.

Recently, the concept of infrastructure has been the object of a renewed interest, to the extent that some have come to speak of an 'infrastructural turn', so much for social science and humanities' turn fatigue. The first step has been that of reconsidering the Marxist, metaphorical use of the concept, normally referred to the 'concrete' economic base of relations of production, which supports the edifice of society all the way to the ideological superstructure (cf. the work of Louis Althusser). Beyond metaphor, various authors have begun considering the physical materiality of infrastructures: the cables, wires, roads, pipes, channels, antennas and all the physical materials that compose the logistics of cities, states and the entire planet. 'Infrastructures shape the rhythms and striations of social life', write Anand and colleagues (2018, 4–5), and have been doing so for a long time, from the role played by railways in shaping colonial (Schivelbusch 2014[1977]) and urban (see chapter 2) imaginaries, to that of contemporary just-in-time logistics in shaping expectations and habits of work and consumptions worldwide. This makes them a compelling 'ethnographic site' to explore the material articulation of race, class, gender, and thus 'how more structural forms of violence often flow through material infrastructural forms, and to remind us that social suffering is often experienced in material terms' (Rodgers and O'Neill 2012, 405). In introducing a dedicated special issue, Rodgers and O'Neill propose the notion of 'infrastructural violence', a term meant to complement structural violence by looking more directly at the concrete forms through which that is mediated and reproduced, insofar as 'completely caught up within the workings of social, cultural, economic and political arrangements, structures and technologies' (idem, 403), with the purpose of revealing how 'relationships of power and hierarchy translate into palpable forms of physical and emotional harm'. Infrastructure, they add, 'is observable, its stakeholders identifiable, and its functions variable' (idem, 402).

The second step has been that of thinking infrastructure beyond its physical constitution, without falling back into metaphor, but rather unpacking its more profound materiality. First of all, recalling Barad's terms introduced above, we could say that infrastructure is more about intra-actions than interactions. As James Ferguson (2012, 559) writes:

> the 'infra-structure' that is of interest here is clearly not conceived as infrastructural in the Marxian sense (underlying, causally primary), nor is it imagined as a 'structure' in the structuralist sense (a symbolically integrated system awaiting decoding). We are rather closer to the domain of engineering, with infra-structure imagined as a set of (often literally) concrete arrangements that both coexist with and enable or facilitate other such arrangements. It is both a support-system that makes it possible (or impossible) for other things to exist and a way of making up a particular kind of social world. And it is 'infra' less in the sense of constituting a 'base' than in the sense of swarming omnipresence that is implied in Foucault's (1980) idea of 'infra-power'.

In other words, infrastructure is not only about connecting subjects, things and spaces—it is about *making*—and being *made* by—them. Not simply planning and engineering, it has to do with a 'multi-species co-engineering', a relational praxis of world-making shaped by history, power and structures, in which notions of 'nature', 'technology', 'environment', 'institution' and 'society' are ontologically entangled (cf. Haraway 2016; Doherty 2019; Castro 2019). Although there has been a long-standing tendency to treat infrastructures as a technological tool employed by human societies on the environmental backdrop of nature, the Anthropocene is only the most spectacular and existentially threatening reminder of the conceptual inconsistency, and indeed lethal consequences, of doing so (Enns and Sneyd 2021). Seriously overcoming ontological separations by gazing directly into this 'in between' (*infra*), to be sure, does not mean unfolding a flat homogeneity, but rather a heterogeneous complexity consisting of beings that are 'made' and 'held' together by all sorts of infra-structures, namely articulations of intra-actions and infra-powers that are historically congealed into given patterns and modes of being that require a novel conceptual, methodological and epistemological attention. A helpful suggestion in this sense has notably come from AbdouMaliq Simone (2004) and his notion of 'people as infrastructure'. Here, the concept of infrastructure is posited decidedly beyond 'the physical channels through which people and object flow' (Rodgers and O'Neill 2012, 405), so as to encompass 'people's activities in the city', that is, the

> incessantly flexible, mobile, and provisional intersections of residents that operate without clearly delineated notions of how the city is to be inhabited and used . . . engag[ing] complex combinations of objects, spaces, persons, and practices' in 'conjunctions [that] become an infrastructure—a platform providing for and reproducing life in the city. (Simone 2004, 407)

Simone's approach has been useful to widen the understanding of infrastructure to the intangible infra-actions which make urban everyday life, paving the way for a convergence, between the notion of commons and that of infrastructure, that holds a remarkable potential in thinking the material, dynamic and processual nature of urban commons as the power-structured, relational and affective matter of which urban life is made (Borch and Kornberger 2015; Berlant 2016). Lately, works on more-than-human multi-species infrastructures have demonstrated the limits of both anthropocentric and state-centric approaches, showing 'how urban infrastructures work and how they are embedded in and constitutive of patchy urban ecologies' (Doherty 2019, S324). A further expansion has been provided by Keller Easterling's

(2014) notion of *infrastructure space*, which encompasses the normative, technological and aesthetic matrix that allows for the standardised reproduction of urban space at the planetary level. Infrastructure space, accordingly, refers to the formulas, models, protocols, manuals, regulations, artistic visions, best practices, renderings, branding, algorithms, logistical procedures, econometrics, global standards: a whole set of discourses, imaginaries and ideas that shape the strategies, expectations and imagination of planning, building, regulating, experiencing and moving through the urban. As she puts it, 'infrastructure is then not the urban substructure but the urban structure itself—the very parameters of global urbanism' (idem, 12), the way in which the global imaginary of urbanisation is aesthetically, normatively and technologically coded (see chapter 4). If Simone's notion emphasises the relational vitality of the urban, Easterling highlights the serial standardisation that characterises contemporary planetary urbanisation—its logistical *formatting* (see Serres 2020[2004]; Pavoni and Tomassoni 2022; chapters 2 and 5). Complementing both notions, infrastructures appear as the intangible, fluid, dynamic forms organising the economy of movement, experience and desire of urban inhabitants in various forms such as an image like the 'smart city', a food-delivery platform, an illegal dump site or a neighbourhood's atmosphere, often evading representation and yet potentially leaving their 'imprint by displacing violence into forms of culture and exchange, into emotional relations and into language' (Aranda et al. 2012).

Infra-Structural Violence

The concept of infrastructure, we have seen, appears as a complex constellation in which more traditional political economy metaphors, and engineering structures, are complemented by a novel ontological understanding in which infrastructure becomes a key notion to explore the way in which the relations constituting the socio-natural *in between* of reality—that is, the shared space of coexistence—hold together, immanently, tensionally and asymmetrically, in intricate arrangements of cables, wires, scaffoldings, wavelengths, practices, habits, norms and affects. As Laurent Berlant intriguingly puts it, the infrastructure 'is the living mediation of what organizes life: the lifeworld of structure' (Berlant 2016, 393), a suggestion that compensates for the limits of structuralist approaches explored above, without neither jettisoning their value nor sacrificing the structure to the alter of 'flatness', by integrating the promises of vital materialism.

While the notion of infrastructural violence has been employed with respect to a more restrained notion of (mostly physical) infrastructure, we propose to reconceptualise it through the recent import of critical infra-structure studies. Merging the tangible and the intangible, the spatial with the aesthetic, the affective and the normative dimension allows the concept of infrastructure to zoom in onto a microphysics of infra-power and infra-politics (cf. Scott 1990) that slip through the net of functionalist-economics and ideology, and through which violence flows as a tensional force that at the same time weaves together, and threatens to disrupt, the fabric of the social. We therefore refer to *infra-structural violence*—where the hyphen is meant to emphasise the relational and tensional in-between—as a way to rework symbolic/economic notions of structural violence towards an onto-epistemological 'statics' of violence, which is attuned to its disrupting, con-structive and preserving quality.

The epistemological potential of this concept for our analysis is vast. Informed by Berlant (2016, 394), applying an 'infrastructural analysis helps us see that what we commonly call "structure" is not what we usually call it, an intractable principle of continuity across time and space, but is really a convergence of force and value in patterns of movement that's only solid when seen from a distance'—a convergence that is inextricably, although always in peculiar ways, tied to violence. Through this conceptual arsenal we are able to properly address 'how violence shapes space, understood in its broad political and processual sense, and how space shapes violence beyond the instrumental way of analysing spatial patterns to help "explain" violence' (Springer and Le Billon 2016, 1). This means exploring violence as distributed across temporal and spatial systems, since we are no longer focusing on 'structures' but more precisely on infra-structural dynamics, processes of 'dynamic structuration' (Barad 2003, 829), that is, 'the move-ment or patterning of social form' (Berlant 2016, 393). Once we understand the heterogenous complexity of infrastructures and their more-than-human, more-than-physical materiality (e.g., Carse 2014; Doherty 2019; Enns and Sneyd 2021), it is also easier to understand the distributed quality of agency, and thus violence. As discussed (see introduction), this is what is at stake with vital materialism: not the naïve provision of a *generic* force, agency or vitality to things, but the exploration of an agency that is understood to be distributed across a complex and power-structured network of relations, rather than causally flowing from deeper structures (cf. Pearson 1999, 171). This also calls for a renewed capacity to bring into view, conceptually and empirically, 'non-human agencies without letting go of human ones' (Jenson and Morita 2017, 622), all the more important given that at the infrastructural level agency and causation occur in ways and according to 'dispositions'—

tendencies, propensities, properties—that are harder to detect, aesthetically and temporally (Easterling 2014).[28]

Rather than limiting our understanding of the working and the violence of infrastructure by reference to all-encompassing frames such as Capitalism or Neoliberalism, that is, by assuming that socio-economic structures would be simply reproduced into the infrastructures, this means looking at the contingent materiality and concrete relations through which these take place. Capitalist structures are not smoothly reproduced onto the urban, they are rather held together by a complexity of infrastructures in which glitches, breakdowns, failures and frictions abound. Frictions, for Anna Tsing, are the 'grip of worldly encounter' (2005), the attritional contingency through which global connections, apparatuses and structures come to life and are actualised, that is, *take place*, within the materiality of the world. Frictions both 'slow down' and 'accelerate', 'allow[ing] universal concepts and norms to get a grip on a particular situation' (Rouse 2009, 207), permitting *simultaneously* for the instantiation of universals into the specific situation and for their diffraction, that is, their never fully successful/smooth reproduction. The violence of logistics for instance, as Deborah Cowen (2014) describes it, cannot be simply presupposed as flowing causally from the abstract working of supply-chain Capitalism. In this view, it emerges from the material contingency of an infrastructure in which different technologies, temporalities, aesthetics, imaginaries and bodies are articulated in specific ways that require to be explored. Exploring the infra-structural violence of urbanisation (see chapter 5), for instance, means understanding this process as always unfolding frictionally, as a patchy, often-chaotic process that is less a reproduction of socio-economic relations onto everyday social space (cf. Lefebvre 1974) than a *disorganisation* of everyday life in socio-economic, spatial, affective and indeed neurological sense (Berlant 2011, 68; Stiegler 2019, Bernard).

How does these messy diffractions hold together, nonetheless? This is the question that infra-structural violence wishes to address: not the smooth reproduction of planetary processes, but their tensional holding together, in the contingency of everyday life, and the potentially toxic effects on the bodies that must endure these tensions. In their attempt to fabricate order, structural forces generate frictions and produce fractures, material and discursive at the same time. Take for instance Feltran's description of São Paulo, where a long history of racial discrimination, economic exploitation and unequal urbanisation engendered a fragmented spatiality that is daily negotiated by inhabitants holding incommensurable 'normative regimes'— i.e., epistemological and aesthetic infrastructures of social patterning offering 'a plausible set of orientations for the empirical action of subjects' (2020,

15)—and inhabiting a fractured space they must share nonetheless, often bridging incommunicability through violence. Around these fractures, where different normative regimes clash, the possibility of violence (of many kinds, from police to mere discrimination, from physical to affective fear) is higher—in other words, these fractures are generators of violence since they are thresholds in which different sets of values overlap and violations become actualised.[29]

Then, while we second Rodgers and O'Neill's suggestion (2012) that infrastructures are 'an ideal ethnographic site' to explore structural violence, we add that they are an ideal ethnographic site to explore the turbulent encounter between structural violence and (urban) experience. 'Frictious sites', as Federico Rahola (2014, 395) puts it following Tsing, namely the sites in which the 'violent and open-ended encounters between capital apparatuses and logics of translation into scalable inventories and the un-reproducible, subjective and non-scalable experience of urban forms of life' do materialise. To be sure, this is not a matter of emphasising the primacy of empirical observation or concrete relation over theory and abstraction, as sometimes it is implied (e.g., Silva 2014). Rather, we intend to explore the affective, normative and material infrastructures of being-together that emerge out of the frictional encounter between structures and experience, the abstract and the concrete, in order to 'decipher global processes through their concrete manifestation in the situated, affective fabrics of human and nonhuman existence' (Arboleda 2020, 20), including 'the frequently violent tensions between what the fractured urban order is and, especially, what it should be' (Feltran 2020, 17).

As we are to see in the following chapters, exploring urban violence on either side of the structure/experience dichotomy is not enough. A deeper understanding can only be achieved by looking at the way violence functions at the level of their frictional encounter, where neither order nor disorder, but rather the infra-structural consistency of the *ordinary* everyday, unfolds (cf. Stewart 2007). The friction, in other terms, may be understood as the excess between the different scales that intersect the surface of the social, the bodies that populate it, the abstractions that insist on and produce its spatiality, and therefore it is also the excess of violence that spills over linear causal explanation: the violence that slowly creeps out of the frictional unfolding of everyday life, in the form of an unequally, socio-biologically asphyxiating gas which fills the socio-natural landscape, affecting and orienting bodies in their complex and anxious adaptation, and wearing them out in the process. In chapters 4, 5 and 6 we will develop this approach in relation to urban violence, where the question of infra-structural consistency will be explored according to three main dimensions: the instituting *imaginary* of urban violence; the planetary *process* of urbanisation; and the *atmospheric* violence through which urban everyday life is breathed through, often with debilitating effects on the vitality of urban life.[30] Prior to do that, however, the notions of urban (in chapter 2) and security (in chapter 3) need be dealt with.

Researching Urban Violence: Health Reductionism (and Covid Redux)

In exploring the occurrence of violence, researchers have recognized the tendency for violent acts to cluster, to spread from place to place, and to mutate from one type to another. Furthermore, violent acts are often preceded or followed by other violent acts. Contextual and social factors play a role in increasing or reducing the risk of violence; such factors might exist at community or individual levels.

> In the field of public health, such a process has also been seen in the infectious disease model, in which an agent or vector initiates a specific biological pathway leading to symptoms of disease and infectivity. The agent transmits from individual to individual, and levels of the disease in the population above the expected rate constitute an epidemic. Although violence does not have a readily observable biological agent as an initiator, it can follow similar epidemiological pathways. Just as with those infected by microbial agents, those exposed to violence have varying levels of resilience and susceptibility. (Patel et al. 2013, 1)

Thus begins a book stemming from a workshop convened in 2012 by the Institute of Medicine (IOM) Forum on Global Violence Prevention to 'explore the contagious nature of violence' (idem, 2). Especially since the 1980s, a public health approach to violence has emerged (see Satcher 1995; Winett 1998), consistent with the more general medicalisation of society under neoliberalism.[31] Promoted by several international institutions, including the World Health Organization, this approach has reached its climax with the Cure Violence model, formerly known as CeaseFire, a Chicago-based organisation launched in 1999 by founder Gary Slutkin, former WHO epidemiologist. Cure Violence is hailed as a remarkable success in addressing urban violence, was successfully championed by an award-winning, 2011 documentary (*The Interrupters*), a widely watched 2013 TED talk, various articles written by Slutkin himself in major newspapers worldwide, and is currently deployed across the five continents.[32] In an article written on *The

Guardian, tellingly reflecting on the 2011 'London riots', Slutkin (2011) summarises the sort of nineteenth-century positivism that seems to be feeding his approach with matter-of-fact style: 'that violence is an epidemic is not a metaphor; it is a scientific fact [. . . it] behaves with the characteristics of an infectious disease'. Therefore, the argument goes, between classic law enforcement and long-term structural action, 'an immediate, middle-ground, public health solution' is needed: namely, 'interrupting the transmission of conflict'.[33] This guiding assumption is meant to challenge the problematic reduction of violence to a moral matter pertaining to an inherently violent individual, something that Slutkin relates to the way in which people infected with a certain disease are often treated, for instance in the case of AIDS/HIV and other infectious diseases, a field in which he extensively worked while at WHO. Hence, the use of 'violence interrupters' to act on 'infected people' to cure them and help preventing the disease from spreading.[34] As Slutkin (2020) observed more recently, 'rather than viewing people at risk of doing a violent act as inherently immoral or bad, we should view them as individuals with a contagious and epidemic health problem, who deserve treatment, compassion and care'. Cure Violence turns violence itself into a disease, postulating an intersection between public health, violence and personal responsibility that subsequently, in the midst of a global pandemic, will become all too common (see chapter 3, Researching Urban Violence).

Assuming violence as contagious, to be sure, is certainly not a preposterous statement. Not only empirical evidence, neurological and psychological studies, or even anecdotical experience may support this thesis. The conception of violence developed in this chapter is not at odds with such an affirmation, as we already hinted when referring to Girard's reflections on violence. The non-essentialist, relational, assembled ontology on which we grounded our discussion is inevitably exposed to multiple contagions, as for instance Gabriel Tarde's social monadology had already elaborated (2012[1893]).[35] This is inscribed within the very etymology of the term, from *cum* and *tangere*, touching together (this is, significantly, also the root of the term 'contingency'). Violence, we argued, can be in this sense understood as a quintessential *pharmakon* vis-à-vis the consistency of the social, that is, an infra-structural force of construction, maintenance or destruction (cf. Esposito 2011[2002]).

A crucial difference between our ontological presuppositions and Cure Violence's (implicit) ones is that the latter develop an epistemology of violence that is simply projected onto an implicit, atomised ontology, in which the role that violence plays—as well as the very definition of violence—remain basically unthought. This is a telling example of both the perils—and indeed the epistemic violence—that follow any attempt to conceptualise violence that takes the underlying ontology for granted. Seen in negative, this is also a reminder of the strategic and ethico-political value that an onto-epistemology of violence harbours.[36] The first consequence for the Cure Violence model is that of resting on the long-held assumption of violence as an exogenous anomaly, a medical condition with respect to a normality (a sort of healthy state of non-violence) that remains unquestioned. An infection, that is, that pertains fundamentally to the individuals and/or groups that catch it and threaten to spread it. Here violence is a *disease* an individual or social groups *has*, rather than an endogenous condition that is present to a more or a lesser degree in a given social configuration (see Rose 1985; and introduction). As a result, a group of people, a place, a neighbourhood, a whole city, may be depicted as *literally* sick—an imaginary that, we will see in chapter 4, in nineteenth century played a prominent role in shaping the notion of urban violence, and that reproduces the fetishisation of certain individuals and places as violent. Once violence is medicalised, the urban is framed into more or less pathological areas that do not so much require to be *cared for*—in the relational, material and ethico-political connotation of the term (see chapter 9)—as to be *cured*: a neutral, non-political, and scientific praxis. Such a reductionism, to follow Malte Riemann (2019, 151), 'obscures any structural, political, and sociological factors that might underpin said violence in the name of a value-free science'.[37]

Indeed, the reductionism Slutkin's model performs is double: not only the medicalisation of violence, but also its fetishisation, since violence is simply assumed to be psycho-physical, direct and visible, just as its mode of transmission. Consider the channels through which the disease spreads: 'visual observation (o) and direct victimization (v)—besides intentional training (t), such as the military' (Slutkin 2013, 106). Direct violence leads directly and indirectly to direct violence. While this affirmation can obviously explain violence in certain contexts and settings, it completely overlooks the role that other forms of indirect violence may play in fostering direct violence, or indeed the way in which indirect violence may spread independently from direct violence (and thus from its treatment), as a thick atmosphere to which a population is, at different degrees, affectively tuned (see chapter 6). Such a reductionist approach is explicit in the text quoted at the beginning of this section, which anticipates that social research has reflected on the 'contextual and social factors' that drive violence, only to move to set out a model that completely disregards them. The resulting model for 'curing' violence is: first, detecting and interrupting conflicts; second, identifying and treating the highest risk individuals; and, third, changing social norms.[38] While the pragmatic nuance of this protocol is interesting, as it is the implicit emphasis on violence-producing habits that is expressed with the reference to social norms, eventually Cure Violence does not really draw the consequences of this assumption, thus reproducing the assumption that violence 'sits' in individuals and places, and that the latter are to be cleansed of it. In other words, the relational, asubjective and endogenous dimension of violence is overlooked. Framing violence as an epidemic disease that must be treated by isolating and treating dangerous individuals reproduces the assumption of violence as a non-social being, surgically separating its unfolding from the socio-material infrastructure through which it takes place. Violence is no disease or a pathological condition, however, it is a *physiological* facet of social existence. While its debilitating effects obviously need to be minimised, violence cannot be eradicated, as this effort only leads to surreptitiously dislocating it elsewhere (cf. Girard 1972). Violence, in other words, cannot be taken for granted. Cure Violence instead, together with seemingly opposite approaches aimed at punitive deterrence, ends up 'divorcing violence from its broader context and placing it in an explanatory vacuum of its architect's own construction' (Apsholm 2020).

Yet, Cure Violence has been considered to be 'effective', in terms of the reduction of the number of reported crimes.[39] This is unquestionable, to the extent that the criteria for defining and measuring violence are unquestionable, which is hardly the case, as we will show in detail in our discussion on official crime data (see chapter 2, Researching Urban Violence). Eventually, the medicalisation of violence draws a separation between the normal and the pathological that, without challenging structural inequalities, simply reproduces them visually and statistically. Georges Canguilhem's analysis comes to mind (1966). Canguilhem maintained that the normal is just an attenuated form of—secondary to—the pathological, a sort of line of consistency that, for a series of reasons, has emerged out of the pathological by means of attenuating multiple variations into a series, a repetition, a routine (see also Cryle and Stephens 2017). The resulting social order is understood as normal, and healthy, regardless of the debilitating effects it may have for many human and non-human others. As Austin suggests and this chapter contends, violence should be understood 'as a "population level" problem that we must come to recognise *all* persons being entangled-with to a greater or lesser degree' (2023, 107; emphasis in original; see chapter 6). In her useful critical discourse analysis of the Cure Violence discourse, Riemann (2019) shows how the medicalisation of violence depoliticises it by pathologising subjects who, on the one hand, are framed through a methodological individualism that ignores the asymmetric infrastructures of the social; and, on the other hand, are collocated into 'at risk' categories, a categorisation that is far from innocent, and in which race plays a disturbingly prominent role. This foregrounds a health discourse of individual responsibility that is perfectly consistent with the rhetoric of self-management and self-improvement that the self-entrepreneurial subjects of neoliberalism are supposed to constantly perform, a discourse that, according to Peter Cryle and Elizabeth Stephens (2017, 357), 'allows subjects to be held personally responsible for their ability to adapt to their social conditions so that . . . twentieth-century public health discourses often held individuals responsible for the health of the nation, rather that ascribing it to governmental policies and practices'.[40]

Finally, not only is Cure Violence's 'medicalisation' problematic in conceptual and analytical terms, but it may also fail its stated goal of contributing to a less militarised, and more 'social', approach to urban violence, rather appearing perfectly compatible with the 'emergency approach' that characterises contemporary politics. Declaring an 'epidemic' of violence is a powerful declaration of crisis,[41] which reduces the room of manoeuvre for dealing with urban violence, most notably by invisibilising its infra-structural dimension.[42] The ultimate consequence of this health model, rather than that of contributing to frame violence as a matter of public health, is the adoption of health instruments (including contact tracing and the like) in a supposedly neutral, scientific manner to deepen the surveillance and control of (racialised, marginalised) populations. While an expanded notion of health, as sketched in the last chapter, can be a promising step in to expand the room to manoeuvre[43] when conceptualising—and dealing with—urban violence, doing so requires to preliminary clear the ground from an interpretation of the relation between health and violence that implicitly draws from an atomistic ontology and a reductionist understanding of violence itself.

Notes

1. Thomas Hobbes. 2002[1651]. *Leviathan.*

2. Available at: www.who.int/violenceprevention/approach/definition/en/. The WHO is a crucial player in the global discourse of violence. It has been directly responsible for the framing of violence as a health concern since the 1980s, a medicalisation that perhaps reached its climax with Gary Slutkin's (himself a former WHO

epidemiologist) Cure Violence model (more on this, in section Researching Urban Violence at the end of this chapter).

3. On the notion of triviality applied to concepts, see Negarestani (2015).

4. Needless to say, the acritical 'celebration' of violence falls into the very same conundrum.

5. Yet this should not authorise threatening violence literally as a contagious disease to be expunged from the social body—we are to see in the Researching Urban Violence section of this chapter an instance of such an epidemiological approach to violence, and the troubles that come with it.

6. Scheper-Hughes and Bourgois write: 'we have proposed conceptualizing violence as operating along a continuum from direct physical assault to symbolic violence and routinized everyday violence, including the chronic, historically embedded structural violence whose visibility is obscured by globalized hegemonies' (2004b, 318). This is a valuable definition that however needs be complemented with a materialist theory of affect, in order to account for the complex interaction between structure and experience, imaginary and normativity of violence, beyond the smooth dialectic the authors instead seem to imply.

7. Austin here is elaborating from Bruno Latour's notion of plasma, namely 'that which is not yet formatted, not yet measured, not yet socialized, not yet engaged in metrological chains and not yet covered, surveyed, mobilized or subjectified' (Latour 2005, 244). Elsewhere we challenged this understanding, on the account of its tendency to de-politicise ontology, and opposed to it Deleuze's notion of the virtual (Pavoni 2018a, ch. 1, pr. 2.4). While this is not the place to exhume such a reflection, it is safe to say that the way in which Austin employs the term—which, admittedly, in Latour is given a rather superficial and cursory introduction—brilliantly avoids this tendency.

8. Theories of nonviolence, for instance, usually strive to avoid a violence which is equated to, following Iadicola and Shupe (2003, 26), 'any action or structural arrangement that results in physical or nonphysical harm to one or more persons'.

9. According to Butler (2020, 18), 'without an understanding of the conditions of life and livability, and their relative difference, we can know neither what violence destroys nor why we should care'. While a solid account of violence can be certainly developed in these terms—and the notion of atmospheric violence we develop below may be a case in point (see chapter 6)—it is important to stress that violence is not 'only' a destructive force. To the contrary, violence may also play a part in creating, maintaining, preserving or nurturing relations (see de Warren 2006; Rodgers 2016; Feltran 2020; Handel 2021). Since there is no innocent or homogenous real—i.e., since any relation is always asymmetrically shaped by all sorts of structures, forces and power relations—one could argue that social bonds are never completely 'free' of violence. This is an important point, since it serves to avoid the dangerous fantasy of positing the political or ethical goal of reaching a 'beyond', e.g., a city without violence (see chapter 4).

10. As François Zourabichvili (2012[2003], 185) acutely explains, this means 'to overcome the alternative between a morality grounded in transcendent values and a nihilistic or relativistic immoralism which, under the pretext of the facticity of all transcendent values, concludes that "everything is equal"'.

11. There is certainly a danger with such an expanded definition of violence and we therefore share Johanna Oksala's worries. As we show throughout this book, however, the strategic attempt to isolate a morally superior space of nonviolence can end up being far more dangerous, as it occurs, at the simplest level, with the notorious projection of a city without violence which feeds the logic of urban security (see chapter 3).

12. Deleuze observes that for an act of creation to occur, violence is necessary, that is, an act of creation can only emerge with a violent encounter with the outside of a given image of thought, that is, to put is simplistically, with the outside of the existent frame of thinking: 'we search for truth only when we are determined to do so in terms of a concrete situation, when we undergo a kind of violence . . . Truth is never the product of a prior disposition [i.e., a good will] but the result of a violence in thought' (2000[1964], 15–16).

13. The root of violence, *vi-*, is also associated to the notion of *vimine*, that is, osier or, more generally, wicker. Violence accordingly has to do with an interweaving, tensional force of holding together.

14. 'There is only a perspective seeing, only a perspective "knowing" and the more affects we allow to speak about one thing, the more eyes, different eyes, we can use to observe one thing, the more complete will our "concept" of this thing, our "objectivity", be' (Nietzsche 1967[1887/1888], 12).

15. 'I understand by the term "apparatus" a sort of—shall we say—formation which has as its major function at a given historical moment that of responding to an *urgent need*' (Foucault 1980[1977], 195; emphasis in the translation used).

16. 'Some epistemologists seek to block any intelligible role for power by sharply separating the normativity of reasons bearing upon judgments from the causal imposition of force upon reasoners. But power is not the same as force. Indeed, the concept of power is best understood as having the expressive role of articulating connections between the causal capacities of agents and institutions and the normative significance of their performances and dispositions' (Rouse 2009, 203).

17. This is what the apparently oxymoronic notion of 'historical *a priori*' by Foucault points to. As Deleuze (2006[1986], 56–57) explains, what allows Foucault to avoid this theory 'from falling into a generally phenomenological or linguistic direction' and thus provides it of this concreteness is the reference to a 'specific a finite body of world and texts, phrases and propositions' which constitute the being of language, whose immediate mediality is therefore at the same time transcendental (vis-à-vis the statements or discursive formations) as well as historical. 'Tthe conditions, or *a priori* of the statements, are themselves historical: the great murmur, otherwise known as the language-being or the "there is" of language, varies in each historical formations and, while being anonymous, is none the less unique, the "enigmatic and

precarious being" which cannot be separated from a particular mode. Each age has its own particular way of putting language together, because of its different groupings . . . The historical being of language never manages to gather this new function in an inner consciousness that founds, originates or even mediates; on the contrary, it constitutes a form of exteriority in which the statements of the corpus under consideration appear by way of dispersal and dissemination. It is a distributive unity'.

18. For a critique of Judith Butler's along these lines, vis-à-vis notions of race and gender, see Saldanha (2006).

19. To explain this concept, Barad (2007, ch. 3) refers to Neils Bohr and to quantum physics' classic account of experimental observation, which denies the separation between subject/observed and object/observed by rather prioritising the relation between them. As the well-known Schrödinger's cat example shows, there is no prior distinction between subject and object but rather a relation out of which, through the working of a given apparatus of observation, an 'agential cut' is produced and therefore an observer and an observed emerge. As this example clearly shows, quantum physics' removal of the *a priori* distinction between subject and object does not amount to a removal of causality or objectivity. I am still able to assess objectively whether the cat is alive or dead, yet this 'objectivity' results from a local process of emergence and intra-actional dynamic structuration, rather than presupposition via deterministic structures. These local emergences and their 'cuts', to be sure, are never simply spontaneous but always filtered *through* spatially and historically situated apparatuses, out of which an 'objective' and yet partial perspective is enacted: 'partial', in this sense, has nothing to do with a relativism premised on the 'free' interpretation of an abstract subject, but rather refers to the *necessarily* partial perspective of a 'situated' body.

20. The work of Barad is particularly useful in this sense. As she puts it, 'matter, like meaning, is not an individually articulated or static entity. Matter is not little bits of nature, or a blank slate, surface, or site passively awaiting signification; nor is it an uncontested ground for scientific, feminist, or Marxist theories. Matter is not a support, location, referent, or source of sustainability for discourse. Matter is not immutable or passive. It does not require the mark of an external force like culture or history to complete it. Matter is always already an ongoing historicity' (2003, 821).

21. This is akin to what Joseph Pugliese and Susan Stryker (2009: 2–3) refer to as a somatechnical assemblage. On technical/technological dimensions, in relation with social imaginaries and the security apparatus, see respectively chapters 4 and 8.

22. We have elsewhere discussed the problems of the idea of the absence of violence, that is, absolute security (Tulumello 2021a); and will come back on this in chapters 3 and 4.

23. 'By insisting on critiquing violence *in itself*, Benjamin challenges the fundamental dogma of jurisprudence, namely, that justice can be attained if means and ends are balanced, that is, if justified means are used for just ends' (Larsen 2013). See also the critique of the 'myth of the balance' in security politics made by Mark Neocleous (2007; see chapter 3).

24. 'The violence criticized by Benjamin is the violence of the status quo' (Herbert Marcuse, apud Hamacher 1994, 135).

25. This is a significative difference also from Hannah Arendt, according to whom violence is always instrumental, while power is productive of an inter-subjective space of possibility, that is, the common 'space of appearance', a trans-historical condition of possibility permitting the mutual intelligibility and communication between subjects. As Maze puts it following Arendt, power 'does not occur *beyond* but *between* subjects' (2018, 128; emphasis in original). Benjamin's understanding instead points to a *mediality* that is not a transhistorical, inter-subjective space of intelligibility, but rather a historical and pre-subjective space *out of which* subjectivation emerges. In this sense, power is neither beyond nor between subjects, it is rather what *makes* them, and the 'common' is never a transhistorical space *between* subject, but rather a space of subjectivation, which is already traversed by stratifications, structuration, apparatuses. Likewise, the 'common' is not a space of appearance (or of civility and expectability), since it does not belong to the domain of presence or to the temporality of the present. It is the opening of historically situated processes of subjectivation whose outcome is always uncertain, since it does not 'take place' within a given linear progression of time but rather puts time itself out of joint (see Benjamin 2005[1940]). Against the Kantian premises of Arendt, which posits a transcendental in-betweenness on which grounding her normative ethics, the Foucauldian insight (Foucault 2010[1969]; see also Deleuze 2006[1986], 48) we follow is that this in-betweenness is already historical, not a presupposed *common* already shared among subjects, but a pre-subjective, pre-individual space out of which the different subjectivities and thus completing sets of values emerges, as per São Paulo's intersecting and conflicting 'normative regimes' that Feltran brilliantly describes (2020).

26. We are to come back in chapter 4 on the complex relation between the symbolic, the real and the imaginary that subtends this discussion.

27. For a punctual critique of Marxist functionalism see Castoriadis (1987[1975]; see also chapter 4).

28. For Easterling (2014, ch. 2), dispositions are those, often implicit or harder to detect, agencies and capacities that organisations and infrastructures are provided by their internal structure and the very activities they perform.

29. In his reflection on Sartre's and Fanon's work on violence, Nicolas de Warren makes a similar argument: 'violence is a praxis that brings together those deprived of speech into a space of possibility in which their own speech becomes a possibility' (2006, 54).

30. Notions like 'slow death' (Berlant 2011), 'slow violence' (Nixon 2011) or 'maiming' (Puar 2017) have taken important steps toward thinking violence beyond the subjective/objective dichotomy, the logics of sovereignty or the spatio-temporal causality of structures, rather looking at slow, attritional, barely perceptible processes of debilitation. These concepts differently point to an affective notion of violence that is not amenable to linear causality and temporality, and whose effects take the form of an intoxication of socio-natural atmospheres—and for this reason, we will

deal with them directly in chapter 6, where the notion of urban atmosphere is intro-duced and that of urban atmospheric violence is proposed.

31. We will engage with the contested meaning of neoliberalism in the next chapter.

32. See https://cvg.org/.

33. The way in which Slutkin (2011) frames the argument is perfectly compatible with the way in which, before the nineteenth-century 'urban crisis', politicians and social scientists were framing the 'problem' of violence, vice and poverty as a matter of inadequate infrastructures (cf. chapter 4): 'to review the events of the past week in London through this lens, we see a grievance (citizens upset that a civilian has been shot by law enforcement officials) that occurs within the context of frustration and general dissatisfaction (poverty, unemployment) serving as the precipitating cause for an outbreak of violence. These conditions set the stage for an outbreak in the same way that poor sanitation, overcrowding, and contaminated water set the stage for cholera'. Slutkin's proposal to secure the socio-material infrastructure of the social is equally mixed with perfectly reasonable considerations (that 'dissatisfaction' may lead to riots, that contaminated water may lead to cholera) and, as we see below, surgically de-politicising solutions.

34. http://cureviolence.org/.

35. Deleuze, for instance, describes the process of coming-together that produces an assemblage exactly in these terms: 'what is an assemblage? It is a multiplicity which is made up of many heterogeneous terms and which establishes liaisons, relations between them, across ages, sexes and reigns—different natures. This, the assemblage's only unity is that of a co-functioning: it is a symbiosis, a "sympathy". It is never filiations which are important, but alliances, alloys; these are not succes-sions, lines of descent, but contagions, epidemics, the wind' (Deleuze and Parnet 1987[1977], 69). We elsewhere dealt with Tarde's social monadology, see Pavoni (2018, ch.1).

36. As we explained in the introduction, it is crucial to develop an onto-epistemic approach to violence, if we are to avoid this depoliticising outcome. It is in this way that our approach, still grounded on a certain connotation of illness as debilitation, is certainly not compatible with Slutkin's.

37. On the troubles with medicalisation with respect to domestic violence, see Rojas-Durazo (2016). In his TED talk (see https://www.ted.com/talks/gary_slutkin_let_s_treat_violence_like_a_contagious_disease), thus Slutkin suggests that science should replace morality (see, for a critique, Aspholm 2020).

38. See https://cvg.org/what-we-do/.

39. For a critique of Cure Violence's self-assessment methodology, see Aspholm (2020). After a very detailed critique of the model's 'failure', Aspholm adds: 'I am friends with a number of current and former Cure Violence workers whom I admire and consider to be mentors, and I have worked with others for whom I have similar admiration. While I remain decidedly unconvinced that Cure Violence is the solu-tion to urban violence that its proponents claim it to be, I consider the work that

many of these individuals do to be important and heroic and their own personal transformations to be deeply inspiring'. We second this comment, stressing that our critique of Cure Violence should not conceal the fact that there are many community workers involved in this and similar approaches, whose important and dangerous effort should not be effaced.

40. See Riemann: 'more specifically, as violent behavior is "acquired or learned" (www.cureviolence.org), individuals that lack the necessary self-governance to acquire immunity or resistance to violence are the problem' (2019, 150).

41. We refer, here, especially to the understanding of crisis as a discursive framing developed by Janet Roitman (2014; see also Mbembe and Roitman 1995) in dialogue with the work of Reinhart Koselleck (2006[1972]). This conceptualisation resonates with the discussions on urban crisis that we are to see later on (see chapter 4).

42. Writing in the context of, and on the use of modelling and simulations on, the Covid-19 pandemic, Warwick Anderson (2021, 169) quotes Koselleck (2006[1972], 37) to argue that declaring a crisis 'is meant to reduce the room for maneuver'. It has been precisely in the context of the Covid-19 pandemic that the circulation of contagion models among health and policing has accelerated (Heimstadt et al. 2020). See chapter 3, Researching Urban Violence.

43. We paraphrase, here, Warwick Anderson, according to whom 'expanding the room to maneuver might be a worthy task for pandemic critique . . . [that is] to recognize social and cultural logics, and ecological settings, often erased from the conceptualization and management of crises, such as the current pandemic' (2021, 170). For a discussion of security and health amid the Covid-19 pandemic, see chapter 3, Researching Urban Violence.

CHAPTER TWO

~

Urban

Hé aquí las razones filológicas que me indujeron y decidieron á adoptar la palaba Urbanizacion, no solo para indicar cualquier acto que tienda á agrupar la edificacion y á regularizar su funcionamiento en el grupo ya formado, sino tambien el conjunto de principios, doctrinas y reglas que deben aplicarse, para que la edificacion y su agrupamiento, lejos de comprimir, des virtuar y corromper las facultades físicas, morales é intelectuales del hombre social, sirvan para fomentar su desarrollo y vigor y para acrecentar el bien estar individual, cuya suma forma la felicidad pública.[1]

What is the urban? A place, a condition, an imaginary, an experience, a process? Perhaps, a bit of them all. Since the Neolithic, the newfound technical and material capacity to live inside a designed built environment has changed dramatically the way we think, sense and relate with human and non-human others. The urban form has played a key role in shaping the ethico-political imaginary, from the Greek *polis*, whose *just* proportions were supposed to reflect the harmony of the *kosmos*, to the imagined cities where the moral architecture of classic utopias was projected. Today, we have become accustomed to the refrain about the global exodus from the rural to the urban, to the fact that: 'the majority of world's population now live in urban areas'. As we are to see more in detail, there is a fundamental problem with this rhetoric: simply put, it takes the urban for granted. This is often a problem urban scholarship shares. Ross Exo Adams provides a useful description of this conceptual blind spot:

The urban today is at once unavoidable and yet curiously undoubted. Almost always taken as a given, the urban appears as a historical constant whose presence, more often than not, serves as a kind of inevitable or static background against which other problems are given visibility. If it is the object of enquiry, its examination tends to remain fixed by predominantly empirical analyses that give it consistency as a matter of the immediate present: through the mapping of the areas of its most rapid transformations, its categorization through perceived abnormalities or disclosure of its most extreme reach into the natural world, the urban nevertheless seems to elide questions about itself. Instead, it is rendered as a condition made visible only through its *effects*, a visibility that affirms broader assumptions that it is the inevitable outcome of a certain naturalized, transhistorical capacity of human cohabitation. (Adams 2019, 5; emphasis in original; see also Roy 2016)

'Naturalised' is the key term here. Assumed as a 'transhistorical capacity of human cohabitation', the urban is removed from history and consigned to a field of a static and statistical reflection, which takes the socio-material process of urbanisation as a self-evident fact that does not need explanation. While, to be sure, critical urban theory has challenged this trend, as we are to see in the next chapters, the question of the *urban* is still often overlooked and taken for granted, playing an implicit and yet fundamental role in articulating the discussion around urban violence, with troubling consequences. Prior to dwell on this matter, therefore, this chapter takes this question seriously, addressing the urban through a tripartite lens, by looking at: first, the explicitation of the city as a novel problem of governance (cf. Foucault 1984[1982]) at the intersection between state, capitalism and liberalism, that is, the urban as a spatio-political *project*; second, the historical, spatial and socio-economic unfolding of urbanisation, that is, the urban as a (planetary) *process*; third, the ontological condition and phenomenological experience that the modern urban condition discloses, that is, the urban as an *atmosphere*. To do so, we take steps from a brief reflection on the trajectory of the discipline(s)—from early urban sociology to recent global urban studies—that have framed and reframed the concept of the urban; and a discussion of the work of Idelfons Cerdá, whose concept of 'urbanisation' has had an immensely powerful, if rarely explicitly acknowledged, influence over the ways the urban is still thought in contemporary times.

What is the Urban?

As suggested elsewhere (Pavoni 2018a, 1–11), 'what is the urban?' is *the* question that underlies, implicitly, urban theory since early reflections. Strongly influenced by changing compositions and practices of social movements, in the 1970s the likes of Henri Lefebvre, David Harvey, Manuel Castells, Ed Soja, have conceptualised the urban in relation to the structures, apparatuses, spaces and temporalities of capitalism. What this fruitful intersection of Marxism, geography and urban theory elaborated is that the metropolis, rather than the factory, had become the quintessential locus of capitalism (e.g., Lefebvre 1974; Harvey 1989; Toscano 2004; Cunningham 2005)—'Operai contro la metropoli [Factory workers against the metropolis]' read the title of *Rosso*, magazine close to *autonomia operaia* in Milan, on April 24, 1974 (see Buitrago-Sevilla 2022, ch. 4).

All too often, however, the crucial attention to the 'real abstraction' of capitalist urbanisation introduced by this approach was developed to the detriment of that fine sensibility for the urban everyday which characterised early reflections on the urban by the likes of George Simmel, Walter Benjamin, Siegfried Kracauer. Replicating the tendency for structural determinism that is typical of certain versions of Marxist thought, the consequence has been that of reducing the everyday to a passive epiphenomenon of the capital, an inert socio-spatial matter on which capitalist structures would be smoothly reproduced—or, at best, resisted—rather than a productive field on its own terms.[2] Arguably, the so-called 'cultural turn' in urban theory, fed by postmodern hermeneutic, sought to address this limit, all too often reproducing, however, a fracture between a supposedly concrete and unchangeable urban matter, and the possibility of its merely literal, interpretative subversion (Watson and Gibson 1995; Dear 2000; Weizman 2010). This contrast soon reached an impasse (Thrift 1993): either overdetermined by the capital or re-interpreted by its inhabitants, the city was equally assumed as 'a bounded unity and a stable object' of research (Farías 2010, 12)—an ontological unity, that is.

This ambiguity, we believe, can be traced to the implicit tension between the 'urban' and the 'city' that haunted urban sociology at the time of its surfacing as a self-conscious disciplinary and epistemological field in the late nineteenth century. A crucial piece of this history, German sociology has been (pre)occupied since its onset with the relation between, on the one hand, rural-to-urban migration, urban growth, industrialisation and metropolisation, and, on the other, the problem of anomy, detachment, disorder, sensory overload, and, therefore, tension, conflict and violence in the city. For very different authors such as Friedrich Engels, Georg Simmel or Walter Benjamin, the city was respectively a *place* of alienation and (sub-)proletarianisation, sensory overload and stress, phantasmagoria and spectacle; dynamics that, in turn, were understood in relation to a wider *process*, namely industrial urban capitalism, 'money economy' and the commodification of urban space.[3] Complementary to these reflections was the exploration of urbanisation through the lenses of a wider process, seemingly shaping urbanising Europe, and ideally the whole world, that is, *civilisation* (e.g., Weber 1958[1905]; Febvre 1930; Elias 2000[1939]).

Where early urban thinkers pondered on the material conditions of urban experience, grappling with the growth, acceleration, intensification, densification and complexification of social relations in the modern metropolis, while also trying to reflect on the wider socio-cultural and economic processes—that is, on the *tension* between the city as a place and urbanisation as a process—the enormously influential Chicago School, founded by Robert E. Park in the 1920s, did 'solve' this tension by conflating the urban with the city. While their genealogy is far older, we argue that it is to this juncture that the core 'problems' with present discussions of urban violence—and particularly the dominant understanding of urban violence as the violence that takes place 'in the city' (see introduction)—can be traced.

Few would doubt that the Chicago School is the place where the mainstream understanding of the relation between space and social processes has been framed. At the core of Park and his colleagues' 'ecological' approach[4] is the attempt at finding a 'natural' definition of the city, that is, those central characters that remain constant in time and space—and to do so through the study of the 'paradigmatic' (American) city, Chicago itself.[5] Quite obviously, deconstructing the possibility of generalising the universal characters of *the* city from, say, Chicago, has been one of the contributions of urban theory inspired by post- and decolonial theory.[6] Where the power of the ecological approach is that of providing an epistemological lens through which every aspect of every city can be systematically analysed, its problem is the creation of a rigidly structural, almost deterministic, a-historical and depoliticised relation between urban form and societal dynamics—including violence. This is particularly evident in one of the founding works of the school, Luis Wirth's 'Urbanism as a way of life'. Wirth explicitly 'avoid[s] identifying urbanism as a way of life with any specific locally or historically conditioned cultural influences which, while they may significantly affect the specific character of the community, are not the essential determinants of its character as a city' (1938, 7). Urban sociability emerges spontaneously (an ecological process) through and throughout the increase of density, intensity, heterogeneity. Relations, therefore, will become more complex, and, at the same time, more superficial and anonymous. Urbanisation will imply a reduction of social solidarity and, therefore, an increase in uncertainty, insecurity and violence.

Much like we saw for the naturalisation of violence, the naturalisation of urban life has implied the reproduction, through their becoming implicit, of a number of normative assumptions, like a moralistic conception of urban life that is seen as a process of weakening of a romanticised, pre-urban social solidarity: a conception that normatively structures urban policy aiming at reconstructing a 'lost' social cohesion, which, however, is neither neutral nor innocent—just as the Greek *polis*, another quintessential locus of pre-urban nostalgia, was not; and is perfectly exemplified by the concurrent ideas of neighbourhood effect and collective efficacy[7] more recently developed at the Chicago School (see Morenoff et al. 2001; Sampson 2011). In epistemological terms, the effect of this ecological approach is a methodological reductionism that, on the one hand, effaces the plurality of *ways* of life that coexist within the city and, on the other, produces a number of problematic equations, like the automatic association between heterogeneity, uncertainty, insecurity and violence—somehow inevitably falling under the influence of a nostalgia for a pre-urban 'community spirit' that must be mysteriously resuscitated.

This process is part and parcel of the essentialisation and reduction of violence to its legalist definition, that is, physical, criminal violence.[8] While we have discussed above the broader implications on the conceptualisation of violence, what we want to stress here is how urban reductionism has provided those that were interested in simplification and generalisation with powerful tools to clearly define, quantify and measure urban violence through statistics on (violent) crime, and draw geographic charts accordingly: an easy solution to the difficulties of 'defining' urban violence (see introduction). We will come back later in this chapter, however, on the many 'problems' of quantitative/positivist understandings of urban violence (see section Researching Urban Violence below).

Overcoming the essentialisation of the 'urban way of life', on the contrary, is a necessary step for overcoming the essentialisation of (urban) violence. In a sense, addressing the former has been a quintessential endeavour of critical urban studies. Where, for instance, Wirth 'call[s] attention to the danger of confusing urbanism with industrialism and modern capitalism' (1938, 7), critical urban theory has clearly shown how this approach effaces those historical, socio-political, cultural and economic-financial processes that not only transcend specific cities but at the same time shape them profoundly and asymmetrically. Different epistemological and conceptual endeavours have been produced in this direction during the last few decades: from 'southern' urban theory inspired by post-, de-colonial and subaltern critique, to the critique of the 'urban age' made through the lenses of planetary urbanisation; from the attempt, in urban political ecology, to overcome the society/nature (and therefore urban/rural) dichotomy, to the import of post-structuralism, affect theory and new materialism. New concepts—among them urban networks, socio-natures, assemblages, infrastructures, materialities, ecologies, metabolism—have been introduced, in the build up of a vibrant field of research aimed, in Ash Amin's words, at 'uncovering the material geographies of urban provision, and the intricate ways in which nature and culture fold into each other' (2007, 108).

As it will become evident in this and following chapters, all these endeavours have systematically problematised traditional presuppositions, thereby fostering a radical rethinking of the urban, while allowing to explore in ever-novel conceptual and methodological ways the peculiar forms into which (global) processes are materialised in the urban contexts. In extreme summary and notwithstanding the various differences, what emerges from this broad and variegated field is the attempt at unpacking a dynamic, relational and processual understanding of urbanisation, while at the same time taking into account the various forms, relations and conflicts through which urbanisation takes place. Moving beyond the unproductive opposition between abstract structures and urban everyday, in this sense, means looking at the entangled ways through which planetary processes and situated atmospheres unfold, so as to be able to account simultaneously for its structures and processes as well as the affective ways through which they are materialised, experienced and lived in urban everyday life. It means, in other words, to explore the infrastructures through which the urban *holds together*, and therefore the infra-structural violence that enacts, keeps in place or disrupts such urban tensegrity.[9]

In order to account for the relation between the urban, urbanisation and violence, then, we propose to focus our attention towards three dimensions of urban(isation) that have been, if at times implicitly, framed in and by critical urban studies: the project, the process and the atmosphere, which we briefly introduce in the remainder of this chapter and will further discuss throughout the book. Prior to do so, however, we critically engage with the work where the notion of urbanisation was first coined, since in it we find the conceptual template of the form said dimensions will take in contemporary times.

Urbanización

Globally known for his plan for the modern expansion of Barcelona (the *Eixample*), while the ideas of Catalan engineer, architect and planner Ildefonso Cerdà have been extremely influential in the field of urban planning, his ambitious theoretical contribution, systematised in *Teoría General de la Urbanización* (The General Theory of Urbanisation), published in 1867, has remained little known (to the Anglophone reader) until quite recently.[10] There, Cerdá coined the neologism *urbanización*, a term through which he intended to frame what he saw as the capacity for cohabitation that is essential to human beings, resulting from two fundamental human needs: protection—i.e., the need to take shelter—and sociability.

In *Variations sur le Corp*, Michel Serres describes the 'intense sense of security' provided by the four-legged posture: 'you inhabit a square', he writes, 'an invisible and mobile parallelepiped' which is the animal's 'first refuge, the original architecture of its primitive building' (1999, 2; our translation). The *homo erectus*, accordingly, emerges out of the destruction of this primary membrane: hands become useless, head in the air, disequilibrium, insecurity, hence the need to build a roof. 'The very first cogito was a plan for a refuge to recover the lost balance' (idem, 4): the need to find a roof, *protection* (from the Latin *tegere*, that is 'to cover', from which the word *tectus*, that is, roof). Cerdá individuates the primordial scene of urbanisation precisely in these terms, understanding the first refuge as the 'urbs-embryo' in which the basic, transcendental rhythm of protection and socialisation that he sees as essential to urbanisation were laid out (2018[1867], 105). Socialisation and, as we are to see, civilisation are for Cerdá almost synonymous to urbanisation.[11]

Cerdà's work must be contextualised vis-à-vis the 'great transformation', as Karl Polanyi termed it, namely industrial revolution, technological innovation and the mass urbanisation that flooded nineteenth-century cities with an enormous mass of people they were vastly unequipped to accommodate. The dire living conditions, lack of basic services and exploitative proletarisation, to which an ever-growing (under)class of urban poor was exposed, formed an explosive mix, with frequent epidemics and urban revolts as simply the most visible outcome of an unsustainable situation. In this context, novel questions concerning social health, standards of living, political conflict, morality of customs, public order and liberal economics were surfacing. The city had become a 'problem', as Michel Foucault argued. While for critical thinkers like Karl Marx, whose *Das Kapital* was published the same year of the *Teoría*, the urban crisis needed to be explained by reference to wider political and economic processes, it was the city itself, within the positivistic ethos of the time, to be looked at as a possible solution, by means of rethinking its own organisation and infrastructure—hence the prominent political role that disciplines such as architecture and urbanism will increasingly come to play (Foucault 1984[1982]). It is in this problematic field, in the midst of an urban crisis he was directly experiencing, and fed by the nineteenth-century belief in the power and civilising mission of science and technology, that Cerdá writes the *Teoría*.

Inspired by Enlightenment thinkers such as Kant and Rousseau, Cerdá intended to translate their values into a pragmatic science: not a social contract was needed, he argued, but a 'system for organizing cities better'.[12] This implied, most of all, making cities compatible with the revolutionary potential of the technological innovations of his time: steam-power and electricity, railroads and telegraphs.[13] These innovations, intersecting the trajectory of capitalism and liberalism, were ushering in a new civilisation, he argued, whose demands were 'more space, greater comfort, and greater freedom', and whose 'distinctive features are movement and communication'. 'Comparing those demands with what could be offered to satisfy them by our old cities, where everything is narrow and cramped', he exclaimed, 'gave me a glimpse of new, immense, expanded horizons, a whole new world for science' (2018[1867], 50–51).

If on the one hand, with feverish enthusiasm, Cerdá saw the unfolding of an epoch 'when everything is movement, expansion, communication' (idem, 282), on the other he saw the city as a disturbing thing of the past: cramped, congested, overpopulated, insalubrious, disordered—and dangerous. Its form, sedimented over strata and strata of history, he found blatantly anachronistic. The word itself, city (*ciudad*), appeared to him far too historically and spatially specific, and therefore of little use, to develop the universal science of human cohabitation he had in mind.[14] At the same time, the city was problematic also for a diametrically opposite reason. As its etymological origin (*civitas*) betrays, the term *ciudad* implicitly refers to a political space, that is, the coming together of citizens (*cives*) under a common law. If the problem of the epoch he was living, Cerdá argued, was a tendency to prioritise 'material, moral, administrative, political and social interests' over those of 'public health and individual wellbeing' (idem, 66), then this was exactly what the notion of *civitas* expressed, incapable as it was to grasp the fine materiality of being together that *actually* constitutes the urban. Cerdá needed a concept that be generic and universal enough to transcend place and history, and at the same time concrete enough to zoom into the actual materiality of living. Avoiding what he saw as idealist abstractions of politics, he was more interested in developing a biopolitical science of the urban infrastructure.

> The first thing that occurred to me was the need to come up with a name for this jumble of people, things, and interests of all kinds, a multitude of different elements which, although they may seem to function independently, at closer observation can be seen to exist in constant interconnection with one another, affecting one another sometimes very directly, which cements them, therefore, as a unit. We know that the sum of all these things, especially in

their material aspect, is called a *city*, but since my purpose was not to express this materiality, but rather the means and systems these groups respond to when they are formed, and how all the elements that constitute them work and are organized—in other words, in addition to the material characteristics, I needed to express the organism, the life, so to speak, that breathes life into the material part. (idem, 66–67; emphasis in translation)

It was yet another Latin term, *urbs*, which in Roman times denoted the material infrastructure and organisation of the city, to provide Cerdá with the inspiration to coin his neologism.[15] Taken 'in its loosest and most general sense possible' (idem, 68), the *urbs* indicates an in-between (*infra*) 'space of connection and integration' (Aureli 2011, 7): neither the physical infrastructure of the city nor the life of the inhabitants, but their functional integration—its living infrastructure, that is. The aim of the relative science, urbanism, is therefore that of rethinking urban infrastructure so as to foster a healthy process of urbanisation, which is in turn understood as a spontaneous process of socio-material aggregation. Such a process was seen as natural and universal, not contingent to any given political or juridical form; and was therefore impaired by the city form itself. The crisis of the city was to be solved by having done with the city altogether, as graphically represented in the plan of the *Eixample*, where the old town of Barcelona is covered, tellingly, with a dark stain. This required the literal and metaphorical demolition of the city walls, to let unfold a continuous space through which the 'natural, immanent fact of human cohabitation' (Adams 2014, 18)—i.e., urbanisation—would be allowed to indefinitely expand.[16] The city, in other words, was to be reduced to the *urbs*, that is, 'to its bare, physical immanence of cohabitation and movement, dismissing the political form which had come to "obstruct" it' (idem, 19).

In this way, *urbanización* overcomes the separation between the urban and the rural, opening up the city to its surrounding region, nation and the whole world. As Cerdá wrote in the frontispiece of his *Teoría*: 'rurizad o urbano, urbanizad lo rural: . . . *Replete terram* [ruralise the urban, urbanise the rural: . . . fill the Earth]'. A ruralised urbanisation 'would designate a system of occupying land no longer bound to the outdated dichotomy of city and country: ruralized urbanisation would be a model of both city and country—both culture and nature' (Adams 2019, 35). As Andrea Cavalletti explains, contrasting the city with urbanisation was for Cerdá a way to substitute the former's static relation between people and place with a dynamic and integrated process: the question, in other terms, 'was no longer that of including life within a determined place, but rather within space itself' (2005, 26; our translation). This is a space that has no boundaries or scale. It potentially coincides with the whole Earth. Cerdá defines it via another neologism: *vialidad*, that is, circulation. In his vision of a world where everything was (in) movement, expansion, communication, the implicit background of urbanisation is the 'greater universal *vialidad*' (idem, 359), the circulation of air, people and goods every *urbs* must be made permeable to, starting from its smaller unit (the household), so as to provide the maximum level of freedom, health, economic and social prosperity.

Circulation

As the attentive reader may have noted, there is more than a resonance, here, with the liberal notion of *laissez faire*, introduced by the physiocrats in the eighteenth century and then championed by the likes of Adam Smith. Just like free market, also urbanisation is presented by Cerdá as a spontaneous process that must be put in the best possible condition in order to unfold without obstructions.[17] As Adams (2019) has shown in his brilliant genealogy of the term, the notion of circulation already played a key role in physiocrats like Roger Cantillon, but also in the work of Claude Henri de Saint-Simon, who developed the notion of *reseau* (network) in a very similar sense. Circulation's modern political significance can be traced, at least, all the way to Hobbes, who introduced the modern conception of freedom as 'absence of opposition': an eminently physical and kinetic notion, with respect to which the key question is that of allowing movement by obstructing circulation as little as possible (Baldissone 2018).[18]

Significantly, to be directly inspired by Saint-Simon was Baron Georges-Eugène Haussmann, whose remarkable works on Paris greatly influenced Cerdá. As Adams (2019, 173–181) notes, Haussmann's notorious demolition *cum* reconstruction of the city centre of the French capital under Napoleon III should not only be understood in the sense of having turned the city into a machine of the capital (Harvey 2004) and a pacified stage for the nascent bourgeoisie (Benjamin 2002[1982]). This was certainly the case, but Haussmann's violent urbanisation should also be understood more generally, in relation to the other logistical works (telegraph cables, railways, roadways) that him and Napoleon III were carrying out at the national scale. Seen in these terms, his work appears to be an attempt at de-territorialising the city from its local place, and re-territorialising it as a node in a wider, national and ideally global network of circulation. As Adams continues, 'Haussmann and Napoleon III had created a paradigm in which the space of the city was made available to planning for the first time . . . distribut[ing] a geometry of power throughout its homogeneous space in which all resources, population, wealth could be measured and their movement could be controlled' (2019, 81).

This 'modern' understanding of space as an absolute, homogeneous, expandable and malleable matter that can be manipulated via an appropriate science, which we find at work in both Haussmann and Cerdá—the perception of 'the city *as a territory* . . . as a single homogeneous mass' (Adams 2019, 158; emphasis in original)—constitutes a fundamental facet of the imaginary that shapes modern urbanisation (see chapter 4) and a central tenet of modernist urban planning (see below). Yet, while praising Haussmann for the success of his work in quelling social disorders (i.e., urban revolts), Cerdá was also very critical of his violent demolitions and the explicitly classist shape of his reconstruction. While he found the *pars destruens* of Haussmann's work both lacking justice and foresight, since no proper provisions for the mass of dispossessed had been planned, he found the *pars construens* to be both unequal and insufficient. As Richard Sennett (2018, 41) observes with reference to the *Eixample*, 'Cerdá's generous original provision of space affirmed, on the contrary, workers' rights to air, light and space'.[19] Differently from Haussmann, an egalitarian utopianism fed Cerdá's vision, framed by the intention to equalise the city by means of equalising its form. At the bottom of Cerdá's theory is the intention to condense urbanism into a few, basic algorithms of urbanisation to be endlessly replicated, and that were centred around a radical rethinking of the relation between *oikos* and *polis*: the house and the *urbs*. Between the urbs and the house, argued Cerdá, there is merely a difference in scale. They are both a set of dwellings and circulation, where the functions of reproduction and production intersect and are opened up to the universal circulation: 'the house/urbs is the original urbs' (2018[1867], 395). Likewise, *intervias*, that is, city blocks, are 'a small world, a small urbs—an elemental urbs, if you will' (idem, 356–359). They are the kernel of urbanisation, which is the task of urbanism to make permeable and communicating with the 'greater universal *vialidad*'.

Out of these units, the basic algorithms of urbanisation are produced: first, by defining precisely, through scientific analysis, the more adequate proportions (up to the required amount of cubic-metres) concerning the domestic space and, more precisely, the city block (*intervias*); second, by replicating this structure in a basic form, that is, the grid, whose homogenous arrangement would both guarantee urban equality and indefinite, context-independent replicability—'[the graph] provides the infrastructural basis on which a single, generalized framework could be made for constructing an *urbe* anywhere' (Adams 2019, 51); third, by articulating the relation between *intervias* across the grid with respect to a basic function, that is, circulation. Movement and rest, production and reproduction, *vialidad* and dwelling: the *urbs* is thought as the infrastructural apparatus that allows for this dual rhythm to unfold. Opening up the city to the 'universal circulation', in other words, means first of all to open up the *domus*, economically and biopolitically: 'urbanization, most succinctly put, is the domesticization of the city' (Adams 2014, 22). *Urbanizácion* is meant to overcome the *oikos/polis* distinction, that is, the one between the private sphere of domestic economy and the public sphere of politics, with a double movement (Cavalletti 2005, 31): on the one hand, the *oikos* is expanded into the *polis*, that is, the urban is produced out of the serial reproduction of the 'domestic' units (*intervias*), a logic we will find later in the work of Le Corbusier or Ludwig Hilberseimer (see Aureli 2013); on the other hand, the *polis* is shrunk into the *oikos*, as a novel political economy (from *oikonomia*, i.e., the administration of the house) infiltrates every level of urban management (see Brighenti and Pavoni 2018).

Project

In the *Teoría* we find the perfect exemplification of, and a powerful inspiration for, the spatio-political *project* of urbanisation as a quintessential 'socio-technical imaginary', a (utopian) projection of a desirable future to be achieved as the culmination of social progress fostered by science and technology (cf. Jasanoff 2015; see chapter 4). The extent to which Cerdá's ideas have shaped the imaginary of urbanisation is exemplified by an excerpt from Vicente Guallart's introduction to the first English translation of the *Teoría*:

> Beyond its historical interest, this translation aims to promote reflection on the process of urbanization today, at the beginning of the 21st century, when a new revolution, the digital revolution, has shown us the need to define rational processes—and if possible scientific processes—for the construction and reform of cities around the world. (2018, 12)

In this vision, the liberal prioritisation of individual freedom, private property, economic prosperity and security is paramount. This is exemplified in Cerdá's anthropology, which pictures an absolutely individualistic 'primitive' human that 'would tend to build an isolated shelter to guarantee his independence, so no one could come to disrupt his delight' (Cerdá 2018[1867], 139). Sociability, in this situation, appears a secondary product of the necessity of security:

> where an individual was forced to recognise his own weakness and impotence, he must have sought the support he required in other individuals: i.e., in a

social group. This is what originally gave rise, in politics, to institutions that sacrifice the individual to the state and, in urbanization, to paltry dwellings and the juxtaposition of buildings, resulting in the consequent densification of the *urbs*. (idem, 158)

In this curious depiction, where both the state and the city are pictured as necessary—that is, as contingent sacrifices the individual must undergo for the sake of security—urbanism is implicitly posited as the infrastructural solution to the exquisitely liberal problem (or indeed, myth: see chapter 3) of the security-freedom balance. The urban, in other words, is the *technology* that allows the coexistence of freedom *qua* security and sociability 'without demanding the sacrifice of one in favor of the other' (Cerdá 2018[1867], 146). A solution, needless to say, that is performed by surgically bypassing the political question, which, writes Adams, 'is displaced by the material fact of an assemblage of buildings and the infrastructure connecting them' (2014, 19). The political is subsumed onto the biopolitical, as evident in the detailed provisions for the management of life all the way to the domestic level.

The biopolitical and technocratic kernel of the *project* of urbanisation finds here its perfect definition, one that is to be put in direct relation with the notion of police (see chapter 3). The police emerges, in the context of the transition towards liberalism, as a novel science that introduces a biopolitical urbanisation of cities, while at the same time feeding the imaginary that will then morph into the notion of civilisation (coined in 1766) and that of urbanisation (one century later). As George Rigakos and his colleagues explain, policing is inaccurately understood if simply framed in the context of criminology. More precisely, it is to be understood as 'a grand intellectual project linked to state formation, prosperity and security in Enlightenment thought' (2009, 2). As we are to see in the next chapter, and already inscribed in its etymological relation with the notion of *polis*, it is crucial to 'equat[e] the *problem of police* with the *problem of the city*' (idem, 3; emphasis in original): police and urbanisation are to be understood as coessential terms. As we argue in chapter 4, they should be also read along an epistemological continuum with the notion of civilisation and must be put in relation with the colonial enterprise, whose logistical, juridical and military flattening of the colonial *space* is directly productive of the spatial imaginary that feeds the *project* of the urban, in the same way as the modern understanding of *time* as an evolutionary line of progress allows the temporal imaginary to feed said project.

The extent to which Cerdà's notion of urbanisation is fed by, and feeds in turn, the 'modern' abstraction of space and time (see chapter 4) is quite evident: a conceptualisation of space as an absolute and homogeneous *tabula*

rasa, on which circulation will smoothly unfold, and time as an arrow of progress, which is the task of urbanisation to achieve. An imaginary, informed by
the intention to domesticate the urban, that would become hegemonic in the
modernist architectural and planning movement through the theorisation of
Le Corbusier—as particularly evident in his vision for a *ville contemporaine*
(2003[1925]) with fast automobility unhampered by the unpredictable chaos
of the urban crowds, and the intermingling of pedestrians and cars.[20] In this
sense, much more than in Haussmann's explicitly authoritarian demolitions,
it is in Cerdá's theorisation that we find a remarkable anticipation of that
technocratic relation, between urbanisation, liberalism and technology, that
will dominate the urban politics to come, all the way to contemporary smart
city solutionism (cf. chapter 8). This is also evident in the way Cerdá frames
the very crisis his theory of urbanisation is supposed to address as a 'profound
malaise', a 'social malady', a 'grave illness', whose fundamental cause is to be
found in 'the organism of our cities': a metaphorical medicalisation of the
urban crisis that, in providing the de-politicising breeding ground for the
proposed *cure*, parallels the literal medicalisation of violence we described
(see chapter 1, Researching Urban Violence).

We may even go further and, with a more speculative suggestion, argue
that in the *Teoría* can also be found an evocative anticipation, in the urban
context, of the future epistemological shift from liberalism to neoliberalism, as far as the relation between (economic) circulation and (political)
intervention is concerned. In classic liberalism, the principle of *laissez faire*
played a key normative role in shaping economic policies and expectations.
As Walter Lippman (1937) argued, however, at the turn to the twentieth
century, *laissez-faire* had become an increasingly naïve and anachronistic
thinking in the face of the complexity of an increasingly industrialised, urbanised, globalised world—that which an author important to him, Graham
Wallas (1914), had called *The Great Society*. With respect to this complexity,
the 'natural' tendency of the market to reach the socio-economic optimum
cannot unfold spontaneously: its conditions must be produced. It is from this
realisation that neoliberalism, a term that was coined at the Colloque Walter
Lippmann, held in Paris in 1938, derived: in other words, from the acknowledgement of the necessity to *intervene* on the society at large so as to adapt
it to circulation itself (Stiegler, Barbara 2019). 'Liberal interventionism',
according to the seemingly paradoxical formula coined by Wilhelm Röpke,
does not aim to 'fix' the distortions of market laws, but rather to produce the
right conditions for their full unfolding (Rehmann 2013, 272). This implies a
shift: from letting be (*laissez faire*), to making be.[21] Education, labour, the legal
system, technology, health, population: in short, the environment in general,
what the ordoliberals called the 'framework', would therefore become the

field of action of a complex governance aimed at achieving the Copernican counter-revolution desired by the neoliberals: *adapting the world to the market.*

What will follow are the strategies we came to know all too well: the attempt to smooth out frictions and conflicts, the emptying out of trade unions, the systematic de-politicisation, precarisation and flexibilisation of society. As Foucault observed, 'to the same extent that governmental intervention must be light at the level of economic processes themselves, so must it be heavy when it is a matter of this set of technical, scientific, legal, geographic, let's say, broadly, social factors which now increasingly become the object of governmental intervention' (2010[2004], 141).

We do not believe it is too far stretched—albeit obviously speculative, and clearly anachronistic—to read Cerdá's *Teoría* through this suggestion. His starting point is similar, namely, the revolutionary changes technological innovation introduced in a fast industrialising, globalising and urbanising world. Likewise, for him, the problem this situation posited was that of adapting the city to the 'universal' *vialidad*, that is, urbanising the city so as to open it up to the planetary circulation, via a technology—urbanisation itself—supposedly able to overcome the obstructions of the political. Needless to say, 'in the process, the political is paradoxically transcribed more deeply on to the everyday processes of life under *urbanización*' (Adams 2019, 63). Regardless of his intention, and the actual impact his concepts had, Cerdá's *urbanización* expresses *in nuce* the urban form of capital, a post-political machine for the extraction and circulation of value, 'anticipating a simplified version of the legal, administrative and governmental paradigm of capitalist urbanization more than a century later' (Adams 2019, 25). While we do not pursue any further this anachronistic parallel, it is nonetheless intriguing to see how, since its etymological birth, the notion of urbanisation appears to contain the germs of both nineteenth-century liberal values and twentieth-century neoliberal pragmatism, framed through a technocratic approach that is still perfectly consistent with the contemporary urban *project.*

Process

The indefinitely expansive, Earth-filling urbanisation envisaged by the *Teoría* also chimes in different ways with the actual *process* of urbanisation we are facing today. If, for Cerdá, the absolute *space* of urbanisation was to overcome the contingent *place* of the city, then we find the same de- and re-territorialising effect in the well-known description of the process of capitalist urbanisation provided by the likes of Simmel, Lefebvre, Harvey, or Deleuze and Guattari. As suggested elsewhere (Pavoni 2018a), while in *urbanización* we can find a kernel of the spatio-political project of (capitalist) urbanisation, this form was to materialise later on, as a process once the economic-industrial machine of the metropolis emerged: namely, the expansion of the urban into urbanisation as a global *process* of networks and flows, expressed in the intersection of the primary (production and trade) and secondary (the built environment) circuits of capital,[22] as per David Harvey's spatialisation of the theory of accumulation (1978). In other words, an urban form that is emancipated from place and ideally connected to a homogenous, global space of circulation, of which the former city is to become a mere node (Cunningham 2008, 255–256).

The metropolis, in David Cunningham's words, is 'the manifestation of a distinctively modern spatial-productive logic . . . which unites a differential whole in which every particular "place" is rendered "*equi-valent*" in a universal circulation and exchange' (idem, 156–157; emphasis in original). This is perfectly consistent with Cerdá's effort to reduce the urban to equivalent spaces, that is, grid squares, a sort of 'infrastructure space'—i.e., the 'parameter of global urbanisation' (Easterling 2014, see chapter 1)—that can be indefinitely replicated.[23] It is through the smooth reproduction of the domestic form onto an indefinitely extensible grid that the city is made permeable to the universal circulation, which is in turn put in direct relation with the biopolitical management of the population (see chapter 3).

In a sense, if Neil Brenner (2013, 90) argued that, today, 'the urban appears to have become a quintessential floating signifier', no longer graspable with the categories of traditional urban theory, we may argue that, more than an epistemological limit, the emptying out of meaning from the urban now appears to be the consequence of the global scale the process of urbanisation has reached.[24] As Brighenti and Pavoni write (2021b, 1), 'the accelerated temporalities, extended scales and contracted geographies of urbanisation have decomposed the solidity of well-known Western dichotomies, such as society/nature, urban/rural, and city/wilderness' (see chapter 4), including the understanding of the city as a static and bounded entity. This limited interpretation of the city has been increasingly overcome by a dynamic, global and, yet, multi-scalar process of continuous socio-ecological transformation (Tzaninis et al. 2021). Following on Lefebvre's suggestion that the city is overcome by a veritable 'planetarisation of the urban' (2014[1989]), Brenner and Christian Schmid (2015; see also Angelo and Wachsmuth 2015; Connolly 2019) have therefore argued for an epistemological approach that shifts the attention of urban theory from the spatial entity of the city and rather focus on the planetary scale of the process of urbanisation: from a static understanding of the urban as a bounded, coherent and discrete unit, towards the 'mutually constitutive moments' of concentrated, extended and differential urbanisation.[25] Brenner understands the urban as a '"concrete abstraction" in which the contradictory sociospatial relations of capitalism (commodification, capital circulation, capital accumulation, and associated forms of political regulation/contestation) are at once territorialized (embedded within concrete contexts and thus fragmented) and generalized (extended across place, territory, and scale and thus universalized)' (2013, 95).

For our purposes, the theses on planetary urbanisation have particular value in their deconstructive component, that is, the critique of the 'urban age' thesis. Since the UN-Habitat first declared, a decade ago, that most of the human population now lives 'in cities', this thesis has been widely trumpeted, becoming, in the academic, political and journalistic discourse, an 'all-pervasive metanarrative' through which urban discourse is implicitly or explicitly framed (Brenner and Schmid 2013, 4). Amid this narrative, urbanisation is a quite simple process: a (dramatic) movement of people from the field to the city, from the rural to the urban, a convenient dichotomy that allows for 'grasping' the process via quantitative statistics. Brenner and Schmid have criticised the urban age thesis both analytically (it is based on extremely problematic and often incomparable national datasets) and theoretically, for the way it naturalises the 'urban' as an unquestioned, pre-assumed, fundamentally universal fact. The reader may at this point have already noticed how the problem of the urban age thesis resonates with some of the problems with urban violence, whose discourse has been oriented, from the nineteenth century to our days, by a similar metanarrative, that is, the conceptualisation of violence as a natural occurrence in, and of, specific and bounded places (i.e., cities), observable via precise statistics (quintessentially: murders), whereby a hierarchy of 'violent' cities around the globe is drawn. Conversely, not only does a focus on the process of urbanisation as a precise historical category linked to the global expansion of capitalism resonate with the arguments against assuming violence as a transhistorical and transgeographical concept (see chapter 1). But, moreover, it is necessary to work toward an understanding of urban violence able to move beyond its static, city-centric bias. Additionally, a lens capable to capture the global and dialectical nature of urbanisation is necessary to overcome the tendency of overly focusing on 'the putatively unique properties of "southern" megacities' (Brenner and Schmid 2015, 4), object of choice of most research on urban violence, by considering the geographical and historical relations within which urban violence locally unfolds (see chapters 4 and 5).

If Cerdá provided us with the template for understanding the *project* of urbanisation that underlines the contemporary urban condition, therefore, the concept of planetary urbanisation is an attempt to critically grasp the

resulting *process*, thereby allowing for its critical as well as empirical exploration. Brenner and Schmid's theses, however, have been hotly criticised,
above all for the risk (at times, indeed, a tendency) to overflow the nature
of *an epistemological lens* and surreptitiously become a homogenising, grand
theory of the urban—critiques have come from any number of perspectives,
including feminist and queer (McLean 2018), post-colonial (Reddy 2018)
and affect-materialist (Pavoni 2018a, 45–55).[26] In line with Tsing's reflection, our understanding is that the process of planetary urbanisation always
'come[s] to life in "friction", the grip of worldly encounter' (2005, 1). This
does not simply mean that there are multiple and 'insurgent' *urbanisations*
(e.g., Holston 1998; Miraftab 2009) that challenge, resist, oppose and tra-
verse totalising *Urbanisation*. More precisely, it is to observe that urbanisation itself always occurs frictionally, in a process of territorialisation and
deterritorialisation that is always problematic, turbulent and sketchy. In a
sense, planetary urbanisation can be read through in the terms of what Theodor Adorno (1973[1966]) referred to as an objective negative universality,
namely, a universalising and totalising process, which must be understood
simultaneously in its general and immediate dimension, where the immediacy of the contingent unfolding can neither be simply explained—as if
smoothly subsumed—by the wider process, and yet at the same time does
not avoid being mediated by it. This complex relation between the universal
and the particular, the continuity and the discontinuities, is missed if simply
reduced to an alternative between dialectical subsumption and irreducible
singularity (e.g., Chakrabarty 2000).[27] Urbanisation, therefore, is not simply
actualised in, and therefore diffracted by, the contingency of an everyday life
that always resists being fully translated into it (Tsing 2012). More precisely,
urbanisation actually emerges out of these frictional instances, not occurring
as a linear, homogeneous, centrifugal process radiating from a centre, but
rather as the very turbulence that is generated by discontinuities that unfold
at the heterogeneous, fragmented and violent thresholds in which it encounters, while simultaneously producing, its outside (Wu and Loucks, 1995; Keil
2018; McFarlane 2018; Tsing et al. 2020; Tzaninis et al. 2021)[28]—and in
chapter 5 we will frame the violence of urbanisation exactly in these terms.

This is why we believe, and will discuss at length, it is crucial to transcend
either/or questions and dichotomous approaches, and rather work to put the
political economic understanding of the *violence of* planetary urbanisation
into dialogue with a materialist understanding of the urban experience *of
violence* (cf. introduction). An immediate implication of the latter approach,
as we just argued, is the attention paid to avoid fetishising urbanisation: similarly, though urban violence is indeed fuelled by, and fosters in turn, global

phenomena, it is perceived, experienced and lived in the urban through specific aesthetic and affective forms. The lens through which we need to conceptualise the urban in urban violence is therefore a bifocal one, made up of a wide-angle to encompass the planetary dimension of the violent process of urbanisation and the socio-spatial configuration it presupposes (see chapter 5), and a telephoto able to capture the material and affective relations in and through which this form is concretely actualised in the urban space (see chapter 6). This is, in a nutshell, the urban equivalent of the argument we made for the importance to focus on the infrastructure of violence (see chapter 1). As AbdouMaliq Simone challenges us to ask:

> For if, as Brenner and Schmid (2015) argue, urbanization extends itself not so much through the imposition of the axioms of capital but through complex processes of instantiation, where the singularities of place and history are experimentally refigured into unsettled articulations with larger surrounds, what are urban processes in such interstices? What is between the peculiar, idiosyncratic features of cities and urban regions and urbanization at a planetary scale? (2016, 8; see also Tsing 2012)

Atmosphere

Where the concepts of *project* and *process* have allowed us to frame our wide-angle, it is through the concept of *atmosphere* that we propose to zoom in onto the fabric of urban co-existence. While this concept will be properly introduced in chapter 6, at this stage we need to anticipate its derivation, from the already mentioned reflections on the materiality of urban experience developed by the likes of Simmel, Benjamin and Krakauer, or, more recently, Jameson, Sloterdijk, Amin and Thrift. These reflections help showing 'the urban public as not simply a site marked by difference, but also as a site where this difference can come to be felt and in some small way made knowable' (Latham 1999, 454)—a conceptualisation, for instance, that has been shown to be immensely productive, in (feminist) geographies of difference, for capturing the multiplex experiences of urban fear, (in)security and violence (see, among others, Grosz 1995; Pain 2009; Machado and Ratts 2017; Kirmani 2020).

The notion of atmosphere is particularly useful in this sense. Atmospheres, we will show, allow to unpack simultaneously the ontological relation, the phenomenological experience and the power-structured ordering that characterise the urban everyday—in other words, its affective, aesthetic and normative materiality—as well as their complex relations with both the project and the process of urbanisation. Moreover, the atmosphere provides an historical conceptualisation with respect to that process Peter Sloterdijk (2013[2005]) refers to as *interiorisation*, namely the gradual integration and organisation of social life into a series of technological, normative, affective and physical infrastructures, through which everyday life has been moulded within safe, comforting, commodified and entertaining spaces, relations and practices—a process we will explore in chapter 7. As we are to see, it is not coincidental that in the same period Cerdá was writing, the modern, bourgeois notion of comfort was surfacing (see Brighenti and Pavoni 2019), a notion that is directly relevant to the '*domesticization* of the urban', and which allows for the exploration of it's aesthetic and affective materialisation in the atmosphere of the contemporary city.

(Urban) atmospheres will help us to unpack the articulation of the political economy and the materiality of violence, or, in other words of the infrastructure and the experience of violence in the urban realm. Before framing and attending to this articulation, however, it is necessary to introduce yet another concept, which, we will show, is crucial for that very articulation to work. The third, and last, of the main concepts of our argument is security (and the police, quintessentially attached to it), which we will discuss in the next chapter by looking at the coexistence, in its logics, of different paradigms—which we will exemplify in the history of (Western) political thought.

Researching Urban Violence: Beyond Quantitative Reductionism

As we have seen so far, the twofold essentialisation of its two terms has mainstreamed a conceptualisation of urban violence as a quantitative relation between (violent) crime, on the one hand, and the social and environmental characters of the city, on the other. While we have so far deconstructed this association, as well as the conceptual problems with the two terms of the equation, we now turn to focus on a more specific problem, the reliance on quantitative data, that is, on crime statistics—the analytical counterpart of some of the problems of the urban age thesis we have discussed above. The use of crime statistics to measure and study crime—and, by extension, violence—brings analytical, definitional and conceptual problems.

Let us start from the empirical and analytical dimension by simply reminding the reader that 'crime statistics' only reflect those crimes that are known to the police and the judiciary. They do not correspond to the social phenomenon of crime broadly, as many (probably most) crimes never get reported or discovered—as early as 1832, Belgian mathematician and sociologist Adolphe Quetelet wrote about 'the dark figure of crime' (Berlinski 2009), all those crimes that remain outside the scope of statistics. Reported crime is influenced by at least three orders of factors. First, for crimes that involve victims, the likeliness that these are actually reported to the police is extremely low for several typologies of crimes (sexual violence, for instance, is known to be among the crimes that are least likely to be reported). Second, reporting methodologies vary dramatically among jurisdictions, jeopardising the possibility for meaningful comparisons. Third, several typologies of crimes, for instance drug crimes, are almost never reported and are thus registered as the result of active police investigation, meaning that police actions influence what crimes will be reported or where they will be reported. In this way, every action performed by the police will influence the statistical distribution of crime data (Hope 2018; 2020) and, through that, the social understanding of crime. In their classic *Criminology*, Edwin Sutherland and Donald Cressey (1978, 30) have argued that police data describe police priorities more accurately than crime—with implications for discrimination and racialisation that have been discussed at length (see the discussion of broken-windows policing in chapter 5, Researching Urban Violence).

Granted, large part of the criminological endeavour has been devoted to 'approximating the truth about crime' (the title of van Dijk 2009), for instance through other sources of data—e.g., so-called 'victimisation surveys', which ask people whether they or any of their acquaintances have been victims of crime in a given period. But this cannot address definitional and political problems, such as the fact that not all activities that cause harm are legally defined as crimes (for instance 'honour killing' is still legal in many countries and was legal in many more just a few decades ago), or that many harmless activities are criminalised for moral or political reasons. More generally, philosophy, anthropology and critical criminology have extensively showed that crime and criminalisation, far from being neutral concepts, are shaped by power relationships, ultimately representing the purview and interests of dominant groups (see Gusfield 1981; Hulsman 1986; Melossi 2003; Agamben 2018[2017]). In other words, 'while crime itself is a social construct, crime statistics are further socially constructed' (Jamieson 1998, 242; see also Coleman and Moynihan 1996; Penney 2014). While this is hardly a peculiarity of crime statistics, it clashes quite evidently with the way crime statistics are commonly used—and even preferred to data, such as those of victimisation surveys, that are more reliable in certain situations—as a proxy for crime in much academic and political discourse.

Now, these sets of issues/problems should act as a cautionary tale for everyone interested in using actually existing data to measure and study crime and, through that, violence. And yet, we have to concede that, thus put, these issues/problems can be partially overcome. Better sets of data can be produced, better ways to address the dark figures of crime can be developed, a better police can be imagined (if, that is, one believes police can be reformed), crime legislation can be reformed, or, at the very least, a better understanding of the relation between the act of criminalisation and the management of social problems can be pushed forward. This notwithstanding, we believe that the reliance on crime data to study violence implies some conceptual and ontological issues that go against the grain of the attempt we are making at de-essentialising both violence and the urban. In part, this is due to the way the dominance of positivist epistemologies—and, with them, of the idea that generalisation is the golden standard for producing knowledge—has made quantitative social research scarcely capable of addressing its own limits and problems, particularly when facing complex social issues like crime (Tulumello 2019). As Tim Hope (2018; 2020) has discussed in depth, much of the patterns that we see through crime data is a 'statistical chimera', irrespective, that is, of the quality of the job of collecting those data in the first place—a discussion that we will further develop in relation to predictive policing (see chapter 8).

Notes

1. Idelfons Cerdá. 1867. Teoría general de la urbanización, y aplicación de sus principios y doctrinas a la reforma y ensanche de Barcelona.

2. Hence the relatively little role these thinkers have played in critical urban theory. Indeed, also Henry Lefebvre's works on 'everyday life' have been broadly overlooked to the advantage of the more 'politico-economic' one (see Goonewardena et al. 2008).

3. In his *The Metropolis and Mental Life*, George Simmel draws a parallel between the *blasé attitude* of the urban dweller, systematically indifferent 'towards the distinctions between things', and the 'money economy', which 'hollows out the core of things', reducing everything to a comparable and measurable quantity (2002[1903], 106).

4. Not to be confused with contemporary urban ecology.

5. A tradition that is far from being lost, as evident from the very title—*Great American City*—of a recent book by former director of the school Robert J. Sampson (2011).

6. Also within the US debate, recent scholarship has noted how the tendency to generalise from few, north-eastern cities has made the complex regional characters of national urbanisation invisible (Rushing 2009; Garner 2018).

7. The neighbourhood effect is, in broad sense, the idea that neighbourhoods (their social and spatial characters) have a decisive impact on individual and collective trajectories—and is widely used in mainstream research to link urban violence with socio-spatial differentiations. Collective efficacy, a linked concept, is the capacity of a local community to control the behaviours of individuals and groups.

8. We believe this association to be self-evident. The sceptical reader, however, may verify in the immense production of, or influenced by, the Chicago School how urban violence always and exclusively defines physical, criminal violence that happens in the city. For a systematic literature review, see Pavoni and Tulumello (2020, 52–56).

9. On the notion of tensegrity, see chapter 6.

10. The first full English translation (Cerdá 2018[1867]) has been published in celebration of the 150th anniversary of the original version.

11. Since, for Cerdá, the infrastructure of urbanisation is the projection of a natural process of socialisation, rather than a socio-material condition that in turns shaped socialisation in significant ways (see chapter 4), his argument misses a more complex genealogy, as shown by archaeologists and anthropologists, concerning the association between novel techniques and materials that, in the Neolithic, allowed to stabilise sedentary life, by building and living inside permanent 'containers' (cf. Mumford 1961), which in turn brought forth a new mode of thinking and experiencing the relation with the surrounding at large: 'whereas the hunter-gatherer (from ethnographic evidence) views the environment as a provider and protector, the builder extracts from the earth itself' (Wilson 2007, 117–118).

12. If Rousseau, rather than speculating abstractly, would have considered the material condition of dwelling in the congested Paris in which he lived, argued Cerdá, 'instead of a social contract he would have dreamt up a system for organizing cities better' (quoted in, and translated by, Adams 2019, 28).

13. This is consistent with Foucault's observation (1984[1982]) that the nineteenth-century city was plunged into a novel spatio-political *problématique* by three key developments: the novel social threats represented by epidemics, revolts and crime; the introduction of railroads; and the advent of electricity.

14. Cerdá (2018[1867], 451–93) also reviews cognate terms to the city (e.g. *villa*, *pueblo*, *lugar*, *aldea*), finding all of them unsatisfying since referring to agglomerations of houses which were too specific in terms of size, scale, regional hierarchy, historical development and so on. As he writes, these 'common names used to designate the various types of groupings of houses are, strictly speaking, today merely an expression of what those groups were at one time, not what they are today. In other words, they are a blatant anachronism' (idem, 454), and therefore of little use with respect to his aim to find 'a more abstract and generic word that could encompass all the different groups under a common name, without classifying them and without forcing them into an unpleasant comparison' (idem, 473).

15. The notion of *urbs* is usually understood as a derivate of *urbum*, which referred to the blade of the plow and, as a synecdoche, to the plow itself: the term *urbs* would

derive from the Roman custom of tracing the outline of the settlement with a plow. Cerdá contests this origin and, with a sweeping etymological suggestion, contends that, rather than a derivative, *urbs* is the original term. More precisely, he argues that the monosyllable *ur* contains 'the root of all those original worlds in primitive Western languages used to refer to groups or combination of houses' (2018[1867], 478–479). Within this word resonates the verb *uro* or *aro* (to plough), which makes the relation between cultivation, civilisation and urbanisation explicit (idem, 482)

16. Incidentally, for all its differences, Cerdá's approach has some resonance with Wirth in the research of the universal coordinates for understanding and managing urban life.

17. The implicit belief in the positive effect of the spontaneous force of urbanisation intersects the invisible hand of the market explicitly when Cerdá argues that enclosing a city within jurisdictional boundaries is 'damaging' vis-à-vis 'the spontaneous, free development of some *urbs*' (Cerdá 2018[1867], 271). Enclosing the development of the city, he argues, limits the amount of space available to each inhabitant, producing high competition and rising rent prices. Moreover, this produces 'a monopoly grounded upon the exclusive privilege enjoyed by the owners of the lands within the wall-line, to the detriment of those who own the outer land, and primarily counter to private tenant's benefit of a free rental market' (idem, 270)—arguments, these, that still dominate neoclassical accounts of housing and real estate markets.

18. Hobbes famously writes: 'Liberty, or Freedome, signifieth (properly) the absence of Opposition; (by Opposition, I mean externall Impediments of motion)' (2002[1651], ch. XXI). Influenced by the science of Galileo, whom he may have befriended, Cartesian mechanisms and William Harvey's demonstration on the system of blood circulation, Hobbes assumed the perfect circulation between the parts that constituted the Leviathan to be central to his scientific body politics (see Adams 2019, 92–96).

19. The plan however could not be developed according to the original aims as it was deemed, Sennett writes, 'an impossible luxury' (2018, 41) for the then poor working neighbourhood of *La Barceloneta*.

20. Quite tellingly, Le Corbusier (2003[1935], 261; our translation) would argue that 'since 1930, military commands ended up giving us [the modernist planners] an unexpected support'—in preparing the *tabula rasa* by relentlessly bombing European cities.

21. This is another way to spell the Foucauldian depiction of the shift introduced by biopolitics: from letting live and making die, to making live and letting die (Foucault 2010[2004]). See on this point chapter 7.

22. Through logistics (Mezzadra and Neilson 2019; Arboleda 2020).

23. Cerdá, here, could build on the long history, from Roman *cardi* and *decumani* all the way to colonial foundation cities, of the use of the grid as a way to create order through human settlements, an imaginary that reached its ultimate expressions in the US grid, the attempt at regularising an entire continent through design (see Corboz 1998, 239–244). See also Foucault (1977[1975], 141–145) on the spatial

operations of the disciplinary state: enclosure (*cloture*), partitioning (*quadrillage*), functional sites (*emplacements fonctionells*) and rank (*rang*)—and, for a discussion of those operations in modernist planning, Tulumello (2017a, 88–91).

24. Cf. the reflections, in the introduction, on how the Anthropocene materialises a 'real decostruction'.

25. Concentrated urbanisation refers to the traditional focus on agglomeration and density; extended urbanisation to the 'operationalization of places territories and landscapes, often located far beyond the dense populations centers, to support the everyday activities and socioeconomic dynamics of urban life' (Brenner and Schmid 2015, 167); and differential urbanisation to the continuous remaking of uneven socio-spatial relations, what Lefebvre (2003[1970], 15) had captured through the metaphor of 'implosion-explosion'.

26. One of the points of debate, which in fact precedes and exceeds the discussion on Brenner and Schmid's work, is whether there is any 'outside' to (capitalist) urbanisation—see Ananya Roy's application (2016) of the concept of constitutive outside to urban studies.

27. As Antonio Vazquez-Arroyo (2008, 463) explains, 'only from the perspective of historical continuities can discontinuities be apprehended, as breaks in such continuums. That is part of Adorno's dialectical contention. But particular events are discontinuous in yet another sense: in the sense of being qualitatively different, non-identical. The particular is thus not a mere instantiation of a larger, universal narrative, yet the particular is mediated by the universal, by the continuous process of domination. If the dialectic is not cut short, the particular mediates the universal as much as the universal mediates the particular. Continuity and discontinuity are thus dialectically mediated and rendered intelligible, in their mutual interruptions, in a negative narrative of universal history'.

28. For an insightful reflection on the operations through which capital constantly produces the very outsides it subsequently seeks to ingest, see Mezzadra and Neilson (2019).

CHAPTER THREE

~

Security

Sollte es nicht der Instinkt der Furcht sein, der uns erkennen heisst?
Sollte das Frohlocken des Erkennenden nicht eben das Frohlocken des
wieder erlangten Sicherheitsgefühls sein?[1]

Security—with related concepts like the 'risk society' (Beck 1992[1986])
or the 'societies of control' (Deleuze 1992[1990])—has recently taken the
central stage in political, policy and media agendas: in the Western world,
security has 'become the *telos* of our government' (Dodsworth 2019, 5). At
the intersection of the dislocations produced by neoliberal restructuring,
and the generalised (if often problematic) perceptions of increasing crime
and violence in European and North-American cities since the 1980s, new
'cultures of control' (Garland 2001) have emerged, pushing towards an increasing centrality of 'crime' within governmental paradigms (e.g., Simon
2007; Reiner 2016). In the early 2000s, terrorist attacks in the USA and
Europe (and above all those to the World Trade Center) have further pushed
the political and public imagination 'toward security', which, Ami Kaplan
(2008/2009) argued, came to supplant freedom as the central concept of
American politics. Similar notes could be written from other geographical
perspectives: the intersection, in Latin American cities, of neoliberal restructuring, exploding inequality, new forms of urban violence and, ultimately,
increasingly 'securitised' politics is a paradigmatic example of a different regional (and temporal) trajectory within the same global trends (e.g., Sanchez
2006; Misse 2008; Goldstein 2010). Indeed, one of the central arguments of

this book is that the category of urban violence is inseparable from the contemporary politics of (urban) security.

At the same time, while acknowledging this recent intensification and its peculiar qualitative characters, is security a 'sign of the times', as Francis Dodsworth (2019) asks, a sign of *our* times? In this chapter, we argue that the specific, to some extent unique, pervasiveness of security in the twenty-first century—and therefore security's role in shaping urban violence in the twenty-first century—can only be understood through the history of security, of its practical and conceptual expansion, and particularly its consolidation at the centre of the project of the (European) liberal state. Borrowing from Michel Foucault's genealogical method, in other words, we suggest considering the present of security through the lenses of discontinuity, that is, ruptures and mutations that intervene between successive discursive formations and policy formulations, but without downplaying the existence of dimensions of persistence (cf. Foucault 1994[1976]; Gutting 1990). On the one hand, we follow Mariana Valverde's argument (2011) that it makes little sense to talk about security regardless of the specific, historically situated security *project* through which it is actualised—one that, we will see, is inextricable from the spatio-political project of urbanisation. On the other hand, we add, it is necessary to explore with as much genealogical attention—that is, without either essentialising or taking for granted—the way a certain *desire for* and the *sense of* security have surfaced in this context and, therefore, the imaginary and aesthetic-affective infrastructure through which the project of security has been actualised.

Prior to unpack this complexity (the goal of chapters 4 and 5), this chapter sets the stage by engaging with some of the main critical approaches to security—therefore making it clear where our approach deviates from this important direction of research. While we endorse the critique of security for deconstructing the problematic assumptions—first of all, the liberal security-freedom balance (see Neocleous 2007)—on which contemporary security logics stand, we believe all too often said critique goes too far, especially when it gets all the way to denying the possibility that security (or freedom, for that matter) may exist, in different forms, outside of Western modernity and its capitalist form, both within and outside the West (e.g., Brauch et al. 2011). Instead, we argue that it is not 'security', but rather *a specific understanding* of security, to be quintessential to liberalism, namely: a precise articulation of the desire of security within a given imaginary, that is, the Hobbesian projection of a society without violence, materialised in the empty city depicted in the *Leviathan*'s frontispiece; a precise articulation of the sense of security, linked to the immunitary (Esposito 2011[2002]) and individualistic understanding of freedom developed within the liberal tradition by the likes of John Locke, Benjamin Constant and John Stuart Mill, among others; and a precise articulation of security mechanisms, technologies and *savoirs*, exemplified by the organisation of power that Foucault has notably described as governmentality.

To understand the modern project of security, therefore, we suggest exploring it as the (often violent) organisation of the desire for security into a set of practices, imaginary and aesthetics, shaped by a peculiarly urban infra-structure. Making sense of this ontological and historical complexity is required if we are to dissect the contemporary paradigm of security and, most importantly, if we are to point somewhere beyond it. But let us start from a brief discussion of what is commonly meant by security—and why this is a limited understanding.

Security

In its most common understanding, security is conceptualised through three main declensions: security as a right, a policy goal and a social demand (Tulumello 2017b). The first dimension, security as *right*, emphasises the normative importance of a certain degree of security for human flourishing, albeit from the viewpoint of an implicit, taken-for-granted understanding of what such a flourishing entails. The second dimension emphasises the fact that actually existing socio-economic and institutional arrangements almost universally attribute to the state, which operates through *policies*, the primary responsibility for guaranteeing that right. Finally, the third dimension serves as a reminder that the understanding of how security should be guaranteed is essentially political, and made up of (contrasting, conflicting) *social demands* and political interpretations thereof. In mainstream understandings of urban security, this political nature is above all manifest in the dichotomies between repression and prevention, and, within the latter, between situational and social paradigms,[2] particularly in balancing these paradigms in the production of policies. In this balancing, as we are to see more in depth in chapter 7, the aesthetic and affective infrastructure of security unfolds.

If the moral imaginary of peace that articulates the desire for security functions via binary abstractions—most notably exemplified in the utopian projections of the city without violence and absolute security that we are to explore in the next chapter—the modern infrastructure of security emerges as a peculiar way to deal with this complexity, organising the desire, sense and practice of security in historically specific ways that need be unpacked. In the following pages we do so by briefly referring to the three main vectors that form, contradictorily so, the infrastructure of contemporary security.[3] We indicate them via the names of the thinkers that most notably express them: Thomas Hobbes, John Locke and Michel Foucault. These dimensions are entangled in multiple contradictions, as Hobbesian absolutism, Lockean liberalism and biopolitical governmentality seemingly coexist in the contemporary framing of security, frustrating any attempt to engage with security only from the side of authoritarianism, liberal legality or biopolitics.

How to encapsulate the 'concept' of security, then? Resonating with reflections on the polysemy of security, its ambiguous, promiscuous and often unaddressed meaning (e.g., Waldron 2006; Zedner 2009; Ranasinghe 2013), Valverde has proposed to start from the practices of security. 'It is dangerous', she observes, 'to go on to the assumption that security actually exists'. Instead, she proposes to understand it as an 'umbrella term under which one can see a multiplicity of governance processes that are dynamic and internally contradictory' (2011, 6). Valverde argues that this multiplicity of practices comes always organised according to specific security projects and it is only in relation to them that it makes sense to ask (critical) questions about security. Elaborating on the Foucauldian distinction between rationalities and technologies (Rose and Miller 1992), she contends that security projects are to be addressed through a tripartite strategy, that looks at the *logic* of the project (including rationale, *telos*, discourse, justifications);[4] the *scope* of the project (including scale and jurisdiction); and the *techniques* of governance, both human and nonhuman, that the project deploys (Valverde 2011, 3–4). This reflection is particularly useful to complement our argument, by underlining the complexity of security practices that, while gradually institutionalised and statalised with the advancement of modernity, have been today diffracted into an overlapping bundle of scales, jurisdictions, logics and techniques—e.g. through the progressive incorporation of non-state actors (from responsabilised citizens to global corporations) in the 'business' of security.[5]

Take for instance the dichotomies between repression and prevention, situational and social prevention. We may call them, following Gabriel Feltran (2020, 10ff), the debate/conflict between 'the Right' and 'the Left', that is, between different understandings of the correct (most just and most efficient) way to achieve 'security'. These understandings, crucially for our argument, are framed within the same 'normative regime', in Feltran's words, which is characterised by the same centrality of 'security' in general and, in particular, by a similar conceptualisation of security as a static condition whereby the state has monopoly over violence—and crime describes the forms of violence that exist outside of the order of the state. On the grounds of many years of ethnography in São Paulo, Feltran argues that crime and criminal violence do not happen 'outside' of that order, but rather alongside and in relation with it; and that they are driven by the clash between that order and other ones. Building on Jacques Rancière, Feltran introduces a third actor, who does not share the idea that the state guarantees security, who believes that it is the 'world of crime' which provides welfare and protection. The third actor largely corresponds to the population of rural-to-urban migrants that has built the large peripheries and slums in São Paolo, whose aspirations to 'modernity' and wealth have been deluded in the age of neoliberalisation, and who have found a path to social mobility and security in organised crime. This actor lives in a different normative regime than the two mainstream actors: violence explodes precisely because there is no space for any deliberative dialogue or democratic conflict between these coexisting regimes—insofar as actors on each side of the fracture do not grant legitimacy to those on the other side (see also Rodgers 2016). Not only does this understanding of crime and violence chime with the infra-structural understanding of violence, by depicting it as a tensional force holding together (through its threat and actualisation) conflicting normative regimes. But it also exposes the limits of a conceptualisation of security (as right, policy goal and social demand) that only makes sense on one side of the fracture.

A more nuanced conceptualisation of security should thus, on the one hand, be flexible enough to encompass the historically changing, and expanding, meanings of security; and, on the other, accommodate the existence of different normative regimes, with their different understandings of security. This will entail deconstructing the assumptions of security as a right, policy goal and social demand by showing what security politics are really about.

Our proposal for this endeavour is threefold: first, from security as a right to security as an aesthetic, understood as the 'sense' of security and, as we are to see, its related 'sense of order'; second, from security as policy goal to security as a practice, the process of making secure as operationalised by different actors, including, but not limited to, the state; and, third, from the social demand for security to the desire for security, and the way this is shaped by a given social, technological and political imaginary. This conceptualisation opens up to acknowledging that, on the one hand, security, broadly understood, is a seemingly universal drive and, on the other, that such a drive can have conflictual, irreducible meanings—opening up to the necessity of building 'agonistic' conceptualisations of security (Tulumello 2021a).

Critique of Security

One of the implications of this sketch is showing the limits of the 'critique of security', by which we refer to a number of strands of scholarship variously concerned with security theory, discourse and practice, an extremely complex and variegated field.[6] At the centre (and to some extent origins) of this field lie Critical Security Studies, which evolved from international relations and war studies as a response to the implicit and explicit violence produced by post-WWII security realism (Booth 1994). Though, within and beyond Critical Security Studies, security has been criticised by numerous epistemological and ontological perspectives, this field has been broadly polarised between two approaches, which João Nunes characterises as deconstructive and reconstructive (see also Nyman 2016; Tulumello 2021a)—a heuristic dichotomy that is of use beyond the field of Critical Security Studies from which Nunes draws.

Let us start with the deconstructive field, which is so broad that delimiting its boundaries is almost impossible. Among others, we would include: critical explorations of the future-oriented nature of security (Anderson 2010b; Aradau and van Munster 2012; Amoore 2013); 'securitisation' theory, with its focus on the construction of the security character, and thus depoliticisation, of public phenomena (Wæver 2011; Balzacq et al. 2015); feminist critique of crime control and prevention agendas (Duff 2018; Shepherd 2020); post- and de-colonial takes on security policies (Barkawi and Laffey 2006; Hönke and Muller 2012); and then the various strands of the critique of policing (and border control and criminal justice), from Foucauldian (Borch 2015; Maguire et al. 2018; Dodsworth 2019), political economic (Correia and Wall 2018; Neocleous 2021[2000]), or anti-racist, feminist and abolitionist (Camp and Heatherton 2016; Duff 2021) perspectives. What all these works have in common is a concern with exposing the 'dark' and violent side of actually-existing security, its role in impeding the realisation of a democratic politics and, more generally, security's crucial role in the maintenance of the capitalist order (with its violence).

The deconstruction of security has had an extremely important role, producing both concepts for scholarship, and instruments for radical and progressive politics. And yet, we argue, it has also shown some important limits, which will become especially evident through a more detailed discussion of one of the most systematic and sharpest versions of this critique. Mark Neocleous has engaged with the problem of security in historical perspective, by tracing back the theoretical roots of contemporary security, from Hobbes to liberal and Enlightenment thinkers such as Mill, Rousseau, Smith and Bentham, as well as early police scientists like Colquhoun, Delamare, Bielfeld, von Justi and so on. Security, Neocleous observes, is, and has always been, the central goal of liberal thought: freedom, the argument goes, in liberal-ism essentially means security, most notably the security of private property and the bourgeois order (2007; 2008). In line with Marx's famous quip on security as the highest social concept of the bourgeois society,[7] Neocleous concludes that security is nothing more and nothing less than the political technology of liberalism, that is, a project of social order (2021[2000]) that needs to be rejected once and for all (2000; 2008, 9–10).

Neocleous' is a remarkable work, which has provided an invaluable his-torical and theoretical platform for contemporary reflections on security. Its main problem, we believe, is its overreliance to the strategy of (deconstruc-tive) critique, as well as a tendency to reduce security to a precise historical context—namely, Western liberalism—thereby overlooking its variety of historical and geographic declensions. While we obviously endorse critique as a fundamental mode of inquiry, we caution against its fetishisation into the only mode to explore a given subject. As Rita Felski (2015) reminds, cri-tique normally functions through a hermeneutic of suspicion that attacks its own target with the aim of demystifying its obscure logic and let emerge, and thus reveal, what is really at stake. In other words, critique ultimately relies on the typical Enlightenment attitude it often, in its contemporary guise, seeks to challenge, namely, an economy of truth and revelation.[8]

As David Bissel and colleagues (2012, 704) summarise with regards to the proliferating critiques to the 'society of control', what this approach implic-itly postulates is 'a hidden logic, a structure of control underpinning diverse collective arrangements that *can* be "exposed", a riddle that can be deci-phered, a thread that can be traced, or a conspiracy that can be unmasked beneath totalising environments of control'. A stance that, all too often, tells us more about 'the will to power and knowledge of their authors', than of the actual functioning of the society they are describing (Birchall et al. 2010).[9] While it would be ungenerous and simplistic to apply these observations to the various iterations of the 'critique of security', examining the latter through the former can be illuminating.

Before we move forward, let us note that the rejection of security—and of concepts that are crucial to the security project, especially policing—is, if in less direct forms, central to many other strands of deconstruction. This is particularly evident in North American abolitionism, but let us take as another example Copenhagen school's securitisation theory, for whom, once a phenomenon is securitised, it is excluded from (democratic) politics; therefore security is, in a way, the opposite of politics and democracy (see, for a critique, Neal 2019): Ole Wæver (2011, endnote 2), for instance, ultimately characterises security as a Schmittian concept. Another example is Daniel Goldstein's argument (2010, 499), based on a critical anthropology of security-making in Latin America, assuming security as antagonistic with human rights. In short, the deconstructive critique of security has argued that abandoning the concept of 'security' once and for all is a necessary step for any radically democratic political project—and, indeed, for guaranteeing the safety of those individuals and groups on the receiving side of state violence.

In order to discuss the limits of this argument, let us come back to Goldstein: arguing that security is antagonistic with rights glosses over the fact that security is a right too—indeed, as just observed, it is coessential to the liberal notion of right. Incidentally, the reliance of security on a grammar of human rights can itself be criticised: as discussed elsewhere, security is understood as a right within a Western/liberal conceptual framework, and this may itself be a problem for building a truly democratic and pluralist security (Tulumello 2021a). What matters here is that, whatever the grammar that one is to adopt, simply locating security as the antithesis to any number of human (and more-than-human) values is as problematic as assuming security in itself as an important value. This is because, as we argued taking inspiration from Nietzsche's genealogy, security is *not* in itself a value, but is always imbricated in specific infrastructure of power, force and value, and therefore the deconstruction of said systems cannot imply the deconstruction of security in itself. Security has to do with a desire, a sense and a practice, which cannot be simply reduced to the configuration they take in the context of contemporary (neo)liberalism.[10]

To sum up—and with some degree of simplification for the sake of the argument. First, constructivist and post-structuralist approaches (e.g., Williams 2003; Huysmans 2011) have focused on security as *discourse*, therefore explaining the discursive roots of the machine of securitisation; but have rarely engaged with those insecurities and violence that exist beyond state violence. Second, the critique to the *theory* of security has successfully demonstrated that actually-existing security is inherently defined by the liberal/Western project of social order, but this, *per se*, does not root out the possibility of finding different conceptualisations of security outside of that very order—security, as a desire, a sense and a practice, has existed, for better or worse, before the liberal order was created and outside of the hegemony of liberal thought within and outside the West. Third, the same limits quite obviously apply to the critique of security *practices*, which, once again, cannot in and of itself exclude the possibility of finding different paths to security. If we agree that each society, human and non-human, is traversed by a desire for, a sense of, and a set of practices that produce some sort of security and order, it follows that the latter cannot be assessed in abstract but always in relation to the discourses and imaginaries through which such desire is shaped, the aesthetic distribution of the sensible through which such a sense is partitioned, and the power-structured relations through which the order is daily *made* and *done*.

Let us stress that the desire for security both transcends, and is part of the explanation of, the history of security as a governmental project. It transcends that history because it locates security, beyond politics, statecraft and policy, as a kernel of (human and non-human) life (see Burke 2011; Harrington 2017), existing beyond the historically-specific forms that it has taken in the history of the European state, liberalism and capitalism, albeit it surely cannot be addressed (either protected or criticised) in isolation from those forms—see Honig's account (1992) of politicisation in agonistic feminism. A basic mechanism of the ideology of security, as evident since Hobbes, is exactly the activation and exploitation of such a desire, and the sense thereof, in order to give the (European, liberal, nation-) state its *raison d'*être (see above and cf. Mandelbaum 2020). In the same sense, freedom cannot be reduced to the 'negative' conception of freedom that was dominant (yet by no means unique) in Western modernity, again courtesy of Hobbes (Baldissone 2018). The 'popular desire' for freedom that emerged out of the demise of feudalism, for instance, certainly does not exactly coincide with its definition within liberalism—one may say, with Deleuze and Guattari (1977[1972]), that such a desire ended up being 'captured' within a constraining juridico-political structure, which defused its relational, affirmative and empowering connotation.[11] Freedom, and security, can and should also be thought beyond the political and legal abstractions in which they are entrapped, that is, beyond their projection as a transcendent and unconditional *a priori* common good (either in the Hobbesian or Lockean connotation).[12]

This is, incidentally, the problem in which reconstructive efforts to think security falls. This much smaller field, which has developed in the Aberystwyth, or Welsh, school of Critical Security Studies, is centred on the concept of security-as-emancipation, which 'seeks the securing of people from those oppressions that stop them carrying out what they would freely choose to do, compatible with the freedom of others' (Booth 2007, 112). Emancipation theory engages with security from a progressive normative standpoint: it starts by emphasising the insecurities affecting people, including, but not limited to, those produced by the state machine of security—and therefore generally embracing the desire for security; and moves to seeking transformative politics. What reconstructive critique has rarely engaged with is the theory of security that supports emancipation. Ken Booth, one of the founders of this field, simply argued that 'the relationship between emancipation and security is more difficult to explain in theory than in practice' (2005, 182). In a more recent piece, João Nunes (2012) relaunched emancipation theory by advocating for a stronger attunement to issues of politicisation and power, but once again without defining a theory of security-as-emancipation. Read through this lens, security-as-emancipation seems to correspond to the flourishing of (individual) human rights. Some critics have suggested that the theory still remains within a liberal framework (cf. Shepherd 2008, 69–71). Ultimately, emancipation theory mirrors some of the key problems of mainstream logics of security: by relying on a grammar of human rights, it risks depoliticising security; it is an essentially individualist approach; and it falls into the trap of universalism. The very notion of emancipation, which literally refers to being 'set free' or liberated, still contains a negative connotation, defined in opposition to a power (originally, the paternal authority). The approach we have proposed so far understands the 'potentiating' role of security not vis-à-vis the abstraction of rights or a transcendent common good, but vis-à-vis the concreteness of material relations and the question of keeping the social together by augmenting its collective *conatus* (see introduction). We will particularly develop this reflection on security and (urban) violence with respect to the notion of vitality and, therefore, the empowering or debilitation thereof (see chapter 6).

To conclude, the deconstructive critique has tended to separate those three dimensions, by overly focusing on either practices, theories or discourses, which are part and parcel of the imaginary, but fail to engage with the aesthetic sense of, and the affective desire for, security. Reconstructive critique, on its side, has engaged with some dimensions of these questions but, unable to overcome the abstractions of human rights, has not been able to address the material, multiple, as well as conflictual dimension of security. We are not interested in challenging notions of order or security *per se*, therefore, since these notions are empty abstractions that are both necessary (against the 'reproach of abstraction', see Osborne 2004) and contingent (against the 'fallacy of misplaced concreteness', see Whitehead 1978[1929]), and require to be explored, we argue, vis-à-vis the debilitating, infra-structural violence they potentially generate in the given spatial and historical context. Security must be dealt with by looking *simultaneously* at its formal quality (i.e., the empty concept of 'security') and the historically-situated socio-spatial relations *in* and *through* which it is actualised (i.e., a given affective, material and semiotic socio-spatial formations) (cf. Cunningham 2005).

As we will show in the final chapter, there is another way to rethink security, and it is through a material approach to care, which is able to mobilise the practices of security by at the same time retuning its desire and its sense. In what follows, by looking at the limits of these approaches in light of our conceptualisation of security, we will open up to the necessity of putting the imaginary and aesthetics of security—which has largely escaped the attention of critique—at the centre of the theorisation of urban violence.

Reconceptualising Security

Seemingly introduced in the Latin language by Cicero in the *Tusculanae disputationes*, the substantive *securitas* is composed by three parts,[13] which provide a clear indication of its complex structure: 'the prefix *sē-* (apart, aside, away from); the noun *cura* (care, concern, attention, worry); and the suffix *-tas* (denoting a condition or state of being). *Securitas*, therefore, denotes a condition of being separated from care, a state wherein concerns and worries have been put off to the side' (Hamilton 2013, 5). The word has many Greek antecedents, similarly composed by a privative particle and a negative term that the given condition supposedly overcomes: *ataraksia*, a state without *-taraksia*, which refers to trouble, disturbance, agitation; *asphaleia*, where to be removed is *sphall*, a verb which comes from the field of wrestling and refers to falling or stumbling; *apatheia*, a state where passions are overcome, a key concept in Stoic philosophy. Fredrick Arends (2011) explains that all these concepts played a role in shaping the meaning of *securitas* which, differently from the existent term, *salus*—literally meaning 'health', as well as welfare, prosperity and preservation (together with its derivate *salvus*, i.e., safe, *salus* is at the root of the word 'safety', and therefore points to the absence of physical harm)—connotes a reflexive condition, a tranquillity of mind and interior peace.[14] This tranquility is achieved by freeing oneself from worries, that is, from all those *curae* (i.e., fear, desire, distress, anger, etc.) that may be of disturbance and disquiet, first and foremost the fear of death, as particularly evident for instance in Lucretius's *De Rerum Natura*. This 'positive' dimension of *securitas* is complemented by a 'negative' connotation, already present in the writings of Seneca, which had to do with the other meaning of *sine-cura*: namely, the condition of being without care, in the sense of being careless. If positively understood, *securitas* refers to a state of being blissfully carefree, negatively understood, it connotes the state of being careless, a term denoting an attitude of irresponsibility and negligence (Hamilton 2013, 61). This negative dimension was implied by another Greek antecedent to *securitas*, namely *a-kêd-eia*, meaning carelessness or indifference, from which the term *acedia* (sloth) is derived, one that in Christianity will be demonised as one of the seven 'capital sins' (Arends 2011, 268).[15]

Besides such an ambivalence, all played within the field of individual ethics, soon the notion of *securitas* will assume a political dimension, at least since the emperor Augustus, as 'public security', with the purpose of improving the good life.[16] We are to come back to the progressive institutionalisation of *securitas* in the next section. Prior to moving on, let us dwell a bit longer on the etymological kernel of *securitas* since in it we find expressed the three aspects that constitute the three-dimensional structure of security.

First, security has to do with a condition that appears to be ontologically constitutive of living. Following Spinoza, essential to every being is an immanent desire to persevere in one's own being, or *conatus*. Following on the discussion made in the introduction, this immanent claim to existence is the essence of every being, which is nothing but a power to act, that is, a power to affect and be affected by entering in potentiating (i.e., flourishing) relations and avoiding debilitating (or toxic) ones (see also Zourabvchili 2012[2003]). In chapter 6 we will see how such an understanding is consistent with a notion of life, health and illness that is dynamic, relational and generative—and therefore rather different from the mainstream, reactive and immunitary understanding of life that also informs the abstract and negative understanding of freedom *as* security we are challenging here. At this stage, we need to emphasise the existential, essential and ontological relation with security that the *conatus* expresses, and with respect to which security may be understood as a protection against, and avoidance of, debilitating, hurting, toxic relations.

A couple of qualifications are in order. On the one hand, providing the 'desire for security' with such an existential and ontological connotation is only a partial move, which must be complemented by taking into account, at the same time, the underlying 'what' that security implicitly addresses. Such a notation is crucial, as in mainstream discourses the 'what' of security remains all too often overlooked, or taken for granted, with the consequence of essentialising security itself as a somewhat 'natural' and a-historical given. This is a classic move of liberal thinking, where security is presented as a self-evident and incontestable need of (human) beings, from the point of view of an atomistic ontology—i.e., liberal individualism—which is in turn presupposed as self-evident. Yet, this ontological presupposition is hardly incontestable. If challenging liberal security without challenging its underlying ontology is an effort bound to get entangled in all sorts of contradictions (see above), the very notion of security is bound to have a very different meaning if applied, for instance, to a relational ontology (see chapter 9). Assuming the desire of security as coessential to living, therefore, does not mean disregarding, or taking for granted, the underlying ontological question. On the other hand, and consequently, it would be as unproductive taking such a desire as being self-evident, objective, spontaneous or 'natural'. Instead, our ontological perspective implies the need to understand desire as being always collective, shaped by socio-material imaginaries, which are historically sedimented, and power-structured accordingly. A desire is never pure or innocent; it always materialises through a specific, historical and sociotechnically constructed imaginary (see chapter 4). Accordingly, it would make little sense to discuss an abstract 'desire for security' without taking into account the imaginary through which it is framed and articulated. At the same time, however, any critique of a given 'imaginary' that assumes such a desire as produced by—rather than articulated through—such an imaginary misses the point. This is precisely the problem of the critique of the ideology of security, when, whilst rightly criticising the imaginary within which the desire for security is imbricated, it ends up concluding that (the desire for) security itself is an alienating concept that must be done away with. This is because desire, although never natural, spontaneous or free, is not simply explainable, and thus reducible, to the 'lack' it supposedly aims to fulfil. Against the Lacanian assumption of desire as stemming from something that is missing, we follow Deleuze in assuming that 'desire includes no lack' but that, at the same time, 'it is also not a natural given. Desire is wholly a part of a functioning heterogeneous assemblage' (Deleuze 2006, 130).[17] In other words, desire is an ontogenetic force, which is always actualised in specific spatio-historical assemblages to which, however, is never fully reducible.[18] The necessary task of deconstructing and dismantling the contemporary paradigm of security, accordingly, does neither entail abandoning security nor reclaiming some pure and unquestionable desire for security. Rather, it means seeking to reconfigure a novel, less debilitating, exploitative and violent imaginary, through which such a desire could be affirmatively enacted. As we are to show in the next chapter, this requires engaging with the specifically urban imaginary that plays a key role in shaping the way security is socially desired and politically projected.[19] We may thus agree with Cameron Harrington (2017, 76), who observes that there is a 'seemingly universal and timeless' desire for security, provided we take into account that such a desire is always articulated in historically contingent ways, materialising a specific, power-structured *partition of the sensible* (Rancière 2004[2000]) through which security is perceived and experienced as such, that is, through which a *sense of security* emerges.[20]

Second, therefore, security is a *sense*, that is, a feeling of being at ease, without worries, *sine-curae*—and, most importantly, without fear.[21] The Stoics had a beautiful term to express a similar condition: *oikeiosis*, namely the process of 'becoming proper to one's own nature' that every animal naturally undergoes. This propriety is to be understood in relation to one's own *constitution* and, in turn, with the environment in which one is immersed: 'the process by which one thing "becomes proper" and "related" to another' (Heller-Roazen 2007, 106), a becoming-at-home (the *oikos* at the root of the term) with the surrounding milieu. If *oikeiosis* is a material, bodily process of becoming, akin to the desire for security we just described—and whose dependence with the 'environment' in which one is immerged testifies of its always relational, or 'assembled', quality (cf. chapter 6)—this process of 'properly' becoming-with is also accompanied by aesthetic reflexivity, that is, an animal's 'indispensable "awareness" (*sunaisthesis, sensus*) of its own constitution" (*suntasis, constitutio*)' (idem, 109). The nature of this ontological awareness is what the Stoic referred to as *inner touch*. While, with undue anachronism, the term is often translated as 'consciousness' or 'self-consciousness', Daniel Heller-Roazen contests this interpretation. Among the Stoics, he stresses, the inner touch is rather akin to a 'sense' or 'sensation' that does not spring from a 'self', but rather brings it into light. It is not a 'consciousness', therefore, but rather a sense of one's own constitution, which is accompanied by a process of 'conciliation' and 'adaptation' to it. As he puts it, quoting Seneca, 'that "the care of myself is before everything" means, among other things, that the care in question "is before" that thing that is "the self"' (idem, 114). *Oikeiosis*, in other words, does not statically unfold from a given self. There is no pre-formed self that the process of becoming-proper is oriented towards: it is the process itself to be generative of a 'self'. A key distinction is posited here, between becoming and sensing, that is, between *oikeiosis* as a process of becoming, and *oikeiosis* as the related sensation or feeling. It is with reference to such a sensation that, we believe, a promising genealogy of what we define as the *sense* of security may be found, namely as a reflexive sensation that accompanies the becoming-proper that the desire for security strives towards.

The relevance of this seemingly 'technical' philosophical qualification can be immediately shown by making reference to Anthony Giddens's well-known concept of ontological security. Elaborating on the notion introduced by R. D. Laing, Giddens (1991, 40) defined *ontological security* as the 'sense of security' which provides a 'protective cocoon' whereby individuals 'create ontological reference points as an integral aspect of "going on" in the contexts of day-to-day life'. Ontological security, in other words, is an aesthetic force that provides continuity and coherence to everyday experience, while fading into the background, as a barely perceptible normality. This process of *anchoring* produces trust about the consistency and coherence of normality—what Erwin Goffman, a key inspiration for Giddens, termed a 'sensing of normalcy' (see chapter 7)—and appears to be shared, at least formally, among cultures. Contrary to much contemporary elaboration, 'ontological' security is not a 'state', let alone an 'objective' one at that, but it rather refers to an 'ontological awareness', that is, a 'sense' of security.[22] Yet, if 'ontological security' is an empty signifier unless its 'ontological' premises are made explicit, to essentialise the 'sense of security' without accounting for its historical, collective and power-structured formation, as Giddens seems to imply, is even more problematic. The result is that of elaborating a sort of static *oikeiosis*, that is, one where the process of becoming-proper is totally resolved into the aesthetic sensation of what is 'proper', whose socio-political constitution is left unaccounted for. The problem with Giddens's conception is the presupposition of an ontological unity (individual, self, identity, community) as the foundation of ontological security, and the implicit reliance on an a-historical understanding of co-habitation (not too dissimilarly from Cerdá's) that not only conceals the structural asymmetries shaping the collective 'sense of security', but also links their contingent erosion—in the context of the so-called 'crisis of modernity'—in conservative terms, that is, as a problem to be reactively addressed by reconstructing the reassuring unity of the now endangered image of the social. The 'sense of security', instead, must be framed historically, and specifically with respect to the surfacing of the modern form of *urban* experience, which has radically modified the pre-urban sensorium (see chapter 4). As we are to see, security can be tied to a precise partition of the sensible that depends on, and materialises aesthetically, a given organisation of power. In chapter 7 we will do so by looking at the way in which the sense of security has morphed into the public notion of *sense of order*, which has increasingly become a direct objective of urban politics, to be actively pursued via legal, technological and aesthetic means, in the context of the so-called societies of comfort. In the complex, deterritorialised and precarious existence of late neoliberalism, we argue, the production of a static *sensation* of being-at-home in the urban space has gradually become *the* aesthetic-political urban question—an exquisitely Cerdian question of domestication, that is (see Brighenti and Pavoni 2018)—shaping urban experience in surreptitious and often violent ways.

Third, security is more than a given state, that is, it is not simply a *static*, but rather a dynamic *practice* of securing, or becoming-secure. Among the Roman Stoics, the notion of *securitas* is discussed in relation to those technologies of the self that Michel Foucault would famously explore in his late works. This means that *securitas*, with an only apparent contradiction, does indeed require care. In a similar way as we may find in some Eastern philosophies, the state of being blissfully *carefree* that the condition of *securitas* expresses does involve practices of *caring*. The Roman neologism already contained this semantic ambiguity, as the term *cura* also referred to responsibility, or office (Dillon 1996, 125).

It is around this ambivalence, between the positive state of being carefree and the negative state of being careless, that the three main dimensions of security—the *desire, sense* and *practice* of security—have been articulated within the structure of the Western political architecture, as we will discuss below. This ambiguity goes deep to the philosophical conundrum that the concept of security expresses, namely its inextricable coessentiality with insecurity: 'security is what is done to a condition that is insecure', reminds Michael Dillon (idem, 127). Not only in the sense that 'security needs insecurity', that is, that within security discourses insecurity is constantly produced, in this way providing security practices with their *raison d'être* (e.g., Sutzl and Cox 2009). More profoundly, security seems to have no meaning without the implicit presupposition of an ontological condition of insecurity (see Burgess 2019). As the Hobbesian model shows all too well, security only exists when it is assumed that reality is fundamentally insecure: this, however, threatens to entrap security in a vicious circle. As many have asked, and empirically shown, is not the very practice of securing bound to reproduce more insecurity? There is evidently a conflict in place at the earth of the task to care for oneself in order to expunge those disturbing *curae*, in other words, between the *practices* of securing and the *condition* of *securitas*. As Hamilton (2013, 57) suggests, from Plato's ideal city onwards the political imaginary of Western politics—an eminently *urban* imaginary—could be read as the unfolding of various institutional orderings aimed at providing a (partial) solution to this conundrum, gradually institutionalising and monopolising the *practices* of security into political projects; this, while at the same time concealing—and reproducing—their inherent violence.

Through this etymological incursion, we proposed to understand security as a three-dimensional concept, including a *desire* for security, a *sense* of security and a *practice* of securing. Security, in other words, is a process that results from the intersection between these vectors, which are always spatially and temporally materialised. This means that, to *make* sense (literally, to be meaningful *and* produce meaning at the same time), the 'critique of security' has to engage simultaneously with both its ontological dimension—namely, its ontological relation with the way life is imagined, felt and practiced— and the socio-material, historical and political relations through which this ontology is actualised. Focusing only on the former leads to dangerously ide-alist positions. Focusing only on the latter leads to as dangerously reductive conclusions. In this book we navigate through this complexity by particularly reflecting on the relation between security, violence and the urban. We do so by proposing to understand security as a dynamic, three-dimensional *process* that emerges as an articulation of desire, sense and practice, and which therefore must always be analysed with respect to the specific (urban) spatio-political *project* through which it is historically actualised, with its 'Hobbes-ian', 'Lockean' and 'Foucauldian' treads. It is to the genealogy of the modern project of security that we therefore move.

Genealogy

Historians of security (and policing) have extensively argued that a new conception of order, protection and security emerges out of the dismantle-ment of the feudal system and the emergence of the nation-state: Neocleous (2008; 2021[2000]) focuses on the production and reproduction of wage la-bour relations and of the capitalist order; Markus Dubber (2005) and Francis Dobsworth (2019) centre their attention on patriarchy and protection—but with different emphasis on matters of continuity and rupture; refusing any causal explanation, Michel Foucault provides a genealogy of the surfacing of the modern state as a novel kind of rationality (*la raison d'État*) which provides a principle of intelligibility in response to the novel *problématique* of government (2007[2004], 227–283). All in all, there is an agreement that, in the emerging order of nation-states, security becomes increasingly statalised and politicised: as the order is understood to be no longer divine but *man-made*,[23] security becomes the state's main purpose. A 'central theme in politi-cal theory in this period', writes Neocleous of the post-Westphalian Europe,[24] 'is that man creates an order (civil society and the state) and simultaneously transfers his creative power to part of his creation (the state), which then uses it to order civil society' (2021[2000], 63).

Nowhere as in thought of Hobbes is this move forcefully posed: the as-sumption, based on the evidence of the tumultuous wars of religion that ravaged Europe at his time, that the natural condition is one of disorder and conflict; and, therefore, that the key political task is crafting an artificial order able to neutralise conflict and guarantee security. This is to be done, Hobbes believed, through a novel political science firmly grounded on a geometric relation between law, desire and fear.[25] Seen through his negative and pessimist anthropology,[26] the human is constitutively unable to control 'a perpetuall and restlesse desire of Power after power, that ceaseth onely in Death' (Hobbes 2002[1651], ch. XI). The quintessential negativity in Hobbes is the coessentiality of fear (of death) and violence that is said to thrive in the anarchic coexistence of humans, and that must be tamed via another negativity, namely the (monopoly of) violence of the sovereign and the subsequent fear he induces (cf. Luhmann 2003[1980]). 'Human society, whatever it may be, is unable to last unless it has an artificial order capable of neutralizing the potential violence that riddles it by nature' (Esposito 2011[2002], 98). There is no attempt to eliminate fear, this quintessential passion Hobbes assumes as fundamental to human nature, but rather to substitute the endemic fear that ravages in the state of war of all against all, with the 'institutionalised' fear induced by the sovereign and his Law, via the ever-present possibility of punishment.

Such an institutionalisation of security, we already argued, appears as the cypher of its modern evolution. Wolfgang Dietrich develops this argument, observing that the Roman se-curus refers to a condition of 'freedom from claims by the state'. This means, he continues, that 'ever since its verifiable appearance, the concept of security presupposes the existence of the institution of the state. It is not thinkable without the state, and it follows its development in the transformation of its own meaning' (2012, 96). We saw that, in its early Stoic use, the notion of security was indeed thinkable without the state—which, once again, reminds us that security does exist outside and beyond a given order. Nonetheless, Dietrich's observation is useful to emphasise the extent to which, within the notion of security, we find a logic that is present since its origin but will become fully mature in Western modernity, what we may refer to as 'institutional delegation', that is, the simultaneous responsibilisation (for one's own security) and de-responsibilisation (for the security of the 'common', which is delegated to the institution) of the individual (see on this Pavoni 2017b; Brighenti and Pavoni 2019).

As Esposito has explained in two key works (2009[1998]; 2011[2002]), within the ontological constitution of every community there is a *munus*, that is, a gift as well as an obligation, which any member of the community has vis-à-vis maintaining and fostering—i.e., *caring for*—the very consistency of the common. With respect to this relational ontology, the modern paradigm of immunity is grounded on the 'exoneration' or 'disbuderning', to use Arnold Gehlen's terms (1988[1974]), of the individual from the 'social circuit of reciprocal gift-giving' (Esposito 2011[2002], 6), that is, from the obligation/responsibility that characterises the *communitas* as sharing (the burden of) a common *munus*. In this sense, to be immune is to be *sine-cura*, that is, literally, in the condition of *not having to care for* the common (more on this in chapter 9). The genealogy of this understanding may be traced to the Roman Empire, when we could argue that a 'political' rather than merely 'ethical' notion of security begins to emerge, according to which 'the *securitas* of the *Imperium Romanum* is the basis of the personal *securitas* of its subjects' (Arends 2011, 270).[27] The institution of the *pax romana*, introduced by Roman law, set the stage for the triangulation between peace, violence and security that still organises contemporary security politics, in which peace is a condition that is statically achieved by the state through a good deal of structural violence (e.g., Arends 2011; Dietrich 2012).[28] In the twentieth-century philosophical anthropology of Helmuth Plessner and Arnold Gehlen, this concept was given perhaps the most systematic elaboration, on the presupposition of the inherent violence of human nature, an excess of violence that must be tamed by an as excessive institutional violence (Esposito 2009[1998]; 2011[2002]). This is what the *Leviathan* is, an artificial monster that, through the authority and the violence of law, is able to tame the monster of the wild *multitude* and its anarchic freedom, by bringing into existence a *population* (Derrida 2009[2008]).

It is in this context that Hobbes introduces the modern conception of freedom, here understood as a *problem* that cannot be decoupled from security and its institutional scaffolding. In the state of nature, he argues, freedom is absolute, while security is absent (2002[1651], ch. LXXI). As a result, the fear of death and of the future dominates, rendering life *'nasty, brutish, and short'* (idem, ch. XIII; our emphasis). Contrary to some simplistic interpretations, Hobbes's political science does not aim to destroy freedom. The Englishman is perhaps the first modern thinker to be directly concerned with the problem of striking a balance between security and freedom, albeit one that is decidedly unbalanced towards the security of the sovereign power.[29] There is freedom in the Hobbesian state. Yet, this freedom can only unfold in the silence of the law. Freedom, in other words, flourishes in the shadows of the social, and will be curbed every time it is assumed as affecting negatively the social. Freedom, in other words, is an eminently negative condition, surgically decoupled from any obligation to positively care for the common. Being carefree and being careless seemingly coincide.

The negative conception of freedom found in the liberal tradition, for instance in John Locke, whose understanding of security pivots 180 degrees with respect to Hobbes, while still maintaining the same fundamental structure. Foucault (2007[2004], 65–67) exemplified this point resorting to the distinction, in French, between the notions of *sûreté* and *sécurité*. While the former concerned the Hobbesian security—first of all, the security and peace of the sovereign, and thus the state as a whole—the latter referred to the security of the individuals that could be jeopardised by *sûreté* itself. Between the *sûreté* or the good health of the sovereign state and, subsequently, of the society, and the *securité* of the individual, therefore, the ambiguity at the core of liberalism unfolds, namely its corrosive effect on the social relation itself. If assuming Hobbes to be an ante-litteram liberal may appear as too much of a stretch (e.g., de Jouvenel 1997[1957]), the genealogy of security/freedom shows that it is to him that liberalism owes its ontological and anthropological grounds (cf. Neocleous 2008, 16ff.). For Hobbes, to be sure, the desire for absolute security projected by the sovereign and imposed through its law is unquestioned: patriarchally speaking, it is done *for the good* of the population, which must accept it *unconditionally.*

Liberal thinking will change the equilibrium of the security-freedom balance, without challenging in any way its assumption, but rather elevating it to its foundational myth (Neocleous 2007). Coherently with the centrality of the 'individual' in the Enlightenment tradition, the analytical conceptualisation of this balance will be devised as one among individual rights, an argument that still organises contemporary society. Take for instance the case of the deployment of CCTV systems as preventative means: in this field, virtually all regulations are concerned with striking a balance of 'proportionality' between crime prevention and privacy. Absent any robust evidence of their capacity to deter or reduce crime, with few exceptions (see Doyle et al. 2012), the CCTV example also opens to the contradictions inherent to the management of the balance.[30] These contradictions are even more evident in the context of contemporary discussions on terrorism, where the security-freedom logic is unbalanced to the extent that pre-emptive strikes, torture (see Ignatieff 2003) and other extremely violent practices may be justified to 'protect our freedom' (see chapter 4, Researching Urban Violence). Accordingly, freedom and security will end up converging, with the latter morphing into former, something that had been implied already by another realist thinker such as Jeremy Bentham, for whom, in Valverde's words, 'security . . . is the necessary complement of liberty; it secures liberty, literally, being essentially future oriented and risk driven. But it is, or at least it becomes, an end in itself as well as a means to the end of liberty' (2008, 28).[31]

Again, the security-freedom equation is predicated on a self-evident understanding of security. If security is inextricable from freedom within the liberal perspective, then security is *not* freedom, but nonetheless remains held together with it in an ambiguous relation. The problem of the security-freedom balance is not solved by putting much weight on the side of freedom, as it is done in an increasingly convergent left- and right-wing libertarianism. Rather, as we will contend in the final chapter, this can be done by challenging the myth of the balance in the first place and, more precisely, the logic of institutional delegation through which it is articulated, as well as the aesthetic-affective infrastructure through which it is materialised: as it will become increasingly apparent, the extent to which the order through which security is communicated to the population cannot be simply guaranteed through law but is also a *common sense* that must be actively produced. Such a proactive dimension is lacking in the Hobbesian model—where order is assumed as necessarily emanating from the sovereign law—as well as in that of Bentham, for instance, where the question of security is tied to the ideal of the elimination of violence that would be achieved through a system of universal legality as a means to achieve 'the total disappearance of crime' (Foucault, 2010[2004], 255; see also 1977[1975], 200–207), an ideal architectonically represented by the ambition to total transparency of the Panopticon. In these modern conceptions there is still a belief in the capacity of law—and the threat of punishment—to achieve absolute security.

Within liberal democracies, as we are to see in detail in chapter 7, security becomes conditional to the development of a certain *sense of security*, which is aesthetically translated into a *sense of order*. This is among the aspects that characterise the novel approach that Foucault will refer to as governmentality: the shift of security, from a presupposed condition, into a *praxis*, a number of enactments, embodiments and operations justified and driven by the scope of reaching that very condition. '*Law enforcement* is more than the application of the law', writes Foucault, it 'is the set of instruments employed to give social and political reality to the act of prohibition in which the formulation of the law consists' (Foucault 2010[2004], 254; emphasis in translation). It is in this sense that we should understand Foucault's conceptualisation of security, within the 'naturalistic' perspective of biopolitical governmentality: stemming from the gradual realisation that the legal system is not able, in and of itself, to guarantee the protection of the dominant interests, and that therefore a series of security *practices* must be devised in order to administer the *gap* between the imaginary abstraction of law (and the absolute security it projects, see chapter 4) and the complex contingency of reality.

Governmentality

There are 'two attitudes to contingency', Alain Pottage observes, 'one which avoids or absorbs contingency (substance), and another which presupposes, and thrives on, contingency (emergence)' (1998, 9). Both the Hobbesian and the Lockean frames (we are of course simplifying) are declensions of the first attitude. The notion of security as governmentality, instead, has to do with the second. Within such an understanding, one may say that security fully assumes its own impossibility: if we understand it as a mechanism of observation that splits the world simultaneously into a reality (insecurity) and an ideal (absolute security), governmentality surfaces once the impossibility to secure the social once and for all is *not* framed as a limit to security, as much critique of security has argued, but rather as its *raison d'être*. With the advent of governmentality, in other words, security is reframed through the rationality of the nascent political economy. Accordingly, it is no longer understood as a supreme and inviolable value, but as a principle of calculation that is immanent to the practice of government itself (Foucault 2007[2004], 106).

This reflection cannot be decoupled from another key Foucaldian intuition, namely, the relation between the surfacing of governmentality as a novel technique of governance and organisation of power, and the 'appearance' of a novel political subject, *population*. Population is a relational whole that cannot be abstracted (into law) or enclosed (into disciplinary spaces). It is 'a reality that has a natural density and thickness' (Foucault 2007[2004], 352), and that must therefore be treated as a living organism: hence, biopolitics. A 'natural' element, with its own regularities, patterns, 'normativities', the population must therefore be governed *in vivo*, that is, in its contingent and material existence, which is understood in inextricable relation to its own environment or *milieu* (see idem, 77–78). This novel epistemology of governance brings about a novel *problématique*, strictly linked to the evolution of liberalism, capitalism and positivism. In this context, notions of freedom, life, knowledge and space assume a wholly novel meaning.

First, as capitalism and liberalism take the place of protectionists economic regimes such cameralism and mercantilism, the novel political and economic requirement of freedom (i.e., the free movement of people, goods and money) opens up a wholly novel problem. In a nutshell, the question of circulation, a concern that, we saw already, was also central in Cerdá's theorisation. The problem of the city, Foucault argues, is a novel problem of governance in which the question of *safe* circulation of air (no epidemics), people (no revolt) and capital (maximisation of profit) becomes paramount. The question, which Foucault summarises with the usual clarity, in a passage that could perfectly feature in the work of Cerdá,

> is no longer that of fixing and demarcating the territory, but of allowing circulations to take place, of controlling them, shifting the good and the bad, ensuring that things are always in movement, constantly moving around, continually going from one point to another, but in such a way that the inherent dangers of this circulation are cancelled out. (2007[2004], 65)

Opening up the cities to the territory—i.e., *urbanising* cities—is a key part of this process.

Second, the life of the population is now directly included within the field of government. If truth be said, we may find a biopolitical kernel even in the theorisation of Hobbes, according to whom not only must the sovereign protect the life of the citizen, but 'he' is also tasked with improving it. However, this is still assumed as a moral task, rather than as part of a political economy in which improving the life of the population is directly proportional to increasing the strength of the state. Moreover, in Hobbes, this improvement is always conditional to both the non-negotiable value of security and the assumption that this value will suffice, indirectly, to guarantee such an improvement (see note 29 above). With governmentality, this is framed within a biopolitical economy in which security becomes a negotiable principle of calculation. Accordingly, improving the life of the population cannot just be normatively presupposed: it must be actively enacted. Again, we saw in the last chapter the centrality this aspect played in Cerdá, where the question was exactly that of envisaging a science able to address simultaneously the material, social and living infrastructure of the urban.

Third, the understanding of the population as a whole organism ordered by immanent regularities and the necessity to address this organism *in vivo* through a logic of calculation make an accurate and detailed knowledge of the population vital. Population-level patterns will have to be recognised, analysed and measured, in order to define, quantify and evaluate the 'good health' of the population—hence a whole new series of '*savoirs*' such as demography, sociology, hygiene, criminology, urbanism (as developed in the last chapter), propelled by the positivistic ethos of eighteenth and nineteenth century, and most notably articulated through *statistics*. Statistics, literally the 'science of the state', is perfectly consistent with the new task of government: neither abstracting individuals into subjects of law, nor 'moulding' them into docile bodies; rather 'modulating'—as well as modelling (see section Researching Urban Violence below)—the population by tweaking its tendencies within the desired, that is, the most cost-effective thresholds. This means that, following Foucault (2003[1997], 246),

> regulatory mechanisms must be established to establish an equilibrium, maintain an average, establish a sort of homeostasis, and compensate for variations within this general population and its aleatory field. In a word, security mechanisms have to be installed around the random element inherent in a population of living beings so as to optimize a state of life.

Biopolitics has to do with the modulation of life, that is, the translation of data into waves and their fine-tuning in terms of amplitude and frequency (cf. Hui 2015; Deleuze, 2006[1986]; 1992[1990]): the management of the life of a population within 'a bandwidth of the acceptable', defined in turn via a principle of economic calculation (Foucault (2007[2004], 21; cf. Murphy 2017). The new science of political economy contains in its very semantic the meaning of a domestic (*oikonomic*) science of administration in which the 'political' is subsumed into the 'economic' (cf. Agamben 2011[2009]).[32]

This deeply realistic, pragmatic, utilitarian and environmental strategy is no longer aimed at fabricating an order but rather seeks to regulate disorder (cf. Agamben 2001) by keeping it in balance. As we can see, the question of *balance* is radically reframed. Not at the static level of rights (that is, the balance between the *right to security* and the *right to freedom*) but at the dynamic level of the population and the statistical calculation of its thresholds: security is exactly such a principle of homeostatic balance, with respect to which *individual freedom* is dependent on the *economics of the population*, rather than simply on the binary code of law or on disciplinary mechanisms. It follows that surveillance and data-gathering practices are not anomalies vis-à-vis liberal regimes: they are constitutive to them, in order to guarantee the security of freedom, and thus freedom *in* security.

Within this logic, crime and violence are no longer possibilities to be eliminated but probabilities to be minimised, in the context of an all-encompassing cost-benefit analysis. On the one hand, potential threats are assessed, calculating the probability and impact of a certain (threatening) event. On the other, security policies are assessed in a cost/benefit curve: the more we invest, the more we increase security, at the same time curtailing other dimensions. 'The essential function of security . . . is to respond to a reality in such a way that this response cancels out the reality to which it responds—it nullifies it, or limits, checks, or regulates it' (Foucault 2007[2004], 47).[33] Nowhere else than in neoliberal economists Gary Becker (1968) and George Stigler (1970)'s proposals to calculate the 'optimal' amount of law enforcement is this approach to security more explicit—making them a central example for Foucault's critique of neoliberalism.[34] 'The goal of enforcement, let us assume, is to achieve that degree of compliance with the rule of prescribed (or proscribed) behavior that the society believes it can afford' (Stigler 1970, 526). The question is how to react to the supply of crime: the focus is the market milieu of crime. Foucault suggests that, for the neoliberal thinkers, even the definition of crime shall be stripped of normative characters: 'Becker gives this definition of crime: "I call crime any action

that makes the individual run the risk of being condemned to a penalty'"
(2010[2004], 251).[35]

Utilitarianism, here, is fully resolved into the calculation of a subject that
is assumed to function as a *homo oeconomicus*.[36] The government of the *homo
oeconomicus* provides a grid of intelligibility that removes the concern for the
singular individual—'the figure of what we could call *homo juridicus* or *homo
legalis*' (idem, 276). This is because the criminal is conceptualised as *anyone
whatsoever*, and therefore crime is framed, rather than as a matter of 'deviant'
individuals, as an increasingly 'situational' dimension of risk and probability.
The notion of environmental crime prevention, we are to see (see chapter
7 and chapter 5, Researching Urban Violence), derives precisely from this
relational, pragmatic and (only apparently) post-moral approach. It is in this
respect that the problem of producing a shared *sense* of security in the social
increasingly becomes crucial, as a common sense of order, or atmosphere, that
must be continuously produced, aroused and guaranteed.[37] The contemporary
aestheticisation of security can be retraced here (e.g., Ghertner et al. 2020).

Fourth, and last, this novel regime also entails a wholly novel epistemology of space. In a sense, if feminist and ecological perspectives propose to
overcome the Cartesian dualisms through an understanding of humanity in
its relation between species and environment (e.g., Plumwood 1993; Haraway 2008; Moore 2015), Foucault shows how this understanding is implicitly at the basis of the very problematic governmentality begins to respond to,
namely as a 'discovery' of that 'natural' being—the population—that is assumed as a conjunct of relations between a species and its milieu. This implies
a key move beyond the a-spatial projections of earlier political theories and
their utopian cities, or empty towns. The attention for the 'fine materiality'
(Foucault 2007[2004], 339) of social life is fundamentally different from both
Hobbesian *sûreté* and Lockean *securité*, both still framed within an atomistic
ontology and an abstract understanding of the individual-society dichotomy.
As an epistemology of power that is deeply relational (it does not atomise
individuals) and dynamic (it does not rely on erecting enclosures, but rather
on allowing the circulation of people, good and money as open as possible),
governmentality entails a complex spatial consciousness. If a population
needs to be managed in the open, then the *milieu* in which a population exists will have to be treated as part of the population itself.[38] This is explicit
in the title to one of Foucault's key courses (2007[2004]), where the notions
of security, territory and population are gathered. Security, in a nutshell, is
to be understood as a principle of calculation applied to an understanding
of a population that is inextricable from the territory—more precisely, an
understanding of a population *as* territory (see Brighenti 2010a). Again, this

shift from the static relation between people and place towards a dynamic relation of a population and its territory does resonate with Cerdá's own notion of urbanisation, which was meant to overcome the 'static' notion of the city by reframing its spatial premises—i.e., by *territorialising* it.

Before moving forward, however, a clarification is in order. As Foucault never tires to clarify, governmentality does not 'substitute' legal and disciplinary mechanisms, but rather complement them—often contradictorily so (see, for instance, section Researching Urban Violence below, and chapter 7). Consider some of the most recent, and extreme, versions of economicist utilitarianism, which applied Becker and Stigler's theories to calculating the correct amount of torture as a 'mechanism for extracting information from a suspect who may or may not be informed' (Baliga and Ely 2016, abstract; see also Mialon et al. 2012), thereby 'rationalising' (Dosi and Roventini 2016), that is, sanctioning the use of torture. It would be disingenuous, we believe, to consider this type of arguments as just another example of the self-referential, indeed esoteric (e.g., Amin 1974[1970]), nature of contemporary neoclassical economics. At the same time, and in line with our epistemological approach, it is not enough to consider utility theory applied to security a 'fetish' (Dosi and Roventini 2016), an expression of false consciousness of wannabe-totalitarian (neo)liberals. It is the historical coexistence of the three paradigms of security that we have discussed, and the way they are articulated through an aesthetic, a practice and an imaginary, that makes it possible that theoretically irreconcilable approaches to security do reconcile in the real world. It is in connection with the specificity of the event of terrorism—and with its politics and imaginaries—that liberal thinking almost systematically ends up sanctioning one of its nemeses, torture (see chapter 4, Researching Urban Violence). But, we shall discuss throughout this book, contradictions and paradoxes of this sort do constitute the very nature of the security/violence nexus.

To sum up, governmentality surfaces as the coming to term with the fact that order is not only a condition to be projected onto the social but also one that must be directly reproduced, within a relational ontology (in which population and territory are inextricable) in 'free' circulation, whose 'life' must be biopolitically improved according to economic calculations that are fully immersed in the relational materiality of coexistence, most notably urban existence. Urbanisation and police are the twin logics through which such a task is carried out.

Police

Consider Foucault's discussion of police in his *Security, Territory, Population* lectures:

> If the governmentality of the state is interested, for the first time, in the fine materiality of human existence and coexistence, of exchange and circulation, if this being and well-being is taken into account for the first time by the governmentality of the state, through the town and through problems like health, roads, markets, grains, and highways, it is because at that time commerce is thought of as the main instrument of the state's power and thus as the privileged object of a police whose objective is the growth of the state's forces. This is the first thing I wanted to say concerning these objects of police, their urban model, and their organization around the problem of the market and commerce. (2007[2004], 339)

As already anticipated, the 'project' of police, which is for Foucault inextricable from the project of the urban, surfaces in the context of the collapse of the feudal order and in the context of the emergence of: an all-encompassing theory of the state, the birth of scientific method and a political arithmetic, with the invention of statistics, that grounds the biopolitical link between the state and the population (Rigakos et al. 2009). The police—of which the modern institution of the police is just an expression—is 'a public thing, a *res publica*, the ensemble of means by which the forces of the state can grow in maintaining the good order of the state, reliant on calculation and technique' (Elden 2007, 572; see also, on police power, Dubber 2005; Neocleous 2021[2000]). Police encompasses a novel form of power, science and regulations, which accompanies a quintessential urban transition towards liberalism. Across this transition, we argue, police may be said to have *mediated* the relation, between the strength of the population and the strength of the state, that the biopolitical epistemology introduces, by translating this relation into a normative and aesthetic question of *order*. We already reflected on the centrality of this notion. If modernity sanctions the disappearance of universally accepted values, social relations can no longer be statically *assessed* with respect to them. The notion of order offers a solution to this conundrum, in the form of an immanent mechanism of *commensuration* with respect to which society can assess itself without reference to transcendent values (Lepenies 1992[1969]). That this is the key purpose of police was already spelled out by the likes of Catherine the Great: 'everything that serves to preserve the good order of society is a matter for police' (apud Foucault 2007[2004], 329, n. 2).[39] Originally, police have to do with the *fabrication* of a biopolitical order in which the health of the state and the health of the population are supposedly linked (Neocleous (2021[2000]); Wall 2021).

Incidentally, also the *necessary* discretionary quality of police may find here a genealogical explanation. There is an ambiguity within police since its advent. Police are a force tasked with fabricating order and therefore one that constantly reminds of a disorder without which, it is evident, police itself would be redundant. The violence of police can be also understood in direct reference to the pragmatic realism of security in the context of governmentality, understood as a technique of government that does not deny or pretend to overcome the gap between the imaginary of absolute security produced by the legal projection of order and the contingent reality, of disorder; and that instead assumes this gap as an inescapable reality which must be directly managed. As Nathan Moore (2007b, 445 and 448) puts it, 'this gap is the zone where law, in all of its technical and historical modes, unfolds'. As he adds, 'what governmentality begins to make explicit is the gap between validity and efficacy, a gap that it is the function of the police to coordinate and manage. It is not the case that this gap does not exist under regimes of sovereignty, but that there it exists only negatively, or even unconsciously'. This fracture, as we will show in chapter 7, is (partially) solved via the surfacing of an increasingly aesthetic and affective dimension of security, that is, of a series of discourses, politics and practices of security that are increasingly aimed at *producing* a shared sense of order, and thus security. What we want to stress here, instead, is the fact that, insofar as being tasked with patrolling the borders defined by law, the police *must* rely on the threat and the exercise of violence (otherwise it would not be needed at all). Police must always exceed the order—be *discretionary* (Dubber 2005)—since every intervention is a demonstration that the law itself has been insufficient in guaranteeing the order. Discretion is a crucial aspect of police power, because that power has among its functions exactly that of 'preclud[ing] efforts to constrain the discretion of the sovereign invoking it' (Dubber and Valverde 2008, 4), on the account that it is a power that is always deployed for the better good of the population. Police, in other words, is *necessarily* violent, expressing a violence that is by definition excessive to the law.[40] The ambiguous and literally *outlaw* violence that instantiates the order (the law-positing violence) is never abandoned once the order is established. The sovereign power must always come back to its violent beginning in order to *maintain* the order, and this is nowhere as evident as in the functioning of the police, whose power, Benjamin writes, 'is formless, like its nowhere tangible, all-pervasive, ghostly presence in the life of civilised state' (1996[1921], 287).

While the likes of Benjamin, Schmitt and Agamben have exposed the essential relation between law, police and exceptional violence in these terms, here we are interested in framing this relation vis-à-vis a specific historical process, namely modern urbanisation, which the police have accompanied since its inception, guaranteeing and greasing its unfolding, as well as haunting it with the permanent possibility of the violent materialisation of state force. The central point for our argument is that police cannot be thought without assuming its co-constitutive relation with urbanisation. There is no (modern, liberal, capitalist) urbanisation without police, and there is no police as such without urbanisation, a relation that is at once juridical, economic and infrastructural.[41] It must be qualified, as we will see further, that, when thinking about modern urbanisation, it is also crucial to keep into account the extent to which this is shaped by colonial urbanisation, in which the role of the police is explicitly administrative and violent at the same time (see chapters 4 and 6).

If, as we explained, urbanisation unfolds frictionally, as a patchy and discontinuous process, then police can be understood as the *necessarily violent* institution that is tasked with the *maintenance* of the given order and its hierarchy, and the *mediator* between urbanisation and its local and discontinuous instantiation. What we are suggesting is that the role of police (and security in the way in which it unfolds in the contemporary city) is that of actualising the imaginary of absolute security by constantly greasing its frictions and contradictions, that is, *by administering the gap between law and order.* Circulation, we already saw, is paramount in this respect, and urbanisation, as Cerdá insisted, is exactly the territoriality that makes circulation possible, and which police are tasked to secure. Foucault goes as far as saying that, by means of regulating and de facto allowing the unfolding of 'cohabitation, circulation, and exchange,' police was 'a condition of existence of urban existence' (2007[2004], 336). To support this argument, Foucault quotes, among others, the seventeenth-century jurist Jean Domat, according to whom 'it is by police that we create towns and places where men assemble and communicate with each other', commenting that 'in the seventeenth and eighteenth century police was thought essentially in terms of what could be called the urbanization of the territory . . . To police and to urbanize is the same thing' (idem, 336–337). The problem of fabricating a manmade order in a world deprived of divine guide, which Hobbes addressed via the introduction of a novel political science, has been translated into police and urbanisation.

A qualification is in order. When introducing the advent of governmentality proper, Foucault discusses the fading out of the post-Westphalian *police state* and its over-disciplinary police. Yet, in the same way governmentality coexists with Hobbesian and Lockean dimensions, the patriarchal, exceptional and discretionary force of the police does not disappear from the picture—quite the opposite, the critique of security would argue. If anything, it was 'police (police regulations, police powers, and police science) [that which] enabled the sovereign power of states to begin to govern differently' (Valverde 2008, 20), by allowing it to be reframed in a more fluid and amorphous form of sovereignty within the liberal regimes. Certainly, this implied that the former, unitary project of police be diffracted into different institutions and mechanisms, most importantly relative to four domains: economic practice, public law (liberal law grounded on respect of freedom), population management (via novel *savoirs*) and 'police' (the organisation, as we now understand it).

This, in conclusion, brings us to where we began, that is, to the question on whether security is a sign of our times. The centrality of the urban-police-security nexus has been widely acknowledged in the present security moment, and often associated with the neoliberal transition (see Garland 2001). This has been grasped with particular emphasis in the Southern European context, where, with a specific terminological turn, the concept of 'urban security' (*sicurezza urbana*, *segurança urbana*, *seguridad urbana*) has achieved increased relevance in the public and legal discourse (Recasens et al. 2013). Focusing on the Italian case, Fabrizio Battistelli (2013, §2) has discussed the shift from *sicurezza pubblica* ('public safety', whose goals are 'people's individual safety and the protection of property') to *sicurezza urbana*, noting how the latter adds up vaster and vaguer concerns with 'the quality of life and the full enjoyment of urban space' (see chapter 7). While, in Anglophone contexts, the terminological shift has been either less relevant (in the USA, public safety remains central) or less linear (in the UK, community safety is the prevalent concept), concepts and practices like quality of life policing, zero tolerance, neighbourhood patrolling have also been the expression of an increasing centrality of 'the urban' (and the urban community; cf. Tulumello and Falanga 2022) for security and policing. The core point, here, is that the relation between police, security and urbanisation is today increasingly tight, needing to be conceptualised in the context of the aesthetic shift in security. At the same time, this relation finds its genealogy in the very original forms that police had taken—in its vast reach and vague, if all-encompassing, scope. The history of security (and policing) has provided us with a fundamental insight: the present of urban violence, for all its specificities and emergence, can only be comprehended by framing it within the long-term surfacing of a specific imaginary, process and atmosphere of the urban—that which we will explore in the next three chapters.

Researching Urban Violence: Hobbes,
Locke and Foucault in Pandemic Times

Two years into the pandemic of Covid-19, the policy and politics of health and safety management that have been put in place offer us a paradigmatic example of how the three logics that we have presented in this chapter—Hobbes' absolutism, Locke's liberalism and Foucault's governmentality, in brief—are always coexisting, and most often contradictorily so, in actually existing security.

If Hobbesian security can be summarised by the necessity to act for the good of the population, to protect it from its own excess, the pandemic has offered an appropriate playground for exercising such a patriarchal urge. This has probably nowhere been more evident than in Italy, the first Western country to be hit by a wave of infections—see Wu Ming I (2021, ch. 21) for a vivid account. The period between March 2020 and the end of the summer has been pinpointed by old (e.g., regulations against *assembramenti*, a fascist-era term for gathering) and new (e.g., the media and political discourse against so-called *movida*) moral panics, including unlikely ones, like that surrounding runners:

> the morning of March 15, on the waterfront in Mondello, in the province of Palermo, a squad of cops has stopped and beaten a citizen who, alone, was jogging close to his residency. An activity that no decree banned at that time. A video, shot from a balcony, showed the runner surrounded and pushed to the ground. 'You have to go back home!', the officers were telling him. (idem, 344; our translation)

This context offered local mayors an invaluable opportunity to exercise with particular intensity the remarkable executive powers provided by more than a decade of security regulations,[42] deploying increasingly arbitrary measures, often beyond any reasonable principle of precaution, accompanied by a *crescendo* of flamboyant video messages. Even after the first wave, despite growing scientific evidence in support of being outdoors (see Tulumello 2021c), public spaces have often remained under strict control, with recurring decisions to hinder or forbid outdoor activity and socialisation, under the deafening noise of the security discourse.

'#*Milanononsiferma*', 'Milan won't stop'. Thus proclaimed a media campaign launched towards the end of February 2020 by an organisation representative of the 'food' sector and endorsed by mayor Beppe Sala as a response to early calls for locking down the Lombardy region, then the most hit by Covid-19 in Italy. In March, while European countries started to lockdown, British Prime Minister Boris Johnson proclaimed that the UK would adopt a different strategy, letting the virus spread with the purpose of achieving herd immunity. Sala later on admitted the campaign was a mistake (Virgolette 2020) and Johnson had to back off from his plan. In these, and many other examples in the pandemic governmental discourse, a Lockean assumption is implicitly foregrounded, namely the championing of individual (and economic) freedoms. In the following months, the highly newsworthy (according to the standards of the contemporary mediascape) no-mask and no-vax demonstrations (and in some cases, in their junction with far-right parties and movements), together with the controversial positions of renowned (Italian) philosophers,[43] made it increasingly visible how the balance of security and freedom is, well, increasingly out of balance. Whatever one may think of no-mask and no-vax rhetoric (and, indeed, of the toxic way in which they have been at the same time overestimated and ridiculed by mainstream media), it seems to us that their primary effect has been that of polarising the debate by deafening both different critiques to the binary alternative, and alternative critical imaginaries that eschewed the public health versus individual freedom alternative—and, for that matter, even attempts at a reasonable discussion on the balance (see Tulumello 2021b).

Again in March 2020, a research team from the Imperial College of London published a report (Ferguson et al. 2020) that estimated the death toll in a hypothetical scenario with no policy response in place—a report that spurred both calls for tightening health measures and accusations of sensationalism (Cepelewicz 2021). This is a paradigmatic example of the intersection between pandemic governance and biopolitics. Warwick Anderson (2021) has shown the extent to which the reliance on abstract modelling and rigid statistical measurement, to abstract the population into a homogeneous whole, dates back to colonial engagement with tropical diseases and still maintains the same problematic biases. While to some extent this is obviously a necessary strategy, its epistemological reification risks de-materialising the social into abstract models that have the purpose of making, 'certain population policies and subject positions conceivable, even necessary, at the same time as it aims to "depoliticise" debate, attempting to silence other voices and alternative imaginations of the future' (idem, 177)—further reducing room to manoeuvre in a crisis.

This necessarily brief overview should had shown how, even in the context of the pandemic—the context of securitisation par excellence[44]— security is everything but a monolith, it is rather a field of tension and contradiction among the three fields that we have identified in this chapter. This is not only a remainder of the necessarily political nature of security (cf. Neal 2019; Tulumello 2021a), but, at the same time, also a reminder for all those interested in criticising both the theory and the practice of security. The key takeaway of this chapter is, in short, that security cannot be criticised for being absolute, liberal or biopolitical—it needs to be engaged with and criticised for the articulation of those three natures.

Notes

1. Nietzsche, Friedrich. 1882. *Die fröhliche Wissenschaft*.
2. The situational paradigm focuses on individual responsibility: it conceptualises the event of crime or violence as the result of the free will of a rational offender, and it therefore prevents by reducing opportunities and/or motivation. The social paradigm focuses on the causes behind the event, thus engaging with structural issues to improve the societal well-being and, hence, reduce motivation. Repression, though happening *after* the fact, is often considered a preventative instrument, in the sense that the possibility of being apprehended and punished would discourage the rational offender.
3. We could indeed state 'the infrastructure of Western security'. And yet, on the one hand, it has become a dominant logic at the global level, with little challenges; and, on the other, we will see that it has been produced in the global travel of ideas and policies, under and beyond colonialism (see chapter 4). This suggests that the North/South dichotomy could be more productively replaced, in this field, by a dialectical lens over global (post-)colonial relations.
4. On contemporary security logics, see also Anderson (2010a).
5. The entrance of new actors into the field of security has been seen by some as signalling the growing 'limits of the sovereign state' (Garland 1996) in terms of its capacity to guarantee security and legitimation to do so. Others have argued that, quite the opposite, the state has deepened its capacity to control their populace precisely by engaging further actors in the operations of security (see Herbert 1999, responding to Garland). We understand the terms of this balance to be both dynamically changing and variable throughout the world. Fabrizio Battistelli (2013) highlights the need for a double set of such coordinates in the field of 'urban security'. On the one hand, the vertical and horizontal relations among a plurality of governmental levels and agencies (governmental or not) in the management of security. In particular, at least four types of dynamics can be traced (Tulumello 2018b, 1138): influence of global political economic shifts (above all, neoliberalisation broadly understood) over national approaches; the international travel of national agendas; local adoptions of global practices; and multi-level policy transfers (e.g., hybridisation between national and local security practices). On the other, the distinction between processes of privatisation (the 'outsourcing' of security activities to other agencies) and participation (the expectation that individual citizens, citizen groups and local communities collaborate in the production of security). As a further confirmation of the complex nature of these restructurings is the simultaneous growth of the punitive and repressive side (Garland 2001; Dikeç 2006; Wacquant 2008; Müller 2012).

6. *Critique of Security* is also the title of an important book by Mark Neocleous (2008). As we will see below, Neocleous understands the critique of security as its rejection as a fundamentally bourgeois, liberal concept, while we use the term in a looser sense to encompass a broader field of scholarship.

7. 'Security is the highest social concept of civil society, the concept of *police*, expressing the fact that the whole of society exists only in order to guarantee to each of its members the preservation of his person, his rights, and his property' (Marx 2008/2009[1844]; emphasis in translation).

8. Journal *Security Dialogue* has dedicated a recent issue (50 [1], 219) to the 'problems' of critique of and in security.

9. It is useful to keep in mind Jacques Derrida's warning: deconstruction is not to be understood as 'a tool or technical device for mastering texts or mastering a situation or mastering anything; it's, on the contrary, the memory of some powerlessness . . . a way of reminding the other and reminding me, myself, of the limits of the power, of the mastery' (1995, 385).

10. Let us qualify that this argument has nothing to do with the Blairite approach to security which, in its Italian version, courtesy of the centre-left, assumes security as 'a value of the Left'—because, once again, security is not a value in itself, but only makes sense within a given system of values and evaluations. In other words, the 'security is a value of the Left' argument renounces to rethink security within a different system of values and rather deploys a concept of security that has already been shaped by the discourse of the Right, with dramatic consequences (see chapter 9).

11. 'The bourgeoisie has never been revolutionary. It simply made sure others pulled of the revolution for it. It manipulated, channelled, and repressed an enormous surge of popular desire' (Gilles Deleuze, interviewed in Guattari 2009[1973], 45).

12. There is no need to go beyond Western modernity to find a different trajectory, one that unfolds through the likes of Machiavelli and Spinoza, with respect to whom security is understood as immanent to—rather than opposed from —the freedom and power of the bodies that constitute the political community (see Del Lucchese 2004; we are to explore this notion of security in chapter 9).

13. As we are to see in chapter 8, Cicero is also responsible for the introduction of the term *decorum*.

14. While most Europan languages use words descending from the same headword—*segurança* (Portuguese), *sicurezza* (Italian), *seguridad* (Spanish), *sécurité* (French), *Sicherheit* (German), *säkerhet* (Swedish), *siguranţă* (Rumanian) and so forth—English is one of few languages that uses a second word with virtually the same meaning, safety, which comes from the Latin *salvus*. For a discussion of the, often fuzzy, distinction between security and safety in the urban realm, see Tulumello and Falanga (2015).

15. Augustinus warned against *mortifera securitas*, that is, lethal indifference (Arends 2011, 269).

16. Seneca would write: *ad propositum bene vivendi confert securitas publica* (Ep. Ad Luc, 73,2).

17. 'It is objected that by releasing desire from lack and law, the only thing we have left to refer to is a state of nature, a desire which would be natural and spontaneous reality. We say quite the opposite: desire only exists when assembled or machined' (Deleuze and Parnet 1987[1977], 96). As usefully summarised by Juan Luis Gastaldi, desire 'is not free or spontaneous, but rather determined by the situations inside which desire finds itself inextricably placed' (2009, 71). This does not mean determinism: 'however, that the machines are desiring machines means that the situations determine us only to desire and to create something new, which does not yet exist in these situations' (idem, ibidem). See chapter 4 for a further exploration of this concept in relation to the notion of social imaginary and Pavoni (2018a, ch. 1) for a more extended discussion.

18. As Deleuze quipped in an interview, this is what an organisation of power is, nothing but 'the unity of desire and the economic infrastructure' (in Guattari 2009[1973], 38).

19. Let us stress once more that we are not implying a relativism of security. We are aware that existence is always dependent on what Spinoza termed *joy*, i.e., the enhancement of the condition that make existence flourish, and a certain degree of freedom from *sadness*, those conditions, affective, psychical and physical, that debilitate and makes it suffer (see introduction). Various authors have explored these aspects: the role of life and bodily integrity in the human capabilities approach (Nussbaum 2011); bell hooks's reflection (1991, 47) on the importance of the home as a space of personal safety for the empowerment of oppressed groups and women; ontological security, from Giddens's original formulation (1991, see above) to recent applications in the field of international relations (Kinnval et al. 2018); the surfacing of a notion of 'safe space'; or the theorisation of security as emancipation that we have discussed above.

20. Security is coessential to the desire to persevere in one's own being that is transversal to the living, and this resonates with Ruth Levitas's definition (2013: xii-xiii) of utopia in terms of desire, according to which security is not simply the projection of a given epoch but also a generative desire necessarily accompanying any quest for better living, namely, the preservation of life through its potentiation, or flourishing—see on this the *Political Treatise* of Spinoza (1677).

21. Hamilton writes that 'for Seneca, all the while mindful of mortality, *securitas* cannot eradicate physical death but only the psychological fear of death' (2013, 54).

22. Anthony Giddens, following Kierkegaard, writes that 'to "be", for the human individual, is to have ontological awareness'. He continues: 'this is not the same as awareness of self-identity, however closely the two may be related in the developing experience of the infant. The "struggle of being against non-being" is the perpetual task of the individual, not just to "accept" reality, but to create ontological reference points as an integral aspect of "going on" in the contexts of day-to-day life' (1991, 48).

23. And we emphasise 'man' to stress the patriarchal genealogy at the core of the emergence of the modern state (see Dubber 2005).

24. The treaties, signed in 1648, that make up the Peace of Westphalia, which ended the Thirty Years War, are often considered to mark the beginning of modern European institutional systems and international relations because of the institution of the principle of exclusive state sovereignty.

25. In this sense, there is a key difference between the administrative logic of the *raison d'etat* and its police state, and the Hobbesian ambition to ground a wholly novel polity based on the social pact that brings into life the sovereign power (see Galli 2011).

26. Hobbes believed of being born, in 1588, 'twinned with fear', because the mother had been traumatised by the news of the attempted invasion by the Spanish Armada (see Neocleous 2019, 27).

27. Arends (2011) emphasises the centrality played in this sense also by the reflection of Thucydides in the context of the Peloponnesian War, a situation of *bellum omnium contra omnes* in which security (Thucydides uses the term *asphaleia*) is presented as a question of Realpolitik, that is, a realistic, a-moral and atheistic matter that greatly inspired Hobbes. The English philosopher knew very well the Greek historian, of whom he published a translation as early as 1629.

28. As Tacitus (Agricola 30.4) synthesised in his famous sentence: '*ubi solitudinem faciunt, pacem appellant* [they make a desert and they call it peace]', a sentence he attributes to the Caledonian chief Calgacus, against the invading Roman army. Interestingly, Tacitus also provided probably the earliest critique of the security-freedom nexus, when referring 'to the antagonism between the old Republican ideal of *libertas* and the new Caesarean value of *securitas*', and stressing their incompatibility (Arends 2011, 270).

29. Hobbes considers *salus populi suprema lex* in the sense of guaranteeing not only survival but also a pleasant life (Fisichella 2008, 80). Yet, this *salus* it only guaranteed through the sovereign, so that the danger for the subject may only come from the others, not from the sovereign.

30. But see the section Researching Urban Violence of chapter 2 on the problems of referring to crime data, even for a critique of security.

31. See for instance what the former Italian centre-left Minister of Internal Affairs Marco Minniti had to say: '*security is freedom*. It is evident that there cannot be an idea of security without guaranteeing individual freedom; and at the same time, there is no true freedom as long as everyday safety is not guaranteed' (apud Giannini 2017; our translation, our emphasis). Through the balance, security and freedom have become one and the same thing—on Minniti's philosophy of security, see Gargiulo (2018).

32. As Valverde puts it 'maintaining security is difficult for modern states not only because people are keen to pursue liberty but also because economic change brings with it new security needs. With the rise of modern economic and social practices and modern knowledges, new entities, such as labor markets, that were unknown to princes concerned only with territories and loyal subjects have to be secured' (2008, 28).

33. The becoming of security as a central engine of policy and politics has gone hand in hand with a specific epistemology of future threats, described by some as the emergence of the 'risk society' (Beck 1992[1986]). Importantly, while the risk society is often considered to be a recent emergence, its genealogies have been traced back

to the very birth of the capitalist society (Rigakos and Hadden 2001). In summary, risk is a governmental practice centred on the measurement and quantification of future dangers, in terms of probability (see Aradau and van Munster 2012, 99–100). It is through this very quantification that security thinking can be centred on the 'balance' between prevention and other dimensions.

34. Foucault briefly discussed this issue, without mentioning Becker, at the beginning of the 1978–1979 lectures *Security, Territory, Population* (2007[2004], 4–5). The following year, he dedicated two of the lectures *The Birth of Biopolitics* to Becker's theory of labour (2010[2004], 215–233), and his (and Stigler's) theory of crime and punishment (idem, 239–260). See also Becker's response (Becker et al. 2013) and a rejoinder by David Newheiser (2016).

35. Becker's article (1968) does not explicitly define crime as such—as noted also by Michel Senellart, editor of the edition of *The Birth of Biopolitics* that we use, who suggests that Foucault was relying on Frédéric Jenny's synthesis of Becker and Stigler's work (see Foucault 2010[2004], 263, n. 25).

36. It is important to keep in mind that the *homo oeconomicus* will gradually be understood in more complex ways than in its classic connotation as an individual that performs choices in purely rational manner.

37. As Foucault famously observed, 'freedom in the regime of liberalism is not a given, it is not a ready-made region which has to be respected . . . Freedom is something which is constantly produced. Liberalism is not acceptance of freedom; it proposes to manufacture it constantly, to arouse it and produce it, with, of course, the system of constraints and the problems of cost raised by this production' (2010[2004], 65).

38. As Gilles Deleuze (2006[1986], 60–61) summarises, governmentality implied the question 'of administering and controlling life in a particular multiplicity, provided the multiplicity is large (a population) and the space is spread out or open'.

39. Since the seventeenth century, the notion of police begins to assume a precise meaning as 'the set of means by which the state's forces can be increased while preserving the state in good order' (Foucault 2007[2004], 313).

40. Foucault (2007[2004], 340) already noted that police are diametrically different from justice, since it has to do with the direct, sovereign intervention into the life of the population in ways that do not stem from the law but, to the contrary, are necessarily *exceptional* to the law.

41. As we will see in chapter 4, arguments that deny this co-constitutiveness by focusing on the role of plantations and slavery patrols in the emergence of police in the USA are simply adopting a limited understanding of urbanisation as the movement of people from rural to urban places (see further chapters 2 and 5).

42. Especially since the Decree of the Minister of Interior 5 August 2008, part of the so-called 'security package' designed by then Minister of Interior Roberto Maroni, increased the power of mayors to issue by-laws.

43. And especially in those by Massimo Cacciari and Giorgio Agamben, whose often preposterous affirmations have been duly debunked (see Bratton 2021).

44. See chapter 4, Researching Urban Violence, for a discussion of securitisation theory.

~

PART II

INTERSECTIONS

CHAPTER FOUR

∼

Imaginary

Let the policeman's club be thrown down or wrested from him, and the fountains of the great deep are opened, and quicker than ever before chaos comes again. Strong as it may seem, our civilization is evolving destructive forces. Not desert and forest, but city slums and country roadsides are nursing the barbarians who may be to the new what Hun and Vandal were to the old.[1]

While the first part of the book is dedicated to setting out the *foundations* of the argument, by way of discussing the three key concepts of violence, urban and security, in this second part, we develop our theoretical argument by focusing on their *intersections*. In summary, we will argue for conceptualising urban violence through three main aspects: first, the *imaginary* of urban violence that feeds the urban project of security; second, the violent *process* of planetary urbanisation; third, the *atmospheric* violence that fills the urban as a result. While, obviously, in the exploration of urban violence these aspects should always be treated together, for heuristic purposes, the next three chapters will deal with each of them individually.

In this chapter, we begin with the imaginary. First, through a recollection of relevant theoretical reflections, we draw a definition of (social) imaginary that is strategically useful for the argument to come. Second, we carry out a genealogical reconnaissance on a foundational binary opposition at the centre of the (Western) urban imaginary, namely, the conceptual and ecological space of the wild. As is well acknowledged by now, the imaginary institution of modernity, as Castoriadis would have put it, is premised on the bifurcation between society and nature, most notably sanctioned by Descartes's philosophy, Hobbes's political theory and Locke's colonial legal theory. What in this section we are more interested in exploring, with a view to link this reflection with the notions of urban, violence and security, is the role played by the notion of wilderness in articulating this separation within the 'modern social imaginary'. Implicitly and explicitly feeding, and being fed back in return, by colonialism, this notion will be reprocessed in the nineteenth-century city into the hidden operator of what we term the imaginary *of* urbanisation, in which planning and police, law and bourgeois aesthetic, converge. Third, consequently, we show to what extent the imaginary of urbanisation must be understood by taking into account the violent encounter with the colonial space and the colonial other, and its consequences in shaping the way in which the nineteenth-century city appeared at bourgeois planners, legislators and police. It is in this context, we argue, that the contemporary notion of urban violence emerges.

Imaginary

The notion of imagination has long played an ambiguous role in Western thought, its epistemological, ontological and political status oscillating between reality and illusion, creation and reproduction, emancipation and alienation, individual and collective. In genealogical terms, a key turning point has been the emergence of modern epistemology—and of the *modern imaginary* (cf. Taylor 2003). It is at this juncture that imagination begins to drift from ancient *phantasia* to modern fantasy, that is, from being understood as an important, if secondary, faculty that partakes in the process of reason, judgement and cognition, to being depreciated as a troubling hinder to rational thought, a dangerous political deception (most notably as *ideology*) and a faculty whose creative potential must be confined to the seemingly innocuous realm of art.[2]

For Plato, imagination (*phantasia*) does emerge from sensation (*aesthesis*), as a capacity to process and produce images, appearances, *phantoms*. It can be deceptive, but, at the same time, it does partake in cognition and judgement. Likewise described as a picturing activity that emerges from the movement of sensation, in Aristotle, imagination is given a more systematic treatment, as a combinatory activity that unifies the data of sensation—an understanding that will remain central throughout the Arab and Scholastic tradition. The pre-modern status of imagination, subordinated to thinking and yet firmly placed within the real, is drastically modified with the advent of modern epistemology and political science, with their prioritisation of rational thought, scientific method and the law of the state. Seen through these lenses, imagination appears as a potentially idiosyncratic, illusory and deceptive activity that, 'being not tied to the laws of matter, may at pleasure join that which nature hath severed, and sever that which nature hath joined; and so make unlawful matches and divorces of things' (Bacon 2004[1605], II, IV.1). An unbound imagination, it follows, is epistemologically and politically dangerous, a literally delirious,[3] monstrous power that threatens the foundations of modern knowledge and the constitution of the modern individual, society and the state, and that must therefore be brought under the control of reason and within the measures of knowledge.

One cannot but notice an ambivalence in the modern framing of imagination, which is implicitly provided with a wildly creative power that, at the same time, is looked with anxiety and fear (cf. Flory 1995), as a potentially devastating force that better be contained and defused. Nowhere such an ambivalence is as evident as in Immanuel Kant, who allegedly *discovered* the productive power of imagination, in the first edition of the *Critique of Pure Reason*, only to *abandon* it, in the second edition, where imagination is firmly secured within the boundaries of the transcendental subject and under the normative control of the tribunal of reason.[4]

This move, we could say, more generally epitomises the role imagination plays in the hegemonic modern imaginary as a creative but dangerous force, both individually and collectively, whose predominance in the present is to be taken as sign of immaturity, illusion, loss of touch with reality, a sign of a mythical, pre-rational stage of evolution still lingering in the present, which must be expunged via the purifying force of reason—the belief therein assuming the form of 'mythical' presupposition (cf. Adorno and Horkheimer 1997[1944]). We are to see below how this contradiction is at play in the Marxist critique of ideology.

Of course, we do not pretend to even slightly encompass the complexity of a genealogy that would require much more space and depth to be undertaken, and that is far from being as linear and homogeneous as we might have unwittingly suggested so far (see Bottici 2014; Lennon 2015). These rough brushstrokes are meant, however, to paint the key *question* that is at play when engaging with imagination, and the reason of its usual devaluation in everyday usage, where it tends to be confined to the immaterial, the mental, the illusional or, at best, to the realm of art. Rescuing imagination to its materiality entails re-anchoring it within the everyday[5]—its relations, practices, habits, atmospheres—that is, understanding imagination as a concrete, collective and ontologically creative, social-historical force. This is what the notion of social imaginary conveys.

Social Imaginary

In both academic and current parlance, the conceptualisation of the 'imaginary' has been often left implicit, with the consequence of defusing its theoretical and strategic potential. An important step beyond this impasse has been the reflection around the notion of social imaginary, which has gained an increasing relevance to the point of constituting a 'field' in its own right (Adams et al. 2015, 19). Usually, authors of the likes of Benedict Anderson, Charles Taylor, Paul Ricoeur, Cornelius Castoriadis, Luce Irigaray, Martha Nussbaum or Arjun Appadurai are associated with this concept. At a first level, notwithstanding their significant differences, most of such theories converge in challenging the long-standing domination of a 'pathological' understanding of the imaginary as a psychological or ideological alienation.[6] In their useful summary, Suzie Adams and colleagues write,

> theories of social imaginaries elucidate the ways in which cultural configurations of meaning creatively configure the human encounter with—and formation (as articulation and doing) of—the world, on the one hand, and, articulate their centrality for the emergence, formation and reproduction of social institutions and practices, that is, of social change and social continuity, on the other. (2015, 19)

In this section we scan through this variegated field in order to highlight six key characteristics of the notion of social imaginary that will inform our discussion on urban violence, at the same time as clearing the ground from as many misunderstandings. In doing so, we will put in communication Cornelius Castoriadis's notion of radical imaginary with Gilles Deleuze and Félix Guattari's notion of desire as presented in the *Anti-Oedipus*. Aware of the significant differences between the two perspectives, we do believe that this frictional intersection expands Castoriadis's concept towards a more explicitly material, affective, heterogeneous and more-than-human understanding—besides offering us an invaluable link to the tripartite notion of security as desire, sense and practice we suggested in the last chapter. At the same time, Castoriadis's theory, and especially his reflection on the process of institutionalisation of the radical imaginary, is useful to draw a link between Deleuzoguattarian desire and the social imaginary, and to make it amenable to socio-historical analysis and critique.[7]

First, let us start by problematising most common definitions of the social imaginary as collectively held representations, shared beliefs or common images,[8] a static understanding of consensual normative visions, as exemplified by the imagined communities famously described by Benedict Anderson

(1983) or in the public imagination Martha Nussbaum (1995) writes about. A problematic implication therein is that the social imaginary remains at a 'reproductive' level, that is, fundamentally a reflection of a deeper reality, the superstructure of a base infrastructure. Of course, the imaginary is also, partially, that. Yet, it is also *more* than that.[9] Collectively held representations—which may indeed assume temporarily stable configurations—can be understood as the 'product' of the imaginary, the *actual imaginary* (or the 'imagined'), to use Castoriadis's terms, the temporary crystallisations of a non-representational, genetic force. Such force is the creative, 'elementary and irreducible capacity of evoking images' that a society holds, its 'ontological' source and condition of possibility—its *radical imaginary* (Castoriadis 1987[1975], 127). This perfectly resonates with Deleuze and Guattari's famous observation as regards the Freudian unconscious being not a theatre, but a *factory*, that is, not a passive re-presentation of a reality out there, but an overflowing and ontologically productive force fed by an impersonal, diffuse and collective desire.[10]

Second: the social imaginary is a *collective* process. In order to hold together, communities have to imagine themselves as such (cf. Anderson, Benedict 1983; Harari 2014[2011]).[11] Yet, to postulate a collective dimension of desire, is not enough: the link between individual and collective imagination should not be left unexplained. This is, however, what happens in Anderson's account for instance, where the imaginary is assumed as the place where individual imaginations converge, rather than 'the place where individuals themselves are made' (Bottici 2014, 44; Çinar and Bender 2007a, xiii).[12] The social imaginary is 'collective' at the same time as it is, or even prior to be, 'individual' and it is a more-than-human relation prior to be reduced onto a human one.[13]

Third, the social imaginary is a social-historical process emerging out of the situated concreteness of a given space and time. A society, for Castoriadis, cannot be thought as separated from a collective process of imagining itself in a socially and historically situated way. This is, he argued, 'the other dimension of the radical imaginary, the social-historical imaginary, instituting a society as source of ontological creation deploying itself as history' (1997[1986], 245). For their part, Deleuze and Guattari stressed this point by reworking the key intuition of another key figure of psychanalysis, Carl Gustav Jung: the collective unconscious is not structured by universal archetypes, but is fully immersed within, and emerges from, the social, the natural and the historical. It is crucial, however, to consider the dynamic interplay between the instituting and the instituted dimension of the radical imaginary, which is neither a simply deterministic or causal relation nor a linear passage between the two. Collective desire 'only exists when assembled or machined' (Deleuze and Parnet 1987[1977], 96), and yet is irreducible to, always overflowing, such instantiations (see chapter 3).

Fourth, the social imaginary has therefore a phantasmatic quality, it virtually exceeds the representations, practices and subjectivities through which it actualises.[14] Castoriadis refers directly to the radical imaginary as a 'magma' in order to emphasise its undetermined quality: an imaginative force that is never fully reducible to, and explainable with, the actual contents it assumes in a given context.[15] The radical imaginary keeps haunting the actual with its overflowing potential, constituting a reserve of potential out of which the actual can be reproduced, contested or transformed. Castoriadis expresses this complex dynamic with the term 'social-historical', in order to stress 'the unity of the twofold multiplicity of dimensions, in "simultaneity" (synchrony) and in "succession" (diachrony) which are traditionally denoted by the terms "society" and "history"' (1987[1975], 285, n42). As he explains,

> the *social-historical* is neither the unending addition of intersubjective networks (although it is this *too*), nor, of course, is it their simple 'product'. The social-historical is the anonymous collective whole, the impersonal-human element that fills every given social formation but which also engulfs it, setting each society in the midst of others, inscribing them all within a continuity in which those who are no longer, those who are elsewhere and even those yet to be born are in a certain sense present. It is, on the one hand, given structures, 'materialized' institutions and works, whether these be material or not; and, on the other hand, *that which* structures, institutes, materializes. In short, it is the union *and* the tension of instituting society and of instituted society, of history made and of history in the making. (idem, 108; emphasis in translation)[16]

This complex interplay between the here and now, and the no longer, the not yet and the not here (cf. Bloch 1986[1954–1959]) feeds the dynamic fermentation of the social imaginary; it does unfold into the affective patterns—or atmospheres—through which an imaginary is differentially felt by each body, often with violent consequences (Gatens and Lloyd 1999; see chapter 6).

Fifth, the social imaginary differs from 'traditional' notions of ideology, understood as an illusionary veneer covering and distorting reality, one that critical thought would be tasked with removing, in this way *revealing* the real functioning of the world. Ideology, to be sure, can constitute an actual imaginary and, more broadly, be understood as a particular way in which the imaginary functions, namely, by positing itself as (the) real.[17] As Claude Lefort effectively put it, 'ideology is the linking together of representations which have the function of re-establishing the dimension of society "without history" at the very heart of historical society' (apud Thompson 1982, 666). While at the superficial level, ideology tends to naturalise power relations and social asymmetries, in this way invisibilising the conflict they produce, however, at a deeper level, ideology is held together by the implicit belief in a 'true' reality, fully transparent to itself and potentially accessible *beyond* mediation (Grusin 2015). This is the ideological 'trap' that naïve critiques of ideology fall into. As Slavoj Žižek argues, 'the concept of ideology must be disengaged from the "representationalist" problematic: ideology has nothing to do with "illusion", with a mistaken, distorted representation of its social content' (1994, 7).[18] We do agree, albeit, as we contend below, the analysis of ideological 'distortions' remain crucial, provided it is rescued from naïve realism and complemented by an affect-centred approach.

Sixth, complementing the distinction with ideology is the importance to not reducing social imaginary to functionalistic explanations. With a detailed and careful critique of traditional Marxist functionalist premises, Castoriadis argues that functionalism is not the *explanans* but rather the *explanandum* as regards social imaginary. The problem is that functionalist explanations do not take into account that needs are historically produced too—that *lacks* themselves are always produced *qua* lacks by a given imaginary. For their part, Deleuze and Guattari state that 'needs are derived from desire: they are counterproducts within the real that desire produces. Lack is a countereffect of desire' (1977[1972], 27). As we have seen (see chapter 3), for Deleuze (2006, 130) desire neither includes lack nor is a natural given. In this sense, what ideology conceals is not 'reality', but rather the overflowing and collective, desiring force of radical imagination. A force that, let us qualify once more, is not necessarily good. Desire can be troubling, toxic or lethal. It can produce violent dystopian imaginaries. The question we are interested in developing is not that of uncritically celebrating radical imaginary over the actual, much like it is not about choosing between desire and lack, but rather to explore the social-historical, abstract articulations through which they are each time assembled.

A brief parenthesis to explain what we mean with 'abstract articulation' is in order. The social imaginary of a given epoch, Castoriadis argues, is insufficiently described if one remains at the representational level. At a more abstract level, he writes, there are 'significations that are not there in order to represent something else, that are like the final articulations that the society in question has imposed on the world, on itself, and on its needs, the organizing patterns that are the conditions for the representability of everything that the society can give to itself' (1987[1975], 143). He terms them *social imaginary significations*, which are called 'imaginary because they do not correspond to, or are not exhausted by, references to "rational" or "real" elements and because it is through a creation that they are posited'; and are called 'social because they are and they exist only if they are instituted and shared by an impersonal, anonymous collective' (1997[1986], 8). These significations work as 'the invisible cement' (Castoriadis 1987[1975], 143) that holds together the real, rational and symbolic dimensions every society is constituted by. Social imaginary significations, in other terms, are certain modes of seeing, sensing and being in the world, they are what 'is operative in the practice and in the doing of the society considered as a meaning that organizes human behaviour and social relations, independently of its exis-tence "for the consciousness" of that society' (Castoriadis 1987[1975], 141). At the level of everyday experience, for instance, they also shape a given society's 'partition of the sensible' (Rancière 2004[2000]), participating in engineering the atmospheres of co-existence (see chapter 6).

This prompts a critique of the imaginary that does neither look for a transparent reality beyond imagination, nor reduce a social imaginary to the representational content (the actual imaginary) through which it becomes conscious to a given society; but rather sets out to explore those 'abstract connections . . . that pervade society and make it cohere' (Virno 2001[1992], 168). That is, those kernels of signification that structure a given social imaginary—for instance, the fact of things being exchangeable in capitalism, of things being right or wrong in morality, or again, as just mentioned, given notions of subject, object, individual, freedom, as well as certain understanding of time, space, epistemology and so on.[19] This understanding has important strategic consequences. For instance, we can analytically distinguish the 'normative violence' that a given representa-tion produces onto the social (e.g., the hierarchical organisation of racism) from the violence of the abstract articulations that sustain it (i.e., the abstract idea of the human that feeds it). Likewise, when exploring urban imaginaries such as the 'smart city', it will be crucial to unpack the linear understanding of time *as* progress and technology *as* solution that feed them, the key abstract articulations of what we are to define as the imagi-nary *of* urbanisation.[20] Understanding such articulations as the infrastruc-tural constitution of social imaginaries, moreover, means to assume them as 'social facts and objects of practical struggle' (Toscano 2011, 91), and thus to explore their strategic value vis-à-vis the production of '"concrete" forms of spatial relationality generative of social meaning' (Cunningham 2008, 465).[21] In other words, the question is not only that of unpacking, analysing and criticising such articulations, but also that of speculatively—

and ontologically—rethinking them (and thus the very notions of human, society, freedom, etc. they underlie) in order to reconfigure different social compositions, via alternative imaginary significations able to organise affective relations differently, in a more flourishing and emancipatory, rather than violently toxic, way (see chapter 9).[22]

This is what an affect-oriented approach to the imaginary might harbour, against over-deterministic, abstracting or reifying readings. As Deborah Gould explains, 'ideologies and discourses emerge and take hold in part through the circulation of affect', that is, in our language, through the socio-material atmospheres through which they are actualised: 'affect, then, greases the wheels of ideology, but it also gums them up. As a result, attending to affect can illuminate how hegemony is affected but also why it is never all-encompassing' (2009, 27). While it tends to posit itself as a coherent, homogeneous and all-encompassing whole, and many accounts remain on a somewhat pacified, homogenous, static and consensual picture,[23] an imaginary is better understood as a metastable formation traversed by frictions and conflicts that keep fermenting beneath their often-smooth appearance, and are differentially felt on bodies. In São Paulo for instance, we saw it already, the lack of a common ground between *asfalto* and *favela* does produce a fractured imaginary, in which different visions of the city encounter and clash without merging, and are somehow held and stitched together *through* violence (Feltran 2020; see chapter 1).

To be sure, the analysis of ideological 'distortions' is not jettisoned by this approach, but rather translated from a revelatory enterprise to an infrastructural analytic of forces, that is, from a critique informed by a hermeneutic of suspicion to a *diagnostic* approach, one that 'aims to disclose how the affective character of presents are (de/re)composed through multiple forces' (Anderson 2021, 206). An affective reading of the imaginary allows one to attend more closely to processes of social reproduction and change—for our purposes, this includes the possibility to consider the role played by violence not against but rather within a given imaginary. Distortion, in this sense, is brought back to its etymology: *dis-torquere*, that is, *twisting*. If the dissimulating force of ideology does not lie in its capacity to cover a 'true real', but rather in positing *this* reality as the only real, then its violence may be understood as a tensional, infra-structural force that crystallises social relations, acting directly on bodies by de-potentiating their *conatus*, that is, hindering their power to affect and be affected, and, therefore, their capacity to sense and move, think and imagine *differently*, in the ways that diverse thinkers such as Frantz Fanon, Laurent Berlant, Bernard Stiegler or Rob Nixon have referred to (see chapter 6).

Once we understand the radical imaginary as being part of any social configuration, then, the question is no longer to be posited in terms of right and wrong, truth and false (i.e., in moral terms), but rather in terms of the effects of capacitation and debilitation that an imaginary's infra-structural violence produces (i.e., in ethical terms; cf. Deleuze 1968). Likewise, it is not a matter of being 'duped' by or 'awakened' from the enchantment of a given ideology, but that of exploring the peculiar atmospheres through which a given imaginary unfold and in which each body is, to a greater or lesser degree, immersed (cf. Protevi 2009; Massumi, 2015; Austin 2023). In chapter 6 we introduce the notion of atmospheric violence exactly as a way to explore—empirically and strategically—the material unfolding of the imaginary *on the ground*, by looking, on the one hand, at the organising, affective patters around which it is held together, and, on the other, the way it affects the bodies that live in and through it. In this chapter, instead, we develop a more genealogical effort, focusing on the surfacing of what we refer to as the imaginary *of* urbanisation.

Prior to moving to this part, however, we link the beginning of this chapter with the concluding reflection of the last one, by showing how the sixfold definition of the social imaginary here proposed can be fruitfully applied to the notion of security, and the imaginary thereof—a similar reflection can be applied to 'cultural' violence (see chapter 1). As we argued, it makes no sense to refer to security as 'ontological' unless the *what* of security is qualified, namely, the implicit ontology that security is assumed to 'secure' (e.g., social imaginary significations such as a certain understanding of 'individual', 'self', 'identity', 'community', 'nation' and so on). In this sense, there is no 'natural' security that be independent from an actual imaginary through which security is each time perceived, experienced, and conceptualised. Yet, we do not want to suggest that security is entirely exhausted by the socio-historical context. Once a magmatic notion of radical imaginary is foregrounded, then it is possible to account for a creative, 'pre-individual', excessive force: this is the desire for security (see chapter 3), which is co-essential to the anonymous collective that composes a given society, and which is directly productive of—rather than secondarily dependent on—those very notions, such as 'individual', 'self' or 'society', that security discourses tend to take for granted. Paraphrasing Bottici (2014, 5; see note 15 above), it is the desire of security that 'makes individuals' in specific ways, depending on specific social, historical and natural determinations, rather than the other way round. At the same time, this approach permits to eschew the symmetrical, equally problematic, functionalist explanation that commonly feeds critiques of security, according to which security is understood as an ideological veneer that expresses a set of relations (of production) that, in turn, are assumed as already structured *before* and thus *independently from* security itself. While the notion of security that emerges in this context does play a key role both as a functional and as an ideological appendage of capitalism and liberalism—security is not *only* that. The desire for security is fuelled by a radical imagination that does not *necessarily* depend on the social imaginary significations that have crystallised with modern liberalism. In other words, the desire for security is indeed ontological, yet in a dynamic, productive and processual sense. It is not bolstered by needs, but rather produces them, as part of that oscillation between resistance and alliance that characterises the *strategy of the conatus* (Bove 1996; see introduction). Thus understood, the desire for security is not a secondary, reactive result of a perceived (e.g. economic) lack, it is rather productive of the socio-material field in and through which actors, needs and lacks are framed.

It is in this sense that Castoriadis's radical imaginary shows its conceptual and strategic value, by allowing to account for both the creation and the disruption (i.e., the possibility for change) of social forms, without sacrificing the political to the altar of the ontological. As Bottici nicely puts, radical imagination 'is radical both politically and ontologically or, even better, it is politically radical because it is ontologically so' (2014, 4; see also Holmes 2008; Haiven and Khasnabich 2014). This is why, at the end of chapter 3, we insisted on complementing the deconstruction of contemporary security with a different imagination of security to counter the risk of depriving the desire for security of any reality. This is the risk critiques of security run, by reducing the imaginary to an illusionary and reactive force that always comes second, after the lack, and produces fantasies, that is, illusionary and phantasmatic imaginaries that have the purpose to fill the gap, thereby implicitly assuming a reality whose basic logics, structures and relations are pre-existent and immutable.[24] In chapter 9, we will speculate on what such a different imaginary may be.

The Modern Imaginary

In Western pre-modern world, space was understood as a heterogeneous complexity whose differences are intrinsic, and 'whose logic and boundaries precede the work and the will of man' (Galli 2001, 19 and 21; our translation). Pre-modern cartography was an embodied practice, a visual translation of the explorers' journey, including the various elements and obstacles encountered along their path (de Certeau 1984[1980], 121). What remained outside, the uncharted, although dialectically produced from the perspective of—as opposed to—the charted, resisted synthetic subsumption. It was an unknown, mysterious or altogether forbidden space, populated by fantastic monsters and feral beasts: *ibi sunt leones*. Self-willed, uncontrollable, un-domesticated, obscure, as the intricate and uncultivated *hyle* (ὕλη) or *silva*, which the Greeks and Romans opposed to the *polis* and the *civitas*. The *silva*, at the root of the term *savage*, is the undomesticated forest, both wildness (with a more experiential and imaginative connotation) and wilderness (with a more territorial connotation) (see Thoreau 1962[1854]; Haila 1997). Etymologically, it refers to a pile of firewood, a similar connotation to the Greek correspondent, *hyle*, that gradually morphed from indicating the 'wild forest' to its material, that is, wood and, from there, metonymically, 'matter' itself. The term composes the notion of hylomorphism, a theory based on the assumption of matter (*hyle*) as a passive, inert and homogeneous substance that is given form (*morphe*) by an external operator, either divine or human.[25] The understanding of 'nature' as being available to be used and disposed of by human beings, which we find for instance in the writings of Bacon and Des-cartes, has therefore implicit hylomorphic premises, which, at least etymo-logically, we can trace back to the very origin of the translation of *hyle* into mere 'matter': the practice of domesticating, and deforesting, the wilderness.

Dario Gentili and Federica Giardini (2020, 92) suggest that the very imaginary of the *polis* is shaped by this relation:

> the absence of form of the *hyle*, of monstrous and dangerous dimensions, is converted into a willingness to be put into shape by human thought, which has now found a 'natural' home in the *polis*. From wild forest, the *hyle* becomes timber to build the city and finally that passive and inert matter on which the shaping activity of the human being is practised.

What we are suggesting is that the abstract articulations composing the imaginary of the *polis* can be said to have originated from its dialectical inter-action with the wild: urbanisation as deforestation, the city as a space carved out of an undomesticated intricacy (*silva diffusa et inculta*).[26] This is arguably the imaginary that the Neolithic revolution brought about: a separation between an inside and an outside, that is, the production of the outside *as* wild.[27] The wild, in this context, is the result of the production of an outside *qua* outside (*fores*, from which 'forest', means 'outside') from an inside, and at the same time an unstable threshold on which this very process hinges. The wild is then in itself a paradox, a space that the *civitas* can never encounter, which must always be pre-emptively domesticated: a contradiction the other, liminal meaning of *fores* ('door') perfectly exemplifies (see Brighenti and

Pavoni 2018). The *silva*, then, is a promiscuous, confused and limitless space of intermingling out of which the humans would *violently* carve a separation (Esposito 2013[2008]).

Yet, although already containing the seeds of future abstractions, such a space was not abstracted, or mapped, in advance, in the modern sense of the term. The pre-modern space remained a territory to be 'occupied without being counted', to 'be explored only by legwork' (Deleuze and Guattari 2004[1980], 362 and 371).[28] Pre-modern 'spaces do not meet the visual condition of being observable from a point in space external to them' (idem, ibidem). Pre-modern wilderness, in other words, is a space where imagination could wander, at its own peril, but that is impenetrable to reason, whose logic belongs elsewhere. This 'qualitative' notion of space, to be sure, was perfectly conciliated with the idea of a transcendent Order of Being—an all-encompassing *kosmos* (the Greek word for order)—that guaranteed the unity of sense (Galli 2001, 25).

The surfacing of modernity, a story told countless times, is to be located exactly at the centre of the dislocation that the crumbling of this 'metaphysical globe' (Sloterdijk 2013[2005]) brought about, as the tectonic outcome of a series of cosmological, religious, political, geographical, aesthetic and scientific revolutions. The modern imaginary, accordingly, is first and foremost an imaginary that is born out of a crisis, indeed an imaginary *of* crisis: an anxiety-laden imaginary grounded on the systematic attempt to find refuge *from* the crisis, by denying its ontological, political and epistemological consequences.[29] Crisis, here, means radical uncertainty—radical, that is, insofar as stemming from the collapse of coordinates that had been hitherto assumed as absolute and eternal. No wonder that the question of *certitudo* (certainty) played such an important role in the work of the first great thinkers of modernity: Galilei, Descartes, Hobbes, Spinoza. It was an epistemological, religious and political question at once: countering the baroque anxiety without surrendering to rampant superstition, esoterism, heresy, sedition or scepticism.[30] Amidst the ruins of the premodern imaginary, *within a forest dark, for the right way had been lost* (Dante), the *project* of modernity was born, as an attempt to find a way out from this wilderness by reasserting a manmade order, grounded on the normative force of reason and the scientific method. While Descartes sought to develop this project at the epistemological level, Hobbes pursued it at the political one.

Reflecting on the myth of *Cura*, narrated by Hygīnus, John Hamilton interprets it as symbolising a human existence that is subjected to impermanence and contingency, that is, *uncertainty*, and therefore doubt, anxiety and worry (worry is one of the ancient meanings of *cura*; see chapter 3).

Thus, he asks, 'is the history of mankind's desire for security nothing other than the history of an ambition to evade time and its contingencies?' (2013, 6). While we are not sure whether the desire for security can only be constructed in opposition to time and contingency, it is evident that modernity, a certain kind of modernity, can be understood precisely in this sense, that is, as a systematic attempt to domesticate contingency through the certainty guaranteed by reason and the security guaranteed by its quintessentially 'statist political imaginary' (Neocleous 2003; see Cassirer 1961[1946]). An attempt that was firmly grounded on the ontological presupposition of 'separation' that the notion of 'individual' embodies.

In this sense, the modernity that became hegemonic through politics and science is a modernity that emerged from the disorientation and uncertainty of *a forest dark*, and more precisely from the interpretation of such an uncertainty *as* insecurity, fear and danger. From the point of view of a supposedly pre-constituted and self-sufficient individual, the conceptual, affective and sensorial entanglement that the 'forest dark' epitomises, its radically immersive, 'common' uncertainty—which is, literally, the ontological negation of certainty, from *cernere*, to separate—cannot but appear as monstrous.[31] While the particular, modern imaginary we are briefly sketching here is by no means unique or homogeneous, it has certainly been hegemonic in shaping the contemporary understandings of the relation between security, violence and the city. This is the purpose of this brief reflection, which is less concerned with either the etymological or historical accuracy of this narration, and more with emphasising the dialectic relation between *civitas* and *silva*, and the role that the question of domestication, understood in the wider sense, has played in feeding a particular imaginary, and normative project, attached to the Western city.

More generally, Pietro Costa (1974) reflects on a 'juridical project' (*progetto giuridico*) of modernity, centred on Descartes's vision of the modern subject. The legacy of the Cartesian move, projecting the hierarchical division between a superior and an inferior domain within the very anthropological fabric of the human, was to provide a normative foundation to the various dichotomies organising modernity (e.g. reason/passion; mind/body; man/woman, rich/poor, adult/child, human/animal, society/nature, civilised/wild) (Del Lucchese 2004, 100–101). This model, at once moral and political, of a normative reason that legislates over an unruly *state of nature* is grounded on the implicit moral distinction between normal and deviant, and on the political fiction of the social contract. It is through the lenses of this imaginary that the aforementioned state of disorientation was brought back to a more determined and, soon, politically charged affect, that is, fear, by thus linking the existential condition of crisis and the epistemological condition of uncertainty to the political promise of security. From this perspective, contingency cannot but be monstrous, insofar as expressing the arbitrariness—the ultimate lack of legitimation—on which any modern attempt at producing order is 'grounded': that is, its unspeakable lack of ground. Contingency is the monstrous wilderness that must be tamed, violently so, in order to instantiate the artificial order of an as much monstrous sovereign, the *Leviathan*.

Society must present itself as a unitary and *instituted* whole, that is, it needs to carefully deny its *instituting* quality—its radical imaginary—since accepting the latter would mean 'accepting the possibility of pure chaos, of social order perpetually standing on the fringes of the abyss' (Bottici 2014, 46). As Galli puts it,

> this is the 'baroque' quality of Hobbes's Leviathan, the fact of being a sovereign power suspended on Nothingness. The state of nature is the operator . . . whereby political reason is made instrumental, politics is made technical, the State is made a machine . . . The State is not a datum but an artifice—which opens onto an abyss of disorder, a Nothingness-of-Order [*Nulla-di-Ordine*]. (2011, xxxv; our translation)

It is for this reason, that is, for the need to deny the Nothingness-of-Order that would utterly compromise it, that the hegemonic project of modernity is structurally articulated as a space of exception. The mechanism of exception is the dispositif that 'takes in' the chaotic, ever-escaping outside (from *ex*, outside, and *capere*, to take), that is, to simultaneously *include* space by *excluding* its inherent difference, via a double move: first, the flattening of space into a *tabula rasa* and then, only then, the projection of (legal, political, epistemological) categories over it.[32] Let us underline this point. At a first level, we argued, modernity can be said to emerge out of the crumbling of premodern *kosmos*, as an immunological project aimed at constructing an artificial order via reason, scientific method, and political science (Sloterdijk 2014[1999]; Esposito 2011[2002]).[33] The imaginary of modernity is not simply an attempt to evade contingency by constructing a certain kind of order, however. Nor is it just the positing of a series of values such as anthropocentrism, rationalism, scientific reductionism, secularism, individualism or an evolutionary understanding of history. At a more profound level, we have seen, what *grounds* the project of modernity is the denial of this very construction *qua* construction. The space of modernity, writes Igor Stramignoni, is premised on the 'prior discovery of some other space—

namely, natural or physical space—and then the abandonment of that space into the background as absolute, universal space' (2004, 225). The construction of the modern scientific and juridical-political order requires first of all the production of an abstract, homogeneous background—a *tabula rasa*, a *terra nullium*—over which the modern geometry could be drawn, a 'homogeneous medium'.[34] As we are to see in detail below, such a gesture was not innocent: not only was the representation of the colony as a *tabula rasa* (populated by what was fundamentally characterised as not pertaining to the human community) necessary to making the colonialist project compatible with the emerging liberal values; but it is also there that such an abstraction most explicitly unfolded in its violent consequences.

This is epitomised by the 'modern' map par excellence, that which Columbus is said to have been carrying in his first journey westwards. Drawn by the mathematician and astronomer Paolo dal Pozzo Toscanelli (1397–1482), this map abstracts the whole Earth into an even grid of equivalent spaces, measuring 250 miles each. There, the city of Quinsai (the modern-day Hangzhou) is shown at exactly 26 *spaces* from the city of Lisbon, along a perfectly straight line, unencumbered by land—an abstraction so violent it could ignore a whole continent.[35] Until the last of his westward journeys, Columbus remained stubbornly convinced he had reached Marco Polo's Cathay, his cartographic reason unwilling to register the invisible continent, striving instead to match the contours of the land he saw with the traits of the map drawn by someone who had never seen that very land (Farinelli 2003; Olsson 2007). That unknown, quintessentially wild space beyond the Pillars of Hercules was no longer a space to be 'occupied without being counted'. It had become a space 'counted in order to be occupied' (Deleuze and Guattari 2004[1980], 399), that is, a space abstractly subsumed in advance by a wholly other sort of all-ingesting imagination. What grounds the juridical project of modernity is the ontological *presupposition* of a society composed by free and equal individuals—an abstraction that, in turn, can only be thought after being pre-emptively grounded by the projection of an abstract space of exception.

Flattened space and vectorialised time—or, more precisely, the flattening of both time and space into a homogenous and empty spatiality—are the 'abstract articulations' that shape the imaginary of modernity, the conditions of possibility for the construction of those categories that appear in the writing of different thinkers such as Grotius and Locke, Hobbes and Rousseau, and for the modern epistemology at large.

This is the role that the dispositif of the 'state of nature' plays. Either as a feral state of violence to be overcome via sovereign law (Hobbes) or as an innocent state marred by civilisation and its violence (Rousseau), in the definition of the state of nature wilderness has been already domesticated, reduced to a homogeneous medium on which political-legal categories could be erected, as well as an empty, pre-historical time on which the civilising mission of the Leviathan could be legitimised.[36] Within this imaginary, wilderness is reframed as the *violent stasis* that will supposedly explode if the institutional order is removed.[37] The conceptual relation among violence, wilderness, order and security is cemented at this turn. The State, tasked with guaranteeing such an order through security, draws its legitimation from its supposed capacity to prevent the resurfacing of violence, as a *kat'echon*, the only power that be able to hold the social together.[38] There is no need to overstate the extent to which these social imaginary significations still implicitly articulate the contemporary, simultaneously feeding pessimistic rhetoric of repression, as well as nostalgic yearning for a peaceful coexistence in the form of mythical images of pre-urban, communal life (e.g., Graeber and Wengrow 2021, 1–27).[39] What we are interested to explore is the way they morphed into what we define as the imaginary *of* urbanisation.

Imaginary of Urbanisation

The notion of imaginary has recently become a hot topic in urban research, and unsurprisingly so, given the extent to which the crafting of urban imaginaries, through dedicated strategies of urban branding, has become fundamental in the global city competition. Hegemonic urban imaginaries have assumed the form of almost ready-made, solutionist ideal cities—the smart, creative, green, safe, healthy city, etc.—which have increasingly become central to urban politics. Used by mayors and local governments as powerful normative orientations for urban administration, these imaginaries have also increasingly been shaping a global hierarchy, whereby cities are categorised for being more or less civilised, developed and, lately, 'liveable'. Critical urban studies have provided systematic critiques of dominant urban imaginaries, all in all emphasising the technocratic policies they foster, at the same time as not addressing, or even strengthening, pre-existing inequalities (e.g. Çinar and Bender 2007b; Vanolo 2017; Lindner and Meissner 2019). From post- and de-colonial lenses, dominant global imaginaries have been exposed for being Western-centric, at the same time as the specific ways in which they are (re-)framed in non-Western contexts have been discussed (e.g. Datta 2015; Melhuish et al. 2016). Other insightful works have explored alternative and performative imaginaries that challenge the racialised, gendered, class and anthropocentric biases of mainstream imaginaries, at the same time as emphasising the role social movements play in re-imagineering urbanisation (e.g., Sites 2012; Haiven and Wilson and Bayón 2016; Florez et al. 2022).

We will engage in more detail with two imaginaries, the liveable (chapter 7) and smart city (chapter 8), that are particularly central in the conceptualisation of urban violence and production of contemporary security politics. At this stage, we are interested in discussing the imaginary *of* urbanisation emerging in the nineteenth century, which we understand to constitute a meta-imaginary that subtends current hegemonic imaginaries. Tightly connected with the project of urbanisation epitomised by the thought of Ildefons Cerdá (see chapter 2), we will argue that the imaginary of urbanisation is something more than the urban counterpart of the surfacing of modernity. Rather it constitutes the *urbanisation* of the imaginary of modernity itself— with crucial implications for our argument.

A simple, and yet useful concept to begin with is Sheila Jasanoff's notion of 'socio-technical imaginary', which she defines as

> collectively held, institutionally stabilized, and publicly performed visions of desirable futures, animated by shared understandings of forms of social life and social order attainable through, and supportive of, advances in science and technology. This definition privileges the word 'desirable' because efforts to build new sociotechnical futures are typically grounded in positive visions of social progress. (2015, 4)

While the socio-technical imaginaries in the urban context can be traced back at least as far as Francis Bacon's *New Atlantis*, it is in the nineteenth century that the convergence of positivism, historicism and technological innovation brought about an optimistic teleology of progress as incremental evolution attainable via science and technology. In this context, we saw it already, the city played a key role, paradoxically as a 'problem' (cf. Foucault 1984[1982]), as well as a solution to this very problem, via urbanisation. It is at this juncture that the surfacing of the socio-technical imaginary of urbanisation may be located, namely, the understanding of urbanisation itself as a 'technology' of social advancement. To be sure, the relation between cities and the betterment of urban life is long-standing, and ancient and modern utopias have typically imagined their ideal of a happier, safer, healthier and better life in an urban form. Yet, in these instances the city is just a secondary product, that is, the geometrical projection of a metaphysical, moral order. As already observed, the modern imaginary is first of all a statist one, in which political science, from Hobbes onwards, is understood as a way to organise society through the institution of the state, its law and the apparatus of security that is tasked with enforcing them. As we also see in the dystopic depiction of the city that appears in the *Leviathan* frontispiece, the urban form is the architectural rendering of a political order.

What the imaginary of urbanisation introduces is the search for a better life not only to be achieved *in* the city as its ideal expression, but *through* the city understood in itself as a technology of power. As anticipated in chapter 2, this is exactly what Cerdá's *Teoría* expresses—and in a much more coherent manner than, for instance, Haussmann's demolitions. Namely, the projection of a desirable future to be achieved as the culmination of social progress, fostered by a novel technology: urbanisation itself—a quintessentially socio-technical imaginary. Technological and technical innovations, from the architecture of the domestic unit all the way to the planning of the urban as an ever-expanding network of circulation, so as to intersect the trajectory of capitalism and liberalism, would therefore usher in, in Cerdá's words, a novel civilisation, whose demands are 'more space, greater comfort, and greater freedom' (2018[1867], 50).

While it is easy to read the twenty-first-century, technocratic rhetoric of the smart city as an ideal continuation of these nineteenth-century premises, what is crucial to highlight here is the extent to which this imaginary—and the imaginary of modernity at large—is in turn shaped by colonial urbanisation. For a long time, genealogies of the Western urban imaginary were developed without much attention to the colonial enterprise, at best assuming the latter as shaped by the former. Post-colonial thinking, however, has shown that, if the seeds of the modern Western imaginary can certainly be found in ancient Greece and Rome, a crucial fertiliser has been colonial violence. As Adams puts it:

> Working *with and across* the heterogeneity of archives, it becomes easier to detach the appearance of urbanisation in nineteenth century cities from the sway of 'modernism' and to instead read it as, to borrow Césaire's notion, the 'boomerang effect' of colonial spatial technologies back into the metropoles. Here, a certain nexus between the spatial ordering of infrastructure and domesticity and a reanimated form of administrative governance becomes legible as a form of power in itself, and the biopolitics of managing population that urban space enables found its first expression in the colonial spaces of plantation. (2020; emphasis in original)

It is no surprise, in this sense, that Hobbes found a real and contemporary model of the state of nature—and, more importantly, of the danger to revert back into that state of nature—in those 'savage people in many places of

America' who 'have no government at all; and live at this day in the brutish manner' (Hobbes 2002[1651], ch. XIII).[40] If Hobbes saw the American frontier as a hypothetical instance of that pre-political wilderness his novel political science would be tasked to tame, Cerdá saw it as the template for his technology of urbanisation. The Catalan drew an explicit relation between urbanisation and domestication, cultivation and civilisation: 'to urbanize means to plow or to cultivate, and cultivation is the origin and the most fertile root cause of civilization' (2018[1867], 482).[41] Nowhere as in the American colony, urbanisation and civilisation became indistinguishable, overflowing their own boundaries in order to violently ingest a wilderness that was cultivated, civilised, urbanised and colonised at the same time (cf. Salzano 1998). Differently from the European cities, built over layers and layers of sedimented history, it was in the American frontier that the homogeneous and absolute space of modernity was more explicitly, if violently, materialised.[42] Cerdá was perfectly aware of that. On the one hand, he lamented the incapacity of his fellow Spaniards to destroy the Arab *urbs* in the Iberian peninsula—after the Arabs had been forced out by the Spanish army during the Reconquista. The Spaniards, he contended, were not willing to pursue radical urban reform 'due to an extreme respect for what already exists' (2018[1867], 204). The same people, however, 'when they were presented with enough space to give free rein to their imagination and their generous instincts, founded vast cities in America', and were thus able to realise the most unconstrained kind of urbanisation, 'the complete destruction of what already exists for the sake of founding a new world where this new civilization could comfortably operate, and where humanity would not be met with obstacles to its action and development' (2018[1867], 204 and 56). As Paul Carter suggestively writes,

> in Australia, in South Africa, in British Guyana or along the western marches of the United States and Canada, explorers and surveyors (not necessarily the same creature) had as their object the haussmannization of the interior . . . Like their Northern European urban contemporaries, these geographical travellers wanted to modernize the land, to make it fit for traffic. (2002, 151)

That *tabula rasa* Cerdá dreamt of, as the only solution to the *silva diffusa et inculta* that he thought the Western city had become, appeared to be materially realisable in the colony, where the 'homogeneous medium' on which modern space is premised could not only be abstractly conceived in advance, via legal means, but also be actually experienced in the 'emptiness' of the frontier, as well as directly produced, violently so, via military force, where needed. It is in the frontier, of course, that John Locke—himself secretary of the Carolinas's Council of Trade and Plantations between from 1673 to 1675—merged colonisation, cultivation and civilisation into the notion of *terra nullius*, which at the same time deprived the 'savage' inhabitants of the possession of the 'wilderness' in which they lived, and reduced such a territory to a malleable and homogeneous matter at the disposal of the colonisers. A colonial hylomorphism, that is, according to which the wild colonial matter could only be given form *qua* property by the colonisers, since they are the one that, by cultivating it, will make it productive.[43] Edward Said famously defined 'orientalism' as a *separation*, between the West and its generic Other, complemented by an *integration* of the latter within the former's imaginary— this double move resonates with the above described grounding of the modern state of exception. Yrjö Haila (1997) suggests that in the context of the American (and Australian) frontier, wilderness is probably more appropriate a notion to grasp the process of colonisation (see also, among others, Perera and Pugliese 1998; Marzec 2007; French 2012).

In this context, Cerdá was particularly impressed by William Penn's plan of Philadelphia, perhaps the quintessential template of the colonial attempt at regularising an entire continent through urban design (see Corboz 1998, 239–244; chapter 2), under the temporal frame of (civilising) progress.[44] Here, the city-countryside distinction is fully overcome into an abstract, *scaleless* grid where economic, disciplinary, legal registers are combined into a model that appears to be perfectly compatible with Cerdá's notion of ruralised urbanisation (Adams 2019, 201). In his vision, the whole earth was turned into an indefinite, homogeneous *hyle* that was to be filled with urbanisation—*replete terram*. Where if not in the colonial city could the full subsumption of the *civitas* into the *urbs* be performed? Fully depurated from political and historical sedimentations, the colonial city could be conceptualised as 'a purely administrative form of power' (idem, 184), whose purposes are expanding into the wild territory, protecting its civilised interiority from the threat of the non-political savage and *de facto* translating itself into a node of a logistical network. 'The colonial settlement', Adams observes, 'was an entity whose existence only made sense as an interchange within a global space of economic circulation' (2019, 203). The 'empty' American frontier provided the smooth background to the colonial city, joining the homogenous *tabula rasa* of the colony with the generic form of the colonial grid—in turn shaped by the topography of plantation (cf. Mendieta 2019; Adams 2020; Macedo 2021; Peano et al. 2023).

Countless examples could be made. Take, for instance, William Glover's (2008) account of the 'making' of Lahore under British rule. Here, the

colonial planners (both English and Indians) shared the belief that the material infrastructure of the city was a technology able to produce (desired)
effects and had, at the same time, the power to shape human conduct. In
this context, the domestic is fully projected onto the wild in two senses:
externally, as the urbanisation and its logistics, most notably railways and
roadways, penetrated the outer wilderness by producing safe and comfortable
interiors within; and internally, as the colonial police—together with its legal scaffolding—is deployed against the threat of the 'savages' that have been
colonised.[45] Through this reflection we can further contextualise the relation
between police, urbanisation and civilisation.

Urban Wilderness

Police emerged as a patriarchal and disciplinary project aimed at governing the state as a household according to what the likes of Adam Smith
or William Blackstone theorised (Dubber 2005).[46] This is the sense of
the police, according to Carl Schmitt (2005[1922]): an administrative
and bureaucratic force that is coherent with the task of the modern state
to produce tranquillity, security and order in its own territory, substituting the political with police itself.[47] The relation between the police and
this civilising mission is already present for instance in the writing of
Jean-Jacques Rousseau, where it is framed in opposition to barbarism—
the French term *policer* still maintains this 'civilising' connotation. More
generally, in the writings of the eighteenth- and nineteenth-century
theorists of police, this function is elaborated through binary couples
such as healthy/sick, useful/useless, civilised/savage (Cavalletti 2005,
118). As Cavalletti (idem, 184) argues, once the meaning of police began to be reduced to its contemporary connotation, a new term came to
substitute its broader meanings, a term able to express the progressive, continuous and processual dimension of security: *civilisation*. As explained by
Lucien Febvre (1930), Norbert Elias (2000[1939]) and Émile Benveniste
(1971[1966]), the term civilisation, introduced in 1766, transformed the
notion of civility by providing it with a processual and dynamic connotation, one that no longer simply referred to a condition but also to a
continuous and indefinite process.[48] It was this dynamic relation, Cavalletti (2005, 194) insists, that was required in the context of a city increasingly understood as an expanding space of circulation. Another neologism
was needed, one in which notions of cohabitation, civilisation and police
would converge onto the urban context: this is what Cerdá's *urbanización*
expresses.

This convergence is particularly apparent in the aesthetic normativity of the metropolis of the nineteenth century, in which the bourgeoisie projected its imaginary of peace, law, order and rationality. At this time, we assist to the culmination of that civilising process already ongoing in European modernity (Elias 2000[1939]). From public executions to defecation (Laporte 2000[1978]), urban reformism accompanied a general moralisation of customs, and 'depuration' of the urban space from those 'savage' and violent habits that, besides having problematic health implications, seemed to belong to a pre-civilised, that is, non-*urbane* past. Animal killing and blood spilling were therefore conveyed in specific places (slaughterhouses) in urban peripheries, while nondomestic animals were gradually exiled from the city (Donald 1999; Kean 2011; McNeur 2014; Brighenti and Pavoni 2021b). Ideas of transparency and control, most notably crystallised in Bentham's panoptical architecture, were projected onto urban bourgeois 'domestic', aesthetic, affective and normative expectations of peace, tranquillity, décor and comfort, a notion whose 'modern' meaning was 'invented' at this time (Crowley 2001; see chapter 7). Coherently, rationalist ideas of planning and hygiene appeared, epitomised for instance by the Sanitary Idea, coined by Bentham's disciple Edwin Chadwick, convinced of the necessity to depurate the city from miasmas via proper system of garbage collection and sewage, as well as from pests (Biehler 2013).

These processes did unfold in direct relation to the nineteenth century's 'urban crisis', as depeasantisation, rural-to-urban migration and industrialisation were turning European cities into overcrowded, insalubrious and turbulent places, increasingly shocked by epidemics and revolts. In this context, scientific rationalism, central to the emerging bourgeois identity, was explicitly opposed to what it saw as an instinctive and vicious violence—thence the emergence of rationalist planning as a tool to scientifically observe and improve individuals and society, and guarantee peace, health and order (e.g., Scandurra and Krumholz 1999; Sandercock 2003; Tulumello 2017a, ch. 5). Within this imaginary, therefore, urbanisation became a veritable 'technology of civilisation', as well as a comparative standard to indicate an evolutionary advancement of society, especially vis-à-vis the condition of the urban poor, at this time increasingly framed as a 'violent savage' in need of being civilised, that is, urbanised. In the notion of urbanisation, therefore, we find the condensation of the concepts of cohabitation, civilisation and police, which are at the same time framed in opposition to a wilderness that is most fundamentally individuated in those visible instances that came to compose the constellation of *urban violence*.

At bottom, of course, this was the precise derivation from the Hobbesian discourse around the state of nature, namely, a distinction between humanity and animality that, by means of having been translated *inside* the human (cf. Derrida 2009[2008]), would be articulated as a distinction between the civilised and the savage, that is, to be progressively overcome via civilisation and, more precisely, urbanisation. If the bourgeois imaginary of peace increasingly framed the city as a space in which violence did not belong—thereby projecting the imaginary of the city without violence onto the urban—if 'bourgeois identity defined itself as the exact opposite of popular [indeed, urban] violence', then, before the imaginary of evolutionary progress, violence was perceived as a contradictory deviance, a reversion of the arrow of time: an *animality* which signalled the regression to a primitive, wild and savage state (Smart 2011, 70; our translation).[49] While violence, in the pre-modern city, was understood as a more or less 'natural' occurrence, it is around this time, in the modern city, that it begins to be perceived as being *out of place* (idem). Urban violence, in other words, begins to appear as an anachronism, an archaism, an atavistic sign that the *silva* is still present, its weeds still infesting the modern urban order, for this reason requiring extirpation. With a vertiginous suggestion, Paul Carter suggests that there is a relation between this attempt to extirpate the wilderness from the urban by producing ordinate clearings and the surfacing of *agoraphobia*, certified by Karl Friedrich Otto Westphal in late nineteenth-century Vienna. Read in this way, agoraphobia would not be simply a symptom of urban estrangement or of psychic displacement but, more structurally, a symptom of the repressed spaces of modernity: 'not so much a fear of wide-open spaces as a fear of their slipperiness, their tendency to incubate uncontrolled, uncoordinated movement' (Carter 2002, 20; see also Aksoy and Robins 1997). A fear of the repressed, that is, symptomatic of an earlier erasure, which keeps resurfacing, often uncannily so (see on this Brighenti and Pavoni 2021b). In the Haussmanesque city of modern planning, just as in the open space of the colony, 'clearing the land only intensified its agoraphobic charge' (Carter 2002, 157), a dialectic Carter also traces to the etymological kinship between the notion of *agorà* (the public square) and *agròs* (the countryside, the 'faraway place'): since its inception, he thus contends, *agorà* is 'twinned with wilderness' (idem, 9; more on this in chapter 7). In this sense, the modern imaginary may be read exactly as a repression of the constitutive wilderness that characterise the social as a space of relation, conflict and radical *uncertainty*. Whether or not one is to endorse Carter's evocative hypothesis, contemporary examples of the ways in which an imaginary may generate unforeseen frictions abound; examples symptomatic of the implicit contradiction at the core of the quintessential juridical (private/public) and aesthetic-affective (comfort/wild) binaries of urban modernity.[50]

What we are interested in stressing here is how the contemporary notion of urban violence emerges at this historical juncture, as the constitutive blind spot of the bourgeois imaginary of peace, law, order and rationality. This violence, while uncannily haunting the urban experience at large, is inextricably tied to the figure of the urban poor: that is, of the colonial savage, back in town. Pierre Clastres (2010[1980]), whom we already encountered (see chapter 1), emphasised the epistemological incapacity of the first 'explorers' to engage with the diversity of the 'Savage', derived from their presupposition of what a society should be and how it should appear. Likewise, in the words of Zygmunt Bauman,

> the anonymous crowd of the urban poor appeared to the bourgeois, and to the agencies of the state to which he looked for protection, as an unruly, obstreperous, rowdy and rebellious mob, which was bound to remain a constant source of danger as long as its conduct was not forced into regular, predictable patterns. To perform this task, a power was needed able to administer human bodies, and not merely the goods which their labor might turn out. (Bauman 1982, 47)

Poor and dangerous became synonymous in the nineteenth-century cities, together expressing the *wild* imaginary of vice, violence and crime that became synonymous with their dark spaces. Think of terms such as labyrinth, obscurity, hidden, dirt, monstrosity, dens, rookeries, slums, which emphasise the dark, shady, savage and primitive people living in an (under)world of violence, danger, crime, vice, misery, stale air, unbearable smell, barbarism, but also sedition, revolt and rebellion. These spaces, these people, composed the counterpoint to the imaginary of urbanisation, an urban experience painted with an ambiguous mix of fear and fascination—the former inspiring draconian measures, the latter urban gothic novels as well as realistic novels, from the Paris of Eugène-François Vidocq, Honore de Balzac, Victor Hugo, Emile Zola or Eugene Sue, to the London of Jack London, Charles Dickens or Jack the Ripper. What linked all urban poor in the emerging imaginary was precisely their association with the spaces they lived: the slums (a world tied to slumber), the *bas-fonds* (literally, the lower parts of a building), terms associated with the low-life, the under-world. For instance, through an analysis of official sources, regulations and novels, Dominique Kalifa (2013) has showed the role played by the imaginary of the *bas-fonds* in the depiction of the urban poor as living a violent and dissolute life in an uncontrolled, undomesticated, *wild* (under)world. A *mala vita* (literally 'bad' or 'evil life') like the one Alfredo Niceforo and Scipio Sighele described in Rome (1898) as a vicious violence that seemingly ferment and proliferate out of the putrid urban underbelly. Their teacher, Cesare Lombroso, notoriously developed the theory of atavism, according to which criminals were individuals who had regressed to the state of primitive savages (1878). In the words of two famous nineteenth-century lexicographers, a class of 'human vermin' (Émile Littré, apud Kalifa 2013), 'degraded by vice and misery' (Pierre Larousse, idem).

At the same time, crowd theorists such as Gustave le Bon were framing urban multitudes in terms of psychological regression, loss of inhibition and irrational degeneration that the human supposedly undergoes in a crowd (cf. Borch 2012). Evidently, this was less a population to be biopolitically included within the governmental apparatus than a 'populace' (Wall 2021), a 'rabble' (Ruda 2011) or 'residue'—as per the definition exposed by the liberal deputy John Bright (see Kalifa 2013)—that needed to be excluded, or repressed. Modern urbanisation, in this sense, appears to be violently shaped by biopolitics as much as necropolitics, to use Achille Mbembe's term (2003; 2019). The latter refers to a whole category of bodies that are not only excluded from within the biopolitical machine, but are rather left exposed to a slow death by exhaustion due to unbearable living conditions. Needless to say, both this imaginary and the strategies employed to deal with it were directly shaped by the place of necropolitics par excellence: the colonial city, where all sorts of planning, law and police tactics were deployed, from North African cities to American plantations to India and beyond, as a macabre training exercise for the metropoles (see chapter 6).

The urban poor was not a homogeneous figure, however. Whereas destitute and non-normative characters (including beggars, vagrants, women living outside the 'traditional household', prostitutes and so forth) were more often associated with vice and savage forms of violence, the urban worker was associated with political violence—being quintessentially representative of that very conflict that modern urbanisation, and police, wished to neutralise in order to fabricate social order (cf. chapter 3).[51] It is more explicitly against the worker that the question of urban violence would be increasingly framed as a 'quasi-mystical war of order against chaos' (Smart 2011, 69; our translation), where what was at stake was the very capacity of the system to hold. All the more so with respect to the urban revolts, which became a central question in the nineteenth-century city, and direct inspiration, in the case of the 1848 revolts, of Haussmann's reconstruction. As Valentina Antoniol and Niccolò Cuppini write, at this time, 'war and its protagonists are no longer locked down within the "external" colonial space or on the rural battlefield of the previous European wars, but rather they bounce back to the heart of the metropolis, and begin to deconstruct the rigid political coordinates adopted up to that point. The city emerges again as the field of political conflict' (2021, 636). The regression to the savage violence of the state of nature and its quintessential threat—the civil war, or *stasis*—are understood as the result of an uncontrolled or 'depraved urbanisation' (to use Cerdá's expression). The promise of civilisation embodied by the *Leviathan* is thus translated into the twin technologies of the spatio-political project of the urban: urbanisation and police, which, shaped by the colonial experience, will be increasingly deployed as a political technology aimed at controlling, civilising and domesticating, that is, *urbanising*. It is from this context that urbanisation emerges as socio-technical imaginary and, in time, as a process unfolding at the planetary scale. At the same time, the connection with the imaginary is that which makes it possible to organise the process into a hierarchy made up of more or less advanced, urbanised or civilised cities.

Incidentally, then, it is in the colony, again, that Foucault's suggestion that the police and urbanisation are essentially the same thing (see chapters 2 and 3) makes full sense. Here, moreover, the violence of this process unfolds in a most explicit and visible way, also in the sense, just suggested, of experimenting a vast array of strategies, aesthetics and tactics, which will then boomerang back onto the metropoles.[52] The emphasis on the coessentiality of police and urbanisation, and the violent, colonial dimension they share, can also be developed referring to Philip Reichel's critique (1992) of historical scholarship on the development of policing in the USA. This scholarship has historically associated police (here understood as the formal institution) and its institutionalisation with 'urbanisation' (we use brackets because urbanisation, in these accounts, is understood in its traditional meaning of growth of cities). Reichel correctly notes that this causal association is weakened once one enlarges the empirical focus from northern US cities like Boston, Philadelphia, Detroit or Chicago, which have historically been privileged objects of studies. Reichel shows that law enforcement structures were developed in the US South prior to those of the North, emerging from slave patrols. On these grounds, he asserts the need to reconsider 'urbanisation' as the main causal driver of policing. By, on the contrary, adopting the understanding of urbanisation developed so far, we can reconsider Reichel's findings in light of an understanding of plantations as a component of what Brenner and Schmid define 'extended urbanisation': 'the operationalization of places, territories and landscapes, often located far beyond the dense population centers, to support the everyday activities and socioeconomic dynamics of urban life' (2015, 1673). Indeed, recent scholarship has argued against the conceptualisation of plantations as 'rural' contexts, and rather retheorised them for their centrality in the production of concentrated urbanisation in Latin America (Castriota and Tonucci 2018; Fenton III 2021) and in transcontinental, planetary relations (Ruddick 2015). From this perspective, rather than opposing the 'urban' history of northern US police and the 'rural' history of southern US police, we would rather reflect on the relations (of uneven and combined development) that put together urban development in the US North with plantation economy in the South; and on the centrality of policing for both typologies of urbanisation.

Police and urbanisation, in this context, can be said to have 'institutionalised' the imaginary of urbanisation itself, with urban violence being its hidden operator as well as lever of evaluation. Subsequently, when the concept of urbanisation, fed by its progressive temporality, will become a measure to assess the degree of urban evolution of any given city, then an implicit, today increasingly explicit, global hierarchy will be drawn, one that is fundamentally framed around the image of *violent cities* and *cities without violence*. This pattern is alive and kicking today, shaped by the implicit presupposition that 'the metropolitan form [is] something that can be organised in advance and whose complexities can be settled or decided by the application of more or less mechanical ideological beliefs onto a reality that is fundamentally elusive' (Nuttall and Mbembe 2005, 195–196; see also Aksoy and Robins 1997). As writers such as Mbembe, Roy, Simone and many others have shown at length, what tends to be taken for granted, in this case, is an equivalence between a special kind of civility and order—with its own juridical, political and aesthetic qualities—with respect to which anything that does not comply is perceived as disorderly, precarious or, at best, 'informal', where a strong 'official' institutional presence is lacking. Violence, in this context, is a powerful operator since its appearance of objectivity—especially if depurated from any discussion on meaning, culture and context via the use of seemingly neutral, quantitative statistics—allows the classification of cities on a ladder constituted by the quantification of murders, robberies, rapes, assaults and so on. If urban violence is to be equalled with 'criminal, physical violence in the city', then it makes sense studying those cities that rank high in crime statistics—i.e., if crime statistics are equalled to criminal violence, which we saw is yet another problem (see chapter 2, Researching Urban Violence). Beyond its analytical conceptual shortcomings, this approach risks reducing urban violence to a problem specific to 'failed', 'feral' (Norton 2003; Kilcullen 2013) or 'fragile' (Savage and Muggah 2012; Muggah 2014) cities of the South, reproducing an evolutionary ladder of civilisation, while overlooking the dependence of such a problem to a wider process of urbanisation, global relations of uneven development and (post-)colonisation.

Sebastian Saborio, for instance, has proposed to link urban violence exactly to the framing of a city *as* violent: 'urban violence is more about the representations that are made of a given city, than the level of violence that is present' (2019, 65; our translation)—that is, the concept of urban violence is inextricable from the everyday experience of, and the discourse about, violence (see also Silva 2008; Misse and Grillo 2014). According to Saborio, to put it in our terms, urban violence is to be understood in relation to a given imaginary, and the partition of the sensible through which this is experienced and lived—configurations that, of course, are in turn shaped by socio-historical power relations. This is an interesting attempt to deal with the conundrum of violence as meaning and the meaning of violence, by showing that the relation between violence and meaning is neither subjective nor objective, neither cultural nor natural, but rather a socio-material emergence (see chapter 1), which is fed by the abstract articulations of the imaginary of urbanisation. This is also useful to grasp the violence of this framing itself, where one may certainly hear the echoes of the nineteenth-century narratives of the 'monster city', applied to London, famously described by William Cobbet as the *Great Wen*, as well as, more significantly, the various colonial cities such as Mumbai, Manila, Shanghai, Tangier, Algiers, Kinshasa, New York, Buenos Aires, Rio de Janeiro and so forth (see Kalifa 2013). We will see in chapters 6 and 7 how this is also the case with the more recent trends of urban liveability indexes, in which statistics on urban violence (i.e., mostly murders and assaults) play a central role. While crime statistics may suggest there is less violence *within* northern cities and that these are supposedly more 'liveable', this does not mean there is no point in studying the specific forms of 'northern' urban violence; looking at the process of urbanisation may well illustrate how the North actively participates in the production of urban violence across the multiple scales through which the global process of capitalist urbanisation is actualised. This will be the matter of the next chapter.

Researching Urban Violence: The Harm of Terrorism

We will chase terrorists everywhere. If in an airport, then in the airport. So if we find them in the toilet, excuse me, we'll rub them out in the outhouse. And that's it, case closed. (Vladimir Putin, 1999)

> I want to put all the nation's resources into protecting our citizens . . .
> We will eradicate terrorism because we are attached to freedom. (François Hollande, 2015)

> These terrorists and their regional and worldwide networks must be
> eradicated from the face of the earth, a mission we will carry out with
> all freedom-loving partners. (Donald Trump, 2016)[53]

'No representation of violence exists apart from its rhetorical opposite or sub-limated counterpart', write Bruce Lawrence and Aisha Karim (2007a, 10). No manifestation of *urban* violence exists apart from its sublimated urban counterpart, namely the imaginary of the city without violence just exposed. As explained, this is not simply a dialectical opposition but, more precisely, a historically situated imaginary. What we want to focus on in this section, however, is the problematic coexistence, within the discourse of terrorism, of two apparently contradictory dimensions. On the one hand, the ideal projection of absolute security and, on the other, the pragmatic realism of actually existing counter-terrorism tactics. Especially in the context of terrorism, the contemporary discourse of security is crafted as an effort in 'communicating' safety by fostering the 'spectacular' promise of absolute security (Boyle and Haggerty 2009). In the promises to 'eradicate terrorism' (François Hollande) 'from the face of the earth' (Donald Trump) that regularly follow terror-ist attacks, security is projected into a spatio-temporal totality, a future in which violence is 'chased everywhere' (Vladimir Putin) and the utopia of absolute security supposedly becomes reality. If we are to take their words at face value, the likes of Putin, Hollande, Trump and countless other leaders around the world are neither interested, as far as terrorism is concerned, in finding the correct 'balance' among security and other rights, nor in keeping the threat under a certain threshold: terrorism is not to be managed, it must be spectacularly obliterated.

Securitisation theory may come to help to make sense of this apparent conundrum. Originally defined in the Copenhagen School (e.g., Wæver 2011; Huysmans 2011), securitisation, in this tradition, is a 'speech act': declaring some issue to be a security problem serves the purpose of depoliti-cising it, that is, bringing it to a plan of governmental action that is outside of democratic deliberation—inasmuch as it concerns (national) security. Now, securitisation theory has been fiercely criticised, for instance for be-ing Eurocentric (Wilkinson 2007) and for neglecting to notice the recent repoliticisation of security (Neal 2019, ch. 1). And yet, it seems to us that securitisation theory, in a more restricted sense, can be of use for making sense of the rhetorics of counter-terrorist politics.

Terrorism, from this point of view, forecloses the discussion to one specific paradigm of security, that of absolute security: in this context, reducing harm, balancing rights or managing risk are not acceptable approaches; one can only be satisfied by the eradication of terrorism. This works in a twofold sense. On the one hand, the possibility to discuss terrorism as a social issue (with its political economy and materiality) is foreclosed; and so is also the discussion on how to deal with it. If terrorism can only be dealt by means of eradication, this in turns entails the unconditional maximisation of counter-terrorist strategies and tactics, all the way to the notorious 'justification' for the use of violence against suspected terrorists, as testified, for what concerns the US forces, by the tortured bodies of Abu Ghraib, Guantanamo or Bagram. On the other hand, politicisation re-emerges in the definition of the single terrorist act, which is far from innocent, or self-evident. Consider, for instance, the attempts at crediting every act of violence carried out by persons identified (and racialised) as Muslims to terrorist networks; or the use of the term 'lone wolf' to emphasise the individual agency of the attacker and shift the case away from the discussion on 'Islamic terrorism'—with the corollary discussion on whether 'Muslim communities' should distance themselves from the act or not. The opposite tends to happen when an attack is carried out by non-racialised subjects: there, the 'right' is preoccupied with defining the act as 'random violence', while the 'left' insists that the logic of terrorism should apply[54]—a particularly interesting case is the discussion surrounding so-called 'incel' attacks in Plymouth (see Townsend 2021).

The rhetorical functioning of terrorism can be read in the Lacanian sense: as fantasy that projects a desirable ideal of how society should be, thereby mobilising communal resources towards its realisation. Further, since the ideal is never actually achieved, the fantasy explains this failure by blaming it on the action of an othered subject (the terrorist) (cf. Tulumello 2021a). In this way, there is a (discursive) power of terrorism in pushing towards this specific form of security politics—transcending the conflicts with the other security paradigms discussed in chapter 3.

There is something, however, that is not captured by critiques that challenge this rhetoric on the account of the unbalanced weight it poses on society—this is a way to buy into a logic (that of the balance) that has been politically foreclosed by the very declaration of an act as terrorist. What is also needed is critical engagement with the *materiality* of terrorism. Terrorism is powerful since it has the capacity to breach an imaginary like no other event. In other words, a terrorist act is immediately capable of reframing the imaginary of a city, and a whole nation, producing that very anxiety that, in theory, is the ultimate goal of 'terrorism'—i.e., a conscious strategy to generate *terror*. A contradiction appears to emerge. On the one hand, counter-terrorism is fed by a Hobbesian imaginary of absolute security: there cannot be an 'accepted' threshold of terrorism—even an extremely minor attack, once it is framed as 'terrorist', is able to plunge a community into fear and to show the State as blatantly vulnerable. A 'random' act of violence like a car thrown into a pavement—terrorism, once it is de-politicised, becomes by definition inexplicable—is scarier than an 'expectable' one, like a robbery. Hence the capillary normalisation of counter-terrorist control, surveillance and restrictions: after all, only the empty city of the *Leviathan* frontispiece can ever by 'safe from terror'. On the other hand, however, this very projection short-circuits the governmental logics of security in the first place. As we showed, security in the context of governmentality means acting on the here-and-now to anticipate, prevent and pre-empt events that are yet-to-happen (Anderson 2010a; 2010b; Aradau and van Munster 2012; Amoore 2013). To paraphrase Tiqqun (2010[2009], 152–153; emphasis in translation), what security strategies 'must circumscribe and put a stop [to] does not exist at the level of the actual *but at the level of the possible*. The discretionary power here is called *prevention* . . . the enemy . . . is within. The enemy is the event'.

To an extent, this is an impossible task: 'we can never be done with securing because this is dependent on invoking the future in a way that disrupts and opens up the here and now' (Anderson 2010b, 229). Yet, this is only the case if we assume 'crime' or 'violence' as an absolute event, rather than an occurrence that is 'translated' into an event only in relation to a given imaginary it supposedly 'breaches'. This means that, differently from the Hobbesian projection, in this context violence is not understood as an already constituted event that must be avoided at all costs but rather as an inevitable uncertainty that needs to be managed within a certain threshold. Faithful to its etymology (*prae venire*, that is, to anticipate, to come before the event), the question of prevention is not that of avoiding any breach, or crime—as per the paradigm of absolute security—but rather that of avoiding that any occurrence would become an 'event'.[55] We can read in this sense Saborio's (2019) suggestion of theorising urban violence by focusing on the way in which given acts of violence are, or not, translated into an event— i.e., in his terms, they are framed as urban violence—therefore shaping the imaginary of a city as a violent city, or not.

It is evident that terrorism presents a peculiar instance of this logic, since as we argued it is the very imaginary of absolute security produced by counter-terrorist rhetorics to preclude any attempt to 'manage' the occurrence of terrorism within a certain threshold: within this imaginary, terrorism does *always* take the shape of an event. In this sense, it is the quintessential threat. As Massumi (2005, 35) explains, 'a threat is only a threat if it retains an indeterminacy. If it has a form, it is not a substantial form, but a time form: a futurity'. Anti-terrorism rhetoric, in other words, appears as a self-defeating strategy, since it crystallises the very imaginary that makes it impossible in the first place. Once it becomes pervasive, a threat is radically deterritorialised, true to its nature, which is indeterminate and temporally linked to the temporality of a futurity that is not actual and yet, albeit not present, it 'has the capacity to fill the present', as Massumi continues (2005, 35;), 'looming casts a present shadow, and that shadow is fear'. Once it is understood as a virtual event, always real even when non-actual, in other words, the risk that the threat expresses becomes an ever-present occurrence whose very potentiality has to be constantly defused and neutralised and yet, because of its radically de-bounded character, is bound to constantly re-produce fear in the present (Beck 2002). Uncertainty is thus radically translated into insecurity, the virtual domain where security is deployed, and which functions spectrally, as a 'quasicause' (Massumi 2005, 35), which always already tilts the social field, thereby legitimising the effort of security while *at the same time* making it impossible and therefore endless.

This may explain the recent 'urbanisation of terrorism' (Fregonese and Laketa 2022), and why have 'low cost' attacks such as random knife assault or driving cars over crowds increased in the past: not only because they are effective tactics to evade ever-tightening security measures, but also because the very tone of political rhetoric provides the possibility for these acts to immediately translate into terrorist events.[56] This mechanism, to be sure, does not function in a merely 'ideological' sense: in our terms, it may be understood with respect to a complex interplay between the abstract articulations that hold the imaginary together (e.g., the ontology of the social underlying it), and its products or representations (e.g., the vision of a city without violence), along clear racial lines. It is in this complexity that the functioning of security, and its infra-structural violence, needs be explored. This approach allows the framing of both discourses and strategies of counter-terrorism—rather than only terrorism—as a form of urban violence, in the sense Ben Penglase (2011, 435) points to, when arguing that 'the very discourse about "urban violence" contains within it a disruptive element which resists order, refusing to allow violence to be "domesticated". For that very reason, violence becomes so much more an object of fear, fantasy, obsession, and anxiety'. It is with respect to terrorism that this observation is at its most effective. Thus, we begin to understand that beneath the apparent contradiction lies an explanation. There is no self-defeating discourse. What the short-circuit between the imaginary of absolute security and its impossibility, in the context of terrorism, produces is an ever-increasing reliance on security and its violent infrastructure.

Kathie Cox (2020) makes this point, in the context of the Australian, post 9/11 counter-terrorist legislation, by applying Laurent Berlant's notion of 'cruel optimism'. Berlant (2011), whose work we are going to explore further in chapter 6, understands optimism as a structure of affective attachment that sustains an inclination, a 'striving' towards a potential fulfilment, one that becomes 'cruel' when this very attachment makes this fulfilment impossible. In a sentimental relation, for instance, this may be the attachment to the promise that a relation will be fulfilling and positive, which remains in place even when the relations is no longer meaningful and sustainable, with the effect of increasing its toxic effects on the partners who, 'optimistically', refuse to acknowledge them. In other words, cruel optimism refers to a structure of affective attachments that keeps holding, tuning and orienting bodies within a situation even once the *content* of this optimism (what had been generative of this optimism in the first place) has dissolved. Optimism is *cruel*, therefore, since it is directly responsible for our incapacity to pursue a 'better' condition, because it keeps us affectively entrapped within a situation even when this has lost any meaning.[57] There is an infrastructural explanation for this functioning, which has to do with the affective role cruel optimism play, beyond meaning and representation: 'whatever the *content* of the attachment is, the continuity of its form provides something of the continuity of the subject's sense of what it means to keep on living' (idem, 24; emphasis in original). It is exactly this *continuity of form*, in the face of its apparent contradiction, that Cox emphasises to explain the proliferation and acceptance of counter-terrorist tactics and regulations: counterterrorism, rather than a self-defeating strategy, appears as a self-fulfilling one, both producing a pervasive atmosphere of fear via Hobbesian rhetorics, and deploying a capillary infrastructure of security, which is in this way justified and legitimised insofar as providing a set of attachments to navigate this very atmosphere.

While we will explore more in depth this aspect in the next chapters, also accounting for the peculiar way in which the relation between harm, right and risk is reconfigured in this context, at this stage we may therefore note that the apparent contradiction between the absolute security of Hobbes, the liberalism of Locke and the pragmatic governance of biopolitcs that we explored in chapter 3 appears to be 'solved' once we overcome the purely logical, legalistic and rational explanation of security, with terrorism being the most remarkable instance. This is not to say that security has become irrational—though, in a certain sense, it has—but, more precisely, that it has increasingly become an atmospheric endeavour. As many suggest (e.g. Allen 2006; Adey 2014b; Pavoni 2018a), it is the very atmosphere of the urban what security increasingly seeks to *secure*, by depurating the city from any 'perturbation'—perturbations, however, that exist within an atmosphere that has been polluted by the imaginary of security in the first place. Evidently, the critique of the 'ideology' of counter-terrorism is a necessary and yet insufficient step in this regard: its discursive construction may be preposterous and racist, and yet the fear it produces is a material reality that cannot be done with only via rational deconstruction. In this last section, we have shown what we anticipated in this chapter, namely, that an analysis of the imaginary needs to be complemented by an affective reading, one that is able to explore it not only as regards its truth-value with respect to a supposedly external 'reality', but through an analysis of affective forces that is able to account for the infra-structural violence of its ideological 'distortions'. Such a materialism of the atmosphere allows one to think about violence as well as the particular and pervasive atmosphere that acts on bodies by wearing them out, slowly and persistently, within the environmental domain of the ordinary, not only in the dramatic instantiation of the event. In chapters 6 and 7, we will pursue just such an analysis, introducing the concept of atmospheric violence.

Notes

1. Henry George. 1883. *Social Problems.*
2. 'The "creative imagination" will remain, philosophically, a mere word and the role that will be recognized for it will be limited to domains that seem ontologically gratuitous (art)' (Castoriadis 1997[1986], 245).
3. *De-lirare*: going beyond the *lira*, i.e., the furrow or boundary.
4. This is, of course, Martin Heidegger's (1997[1929]) by now classic interpretation of Kant's alleged retreat from unfolding the productive power of imagination (see Žižek 1999, 42). Kant's *de jure* solution would in this way prevently neutralise imagination (e.g., Deleuze 1985[1967]; Sartre 1957[1933–34]). 'There is nothing more deprived of imagination than the transcendental imagination of Kant', utters Castoriadis, bound as it is, 'always producing the Stable and the Same' (1997[1986], 245). Likewise, in Aristotle, Castoriadis contends, we may find a similar ambivalence in the Book III of *De Anima*, where two theories of imagination are foregrounded. The first, fully developed by Aristotle, understands imagination as a picturing activity, 'that in virtue of which we say that a particular image comes about for us', so that

'imagination would be a motion effected by actual perception (Aristotle, *De Anima* III 3, 428a 1–2, 429a, 31–32; Shields 2016). In the second, that will remain only hinted, imagination is no longer subordinated to thought and sensation, but rather becomes a sort of inescapable background of thought: 'the soul never thinks without an image [*phantasma*]' (Aristotle, *De Anima*, III 7, 431a, 16–17; Shields 2016). Thinking, in this sense, is envisaged as an always phantasmatic activity.

5. An important role has been, in this sense, the contribution of phenomenologists such as Edmund Husserl, Jean-Paul Sartre and Marcel Merleau-Ponty.

6. The first reference in terms of imaginary is, of course, Jacques Lacan, whose complex conceptualisation of the Imaginary, as a third term in his psychoanalytical triangle—together with the Real and the Symbolic—understands it as an inescapable dimension of subjective development, yet one characterised by illusion, deception and alienation. Such a reduction or denigration of the imaginary we will also find in its socio-political adaptation, via structuralism and Marxist notion of ideology, as the locus of a social alienation that must be 'cured' via critique.

7. Both Castoriadis's notion of radical imagination, and Deleuze and Guattari's notion of desire are employed in order to politicise the Freudian notions of drive and unconscious beyond Lacan. There are resonances, but also many differences between these authors. This is not the place to explore their missed encounter.

8. A well-known example is Sheila Jasanoff's definition of 'socio-technical imaginary' (2015), which we will discuss below.

9. Josh Watkins for instance finds that in the geographic interpretation, the main tendency has been that of 'explain[ing] spatial imaginaries as representational discourses about places and spaces' (2015, 508). Watkins then moves to illustrate, and advocate for, a less common use of spatial imaginaries as a performative act capable of reproducing and contesting socio-spatial relations.

10. 'If desire is productive, it can be productive only in the real world and can produce only reality' (Deleuze and Guattari 1977[1972], 26). We already explained, in the last chapter, that desire is never natural, free or spontaneous, but only exists in and through a given socio-historical situation, while at the same time being irreducible to such a situation: this is where the magmatic reserve of potential for social change lies (see below).

11. According to Yuval Harari (2014[2011]), homo sapiens did survive other species of hominids thanks to collective imagination, that is, their capacity to create a common imaginary made of myths, legends, gods and other fictions through which a common understanding, sense of belonging and capacity for cooperation and coordination—a common *world*—could unfold. This is certainly an evocative hypothesis, whose value rests more on the inspiration it provides for the subsequent discussion, than on its accuracy, which is (perhaps unavoidably) rather shaky. On the more general controversies on the methodology—or lack thereof—supposedly informing Harari's work, see Narayanan (2022).

12. Bottici also moves the same observation to Martha Nussbaum's notion of public imagination (1995). For Castoriadis himself, the relation between individual

imagination and social context is not always very clear, and for some (e.g., Bottici 2014, 5) it risks leading him to 'highly problematic, and thus untenable, metaphysical opposition'. For others, Castoriadis does not see imagination as an individual faculty but as 'the way of acting of an anonymous or impersonal collective', a notion that seemingly move beyond the individual/society opposition (Ferrari 2021, 8; our translation). In any case, this is exactly one of the potential problems that are overcome by complementing Castoriadis's approach with Deleuze and Guattari's more advanced reflection on the question of relation, emergence and distributed agency, that is, on how such an 'anonymous or impersonal collective' actually exists and acts.

13. 'Fantasy is never individual: it is *group fantasy*', (Deleuze and Guattari (1977[1972], 30; emphasis in translation). 'We "délire" about the whole world. That is, one "délires" about history, geography, tribes, deserts, peoples . . . delirium is geographical-political' (Gilles Deleuze interviewed in L'Abécédaire de Gilles Deleuze, avec Claire Parnet, documentary directed by Pierre-André Boutang, 1996; excerpt from the transcription by Charles J. Stivale, https://deleuze.cla.purdue.edu/sites/default/files/pdf/lectures/en/2-ABC-MsRevised-Notes%2002052020.pdf).

14. On the notions of virtual and actual, see introduction, note 14.

15. This is an aspect that is often missed by critiques that consider Castoriadis's notion of social imaginary as excessively abstract, reified and homogeneous (e.g., Strauss 2006; Lennon 2015). Castoriadis does not reify the imaginary; rather, he is interested in the process of its reification. He does not believe that an imaginary *is* homogeneous, but he is interested in exploring the process of 'institutionalisation' through which an imaginary becomes to some extent—and is experienced as being—'homogeneous'. In other words, for him it is a question of process and hegemony, rather than substance and homogeneity. Likewise, with his insistence on the magmatic, indeterminate and irreducible quality of the radical imaginary, Castoriadis is not 'abstracting' the concept, he is rather emphasising the fuzzy, blurred, never clearly defined contours of an imaginary, in which all sorts of ghostly spatialities and temporalities are included. Claudia Strauss misses this point when she caricaturises Castoriadis's tendency to envisage the imaginary as a 'ghostly abstraction' (2006, 326). We do endorse this term, although we give both 'ghost' and 'abstraction' a rather different, materialist nuance. A few lines later, Strauss provides one of the reasons for her misunderstanding, when arguing that 'societies are not creatures who imagine, but people do', and that meanings 'can only, in the end, be mental entities, the significance imparted by people' (idem, ibidem). We tried to show how our approach resolutely challenges such a mentalist interpretation, by stressing the material-discursive surfacing, affective patterning and embodied reproduction of imaginaries. The imaginary is not produced by a transcendent 'society', nor it is 'in the minds' of its members, but emerges out of pre-individual relations. Nobody 'creates' a social imaginary. It is the creation itself to be the 'mode of being' of a society: 'society is self-creation deployed as history. To recognize this and to stop asking meaningless questions about "subjects" and "substances" or "causes" requires, to be sure, a radical ontological conversion' (Castoriadis 1997[1986], 13–14). That

also solves the apparent impasse that seemingly puzzles Bottici: 'if we begin with the imagination as an individual faculty, the problem is how to explain the influence, at times overwhelming (because it is constitutive), of social contexts. If we begin with the imaginary understood as a social context, the problem is how to account for the emergence of the free imagination of individuals' (2014, 5). The problem disappears when we understand that this very division between individual and social context is itself dependent on a specific imaginary.

16. There is an interesting resonance between this concept and that of 'historical *a priori*' developed by Foucault (1994[1966]) in the context of his reflections on language. Language, he explained, has an *a priori* structure constituted by abstract articulations that provide the condition of possibility for producing statements: not 'the syntax with which we construct sentences but also that less apparent syntax which causes words and things (next to and also opposite one another) to "hold together"' (idem, xix). *A priori* since they are the conditions of possibility to build statements, these abstract articulations are nonetheless historical: contrary to Noam Chomsky's universal structures, they emerge out of the relational complexity of a given epoch.

17. Paul Ricoeur (1986, 14–17), for instance, following Karl Mannheim's *Ideology and Utopia*, distinguishes between ideology and utopia as two different ways in which an imaginary functions, with ideology signalling the closure of the imaginary by assuring its tight integration with the existing system of authority and utopia signalling its potential opening by introducing 'imaginative variations'.

18. Ideology in this sense can be understood as the crystallisation and naturalisation of a social imaginary, while the critique of the ideology is the deconstruction of this naturalisation, a necessary step that is always at risk of falling into another form of naturalisation: 'if the role of the imaginary was glimpsed by Marx, it was nevertheless distorted by his claim to determine, through the procedures of positive science, the nature of social reality' (Thompson 1984, 25).

19. Manfred Steger and Paul James (2013, 31–32) differentiate between 'ontologies'—that is, the 'most basic framing categories of social existence: temporality, spatiality, corporeality, epistemology and so on'—and 'imaginary', which they more generally refer to 'the calling together . . . of an assemblage of meanings, ideas, sensibilities–that are taken to be self-evident . . . the way in which certain apparently simple terms such as "our society", "we", and "the market" carry taken-for-granted and interconnected meanings'. We believe both definitions can be included in a properly ontological notion of social imaginary.

20. We will engage with racism and the smart city, which we consider particularly useful fields to exemplify the strategic consequences of this understanding, respectively in chapters 6 and 8.

21. One may find here a resonance with Marx's notion of 'real abstraction' (e.g., Finelli 1987; Toscano 2008a; 2008b; McCormack 2012; Pavoni 2017).

22. Spinoza's 'materialist' notion of imagination, which we have no room to explore here (see Gatens and Lloyd 1999; Vinciguerra 2012), implied that an imaginary is never overcome simply by rational 'deconstruction', but only by another,

affectively stronger one (cf. Spinoza 2002[1677a], p. IV, pr. 1, *scholium*; see also part III, pr. 13, *demonstration*).

23. We refer to broad commonalities among otherwise different accounts like those by Benedict Anderson (1983) and Charles Taylor (2003), but also otherwise valuable reflections (e.g., Gaonkar 2002; Hargreaves 2004; Steger and James 2013).

24. This is the case of otherwise fine readings, for instance Lacanian approaches (e.g., Meyer 2021) that understand security as a phantasmatic imaginary that fills the constitutive gap in the symbolic structure of the Real. In Lacanian psychoanalysis, fantasies render reality possible through a double movement (see Mandelbaum 2020, 51–60). On the one hand, fantasies project a desirable ideal of how society should be, therefore mobilising communal resources towards its realisation. On the other hand, since the ideal is never actually achieved, fantasies explain this failure by blaming it on the action of an othered subject. For instance, Charlotte Heath-Kelly (2018) has mobilised psychoanalytic fantasies to explain how, in the field of counter-terrorism, defeating enemies (Bin Laden and the Taliban, ISIS and so forth) never brings the perception that security is achieved—quite the opposite, there is always a new threat emerging from the demise of the previous one. The 'repetitive constitution' (idem) of terrorist threats reminds us that securing is a never completed task: there is always another potential threat, disruption and another othered subject to be blamed.

25. As we argued in chapter 1, it is exactly such a separation that is revoked by a vital materialist approach, according to which the form/matter separation is overcome in favour of an ontology of form-matter, matter-discourse, formation. The hylomorphic model assumes a distinction between a genetic form and an inert matter, where the former shapes the latter in the same way as in Genesis, God shapes Adam from clay. Form and matter cannot be separated though, they are rather joined in processes of formation that cannot be presupposed, but only followed.

26. That a limitless *silva* was at the origin of civilisation, Gianbattista Vico's *Ingens Silva*, famously appears in James Frazer's mythical account: 'at the dawn of history Europe was covered with immense primaeval forests, in which the scattered clearings must have appeared like islets in an ocean of green' (1922, ch. IX, § 1). These 'natural' clearings, where the humans would first gather, were perhaps the blueprint for what the Greeks called ἄλσος (*álsos*) and the Romans called *lucus*—with reference to the light (*lux*) of the Sun that would illuminate it—that is, a holy space, or sacred wood—albeit the more precise definition would be that of 'sacred clearing in the wood' dedicated to the worship of gods. The humans subsequently would begin to open their own clearings, the *nemus*. While the two terms are often treated as synonymous, in his commentary to Virgil's *Aeneid*, Servius distinguished between the sacred status of the *lucus* (*arborum multitude cum religone*), the ordered and regulated, yet profane quality of the *nemus* (*composita multitudo arborum*), and the intricate and uncultivated *silva* (*silva diffusa et inculta*) (see Gentili and Giardini 2020).

27. Peter Wilson (2007, 117–118) suggested, at least since Neolithic, life within the exclusionary inclusion of durable walls meant that thought itself would be domesticated. *Inside*, new experiences and practices of security bring about the seeds of

an imaginary, whose building blocks are walls themselves. Building physical and symbolic interiors was the primordial technical enterprise: walls and words, the primary technologies to ward off the outside (Leroi-Gourhan 1993[1964]; Mumford, 1961).

28. We are employing Deleuze and Guattari's definition of smooth space. See Pavoni (2018a, ch. 3).

29. A denial that prompted Bruno Latour's famous quip: *we have never been modern* (1993[1991]).

30. Baroque here, following François Zourabichvili's 'minimal definition', indicates 'that acute relation that the mind undergoes as it is affected by the infinite vis-à-vis the unstable, the confused, the disproportionate, and which characterises in different ways in space and time the European culture between the end of sixteenth century to the second half of seventeenth century' (2017[2002], 216–217, our translation).

31. On the troubling relation between monstrosity and boundaries, see Brighenti (2021).

32. This is what Castoriadis refers to as the 'original investment by [modern] society of the world and itself with meaning', and 'the operative condition for every subsequent representation' (Castoriadis 1987[1975], 128, 142): the erasure of space as *tabula rasa* and the vectorialisation of time as *progress*. We expanded on this reflection elsewhere (Pavoni 2018a, ch. 3; see also Agamben 2005[2003]).

33. This is, in a sense, what is implied by Charles Taylor when describing the 'modern social imaginary' as a social ordering grounded on 'the mutual respect and mutual service of the individuals who make up society' (2003, 12), in which natural rights provide a moral background of obligations and a willingness to collaborate for the achievement of the 'two main ends, security and prosperity', via the twin instruments of a common law and a common market.

34. We are borrowing the term from Carl Schmitt: 'every general rule demands a regular, everyday frame of life to which it can be factually applied and which is submitted to its regulations . . . : a homogeneous medium. There exists no norm applicable to chaos' (2005[1922], 13; see also Agamben 1998[1995]). We expanded on this aspect elsewhere (see Pavoni 2018a, ch. 3, pr. 1.3).

35. Toscanelli sent the map to king Alfonso V of Portugal, and probably it was through Fernando Martins, a Portuguese clergyman, that the map reached Columbus. There is a historiographic debate on this matter (see Farinelli 2016).

36. 'The Leviathan is the *kat'echon*—the great power that holds the conflict back . . . but also the promise of civilisation, the project of the improvement of the human condition' (Galli 2011, xxxiii; our translation). As Benjamin observed in his essay 'On the Concept of History' (2005[1940], § XIII), 'the concept of the progress of the human race in history is not to be separated from the concept of its progression through a homogenous and empty time'.

37. As Giorgio Agamben (2015) argues in an essay dedicated to the concept, *stasis* is an ambiguous notion reflecting the ambivalent status of the *oikos* within the *polis*, and more precisely to the threshold in which the political dramatically dissolves into the domestic realm of blood ties and, conversely, where the household overflows into the *polis*, bringing its unspoken violence onto the political space. In a sense, *stasis* is

the possibility that the excess that is constitutive to any community would violently overflow (Esposito 2010[1998]).

38. A template we may see today for instance in the anti-abolition rhetoric, where the removal of the police as we know is pit against the apocalyptic mayhem that would unavoidably ensue. 'Abolish the police? Those who survived the *chaos* in Seattle aren't so sure' (Bowless 2020; our emphasis) recently titled a *New York Times* article. Or take the conclusion of a review of *A World Without Police*, by Geo Maher (2021), on conservative *City Journal* (Lehman 2021): 'this is the grim reality beneath the abolitionist fantasy. Drawing down the police will weaken communities, not empower them. It is no accident that the militias that Maher seems to prefer spring up in failed states—they are not a triumphant fulfilment of social order but an evil made necessary by its collapse' (Maher, it should go without saying, defends everything but 'militias').

39. See, for instance, Carl Abbot (2006) on movies and novels that depict the destruction of US cities. Abbott shows that this fiction is centred on the representation of the city as a place of corruption and sin; and on its destruction as the ultimate chance for regeneration and (re)construction of a non-urban society.

40. Hobbes's picture of the *bellum omnium contra omnes*, of course, was influenced by the writing of Thucydides and Lucretius. Later in life he will admit its fictitious meaning: 'it is very likely to be true, that since the creation there never was a time in which mankind was totally without society' (1841[1656], 183–184).

41. As already mentioned, an etymological relation holds these terms together around the Latin word *urbum* (plow), but also, as Cerdá adventurously speculates, the monosyllable *ur* that he relates to the Latin *aro*, i.e., to plough (see chapter 2).

42. As Adams writes, 'the actual practices of occupying and controlling the "empty" land of the Americas differed radically from those used to order the interiors of a landscape of competing European state territories, precisely because, to the colonizers, they lacked the same ontological qualification of interiority so crucial for the territorial state' (2019, 201). This empty space played the same role of the ocean, whose apparently smooth surface had modelled the fantasy of a homogeneous space, free of obstacles and barriers, which grounds the logistical imaginary of frictionless circulation we already encountered (see Schmitt 1986[1942]; Steinberg 2001).

43. For Locke (2003[1690], §V), those who cultivate/civilise the land and make it productive should be granted the right to property over those undeserving 'common' hands usually inhabiting the *terrae nullius* of the New World: 'as much land as a man tills, plants, improves, cultivates, and can use the product of, so much is his property. He by his labour does, as it were, inclose it from the common'.

44. The example of Philadelphia is part of a series of considerations through which Cerdá sees the American grid as the quintessential template of urbanisation. Cerdá also notes that American people had their own urbanisation, and a particularly advanced one, which shows that they 'were not, especially in some regions, as barbaric as they were thought to be' (2018[1867], 205).

186 ~ Chapter Four

45. On the double projection of domestication, simultaneously towards the 'social' (the public) and the 'natural' wild, see Brighenti and Pavoni (2018).

46. E.g., Blackstone's well-known definition of police as 'the due regulation and domestic order of the kingdom: whereby the individuals of the state, like members of a well-governed family, are bound to conform their general behaviour to the rules of propriety, good neighbourhood, and good manners: and to be decent, industrious, and inoffensive in their respective stations' (1791[1765], 162).

47. This technocratic nuance is also implied by Foucault in another context, when he observes that 'the marginalistic integration of individuals in the state's utility is not obtained in the modern state in the form of ethical community which was characteristic of the Greek city. It is obtained in this new political rationality but a certain specific technique called then, and at this moment, police' (Foucault 1988, 153). On the opposition between the political and police, with the latter term understood as indicating the given order more generally, we point readers to the work of Jacques Rancière.

48. As Emile Benveniste (1971[1966], 292; emphasis in translation) explains, 'from original barbarity to the present state of man in society, a universal and gradual development was discovered, a slow process of education and refinement, in a word, a constant progress in the order of that which *civilité*, a static term, was no longer sufficient to express and which had to be called *civilisation* in order to define together both its direction and its continuity'. See also Adam Ferguson's classic observation (1792, 252): 'the success of commercial arts, divided into parts, requires a certain order to be preserved by those who practise them, and implies a certain security of the person and property, to which we give the name of civilization'.

49. In the same way as the beastly urban rabble appears as an inacceptable deviation with respect to the Hegelian dialectic of history (see Ruda 2011).

50. See for instance the case of extremely 'domesticated' spaces ('safe spaces', in the words of Epstein 1998) such as gated communities, born in the USA and then proliferated above all in 'Global South' megalopolises, that often exist in the form of a disembedded network (Rodgers 2004), an archipelago (Petti 2007) that literally provides a domestic channel to live the city by utterly bypassing its uncomfortable wilderness. A more explicitly violent example is the elastic geography of Israeli colonisation, characterised by fortified settlements connected by roads that, at the same time, disconnect the Palestinian territory (Weizman 2007). As the literature shows, the urban uncanny tends to resurface in the form of a fear, vis-à-vis the ungated outside, that is directly proportional with the closure through which gated life is experienced: attempts to eradicate violence from the insulated comforts of gated suburbs, shopping malls and other armoured bubbles only reinforce the perception of the outside as menacing and insecure (Epstein 1998; Klauser 2010; Pavoni 2011; Zeiderman et al. 2015; Tulumello 2017a, ch. 4), besides, of course, excluding (thus generating further violence against) those unable to afford entering such a 'comfort-animated artificial continent' (Sloterdijk 2013[2005], 195). In chapters 6 and 7 we

will expand on this aspect by focusing more precisely on the affective and aesthetic—that is, atmospheric—dimension of urban space, and its violence.

51. In this imaginary, the urban worker mirrors the contemporary stigmatisation of the figure of the 'terrorist', or that of the 'black bloc', bestialised but at the same time diabolised, their violence understood as the most dangerous since, so to speak, anti-systemic. Even Marx, though from a radically different viewpoint, reproduced such a duality: while finding in the urban proletariat the potential power to build socialism, he famously identified counter-revolutionary forces in the *Lumpenproletariat*, who he described as degenerate and criminal. Another version of this dichotomy is the one that opposed, in the viewpoint of socialist intellectuals, class-conscious urban workers of the industrialised Northern and reactionary peasants of rural South in reunified Italy between late eighteenth and early nineteenth century—a dichotomy that Antonio Gramsci firmly opposed (see Urbinati 1998). At the same time, the lines of distinction are often blurred, especially for women, as reconstructed, for instance, by Hallie Rubenhold (2019) in her account of misconceptions and gender commonplaces in Victorian London and in the contemporary reception of the history of Jack the Ripper.

52. We will engage with this point through the account of Frantz Fanon in chapter 6. See also Sarmento and Linehan (2019).

53. Excerpts from speeches, transcriptions/translations available at: www.telegraph.co.uk/news/worldnews/vladimir-putin/11588182/Fifteen-years-of-Vladimir-Putin-in-quotes.html; www.wsj.com/articles/frances-hollande-extends-state-of-emergency-for-three-months-1447690309; www.independent.co.uk/news/world/europe/berlin-attack-germany-donald-trump-isis-terrorism-blame-latest-news-updates-lorry-a7485936.html.

54. Our use of 'left' and 'right', here, resonates with that made by Gabriel Feltran (2020, 10ff) in his discussion of normative regimes (see chapter 3 for a discussion in the context of security politics more broadly).

55. This is consistent with Gilles Deleuze's reflection on the logic of control (1992[1990]). For an account of the difference between control and governmentality, see Pavoni (2018a).

56. We are grateful to the team of project 'Atmospheres of Counterterrorism in European cities' (see https://atmoct.org/) for pointing us to the urbanisation of terrorism and the case of 'incel' attacks mentioned above.

57. In the context of contemporary neoliberal rhetorics, writes Berlant, cruel optimism 'is an incitement to inhabit and to track the affective attachment to what we call "the good life", which is for so many a bad life that wears out the subject which nonetheless, and at the same time, find the conditions of possibility within it' (2011, 27).

CHAPTER FIVE

~

Urbanisation

Dissolving city, planetary metamorphosis.[1]

In this chapter, we address the second link at the core of our theory of urban violence, that is, the one between violence (understood in its manifold structures and materialities; see chapter 1) and the urban (and in particular its processual and relational understanding as urbanisation; see chapter 2). In other words, we move to 'urbanising' violence, fleshing out our understanding of the mutual interwovenness of these two concepts—and of the way their relation is mediated by security (and policing). We begin by reviewing the way the 'urban' tends to (not) be conceptualised in research on urban violence: the fact that literature has generally taken the urban for granted—using 'urban' as a mere adjective, synonymous of 'city'—with significant implications for the possibility to theorise the specific qualities of 'urban violence'. Then, we argue that this problem is linked to the way urban violence is overly understood in relation with—and generally as a consequence of—the 'urban age', in line with long-held ideas about urban life (see chapter 4), and their renewed actualisations in an age of mass, capitalist urbanisation. By referring to the critique of the urban age, and our threefold understanding of the urban as project, process and atmosphere (see chapter 2), it is through the lenses of political economy and political theory that we begin, in this chapter, to move beyond the problem of the urban, and argue for the co-constitutiveness of urbanisation and violence. In particular, we show the promising steps taken by the literature that has discussed the (direct and indirect) forms of violence of capitalist urbanisation; and high-light the limits therein, adding that a politico-economical approach to the dialectical relation between urban space and the planetary process of neoliberal urbanisation needs to be further integrated by a sensibility to the affective relations through which this materialises in the urban, which is the purview of the next chapter.

Urban in Urban Violence

In chapter 2 we have begun to show how a rich tapestry of epistemological and theoretical endeavours has for long time, and with renewed energy dur-ing the last few years, engaged with the 'urban', proposing from both analyti-cal and normative standpoints to overcome the simple association with the locus of the 'city', and rather bringing to the fore the projectual, processual and atmospheric dimensions of the urban. While in the field of critical urban theory this direction is being fruitfully pursued, little of this endeavour has been incorporated within scholarship on urban violence, which has rather tended to take the urban for granted and, as a consequence, to explore urban violence as just an (epi-)phenomenon of the city (Saborio 2019; Pavoni and Tulumello 2020)—that is, as whatever violence that happens to take place *in* the city and/or is produced *by* the city.

Let us move now to see precisely how this happens, starting with the first dimension, the equalisation of urban violence with 'violence in the city'. Consider, for example, a very influential contribution: Caroline Moser's in-troduction to a 2004 special issue of *Environment and Urbanization*. Moser sets out a 'roadmap' to urban violence and insecurity, a conceptual framework with the goal 'to define and systematically categorize the multiple forms of [urban] violence' (2004, 4). Since Moser does not explicitly define urban vio-lence—a typical feature of literature on urban violence (see introduction)—we can take steps from the forms of violence included in her taxonomy of 'categories, types and manifestations of violence in urban areas' (idem, 5): political, institutional, economic, economic/social and social. Moser sets out a large, complete list of direct manifestations of violence, including a number of typologies of actions that are not peculiar to urban space—from 'guerrilla conflict' to 'lynching of suspected criminals', from 'kidnapping' to 'physical or psychological male-female abuse'. Later on, Moser reviews literature on causes and causal factors of urban violence, focusing on the interplay of 'structure, identity and agency' (idem, 8), and particularly on the intersection of poverty, inequality, exclusion, politicisation of crime (and political violence) and privatisation of security (and violence thereof). And yet, neither within the taxonomy of manifestations nor in the discussion of causal factors does the 'urban'—in its manifold characterisations—seem to be playing a specific role: 'urban violence' is understood as the violence that happens in the city.

Ten years later, Moser joined forces with Cathy McIlwaine to edit another issue of *Environment and Urbanization*, guided by the perception that fundamental changes, including the ongoing increase in urban violence, had made it necessary to broaden the agenda by exploring 'the symbiotic relationship between urban conflict and violence' (2014, 334). Moser and McIlwaine put forward important insights. On the one hand, they acknowledge that violence is part and parcel of 'the current model of development', arguing that scholarship on violence should above all contribute to empower the people affected to 'contest and confront' its structural causes (idem, 332). On the other, they embrace insights of global urban studies in noticing that the 'city' has transcended a purely local level, becoming a central scale—possibly even more relevant than the national one—in shaping dynamics of conflict and violence. Therefore, acknowledging that 'cities are inherently conflictual spaces' (idem, 336), Moser and McIlwaine move to emphasise the relevance of conceptual tools such as conflict-to-violence transient 'tipping points' and 'violence chains', that is, an epistemological focus on the emergence and then generalisation of social processes (see also Moser and Rodgers 2012, 1). While these insights point a processual understanding of urban violence, there remains a tendency to implicitly refer the inherent conflictual nature of cities to their ahistorical, 'violent' quality, rather than to the historically and geographically specific violence of urbanisation. Moser and McIlwaine do emphasise the relation between the 'rescaling' of cities and forms of violence (e.g. organised crime) (2014, 336). Yet, they fail to note that not only are such forms of violence rescaled as a result of the rescaling of the former, but that violence emerges from the process of rescaling—that is, urbanisation—in the first place.

These examples are symptomatic of a wider tendency in existing literature to link violence with the city, and more precisely, with usually quantitative characterisations of cities, generally surrounding its size, density and so on. If the reader were to find more than a resonance with the approach epitomised by Louis Wirth (see chapter 2), that would not be odd. Traditionally, direct, psycho-physical violence has been associated with the very fabric of urban life, a link which is usually presupposed as directly propositional to the extension, in size and complexity, of the city itself. Interestingly, the recent influx of data scientists into social and urban studies has inspired a 'new urban science' (see Townsend 2015, for a critique), which has refashioned these ideas.

Take one of the most paradigmatic examples, Luis Bettencourt and Geoffrey West's 'unified theory of urban living' (sic):

> the bigger the city, the more the average citizen owns, produces and consumes, whether goods, resources or ideas. On average, as city size increases, per capita socio-economic quantities such as wages, GDP, number of patents produced and number of educational and research institutions all increase by approximately 15% more than the expected linear growth. There is, however, a dark side: negative metrics including crime, traffic congestion and incidence of certain diseases all increase following the same 15% rule. The good, the bad and the ugly come as an integrated, predictable, package. (2010, 913; see also Bettencourt et al. 2007)

In this type of mainstreamed discourses, violence *in* the city is assumed to be a (the?) natural consequence of the condition of urban co-habitation; and hence the observed increase of violence is considered to be a much natural outcome of the growth of cities. 'The city is a dark force', the protagonist of Aleksei Balabanov's movie *Brother* (1997) utters: 'the strong comes here and becomes weak'. We already saw in the last chapter the extent to which this imaginary of violence has been attached to the city since the inception of urban modernity, populating public discourses, literature and early urban theory. This trope, we believe, albeit often implicitly, is still alive and kicking as of today. As we have seen with Moser and McIlwaine, critical scholarship has moved beyond pure size—and the simplistic association between urban life and violence. Yet, what seems to persist is a not so dissimilar, although certainly more nuanced, attempt at drawing linear relations between violence and (some characters of) urban growth. Another example is provided by Robert Muggah, who dismissed, in a 2014 TED talk, the correlation between urban density and violence as empirically untenable, only to suggest a correlation between the speed of urbanisation (what he defines 'turbo-urbanisation') and violence.[2] Note that, for Muggah, urbanisation is synonymous with urban growth. Problematic here is that attributing violence to the modes ('rescaling') and speed ('turbo-urbanisation') of urban growth tends—absent a reflection on the process, drivers and causes of the urbanisation in its uneven and patchy planetary unfolding—to provide an overly homogeneous picture of it, and therefore an overly simple and quantitative equation with violence: hardly a significant change in perspective. More promising is Williams's suggestion that 'the rapid and chaotic nature of contemporary urbanization in the Global South has created a set of conditions and dynamics that increases the risk of violence' (2022, 23). While we have already addressed the problems with the centrality of the Global South in literature on urban violence (see introduction), we want to focus here on the way Williams frames the causal relation between urbanisation (understood explicitly as urban growth) and violence, in terms of how the former shapes the context in which the latter may or may not proliferate, thereby breaking up a simple, linear causality. However, Williams's chapter, together with the other works in the collection that the former theoretically grounds (Glass et al. 2022), end up not considering the process of urbanisation in the explanation of the forms of violence they study in cities across the Global South. While this approach contributes to overcoming the understanding of violence as a natural occurrence of the city, it does so by considering violence in the city as being shaped, *prima facie*, by dynamics other than urbanisation.

The equalisation of urban violence with violence that happens in the city is accompanied by an empirical blind spot with significant analytical implications, that is, the virtual absence of comparative studies of violence in the city in opposition to violence outside the city—in other words, in opposition/relation to the rural. One of the rare exceptions is a study by Matthew Lee (2011) that compares homicide among 'urban Blacks' and 'rural Whites' in the USA. Quite interestingly, in his research of a common linkage among forms of violence in the two contexts, Lee ends up focusing on a dimension that points in the direction of transcending the urban/rural dichotomy. For Lee, violence is above all driven by an institutional dimension, what he calls the 'stateless environments': the result of the socio-economic problems of (North American, minority-majority, 'inner') cities and of the isolation of rural areas. On the one hand, this perspective—which resonates with widespread ideas on (criminal) violence as the result of the incapacity of the state to maintain its monopoly over (legitimate) violence—runs against our conceptualisation of the role of security (and state policies therein) in shaping (urban) violence (see chapters 3 and 4), as well as of empirical studies, carried out above all in Latin America, that have shown how urban violence is shaped at/by the interplay of state and non-state actors, and of coexisting normative regimes (e.g., Rodgers 2006; Silva 2010; 2011; Auyero et al. 2014; Auyero and Berti 2015; Feltran 2020; Mauloni 2021). On the other hand, by refraining from exploring the linkages among those 'stateless environments' in their own terms, Lee ends up leaving the rural/urban distinction unquestioned. While his effort is surely valuable, his description of the difference between urban and rural environments takes into account only the specific cultural contexts—and patterns of socio-economic marginalisation thereof—without taking into account the role played by urbanisation itself.

A further, interesting example is constituted by recent works on Latin America where urban violence refers to the growth and concentration of 'new' forms of violence in urban areas, and the social stratification of the phenomenon of violence (Auyero et al. 2014; Auyero and Berti 2015; Larkins 2015). These works bring forward important insights in exploring the origin of violence, beyond structural, socio-economic dimension, also in the actions/inactions of the state, including the 'intermittent, selective and contradictory' (Auyero et al. 2014, 95) forms of governance and policing. These authors focus above all on the 'urban margins', where they observe how violence appears to increase as the result of the collusion and 'connections between state actors and perpetrators of violence', affecting disproportionately the urban poor—to the extent that those very 'margins' are defined by violence as much as by poverty (Auyero 2011; Auyero et al. 2014, 108; see also Moncada 2013). Yet, it seems to us that in these otherwise valuable works the urban still remains a significant *context* of wider processes producing violence, rather than the actual *process* that, as we have argued, unfolds through these heterogeneous, fragmented and violent thresholds. As exposed in chapter 2, we see the urban margins as not simply a place where violence occurs, but the actual product of urbanisation—understood as a process that constantly produces and fills its own margins, and violently so. In other words, we understand urban margins as not simply the 'actual', spatial and socio-economical realms of urban marginality, as they are commonly understood, but more precisely as the multiple frontiers or thresholds that the process of urbanisation constantly generates, negotiates and ingests. These margins, in this perspective, should not be considered 'marginal' with respect to spatial and socio-economical geographies of the city; rather we see them as being marginal to, and produced by, the process of urbanisation, implying that they may actualise transversally with respect to urban geographies. This is what, for example, Ana Villarreal (2021) suggests, in her proposal to conceptualise urban violence, in the context of the Global South, 'beyond the margins', that is, beyond the context of 'marginality' where it is usually explored, in order to explore also the way in which it affects the wealthy, and shapes their urban spaces into increasingly disembedded and fortified enclaves (see also Rodgers 2004).

As a way to capture this dynamics we suggest a parallel with Sandro Mezzadra and Brett Neilson's reflection on capital's politics of operations:

> The multiple outsides of capital take on a rather paradoxical character against the background of this conceptual analysis. Far from being limited to spaces (which also means forms of economic and social activity) that have not yet been subdued to the domination of capital, they are also continually produced *from within* capital, both through its initiative and through resistance to its

logic. These outsides are privileged sites for the investigation of the operations of capital and their contestation. (2019, 66; emphasis in original)

Likewise, capitalist urbanisation constantly 'draws' into its own ever-expanding orbit all sorts of relations, spaces and bodies, virtually 'urbanising' them from within, well before the actual process of urbanisation, with its frictional violence, unfolds in its context-specific ways, and through all sorts of mediations, filters and transformations (e.g., Williams 2022). Another compelling avenue to explore this process, as we are to briefly expand on below, is that concerning the way in which non-human nature is constantly produced and urbanised at the same time, first by being abstractly ingested within logics of valorisation, and subsequently by being concretely affected via violent processes of expansion and extraction. It is for this reason that such complex dynamics require to be explored through a situated attention that is simultaneously focused on the process that produces them, and the atmosphere through which they are experienced, lived and endured (e.g., McFarlane 2018).

In summary, the works we have reviewed here are exemplary of two common limits of literature on urban violence. First, the label 'urban' tends to be a merely physical container, a synonymous with 'city' as the geographic location where manifestations of violence happen and are concentrated (see for Brazil: Zaluar 2004; Cunha 2012; Landim and Siqueira 2013)—quite often, with specific reference to those urban areas that are labelled or understood as particularly 'dangerous' such as slums and 'peripheries' (see Moser and McIlwaine 2004; Silva 2010; Feltran 2014; 2020). Second, when the label 'urban' exceeds the purely spatial dimension to take on a socio-economic one, this is mostly contingent to the explanation of specific forms of violence. This is particularly evident in 'mainstream' research on urban violence, which generally adopts a conceptual framework that could be, *ceteris paribus*, adopted under different labels like social violence or communal/intra-communal violence—a term more or less synonymous with urban violence in research on Black-majority neighbourhoods in North America is an exemplary case in point. In this tradition, a common goal is finding the 'variables' that correlate with violence in different socio-geographic contexts—with the 'pragmatic' goal of seeking the correct variables on which to intervene to reduce violence. The most prominent example of this approach is the literature on US 'inner city' violence and most prominently that which follows the environmental tradition of the Chicago School (e.g., Shishadeh and Flynn 1996; Morenoff et al. 2001; Harpaz-Rotem et al. 2007; Jacobs and Wight 2010;

Sampson 2011; Doucet and Lee 2015; Levy et al. 2020)—but examples exist also from other contexts (Vilalta et al. 2020).

This brings us to the main conclusion of this critical review. In scholarship on urban violence, urban and violence tend to be systematically conflated, while their co-constitutive nature is left unexplored. The aim of this chapter, in this sense, is to explode this conflation through the lens of political economy.

Urbanisation and Violence

Resonating with the discussion we developed in the last chapter, Feltran writes that: 'the representation of "urban violence" is fundamentally construed in time . . . through an *arbitrary process* of association of distinct concepts and phenomena, which end up constructing a single apparatus, which becomes reified—through various mechanisms—and, hence, "reality"' (2014, 301; our translation, emphasis in original). Within this 'constructed reality', or imaginary, of urban violence, the urban is naturalised as fact, namely the background out of which violence emerges. How this process emerges, and the role played by this background in orienting it, however, is rarely addressed.

In line with what we have discussed so far, let us point out that Feltran's use of the term 'arbitrary' may appear misleading. Indeed, on the one hand, the (discursive, epistemological) construction of urban violence is a matter of socio-historical power relations—at its most simple, the relations that separate who has the power to define what is urban violence and who is framed as 'violent' in opposition (see Auyero et al. 2014; Silva 2014; Saborio 2019).[3] On the other hand, the construction of urban violence is in turn shaped by the security imaginary of the 'city without violence', which is linked to the nineteenth-century convergence between urbanisation, colonisation and police (see chapter 4). Therefore, while *contra* traditional sociological views, we endorse Feltran's observation that urban violence is not a 'native' category of the city (2014, 301), of the places and actors to which it is associated; at the same time we believe it is fundamental to acknowledge that urban violence ('actually existing' urban violence, that is) is coessential to urbanisation. If violence has been part of cities since their foundations, urban violence is best understood, for both conceptual and strategic reasons, as a precise historical category emerging out of the modern process of (capitalist) urbanisation.

It is thus by briefly recalling the tight relation between urban and urbanisation, which we have developed in chapter 2, that we can move on. With Brenner and Schmid (2013), we have seen how the urban age thesis paints urbanisation as urban growth, that is, a simple, if dramatic, move-ment of people from the rural to the urban, a dichotomy that is naturalised and measured via quantitative statistics. In this chapter, we have seen how a similarly biased metanarrative seemingly orients the discourse on urban violence: the conceptualisation of violence as an occurrence in specific and bounded places (i.e., cities), observable via precise statistics (quintessen-tially: murders), whereby a hierarchy of 'violent' cities around the globe is drawn. Conversely, Brenner and Schmid's argument on planetary urbanisa-tion, on the path indicated by Lefebvre (2014[1989]), permits us to challenge Cerdá's symmetrical argument: urbanisation may indeed be planetary, and yet this is far from being a transhistorical and transgeographical concept. The same can be said as regards the violence of urbanisation, which cannot be un-derstood without taking into account the specific socio-economic infrastruc-ture through which it is enacted and reproduced. In other words, we call for a processual understanding of both violence (e.g., Lawrence and Karim 2007a, 11) and the urban (as urbanisation), which we believe necessary to craft an un-derstanding of urban violence able to move beyond its static, city-centric bias.

Violence of Urbanisation

A first step toward a processual understanding of urban violence, the one that more directly stems from the critique of urban age and chimes with the conceptualisation of planetary urbanisation, is the exploration, from a politi-cal economic perspective, of the intrinsically violent nature of (capitalist) urbanisation—and the centrality that policing has played therein. Above we have traced the role played by security, mainly through policing, beyond the 'preservation, management or control of order', in the 'fabrication' of liberal order (Neocleous 2021[2000], 48); and, with the work of Michel Foucault, the relation between policing, security and urbanisation, especially vis-à-vis the 'question of the spatial, juridical, administrative, and economic opening up of the town' (2007[2004], 13), that is, a twofold problematic of ensuring the relentless *circulation* of goods and people, and at the same time guaran-teeing its *security*—which implies at times the capacity to selectively disrupt that very circulation (see also Elden 2007). There are obviously differences between the two. Foucault does not understand security as a merely capital-ist question, but rather frames it within a wider problematic of governance in which capitalism, liberalism and urbanisation are to be explored in a less deterministic fashion. Other differences depend on Foucault's somehow con-tradictory treatment of the notion of police, as explained in chapter 3—see, for instance, the distinction between the police state and the rule of law (2010[2004], 168ff).

All in all, however, Marxist and Foucauldian insights can be usefully complemented to unpack the capitalism/urbanisation/policing nexus, for instance in order to develop critiques of various paradigms of urban planning for their participation in projects of social engineering and control (e.g., Sandercock 2003; Pløger 2008; Yiftachel 2009; Tulumello 2017a, ch. 5). What we propose is taking a step beyond and aside this literature, and towards overcoming the 'city' bias of urban violence scholarship—a move made possible by reflecting on the specific *violence of (capitalist) urbanisation*, particularly the way the it is driven and shaped by the dynamics of policing. As Ariel Handel puts it, 'urban violence is not only happening in the city, it is also inherently urban, as part of the city's making and unmaking' (2021, 24).The first step for studying the being urban of urban violence is building on the vast field of literature that has exposed the forms of precariousness and insecurity produced by the uneven dislocations and dispossessions of urbanisation (e.g. Harvey 2003; Sassen 2014).

While this literature is manifold and has fully explored the relation between urbanisation in the wide sense we have proposed here (more on this below), let us start with a pretty 'urban' (in the reduced sense as that which is typical of the city) example, as this is probably the field in which the violence of urbanisation has been expressed more explicitly and through a wider set of perspectives. We are referring to literature that has articulated around the conceptual umbrella of gentrification, at least since Neil Smith's classical reflections on the 'new urban frontier' (1996). The link between gentrification and (state, urban) violence has been unravelled among two, interlocked, dimensions. The first, and more general, is the violence that stems from gentrification—and cognate processes like touristification—in terms of displacement, harassment and expulsion. While, traditionally, critical scholarship has not explicitly dealt with this violence, which emerges as an implicit component of accounts of gentrification (e.g., Lees et al. 2015; Peyrefitte 2020), the gentrification/violence nexus has been directly addressed more recently, with the adoption of a quite explicit language. This is the case of: discussions on the violence of un-homing and displacement (Elliott-Cooper et al. 2020; Gillespie et al. 2021); the link between gentrification, public space activation and slow violence against the homeless made by Lauren Brown and Jeff Rose (2021); the reference by José Mansilla (2018) to the 'symbolic violence' of touristification;[4] the reflections on the violence imposed on urban life by the rich and super-rich (Pinçon and Pinçon-Charlot 2013; Paone and Petrillo 2019; Atkinson 2020);[5] studies on the violence of, and racialisation in, the finance/housing/real estate nexus (Aalbers 2016; Fields and Raymond 2021); and, finally, a recent special issue on infrastructural violence and urban stigma (Baumann and Yacobi 2022; Martén and Boano 2022). The second dimension, which is at the same time more specific and more recently object of critical engagement, is the discussion of the central role played by policing in gentrification, touristification, night-life development and so forth. See, for instance, Stefano Bloch and Dugan Meyer (2019) on the implicit revanchism of liberal gentrifiers, and Terra Graziani and colleagues (2022) on public nuisance laws and the production of property relations, in Los Angeles; Jackson Smith and colleagues (2021) on the policing of dispossession along the gentrification 'frontier' in Philadelphia; a large literature on policing and the military occupation of *favelas* in the contexts of gentrification and global events in Brazilian cities (e.g., Saborio 2013; Amaral and Andreolla 2020; Di Bella 2020); or Margo De Koster on the policing of night-life in Antwerp (2020).

Especially in light of discussions on the inter-contextual, global, ultimately planetary nature of gentrification (Atkinson and Bridge 2005; Lees et al. 2015; 2016; but see, for critiques, Ghertner 2015; Maloutas 2018), the literature on and around gentrification provides us with a consolidated entry point on the link between a central component of contemporary concentrated urbanisation, and the forms of direct, indirect and state violence that stem from it. In this sense, Dugan Meyer's suggestion—which implicitly mirrors Marx's quip on security—that gentrification '*is* a security project' (2021, 271; our emphasis) perfectly fits our discussion, since it highlights how the structural violence of gentrification is, on the one hand, produced by policing (*latu* and *strictu sensu*) and, on the other, mediated by a feeling of insecurity (see also Kern 2010).

In line with our conceptualisation of the urban, we need, however, to widen up our lens to understand the violence of urbanisation 'outside' the city. Quite interestingly, gentrification still provides us with examples, as the literature on rural gentrification (Phillips 1993; Lópes-Morales 2018) has very recently started to 'blur' the traditional distinctions between urban and rural, for instance questioning the idealised dichotomy between gentrifiers looking for urbanity vs. those looking for the availability of green spaces (Bernt 2018). A parallel thread is that on how conservation planning and ecotourism have, especially in the Global South, often gone hand in hand with processes of land grabbing and the expulsion of local populations (e.g., Hughes 2005; Gardner 2012; Ross 2017; Trogisch and Fletcher 2020). David Hughes shows, in the case of the Great Limpopo Transfrontier Conservation Area (which spans territories in South Africa, Mozambique and Zimbabwe), a perpetuation of 'structural and spatial racism' (2005, 174), especially evident in the deployment of arguments on the 'unsustainability' of the practices of local populations like seasonal mobility following the availability of natural resources. Not only do these arguments perfectly exemplify the persistence of the tropes about 'wilderness' and 'savage' natives to be tamed we have seen to be central to the imaginary of security/violence (see chapter 4),[6] but they also capture the violence that is embedded in the contemporary—extended—urbanisation of nature.[7]

More broadly, the conceptualisations of infrastructural and logistical violence we have touched upon in chapter 1 have inspired a recent, but growing, scholarship that has articulated urbanisation and structural violence beyond specific forms like gentrification. One example is Gerald Roche and his colleagues' discussion of how China uses urbanisation in Tibet as an instrument of differential inclusion, 'which includes elements of assimilation, marginalization and subordination, but cannot be reduced to the eliminatory logic typically associated with settler colonialism' (2020, 2). Explicitly inspired by planetary urbanisation, Martin Arboleda (2020, particularly ch. 3) articulates territories of extraction, land grabs, global depeasantisation (as forms of structural violence) and their manifestation in the growth of informal settlements (themselves most often the focus of discourses on urban violence), thereby opening up to a dialectical understanding of the violence of urbanisation in the relation between the city and the rural. Arboleda's dialectical materialism is also inspiring for its capacity to articulate the violence of the state and the impersonal relations of capitalism, or, in his words, 'the violence of capitalism and the opportunism of capital' (idem, 142).

The conceptual broadening of urbanisation helps us to capture yet another dimension of (structural, urban) violence, the one that links environmental conflict, activism and its policing. Let us take as example two long-standing environmental conflicts: the No TAV movement against the high-speed train in Val di Susa in Italy, ongoing since 1991, and the struggle in Notre-Dame-des-Landes against the Grand Ouest Airport in France, launched in 2000 and concluded in 2018 with the abandonment of the project. The relevance of these cases for our argument is manifold. To begin with, the arguments of the activists have long been centred on the violence that infrastructural development and logistic—or, in other words, extended urbanisation—impose over nature and local populations. At the same time, among the strategies of the activists, the one that has been crucial for the long-term duration of the struggle has been that of creating 'temporary' cities—reflecting on the French case, Frédéric Barbe (2016) has talked of 'conscious inhabitation' as politics. Even more interesting are the strategies and tactics the police and the judiciary have used for repressing and criminalising the struggles, which go beyond direct (police) violence and the traditional framing of political struggle as a threat for order (cf. chapter 4). In the Italian case, we can see two further tactics: on the one hand the attempt (and failure) by prosecutors at framing a sabotage action as terrorism (Chiaramonte 2019)—a framing, as we have seen (chapter 4, Researching Urban Violence), that is particularly powerful in shaping the imaginaries of security; and, on the other, the use of preventative measures (e.g., restraining orders, including bans from the areas of the conflict) typical of police power (cf. Dubber 2005). In the criminalisation of these environmental struggles, in summary, we see a perfect exemplification of the violence administered by the police in its efforts for urbanising the rural and ruralising the urban: in a sense, the nemesis of Cerdá's dream of pacification via urbanisation (cf. Adams 2014).

Expanding further, conceptualising the violence of urbanisation also implies capturing the ecological and more-than-human implications of socio-spatial transformation, a field to which an ever-growing literature has been contributing indirectly (e.g., Moore 2015; Huggan and Tiffin 2015) and directly. Urban political ecology, a field born from the observation of uneven effects of urban pollution on different urban areas and social groups, has more recently explicitly engaged with broader implications of global urbanisation linked to the commodification of nature and restructuring of human/nature relations (e.g., Arboleda 2016; Connolly 2019; Connolly et al. 2021). In particular, the recently surfacing area of research on 'urban animals' has explicitly engaged with the need to reformulate conceptions of the urban:

> The urban cannot be confined within one side of the urban/wild opposition. It should instead be understood as emerging out of the constant, semiotic, and material reformulation of their threshold. If the radical modification of the planet as a result of human activity is by now a certified fact, and if this is fundamentally tied to the global process of urbanization, it follows that all animals are to some extent directly or indirectly, implicitly or explicitly, in the process of being urbanized (Brighenti and Pavoni 2018, 583; emphasis in original)

Crucially for our purposes, research on urban animals has been documenting the unequal and asymmetric violence this very process produces (e.g., Holmberg 2015; Braverman 2016; Brighenti and Pavoni 2016; 2018; 2021b; Narayanan 2017; Barua and Sinha 2019).

At the intersection of, and moving beyond, the field of studies here reviewed, the violence of urbanisation, in its many forms, has been indirectly captured by theorisations on the convergence of the planetarisation of the urban and of its historical counterpart, the plantation (see chapters 2 and 4). Eduardo Mendieta has recently discussed this convergence by weaving together the concepts of the Urbanocene and the Plantationocene, which he defines as 'the Urbanocene face of the Capitalocene, its necropolitical face' (2019, 86). The concept of the Plantationocene has been introduced by Donna Haraway (2015; see also Haraway et al. 2016), the Capitalocene first by Andreas Malm[8] and then by Jason Moore (2015). With all the problems with contemporary academia's need to invent neologisms,[9] the question of 'naming' seems to us to be indicative of the acknowledgement of the necessity to capture the urban(ising) dimensions of historical and contemporary formations (cf. Haraway 2015). Mendieta thus summarises the embeddedness among the parts of this formation:

> Cities preceded capitalism and arguably without cities there may not have been capitalism. Capitalism is as much a product of the plantation and the rise of global trade it enabled, as the modern city is the product of racial capitalism. (2019, 93)

The foundational relation between urbanisation and plantation (and racism; see chapter 6, Researching Urban Violence) points in the direction of the wide lens that we argued is necessary to grasp the globalising dimensions of urban violence. Diren Valayden precisely captures this co-consitutiveness when arguing that 'the organization of violence is shaped by the discourse and social imaginary of racial feralization as a problematic of government amidst the dislocations created by "planetary urbanization"' (2016, 166).[10]

Finally, the conceptualisation of the violence of urbanisation we have developed here can also be used as a lens to focus on the multi-scalar dimensions of forms of violence that have long been at the centre of studies of urban violence. This is done, if implicitly, in a recent collection, edited by Gabriel Feltran (2022), which traces the global ramifications of 'stolen cars' in São Paulo, a privileged perspective to observe the integration of local conflict with transnational drug traffic and global insurance corporations, always at the border between legal and illegal markets. More broadly, the work of Feltran and his colleagues points to the possibility—yet to be fully explored—to use the lenses of concentrated, extended and differential urbanisation (Brenner and Schmid 2015; see chapter 2) to connect, through the logistical implications of the travel of illicit drugs, political conflict in rural regions of producing countries, the territorial control of gangs in cities where drugs are commercialised and sold (see Basu 2014; Rodrigues et al.

2017; Fraser and Hagedorn 2018; Madarie and Kruisbergen 2020), and the political economic implications of drug trafficking as an example of global, 'gore' capitalism (Valencia 2018).

Urban Criminology?

The scholarship and ideas that we have discussed so far provide a crucial compass to study the *process* through which urban violence proliferates; and yet, they cannot encompass the entire problematic of the *atmosphere* of urban violence—they cannot say much beyond the (direct) impact of (state) policies and real estate development, and resistances thereof. In particular, a political economic approach can indeed explore the way the imaginary of urban violence and absolute security produces and justifies state violence through urban development and extended urbanisation; but cannot take into account its relations with the desire, senses and practices of security that exceed this imaginary. This is the direct equivalent, in the field of violence, of the limits of theories such as planetary urbanisation (see chapter 2), which do grasp the global scale of the problem, but have less to say on the way this same problem is actualised in and through concrete and contingent spatio-historical relations. We have argued for the importance of adopting a bifocal lens, pointed simultaneously at the planetary dimension of the violent process of urbanisation and the socio-spatial configuration it presupposes, and at the material and affective relations (atmospheres) in and through which this form is concretely actualised in the urban space. In terms of urban violence, this means that the political economic approach that we have developed here needs to be integrated with a materialist exploration of the forms into which violence comes to be perceived, experienced and lived in the urban.

Some steps in this direction have been taken under the lenses of 'urban criminology' (Atkinson and Millington 2018; 2020; Peršak and Tulumello 2020), a pretty recent field whose endeavour has been precisely that of meshing the more traditional, structuralist instruments of critical criminology (labelling, social structures) with the sensory, aesthetic and affective dimensions of urban space and its social control (e.g., Carrabine 2012; Ilan 2019; Peršak and Di Ronco 2021). However, also this literature has its limits in light of our conceptualisation, which we can summarise as pertaining to two dimensions. The first, and more contingent, is the persisting hegemony of 'northern' perspectives as urban criminology has just started to embed the recent developments of southern criminology (e.g., Carrington et al. 2016; Travers 2019)—a quintessential example is the otherwise intriguing attempt by Jon Bannister and Anthony O'Sullivan (2020) at theorising a planetary urban criminology (see also Peršak and Tulumello 2020, 5). The second, and more structural, is that urban criminology has only incipiently worked its understanding of the urban and developed a theory of it. Granted, these issues may above all be the result of the very recent emergence of urban criminology, which has just begun to dialogue with global and post-colonial urban studies, as well as with urban theory.

To move forward, in the next chapters, we will suggest reframing the planetary, political economic relations sketched in this chapter under the framework of security logics; and to focus on the affective and atmospheric configurations of fear—through the lenses of comfort—as a key lens through which the co-essential relation between security, violence and the urban can be unfolded. By doing so, we will move from a structural to an infra-structural understanding of urban violence.

Researching Urban Violence: Broken Windows

In 1982, criminologist George Kelling and political scientist James Wilson summarised, in *The Atlantic*, a study by Philip Zimbardo (1970), giving birth to the 'broken windows theory':

> Philip Zimbardo, a Stanford psychologist, reported in 1969 on some experiments testing the broken-window theory. He arranged to have an automobile without license plates parked with its hood up on a street in the Bronx and a comparable automobile on a street in Palo Alto, California. The car in the Bronx was attacked by 'vandals' within ten minutes of its 'abandonment'. The first to arrive were a family—father, mother, and young son—who removed the radiator and battery. Within twenty-four hours, virtually everything of value had been removed. Then random destruction began—windows were smashed, parts torn off, upholstery ripped. Children began to use the car as a playground. Most of the adult 'vandals' were well-dressed, apparently clean-cut whites. The car in Palo Alto sat untouched for more than a week. Then Zimbardo smashed part of it with a sledgehammer. Soon, passersby were joining in. Within a few hours, the car had been turned upside down and utterly destroyed. Again, the 'vandals' appeared to be primarily respectable whites. (Kelling and Wilson 1982)

In the years following that study, Zimbardo further pursued his attempt at 'understanding how good people turn evil'—as the subtitle of his most famous book goes (2007)—in the notorious Stanford Prison experiment (Haney et al. 1973). There, a group of students were divided between 'guards' and 'inmates' in a prison environment simulation that was to last two weeks, but was interrupted after only six days, due to the 'guards" increasingly sadistic and cruel behaviour. The study has become a template for the socio-psychological emphasis on the role played by external conditions, viz. the *situation*, over personal *traits*, in prompting violent behaviour—it also became, arguably, a template for how *not to do* a psychological experiment.[11] Regardless of its validity, what was central in the Stanford experiment, as in the famous experiments carried out by Stanley Milgram (1974) in the 60s, was the notion of responsibility, and the 'dehumanising' effect that institutional delegation, authority and technological mediation might have on the individual vis-à-vis indulging in cruel and violent behaviour (Zimbardo and Haney 2020).

A similar question is at the core of Kelling and Wilson's theory, which intends to explore the criminogenic effects that urban environments might exude, once they are no longer perceived as kempt, tended and under control—that is, once they undergo a process of 'urban decay'. While in chapter 7 we are going to discuss more generally 'situational models' of crime prevention, here we are interested in emphasising, through the lenses of an 'urban criminology', the characteristics and limits of this enormously popular theory, since it epitomises the (violent) relation we have been discussing so far, between policing, the imaginary of order and the process of urbanisation.

At bottom, this is a question of normalcy: the everyday life of an urban neighbourhood, as Erwin Goffman (1971) would say, is organised around 'normal appearances', that is, the shared, taken-for-granted expectations that urbanites have as they go about in their lives and that shape their ontological security, that is, their common sense of order (Giddens 1991, 37; see chapters 3 and 7). When these expectations crumble, uneasiness, anxiety or altogether fear *might* ensue—'might' since unravelling the causal dynamics is what Broken Windows and similar theories allegedly do. This is the question behind Broken Windows, whose focus is not crime *per se* but rather what happens when such expectations are no longer met, when the belief that things will go as they should is broken—when order decays into disorder. 'Vandalism can occur anywhere once communal barriers—the sense of mutual regard and the obligations of civility—are lowered by actions that seem to signal that "no one cares"' (Kelling and Wilson 1982, 31). *Sine cura*, indeed.

This is where the 'broken windows' come in: just like graffiti, uncollected garbage, for Kelling and Wilson, disorderly people are broken windows in human form, actants that are able to re-signify the atmosphere of a place, communicating a breakdown of mutual trust, providing the 'inescapable knowledge that the environment . . . is uncontrolled and uncontrollable' (Glazer, *apud* idem, 33).[12] Broken windows, in this sense, are the uncanny symptoms of that 'abyss of disorder' that lies beneath everyday 'normality', the sign that the repressed wilderness could spring back at any time, compromising the civilising project of urbanisation (see chapter 4).[13] Just like weeds in a garden, disorder may proliferate in an unkempt neighbourhood, bringing forth new savages, 'not violent people, nor, necessarily, criminals', Kelling and Wilson (1982, 30) clarify, 'but disreputable or obstreperous or unpredictable people: panhandlers, drunks, addicts, rowdy teenagers, prostitutes, loiterers, the mentally disturbed'. When their presence is unchecked or untended, 'a stable neighborhood . . . can change, in a few years or even a few months, to an inhospitable and frightening jungle' (idem, 31). Crime, unavoidably, will follow, since 'serious street crime flourishes in areas in which disorderly behavior goes unchecked' (idem, 34).

What the theory fundamentally argues is that cycles of order or disorder function as self-fulfilling prophecies: if control seems to be lacking, it will be lacking; if control seems to exist, it will exist. Let one minor crime happen and more crime will happen, let many small crimes happen and serious crime will happen. Let one window remain broken and you will find yourselves in a 'crime infested' neighbourhood. If you want to stop the cycle of vandalism and crime, the argument goes, you have to act at the aesthetic level of the urban façade: repairing broken windows, erasing graffiti, and criminalising deviant behaviour, even minor ones, such as loitering, panhandling, public drinking, rough sleeping—in sum, you have to keep the normal appearances and the shared sense of order in place. This is, Kelling and Wilson stress, the 'original function' of police, that is, not so much fighting crime as 'maintain[ing] order against the chief threats to order—fire, wild animals, and disreputable behavior'. This is what has been forgotten, the authors argue, 'the link between order-maintenance and crime-prevention, so obvious to earlier generations', which Broken Windows intends to restore (1982, 33; see chapter 7). Sure, this might lead to discrimination, and Wilson and Kelling—the racist overtones of their reference to 'clean-cut' and 'respectable' Whites notwithstanding—have a word of caution about the danger of disproportionately affecting certain categories and punishing seemingly innocuous behaviours that 'harm no ones'. Yet, the implicitly epidemiological approach to urban violence that feeds this theory allows one to trump such questions of ethics or justice. Perverting the Kantian categorical imperative, thus they write:

> Arresting a single drunk or a single vagrant who has harmed no identifiable person seems unjust, and in a sense it is. But failing to do anything about a score of drunks or a hundred vagrants may destroy an entire community. A

particular rule that seems to make sense in the individual case makes no sense when it is made a universal rule and applied to all cases. It makes no sense because it fails to take into account the connection between one broken window left untended and a thousand broken windows. (Kelling and Wilson 1982, 35)

The theory was so appealing it was taken seriously by any number of politicians and policy makers, first in the USA and then throughout the world. Unsurprisingly, it particularly throve in New York City when, in 1993, Rudy Giuliani appointed William Bratton as police commissioner. Bratton was a convinced supporter to this approach: on its grounds, he restructured police work in the city through two concepts. On the one hand, zero tolerance: no windows shall remain broken, all crimes shall be punished harshly, because small crimes bring to more serious crimes—in Kelling and Wilson's words, 'public drunkenness, street prostitution, and pornographic displays can destroy a community more quickly than any team of professional burglars' (1982, 38). On the other hand, directly following from Kelling and Wilson's emphasis on the order-maintenance function of the police, Bratton's second innovation was the introduction of quality-of-life policing. In other words, the idea that policing must become all-encompassing, encircling the urban as an omnipresent atmosphere of peace and tranquillity, with respect to which any potential harm or disturbance should be prevented (see chapter 3). 'Just as physicians now recognize the importance of fostering health rather than simply treating illness, so the police—and the rest of us—ought to recognize the importance of maintaining, intact, communities without broken windows' (Kelling and Wilson 1982, 38).

In more concrete terms, one of the main operational tools of zero tolerance, whose use further increased under the tenure of Michael Bloomberg in the 2000s, was the systematic use of stop and frisk, in search of illegal guns, small quantities of drugs and so on.[14] As the story goes, crime in New York City dropped dramatically during the 1990s: Broken Windows worked! But did it? As it is often the case with seemingly self-evident theories, Broken Windows does neither explain crime nor help meaningfully address it. Sure, it does provide a model that assumes crime will be more likely where windows are broken. This may certainly be the case. Yet, this is a clear example of a bad inference: street crime could be more likely in a socio-economically deprived neighbourhood, which, exactly for being socio-economically deprived, will also be more likely to have 'broken windows'. Correlation does not mean causation.[15] More poignantly, even if we were to assume that disorder *does* breed crime (see Kelling and Bratton 2015), this would tell us little as regards the underlining causes of the unequal distribution of 'disorder' in the city and thus about the violently disordering role the process of urbanisation has on the urban fabric.[16] In any case, while Kelling and Bratton (2015) argue that 'ample evidence makes clear that Broken Windows policing leads to less crime', the very association between small incivilities, 'disorder' and crime does not stand empirical scrutiny (Harcourt 1998; O'Brien et al. 2019). Moreover, while we already saw that crime statistics are far from being an uncontroversial means of urban policy evaluation, it is worth noting, against the claims of their supporters, that there is no evidence that policing strategies inspired by Broken Windows contributed to reducing crime. Though crime did go down during Bratton's tenure, it had already been going down since the late 1980s (Schneider 2014, 138–139)—as reminded by Michael Tonry (2011), in the 1990s, when crime was going down throughout the USA, 'everything worked', you could find evidence of 'success' of every policy, and of its opposite.[17]

Quite simply, while we certainly agree with the significance of inquiring the general hypothesis on the relation between environment and social dynamics—in abstract terms, the theory of atmospheric violence we will develop (see chapter 6) contributes to this inquiry—it is when it moves to building specific causal relation to transform the hypothesis into a general theory that Broken Windows loses explanatory power. In their original text, Kelling and Wilson remained on the level of suggesting hypothetical inferences. Let us see how:

> if the neighborhood cannot keep a bothersome panhandler from annoying passersby, the thief *may reason*, it is even less likely to call the police to identify a potential mugger or to interfere if the mugging actually takes place . . .
>
> But failing to do anything about a score of drunks or a hundred vagrants *may destroy* an entire community . . .
>
> But in cases where behavior that is tolerable to one person is intolerable to many others, the reactions of the others—fear, withdrawal, flight—*may ultimately make matters worse* for everyone, including the individual who first professed his indifference. (Kelling and Wilson 1982; our emphasis)

Thieves may feel empowered, failing to harass vagrants may destroy communities, withdrawal may make things worse: or they *may not*. While this may have opened to a precise inquiry of the conditions for these hypotheses to verify, Kelling and Wilson soon move to the normative dimensions by fundamentally assuming that those causal relationships have been proved once and for all; and they have not. The burden of evidence is inverted: while Broken Windows theory may have provided useful analytical lenses, it has been used as a normative guide despite an enormous amount of critical research that has shown those causal relationships are fundamentally wrong.

Also with regard to wider implications, Kelling and Wilson were relatively cautious in suggesting that, 'our crime statistics and victimization surveys measure individual losses, but they do not measure communal losses' (1982, 38). We certainly agree. Yet, the problem with their theory concerns the 'communal losses' that Broken Windows causes in the first place, exactly *by means of being successful*. Let us qualify. If we understand Broken Windows's quest for order as the reduction of a certain kind of visible signs of disorder, it is probably the case that the quality-of-life policies it inspired around the world have been for the most part successful, insofar as being able to generate, in certain parts of the city, an aesthetically and affectively pleasing 'sense of order'. This is confirmed by Kelling and Bratton's own defence of the theory: 'our experience suggests that, whatever the critics might say, the majority of New Yorkers, including minorities, approve of such police order-maintenance activities' (2015). They may surely be right, and they have polls supporting them—after all, populist, tough-on-crime rhetorics have been extremely successful in the last decades across the political spectrum, therefore their capacity to attract popular support should be no surprise. That the approach is popular, however, hardly shows it is desirable. If anything, it shows that it feeds on the powerful imaginary we already discussed—that of absolute security—and that it provides with a fitting aesthetic complement (see chapter 7). It is the urban violence of such an order, as discussed in this chapter, and further explored in the next two, that is of concern. What the reproduction of such a visible order does, in reality, is crystallising the underlying political economy discussed in this chapter, that is, the violence of urbanisation, unequally redistributing via the discrimination and criminalisation of (racialised) groups and minorities (Merrifield 2000; Schneider 2014; Jefferson 2016; Camp and Heatherton 2016). This is an unavoidable outcome of the conceptual basis that implicitly feeds Broken Windows, which presupposes the 'effects' a given situation has on abstract individuals, that is, homogeneous subjects without race, gender or class, that are assumed as reacting uniformly across the population. The outcome, unavoidably, is that of distributing *unequally* the burden—indeed the violence—of such a policy. The violence of urbanisation/policing has been clearly exemplified, moreover, by the critical literature that has exposed the political economic links among the 'return to the centre', gentrification and broken windows—in 1990s USA (idem) and now, in the USA (Smith et al. 2021) and beyond (Sclofsky 2021).

At the same time, it is the very success and persistence of Broken Windows, despite its inherent contradictions and the amount of evidence against it, that interests us. If we discount for a moment the false consciousness that may animate at least some of its advocates—after all, for some, it may just be a good way to maintain the racialised system of policing—it is worth questioning how is it possible that, despite the mass of counter evidence, many, including in the social sciences—its author and major executor included (Kelling and Bratton 2015)—still honestly believe that Broken Windows is effective against crime and that it is not structurally discriminatory. Rachel Herzing argues that Broken Windows seems to have taken on a 'magical life' of its own, as an all-purpose approach seemingly applicable to everything, regardless of its blatant inadequacy, countless times proven. It is a magic, she argues, that is deployed to 'dazzle and amaze—to demonstrate how the systems of subjugation actually protect us . . . The magic of policing rests in its ability to appear as the remedy to the very harm it maintains' (2016, 267). Broken Windows is compelling precisely because it works through untested causal relations: 'the construction of the broken windows theory constantly shifts among imagined, imaginary, possible and real arguments'.[18] It is for this reason that debunking it, and exposing the fallacies of its practices, is not sufficient, unless this is complemented by addressing the imaginary that feeds Broken Windows, and the way this articulates the desire and sense of security in the social field. This cautions us from the illusory temptation that debunking the false promises of actually-existing security is enough. In its deeply problematic way, Broken Windows offers a response to the perceptions of the 'visible signs of a city out of control' (Chesluk 2004), providing a *continuity of form*, in the face of its apparent contradiction, in the manner of the 'cruel optimism' of security described by Kathie Cox (2020; see chapter 4, Researching Urban Violence): the critique of security alone is unable to address such a demand.

A further argument, recalling the discussion developed in chapter 3, may provide another explanation for the 'resistance' of Broken Windows in the face of its failures and contradictions. The theory appears to sit at the intersection of two coexisting, and yet fundamentally different, paradigms: the (Hobbesian) 'zero tolerance' rhetoric and the (Foucauldian) managerial pragmatism (see chapters 3 and 7). The approach inspired strategies pointed at both paradigms: no tolerance for any minor incivility (because of its potential to generate mayhem), pragmatic management of minor crimes— through quality-of-life enforcement and predictive instruments (see chapter 8), 'crime is actively managed in New York City every day', argued Kelling and Bratton (2015). While certain events—and particularly terrorism, as we saw—can temporarily 'resolve' this coexistence, the inconsistency between zero tolerance and pragmatic management has puzzled several thinkers. It is easy to see the extent to which zero tolerance rhetorics appear as directly contradictory to the very task they seem to be pursuing in the first place. Michalis Lianos and Mary Douglas (2000) termed it the 'safety-paradox': the more the society is sought to be purified into a given normality, the more 'variations' from the norm will be singled out as impure, and dangerous—let one single window remain broken and order will be jeopardised. What is key here is not the logical impossibility of actually eliminating violence *in the future*, however, but the material and affective violence this very projection produces *in the present*.

Shifting the question in this way, we may see that, after all, populist rhetoric and pragmatic governmentality are not so incompatible as they appeared in the first place. In chapter 7 we will show to what extent this problematic coexistence is held together by reworking the other, 'Lockean' dimension of security, as the liberal 'right to be left alone' appears to be gradually reworked into a 'right to be free from fear', that is, a right to be at ease or, as we are to see, a right to be comfortable. The consequence is that security itself shifts towards an affective dimension—as we have started to discuss with the example of terrorism (see chapter 4, Researching Urban Violence), it is the very atmosphere of the urban to become what security increasingly seeks to *secure*. Prior to discuss these aspects more in depth in chapter 7, however, we need to introduce more precisely the notion of (urban) atmosphere and the violence thereof: this is next chapter's task.

Notes

1. Henri Lefebvre. 2014[1989]. "Dissolving city, planetary metamorphosis." This is the English version of the title of the article in which the expression 'planetarisation of the urban' first appears. Copyright © 2014 by Pion and its Licensors. Reprinted by Permission of SAGE Publications.

2. See www.ted.com/talks/robert_muggah_how_to_protect_fast_growing_cities_from_failing.

3. But see Feltran (2020) on how this construction is everything but monodirectional.

4. See also Agustin Cocola-Gant (2016) on short-term rentals as a 'battlefront' of gentrification.

5. Atkinson's argument is even more explicit in an interview at the *City Road Podcast*, available at https://cityroadpod.org/2020/05/25/alpha-city/.

6. See, more broadly, on the link between wilderness and the legacy of colonialist spatial development, Guernsey (2008) on British Columbia and Caprotti (2008) on Italy.

7. The central relation between colonisation and spatial development (and the violence therein) is also evident in the systematic imposition of Western/liberal forms of property over other systems of tenure—particularly over liminal, cultivated and common spaces—issues that have remained battlegrounds in shaping statecraft and urbanisation also in post-colonial contexts (e.g., Yiftachel 2009; Ghertner 2015).

8. In a seminar in 2009 (see Haraway 2015, 160, note 5).

9. Franciszek Chwałczyk (2020) has identified eighty (80!) alternatives to the Anthropocene.

10. 'Racial feralization' refers to 'an apocalyptic eschatology of regression and the unraveling of the species', and, Valayden argues, 'has now entered the realm of power as a way to problematize heterogeneous populations defined by their relation to global risks and urban agglomerations' (2016, abstract).

11. The experiment has been widely criticised since the subjects were seemingly prompted to behave in a certain way, that is, to play a certain kind of role, by the scientists (e.g. Banuazizi and Movahedi 1975; Le Texier 2019).

12. Nathan Glazer's quote particularly refers to the proverbial sight of graffiti in the New York subway. Since at least mayor John Lindsay (1971–1976), and particularly under Ed Koch (1978–1989), New York public authorities waged a veritable war against graffiti, implicitly, as well as often explicitly, framed as the 'cause' of the crisis the city underwent in the 1970s and 1980s (Huertas 2015).

13. This is directly suggested, referring more generally to hip hop, by RUN-DMC's Darryl McDaniels, when noting that, although it looked 'different to the civilised world . . . to everybody uncivilised it was the familiar thing, and that's why it worked' in *Hip Hop Evolution*, HBO (season 1, episode 3), 18 September 2016. See Pavoni (2021).

14. Granted, Kelling and Bratton (2015) argue that stop and frisk is completely distinct from Broken Windows, because the former is 'based on reasonable suspicion that a crime has occurred, is occurring, or is about to occur', while the latter, as we discussed, acts on the environment in which crime and incivility may develop. However, first, stop and frisk was in practice considered in New York to be an application of Broken Windows. Second, and more poignantly, decades of critique of stop and frisk have shown how its indiscriminate use was not oriented at preventing specific crimes, rather at creating an atmosphere of control hovering over certain specific groups—fundamentally, Black youths.

15. Kelling and Bratton (2015) argue that two recent randomized experiments do confirm some of their causal claims. While a specific discussion of these studies is beyond our scope, let us remind that studies that have argued the opposite count on the dozens—the 'scientific consensus' on the causality nexus is certainly not existing.

16. Again, Kelling and Bratton emphasise the uncontroversial quality of their notion of disorder by appealing to the 'broad consensus' it finds among the popula-

tion, an argument that assumes said consensus to be somehow self-sufficient data, independent from the imaginary of order which instead feeds it and was produced by zero tolerance rhetorics in the first place. Here's how they put it: 'far from being a divisive issue, concern about disorder brings people with different backgrounds together. They [the communities] know what disorderly behavior and conditions are, and they want something done about them' (2015).

17. Just a few years ago, Kelling, and Bratton (2015) were still advocating for Broken Windows in conservative *City Journal*, which has long been active in defending the theory, by reproducing the same argument: 'New York is a vastly safer place than it was 20 years ago'.

18. In the words of Wolf Bukowski. See https://www.youtube.com/watch?v=ovw6loFfOnE&ab_channel=AlegreEdizioniAlegreEdizioni (minute 20:00; our translation).

CHAPTER SIX

∿

Atmosphere

Stadtluft macht frei.[1]

Id, quod Corpus humanum ita disponit, ut pluribus modis possit affici, vel quod idem aptum reddit ad Corpora externa pluribus modis afficiendum, homini est utile; & eo utilius, quo Corpus ab eo aptius redditur, ut pluribus modis afficiatur, aliaque corpora afficiat, & contra id noxium est, quod Corpus ad hæc minus aptum reddit.[2]

The discussion on urban violence seems to be oriented by a common quest: the attempt to make violence visible, either through the inventory of its physical manifestations, the examination of its structural instantiations or the deconstruction of its discursive representations. In chapter 4, we showed that urban violence cannot be discussed without taking into account the way in which it is articulated in and through a specific imaginary coalescing at the intersection between security and the urban. In chapter 5 we maintained that, whether urban violence is to be an effective concept, such dimensions should be framed dynamically vis-à-vis urbanisation as a planetary process. How is such interspersion concretely actualised into the urban, however? How do the imaginary of urban violence and the violence of capitalist urbanisation take place in, shape, and are shaped in turn by, the affective infra-structure of everyday urban life?

In this chapter we provide answers to these questions via an infra-structural analysis of affective forces. In particular, we introduce the concept of urban atmospheric violence,[3] to explore the gaseous consistency urban violence takes in the contemporary city, often in the form of an asphyxiating force that debilitates urban bodies and their capacity to think, sense, imagine, move and live. While in chapter 7 we will take a genealogical approach to atmospheric violence by exploring the surfacing of the so-called society of comfort—understood as an aesthetic-juridical *dispositif* through which security, violence and the urban are articulated in the contemporary city—in this chapter we unpack its ontological and strategic value in relation to a material and not metaphorical understanding of breathing, a speculative effort that will require some theoretical elaboration. Building on the notion of affect as presented in the introduction and chapter 1, we begin by introducing the concept of atmosphere.

Atmosphere

A concatenation of affections that achieves a certain degree of consistency, a relatively constant rhythm of oscillation between composing and decomposing forces: this we define atmosphere. On the escort of the work on *Atmosphäre* by German scholars (e.g., Hermann Schmitz, Gernot Böhme, Peter Sloterdijk and Jürgen Hasse) and on *ambiance* by the French ones (e.g., Jean-François Augoyard and Jean-Paul Thibaud), the notion of atmosphere has gradually reached popularity also in the Anglophone world (e.g., Ben Anderson, Dereck McCormack, Steven Connor), where it has been processed through affect theory, integrating the previously dominant phenomenological nuance with a finer attention for the ontological emergence of the atmospheric condition. As we discussed, the notion of affect permits to explore the circulation of feelings and emotions in socio-natural configurations, removing ontologically the separation between subjects and objects, individuals and environment. This is not completely achieved by more traditional phenomenological approaches, which tend to leave unquestioned the unity of the subjects and their ontological independence from the atmosphere, still understood as something that lies in-between bodies, influencing social interactions accordingly. In this context there is often, moreover, a tendency towards a socio-cultural reductionism of the atmosphere—understood as an aesthetic, psychological and gnoseological phenomenon—which misses the fact that the atmosphere is an emergent configuration directly composed by the intra-actions of socio-natural bodies: not a pre-existent sphere (σφαῖρα) of vapour (ἀτμός) in which subjects are but a common breathing through which bodies become (see Anderson 2014; Philippopoulos-Mihalopoulos 2015; McCormack 2018; Pavoni 2018a; and, for recaps, Adey et al. 2013; Bille et al. 2015; Gandy 2017).

An ontological approach recognises that natural existence, being it social or biological, human or nonhuman (merely heuristic distinctions, it goes without saying) produces the atmosphere through which it unfolds: beings exist by entering in relations, that is, they become together by co-engineering their own atmosphere. In biological terms, the earth's atmosphere is the product of the co-respiration of vegetable life, which has transformed solar energy into oxygen up to the point that oxygen, overcoming the threshold of oxidation, did stabilise into the earth's atmosphere, allowing organisms to move from one fluid existence, water, to another, the 'atmospheric sea' of earthly cohabitation (Adey 2014a; Coccia 2019[2017]). If immersion in this atmospheric sea is the only possible condition of life—for the vast majority of species, at least—then the idea of a separation from the environment loses meaning, as Jakob von Uexküll (2010[1934]) already understood. The environment and the living produce each other, in a mutual interpenetration: atmosphere. The revocation of the individual-environment separation, and thus the notion of their entangled becoming or 'individuation', is a key premise of atmospheric thinking. It implies revoking, as Jean-Baptiste Lamarck already understood, the static evolutionary understanding of adaptation, which assumes the individual as changing vis-à-vis a fixed environment. 'We must begin with individuation'—wrote Gilbert Simondon—'with the being grasped at its centre and its relation to its spatiality and its becoming, and not by a realized [*substansialisé*] *individual* faced with a *world* that is external to it' (1992[1964], 310; emphasis in translation).

One always begins in the middle, as Gilles Deleuze never tired to stress. Beyond the individual-society dichotomy, then, we begin from the atmosphere and, more precisely, from the immanent tensions through which a given atmosphere 'holds together'. The tensional question, we saw it already (see chapter 1), is a particularly cogent one, and suggests an infra-structural way to think the immanent relation between an atmosphere and the bodies that compose it (no atmosphere without bodies, no bodies without atmosphere). This allows the response to a classic ontological question— 'what holds things together?'—without resorting to downward causality or structural determinism (cf. Deleuze and Guattari 2004[1980], 327). What holds things together, in this sense, is the immanent tension between its composing parts, tangible and intangible, humans and nonhumans. Further, the notion of infra-structure also helps to stress that an atmospheric depiction of reality entails neither separation nor fusion. Thinking atmospheres infrastructurally, as we are to see, overcomes the false dichotomy of atomism and organicism, eschewing the 'spatialisation' Henri Bergson lamented as regards modern thought[4]—without falling, however, into a homogeneous and flat confusion. Atmosphere is 'the space of mixture' in which bodies are entangled (not separated) without losing their singularity (not fused): 'to be mixed without being confused [from *cum* and *fusion*] means to share the same breath', the *pnéuma*, as the Stoics, the first thinkers of the atmosphere, called it (Coccia 2019[2017], 51). While obviously we are never isolated in this co-immersive condition, therefore, what we *hold in common* is not a homogeneous substance, as a Durkheimian view would hold, but rather, a rhythmical vibration that 'radiates' from situated bodies.

According to Peter Sloterdijk's Heideggerian elaboration, being-in-the-world means inhabiting-the-world, which in turn is nothing but a praxis of world-making (Sloterdijk 2007[1998]); and this occurs in the always co-constitutive coming together of humans and nonhumans, individuals and environments, a process that the mutual cannibalism of breathing makes explicit.[5] This requires foregrounding some kind of distinction between air and atmosphere (cf. Gandy 2017), with the latter emerging as a situated configuration of the former, at once produced and experienced, through breathing. Breathing, here, neither is a metaphor, nor refers simply to the 'act' of breathing. As Emanuele Coccia (2019[2017], 56) writes, breathing is something more than one of the activities of the living: 'it defines the consistency of the world', that is, it is an ontogenetic process whereby we co-produce the common as a space of co-mingling. This is literally a *commoning* that puts into question taken-for-granted notions of individuality, security and propriety, as well as boundaries between body, environment, matter and feelings (Brennan 2004; Ingold 2015).[6] Breathing together means, among other things, accepting the inevitable *contingency* of *contagion*, hence the realistic impossibility of absolute security.[7] Breathing is not something we have, but something we share and through which we become, as underlined by Roberto Esposito's etymological excavation on of the term *munus* (2009[1998]): *munus* simultaneously refers to gift, obligation and duty, and its positioning at the core of the notion of 'community' shows the back-and-forth, give-and-take relation of co-immunity and mutual vulnerability that ontologically grounds our being in common (see chapter 3). Understood in these terms, then the atmosphere is not something we enter as pre-formed individuals, but something we generate together by *ex-propriating* ourselves and becoming-with, as 'a fully transformative practise in which humans [and nonhumans, we add] find themselves fully immersed in the materiality of air' (Nieuwenhuis 2016, 504). What is breathing if not a process of incessant differentiation, inhaling and exhaling the world, adding and losing something, at each breath?[8]

Increasing pollution, tear gas and other chemical weapons, the planetary modification of the atmosphere due to climate change, a global pandemic tied to an airborne disease: we do not have shortage of events to become aware of the inherent danger that the ontological condition of breathing-together—i.e., being-in-an-atmosphere—entails. Breathing, increasingly, shows its quality as a quintessential *pharmakon*: simultaneously a *remedy*, what makes a common emerge, and thus a *remediation*, that is, the ongoing composition, adjustment and attunement to such a common;[9] and, at the same time, a *poison*, what threatens the common, whose members are thus exposed, simultaneously, to this ambiguous source of life and danger. Rafael Lozano-Hemmer captured this ambiguous condition with precision in *Vicious Circular Breathing*,[10] an installation consisting of a sealed, glass decompression chamber in which the visitors enter, one at a time, accepting the anxiety and the risk of breathing through the breath of the other visitors, which is kept in *vicious* circulation through a system of tubes, filters and paper bags. As curator John Hanhardt put it, this work 'makes tangible a resource we all share and need—the air we breathe', so that, by taking part, 'we give our bodies, our selves, to the risk and power of the intangible presence of the breath of life, but in sharing the breath of life, we open ourselves to the germs and bacteria in each other's bodies' (2013, 23–24).

Perhaps the reason of the 'forgetting of air' that Luce Irigaray (1999[1983]) famously diagnosed in Western thinking is dependent on the very capacity of air, through breathing, to overcome boundaries, problematise long-standing ontological dichotomies and question the immunitary paradigm on which Western political thinking is grounded. By prompting a shift towards a 'medial mode of being' that 'implies that the surrounding medium loses its object status' (ten Bos 2009, 77–78), atmospheric thinking unfolds a condition of living as *suspension*, being-in-the-atmosphere, that is, constantly having to 'attune' or 'acclimatise' to something else, with the consequence of radically putting into question long-held assumptions about notions such as decision, autonomy, causality, agency and freedom (Choy and Zee 2015). In a world of co-immersion, the certainties (from the Latin *cernere*, that is, 'to separate') that fed the project of modernity (see chapter 4) literally melt.

Once the ontological quality of atmospheres has been underlined, it is important to stress that the atmospheres of coexistence are not to be understood as being 'natural' or 'fixed', but rather socio-natural, processual and historical (Chakrabarty 2009). Being-in-the-atmosphere means attuning to its air-partitioning (Philippopoulos-Mihalopoulos 2016), and thus to its unequally enlivening or exhausting, empowering or debilitating, 'breathability', which in turn depends on the contingency of bodily encounters and the histories of structures, violence and power relations (e.g., Graham 2015). Historicising air: this is another key insight from atmospheric thinking (Adey 2014a), an important antidote against the fallacy of 'transparent immediacy'—i.e., the naïve realism presupposing that the 'the subject's contact with the real depends upon the erasure of the medium, which correlates and thereby obscures the relationship between subject and the world' (Grusin 2015, 131)—and a necessary step to move towards a properly atmo-political analysis.[11]

Emergent/Engineered

Not simply flat, symmetrical and spontaneous, therefore, atmospheres are both emergent *and* engineered: they emerge from the coming-together of bodies, but are simultaneously shaped by wider forces, structures and power relations (Philippopoulos-Mihalopoulos 2015, 129). Following the work of Buckminster Fuller, Sloterdijk suggests thinking about atmospheres as tensegrity structures, that is, structures that are held together by the co-tractions between their internal tensions: literally, infra-structures.[12] Just like a foam, the consistency of an atmosphere depends on the capacity to oscillate between rigidity, which decreases the resilient capacity of the foam to adapt to change, and flexibility, which decreases the internal cohesion of the foam, threatening dissolution (Sloterdijk 2008[2007]; see also Borch 2008; 2010). This rhythm, which provides the atmosphere with 'stabilisation through internal normative tensions', is what Sloterdijk terms the *nomotop*, that is, the affective and normative infrastructure of co-existence, a tensional force-field that holds the social together in the form of a mutually affecting co-traction among its bodies, via the functioning of customs, laws, rules, relations of production, language games, emotions, senses, institutions and habits (2006; Stewart 2011, 452; see also Pavoni 2018a, ch. 2). Attuning to an atmosphere means to be taken in power-structured orderings, shaped by emergent (contingent) and sedimented (historical) relations, and exposed to various degrees of tensional force and its inherent violence.

All of that, at the same time, melts into air. While atmospheres are always 'tuned' or 'dyed' in specific ways, thereby orienting and influencing—without determining—the way bodies move, breathe and live through them, this tuning normally fades into invisibility: 'atmosphere dissimulates itself as emerging and not engineered', presenting itself 'only as an emergence' (Philippopoulos-Mihalopoulos 2015, 129 and 145). A radical atmospheric thinking, therefore, aims to disarticulate experience from its reduction to the phenomenological, the subjective, the personal, the proprietary and the human dimension—that is, from the tendency to take senses as something we individually 'own', rather than a relational emergence resulting from an immersive condition to which we are attuning (Brighenti 2010a). Fear, enthusiasm, anxiety, boredom: these are not external emotions we subjectively feel, but rather affective relations through which we become by materially *breathing* them (see Brennan 2004; Ahmed 2004). In this regards, Dereck McCormack, in a perhaps schematic and yet useful way, distinguishes between 'affect (as a pre-personal field of intensity), feeling (as that intensity registered in a sensing body) and emotion (as that felt intensity expressed in a socio-culturally recognizable form)' (2008, 426). While atmospheres obviously tend to blur this distinction (Anderson 2009, 77), it is important to keep it in mind, since it avoids either collapsing atmospheres within the individual and subjective dimension, or reifying atmosphere into a sort of determinist mechanics of forces. At the same time, it also permits to keep a firm historical and geographical gaze fixed on the way urban atmospheres have surfaced, as a socio-political and existential question, especially in the colonial city and the nineteenth-century metropolis (see below and chapter 7). In this sense Brian Massumi, reflecting on the Deleuzian interpretation of Spinoza, offers an insightful way to grasp this interspersion between sensing and becoming, and the consequences, which we are to explore soon, in terms of the capacitation or debilitation of a body's power to act:

> a power to affect and be affected governs a transition, where a body passes from one state of capacitation to a diminished or augmented state of capacitation. This comes with the corollary that the transition is felt. A distinction is asserted between two levels, one of which is feeling and the other capacitation or activation. But the distinction comes in the form of a connection. This separation-connection between feeling and activation situates the account between what we would normally think of as the self on the one hand and the body on the other, in the unrolling of an event that's a becoming of the two together. (2011, 48; see also Deleuze 1968)

In the following pages we will explore this oscillation between the aesthetic and the affective dimensions of urban atmospheres, and particularly the way in which the aesthetic politics of urban security violently and unequally affects bodies and their capacity to act. To do so, however, it must be qualified that the fact that atmospheres are 'engineered', that the sensible is 'partitioned', that the urban is 'ordered'; should not be read as problem *per se*. Indeed, it is an unavoidable outcome of being-together. Socio-material relations are *never* simply flat, symmetrical and power-neutral. That there would be an authentic space, or authentic relations and practices—lying *beneath* social structures, norms, order and power relations—is a long-standing temptation of critical theory, and a dangerous one at that. While it is certainly crucial to analyse, criticise—and strive to overcome—a given status quo and its asymmetric order, it is extremely problematic to do so on the assumption that beyond would lie some kind of differential space (cf. Lefebvre 1974), vibrant matter (Bennett 2010) or enlivening disorder (Sennett 1992[1970]) that be emancipatory *per se* (for a critique of these tendencies, see Doel 1999; see also chapter 4). Even conflict, the favourite notion of critical political theory, is far from being self-evidently emancipatory or empowering—it is experienced by the majority of the world population as stressful, painful and dramatic (e.g., Mosselson 2019). Nonetheless, it is important to qualify that conflict cannot be surgically removed from the social, since pretending to do so is bound to reproduce it in increasingly uncontrollable, unequal and violent forms. As Jacques Rancière's reflection (1999[1995]) showed, and Machiavelli well before him, conflict is not a normative ideal that would paradoxically heal the social from its asymmetries and troubles: it is an ontological reality that cannot be eliminated and therefore must be *realistically* dealt with. We understand conflict, in other words, as a neither pathological nor positive, but rather physiological element of politics and urban life at large (cf. Lucchese 2004). After all, is not the more or less implicit yearning for a reality beyond power, class, order, the inverted, optimistic mirror of the Hobbesian projection?[13] A critique of the atmosphere, and thus of its violence, therefore, cannot stop to the dialectics of emergence and engineering. A third aspect must be introduced.

Excess

Besides ontologically co-engineered and immanently ordered, atmospheres are *structurally excessive*. From physics to philosophy and art, more than a century of visionary thinking has shown that reality is not simply coincident with itself, and that an 'actual' state of affair is always haunted by a 'virtual' cloud of potentialities which neither belong to the status of presence nor inhabit a temporal present—a cloud, that is, that does not exist and yet *insists* on the actual. Differently from the possible, which is by definition what is *not* real, this virtual, despite not being actual, is real: it has real effects on the actual. In other words, it is *material*: it 'haunts' the actual, intensively affecting the extensive, structurally excessive quality of the real (Deleuze 1991[1966]; Derrida 2006[1993]; DeLanda 2005; for a discussion see Pavoni 2018a, ch. 1). This conception jettisons, at the same time, an understanding of reality as either an absolute objective exteriority or an idealist subjective interiority. Beyond these equally problematic alternatives, reality is understood as a 'metastable' field of pre-individual potentialities that are always excessive vis-à-vis the historically contingent and power-structured configurations they take in each place and epoch. Stability, in physics, indicates a system of equilibrium in which forces are no longer in agitation. Metastability, instead, refers to a pre-individual field of intensities that is pregnant with becoming, an understanding we already encountered when exploring the *magmatic* quality of the radical imaginary (see chapter 4). An atmosphere is, accordingly, an emergent configuration that always carries an excess of potential, what in quantum physic parlance would be termed a cloud of probabilities—a potential that holds the atmosphere in a tensional, metastable equilibrium in turn. Not a metaphor, this reflection opens the possibility for a veritable chemistry of the social.[14] It is worth quoting Simondon (1992[1964], 300) at length:

> the individual is to be understood as having a relative reality, occupying only a certain phase of the whole being in question—a phase that therefore carries the implication of a preceding preindividual state, and that, even after individuation, does not exist in isolation, since individuation does not exhaust in the single act of its appearance all the potentials embedded in the preindividual state. Individuation, moreover, not only brings the individual to light but also the individual-milieu dyad . . . Thus, individuation is here considered to form only one part of an ontogenic process in the development of the larger entity. Individuation must therefore be thought of as a partial and relative resolution manifested in a system that contains latent potentials and harbors a certain incompatibility with itself, an incompatibility due at once to forces in tension as well as the impossibility of interaction between terms of extremely disparate dimensions.

Since atmospheres are emergent, there neither are pre-formed individuals preceding them, nor can a separation between individual and the environment be postulated. Since atmospheres are dynamic, they are metastable configurations whose life is marred with 'problems' of (de)stabilisation, which in turn trigger processes of individuation or, at the collective level, 'trans-individuation'. Through the latter, atmospheres may or may not gain a certain degree of temporary stability, or consistency, through repetition, habituation and institutionalisation. Yet, whatever the degree of stability that is achieved, a latent spatial and temporal excess always remains, a residue that is at the same time a reserve of potentiality. It is here that the potential for change resides and, we will argue, that contemporary atmo-politics is played out.

Let us sum up: atmospheres are emergent, ordered and excessive. First, an atmosphere is never external to the bodies immersed in it, but is composed by them as an emergent, co-engineered normativity. Second, atmospheric emergence is not a flat and frictionless process; rather, it is always tilted and tuned by historical, power-structured configuration of force and value. Third, atmospheres are always excessive to their *actual* configuration, harbouring a creative, 'normative power' that is excessive to the actual state of affair.[15] Neither stable nor unstable, neither chaotic nor structurally determined, atmospheres are metastable configurations in and through which structures, representations and power simultaneously take place and are displaced by all sorts of adjustments, fractures and frictions. Understanding the atmosphere as structurally excessive, therefore, allows for explaining how, even though atmospheres are always emergent *and* ordered in some way or another, change *does* occur—an explanation that avoids resorting to voluntarism, spontaneism, decisionism, downward causation or structural determinism. This is not a minor import, and it is somehow missing from other relational accounts such as Latour's and, to some extent, Sloterdijk's, whose agglutinative relational models tend to remove both structures and excess from the picture.[16] Atmospheres are in a state of metastable equilibrium, always ordered (engineered) in some way or another, and yet always simultaneously 'excessive' to that ordering. We insist on this point since it is particularly central to counter a certain tendency in social theory to understand the ordering of the social as always conditional on the suppression of excess. Instead, we stress that atmospheres are not relations emerging out of the neutralisation of the excess, but rather intensive spaces that overflow 'lived or conceived space-time' (Anderson 2009, 79), that is, affective configurations through which 'this excess, collectively yet autonomously' (Philippopoulos-Mihalopoulos 2013, 8) is rhythmically tuned (see Pavoni 2018a).

This understanding chimes with what Ben Anderson defines as affective life, namely a life that is 'imbued with relations of power' without being reducible to them (2014, 8). This notion, which resonates with the concept of vital materialism we developed above, synthetically ties together the threads of our discussion, by conveying the interspersion between the excessive dynamism of life (see introduction) and its atmospheric organisation. Anderson cautions against contemporary tendencies to celebrate the dynamism of affective life without considering the forms and structures that organise affect. We do strongly agree: as already observed, the excessive force of affective life is an ambiguous quality that should not be uncritically celebrated. We add, however, that it is exactly this dynamism, to the extent to which it overflows the organisation, to be the target of contemporary biopolitics, which aims to both foster it (e.g. logics of capitalisation, valorisation, eventification) and control it within desirable and safe thresholds (see Pavoni 2018a).[17] The excess, in a formula, is the *vitalism* of the atmosphere, as well as its biopolitical battleground.

Atmospheric Violence

While, to clarify our usage of the terms vitalism and vitality, we refer the reader to the introduction, we anticipate that in chapter 7 we will deal with the peculiar way in which the notion of urban life has been lately translated in global city charts, through the notion of 'liveability', where a narrow statistical definition of violence, unsurprisingly, is among the key indexes sanctioning the extent to which a city is more or less 'liveable'. In a sense, urban liveability is the antithesis of our concept of (urban) vitality, which refers to the excess potential any urban atmosphere holds, that is, its capacity for (trans)individuation in response to 'vital' problems and, therefore, its immanent potential to create norms. In the introduction we explained that, in our terms, vitalism has nothing to do with the essentialisation of life as an absolute value, as it is the case for various instances of contemporary, religious and secular vitalism. Instead, against these substantialist interpretations, we propose a notion of vital materialism that emphasises the 'vital', relational and creative tendency of life, that is, its potential to *exceed* itself: its 'dynamic livingness'. It is this reserve of potential that is depleted—literally 'devitalised'—when a social or biological body falls ill. Following the likes of Spinoza, Canguilhem, Villarreal and Rose, we proposed a concept of 'illness' understood as the weakening of a body's capacity for integration and transformation. If we apply this reasoning to the affective life of an atmosphere, a question of 'breathability' is foregrounded, one that is sociopolitical and ecological at once. An atmosphere is debilitated or devitalised, in our terms, when it becomes less 'breathable', that is, when its potential to become is reduced, or atrophied, at the biological, social, normative, sensorial and other levels.

This may depend principally on two factors. On the one hand, the degree of toxic pollution that may penetrate an atmosphere, for instance the particulate matter that fills the urban atmosphere at the bio-chemical level, poisoning the bodies and their capacity to breathe; or, for instance, the terror that fills post-colonial spaces of death (Taussig 1987), or the fear that Ingmar Bergman describes in Weimar Berlin, which 'rises like vapour from the cobblestones . . . like a pungent smell . . . a nerve poison, a slowly working poison, felt only as a quicker or slower pulse, or as a spasm of nausea'.[18]

On the other hand, it is the degree of saturation that a given atmosphere achieves for lack of variation, difference and change—that is, the suffocation caused by more or less oppressive homogenisation, from the stale air that suffocates migrants entrapped inside cargo containers or in the ship holds (see Marsi 2021), to the 'affective ankylosis' produced by racism (see below) or quality-of-life policing (see chapter 7). In chapter 9 we will draw some consequences from this reflection with respect to what Wolfgang Dietrich (2012) refers to as an 'energetic'—as opposed to 'moral'—notion of peace. In this section, instead, we bring together this atmospheric reflection with the notion of biopolitics (see chapter 3) in order to unpack what we define as atmospheric violence.

From CO_2, particulate matter and other forms of atmospheric pollution to SARS epidemics, atmospheric violence is literally a violence *of* and *through* the air. Sloterdijk (2016[2004]) situated the paradigmatic instance of what he termed the 'violence against the air' in the so-called second battle of Ypres, fought on April 22, 1915, where the 'phenomenon of unbreathable space' was explicitly pursued as a way to control and eliminate the enemy. Never a toxic gas had been used on such a scale like the German troops did on that day, with what will become notorious as mustard gas (or Iprit, from the name of the city around which the battle was fought). While Sloterdijk focuses on Western soil, however, it was the colony, as it is often the case, to provide the laboratory for the deployment of explicit forms of 'atmoterror'. Whether by the British in Palestine, French in Algeria or Italians in Ethiopia, colonising powers experimented with various strategies against the biological and moral consistency of the colonial atmosphere, from the strategic use of excessive violence as a 'show of force' to intimidate the colonised, to the direct use of lethal gases to asphyxiate them. Illan Rua Wall (2021, 103–104), for instance, analysing police manuals, shows how British tactics aimed at modulating the atmosphere of urban protest migrated from post-WWII Hong Kong (where in turn they had been influenced by classic crowd theorists such as Le Bon) to the 1980s UK, in response to the 'growing racial and industrial unrest' that Great Britain was experiencing at the time. In this context, such 'atmo-technics' played the same saturating and atrophying role as in the colony, namely: 'the intention to trump any desire for change' (idem, ibidem). Likewise, Pierpaolo Ascari reminds how the French colonial territories, from urban planning to policing, where understood as 'champs d'experience, that is, laboratories where to experiment with solutions to the problems of political, aesthetic and social order that were emerging in France' (2020, 95; our translation). Western logics of governance have been directly shaped by the 'matrix' of power, the imaginary and the atmo-technics that unfolded in the colony (Mignolo 2017).

In her powerful work, Christina Sharpe (2016) similarly defines the violence of what she terms antiblackness as a 'total climate', which has sedimented from slavery onwards as a pervasive 'hostile weather' that continues to affect and asphyxiate the black body. As she explains, following Fanon, this weather 'is not the specifics of any one event or set of events that are endlessly repeatable and repeated, but the totality of the environments in which we struggle' (idem, 138), 'the archives of breathlessness', that is, that debilitate black bodies all the way into contemporary struggles, what Fanon (1963[1961]) himself had termed 'atmosphere of violence', endured and sensed by the black body even when not explicitly actualised, or consciously experienced. No other than Thomas Hobbes already emphasised this aspect of violence when comparing the war of the state of nature to weather:

> For WARRE, consisteth not in Battell onely, or the act of fighting; but in a tract of time, wherein the Will to contend by Battell is sufficiently known: and therefore the notion of Time, is to be considered in the nature of Warre; as it is in the nature of Weather. For as the nature of Foule weather, lyeth not in a showre or two of rain; but in an inclination thereto of many dayes together: So the nature of War, consisteth not in actuall fighting; but in the known disposition thereto, during all the time there is no assurance to the contrary. All other time is PEACE. (2002[1651], ch. XIII)

If, according to Hobbes, the atmosphere of peace and tranquillity will have to be produced by the State through security, it is especially post-colonial critique that allows the reversal of this equation. Kristen Simmons (2017), for instance, describes the atmosphere of violence that the 'US settler state' produces within the Oceti Sakowin (Great Sioux Nation), in the context of the recent events surrounding the project for, and resistance against, the Dakota Access Pipeline (DAPL). As she writes,

> settler atmospherics are the normative and necessary violences found in settlement—accruing, adapting, and constricting indigenous and black life in the U.S. settler stat . . . Our attunement to settler atmospherics . . . can be pathologized as anxiety, paranoia, or conspiracy in an atmosphere of uncertainty and half-knowing. At Oceti Sakowin, too, we experienced various suspensions: of time, bodies, affects. Anticipation of state violence became a rhythm, with constant low-flying helicopters, floodlights, and a large militarized police presence creating a tension that settled deep into muscles.

At times, this may outburst by literally poisoning the air, as in the case of so-called Non-Lethal or Less-Lethal Weapons such as tear gas, that can be paradoxically deployed in urban contexts, though forbidden in warfare under the Geneva Convention (Feigenbaum 2017). A particularly pernicious instance is the Israeli use of Skunk—a stinking liquid—against Palestinian protestors in the Occupied Territories. This weapon of 'olfactory violence', as Jean-Thomas Tremblay and colleagues put it (2023), is one instance of a series of 'less-lethal loopholes' that are deployed to circumvent national and international regulations, as well as to provide a 'less violent' image of police action, reproducing 'the continued fiction that riot control agents are safe' (Feigenbaum 2015, 109). Skunk's allegedly non-lethal and 'eco-friendly' quality—as the makers remind—makes it adaptable to all sorts of contexts, from the Occupied Territories, to Black Lives Matter demonstrations or the management of the US-Mexico border, as a technological solution to the legal and ethical troubles of crowd control.[19] On the one hand, the marketing of Skunk capitalises on a reductionism we extensively discussed, that is, the reduction of (urban) violence to visible and measurable events (quintessentially, death and murder), in this way 'perpetuat[ing] a human rights framework wherein deaths are the only significant statistic, and other, less quantifiable modes of trauma and debilitation become simultaneously obscured and revalued as techniques of "psychological deterrence"' (Tremblay et al. 2023).[20] On the other hand, its 'atmospheric' scope, the fact of apparently affecting a crowd's air, its smell, rather than its bodies, provides the impression of not being actually violence. 'It is precisely this insensitivity to the truly debilitating power of smell', Marijn Nieuwenhuis notes, 'which seems to have granted Skunk such popularity that now US law enforcement agencies are also interested' (2015). Smell, however, belongs to an atmosphere and therefore materially affects the bodies that constitute—and breathe through—it. While it is presented, allegedly, as neither lethal nor toxic, Skunk's effect is indeed remarkable, both aesthetically and morally, as its disgusting stench is said to persist for days, even months, with obvious consequences in the personal and social lives of the victims, and the breathability of the everyday atmospheres they inhabit.[21] Not only is this 'atmospheric' form of violence pervasive, moreover, but also further reproduces, and inscribes on bodies, a long colonial and post-colonial history of olfactory racism (Reinarz 2014; Kettner 2020; Philippopoulos et al. 2023). Such olfactory violence, together with other allegedly less-lethal tools like acoustic weapons (i.e., long-range acoustic devices), water cannons, disorientation devices, rubber bullets and the like, as well as associated practices, including that of the Israeli forces shooting to maim, are pernicious instances of the 'right to maim' Jasbir Puar compellingly explores as 'part of a biopolitics not of disability alone but a biopolitics of debilitation', emphasising the notion of debilitation 'because it foregrounds the slow wearing down of populations instead of the event of becoming disabled' (2017, xiii-xiv). A similar reflection can be made as regards the debilitating effect of 'psychological deterrence' produced by recent anti-protest legislation such as the UK Government's Police, Crime, Sentencing and Courts Act 2022, where the disrupting noise generated by protesters is given a particular prominence, or the Italian 'anti-rave' decree.[22] 'Atmospheric governance', as Nieuwenhuis suggests, 'has made it difficult to disentangle where life/nature ends and law/culture begins' (2018, 88). As we are to see more in detail in the next chapter, these regulations, albeit crafted with the stated intent to limit violent protests, are a telling instance of what we term atmospheric violence. In a not so dissimilar way from so-called 'less-lethal' weapons, they both allow for discretionary (and often violent) crowd control, as well as generate a climate of anxiety and deterrence on those willing to exercise their own right to protest—that is, they have a debilitating effect on the exercise of this very right—due to the harsh and disproportionate sentences they threaten.

Moving beyond these examples, however, what we are interested in stressing here is that the notion of atmospheric violence is not only confined to these more or less explicit instances of 'atmospheric governance', but can rather be understood as a way to explore the affective, infra-structural unfolding of urban violence at large. Foucault had already observed that governmentality is an organisation of power that does not deal with the abstract subjects of law or the individual bodies of discipline, but rather with the relational dimension of the population, which is inextricable from its environment or milieu, what he defines as 'the medium of an action and the element in which it circulates' (Foucault 2007[2004], 21). As Anne Sauvagn explains, distinct from disciplinary 'moulding', this ushers in a non-hylomorphic logic of 'modulation', which 'consists in substituting the abstract confrontation of matter and form with a new analysis of form, understood as intensive variation of forces and materials, as information, that supposes that the existence of a system in metastable equilibrium can be individuated' (apud Hui 2015, 77; see also Deleuze 1992[1990] and chapter 3).[23] This is consistent with the ontological presupposition that informs neoliberalism, whose concern, at least theoretically, are not individuals but processes of individuation. The 'normal body' of neoliberalism, in the words of Peter Cryle and Elizabeth Stephens (2017, 354), 'is not the standardized body but the flexible body, the one best able to adapt to constant change to manage fatigue and maintain fitness'. Evidently, this means that that 'individuation . . . is not to be understood as liberatory, in opposition to the violence of enforced homogenisation. Individuation also allows subjects to be held personally responsible for their ability to adapt to their social conditions' (idem, 357).

In this sense violence, as a weather, recalling Sharpe's suggestion, does not (always) result from an explicit violation of some kind of individual immunity, but more often from the seemingly *unavoidable* necessity each body has to attune to, and to breathe through, a violent atmosphere. A necessity, it goes without saying, with respect to which the possibilities of, capabilities for, and modalities of acclimatisation are highly unequal. Thus understood, the affective materialisation of the social imaginary we discussed in chapter 4 becomes more apparent, as a diffuse and pervasive atmosphere in which we all, differently and with different consequences, have to breathe through.[24] It is in this sense that atmospheric thinking provides a further, affective dimension to Foucault's attention to the milieu. Moreover, it provides a complement to the rigidity notions such as structural or symbolic violence betray, allowing to account for the less obvious, more surreptitious ways through which violence circulates, flows and sediments within and through bodies. In other words, it allows one to capture violence's infra-structural unfolding in the current urban condition by exposing its *neutralising* and *chronic* effects vis-à-vis the vitality of urban atmospheres.

The concept of atmospheric violence gains relevance in this sense, insofar as it expands the analysis to forms of violence where notions of causality, intentionality and agency are not obvious, and which do not take place in specifically identifiable locales. While structural violence—which does engage with these problems—is surely crucial for understanding atmospheric violence, the latter is meant to challenge the former's bias towards causality, which often emerges in accounts of the violence produced by the State, Capital, Neoliberalism and so on. Atmospheric violence opens up to more subtle forms of violence that surface as planetary processes, structures and imaginaries frictionally materialise, ordering and disordering at the same time, into the affective fabrics of the urban (cf. Arboleda 2020). Calling on McCormack, our attempt is not to jettison the value of 'structural' investigations, but that of complementing them with a focus on 'a range of more-than-human processes and relations while also remaining attentive to how these processes and relations are potentially sensed in moving bodies' (McCormack 2008, 414). For instance, the way in which a normative imaginary of how the city should be—one that is institutionalised via law, security and police—becomes a pervasive, phantasmatic atmosphere that pervades the urban, providing a repertoire of violent narratives, discourses, regulations and practices in which everyone is immersed and that can be actualised into the urban everyday in all sorts of ways. Thinking violence atmospherically allows one to eschew deterministic readings and to consider urban violence, to paraphrase again Austin, 'as a "population level" problem that we must come to recognize *all* persons being entangled-with to a greater or lesser degree' (2023, 107; emphasis in original; see below).

This pervasiveness, and the corollary necessity to acclimatise as if in a condition of 'suspension',[25] captures precisely the contemporary condition, in which violence, from CO_2 to toxic waste, from hurricanes to 'quality of life' policing, from systemic racism to austerity politics, generates a socio-biological pollution one must breathe through nonetheless. Daily breathing in an increasingly toxic atmosphere is evidently debilitating, from lethal diseases such as cancer or Covid-19, to psycho-affective pathologies such as anxiety, stress (on the rise in urban society, cf. Brighenti and Pavoni 2019) and depression (Stiegler 2016[2015]; Lovink 2019b). Debility is 'already here', Puar writes, 'in neoliberal, biomedical, and biotechnological terms, the body is always debilitated in relation to its ever-expanding potentiality' (2017, 13; cf. Pasquinelli 2015). Under neoliberalism, she continues, 'health itself can then be seen as a side effect of successful normativity' (2017, 13): the calls to sacrifice lives in order to maintain a high level of productivity during the pandemic are a macabre instance of just that.

In a wholly other context Frantz Fanon (1965[1959], 65), whose atmospheric work we delve deeper into atthe end of this chapter, already captures this pervasive, all-encompassing quality, when describing the 'atmosphere of violence' in the French-occupied Algeria:

> There is not occupation of territory, on the one hand, and independence of persons on the other. It is the country as a whole, its history, its daily pulsation that are contested, disfigured, in the hope of a final destruction. Under these conditions, the individual's breathing is an observed, an occupied breathing. It is a combat breathing.

Suvendrini Perera and Joseph Pugliese, taking inspiration from this passage, explore the relation between violence and breathing in order to account for the way state violence, at the 'somatechnical' intersection between technologies and bodies, turns individuals to the state of expendable bodies, whose political life is reduced to the bare struggle for survival: 'combat breathing names the mobilisation of the target subject's life energies merely in order to continue to live, to breathe and to survive the exercise of state violence', whose 'logic is predicated on ensuring that the subject cannot begin to expend their energies in resisting, contesting or subverting the power of the state' (2011, 1–2). Our approach widens this notion in two senses, adding to their necropolitical lens an attention to the everyday biopolitics of atmospheric violence; and expanding beyond the seemingly purposeful logic of state violence towards a more diffuse and less unidirectional understanding of violence that 'flows like a viscous plasma around us all' (Austin 2023, 120), not causally stemming from institutions, although often being reified and reproduced by them. It is also the atmospheric violence that is imbricated in the seemingly more mundane 'patterns of undramatic attachment and identification' (Berlant 2011, 100) that we are interested in highlighting, that violence nested in the ordinary infrastructure of life, which slowly and unequally suffocates urban bodies in their lungs, gestures, habits.

Atmospheric violence is also inspired by the emphasis on 'slowness' that has been, if differently, at the centre of two recent contributions, by Rob Nixon and Laurent Berlant. Nixon's slow violence is that 'violence that occurs gradually and out of sight, a violence of delayed destruction that is dispersed across time and space, an attritional violence that is typically not viewed as violence at all' (Nixon 2011, 2). Nixon intended primarily to emphasise the violence of environmental devastation and climate change, an 'incremental and accretive' violence whose temporality is slow, whose aesthetic is unspectacular, and whose 'calamitous repercussions pla[y] out across a range of temporal scales' that escape linear explanations (idem, ibidem). At the same time, atmospheric violence further problematises the 'invisibility' of slow violence, following Thom Davies's observation (2019) to not fetishise it, rather asking 'out of sight to whom?' Slow violence such as toxic pollution, for instance, is quite 'visible' to its victims. While we agree and second Davies's suggestion of 'slow observations' as an ethnographic practice attuned to the ambiguous temporality and 'deferred causalities' of slow violence, atmospheric violence helps to take the question of invisibility not literally: often this and other forms of violence are perfectly apparent, and yet, their being part of an atmosphere may make so they are not perceived and understood as violence (see also de Leeuw 2016; Davies et al. 2017; Cahill and Pain 2019).

Where Nixon's concept makes the political and toxic materiality of the atmosphere of everyday breathing explicit, Laurent Berlant addresses a violence that, neither belonging to an oppressive order nor to an anarchic disorder, pertains to the infrastructure of the *ordinary* everyday. The ordinary, in a nutshell, is the way things go (cf. Stewart 2007), the way reality flows, synched into everyday routines, power-structured relations, socio-technical assemblages, affective patterning, as an emergent wavelength (e.g., Pavoni 2011) through which urban atmospheres are *affectively tuned* and *aesthetically sensed* in more or less enduring, empowering or debilitating ways. The ordinary is the daily 'activity of reproducing life', the everyday process of 'getting by, and living on, where the structural inequalities are dispersed, the pacing of their experience intermittent, often in phenomena not prone to capture by a consciousness organized by archives of memorable impact' (Berlant 2007, 759). According to Berlant, the increasingly precarious existence under neoliberal condition takes shape among the ruins of the post-WW2 imaginary of a 'good life' that, despite having crumbled since the neoliberal turn of the 1980s, still shapes, orients and colours our everyday urban experience, structuring the world *in absentia*, with its promises now rationally and realistically dissolved, and yet still lingering in the air, with its affective attachment still colouring the ordinary atmosphere of coexistence even if its contents are no longer believed, nor rationally believable (cf. Fisher 2014). As a result, the everyday activity of reproducing life all too often unfolds as, Margrit Shildrick (2015) caustically put it, 'living on, not getting better', that is, a daily 'hanging on' and 'wearing out' that characterises the precarious life under neoliberalism, where bodies are slowly depleted in physical, normative, affective sense, as they go about in their everyday effort to keep afloat, in their everyday quest to *adapt* (see Stiegler, Barbara 2019).[26]

Atmospheric violence, in this sense, may be seen as the gaseous outcome of the structures' turbulent instantiation: if planetary urbanisation and urban imaginaries alike always materialise through frictions, then atmospheric violence is the toxic by-product of these frictions, unequally affecting urban bodies as they are forced to flexibly cope with, and adapt to, this everyday turbulence.[27] Surely, violence can outburst in all its manifest evidence, actualising its structural fractures—take, for instance, the case of the death of Paul Alphonse and the other Aboriginal deaths in custody described by Sherene Razack (2011), or the cases of Eric Garner in 2014 and George Floyd in 2020, whose death by literal suffocation triggered a wave of global protests under the slogan 'I cannot breathe'. Yet, these deaths are only the most brutal—and consequential—actualisations of a pervasive violence that is experienced, along racial, gender, sex and class lines, on a daily basis, in neither spectacular nor punctual way, as the violence of *having to* acclimatise, unavoidably so, to an atmosphere that, in turn, is normalised and legitimised as a commonsensical, ordinary background. As the uneventful and *ordinary* violence of everyday breathing in unequally toxic atmospheres 'in which certain bodies are psychometrically forced to suffer from "saturated air" and "dry air", while others delight in more hospitable milieux of "clean air'" (Nieuwenhuis 2016, 505). Challenging the reductive equation we saw already, between violence and death, Berlant refers to this process of wearing out as *slow death*, namely as a *chronic*, endemic, gaseous violence 'in which structural conditions are suffused through a variety of mediations, such as predictable repetitions and other spatial practices that might go under the radar or, in any case, not take up the form of event . . . Slow death . . . is neither a state of exception not the opposite, a mere banality, but a domain where an upsetting scene of living is revealed as interwoven with ordinary life' (2011, 101–102).[28]

It should be by now clear then the 'atmospheric' quality of violence is no mere metaphor or terminological redundancy. Rather, it is an epistemological lens that provides concrete instruments to explore the ontology of violence beyond the categories of repression, subjection, ideology, domination, as well as beyond the deterministic causality of structural violence, by looking at the gaseous consistency of urban violence as an atmospherics that percolates through the urban, differently but equally weighting on bodies and their thinking, imagining, moving and sensing through the city. Breathing differently, struggling to breath, in this sense becomes an inevitable fact of life as well as a platform from which other forms of violence might actualise.

It is in this respect that Achille Mbembe's suggestion is particularly valuable. Writing at the beginning of the Covid-19 pandemic, Mbembe suggested that breathing should be thought 'beyond its purely biological aspect, and instead as that which we hold in-common', calling for a universal right to breathe. 'As that which is both ungrounded and our common ground', he continues,

> The universal right to breathe is unquantifiable and cannot be appropriated. From a universal perspective, not only is it the right of every member of humankind, but of all life. It must therefore be understood as a fundamental right to existence. Consequently, it cannot be confiscated and thereby eludes all sovereignty, symbolizing the sovereign principle par excellence. Moreover, it is an originary right to living on Earth, a right that belongs to the universal community of earthly inhabitants, human and other. (Mbembe 2020)

What is still needed for our reflection on atmospheric violence is a more explicit accounting for its peculiarly *urban* quality, vis-à-vis the aesthetic-affective infra-structure of urban modernity. With respect to the urban, we believe this can be analysed by exploring the *explication* of the aesthetic and affective materiality of urban everyday life, that is, the way in which the common spaces of coexistence have simultaneously become more explicit *and* have been produced (via a series of novel *savoirs* and techniques and technologies) as the battlefield of a novel form of environmental power, at the intersection of the fields of security, marketing, design and politics at large. What Matthew Gandy refers to as the 'tension between the role of atmospheres as a focus of political or scientific contestation and the presence of tangible atmospheres in everyday life' (2017, 364), a tension that, as we are to see, gradually unfolds in the urban context from the nineteenth century onwards. What we are particularly interested in is how this process has been accompanied by a particular *apparatus* (a material-discursive set of practices, laws, ideas, technologies, etc.) shaping everyday life in the city, what Wall terms the 'sense of order' (2021), that is, the silent background of sense-perception—the aesthetic-affective infrastructure—that shapes without determining urban everyday life. While obviously any socio-natural formation is characterised by a process of organisation and by an accompanying set of senses and affects, as for instance explored by Giddens vis-à-vis ontological security, what is particularly important in this case is the gradual amplification of an apparatus of acclimatisation, so to speak, that is, an atmo-politics in which regulations (e.g., quality of life, *decoro*), technologies (e.g., ambient computation) and the strategies of aesthetic capitalism at large, converge in shaping directly the atmospheric ordering of the city, with dynamics of valorisation and debilitation which are in need of dissection. This is what the next chapter sets out to do.

Researching Urban Violence:
Colonial Atmospheres of Violence

To exemplify ways to research urban violence atmospherically, we now briefly engage with the explorations of the 'atmosphere of violence' developed by Frantz Fanon, through two of his most famous examples.

Without a veil, the Algerian woman in the European metropolis finds herself 'naked', wrote Fanon in his controversial essay, *Algeria Unveiled* (1965[1959]). Therefore, she is forced to reconfigure her way of thinking, sensing and moving by managing the violent encounter with a panoply of affects (exhilaration, shame, pride, fear, etc.) that have been released from the veiled structure of the 'traditional' city. A metastable situation, a 'new' urban *problématique*, which the woman is prompted to temporarily 'solve' through a process of individuation, that is, by becoming a different formation of body, clothes and movement in space, so that the veil may end up being reconfigured in this novel assemblage, from a tool of restraint, or even oppression, to one of resistance, or even defiance. Fanon's example shows how thinking race, gender, class and other socio-political asymmetries through an atmospheric gaze allows the recognition of them as something more than a symbolic violence (injected on neutral bodies by language, culture and ideology) or structural violence (resulting from socio-economical inequalities), but also as a form of atmospheric violence that poisons, across space and time, the air of urban coexistence that everyone has to breathe through, and acclimatise to. 'Thinking atmosphere racially', Renisa Mawani (2019) suggests, enables the understanding of race not only 'as biology, corporeality, or ideology' but rather as 'a regime of power that works ontologically and epistemologically', that is, 'as an affective movement, a force rather than a thing, a *current* that reconstitutes and reassembles itself in response to its own internal rhythms and to changing social and political conditions', and which sediments into the 'rhythms and habits of history', producing long-standing, calcified, more or less suffocating rhythms and patterns of habituation and acclimatisation.[29] With this approach, to be sure, the critiques of the symbolic and structural violence of racism do not lose their value; yet, they are complemented by an attention to the present materiality of the aesthetic-affective infrastructure of racism and the way it orients, shapes and wears out bodies, regardless of their conscious acceptance, or refusal, of racist ideology (see Saldanha 2006). Austin, we saw it already, similarly proposes to understand violence as a viscous substance that is not simply processed, rationally or representationally, by individuals, but rather flows between and through them, humans and nonhumans alike, as a dense imaginary that is affectively felt on bodies. Focusing on the use of torture, through a series of empirical examples and interviews, he shows 'how practices of violence are embedded at a distributed ontological level through the historical accumulation of (popular) cultural, textual, technological and other epistemic objects' (2023, abstract; see also Austin 2016; 2017). 'That process of accumulation', he continues with reference to Latour, has generated a '"reserve, a reserve army, an immense territory" of violence' whose 'effects are differentially felt by each and every person and in each and every situation that person may find themselves' (2023, 116). This is all the more evident as we move to the second example, set in colonial Algeria.

The bodies of the colonised move slowly in the colonial city, Fanon writes in *The Wretched of the Earth* (1963[1961]). The colonial atmosphere is thick with a sedimented archive of violence that slowly poisons them, that is felt as a persistent mood of suspicion, the feeling of being constantly out of place, in the wrong place, shaping their perceptual and proprioceptive habits into a stressful contraction. The colonised body moves through the colonial city as if walking at high altitude: shortness of breath, dizziness, lower threshold of fatigue. In this condition, with its toxic saturation of stress, anxiety and pain, the colonised body struggles to breathe, her breathing becomes 'combat breath-ing'. This 'atmosphere of violence' is produced by a conjunction of violent practices, discourses, regulations, which are embedded in the space-times of the city, encompassing gestures, attitudes, perceptions and, in general, stifling the socio-biological 'breathability' of the urban.[30] By reading (the violence of) racism atmospherically, the focus shifts from representation to capacitation, from regimes of discourse to matter-discourse constellations.[31]

Fanon spoke elsewhere of an 'affective ankylosis' (Fanon 1970[1952]), a term that effectively expresses the calcifying effect of atmospheric violence on the habits of thinking, perceiving and feeling. This ankylosis debilitates the capacity 'to be affectively open to the difference and becoming of the lived body'—our *conatus*, that is—as Alia Al-Saji writes (2014, 139), in the sense of atrophying one's ability to see and think otherwise (see also Dodd 2009). Violence is not merely linear, causal, unilateral. It can, and does, lin-ger over the urban as a pervasive atmosphere that everyone is 'entangled-with to a greater or lesser degree' (Austin 2023, 107). In this sense, atmospheric violence may also be said to be 'breathed through' by police officers or racist subjects, when they are prompted towards drawing 'automatic' reaction or unthought correlations—for instance by actualising racist correlations and violent practices without hesitation. This resonates with that 'incapacity to think' that Donna Haraway describes as regards Hannah Arendt's reflection on Adolf Eichmann, where the banality of evil corresponds to this 'surrender of thinking', that is, an incapacity to think otherwise, to let in hesitation and ambivalence, 'to make present to himself what was absent', to be able to respond, that is, to be response-able (2016, 35–36).

This is a peculiar instance of that suffocation that atmospheric violence produces on bodies. As Austin observes, 'if we are already trapped by a set of asubjective relations that enforce that kind of thoughtlessness upon us, the possibility of *choosing* to escape those relations is severely limited' (2021, 24; emphasis in original). Elsewhere, following classic studies on police theory and training, Austin (2023) notes that police officers tend to make judge-ments that are neither deductive nor inductive, but more precisely abductive (cf. Peirce 1929), that is, based on a repertoire that is mostly unconscious, drawn from by inference, guessing, unthought reaction, automatic correla-tion, and which derive from all sorts of sources, from popular culture to training manuals. Obviously, this move is not to eliminate distinctions be-tween the violence that is endured and the violence that is perpetrated, but rather to zoom in on the a-subjective breeding ground out of which (urban) violence emerges, in order to think strategically about ways to minimise its occurrence and effects.[32] For instance, this 'materialist' approach shows, as Al Saji (2014, 139) observes, why 'ideals of postracial colour-blindness do not overcome but rather repeat and confirm . . . racist disavowal'. The same happens with romantic ideals of urban multiculturalism since, one the one hand, to presuppose that there is no difference, or that difference *does not count*, means to pretend that there is no aesthetic field already titled by power structures and affective infrastructures—it means, in other words, to fall once again into the fallacy of transparent immediacy; on the other hand, this removal of difference is an idealised abstraction that overlooks the fact that we are all immersed in atmospheric violence, materially so, and this is a condition that must be challenged from within, rather than simply erased through wishful thinking. Dealing with a 'racialised assemblage' (Weheliye 2014), 'means that antiracist practice needs to be more than a discursive or cognitive intervention' (Al-Saji 2014, 142)—more precisely, it must address the dense materiality of the urban atmosphere and its debilitating effects on the way bodies move, sense, breathe.[33] Evidently, this is a material and bodily engagement that cannot be captured, and overcome, via dialectics of recognition, critique of ideology and practices of revelation. It rather requires to 'find modes of intervention that work through affect, aesthetics, emotion and technology and so tackle the drivers of violence *on their own asubjective terms*' (Austin 2021, 27; emphasis in original).

This is implicitly suggested in the 'atmospheric materialism' of Fanon. Ernesto Che Guevara once argued that in the struggle of liberation there are two key 'subjective conditions' that need be achieved by the oppressed population: there must be consciousness of the necessity of revolutionary change, *as well as* of its possibility (see Lowy 1970). Fanon provides an atmospheric complement to this suggestion: not simply a subjective consciousness, what triggers the revolutionary moment is the attainment of a critical tipping point that is materially felt on the bodies—a 'revolutionary atmosphere', as Karl Marx (1978[1856], 577) once put it. The infra-structural violence of colonial power requires more than being rationally understood as oppressive and unjust. Its injustice must be collectively felt on the very materiality of bodies as a toxic, unbreathable atmosphere (cf. Mezzadra 2013). 'When we revolt', as one of Fanon's most famous quotes goes, 'it's not for a particular culture. We revolt simply because, for many reasons, we can no longer breathe' (apud Ros 2014). When this threshold is reached, when people find themselves in a bottleneck, the *atmospheric violence* of the colonial city becomes at once absolutely tangible and thus no longer bearable.[34] By gathering in the streets and the squares, by occupying the urban space, the colonised bodies begin to challenge and disrupt the aesthetic-affective infrastructure of colonial order, both in the phenomenological contingency of their actual occupation, and vis-à-vis the history of violence inscribed on the bodies and spaces of the city

(Bhabha 1994; Chakrabarty 2000; Ascari 2020). By doing so, writes Fanon, the colonised realises that the colonial separations, and the 'theory of individualism' that informs them, are false. This is not only an intellectual realisation, however: it is a corporeal one, performed through the bodily experience of 'becoming common'.[35] A process of trans-individuation thus ensues: through this experience, the bodies undergo a transformation, from fearful and disciplined individual bodies, to an empowered and defiant becoming-common.[36]

Recalling what has been argued in chapter 1, the latent excess that any atmosphere harbours also includes the violence that is excessive to any ordering, and which provides a reserve of potentiality that has the capacity to shatter the apparatus through which a given infra-structural violence is held in place. As Illan Rua Wall (2021, 180; emphasis in original) puts it,

> when Fanon describes it as an *atmosphere* of violence he points to the way in which violence seems to be hanging in the air. He identifies a latency, potentiality or virtuality of violence. It is 'operative' in the sense that it shapes the capacity of those within the atmosphere to act. The 'atmosphere of violence' increases the potentiality of the colonisers over the colonised, but at the same time it increases the potentiality of the colonised to overthrow the colonisers and being effected by the changing situation.

It is, in other words, a vast, ambiguous, 'plasmatic reserve of violence [that] risks flowing into all domains of life, irrelevant their institutional configuration, if circumstances present themselves appropriately' (Austin 2023, 116). Recalling McCormack's triadic schema, we may say that, while in this example a structural notion of symbolic or normative violence would refer to the socio-cultural shape of emotions in the colonial city, an affective notion of atmospheric violence points to the intensive force of the colonial matrix, and the way in which it literally *weights* on and *asphyxiates* bodies as they breathe through their everyday life. Applying atmospheric thinking to violence allows a closer examination of the way in which 'the political becomes directly felt' (Brian Massumi interviewed in Evans 2017; see also Protevi 2009). This approach explores questions of power, knowledge and violence without clinging on notions of intentionality, consciousness and ideology, and rather focusing on the encounter between what is sensed and what is known (cf. Berlant 2011), that is, the way in which a given imaginary is materially sensed through an aesthetic and affective infrastructure that holds the urban together (see chapter 4).[37] One may similarly think about the everyday 'fearscapes' (Tulumello 2017a, ch. 3; Trogisch 2022) of the contemporary city, in which 'bodies are slowly transforming, readapting themselves to security policies requests' (Tedeschi 2020, 33); the debilitating atmosphere of urban neoliberalism's existential precarity, as discussed above;

or the poisoning of 'animals' atmospheres' in the context of pervasive urbanisation (cf. Lorimer et al. 2017; Brighenti and Pavoni 2021b). In a fleeting passage of his seminal article on structural violence, Johan Galtung gestures towards such a dimension when referring to structural violence as what 'is present when human beings are being influenced so that their actual somatic and mental realizations are below their potential realizations' (1969, 168). It is this lowering of potential, this atrophy of conatus, in relation to the process and the project of urbanisation, that we understand as urban atmospheric violence.

Notes

1. 'Town air sets you free', German proverb.
2. Baruch Spinoza. 1677. *Ethica, ordine geometrico demonstrata.*
3. Although from now on we will refer to 'atmospheric violence', the adjective 'urban' is implicit, since it is in the urban experience that atmospheric politics will become particularly relevant.
4. I.e., the tendency to perceive reality as made by isolated and independent points localisable in space and time (see also Whitehead 1929).
5. There is a clear difference between this ontological understanding of cohabitation and that of Cerdá: while the latter understands this process as self-evidently stemming from pre-formed individuals, in Sloterdijk, and atmospheric thinking at large, this is always an ontologically generative process in which there are no pre-formed individuals but relata that 'have no independent existence outside of the relation' (Morin 2009, 61) or, more precisely, dynamics of individuation.
6. The notion of commoning has been developed to provide a processual elaboration to what was perceived as a somewhat static and reified understanding of the commons, among the others, for instance by David Harvey (2012), Peter Linebaugh (2008) or Stavros Stavrides (2016). Elaborating on this understanding, Christian Borch and Martin Kornberger have provided an explicitly atmospheric approach to the commons (2015).
7. Both 'contingency' and 'contagion' have their etymological root in *cum* (with) and *tangere* (to touch), literally, 'touching with' or 'touching together'.
8. Margrit Shildrick (1997) points to something similar when defining bodies as 'leaky', their unstable boundaries constantly negotiated and overflown.
9. Compare with Goffman (1971), on the remedial work of public life, and Stewart (2011), on atmospheric attunements.
10. See www.lozano-hemmer.com/vicious_circular_breathing.php.
11. Although, as Matthew Gandy notes (2017, 368), all too often phenomenological approaches to atmospheres overlook this historical aspect, together with those of gender, race and so forth.

12. Sloterdijk develops his spatial ontology in the trilogy of *Spheres* (2007[1998]; 2014[1999]; 2016[2004]). For a creative use of the notion of co-traction in the sense of a natural contract, see Serres (1990).

13. Cf. Chantal Mouffe's critique (1999) of Habermas's deliberative democracy, and our remarks on agonism and the critique of security (Tulumello 2021a). Even agonistic approaches, it should be said, can fall in yet another version of the normative trap. Indeed, Mouffe's approach is above all pragmatic: conflict is inevitable in pluralist societies, therefore a radical democracy should aim at reframing it as one engaging 'adversaries' that 'share a common symbolic space', rather than enemies (2000, 13). The problem lies, at a meta-level, with the definition of the common symbolic space—and, therefore, of the conflict. In this sense, Mouffe's distinction between antagonism (among enemies) and agonism (among adversaries) reminds Feltran's argument (2020; see chapter 3) on how violence explodes when the mutual recognition in a same normative regime is lacking—a lack of mutual recognition that becomes an increasingly unavoidable condition, especially vis-à-vis more-than-human relations. In this sense, the simple scaling up of the problem of recognition (from the rational deliberation to the symbolic space) does not seem to us to ontologically change the core of the matter, since there seems to be a deeper problem with the notion of recognition itself (cf. Rancière 1999[1995]).

14. Simondon (1992[1964]) made the example of salt, which materialises out of a process of crystallisation once, in a sodium chloride solution, a certain critical threshold is overcome and new chemical bonds begin to be formed (cf. Hui 2016). Salt, in other words, is formed once a metastable solution undergoes an *individuation*, overcoming a metastable condition into a novel, temporary stable configuration.

15. The notion of normative power has been coined by Kurt Goldstein (1995[1934]; see chapter 7). Here we employ the term to refer to the norm-producing creativity it suggests, while at the same time moving beyond Goldstein's individual ontology (see below).

16. Whilst useful when describing 'the steely accumulation' of social associations—i.e., the way social components get together crystallising in assemblages—are Latour's and Sloterdijk's ontologies able to account for the 'lightning strikes' of change (Thrift 2008, 110)? According to Philippopoulos-Mihalopoulos, Sloterdijk assumes 'the undoubtedly true fact that atmospheres are engulfing and producing of their own inescapable immanence. But in so doing, he leaves out the excess of the totality' (2013, 155). Informed by an 'attenuated notion of the event' (Thrift 2008, 111), these perspectives seem unable to account for the overflowing potential that every configuration carries with it. See also Bryant (2011, 271) and Pavoni (2018a, ch. 1, section 1.3). This is all the more important once we understand that urban politics implicitly and explicitly revolves, for a great part, around the simultaneous exploitation and neutralisation of such a potential.

17. The ambiguous oscillation of urban atmosphere between order and chaos has obviously been described at large by crowd theorists. At the urban scale, public rituals for instance have always been characterised by a conundrum. On the one hand, the

need to stimulate, reinforce and confirm the common, affective and material getting-together of bodies that constitute any community: the ritual as a strategy to rendering more 'tangible' and effective the urban being-together, 'mobilising people, publics and crowds in order to transform them' (Boullier 2010, 93; our translation). On the other, the necessity for the collective to self-immunise, through a series of codified and performative procedures, against the excess of this very common (cf. Nancy 1991; Esposito 2011[2002]). Likewise in contemporary public events, whilst the affective quality of the event is key to neoliberal urbanisation, its disruptive and conflictual potential is most feared. The 'resonant fusion' of the crowd is at the same time the dream and the nightmare of event organisers, who rely on this 'fusional instant that produces the event', but at the same time are aware of the danger of this 'explosive mixture' (Boullier 2011, 10; our translation).

18. This is a voiceover from Ingmar Bergman's *Serpent Eggs* (1977).

19. Albeit there are no certified uses of the weapon in USA, Skunk has been already sold to several US police departments (see Tucker 2015).

20. The expression 'psychological deterrence' is taken from a no longer accessible report by Mistral Security, an Israeli manufacturer that has sold Skunk to various US police departments.

21. 'Although Skunk's developers present it as a humanitarian, "less-lethal" weapon . . . the malodorant is also more-than-lethal in its unbearable, dehumanizing effects on civilians' bodies and minds' (Tremblay et al. 2023).

22. Legislative Decree 150/2022, converted into Law 199/2022.

23. On 'environmental governmentalities', see Luke (2016). Matteo Pasquinelli for instance, elaborating on the classic Spinozist distinction between *potentia* and *potestas*, proposes to understand the advent of governmental biopolitics in the sense of a shift 'from normative potentiality (*potentia, puissance*) to normative power (*potestas, pouvoir*)' (2015, 87). If life can be understood as a differentiating, norm-creative *potentia*, then governmental biopolitics may be framed as an organisation of power aimed at controlling, channelling and thus defusing the vitalism of (urban) atmospheres within economically-viable thresholds.

24. This is, incidentally, a way to avoid the risk that Chiara Bottici laments, in theories of the social imaginary, that 'by overly emphasizing the role of social contexts, one risks exchanging a problematic philosophy of the subject for an equally problematic metaphysics of the context' (2014, 4). See chapter 4.

25. Atmospheric violence is particularly adequate to understand this condition of suspension, the 'becoming-open in an atmosphere of violence', in which 'porosity thus becomes a site of potential, exposure, and entanglement all at once, questioning the stability of our worlds, human and nonhuman' (Simmons 2017; see also Choy and Zee 2015).

26. This resonates with that 'secret of everyday violence', as Alison Young put it, 'raining down upon individuals as they attempt to move through everyday life' (2019, 17).

27. This approach also permits to circumvent the risk of over-simplified, rigidifying, deterministic as well as over-paranoid and subjectivist accounts of contemporary society (cf. Birchall et al. 2010), including the tendency to employ *a priori* assumptions and over-encompassing prophesies, instead of performing the task to actually explore what security, neoliberalism, commodification, gentrification and urbanisation at large 'look and feel' on the ground (see Shearing and Johnston 2010; Ranasinghe 2013).

28. Thus Berlant: 'a materialism of the atmospheres points to something more solid [than the notion of "event"], like "environment"' (2011, 100).

29. We are grateful with Renisa Mawani for sharing the draft of this unpublished lecture with us.

30. It is useful to follow Illan Rua Wall's insight on this matter. 'Fanon', as he writes, 'suggests a relation between the general (affective milieu) and the particular. Atmosphere does the theoretical work of connecting different events spatially and temporally. This gives rise to a dynamic tension where the "atmosphere of violence" can retain an apparently stable sense, while still causing and being effected by the changing situation' (2021, 182).

31. As Mawani observes, it allows direct 'attention to the ways in which racial meanings are produced through specific and momentary affective collisions and co-agulations of bodies and objects' (2019).

32. Joshua Oppenheimer's two documentary films on the Indonesian mass killings of 1965–66—*The Act of Killing* (2012) and *The Look of Silence* (2014)—are compelling instances of an approach that seeks to explore violence and its enactment as something that is performed by subjects but that is, at the same time, beyond them. Dimensions, these, that notions of truth, guilt and justice that feed the process of reconciliation, in this as in other similar contexts, often fail to grasp (see on this, e.g., Baldissone 2018).

33. Alexander Weheliye defines 'racialised assemblages' as 'complex relations of articulations that constitute an open articulating principle—territorializing and de-territorializing, interested and asubjective—structured in political, economic, social, racial and heteropatriarchal dominance' (2014, 49).

34. The production of a revolutionary subjectivity is the creative act of a radical imaginary that, *pace* Alain Badiou, does not occur in a vacuum, but rather requires such an atmospheric limit-experience. As Gilles Deleuze observed more generally, 'a creator who isn't grabbed around the throat by a set of impossibilities is no creator. A creator's someone who creates their own impossibilities, and thereby creates possibilities' (1995[1990], 133).

35. Elias Canetti described in his *Crowds and Power* (1962[1960]) the 'enormous relief' bodies experience when, in the crowd, they overcome the invisible boundaries and the fear thereof, unfolding an overflowing force which provides them with the material awareness of something (e.g., the reality of colonial oppression) they were consciously aware but that, we would argue, still held them bound to an aesthetic-affective infrastructure which somehow thwarted their desire for liberation.

36. Following Rancière (2001), the collective political subject is not pre-existent to this moment, it rather *emerges* out of this process as the immanent re-engineering of the colonial atmosphere performed by mobilising its excessive potential. It is in this way that the atmospheric violence of the colony is broken, by turning colonial violence into revolutionary violence (see also Wall 2021), a task that is political, affective and aesthetic at once.

37. With Laurent Berlant, we may say atmospheres are an aesthetic-affective infrastructure that emerges 'from the space of time and practice that not only made people historical but made them feel responsive to and shaped by something historical in the atmosphere they've lived, whether in the flesh or through mediated inheritances of what is always bodily memory' (2011, 66).

PART III

~

EXTENSIONS

CHAPTER SEVEN

~

Comfort

Τεῖχος δὲ περιβαλοίμεθα, ὃ πρῶτον μὲν πρὸς ὑγίειαν ταῖς πόλεσιν
οὐδαμῶς συμφέρει, πρὸς δέ τινα μαλθακὴν ἕξιν ταῖς ψυχαῖς τῶν
ἐνοικούντων εἴωθε ποιεῖν, προκαλούμενον εἰς αὐτὸ καταφεύγοντας
μὴ ἀμύνεσθαι τοὺς πολεμίους, μηδὲ τῷ φρουρεῖν ἀεί τινας ἐν αὐτῇ
νύκτωρ καὶ μεθ' ἡμέραν, τούτῳ τῆς σωτηρίας τυγχάνειν, τείχεσι δὲ καὶ
πύλαις διανοεῖσθαι φραχθέντας τε καὶ καθεύδοντας σωτηρίας ὄντως
ἕξειν μηχανάς, ὡς ἐπὶ τὸ μὴ πονεῖν γεγονότας, ἀγνοοῦντας δ' αὖ τὴν
ῥᾳστώνην ὡς ὄντως ἐστὶν ἐκ τῶν πόνων· ἐκ ῥᾳστώνης δέ γε, οἶμαι, τῆς
αἰσχρᾶς οἱ πόνοι καὶ ῥᾳθυμίας πεφύκασι γίγνεσθαι πάλιν.[1]

At the end of chapter 4 (section Researching Urban Violence) we explored
the contradiction between the utopian imaginary of absolute security that
feeds counterterrorism discourses and the pragmatic realism of actually existing counterterrorist strategies, concluding that this paradoxical coexistence
should be explained by zooming in on its atmospheric consequences for the
urban. In this chapter we aim to expand this aspect with respect to urban
security at large, by complementing the investigation developed in chapter
6 with a genealogical gaze. In the last chapters we saw how the nineteenth-
century 'urban crisis'—including its very framing *as* crisis—was crucial in
shaping both the project and the process of contemporary urbanisation, and
the related emergence of the contemporary notion of urban violence. Here
we argue that also the surfacing of the aesthetic and affective infrastructure
of the contemporary urban atmosphere—what we refer to as the society
of comfort—can be traced to this fateful turning point. It is in this way,

exemplified with specific reference to the precise juridical and aesthetic dispositif recently introduced in the Italian context—i.e., *decoro urbano* (urban decorum)—that we intend to read the current unfolding of urban security, the notion of urban violence that has been in this way implicitly constructed and its atmospheric violence. Let us proceed in order, starting from the (apparent) contradiction we have referred above.

Environment

What the context of (counter)terrorism brings to the extreme is the awkward coexistence of two seemingly antithetical approaches to crime, and criminal violence, at large. These approaches have been converging, and indeed clashing, since the last decades of the twentieth century (see Garland 2001; Borch 2015; chapter 6, Researching Urban Violence): on the one hand, the emphatic 'zero tolerance' rhetoric, most notably popularised by the controversial stint of Rudy Giuliani as New York mayor (1994–2001) and eagerly implemented by cities all around the world (Wacquant 1999); on the other hand, the surfacing of that post-moral approach to crime control that Foucault so carefully described. The latter encompasses an alleged 'transition' from a 'transformative' to a 'managerial' paradigm, according to which the quest for the social, moral and psychological roots of crime is subordinated to an analytic calculation that poses at its centre a *homo oeconomicus*, that is, a rational actor engaged in purely utilitarian decisions and assessments with respect to the cost and opportunities offered by a given situation (cf. Foucault 2010[2004], 249; Lianos 2003; see chapter 3). In this way, the neoliberal understanding of the individual as self-entrepreneur focused on maximising her own human capital has been translated into criminological theory. It is around notions of situation, environment, space and, implicitly, atmosphere that the awkward coexistence of zero tolerance and managerialism did unfold.

Since at least the seminal work of Jane Jacobs (1961) on the 'eyes on the street', approaches to crime management have been developing an awareness of the role played by the environment in producing conditions that are conducive, or not, to the perpetration of crime. In this context, the crisis of the rehabilitative and structuralist frameworks (see Garland 2001; Borch 2015) paved the way to the emergence of 'situational' models aimed at tweaking such 'conditions' by erasing the supposedly criminogenic ones. Crime Prevention Through Environmental Design, or CPTED (Jeffery 1971), defensible spaces (Newman 1972), situational crime prevention (Clarke 1983) and, indeed, Broken Windows (Kelling and Wilson 1982; see chapter 5, Researching Urban Violence) are among the most famous early reflections on this matter. Whilst different in their emphasis (e.g., architecture, the 'situation' or a wider urban aesthetics), these approaches converged in championing, to borrow again from Foucault, 'an environmental type of interventions instead of the internal subjugation of individuals' (2010[2004], 260; see Luke 2016).

As these approaches seemingly suggested a post-moral and pragmatic way to address crime prevention, however, an emphatically moralist stance to crime eradication was complementing them. Not that this was necessarily a contradiction: promising extremely harsh punishment for instance, as was the case of the notorious Reagan's war on drugs, could certainly be read as a measure aimed to raise the costs of crime with respect to its opportunities.[2] One may also argue, moreover, that rhetorically moralising the society against committing crime may not be at odds, after all, with situational approaches. Granted, situational prevention advocates have always been adamant in defending that theirs was 'a practical versus a moralistic approach' (Sorensen et al. 2008, 75). And yet, situational prevention has been criticised precisely as a practice centred on moralising citizens through civilizing actions, what Leonie Sandercock (2002) defined 'moral reform' actions to manage urban fears (see Parnaby 2006; Tulumello 2017b, 399–400).

At any rate, the inconsistency among zero tolerance and pragmatism puzzled many: David Garland (1996) went as far as referring to it as a 'hysterical denial', were the 'old myth of the sovereign state' did rhetorically resurface in the face of a seemingly opposite tendency to deal with crime in terms of prevention, opportunity and costs. According to Loïc Wacquant (1999), there was no denial whatsoever, let alone 'hysterical'. To him, this was a deliberate strategy aimed to turn security into an all-encompassing lens through which framing nearly every aspect of social life—governing 'through crime', that is (Simon 2007). This was what Foucault had already understood: what is key to governmentality is the fact that security becomes the quintessential political economic framework through which interpreting and acting on reality—it is in the specific understanding of the nature of security as a principle of calculation that Foucault's approach is distinct from others like, say, securitisation theories (see chapter 4, Researching Urban Violence). There is another aspect that was seemingly overlooked by Garland, however.

As we discussed already, the question of order—that is, of a 'man-made' order, which is to be built up and maintained, in a world where order can no longer be guaranteed by a transcendent God—played a fundamental role, since at least Hobbes, in allowing Western modernity to deal with the anxiety that the collapse of pre-modern values had left behind. Following the suggestion of Wolf Lepenies (1992[1969]), we noted that amidst the anxious experience the bourgeoise was undergoing before what it saw as the savage and disorderly city of the nineteenth century, the question of *order* became paramount in providing an adequate mechanism of commensuration, and a novel aesthetic and moral compass with respect to which society could evaluate itself (see chapter 3). Fast-forward to late twentieth century, and in the writing of the likes of Anthony Giddens, Ulrich Beck and, to some extent, Zygmunt Bauman, we find again the question of a collapsing order—the modern order, now seemingly threatened by post-modern liquefaction. In this case, renewed anxieties prompt novel calls for an 'ontological security' to be re-established. Looking at environmental approaches to crime prevention through this lens may prove fruitful.

At bottom, environmental crime prevention models, especially for what concerns the first, design-oriented generation,[3] are yet another attempt to move beyond the occurrence of crime, with the aim of climbing up to its sources. Such sources, in this approach, at least superficially, are not to be found on the moral psychology, genetic material or socio-economic condition of the individual, but rather on the precise forms and affordances provided by the 'environmental' situation. Yet, as it was performing its own 'spatial turn', criminology was not abandoning the moral and normative bases—and biases—it had been accumulating for over a century. They remained in place, although made invisible, concealed beneath a supposedly objective notion: disorder. This is where the apparent 'contradiction' we referred to dissolves. What implicitly feeds the managerial approach to environmental crime prevention is a moral normativity of order, complemented by an urban political economy in which the process of capitalist urbanisation seemingly provides yet another surreptitiously normative lens: what is disruptive vis-à-vis such a process is by definition labelled as disordered.[4]

As discussed in chapters 4 and 6, the way in which a given society is 'held together' and perceives this 'holding together' as being 'ordered'—in other words, the way a given urban atmosphere is engineered and the aesthetic 'sense of order' that complements it—is never innocent. Instead, that depends on an affective, aesthetic and normative infrastructure shaped by all sorts of power relations, forces and histories. In other words, there cannot be a strictly post-moral approach to crime—since there is no notion of crime *beyond* morality in the first place, as the likes of Spinoza, Nietzsche or Benjamin already understood, and critical criminology has discussed at length (e.g. Sutherland and Cressey 1978; Hulsman 1986). By pretending to overcome the subjectivity of individual psychology onto the seemingly objective spatial context, therefore, environmental crime prevention *de facto* reproduces social biases, albeit in a less evident and therefore even more pernicious way, insofar as invisibly embedding them within its forms, objects, appearance and practices—something that will be replicated and doubled down on, as we are to see in the next chapter, when digital technologies will usher in another supposedly post-moral and objective approach to crime prevention, predictive policing. While we already discussed the relation between social control and capitalist urbanisation, seen through the lenses of our ontology, what environmental crime prevention models bring about in unprecedented fashion is the aesthetic dimension of this relation, codified in novel regulations, security tactics and technologies.

Danger

As per Foucault's famous remarks, the novelty of biopolitics, with respect to so-called disciplinary societies, is a shift from the sovereign that 'lets live and makes die' to the government that 'makes live and lets die'. Biopolitics directly links the (improvement of the) welfare of the population with that of the State, through a principle of calculation, which is nothing but security itself. If biopolitics sanctions the fact that every aspect of life must become the concern of the government, then, it is through the lenses of security that this must occur. The extent to which this was also, at least symbolically, posited as an 'aesthetic question' is made clear by Foucault when he notes that early police treatises linked the question of improving the strength of the state force by improving the coexistence of the population to that of producing and *showing* a 'good order'. For instance, in the work of authors such as Saxon minister and police scientist Peter Carl Wilhelm von Hohenthal, this was referred to as the *splendour* of the state.

> What is splendor? It is both the visible beauty of the order and the brilliant, radiating manifestation of a force. Police therefore is in actual fact the art of the state's splendor as visible order and manifest force. (Foucault 2007[2004], 314)

Foucault argued that there was a contradiction in place, however, between the biopolitical task to improve the life of the population and the sovereign right to kill, a contradiction that was far more explicit, for obvious reasons, in the colonial and post-colonial contexts, as Achille Mbembe (2003; 2019) explains. While the life of the population is biopolitically improved to an economically viable threshold, there remains a leftover, a part of the population that is necro-politically abandoned, exhausted, a part that is *let die*. We saw already how the urban poor was framed exactly in this way, literally as a 'residue', in the nineteenth-century city. Foucault believed that 'racism' was the dispositif that allowed to keep together the seemingly uncoherent coexistence of biopolitics and necropolitics. The question, then, is what happens to racism when racism can no longer, at least in theory, be juridically implemented in explicit terms. It would be danger, Foucault argued, to play the trick.

It may be useful to refer to a work that played a key, if often overlooked, role in shaping contemporary approaches to crime prevention. In *The Unheavenly City Revisited*, Edward Banfield sketches the contours of his own biopolitical recipe for improving the 'welfare' of individuals and the 'good health' of the society. A task that may be contradictory since, Banfield argues, it might be that 'the essential welfare of individuals must be sacrificed for the good health of society' (1974, 9).[5] It does not take many pages to see whose welfare he believes should be sacrificed. Making our way through a style littered with a remarkable amount of racist stereotypes, we find a description of lower classes as being impulsive, irrational, luxurious, present-oriented. These people 'feel little attachment to the society' (idem, 13), they lack ambition, future-thinking, rationality, mental health, to the extent that their very freedom should be limited for the 'good health' of the social whole. Perhaps nowhere Banfield's programmatic account of urban savages, and what to do with them, is more explicit as when he candidly writes: 'in the chapter that follow, the term *normal* will be used to refer to class culture that is not lower class' (idem, 63; emphasis in original).[6] Banfield's Lombrosian account[7] could hardly have a future in this form. If today racism cannot be mobilised, at least explicitly, without accusations of discrimination, then other notions provide a way to circumvent the problem by keeping its structural violence in place.

Danger serves this precise purpose. A part of the wider shift in the logic of social control introduced by biopolitics is the fact that the main target of governmental strategies is not only the link between individual action and personal responsibility, but widens to encompass a much fuzzier region, that of potentiality. The category of 'dangerousness' introduces an understanding of social control that does not target 'acts' but rather the 'potentialities' of an individual: not so much what one does, as what one is *capable* of doing (Foucault 1998[1973]). This overcomes the 'conundrum of discrimination' of racism, while fully integrating crime control within a wider (bio)political economy of the state. Michalis Lianos and Mary Douglas proposed to term *dangerisation* this tendency 'to perceive and analyse the world through categories of menace' (2000, 267–268). Dangerisation, in other words, is the tendency to categorise discrepancies vis-à-vis *normalcy* as dangerous since

potentially leading to crime, and, therefore, within a coherent epidemio-
logic, to act (through law, police, technology or design) on them as a way
to pre-emptively extinguish the sources of danger. Race, class and other
discriminants are in this way substituted by an 'objective' category, which
'produces normality via the constant re-definition of the abnormal, and thus
dangerous, allowing for *de facto* discrimination whilst escaping' *de jure* accu-
sation (Pavoni 2018a, 139). No other than Rudy Giuliani himself provided
a blatant example of the extent to which this logic is being deployed at the
highest stages, referring to Donald Trump's controversial 'Muslim Ban',[8] with
candid sincerity:

> So when he first announced it, he said, 'Muslim ban'. He [Donald Trump]
> called me up. He said, 'Put a commission together. Show me the right way to
> do it legally' . . . We focused on, instead of religion, *danger*—the areas of the
> world that create danger for us. Which is a factual basis, not a religious basis.
> (apud Kertscher 2017; our emphasis)

It should be evident how this logic dissolves the contradiction that the
coexistence of environmental crime prevention and zero tolerance moralism seemingly implied—both paradigms are different lenses aiming at the
same focus, danger. One perhaps may argue that 'risk' is an even more accurate concept than danger to describe crime prevention strategies. While
danger refers to the inherent potential for harm, adversity or injury in some
person, event or thing, risk is a *measure* of that potential's likelihood and
consequences/impact (Garland 2003, 50; Hacking 2003), and therefore more
appropriate a notion to describe a pre-emptive approach to crime. Be it as
it may, at bottom remains the question of (dis)order, as Giuliani explicitly
stated. A question whose genealogy is instructive: as is well known (dis)order
was central to Giuliani's tenure in 1990s New York and his nomination of
police commissioner William Bratton to implement Broken Windows, the
theory coined by criminologist George Kelling with a political scientist,
James Wilson, who was a student of Edward Banfield in Chicago, where he
completed his PhD. As already discussed (see chapter 5, Researching Urban
Violence), Broken Windows theory mixes Banfield's stress on the need to
control the lower classes' anti-social impulses with a heavy dose of simplified
social psychology and urban aesthetics, positing the basis for a reconfiguration of the relation between danger, risk and fear that will greatly influence
the next decades of urban security.

Here, the seemingly 'innocent' and self-evident notion of disorder—the
'objective' disorder that graffiti, waste or broken windows supposedly ex-

press—becomes a powerful affective actant, which links bodies, practices and spaces in a novel constellation, reconfiguring the atmosphere of a place by polluting its 'sense of order', to the extent of making its very atmosphere *criminogenic*. This is explicitly stated by Kelling and Wilson, as noted already (see chapter 5, Researching Urban Violence), when insisting that, upon assessing the necessity to punish individual behaviours, one needs to 'take into account the connection between one broken window left unattended and thousand broken windows' (1982).

This epidemiology of crime, perfectly compatible with the epidemiological approach to violence discussed through the example of the Cure Violence model (see chapter 1, Researching Urban Violence), rests on two fundamental presuppositions: first, that the 'sense of order' is, to paraphrase Giuliani, a 'factual basis', objectively shared among the community; second, that it is neither actually crime, nor even a question of order but, more precisely, the maintenance of a shared 'sense of order' itself that constitutes the first and foremost concern of (urban) security.[9] The corollary 'sense of security'—implicitly assumed to *necessarily* stem from a 'sense of order'—will become the quintessential domain where the politics of urban security unfolds, either via discursive manipulation through populist rhetoric, or via direct management through aesthetics and affective measures. The notion of 'urban security' should be emphasised here, since it does not simply refer to the security politics that occur in the city but, more precisely, to such a widening of the field of application of security and prevention, a shift captured by Fabrizio Battistelli's definition:

> while *public safety* has, among its objectives, highly institutionalised goods, formalised by a long and consolidated legal tradition, including personal safety and the protection of property, *urban security* adds to those objectives the quality of life and the full enjoyment of the urban space, goods that are by far less institutionalised. (2013, §2; our translation, emphases in original)

If prevention is about 'breaking down the boundaries of what can be done in the name of fighting crime' (Borch 2015, 147), the widening of urban security to literally every aspect of urban life is a crucial step toward the construction of the totalitarian biopolitical character of crime prevention (idem, ch. 5).

(Sense of) Order

Peter Sloterdijk writes that 'culture is primarily and normally the nonrelaxation of tensions generated by a pull through which the members of a group are bound to the regularities proper to that group' (2006, 6). Every social formation is held together by an infrastructure made of relations between humans and nonhumans, tangible and intangible bodies, ideas, affects, laws, held together by immanent tensions: an atmospheric tensegrity. Considering order to be just produced from above is, in this sense, unproductive: we are interested in exploring the dynamic emergence of order, the way it is *made* and *done* at the intersection between power-structured forces, all-encompassing imaginaries, partitioned aesthetics, affective attachments and accustomed practices. We already discussed this aspect in chapter 1, when introducing our understanding of the notion of infrastructure and the role that infra-structural violence plays in this regard. As we had the chance to stress more than once, a key aspect of urban atmospheres is that the tensional, pull and push of their infra-structural forces tend to fade into the background, as order dissolves into the *ordinary* (see Stewart 2007), and the sense of order is naturalised and invisibilised as the air we breathe. This is literally the point made by Sir Carleton Allen in his 1953 *Hamlyn Lectures*:

> The 'peace of our Sovereign Lady the Queen' [public order] has been described by . . . Maitland, as an 'all-embracing atmosphere' in our law, and, we may add, in our whole social life. We could not breathe in any other atmosphere, and we take it for granted as if it were part of the order of nature. (apud Wall 2021, 112–113)

The classic account of the immanent surfacing of order in the urban space of course belongs to Erving Goffman. While Goffman did presuppose the existence of social structures and systems, his account was more concerned with the way order surfaces 'from below', and how social peace is made every day, in the city, via a constant adjustment and negotiation of daily interaction and occasional conflicts via interpersonal visibility, accountability and trust.[10] The 'normal appearances' emerge in this way, aesthetically shaping urban interactions by communicating to the individuals 'that it is safe and sound to continue on with the activity at hand with only peripheral attention given to checking up on the stability of the environment' (1971, 239). Normal appearances, in other words, are the 'sense of order' that urbanites have as they go about in their lives, the ordinary atmosphere of urban everyday life that fades into the background, barely perceptible, while providing the condition of possibility for the smooth and peaceful unfolding of life in the city. This implicit 'sensing' of normalcy, as Goffman puts it, is fundamental for the social processes of habituation and ordering, a counter to the proverbially stressful atmosphere of urban life, since 'when a subject senses that things are normal, he is likely to exude signs of calmness and ease' (idem, 270). The subject, in other words, feels *comfortable*.

Its value notwithstanding, the limits of this account have been widely exposed by critical theory from the point of view of race, gender, class and so on. Goffman's intriguing urban choreographies are premised on an individualistic ontology at the centre of which is an abstract individual that, exactly due to this abstraction, ends up being implicitly filled by very concrete qualities: White, male, heterosexual, middle class and so forth. Moreover, it has been noted that an implicit normative stance was present in Goffman, one that champions a rather rigid picture of the social, in which disorderly excess tends to be categorised as a negative occurrence—a premise that arguably feeds his ultimately conservative understanding of the social, where 'excess' and 'deviation' from the social norm is instinctively seen as suspicious (see chapter 6). The consequence is that the 'sense of normalcy' emerging out of this smooth interaction is depicted as far more consensual, homogeneous and non-conflictual than is actually the case (Law 2004; Borch 2005). The 'sense of normalcy' is more akin to what Jacques Rancière (1999, 29) famously defined as 'police', namely 'a rule governing their [bodies] appearing, a configuration of occupations and the properties of the spaces where these occupations are distributed', that is, the rule organising the partition of what is sensible for a given society at a specific time. If, as we explored earlier (see chapter 3), the sense of security depends on a power-structured distribution of the sensible—Rancière's police—such a distribution is in turn dependent on the more specific work of police *qua* institution, whose role in both reproducing as well as cementing a given 'sense of normalcy', and thus order, is paramount. Police are always on the side of order, whatever the order might be. Their most essential role, as Benjamin indicates in his essay on violence (1996[1921]), is that of preventing and repressing any attempt to *challenge* and *reconfigure* the order itself, first and foremost at the aesthetic level of the correlate *sense* of order. This may be perfectly observed in those instances (e.g., occupations, demonstrations, revolts) in which police discretionality is the norm.

In his genealogy of (sovereign) peace in the British context, Illan Rua Wall (2021) makes this point effectively, showing the way in which the 'sense of (public) order' has been gradually framed as something that must appear as natural *and yet* must at the same time be constantly (re)constructed—hence the key role played by police in radiating, and indeed building, 'the feeling which, on the part of the public, means security'.[11] As Foucault (2007[2004], 326) argued: 'what police has to govern, its fundamental object, is all the forms of, let's say, men's coexistence with each other. It is the fact that they live together, reproduce, and that each of them needs a certain amount of food and air to live, to subsist . . . Police must take responsibility for all this kind of sociality', its 'well-being' at large, including convenience or comfort (*commodité*), while assuring this is done within the boundaries of order and peacefulness. This peacefulness is not simply a condition but a shared atmosphere that the police are tasked to constantly manufacture in order to keep in place a common atmosphere of reassurance so that the 'honest citizens . . . may go about their affairs in peace'.[12] As Andrea Mubi Brighenti puts it, 'the police system is not simply an unseen seeing eye; it also exercises an exemplary visibility through its own visibility . . . to create and stabilise a certain definition of contextual situations' (2010b, 154; see also Harper 2013; Adey 2014b; Pavoni 2018a, ch. 5). If the police and the law produce order by means of their normative and disciplining activity, at the aesthetic/affective level they are also tasked with keeping in place the sense of order: normal appearances must be simultaneously *constructed* and *naturalised*.

In this context (social) peace means an atmospheric and amorphous condition that, according to Wall, is 'liminal to the legal system in two ways: a symbolic form without substantive power and substantive power without a formal structure' (2021, 71). This means that the immanent and performative daily making and doing of social peace—which Goffman described as surfacing out of daily urban interactions—comes to be framed as an atmosphere (of peace, see chapter 9) that must be actively engineered by *law and order*. A breach of the latter is a breach of the former and must therefore be repressed or, ideally, prevented. This relation has a long genealogy: from its early appearance in the Latin world, the political connotation of the notion of *securitas* 'denotes the "atmosphere of peace and tranquillity" entering Rome during Augustus' (Anders 2011, 270). Similarly, this implicit, atmospheric valence of security can be observed in the Middle Ages, as it is the case of the Queen's peace in the British context. Wall (2021) shows how, with the consolidation of modern nation-states, the notion of peace gradually expanded from the immunity of the sovereign to that of the whole territory, so that any breach of the law came to be seen as a breach *to* the law. Benjamin (as mentioned in chapter 3) suggested that the quintessential 'problem' constituted by crime is that it implicitly challenges the authority of the law: a crime somehow demonstrates that the law is insufficient forguaranteeing social order (see also Agamben 2018[2017]). 'If the general sense of the Queen's peace is a form of power without substance, then the "breach of peace" is power without form' (Wall 2021, 71), that is, a form of 'violence' that can be indefinitely stretched. Put otherwise, pretty much *anything* can be framed as a breach of peace and, by consequence, as violence, depending on the way in which a given imaginary of peace, order and security is structured. As a result, room for action is released for the discretionary power of that 'formless . . . all-pervasive, ghostly presence' that Benjamin (1996[1921], 287) referred to as the police (see also Kann 2008). As put by James Fitzjames Stephen in his classic *History of Criminal Law in England* (1883), 'every crime is to a greater or less extent a breach of the peace' (apud Leung 2013, 46). In short, the awareness of the atmospheric dimension of peace and security, and the necessity to keep it in place, has been a long-standing feature in political theory. What is of interest to us is the gradual explicitation of this dimension in relation with urbanisation, an historical process through which Stephen's assumption undergoes a remarkable inversion, according to which, implicitly, *every breach of the peace is to a greater or lesser extent a crime*. This, in a nutshell, is the formula of the aesthetic-affective configuration that we define as the society of comfort.

Comfort

In his seminal book, John Crowley (2001, ix) defines comfort as a 'self-conscious satisfaction with the relationship between one's body and its immediate physical environment'. If Kurt Goldstein (1995[1934]) coined the notion of 'normative power' to refer to the organism's ability to create new norms out of 'the constant antagonism of the organism *against* its environment' (Pasquinelli 2015, 83; emphasis in original; see chapter 6), comfort appears as the pacification of such an antagonism, 'a sensation of being-at-one with the immediate environment', that is, a sensation of *fitting* with the surrounding (Bissel 2008, 1700). Comfort may be read as the process of becoming-with the environment—i.e., individuation—and, at the same time, the reflective sensing of such a process as fitting, suitable, convenient, *proper*, 'at home'.

We already found (see chapter 3) a notion that precisely expresses this process: *oikeiosis*, 'the process by which one thing "becomes proper" and "related" to another' (Heller-Roazen 2007, 106). In the words of Diogenes Laertius—which clearly resonates with the Spinozian epigraph that opens chapter 6—'it is in this way that harmful things are thrust away and proper things [*ta oikeia*] are permitted to approach' (apud Heller-Roazen 2007, 108).[13] This notion may be understood in two senses, that is, as a process of becoming, as well as the related sensation or feeling that accompanies it. Both dimensions, becoming and sensing, are material and relational, and provide a useful cartography to map comfort in its ontological and phenomenological dimensions. In other words, they provide an ontological angle—the relation of comfort with the process of living, becoming and flourishing—that clears the ground from moralistic critiques of comfort *per se*.

As Brighenti and Pavoni suggest (2019), comfort should be read at least through a three-fold lens. First it has to do with a process of becoming that is relational, ontological and coessential to living. In this sense, comfort is certainly compatible with the Spinozist notion of *conatus*, as the striving through which each body perseveres in its own being, increasing its capacity to affect and be affected, by entering in potentiating relations (joy) while avoiding debilitating ones (sadness) (see introduction). That comfort, a notion we associate with the passive relaxation of the body, is associated to *conatus*, a notion that emphasises an essential relation between body, force and power, should not sound outlandish.[14] This is what comfort originally meant. In the medical and religious contexts out of which it originates, comfort was mostly assumed as a transitive verb (comforting someone) indicating the *comforting* action that one performed on another—for instance, the spiritual comfort provided by a priest, or the medical comfort provided by a doctor—rather than a condition of passive relaxation (being comfortable). This is indicated by its very etymology, in which *fortis*, meaning strong, is propelled by the particle *cum*, here indicating an intensification: in other words, a process of strengthening, corresponding to the need for every being to find a safe milieu wherein one is preserved by means of nurturing empowering relations. Moreover, the process is constitutively—i.e., ontologically—relational, as implied by the other meaning the particle *cum* (meaning 'with') harbours. Second, comfort is a phenomenological *mood* whose characteristics are not fixed or pre-determined, but rather depend on the particular constitution one has, together with the historical and socio-cultural distribution of the sensible in which one is thrown: one can feel comfortable in a damp cave and uncomfortable in a shiny suite, and vice versa. Third, comfort is a precise urban condition that has historically emerged in the nineteenth century, and fully unfolded in the twentieth century, with the advent of the so-called society of comfort. It is this historical and material—urban—dimension, we are most interested with.

In the midst of the nineteenth-century urban crisis, as the 'wilderness' of the urban *bas-fonds* was threatening urban experience (see chapters 2 and 4), a novel sensibility about the aesthetic, affective and immunological climate of the 'interiors' of existence emerged. In a sense, urban comfort was an aesthetic way to cope with the frictions that industrial urbanisation produced when it came to grip with the materiality of the urban. One that, however, was greatly shaped by class, gender and race, and increasingly informed by the nascent consumerist society and the violent process of (capitalist) urbanisation. As Crowley (2001) suggests, since the eighteenth century the phenomenology of comfort was increasingly framed with respect to the relation between body, material culture and environment, and profoundly tied to the new bourgeois house and the novel quality of its interior climate in terms of light and temperature (the popularisation of windows and heating), privacy (in opposition to lower classes' promiscuous conditions) and convenience (let us remind that *commodus*, the Latin term for convenient, suitable or cosy, is also the root of the term *commodity*).[15] If we were to stretch the use of the Stoic term, we would say that in this context *oikeiosis* gradually became a socially shared process articulated around an artificial environment produced by all sorts of old and new savoirs (e.g., architecture, urban planning, interior design and, later on, experience economy) and technologies, in turn influenced by the nascent (urban) aesthetic capitalism.

What is particularly interesting for our purposes is not so much the evolution of the private comfort of the bourgeois interior, but rather its overflowing onto the urban space at large. A sort of aesthetic complement to the *domesticisation* of the city that was the cypher of that *project* of the urban epitomised by Cerdá and that Sloterdijk efficaciously framed as *interiorisation*.[16] In what is one of the most convincing genealogies of the urbanisation of comfort available—his neglect of the role played by colonialism notwithstanding[17]—Sloterdijk (2013[2005]) defines *interiorisation* as a process that emerges since the end of nineteenth century out of different developments in various domains—from design to planning, from architecture to experience economy, from criminology to war—all under the influence of a novel awareness of the material quality of the common spaces of co-existence, and therefore of a novel question of how to organise them aesthetically and affectively.[18] Interiorisation, therefore, is described as the gradual integration and organisation of social life into a series of technological, normative, affective and physical infrastructures through which everyday life has been moulded within safe, comforting, commodified and entertaining spaces, relations and practices, in the context of urban capitalism.[19] This is a process Benjamin (2002[1982]) had already begun to understand; wandering through Paris, he developed his aesthetic methodology concerned with exploring capitalism. His approach did not course through a critique of capitalism's abstract ideology but rather through an aesthetic account of its expressive surfaces: that is, the concrete forms and experiences through which it is materialised. Among them, the Parisian *passages couverts*, the arcades, famously attracted him. These arcades, in Sloterdijk's account, are just one among the many socio-cultural, technological, imaginary and aesthetic 'containers' through which modern interiorisation unfolded, as the material project to produce safe, commodified and entertaining spaces, relations and practices, from which risk, danger and uncertainty had to be expunged (Brighenti and Pavoni 2019). An aesthetic and affective infrastructure, that is, shaped by increasingly converging strategies and discourses of design and law, security and marketing, warfare and epidemiology.

Comfort, in this context, appears as one of those terms Fredric Jameson refers to, namely, 'words which have historically articulated undiscovered states of being which, while perhaps not newly emergent, were at least dormant if not unconscious in everyday human existence, and which then begin to play their own role as agents in a reorganization of life' (2013, 30). In the specific, comfort, we argue, gradually became the aesthetic and political cypher of urban politics, an implicit paradigm around which the statement ending the previous section would increasingly find juridical and technological expression: *every breach of the peace is to a greater or lesser extent a crime.*

Discomfort

After a spatial turn in the 1970s, criminology and critical urban studies have been undergoing a more recent affect turn (e.g., Åhäll and Gregory 2013; Adey 2014b; Pavoni 2018a; Nyman 2021; Peršak and Di Ronco 2021). Let us take Timothy Mitchener-Nissen's observation (2014, 76) that contemporary security appears to be increasingly targeting 'harms that are not crimes'—i.e., fear of crime, feelings of unsafety and so forth. In light of the argument developed in this chapter, it would be more accurate to say that security does reconfigure those very harms *as* crimes. The consequences are remarkable, as may be shown by referring to Douglas Husak's (2008) notion of 'public wrongs'. In order to address the liberal separation between public and private sphere, Husak argues, the State has a legitimate interest to punish not only wrongs that are done to individual victims but also those that harm shared values and interests of communities, that is, public wrongs. Yet, 'harm' and 'public wrong' are floating signifiers to which many 'things' can be attached. What happens, for instance, when floating affects such as fear, anxiety, unease and discomfort are perceived as a public wrongs *per se*? What happens, then, when the sense of order, or public 'peace', is both naturalised *and* legally codified?

What happens, it seems, is that the quintessential liberal abstraction, *the right to be left alone*, is affectively reworked into a *right to be free from fear*, in turn prompted by an implicit and yet ever-expanding category of disorder. Peace gradually becomes tautological with an atmosphere of order. This is because it is not simply crime but, more profoundly, unrest and disorder that are assumed to be threats to the stability and legitimacy of the law and the state: an amorphous atmospheric condition, which feeds amorphous and discretionary police action. Peace 'is the very end and foundation of civil society', wrote William Blackstone, and 'the great End of all Governments' (apud Wall 2021, 72). To this, Wall adds: 'the peace is the ground upon which the interiority of the modern state is built' (idem, ibidem; see also Leung 2013). If this is undeniable, since ancient times, the key question here is that, while peace remains a key political concept across history and, arguably, geographies, its political ontology and aesthetic phenomenology do not, especially vis-à-vis urban violence. What interests us to emphasise then, is the way in which, with the advent of urban modernity, such an expectation of peace comes to be entangled with the aesthetic and affective organisation of urban space.

In chapter 9, taking inspiration from Wolfgang Dietrich (2012), we will come back to this aspect in order to point to an understanding of security grounded on a different articulation of the relation between peace, violence and the urban. At this stage, however, let us continue exploring what no-tion of peace implicitly (as well as explicitly)[20] emerges in the context of the comfort society. To do so, let us remain a bit more in the UK. As formulated in a British decision from 1982,

> We are emboldened to say that there is a breach of the peace whenever harm is actually done or is likely to be done to a person or in his presence to his property or a person is in fear of being so harmed through an assault, an affray, a riot, unlawful assembly or other disturbance.[21]

The all-encompassing character of this statement exemplifies the sublima-tion of police power into a 'formless' and 'ghostly' presence that characterises contemporary *urban* security, with respect to which order does not tautologi-cally coincide with law. Rather, order more generally refers to the aesthetic and affective dimension of peace, understood as not simply the absence of violence and crime, but as a positive and reassuring *sense of order* that gradually melts into the air we breathe. This is exactly how Žižek describes symbolic-structural violence: 'the spontaneity of the milieu in which we dwell, of the air we breathe' (2008, 31), whose debilitating, toxic quality we referred to as 'atmospheric violence'. Whether, as Ian Hacking (2003) ob-serves, risk could be understood as a modulator of the relationship between fear and harm; if fear becomes a harm in itself, this configuration collapses into a self-referential circularity. Once pervasive, a threat is radically deterritorialised, true to its nature, namely, as an indeterminate probability that is temporally linked to a futurity (Massumi 2005, 35; see chapter 4). Once it is understood as a virtual event, always real even when non-actual, risk becomes an ever-present occurrence whose very potentiality has to be constantly defused and neutralised, and yet, because of its radically de-bounded character, is bound to constantly re-produce fear in the present (Beck 2002; Boyle and Haggerty 2009).

Urban violence, in this sense, is turned into a spectral concept. As Ben Penglase (2011, 435) observes, 'the very discourse about "urban violence" contains within it a disruptive element which resists order, refusing to allow violence to be "domesticated". For that very reason, violence becomes so much more an object of fear, fantasy, obsession, and anxiety'. This can be observed at its most explicit in the UK Anti-Social Behaviour Orders (ASBO), introduced under Tony Blair in the 1998 Crime and Disorder Act, and substituted by Criminal Behaviour Order (CBO) and Injunction in 2014.[22] In the Crime and Disorder Act of 1998, anti-social is a manner or course of conduct that 'caused or was likely to cause harassment, alarm or distress'.[23] Evidently, as Peter Ramsay observes, this means that 'it is not the offensiveness of the conduct which causes "harassment, alarm or distress" that is the problem, even where the conduct concerned is offensive, but rather it is the underlying threat to others' sense of security' (2008, 9; see also ICHRP 2010, 6). To be criminalised, in the words of a communication of the European Commission, is a conduct 'which, without necessarily being a criminal offence, can by its cumulative effect generate a *climate* of tension and insecurity'.[24]

It should be stressed that, as notions of crime and order are implicitly read through the lens of comfort, also the presupposition of the criminal as a rational actor involved in a cost-opportunity assessment, central to environmental crime prevention models, seems to blur. What is criminalised is the perturbation one's conduct is 'likely to cause' to the atmosphere of peace, order and tranquillity: one's *violence against the air*.[25] Social control strategies thus shift away from individual agency and situational cost-opportunities evaluation, beginning to target impersonal, collective, intangible affects and their atmospheric articulation, where notions of 'peace', 'tranquillity' and the likes come to indicate a precise 'holding-together' of the atmosphere, which becomes, in the end, the very *purpose* of crime prevention. As a result, crime prevention 'overflow[s] the concern with preventing crime and violence (or, to use the cumbersome jargon of the field, with "objective security")', becoming 'an atmospheric endeavour, with the task of producing reassurance, or the conditions of being at ease, in "peace of mind" and "absence of fear" (namely: "subjective security")' (Pavoni 2018a, 140; see also Baldwin 1997, 14). Ramsay made precisely this point when observing,

> The key to the ASB [anti-social behaviour] that renders a person liable to the imposition of an ASBO is that the disposition of contempt or indifference, made manifest by the defendant's conduct, *fails to reassure* others with respect to their security in the future. (2008, 8; emphasis in original)

Goffman's mechanisms of 'reassurance' are in this sense legally codified, so that the very *failure* to reassure may become an offence in itself. These relations have been described, by Renzo Carli and Rosa Maria Paniccia (2003, 212–225), as being typical of relations of control, in which the 'other' is assumed as being inherently inclined to transgression and, therefore, having the responsibility to continuously prove their innocence. Incidentally, making reference to a psychosocial lens, here, also serves to remind that security logics, beyond being mere ideology, often takes steps from—and/or reframe to their advantage—psychological dimensions that are central to individual and social life (cf. Tulumello and Falanga 2022).

What matters the most for our argument is how anti-social behaviour measures seemingly complete the boomerang effect of the mechanism Fanon described in the colonial context. In the *Wretched of the Earth*, Fanon showed how the colonial organisation of power produced an atmosphere of violence that filled the colonial city with a toxic gas affecting the gestures, attitudes, perceptions and habits of the black bodies, slowing them down in a sort of affective ankylosis (see chapter 6). 'The native', writes Fanon, 'is always on the alert, for since he can only make out with difficulty the many symbols of the colonial world, he is never sure whether or not he has crossed the frontier. Confronted with a world ruled by the settler, the native is always presumed guilty' (1963[1961], 53). While the settings are obviously different, the underlying logic appears to be the same: both in the colonial city and in the contemporary metropolis, reassurance, or the failure to do so, is a performative role play that depends on the simultaneously power-structured and naturalised way in which the urban atmosphere is engineered. Its atmospheric violence, it goes without saying, varies greatly depending on the bodies that are breathing through it. In today's European city, for instance, Abdelmalek Sayad (2004) wrote, the migrant body undergoes a constant 'experience of suspicion', an atmospheric urban violence that normally falls under the radar, failing to manifest as such.

In a temporal sense, this logic 'reverses the onus of proof in respect not of accusations about the past, but of *fears about the future*' (Ramsay 2008,

12; our emphasis).[26] Agency is further removed from certain bodies, since race, sexual orientation, class and so on may be sufficient, regardless of the actual 'conduct' of the individual, to already electrify the urban atmosphere towards a potential perturbation.[27] This discussion obviously falls back onto our reflection of urban violence, which is not only framed with respect to the normative projection of the 'city without violence' that characterises the imaginary of (absolute) security we already explored, but also with respect to the affective tensions organising the ordinary infrastructure of coexistence through which this very imaginary materialises. Within comfort societies, be they partitioned via explicit militarisation (e.g., Graham 2010) or 'soft' aesthetics (e.g., Thörn 2011; Hentschel 2015), violence is rhetorically opposed to a phenomenological right to be comfortable, in turn framed in reference to such states as 'peace of mind' and 'absence of fear', to be achieved through various (discursive, technological, legal) means: an affective infrastructure (the ordering) and an aesthetic perception (the sense of order) that are taken for granted. Consequently, the categories within which 'manifestations' of urban violence may be included dramatically expand,[28] justifying the (direct and structural) mechanisms to repress them, while simultaneously invisibilising the urban violence this juridical-aesthetic apparatus puts in place.

With the society of comfort, a perverted kind of a social *oikeiosis* thereby unfolds: an aesthetic of the domestic interior—a *'domus'* that, of course, has a precise socio-economical and racial definition—is gradually projected onto the urban,[29] whose underlying *sense of order* is simultaneously naturalised and codified via legal regulation, security practices, and that convergence of planning, design and branding that is usually indicated as regeneration.

A remarkable instance is the already mentioned UK Government's Police, Crime, Sentencing and Courts Act (the Policing Act), which has introduced novel restrictions to the right to protest by following the same wording. The act targets public assemblies if they generate 'serious disruption to the life of the community', a category that is extremely wide, including transport facilities, places of worship, commercial activities, educational institutions. As already mentioned in the last chapter, an interesting category that is particularly emphasised by the act is that of the protest's noise, which is deemed to become 'disruptive' when it is assumed as having 'a significant impact on persons in the vicinity of the assembly' by causing 'intimidation or harassment', 'alarm or distress'—the very characters of *anti-social* acts according to the 1998 Crime and Disorder Act we just discussed. It should go without saying that the production of some sort of 'disruption' is part and parcel of any protest strategy, and that this disruption, from a roadblock to a school occupation, is likely to produce alarm or at least distress in those

whose activities and expectations are thus 'disrupted'. While, of course, setting some sort of thresholds beyond which a public protest is said to become
inacceptable is completely reasonable, any disruption is criminalised here.
The Policing Act generates an atmospheric violence, both in the sense of
fundamentally denying the right to protest, and as a tool that enacts police
violence and deprivation of liberty (see chapter 6). The mechanism of this
violence is the criminalisation and pre-emptive neutralisation of those
'breaches of peace' that 'the life of the community' draws on, especially
when seeking to challenge and resist the atmospheric violence the ordinary
urban peace generates. A violence, in other words, that seemingly targets
the excess 'life of the community', here negatively reframed as 'disruption',
and dealt with accordingly. Through the genealogical lenses deployed in
this chapter so far, we can now understand the articulation of the aesthetic
relation between peace, violence and disruption, with the domestication of
the 'sense of order' in the urban that we are exploring through the notion
of comfort.

Another, almost didactic example, already explored elsewhere (Pavoni
2018a; Pavoni and Brighenti 2019), has been provided by Catharina Thörn
(2011) with reference to the public space campaign THINK in Gothenburg,
Sweden. The campaign's purpose was encapsulated in the following statement: 'we want to create a feeling of being "at home" by making everyone
seeing the city as our "common living room"'. Within this intention to 'make
the city safer, beautiful, and comfortable'—as the Swedish notion of *trivsam*
expresses—practices of security, design and branding overlap (see Berglund-
Snodgrass 2016). Likewise, in Rotterdam, as Marguerite van den Berg and
Danielle Chevalier write, 'the city planning programme that ran until 2018
was guided by the concept of a "City Lounge" geared towards making the city
a "soft, warm and hospitable" space that is attractive for middle-class families
to settle' (2020).

It should go without saying that urban public space—the quintessential
locus of anonymity, heterogeneity, unpredictability and otherness—is by
definition at odds with the familiar domesticity of a 'living room', which
moreover is normally the expression of a precise socio-cultural and economic
background. The aspiration of being 'at home' in the public, especially after
being translated into all sorts of architectural, aesthetic and juridical configurations, is bound to be a divisive and exclusionary experience, gradually
leading to the construction of a 'comfort-animated artificial continent' that
excludes those unable to afford entrance, those left floating 'in the ocean of
poverty', as Sloterdijk puts it (2013[2005], 195). More generally, exclusion
will concern all those socio-economically, racially or sexually marginalised,

or *different* people—not to mention many non-human undesirables—who are likely *not* to feel 'at home' in these public spaces (see Young 1990, 199ff; Epstein 1998).

That the quest to immunise space from discomfort is bound to reproduce discomfort at its various thresholds was already evident at the initial stages of the society of comfort. An argument could be made, for instance, for reading in this sense the nineteenth-century appearance of agoraphobia (see chapter 4). As Camillo Sitte (1986[1889]) observed at the time, agoraphobia was a symptom of the alienation produced by the 'inhuman' quality of modern planning, with its disquieting scale, labyrinthine illegibility and geometrical voids. In this reading, the attempts of modernist planning to domesticate the city backfired and the linear order of the rational urban form ended reproducing the spectral fear of the wild it had sought to tame in the first place—a contradiction that was experienced, with debilitating effects, by the most sensible, agoraphobic bodies (Carter 2002). One of the implications of this contradiction was the 'urbanisation' of the concept of uncanny. Not uncoincidentally, as for the modern concept of agoraphobia, born in late nineteenth-century Berlin, also the 'uncanny' was coined in one of the centres of urbanisation at the time, early twentieth-century Vienna, by Sigmund Freud. A quintessentially bourgeois anxiety, the uncanny is inextricable from the surfacing of the domestic paradigm of comfort. The term—which in the original, German spelling, *Unheimlich*, literally means un-homely—may be understood, following Anthony Vidler's useful definition, as 'a domesticated version of absolute terror, to be experienced in the comfort of the home' (1992, 3). It has to do, more precisely, with a spectral feeling, an awareness that 'something is not right' within the space—i.e., the home—where everything is supposed to be (in the) right (place). Uncanny, in other words, is the process whereby the homely and its expectations are translated into the un-homely. When, with modern urbanisation, the homely is projected onto the urban, the uncanny expands indefinitely, as a background anxiety, symptomatic of the contradiction nested within assuming the urban as homely in the first place. 'The uncanny finally became public in the metropolis' of the nineteenth century, writes Anthony Vidler, as the domestic expectations of a rising bourgeois were projected onto a space that in turn was increasingly unfamiliar, unknown and unreadable, a space that 'became identified with all the phobias associated with spatial fear' (idem, 6). This contradiction will remain in place, only further complexified, in the next century of urbanisation.

Resonating with this reflection, Leopold Lambert (2010) moves a critique to modernist comfort when reflecting on what he terms a 'Spinozist architecture', that is, one that is joyous insofar as prompting an increase of the capacity of feeling and acting (*potentia*), even at the price of 'challeng[ing] the body, put[ting] it in danger and leav[ing] it without any other alternative than to react to this delicate situation'. Spinozist architecture, specifies Lambert, is incompatible with modernist comfort and its 'weakening of the body', since: 'comfort and joy are not synonyms. We might even wonder if they are not antonyms' (2010). As we anticipated (and will see in more detail in chapter 9), comfort contains a rather more multiple and overflowing set of meanings than its specific historical—'modernist'—construction betrays. As observed elsewhere (see Brighenti and Pavoni 2019), Lambert's is a useful suggestion, since it contains a critique to comfort that is neither moralistic (as for instance in the context of the heroic and Fascist critique of comfort) nor nostalgic (as in the critique of the alienating role of comfort and its 'artificial mediations' vis-à-vis a more authentic and un-mediated life, e.g., Boni 2014). Lambert instead suggests a strategic critique, which has to do with the potentially debilitating effect comfort may have vis-à-vis a body's capacity to think, sense and feel. In other words, he implicitly highlights the atmospheric violence comfort may hold. To be sure, this observation would be of little use if kept at the level of individual psychology. Were this the case, there would not be much difference with self-help injunctions to get out of one's 'comfort zone'—a rather common suggestion in the neoliberal mood of universal competition. Instead, by proposing an approach that looks at comfort simultaneously as a phenomenological sensation, an ontological process of individuation and an historically specific urban configuration,[30] ours is an eminently materialist, affective and ontological critique that avoids moralism and its conservative undertones, and rather situates comfort within the wider trajectories this book so far developed: those of security, violence and the urban.

Liveability

The notion of urban security aptly encapsulates the juridical, tactical, technological as well as 'atmospheric' expansion of security into the urban experience, and the violence thereof.[31] This is particularly evident in the Italian context, where the definition of 'urban security' has been codified by law, in relation to a vague notion of liveability (*vivibilità*) and a novel juridical dispositif (*decoro urbano*), whose provenience from the realm of art and heritage is a particularly remarkable exemplification of the aestheticisation of contemporary security (e.g., Ghertner et al. 2020). The notion of liveability in relation to the city, together with that of 'quality of life', although present since early Greek theorisations around notions of happiness, pleasure and well-being in the life in the *polis*, emerges as a category of urban politics in the second half of the last century (Kaal 2011; McArthur and Robin 2019). Its genealogy is variegated and surely influenced in its methodology by the Social Indicators Movement, born in the 1960s from the idea that 'it is important to monitor changes over time in a wide range of quality of life . . . because such information, when combined with other data, can generate new knowledge about how to increase quality of life through more effective social policies' (Andrews 1989, 401).[32] What is most significant for our argument is the extent to which the concept of liveability/quality of life has become increasingly central in *city branding* politics, within the planetary competition among so-called global cities (Anttiroiko 2014; Vanolo 2017). In other words, urban liveability has become a quantitative means of commensuration that allows the direct comparison of cities through charts, which in turn certify their 'success' in terms of visibility, prestige, and therefore attractiveness to investors, tourists and creative classes.

As the notion assumes a global relevance by appearing in programmatic documents of organisations such as the World Bank, UN-Habitat, OECD and so forth, an increasingly important role is played by the *liveability indexes* published annually by the likes of the Economist Intelligence Unit, Mercer, Monocle or PwC. Perhaps the most famous, the *Economist*'s Global Liveability Index ties the notion of urban liveability directly to what it defines as 'relative comfort'. Every city is assigned a rating of relative comfort for over 30 qualitative and quantitative factors across five broad categories: stability, healthcare, culture and environment, education, and infrastructure. The highest level of liveability corresponds to the highest level of relative comfort, inversely proportional to the amount of challenges urbanites endure to such 'standards of life'. For instance, in cities scoring 80 (out of 100) or more, it is considered that 'there are few, if any, challenges to living standards' (EIU 2021, 7), resonating squarely with the paradigm of urban comfort understood as a static condition of being at ease, without challenges.

Let us be clear. First, as already suggested, we eschew any neo-ascetic, heroic and fascist forms of contempt for any sort of bourgeois comfort. Living a comfortable life is not a bad thing in itself: it is indeed a legitimate desire for many. The problem here is not that of the pursuit of a comfortable life but, more precisely, that of fetishising a normative, historically specific (i.e., with precise exclusionary connotations as a result of its history), and yet superficially aesthetic and ethically passive notion of comfort, and make it coincide with a concept of urban liveability understood as the minimisation of challenges, conflict and unpredictability from the urban. Likewise, as in other parts of this book, also in this case we stress that here we are not interested in proposing an acritical exaltation of conflict, 'challenge' or unpredictability against the liveability concept. In the same way as we reflected on the excess of urban life more generally, the former are not self-evidently emancipatory or empowering *per se*—they can be extremely debilitating and they tend to be particularly so for the marginalised populations that have to endure them the most. Making urban life more 'comfortable' or 'liveable' is a valuable desire and political objective, one that, however, may require questioning the peculiar ways in which notions such as comfort or liveability—with their very precise specific, historical and political, genealogy—have been constructed, and the troubles thereof.

In this sense, the concept of urban liveability may be criticised from many points of view, for instance insofar as providing a homogenising depiction of a city that conveniently erases its internal differences, or for the fact of re-enacting an old and problematic narrative, according to an implicit definition of linear urban progress, in which the colonial nuance of the notion of *civilisation*—that directly fed the very notion of *urbanización* coined by Cerdá (see chapter 2)—is substituted by the apparently innocent and self-evident notion of liveability. It is at the same time too vague and too rigid a notion, reductively framing the evaluation of the individual and the (physical, socio-cultural, economic) environment to a series of quantitative indicators, which are very practical in allowing easy inter-urban comparisons, while hardly capable of providing a picture of urban life in a given city—thus resonating squarely with the problem of capturing, and comparing levels of, urban violence through quantitative indicators (see chapter 2, Researching Urban Violence). Moreover, one may note the extent to which such charts are far from being innocently produced and rather feed an ever-expanding market of urban experts. Experts who, in turn, feed the urban imaginaries that influence a selective approach to urban politics, which, seeking to improve the global perception of certain standards of life, are directly detrimental with respect to the possibility of expanding access and enjoyment to such standards in the first place (see McArthur and Robin 2019).

What is especially worth noting, moreover, is the extent to which the notion of liveability is conceived as something that is both *measurable* and *applicable* to every city, and therefore as something that can be produced, governed and managed. Liveability emerges as a powerful epistemological lens that inserts a city within a pre-structured problematic field. In this way, *any* urban politics would be understood (and assessed) as regards the positive or negative effects on liveability itself, pre-emptively defusing any attempt to challenge this notion and its values, and therefore to imagine alternative values and standards to urban life (cf. Simone and Broto 2022). If, above, we defined urban vitality as a normative power of differentiation that is structurally excessive to the living, urban liveability could be understood as the systematic eradication of any differential, excessive and creative potential from life, through its reduction into precise categories, and whose normative force barely hides its colonial background. In a sense, liveability indexes show the way an urban imaginary—urban life and its 'quality'—is naturalised as a seemingly self-evident point of reference, around which specific normative arrangements are articulated, producing in turn a silent and invisible atmosphere capable of debilitating life in its multiple variations, that is: urban violence.

In the Researching Urban Violence section that follows, we briefly explore the genealogy of a concept that crystallises in juridical form the convergence, which this chapter sought to unpack, between liveability, comfort and violence, a convergence that the becoming atmospheric of urban security seemingly encapsulates: *decoro urbano* (urban decorum).

Researching Urban Violence: *decoro*

The notion of *decorum* is the Latin translation of the Greek τὸ πρέπον (*to prepon*), meaning propriety or appropriateness in the domain of rhetorics. Since its appearance in the Roman context, the term overflew this domain, by referring more generally to the normativity of social relations.[33] Decorum refers to a condition of 'orderliness', being proper, seemly, decent, convenient, appropriate, suited or fitting (in Italian, *addirsi*, *confarsi*) with respect to an *unspecified* standard: being decorous is the condition or the act of being 'suitable to a character or time, place, and occasion'.[34] Decorum does not refer to the characteristic of a subject, an object, or a behaviour *per se*, but rather to the formal relation these have with a specific (social, cultural, artistic, moral, etc.) background. If the notion of decorum appears terminologically fuzzy, then, this is not due to a polysemy or a vagueness of the term, as it is sometimes implied, but more precisely because of its parasitical structure vis-à-vis a given system of values. To be decorous means to aesthetically conform to a given order, something that will formally and normatively cement the link between an order and the *sense* of order, once translated to the realm of urban regulation, as it particularly occurred in the Italian context.

While decorum has long belonged to the overlapping fields of art and morality, in Italy its legal codification is recent. Decorum first appears in the 2004 Code of Cultural Heritage and Landscape (Codice dei beni culturali e del paesaggio), where it is presented as a self-evident complement to other expressions such as the 'appearance', 'fruition' and 'enjoyment' of places of interests, which the law is supposed to protect and guarantee.[35] The 'becoming urban' of the concept may be said to accompany the 'becoming atmospheric' of cultural heritage as codified at the global level by the concept of 'intangible cultural heritage'.[36] It is with respect to this atmo-cultural connotation (see Brighenti and Pavoni 2020; 2021a) that the notion of decorum assumes a peculiar significance, providing a correlation of cultural heritage with the question of national identity, a greater awareness about the 'civic and social duty' involved in protecting this heritage, and therefore the necessity of its valorisation, in turn linked to the development of the tourist industry (cf. Marzocca 2001).

While never clearly defined, in the 2004 Code 'decorum' seems to refer to the need to protect something more than the physical/material dimension of the good. It is the atmosphere of a place that must be *appropriate*. *Decoro*, in this way, is provided with a contagious force. If present, it colours the atmosphere of a place in moral sense, making a place more beautiful, prestigious and decent. Conversely, if absent, the place will be thrown into degradation and decay. This also sanctions the fragility of the 'decorous atmosphere': where the physical 'dignity' of a monument remains unaltered unless an explicit act of vandalism is performed, the decorum of a place is much more vulnerable, to the extent that even a single indecorous behaviour may be able to poison its atmosphere.[37] This will be all the more evident as decorum migrates from the domain of cultural heritage to that of urban security.

In this field, *decoro* emerges in the early 2000s as a counterpoint to rhetoric on the *degrado* (decay) of central and peripheral urban areas.[38] A turning point is the Decree of the Ministry of Internal Affairs of 5 August 2008, dedicated to 'public safety and urban security [*incolumità pubblica e sicurezza urbana*]'. In line with the discussion developed above, the decree defines public security as a 'public good' directly tied to liveability: 'urban security [is] a public good that must be protected' by guaranteeing 'the respect of the norms that regulate the civil life, in order to improve the conditions of liveability in the urban centres, civil coexistence and social cohesion' (art. 1). In this context, *decoro urbano* (urban decorum) is introduced among the areas for mayoral intervention: it is an undefined condition that, if tampered with, must be addressed. Though providing specific reference to street vending, the legal formulation of *decoro urbano* remains open to any number of interpretations[39]—those 'less institutionalised' goods mentioned by Battistelli (2013; see above). Perfectly in tune with the Broken Windows framework, the decree provides a symptomatology of urban life, indicating decay or isolation as direct causes of 'criminogenic phenomena', which therefore require to be addressed and prevented by also tackling *all* the 'situations that alter *decoro urbano*'. Mirroring the experience with the protection of intangible cultural heritage, therefore, what urban security addresses via *decoro urbano* is not damage or crime but, more profoundly and discretionally, a sort of 'spiritual dignity' of the city (Videtta 2019), that is supposed to be protected by maintaining in place a seemingly shared and consensual *sense* of what this dignity may be: a perfectly tautological aesthetic at the centre of which is decorum itself, a shortcut for the 'objective' sense of order.

The term would take a much more prominent role a few years after, in the Decree-Law 14/2017, tellingly titled 'urgent measures concerning security in the cities'.[40] Here, a far closer relation between urban security, decorum and liveability (*vivibilità*) is underlined since the very definition of urban security that is provided, namely as 'a common good concerning the liveability and the decorum of the city' (art. 4). Urban security, the decree continues, shall be pursued also 'via interventions of urban, social and cultural regeneration, and the recovery of degraded areas, or sites' (idem). Urban regeneration, in other words, is presented as having the capacity to 'improve liveability (and most notably decorum), providing the urbanites with an environment that is comfortable and "liveable" (and therefore safe, according to the decree's connotation)' (Videtta 2019, 55; our translation). Notions of comfort, liveability and decorum are articulated in an ideal vision of the city, framed by an ever-extended concept of urban security that encompasses urban planning and politics at large.

In this very notion, it seems, the *project*, the *process* and the *atmosphere* of the urban converge. Here, the criminogenic premises of Broken Windows are provided with a coherent aesthetic and juridical complement, according to which what does not correspond to the shared sense of order is the not-conforming, the 'not proper' and 'inappropriate'—that is, indecorous. The indecorous act, behaviour or being is at the same time assumed as always potentially contagious, since the sense of order is a fragile atmosphere, vulnerable to pollution.[41] Urban security is thus articulated as a symptomatology aimed to individuate (and if possible, *prevent*) any excess, an approach with respect to which *decoro urbano* appears as a particularly strategic dispositif.[42] Because of its tautological normative structure, *decoro urbano* is inherently repressive vis-à-vis the excessive potential of urban life. If urban vitality, as argued above, can be referred to as life's tendency to exceed its own *form* (per Deleuze's own notion; see introduction and chapter 6), then it is evident how a dispositif such as *decoro urbano*, seeking to produce a static and predictable—and, crucially, marketable—urban atmosphere, has a defusing and neutralising effect, filling the urban with atmospheric violence.[43] Besides the necessary critique of decorum as a dispositif consistent with the unequal process of neo-liberal urbanisation (e.g., Pitch 2013; Pisanello 2017; Bukowski 2019; Ascari 2020), therefore, we emphasise its inherent incompatibility with any emancipatory urban politics whatsoever. In concluding her insightful analysis, Videtta argues that the concept could have potentially become 'a transversal value in urban liveability politics, and a functional tool to the objectives of inclusion and therefore social equality' (2019, 64; our translation). This did not occur, Videtta continues, due to the vagueness of its codification, the lack of clearly indicated financial instruments to its application, the absence of precise indication as regards the measures to be implemented and the reduction of decorum to a mere tool for situational prevention. Granted, these are all problems with the actually existing *decoro urbano* in Italy. Yet, in light of our discussion, the notion of *decoro urbano*—that is, the juridical urbanisation of decorum—appears to be problematic: its systematically anti-excessive structure makes it constitutively debilitating, albeit asymmetrically so, as it atrophies the excessive potentiality of urban coexistence, decaying its differential vitality to the extent that it cannot be subjected to any 'good use'.[44]

Notes

1. Plato, Νόμοι. 'A wall is by no means an advantage to a city as regards health, and, moreover, it usually causes a soft habit of soul in the inhabitants, by inviting them to seek refuge within it instead of repelling the enemy; instead of securing their safety by keeping watch night and day, it tempts them to believe that their safety is ensured if they are fenced in with walls and gates and go to sleep, like men born to shirk toil, little knowing that ease is really the fruit of toil, whereas a new crop of toils is the inevitable outcome, as I think, of dishonorable ease and sloth' (Plato 1967/1968, 778e-779a). Translation available through the Annenberg CPB/Project (http://www.perseus.tufts.edu/hopper/text?doc=urn:cts:greekLit:tlg0059.tlg034.perseus-eng1:6.778e) and licensed under a Creative Commons Attribution-ShareAlike 3.0 United States License.

2. As it happens, there is no evidence that harsher punishments work to deter crime (see Tonry 2011). Though this is a necessary notation; it should be obvious, at this point, that the fact that repression advocates have never been themselves deterred from this evidence is yet another reminder of the limits of political economy critique to security politics.

3. Three generations of CPTED and environmental crime prevention models have been identified (Crowe and Fennelly 2013[2000]): the first is explicitly focused on environmental design; in the second, the notion of environment is expanded from the physical to the social one, with the involvement of the community, and the promotion of mutual identity, trust and 'civic' duties (Saville and Cleveland 2008);

the third generation, whose theories are less consolidated, encompasses a number of ideas—including sustainability and liveability—but is generally characterised by the mathematisation of the environment as a space of (ambient) computation, throwing digital technologies into the mix (see chapter 8).

4. The relation between capitalism and the process of (urban) ordering is much more complex than any linear, causal correspondence would suggest. Berlant (2011), for instance, notes that, differently from classic Marxist everyday life theory, capitalism does not really 'organise' everyday life in the city as much as it 'disorganises' it, *de facto* engendering an affective and existential dislocation that security politics tend to make up for, by providing a way to 'make sense' of this disorder through their own 'sense of order' (see on this Cox 2020).

5. Banfield defines the welfare of individuals as the possibility to live without 'serious impairments' to physical and psychological health, and the 'good health' of the society as 'its tendency to produce desirable human types', not only by staying alive but also moving 'in the direction of giving greater scope and expression to what is distinctively human' (1974, 9).

6. Banfield predated by about a decade the popularisation of the concept of underclass prompted during Reagan's tenure by Charles Murray's 'scientific' endeavour at demonstrating the inferior nature of the (racialised) 'inner city' residents—see particularly *The Bell Curve* (Herrnstein and Murray 1994) and, for an intellectual history of the concept, Wacquant (2022).

7. Let us remind that, much like the infamous Italian criminologist, Banfield (1958) had developed his understanding of the underclass in Southern Italy.

8. President Donald J. Trump Executive Order 13780: Protecting the Nation from Foreign Terrorist Entry into the United States.

9. As summarised by Bruce Shapiro, Broken Windows is 'an illusory obsession with order at all costs' (1997, 23).

10. Here is Anthony Giddens, whose debt to Goffman we already mentioned (see chapter 3): 'the observing of "civil indifference" between strangers passing on the street, so brilliantly analysed by Goffman, serves to sustain attitudes of generalised trust on which interaction in public settings depends. This is an elemental part of how modernity is "done" in everyday interaction, as we can see by comparing the phenomenon to typical attitudes in pre-modern contexts' (1991, 46).

11. This is Arthur G. Keech (the inspector in charge of training the Kent County Constabulary in the early 1950s), quoted in Wall (2021, 112). Keech adds that, accordingly, 'the police officer should radiate this feeling, leaving his affective trace as he moved through the populace' (idem, ibidem).

12. Justice McCardie in *Fisher v. Oldham Corporation [1930] 2 KB 364*, apud Wall (2021, 112).

13. 'As soon as it is born,' observes Cato in Cicero's *de Finibus*, 'an animal is conciliated to itself and it is commended to preserve itself and to love its own constitution and things that tend to preserve that constitution, while it is alienated from destruction and things and seem to bring about destruction' (apud Heller-Roazen 2007, 108).

14. On the relations and differences between the Stoic notion of *oikeiosis* and Spinoza's *conatus*, see Miller (2015).

15. This was also tied with a Victorian concern with increasing the comfort of lower classes.

16. It is certainly not a coincidence, as we suggested, that the modern, bourgeois notion of comfort did surface in the same period Cerdá was writing: the *domesticisation* of the urban pursued in Cerdá's project was to be complemented by a set of aesthetic expectations which were framed around notions of order, cleanliness and civilisation— 'urbanisation', in Cerdá's terms (see chapter 2).

17. The relation between comfort and wilderness was also prominent in the colonial experience, where the railway played a key role in shaping the aesthetics of the colonial imaginary, as a voyage of civilisation experienced from the pleasure of a comfortable couch, at a speed that allowed only a fuzzy impression of the surrounding landscape, while the remainder of this civilising process and its violence was crammed in the uncomfortable spaces of the third class. See for instance Schivelbusch (2014[1977]).

18. For a different and yet compatible perspective on the transformation the sensorium underwent around this time, see Jameson (2013).

19. This development can be captured through the concept of atmo-culture, developed by Pavoni and Brighenti (2017; Brighenti and Pavoni 2020; 2021a) to bring forth an ontological understanding of culture *as* atmosphere, while at the same time referring to the surfacing of a culture *of* the atmosphere.

20. Among countless examples, see for instance *Deneys Reitz v SA Commercial, Catering and Allied Workers Union and others 1991 (2) SA 685 (W)*, when a workers' protest in Johannesburg was forbidden on the ground that it was infringing the 'right to peace and quietness' of the residents (see Grant 1991; van der Walt 2007). Notions of 'peace' and 'tranquillity' play a key role in 'qualifying' affectively and aesthetically the notion of (urban) order that frames the 'normal background' with respect to which questions of disorder, and therefore danger, risk and fear, are played out in urban security politics.

21. *R v Howell [1982] QB 416; [1981] 3 All ER 383*, see Leung (2013, 38).

22. Initially the Injunction was named Injunction to Prevent Nuisance and Annoyance (IPNA), and went under considerable controversy since, as Kevin Brown writes (2020, 99), 'the test for imposition of an IPNA was to have a lower threshold than that for either the ASBO or the CBO. Rather than the latters' test of causing harassment, alarm or distress to any person, the test for the IPNA was to be that the behaviour had caused, or was capable of causing, nuisance or annoyance to any person'. Brown further discusses the problems that CBO and Injunction still present, and the changed cultural context that, he argues, allowed for their far less critical acceptance by the public, 'despite being just as troubling, if not more so, than their predecessor' (idem, 104).

23. Part I, ch. I, art. 1 (1). See also Part I, ch. II, art. 19 (1).

24. COMMUNICATION FROM THE COMMISSION TO THE COUNCIL AND THE EUROPEAN PARLIAMENT–The prevention of crime in the European Union–Reflection on common guidelines and proposals for Community finan-

cial support /* COM/2000/0786 final */. https://eur-lex.europa.eu/legal-content/LT/ALL/?uri=celex:52000DC0786. Our emphasis.

25. José Antonio da Conceição defines public safety (*segurança pública*) as the situation in which 'everyone enjoy their rights and practice their activities without perturbation from others' (2008, 17; our translation).

26. Evidently, there is a clear difference with classic situational crime prevention models, where the individual is responsibilised in two senses. On the one hand, s/he is responsible vis-à-vis committing crime (although the environment may be assumed, at least indirectly, as an extenuating circumstance). On the other hand, the individual is also responsible to avoid providing a favourable environment to crime itself. Dean termed 'new prudentialism' 'the multiple "responsibilisation" of individuals, families, households, and communities for their own risks' (1999, 162; see also Hay 2006).

27. This process has been described for instance by Massumi (2005) in the context of the US Terror Alert System (a warning system tailored around colours or words which indicate increase or decrease in the level of a given threat). As he contends, the effect of this system is that of affectively modulating the *socius*, not in a deterministic sense (evidently not everybody would act in the same way once the terror alert is shifted to, say, orange), but more precisely insofar as producing a state of common attunement, by activating direct bodily responses (e.g. anxiety, fear, uneasiness) depending on given levels.

28. One of the very reasons why we argue urban violence cannot be defined by defining the set of manifestations that the concept should encompass (see introduction).

29. We agree with Regan Koch and Alan Latham (2012) that the notion of domesticisation—just like that of comfort, as we just maintained—should not be presupposed as negative, repressive or oppressive. Domesticisation is an unavoidable process of becoming-at-home, individually and collective, that everybody undergoes. Moreover, it is not a unilateral process of subjection: as many anthropologist and ethologist have shown, it is a much more complex and multilateral relation in which the distinction between tamer and tamed is far from being clear (e.g. Cassidy and Mullin 2007; Pearson 2021). Our question is more precisely that of framing domestication and comfort within a precise socio-economical and cultural articulation, in order to be able to assess its consequences.

30. We believe it is crucial to avoid conflating the three dimensions of comfort as individuation, phenomenological sensation and historical apparatus. This is for instance what is done in an otherwise intriguing anthropological exploration such as Stefano Boni's *Homo Comfort* (2014), whose central thesis is that the yearning for comfort has produced a scission among human beings, and between humans and the broader environment. As can be seen from this sentence, Boni tends to conflate the three qualities of comfort, ending up criticising its phenomenological and ontological qualities—at times, with an overromantic, techno-phobic perspective—instead of exploring what is actually problematic with comfort, namely its peculiar aesthetic-affective configuration in the context of the society of comfort. Comfort is not a hyper-technological mediation that seeks to control, screen off and neutralise sense, as he contends (the fallacy of transparent immediacy is here to be seen), but rather it

is part of a necessary process of common habituation/ordering—the generation of a common nomotop—that makes no sense to criticise *per se*, that is, in isolation from the given epoch and society in which it materialises.

31. This is also evident in the way the CPTED (Crime Prevention Through Environmental Design) acronym has been at times substituted by CP-UDP (Crime Prevention through Urban Design and Planning), where the relation with an explicitly *urban* understanding of security—and thus the integration of security strategies with urban politics at large—is evident.

32. See also *Social Indicators Research*, founded in 1974 and self-described as 'the leading journal on problems related to the measurement of all aspects of the quality of life' (from the journal homepage, see www.springer.com/journal/11205).

33. As for the term *securitas*, it is again in the work of Cicero that we find the first appearance of the term *decorum*, in the *De Oratore*. Since then, Ethan Stoneman writes, decorum would begin to refer to a 'more abstract awareness of the arbitrary social codes that shape any particular arrangement of propriety' (2011, 132): rules of conduct, that is, aimed to configure the relation between place and behaviour, signs and situation, as well as 'providing social cohesion and distributing power' (Hariman 1992, 156).

34. Webster's Unabridged Dictionary (1913). According to the main definition in Italian Treccani vocabulary, *decoro* is a 'dignity that, in the appearance, manners and acting, is suitable [*conveniente*] to the social condition of a person or category [*dignità che nell'aspetto, nei modi, nell'agire, è conveniente alla condizione sociale di una persona o di una categoria*]' (our translation). See www.treccani.it/vocabolario/decoro2/.

35. Legislative Decree 42/2004. The law refers to 'the appearance, decorum and public fruition [*l'aspetto, il decoro o la pubblica fruizione*]' (art. 49.1) and 'the decorum and enjoyment [*il decoro e il godimento*]' (art. 96.1) of a given good.

36. The 2003 UNESCO Convention for the Safeguarding of the Intangible Cultural Heritage defines intangible cultural heritage as the 'practices, representations, expressions, knowledge, skills—as well as the instruments, objects, artefacts and cultural spaces associated therewith—that communities, groups and, in some cases, individuals recognize as part of their cultural heritage. This intangible cultural heritage, transmitted from generation to generation, is constantly recreated by communities and groups in response to their environment, their interaction with nature and their history, and provides them with a sense of identity and continuity, thus promoting respect for cultural diversity and human creativity' (art. 2). In Italy, consider the disappearance of the term 'material' from the expression '*testimonianza avente varole materiale di civiltà* [patrimony bearing material witness of civility]' in the 1967 proceedings of 'Commissione Franceschini' (created by Law 310/1964 and which elaborated the normative and cultural guidelines for the management of cultural heritage as an autonomous field of public action) to '*testimonianza avente varole di civiltà*' enshrined in Legislative Decree 112/1998, art. 148.

37. The recent crusades of Italian mayors against the packed lunch (*pranzo al sacco*), on the account that eating sandwiches while sitting somewhere in the historical centre is indecorous, is a perfect case in point. It goes without saying, if packed lunch is for-

bidden, then the only option is eating at the (overpriced) restaurants of the historical centre, revealing quite clearly which classes of tourists the mayors are interested in attracting (see Bukowski 2019).

38. For instance, Nick Dines (2014) shows how *degrado* was central to the representation of popular classes during the third way transition of the Partito Comunista Italiano in Naples.

39. The 2008 decree refers to 'those situations that constitute a hindrance to traffic circulation [*pubblica viabilità*] or alter *decoro urbano*, and in particular those [situations concerning] unauthorised retail or occupation of public land', as well as 'those behaviours, like street prostitution or harassing panhandling, that can offend public decency, even for the modalities they are manifested, or rather seriously disturb the free use of public spaces' (art. 2; our translation).

40. Converted, with modifications, into Law 48/2017—from which are taken the following excerpts.

41. Consider the words of the 1996 European Sustainable Cities Report for the European Commission: 'physical problems, like decline, decay and pollution of cities, contribute to serious human and social problems, including alienation and violence. It is necessary to deal with both physical and social problems' (Gruppo di esperti sull'ambiente urbano 1996, 156; our translation).

42. As Coomaraswamy (1939) observed, as regards the artistic field, decorum has to do precisely with 'the condemnation of an excess'.

43. Danger has not simply to do with crime but also, coherently with the Foucauldian reflection, with a wider economy of urban valorisation (see also Ascari 2020). This is explicit, for instance, in the association, in the 2017 Italian decree, of places of cultural interest with those 'interested by significant touristic flows' (art. 5) among the ones deserving protection, *de facto* legally sanctioning a hierarchy of deserving and undeserving urban areas.

44. See Stoneman (2011) for a reading, in the field of rhetorics, consistent with our approach, employing the *police/politique* dyad of Jacques Rancière.

CHAPTER EIGHT

∼

Smartness

Woher die Dinge ihre Entstehung haben, dahin müssen sie auch zu-
grunde gehen nach der Notwendigkeit; denn sie müssen Buße zahlen
und für ihre Ungerechtigkeiten gerichtet werden gemäß der Ordnung
der Zeit.[1]

On August 9, 2014, police officer Darren Wilson shot and killed Michael
Brown Jr. at the Ferguson Market and Liquor in Ferguson, Missouri. Brown
was suspect of a petty robbery, the stealing of a box of cigars; and was to become one of many Black and Brown victims of police violence in the USA.
In the following days, civil unrest inflamed the city. On November 24 of that
same year, when a grand jury decided to not indict Wilson, protests erupted
again in 170 cities across the USA. Eventually, the killing of Michael Brown
was one of the triggers of the national growth and consolidation of Black
Lives Matter (BLM) and further social movements that argue for police
reform and/or abolition.

What if Michael Brown had never encountered the agent of his death?
What if a technological fix could have prevented the crime in the first place?
This is the question Mark Maguire (2018, 154) poses:

if the critical social sciences simply engage with new policing and security technologies in terms of their possible nefarious uses, we will lose the possibility of
genuine critique, by which I mean an understanding of the core assumptions
from which those technologies emerged and the alternatives available at root
. . . Even if we distrust technological governance and despise the advocates of

predictive solutions, we must ask ourselves this: what if the robbery in the Ferguson Market and Liquor had never occurred?

Very much in line with our proposal to think about security (and violence) beyond the critique of ideology, this question indirectly suggests that the potential of new technological developments—in policing and beyond—should not be *ideologically* dismissed in advance. Yet, at a closer look, its problematic presuppositions emerge forcefully. The robbery at the Ferguson Market and Liquor is not an isolated event that can be surgically separated from the imaginary and atmosphere out of which it emerges. Likewise, technology cannot be assessed with a merely instrumental gaze. In this case, it is the wider conceptual field informing this whole discourse—i.e., the intersection between smart city ideas and policing practices, converging in the technologically intensive and future-oriented approach known as predictive policing—to be problematic in itself. As we will see, there are several reasons why this question risks obscuring this very field rather than pointing to its clarification. At a first level, as we discussed (especially in chapter 2, Researching Urban Violence), police and the security apparatus at large are responsible for defining crime: the question of whether they are or not effective in reducing crime is therefore controversial in the first place. At a deeper level, as Louise Amoore (2020, 5–6) puts it, 'algorithms are implicated in new regimes of verification, new forms of identifying a wrong or of truth telling in the world'—in other words, new regimes of truth are ushered in with the advent of algorithmic computation, to the extent that uncritically engaging with Maguire's question risks overlooking the consequences of this epistemological shift, reproducing the very opacity that characterises the age of the algorithm. By unpacking these observations, this chapter engages with the specific (urban) atmosphere of violence this novel configuration and emerging urban security instruments imply, providing another lens to the conceptual argument developed in chapter 6.

Prior to do so, however, a brief introduction is in order. What Maguire's question implicitly points to is the possibility that the Hobbesian dream of absolute security will be finally realised, or indeed *solved*, courtesy of digital technologies. The 'city without violence', would find its earthly materialisation in the smart city. Therefore, by examining the smart city we are able to reflect on the ultimate, if at this stage still incipient, implications of the imaginary of (absolute) security for the materiality of urban violence. It is with the smart city and its genealogies, then, that we shall begin.

Smart/Cybernetics

Orit Halpern's *Beautiful Data*, exploring the post-WW2 history of the relation between communication, perception, reason and cybernetic in the urban space and beyond, begins with a description of Songdo, a new city built from scratch on reclaimed land close to Seoul, South Korea. Developed by US real estate company Gale, with the collaboration of the multinational technology corporation Cisco, Songdo is the quintessential smart city, 'an entire territory whose sole mandate is to produce interactive data fields that, like the natural resources of another era, will be mined for wealth and produce the infrastructure for a new way of life' (Halpern 2014, 3). Key to this project, and to the smart city rationale more generally, is that the city is envisaged as a self-regulating organism capable of smoothly ordering itself through the coordination between human and non-human perception, information and the urban space. Smartness and intelligence, Halpern observes, are in this context understood as a 'sensorial capacity for feedback between the users and the environment' (idem, 4). Key to this fantasy is the assumption that digital technologies and, more precisely, machine vision and big data, thanks to their capacity to break with traditional epistemological limits, [2] be 'the solution to economic, social, political, and ecological problems; a new resource to extract in a world increasingly understood as resource constrained' (idem, 5).

Technocratic fantasies inhabit the urban imaginary at least since Francis Bacon's *New Atlantis* (1626). As we have seen, both Hobbes's new political science and Cerdá's new urban science may be read as attempts to overcome the conflict and messiness of (urban) life via (de-politicised) scientific praxis: a quintessentially technocratic urban project. The advent of digital technology follows and drastically updates this project, prompting the 'reorganization of planning and architecture around computing' (Halpern 2014, 10–11). The smart city thus emerges, as an urban imaginary premised on the power that big data and computation might harbour vis-à-vis harmonising every aspect of urban life (municipal services, public safety, health, education, quality of life, transport, communication, water, energy, etc.) within an integrated and dynamic infrastructure.

Countless are the critical accounts of the smart city, as well as the perspectives from which they have been developed. What interests us here, because of its direct relevance for the imaginary of urban violence and the (policing/security) policies that feed it, is the epistemological field that grounds the smart city concept and its actualisation. At its core is, in the words of pioneer MIT designer Gyorgy Kepes, the notion that 'the essential vision of reality presents us not with fugitive appearances but with felt patterns of order' (apud Halpern 2014, 14). In the last chapter we explored the 'sense of order' in the contemporary city as an urban aesthetics shaped by the encounter between the modern urban imaginary, bourgeois sensibility and mass urban-isation. Within this understanding, instead, order appears to assume a much more ontological quality, as a quality that is intrinsic to the real and whose patterns require machine vision to be fully unlocked. Smart city imaginaries foreground a novel aesthetic of perception, communication and information, one that is produced by the mining, gathering and patterning of data, through various processes (featurisation, translation, labelling, etc.), which engender a novel *logistics of perception*, to use Paul Virilio's famous expression.[3]

In 1967, the first US drones flew over Laos, sending information to IBM centres in Thailand and South Vietnam. Reflecting on this event, Virilio (1989[1984]) sees a novel logistical paradigm in the making: the shooting (in terms of weapons) field transformed into a shooting (in terms of camera) field. As a result, more than the actual movement of bodies, it is their *potential* mobility that becomes the object of calculation, projection and control at a distance: 'space is no longer separated from the trajectory; the relation to that space is precisely defined by this "navigation", and this relationship creates a kind of behavioural ballistics' (Virilio interviewed in Ruby 2001[1996], 60).

War was the training ground of another MIT professor, Norbert Wiener. During World War II, he worked on enhancing the precision of anti-aircraft missiles and devised a system 'based on constantly updating their trajectory, comparing the real trajectory of the target with prior estimates' (Cardon et al. 2018, 9). This was, in a nutshell, the idea of feedback loop at the grounds of the theory of cybernetics, which Wiener defined as the 'science of communica-tion and control' (1948). What is key to cybernetics is the 'control or predic-tion of future events and actions' (Halpern 2014, 25). A novel relation with space and time is implied, one that is based on anticipation, calculation and probability. Foucault described in these very terms the logic of security that informs governmentality, as a rationality that does not target bodies but rather populations, and whose knowledge is informed by data-gathering and statisti-cally organised around desirable thresholds. Governmentality indicates a novel epistemology of governing—a word that, as countless times told, stems from the Latin *gubernator*, in turn derived from the Greek *kybernetes*, i.e., steersman, from which Wiener had crafted the name of his novel science[4]— grounded on a novel way to visualise and organise information in order to control and steer socio-economical tendencies and probabilities. What Foucault did not and, indeed, could not explore, however, were the profound changes that digital technologies would have brought about to this model.

Control/Visualisation

It is in the form of an afterthought to Foucault's work on governmentality that his friend Gilles Deleuze wrote his famous, enigmatic *Postscript on the Societies of Control*. This short text, commented upon a thousand times (including by us: see Pavoni 2018a), speculates on what may become of governmentality after the digital revolution, whose contours were still rather sketchy at the time of his writing (1992[1990]). In Wiener's theory of cybernetics the notion of 'control' refers to the 'maintenance of a goal by active compensation of perturbations' (Heylighen and Joslyn 2003, 155). It indicates the given state that a system, either physiological or technological, seeks to achieve 'in the form of self-regulation produced through formally equivalent circuits or closed loops of negative feedback' (Clark 2016, 2). We can obviously recognise here the homeostatic and recursive logic feeding both the smart city rhetoric and its technological infrastructure: the capacity that machine learning algorithms have 'of integrating contingency into their operations' (Yuk Hui interviewed in Lovink 2019a; see below). Again, we find echoes of Foucault's definition of governmentality, premised on the setting up of

> regulatory mechanisms . . . to establish an equilibrium, maintain an average, establish a sort of homeostasis, and compensate for variations within this general population and its aleatory field. In a word, security mechanisms have to be installed around the random element inherent in a population of living beings so as to optimize a state of life. (2003[1997], 246)

It was not from Wiener however, but from the writings of William S. Burroughs, that Deleuze borrowed the term. Control, to Burroughs, is the repressive power the 'word' has with respect to thinking. Insofar as tied to a linguistic structure, the word 'prevents expansion of consciousness' by 'controlling thought feeling and apparent sensory impressions of the human host' (interviewed in Corso and Ginsberg 1992[1961]). What the word does, then, is entrapping human thought within pre-given channels of designation, manifestation and signification, in this way pre-empting the expression—the *event*—of sense (Moore 2007a; 2007b; Deleuze 1990[1969]). Control, in other terms, is the way language *speaks* through us. Burroughs was concerned with a form of power that is inscribed within the very linguistic structure through which we think—hence his attempts to 'escape' it by reinserting an aleatory logic, via the cut-up,[5] in a similar way to the situationists sought to 'escape' the pre-determination of urban space through the *dérive*.

A note of caution is needed. All too often the study and interpretation of the society of control entails the risk of falling into the trap of paranoid thinking (Birchall et al. 2010; Bissel at al. 2012; Pavoni 2018a). Instead, we believe it is more interesting exploring how these two understandings of control, Wiener's and Burrough's, merge in Deleuze's cryptic text. In the 'societies' the *Postscript* is concerned with, control appears as having a two-fold character: an immanent logic of self-regulation between increasingly interconnected systems at the linguistic, biological and technological level (see also Deleuze 2006[1986]); and a logic of 'literal' prevention, consistent with the etymology of the term we already touched upon in chapter 4 (from *praeevenio*, i.e., coming before the event). The smooth self-regulation of the system requires preventing any possible disruption, that is, event, from taking place. What this crucially entails, differently from 'traditional' governmentality, is that control is concerned with possibility rather than probability (Amoore 2013).

As we will discuss at length below, where these new governmentalities of control—inherent to the logic of the smart city—intersect with the expansive nature of policing, the conceptualisation of crime (and violence) seems to undergo another variation: crime, no longer just a probability that must be *governed* under a certain threshold, is now framed as a possibility that must be prevented (Clear and Cadora 2012[2001]; Amoore 2013). The Hobbesian fantasy of absolute security, which the pragmatism of governmentality attempted to dismiss—barred exceptions, such as in the case of terrorism (see chapter 4, Researching Urban Violence)—makes a comeback as a 'realistic' objective of governance, thanks to digital computing's unprecedented capacity to visualise, articulate, act and react upon the social field.[6] This novel capacity to visualise the social—and therefore to extract, gather and organise spatial and temporal information about it—is the power that predictive policing promises.

Visualisation, in this sense, means 'making data actionable through representation while also facilitating the ongoing analysis of data' (Halpern 2014, 22). This is how IBM defines it, namely as 'the language for the act of translation between a complex world and a human observer', that is, 'the formulation of an interaction between different scales and agents—human, network, global, nonhuman', as well as between different temporal scales (apud idem, ibidem). Visualisation, understood as a complex ensemble of extraction, translation and patterning, is the way in which machine vision functions and, as we are to see, its violence is deployed. In pre-digital times, visualisation had been a main concern of yet another MIT professor, prior a student under Kepes.

In his seminal work, *The Image of the City*, Kevin Lynch proposed a cybernetic, albeit obviously still analogical, approach to the city, envisaged as an ensemble of individuals whose imaginations were harmonised within a coherent, shared imaginary. In the growing complexity of contemporary ur-ban life, Lynch observed, the individual is exposed to the risk of alienation, that is, disorientation, in a landscape whose aesthetic is increasingly harder to process. Lynch devised two key concepts to counter urban alienation: *legibility*, which measures 'the ease with which [city] parts can be recognized and can be organized into a coherent pattern' (1960, 2–3); and *imageability*, that is, 'that quality in a physical object which gives it a high probability of evoking a strong image in any given observer' (idem, 9). What Lynch aimed to achieve, via the aesthetic reconfiguration of cities by means of signposts (paths, landmarks, edges, nodes, districts), was coordinating the relation be-tween the collective and individual dimensions of the urban imaginary, un-derstood as the coming together of perception, imagination and movement. Not unlike Cerdá, Lynch was interested in taming the wildness of public space via the use of specific *savoirs*—in his case, system theory, psychology and cybernetics—with the aim of both unfolding and prompting those 'felt patterns of order' that are assumed to emerge through distributed interac-tion and feedback mechanisms, and that were to be subsequently coded into algorithmic protocols.

Lynch did not intend to address urban disorientation—that is, alien-ation—via the normative, top-down model of an ideal city, but rather by gathering data via empirical surveys (questionnaires, interviews, mental maps, etc.), finding patterns and reconfiguring the aesthetics of the urban surface accordingly. 'The city must be plastic to the perceptual habits of thousands of citizens, open-ended to change of function and meaning, recep-tive to the formation of new imagery' (Lynch 1960, 119). As Brighenti and Pavoni (2021a, 7) note, 'by developing an approach in which data-gathering and pattern-finding precede policy decisions (contrary to what happens with normative approaches), Lynch aimed at unfolding a recipe, or algorithm, for successful urban-psychic orientation'. A purely scientific approach to the urban, therefore, aimed at finding solutions to given problems via pragmatic fixes, without questioning the constitutions of the problem in the first place.[7] Lynch did so by foregrounding matters of perception, aesthetics and psychol-ogy, while at the same time displacing matters of class, social structure and inequality (Halpern 2014). As with Cerdá one century earlier, however, Lynch's apparently non-normative, post-moral approach to urban planning does contain an implicit normative orientation, one that presupposes that the smoothness, efficiency and efficacy of urban circulation must take the pride of place over improvisation, unpredictability and *dérive*. This presuppo-sition, we are to see, can be found as implicitly articulating the tendency to coalesce notions of 'unusual', 'unexpected' and 'suspicious', that informs predictive policing and feeds its algorithmic logics.[8] In both approaches, whatever the differences, urban problems are not supposed to be questioned for the (social, political, economic, etc.) way in which they emerge and the violent structures that keep them in place, but are rather taken as a self-evident urban environment with respect to which a solution—a technological fix—must be found. In Cerdá's and Lynch's depoliticised urban aesthetics, in other words, we find the seeds of the *solutionism* that feeds the contemporary imaginary and aesthetic of the smart city, as well as the implicit logics orienting predictive policing, to which we may now turn.

Prediction/Prevention

As the previous discussion showed, the genealogy of both the smart city and predictive policing is the nth expression of the long history of the *project* of the urban, that is, the desire to make the city object of data calculation, prediction and control. This history seems to proceed in cycles (Townsend 2015; Mattern 2015; Angelo and Vormann 2018), according to which emergent socio-technical paradigms create hopes for technological solutions to old problems, however leaving untouched their structural conditions, as the technocratic rationale through which 'solutions' are applied tends to bypass political considerations as regards social asymmetries and inequalities, and it is in this way bound to reproduce them. This creates new iterations of old problems, and novel forms of exploitation and inequalities that add up to the old ones, calling for further innovation, and so on. The version of this imaginary that informs predictive policing, at the intersection of the smart and safe city, seems to be particularly powerful: on the one hand, the global imaginary of the smart city offers 'a general but flexible narrative' (White 2016, 3), whereas technology is framed as the adequate response to any number of impending yet unavoidable 'crises' (mass urbanisation, climate change, and so forth; see Nugent and Suhail 2021); on the other, the imaginary of the safe city focuses on a specific, yet particularly sensitive field, by promising to prevent crime and violence from happening in the first place.

This convergence is evident for instance as regards the role played by IBM, probably the major global player in smart city developments. When Sam Palmisano famously delivered the 'A Smarter Planet' speech at the Council on Foreign Relations in 2008, IBM had already been working for at least two years on predictive policing in Memphis, and would in a few years consider crime detection and prevention a core business activity (see McNeill 2015). In line with the logic of the smart city, predictive policing deploys technology, and puts governments in partnership with private companies, to offer a future-oriented, technically neutral solution to crime and violence. It should not come as a surprise that predictive policing emerged in the USA, where crime is not only entrenched in socio-economic relationships (including racial and class strife) in a particularly evident way, but is also an extremely politicised and contested issue (see Tulumello 2018a). In this context, predictive policing's promise that 'chaos can be controlled with information and technology' (Rosin 2008) was particularly appealing to policy makers.

In operational terms, predictive policing has to do with 'the application of statistical methods to identify likely targets for police intervention (the *predictions*) to prevent crimes or solve past crimes, followed by conducting interventions against those targets' (Hunt et al. 2014, iii; emphasis in original). It promises to reduce crime in the present by anticipating future crimes through technologically intensive analysis of past police reports interfaced with predictive analytics. In this sense, predictive policing is the natural evolution of the premises of contemporary security and the particular relation with the event—i.e., prevention—that it introduced (see chapter 3 and chapter 4, Researching Urban Violence). At the same time, predictive policing has a different ambition. It is concerned with acting at the level of the possible, rather than the probable. It dreams of eradicating crime by acting *before* this happens, rather than simply reducing its likelihood.[9] Technology, in the shape of an ever-increasing, massive field of heterogeneous datasets, and the development of machine learning algorithms able to see and sieve through them, thus 'appears to harbour new capacities of peering into the future and revealing the unknowns to be tamed and governed' (Aradau and Blanke 2017, 374). It is the very notion of 'prediction', in other words, to undergo an epistemological and strategic shift with respect to the meaning it assumed vis-à-vis traditional governmentality.

Differently from the Hobbesian dream of absolute security, we argued, governmentality introduces a more pragmatic stance vis-à-vis contingency, which does not seek to eliminate, but rather 'presupposes, and thrives on' (Pottage 1998, 9). In this sense, 'prediction does not focus on stopping or avoiding an event, but on managing its consequences within a milieu' (Aradau and Blanke 2017, 378), that is, on keeping the statistical curve under a desirable threshold. Yet, as societies grow complex and security politics generate imaginaries that fill them with fearful atmospheres, 'Beck's (2002) notion of de-bounded risks assumes a new meaning; not only are risks spatially, temporally and socially de-bounded, they are also de-bounded from quantitative, predictive actuarialism and invigorated with cultural constructions and speculative popular imaginations about what could potentially transpire' (Boyle and Haggerty 2009, 261). As Philip Boyle and Kevin Haggerty were observing more than a decade ago, this means that, especially in counter-terrorism scenarios, a different approach to risk control seemed to be surfacing, namely a 'non-actuarial planning orientation focused on what could *potentially* happen independent of probability assessment' (idem, ibidem; emphasis in original; see also Anderson 2010a; Amoore 2013).[10] Predictive analytics promises to overcome this apparent contradiction, by 're-binding' risk and thus restoring the centrality of prediction through a novel approach that is not based on statistical modelling but on the power of big data (Abbott 2014) and on the capacity of machine learning algorithms to sort out the information overload of the hyperconnected society.

The emergence and consolidation of this promise can be traced through a brief history of predictive policing. Early experiments of crime mapping can be traced back to the 1960s, with experiences in Philadelphia, Cleveland and California (Hinton 2016, 91). But it is during the 1990s, in New York City, that a major step forward was taken. Among the novelties introduced by Police Commissioner William Bratton, whom we met already (see chapters 5 and 7), was the program CompStats (short for Compare Statistics), launched in 1994. CompStats, developed by the New York City Police Department, was originally thought to be an accountability instrument, useful to hold precinct commanders to account for crime spikes. However, not only did the weekly meetings served to discuss past statistics, but, on their grounds, geo-referenced patterns and regularities were identified to map high-crime areas and 'rationally distribute' patrols (Jefferson 2018a, 1254). Indeed, CompStats came to be considered also a tool, and a successful one, for crime reduction: in 1996, it was acknowledged with an Innovations in American Government Award by the Harvard Kennedy School Ash Center as a 'crime reduction management tool'.[11] During the very same period 'zero tolerance' was also praised as an effective crime reduction strategy: since crime was going down for structural reasons, police could claim success for any tactic or strategy (see chapter 5, Researching Urban Violence).

Predictive policing proper was born sometime around 2006, when University of California criminologist Jeffrey Brantingham and mathematician and computer scientist George Mohler teamed up with the Los Angeles Police Department to create PredPol, a proprietary software owned by the homonymous company founded soon after. That same year, the partnership between the Memphis Police Department and IBM launched Blue CRUSH (short for Crime Reduction Utilizing Statistical History), a system on which University of Memphis criminologist Richard Janikowski had been working for some years. Thanks to the emerging logics and techniques of the smart city, predictive policing pushes crime mapping and analysis one step further by adopting (near) real-time analysis, and promising to map future high-crime areas by extracting data and seeking to 'discove[r] interesting and meaningful patterns' in them.[12] This is done by combining GIS, algorithmic analytics with state-of-the-art mapping and visualisation (see Fittered et al. 2015), and relies heavily on partnerships with private companies (IBM in particular). PredPol is by now the most popular technology, used by dozens of departments all around the USA (Hvistendahl 2016). A more recent, if less common, version of predictive policing works, instead that with time/space crime patterns, with individual risk assessment. This is the case of the Strategic Subject List created in 2013 by the Chicago Police Department (Saunders et al. 2016) and of the system controversially developed by Palantir in New Orleans (Winston 2018b), which assess the likeliness that individuals may be involved in crimes in the future on the grounds of their criminal records, socio-economic status and networks of relations—similar predictions are also used in the US criminal justice system to support decisions on bails, sentencing, release, probation and parole (see O'Neil 2016).

Predictive policing is also central to the third generation of CPTED, in which the aesthetic concerns of the *first* and the 'community' orientation of the *second* are reworked through digital technologies (see chapter 7, and especially note 3). More generally, it can be said that predictive policing is meant to overcome the contradictions of the classic situational/social dichotomy of crime control. On the one hand, where social prevention, by changing the structural determinants of crime and violence, promises improvement in the medium- to long-term, predictive policing promises to disrupt crime in the here and now, preventing the event of crime by means of severing the relation between causes and effects, while leaving said causes for the most part untouched. On the other hand, where situational prevention acts on generic future threats, predictive policing promises to surgically act on specific threats, supposedly individuated via data analytics. In this sense, there is a significant epistemological shift vis-à-vis the understanding of risk in situational prevention. A locker, a fence, a bullet-proof glass are designed to prevent generic threats, and their strength should be 'calculated' by balancing the cost of their production and use versus the risk of loss (which is itself a function of the assessed probability of the threat and of the value of the things protected). Similarly, the deployment of preventative patrols in traditional fashion can be calculated through a function of their cost and the expected benefit in terms of the total of crimes expected to be prevented.[13] Traditional risk assessments are generic (a cost versus an average value in terms of benefit), quasi-static (the locker is what it is until it is replaced or

292 ~ Chapter Eight

broken; police patrols are assigned once a day, with some possibility for adjustment, but most often only after a crime has already happened) and probabilistic. Put otherwise, situational approaches such as Broken Windows, whose contradiction we fleshed out already, project a generic individual who is engaged in cost-opportunities evaluation within a generic urban space,[14] and set out to develop a strategy that is aimed at designing (in aesthetic, legal, and social sense) this space in a way that will 'persuade', either rationally or emotionally, the individual not to commit crime. Accordingly, situational prevention works by disrupting the 'favourable' context and prompting the criminal to choose to not commit a crime. Their problem, in other words, is that of *depurating* urban space from its criminogenic potential, that is, from those environmental affordances that are assumed to offer 'opportunities' (in the wider sense) for criminal activities to a generic individual. As the old saying goes, it is the opportunity that makes the criminal. The aim is therefore that of modifying the generic 'situation' by either reducing opportunities (e.g., by encouraging people to not walk alone at night or carry large amounts of cash) or increasing risks (e.g., by placing surveillance cameras or deploying police patrols). Granted, Brantingham (2013) has suggested a more complex theory for car thefts, arguing that criminals follow sub-optimal choices guided by evolutionary patterns (see also Maguire 2018). At any rate, positivist criminology has long discussed most property crimes, and quintessentially burglary, as following rational choice patterns. And, more importantly for our discussion, in the framework of predictive policing the use of police patrols as preventative means is presented in the framework of a paradigm of situational prevention.

Differently from traditional situational prevention, however, predictive policing does engage with a wholly different space, not the tangible and aesthetic materiality of urban space, but a sort of mathematically abstracted space. In a sense, predictive policing, and predictive analytics more generally, are the quintessential materialisation of the epistemological revolution announced by René Descartes in his *Discours sur le Method* (1637): the complete mathematisation of the real, that is, the reduction of every bits of reality to points within a coordinate system. As for Descartes, also predictive analytics purports a geometrical form of knowledge deployed onto an abstract space, where data are made available and 'labelled' for algorithmic processing. As we will see below, the very production of such an abstract space (so-called 'featurisation' or 'vectorisation') may be understood as a violent process in itself. Differently from situational prevention (which works, we may say, in a more Aristotelic fashion, by addressing the domain of aesthetic sensibility), predictive policing unfolds on an abstract space populated by data points, which are patterned, and therefore recomposed, with the purpose of profiling criminogenic spaces (deployed to draw 'hot spots', 'heat maps')[15] and certain individual patterns-of-life (known as 'POLs'),[16] which are in turn understood as potentially generative of criminal activity in actual urban space. At its most striking, literally so, this can be observed in the 'machinic vision' (Johnston 1999) of new generation, twenty-first-century drones, which survey the terrain and process the information they gather looking for anomalous patterns that can prompt so-called *signature strikes*. Here, a wholly novel logistics of perception is at play: machine vision emerges through the recursive de-/re-composition of a constellation of bits of information that are processed according to POLs models that bypass both the object of the observation (the human target) and the subject of the observation (the drone-operator) (Kosek 2010; Bousquet 2018; Bloomberg 2019; Brighenti and Pavoni, 2020, 432). More prosaically, this is what occurs in contemporary predictive policing, courtesy of video analytics tools that scan the countless images coming from public and commercial cameras in search for unusual behaviour. This logistics of perception—or 'algorithmic vision' (Brighenti and Pavoni 2020, 431–433)—is at play in today's platform cities, increasingly shaped by ambient computing, itself ushered in by the triangulation of portable-wearable devices, social networks, mapping and GPS location system (e.g., McCullough 2013).

While environmental models assume, and seek to shape, an aesthetic relation between individual and urban space, therefore, predictive analytics is premised on their decomposition into 'dividuals', that is, data and their recomposition into patterns via algorithmic sieving. It is in this sense that, as Antoinette Rouvroy observes, 'algorithmic governmentality is without subject: it operates with infra-individual data and supra-individual patterns without, at any moment, calling the subject to account for himself' (2013, 144–145). In other words, the logic of predictive policing appears as more open, heterogeneous, unstructured and all-encompassing than traditional models of population statistics, prefiguring a proactive rather than reactive approach to crime that unfolds out of the ocean of data produced by an increasingly on-life society.[17] As for instance pointed out by the then IBM's responsible for public safety Mark Cleverley: 'historically policing has been involved with trying to "do better" the job of reacting. What people are starting to do now is a new approach from getting better at reacting to getting better at predicting and becoming proactive' (apud Scannell 2015). The result is that agency is further removed from the 'crime suspect', and rather distributed on a mathematised space where subjectivity is recomposed by machine learning algorithm able to detect patterns that often escape human attention and, indeed, cognition.[18]

To be sure, the base logic is not dissimilar. Although, through its data analytics, predictive policing also inserts a crucial temporal variable—the capacity to freeze individual histories into given trajectories via network analysis—which is especially critical for visual detection functions like first-generation CPTED models, concerned with scanning the environment in search of aesthetic performances that do not match expectations. This is why it is usually referred to as a third generation CPTED. The key difference, of course, is that such a scanning, and the finding of patterns, is increasingly left to the capacity of machine vision, foregrounding a notion of 'deviation' that is different from the traditional, normative concept of 'deviance', since it is concerned with variations vis-à-vis a given set of patterns to be flagged by an automated video analytics (Pasqunelli 2017). Machine learning attends to 'anomaly detection' and, as suggested, tends to freeze urban life within pre-determined behavioural patterns. The deviation from such patterns—even if only an 'unusual' pattern linking race, class and place—may trigger an encounter with the police, which, as we know all too well, is a dangerous event even when the 'suspect' turns out to be perfectly innocent.[19]

This introduces a novel form of (urban) violence in the practice of policing, one that may be referred to as 'algorithmic', following Bellanova and colleagues' suggestion:

> We argue that it is important to foreground, unpack, and examine critically how algorithmic systems feed (into) specific forms of violence, and how they justify violent actions or redefine which type of violence is considered legitimate. (2021, 123

The discourse of predictive policing overlooks—either naively or, more often, strategically—these aspects, since its rationale presupposes that data-gathering and pattern-finding will drastically increase the accuracy through which police are able to know the causes from which certain (violent) effects naturally follow: it is the system that is *aware* of this future trajectory (as explicitly suggested by the name of the largest digital surveillance system in the world, NYPD's Domain Awareness System, built in partnership with Microsoft), even if the criminal may not be. As put bluntly by the Modesto Police Chief Galen Carroll:

> the theory is that you prevent them from committing the crime to begin with . . . Burglars and thieves work in a mathematical way, *whether they know it or not*.[20]

Effectiveness/Fairness

Prior to engage more specifically with the algorithmic rationality of predictive policing and its (urban) violence, however, let us come back to
Maguire's question. We may be distrusting predictive policing, yet, what if it
does work? In light of what has been written so far, there are many reasons to
believe this is the wrong question. From an epistemological standpoint, the
question cannot but be engaged with through those supposedly self-evident
crime statistics we have already problematised (see chapter 2, Researching
Urban Violence). At the same time, the question engages with whether
predictive policing 'actually works' independently from the way in which
the very problem, with respect to which predictive policing purports to be
the 'solution', has been framed in the first place. Evidently, the 'event' of the
robbery cannot be artificially separated from the spatio-temporal density out
of which it emerges. From an ontological standpoint, the question is as much
problematic, since it understands time as a linear flow on which events occur, and according to which future events naturally unfold from present conditions and can therefore be prevented, if their present causes are disrupted,
without perturbing the wider flow of time.[21] Regardless of its capacity to actually 'prevent' a given crime, predictive policing always already acts on the
present in invasive, ontogenetic and violent ways. More precisely, it does so
by reinforcing and reshaping the trade-offs between present and future that
characterises contemporary security at large, trapping the urban within a past
that is supposed to necessarily reproduce the future: a veritable 'dictatorship
of the past, of past taxonomies and behavioural patterns, over the present'
(Pasquinelli and Joler 2021, 1275; see also Chun 2021). The urban violence
this model produces in the present—we will see below—goes far beyond its
actual capacity to curb the specific sort of 'urban violence' it purports to
prevent and for the definition of which, moreover, police are responsible in
the first place. Finally, from a strategic standpoint, if we address predictive
policing only on the side of its effectiveness, we are bound to meet a hardly
contestable reply: if it fails, then it fails because there are not enough data or
algorithmic power. We only need, the argument goes, to develop technologies that are more powerful and more intrusive, which means we also need to
lift the restrictions to our capacity to extract data. This is a quite dangerous
slope. Once we have clarified that the game is rigged, however, and before
exploring more precisely what is the violence predictive policing produces
and reproduces, it may be still worth it to call the bluff. Even if we are to
play within the discursive frame and data through which predictive policing
is 'sold' by its proponents, it is still possible to debunk it.

Predictive policing has been widely advertised as a successful experience. Take for instance Blue CRUSH: in 2009, Memphis Police Department received the award for Excellence in Law Enforcement Communications and Interoperability (Large Cities) by the International Association of Chiefs of Police; while in 2010, Richard Janikowki was designated, by the Memphis newspaper *The Commercial Appeal*, 'as one of the 10 people who helped shape the past decade for Memphis for his work on Blue CRUSH' (Poe 2021). The frenzy around Blue CRUSH's success developed around data released by Memphis Police Department, according to which serious property and violent crimes had dropped 26% between 2006 and 2012 (Vlahos 2012), and similar data reported by other sources (e.g. Smith 2010)—2011 was the last year of full implementation of Blue CRUSH, which was scaled down afterwards. Since Blue CRUSH has scantly been object of empirical scrutiny, virtually all the few academic or journalistic works that have discussed the program report those data without much comment, most lately in occasion of the death of Richard Janikowski (Poe 2021; see Hickman 2013; Perry et al. 2013, 67–69; Dinale 2014; Djukanovic et al. 2015, 103). However, the only two studies that have scrutinised available police data (Vlahos 2012; Tulumello and Iapaolo 2022) have shown that: first, during the period of full implementation of Blue CRUSH, some crimes have gone down, while others have gone up; second, contrary to allegations by policy makers, crime did not start increasing again after the scaling down of the program; and, third and most important, once considered in the long run, the drop of crimes observed in 2006–2011 is in line with an already ongoing crime drop, which can be associated with the national crime drop (see above). Additionally, these conclusions are based on analysis of official police data, without taking into consideration some allegations, made in 2012, that tens of thousands of police memos were not included in police reports between 2006–2011.[22] In other words, irrespective of the problems we have discussed with using police data to study crime trends, what we want to stress here is that official data themselves do not provide any empirical ground for the claim that Blue CRUSH caused a reduction of crime.

Doubts exist well beyond Memphis: a recent review (Meijer and Wessels 2019) has found two papers backing up claims on the effectiveness of predictive policing. These two papers have something in common: the first is authored by the developers of PredPol (Mohler et al. 2015) and the second, on the NYPD's Domain Awareness System, by members of the same department (Levine et al. 2017). This is to say, the only empirical works that have argued that predictive policing reduces crime have been carried out by practitioners invested in the development of the very programs they evaluated. Findings produced by independent research have been quite different. Even two reports by RAND Corporation (one of the major private players in security/safety research in the USA) on the predictive policing program used by the Shreveport Police Department (Louisiana) and on the Chicago's Strategic Subject List (in this case, an individual risk assessment tool) found no significant effects in crime reduction (Hunt et al. 2014; Saunders et al. 2016). In summary, no empirical evidence based on those very data backs, to this day, the effectiveness of predictive policing (Moses and Chan 2018; Meijer and Wessels 2019; Tulumello and Iapaolo 2022).

Yet, could this model provide a way to make police work more 'objective' and bias-free, that is, less influenced by (racial, above all) politics? Needless to say, this is a particularly powerful argument especially in the USA. See for instance the following claim:

> PredPol uses only three data points in making predictions: past type of crime, place of crime and time of crime. It uses no personal information about individuals or groups of individuals, *eliminating any personal liberties and profiling concerns*.[23]

It may not come as a surprise that the only study that, to the best of our knowledge, has partially confirmed this affirmation through an empirical scrutiny of PredPol was authored by Jeffrey Brantingham and his affiliates (2018).[24] And it may not come as a surprise either, that independent research has suggested a quite different panorama. On a general level, research on the relation between scientific evidence and racialisation of policing has long problematised the idea that the use of data (and crime data in particular) prevents or reduces bias or profiling (racial or otherwise), for instance in the history of mass incarceration (Hinton 2016, 17–26). In the field of crime mapping, Brian Jefferson (2016; 2018a) has discussed the embeddedness of racialisation in practices of the New York Police Department, including CompStats.

With specific regard to predictive policing, a growing academic and journalistic literature has emphasised a number of problems (Ferguson, A. G. 2012; Vlahos 2012; Stroud 2014; Townsend 2015; Lum and Isaac 2016; O'Neil 2016; Shapiro 2017; 2019; Jefferson 2018b; Moses and Chan 2018; Munn 2018; Winston 2018b; Alikhademi et al. 2021; Tulumello and Iapaolo 2022; Gatti 2022a). First, research on issues of accountability and transparency, and therefore the possibility to verify claims about the neutrality of predictive policing practices, is hampered by the proprietary nature of algorithms. This issue has been discussed for the smart city, and the so-called 'black-box society', in general (Pasquale 2015; Richardson

2019), but seems to be particularly problematic in the field of predictive policing, and especially in the USA, where police departments and corporations have tended to implement predictive policing either without much political discussion or even secretly—in New Orleans, for instance, Palantir has been testing its predictive technologies without even informing the city government.[25] Second, at a general level, the collection and storage of sensitive data about crime creates significant issues of privacy and data handling, and this is especially relevant in programs where such data are shared among the government and private actors. Third, irrespective of the problems that may or may not exist with their elaboration, as we have already hinted at, the data predictive policing use is collected by the very agency whose biases predictive policing is supposed to overcome: if enforcement, hence reporting, is influenced by class and racial biases (something that has long been discussed and proven, especially in the USA), its algorithmic elaboration will inevitably reproduce, at the very least, the biases that the data contain to begin with. Hence, fourth, a policing practice based on the elaboration of geographic concentration of reported crimes will, if influenced by police biases, provide an aura of neutrality, while deepening pre-existing processes of territorial stigmatisation.

In short, when and where it has been applied, predictive policing has fundamentally implied doubling-down on pre-existing socio-spatial injustices in police activity—for instance, in Memphis, the geography of predictive policing has been a dual one, made up of CCTV cameras placed in wealthy (and White) neighbourhoods and police 'occupation' in poor (and Black and Brown) neighbourhoods.[26] Similarly, an internal PredPol report obtained by Lucy Parsons Labs shows that the company, in contrast with its own public communication, considers predictive policing to be a contemporary form of Broken Windows[27]—a telling fact, irrespective of the differences between traditional situational prevention techniques and predictive policing that we have discussed above. Predictive policing, much like Broken Windows, appears as yet another example of a delusional praxis: 'the ambiguities and contradictions of the patrol are not resolved through algorithmic remediation. Instead, they lead to new indeterminacies, trade-offs, and experimentations based on unfalsifiable claims' (Shapiro 2019, abstract). In the next section we are to come back to this aspect, showing at the more general level the extent to which procedures of data extraction and algorithmic patterning are intrinsically violent.

Prior to do so, let us expand the critique of predictive policing developed so far by considering its political economy, which, we argue, is part and parcel of a broader restructuring of urban government towards technocratic and neoliberal approaches—therefore resonating with broader critiques to strategies of urban entrepreneurialism and technocratic configurations of governance in the smart city discourse (see, among others, Hollands 2008; Kitchin 2014; Rossi 2016). As argued by Hillary Angelo and Boris Vormann (2018, 16):

> We repeatedly see reform agendas framed in terms of beautification and optimization which tend to distract us from what they ultimately are, namely the expression of underlying political and social transformations, and the reproduction of the same problems in new guises.

Moreover, this argument is often framed within a political economy of (alleged) austerity for police departments, making the case for its utility in the context of budget cuts and as an instrument of cost reduction more generally (see also Beck 2009). The following quote from Los Angeles Police Chief Charlie Beck is telling:

> I'm not going to get more money. I'm not going to get more cops. *I have to be better at using what I have,* and that's what predictive policing is about.[28]

We have elsewhere shown how predictive policing has been a piece of broader political arguments that have made so police funding has expanded even in contexts of long-term austerity (Tulumello 2018a; Tulumello and Iapaolo 2022). We may argue that predictive policing reinforces the justification of historical patterns of state and police violence by normalising the structures of power at their core (cf. Datta and Odendaal 2019). At the same time, in order to do so, predictive policing feeds into mechanisms that determine, and therefore reshape, patterns of police and state violence by shifting the ideal scope, indeed the imaginary, of policing itself. The particular configuration and field of intervention of predictive policing also imply specific impacts that can be understood through the lenses of (state) violence or, more precisely, of the violence of (capitalist) urbanisation as we have previously defined it (see chapter 5). Whereas predictive policing becomes a discursive and operational tool for the expansion of (racialised) policing at the expenses of other forms of urban and social policy, it can be understood, above all, in continuity with programmes such as Broken Windows and the long history of violence stemming at the urbanisation/policing nexus we widely discussed in previous chapters. Beyond the police context, such a violence should be also framed with reference to the way data extraction and algorithmic analytics shape urban life, both in respect with their functioning and the (smart city) imaginary they reproduce. It is to such algorithmic analytics that we therefore move, considering through our ontological and epistemological lenses the violence that is thus produced.

Algorithmic Violence

The smart city discourse and algorithmic governance more generally (cf. Coletta and Kitchin 2017; Danaher et al. 2017) are informed by two main assumptions. On the one hand, that urban problems be made the target of objective, politically neutral, technological fixes. On the other, that data analytics may allow to anticipate uncertain futures so as to improve policy in the present. Among other things, these assumptions feed the promise of an algorithm-powered solution(ism) to urban violence. A solution that, however, is inherently flawed and indeed violent: this is not only due to the already flawed and violent practices and political economy of police, but also because of the way in which big data infrastructure and algorithmic computation reconfigure urban life, as it undergoes a so-called platformisation, at the convergence of built infrastructures, information protocols and algorithmic governance (Easterling 2014; Bratton 2015; Srnicek 2017; Strüver and Bauriedl 2022).[29] Movement, leisure, sociality, work: urban life at large is increasingly unthinkable without the mediation of the socio-technical infrastructure of computation. It is especially in this context that technology, as the ubiquitous 'embedding of computing into the background environment of cities' (Crang and Graham 2007, 790), cannot be understood passively as a device or instrument, but rather as a constitutive infrastructure of mediation which increasingly 'holds' the urban space, and planetary urbanisation at large, together (Kitchin and Dodge 2011; Beverungen and Sprenger 2017).

In chapter 1 we presented the notion of infra-structural violence as a way to explore violent processes of socio-material structuration by attending to their composition, orientations and consistency vis-à-vis the tensional holding together of the urban. Today, this tensegrity is increasingly enacted and shaped by the dispositions and propensities (Easterling 2014)[30] generated by an infrastructure of software, protocols, wearable devices, social networks, augmented reality cameras, GPS location systems, data centres, algorithmic analytics, which produce significant modifications in the way urban life unfolds. While exploring this crucial dimension in depth is far beyond the scope of this chapter, in this last section we are interested in highlighting the specific violence this socio-technical infrastructure generates, expanding on the urban violence produced by predictive policing so as to encompass the inherent dynamics of the technological tools of algorithmic prediction proper.

In the interviews with police officers and expert consultants working on predictive policing systems in cities like New Orleans, New York, Los Angeles and so on, collected by Luis León and Jovanna Rosen (2020), one is struck by the naïve techno-optimism and the instrumental understanding of technology that feeds it.[31] The words that keep resurfacing on and on are *efficiency* and *effectiveness*: data analytics, algorithmic vision, real-time crime centres, wearable devices and all the tools constantly crafted by companies such as Motorola (New Orleans), Microsoft (New York), or IBM (Memphis) are sold as capable of increasing accuracy and minimising human error and bias in a surgical way.

Smart city solutionism, the argument implies, will be ultimately able to achieve the old Hobbesian utopia of absolute security. The 'risks' this approach may entail—discrimination, bias, privacy violation and so on—are obviously taken into account, but this is normally treated as just another technical problem that the police force is absolutely aware of, and which is usually considered the result of an *improper* use of technology, rather than depending on its *proper* functioning in the first place. As we already reflected, the critique certainly cannot be content with assessing whether 'the algorithm is right or wrong', nor with painting one of the traditional Orwellian, or more up-to-date *Minority Report* or *Black Mirror*, dystopias. As Josh Scannell (2015) puts it, referring to Deleuze's famous Spinozist question—what can a body do?—beyond the 'does it work?' question, we need to ask what an algorithm actually does and what it can do. This means, first of all, exploring algorithms as not simply external forces that shape culture, but as a 'culture' in itself, one that is 'composed of collective human practices' (Seaver 2017, 5). Likewise, as Scannell (2015) suggests, we should explore algorithms as political objects that 'are concrete, mobilise and reshape social relations while also occluding them into a functionalist invisibility managed by machines in which relations of power are at ones made opaque (and reduced to concerns of efficiency) as well and inscribed into coding itself'.

A parenthesis may be of help. Far more than a merely linguistic or informatic instrument, a materialist approach to algorithms allows framing algorithms vis-à-vis the social, cultural and political practices out of which they are composed. Algorithms, to be sure, far predate the digital era, belonging to a millennial history of ritual, codification and automation. According to the definition given by Jean-Luc Chabert in his seminal work, an algorithm is 'a set of step by step instructions, to be carried out quite mechanically, so as to achieve some desired result' (1999[1994], 2). An algorithm, therefore, can be understood as a process of organisation that is not projected 'from above' but rather 'materialises' from below, as a crystallisation of real practices—they are an abstraction, in other words, that is composed of social matter (cf. Sohn-Rethel 1978; Virno 2001[1992]). The algorithm 'emerges', Pasquinelli writes, 'from the repetition of a process, an organization of time, space, labor, and operations: it is not a rule that is invented from above but emerges from below', as the efficient solution to a problem, that is, as 'an economic process [that] must employ the least amount of resources in terms of space, time, and energy, adapting to the limits of the situation' (2019). As Wiener had already argued, 'the process of receiving and of using information is the process of our adjusting to the contingencies of the outer environment, and of our living effectively within that environment' (1950, 17–18).

Algorithms are indeed *recipes of* and *for living*: they surface out of, and seek to economise, a repetitive trial-and-error process sustained by negative feedback—i.e., the incorporation of previous errors into an overall adaptive effort—that gradually crystallises into a coherent adaptive sequence, which expresses the most convenient, and therefore most efficient and cost-reducing, way to achieve a result (see Brighenti and Pavoni 2021a). The philosophy of machine learning algorithms, which feeds predictive policing, encompasses the extraction, recognition and prediction of patterns via recursive, comparative and statistical computation performed within a field of contingent events.[32] Needless to say, what is often left unsaid in the rhetorics that surround their deployment is the fact that the 'problems' they purport to address are never innocent or natural, but always shaped by all sorts of forces, structures and power relations, as our discussion on crime, violence and police has amply shown. The immanent normativity of the algorithm, whose 'purpose' is the maximum efficiency of the operation itself, carries with itself, and reshapes in turn, the asymmetries and power-structured relations of a given society.[33]

We thus propose to explore algorithms in their actually existing, world-producing praxis, according to the infrastructural analysis introduced in chapter 1, that is, as 'the living mediation of what organizes life' (Berlant 2016, 393), dissecting the 'propensities and possibilities that algorithms embody' (Amoore 2020, 7), their 'pragmatic functioning' (Goffey 2008, 19), and, therefore, the violence these processes produce and reproduce. To do so, in a recent paper-discussion, Rocco Bellanova and colleagues introduce the notion of 'algorithmic violence', which they see as 'a situated, all too material and coercive use of force—not only the claimed reaffirmation of a monopoly of violence by state authorities, but also the computational force of the infrastructure' (2021, 130). This form of infra-structural violence may be explored by looking at the way the data infrastructure is created via procedures of data collection, data training, data labelling and translation;

the way these data are acted upon via machine learning algorithms; and the aesthetics through which this information is translated back to humans, for instance in the urban in/visibilities generated by the cartography of 'hot spots' and 'heat maps'.

First, it is important to emphasise that not only do violent procedures remain in place at the level of data collection—i.e., at the pre-algorithmic phase when information is actually gathered—but they are drastically amplified in scope, intrusiveness and opacity. Not only because the extraction of fingerprint, iris pattern, face coordinates, localisation, DNA samples and so forth is never innocent, but also because ubiquitous computing and big data analytics constantly threaten to overflow the frontier of urbanites' awareness and trust. Data collected and algorithmic systems developed for military, humanitarian, health or retailing purposes, for instance, are often weaponised in police activities. Moreover, not only are data gathered with the population being unaware of, but there is also a remarkable amount of information, consensually given away for non-security purposes, that ends up being illegally employed for security purposes: the databases of images amassed by Clearview AI by scraping social media and then used to sell facial recognition software to law enforcement is a paradigmatic a case in point (Hill 2020).

This constant de-/re-composition of bits and pieces of social and urban life raises novel concerns that the traditional discourse on rights is hardly able to engage with. This violence for the most part unfolds silently, as a latent, infra-structural force that remains impersonal and hypothetical, until a given event, chance, opportunity or state of emergency make it precipitate and affect a given individual. Likewise, its effects are barely detectable, since unfolding at the level of those infrastructural propensities, dispositions and possibilities that tend to appear as almost 'natural' facets of urban life: infra-structural violence draws its own force from its merging with, and disappearing into, the urban, becoming natural as the air we breathe. All too often, the data we give away appear to us as absolutely innocuous and not worthy of our concerns: the *I've got nothing to hide* assumption is still a very effective misunderstanding in this sense (Solove 2007). The problem, as we see it, is that this assumption is still framed—as security, more generally, see chapter 7—from the standpoint of possessive individualism, namely as a question of being able to *protect* the precious information we supposedly hold *inside* from any intrusion from the *outside*: information, that is, as a 'property' to be safeguarded from those who want to 'steal' it, depending on its perceived value. In a similar way as we observed in the last chapter, understanding the violence of data analytics requires having done with possessive individualism

(Macpherson 1962) and its implicit presupposition that the individual has a proprietary relation with her own data. From the standpoint of a relational ontology, privacy cannot be decoupled from the sets of practices, relations, affects, customs and so forth that constitute the fabric of everyday urban atmospheres, and therefore the unfolding of urban lives therein. What should be considered violent, in this sense, is not simply the act of intrusion into a 'hidden' space, or the gathering of 'sensible' information, but, more pervasively, the infra-structural way in which these practices, and many others, slowly erode individual life paths, asymmetrically diminishing our capacity to flourish, even without being explicitly 'intrusive' or perceived and understood as such (see Curry 2000; Solove 2007; ICHRP 2011). The peculiar quality of machine learning algorithm, their capacity to analyse enormous datasets of heterogeneous data, means that it is increasingly harder to dismiss specific data collections as innocent or innocuous, since it is the way in which data is organised, labelled, patterned and subsequently deployed that counts (Hildebrandt and de Vries 2013).

At a second level, it is the translation of information into data, that is, the mathematisation of reality, to be a potentially violent process in itself. 'Algorithmic violence is indeed located not only in the acts of collecting or processing data, but rather in the technical operations of translation' that make the world actionable, computable (Bellanova et al. 2021, 142). Normally, this process tends to be naturalised: reality is supposedly made of 'raw' data that are 'harvested' via machine vision. This agricultural jargon conceals the fact that there are no raw data in reality and that every 'harvesting' is an extraction that is premised on a preliminary reduction. Every dataset must be *worked* in advance: 'algorithms need data(ification) to operate' (idem, 124). Data are semio-material constructs, formed by *production* (labour, phenomena), *captured* via encoding, *formatted* into a dataset and *labelled* in categories, that is, metadata.[34] Capturing the complexity of the world requires granulating it into data and transform it into a calculable format through 'embedding' operations. The world, in other terms, must always be coded in advance in the form of a purely digital vectorial representation (Cardon et al. 2018: 195).[35]

As Dominique Cardon and colleagues observe:

> data is not made available to the perception of calculators in a 'raw' and 'immediate' form, but rather is subject to atomization and dissociation in order to transform it into the most elementary possible standardized digital signs. To create these inputs, a new metrology of sensors, recordings, and databases constitutes an essential infrastructure for transforming images, sounds, move-

ments, clicks, or variables of all types into these giant vectors required by con-nectionist machines. (idem, 201)

As result of this process, termed vectorisation or featurisation, 'data are never really raw, and data labelling procedures are prone to confirm and reinforce already existent skews of visibility' (Brighenti and Pavoni 2021a, 13).[36] Racism, classism, ableism, misogyny and other tilted power relations are often ingrained within the algorithmic language, and are in this way made more 'infrastructural' and invisible at the same time (see Noble 2018; Benjamin 2019; Espeland and Yung 2019). This is why the argument that 'through the featurization of time and space, PredPol has, for example, pre-emptively dis-activated accusations of discrimination' (Aradau and Blanke 2017, 386) does make sense, but only at the strategic level. *Strategically*, Pred-Pol has indeed done so, yet this does not mean that the critical vocabulary of discrimination and exclusion is no longer valid to criticise it. More precisely, such a vocabulary must be rescued from, and updated to, the invisibilisation to which it is subjected by the opacity of the algorithmic process.

At a third level, data are translated 'back into discursive and sensorial outputs that can be acted upon by professionals of security and warfare' (Bel-lanova et al. 2021, 142). It is here that the 'semiotic violence' of algorithm fully unfolds, ingrained in the process of extraction, translation, labelling and algorithmic training. What is particularly interesting in Rocco Bellanova's stress on the 'semiotic violence' of algorithms is the way in which it tends to suppress the polysemy, as well as the cultural and historical contingency of meaning. Since the machine is trained to assume correlation as truth, 'the force of computer vision systems is predicated on a semiotic violence that is the suppression of the always dynamic intersubjectivity on which visual social relations develop by a vision that is cypher and not sense' (idem, 138).

The result is the engendering of a violent calcification of the urban, which is consistent with the de-potentiating force of atmospheric violence we discussed in chapter 6. There, we encountered Fanon's notion of 'affec-tive ankylosis', through which he expressed the effect that the atmospheric violence of the colony has on gestures, thoughts, in the ways of feeling and perceiving of the colonised bodies. This ankylosis, we argued through the re-flection developed by Al-Saji (2014), tends to atrophy one's ability to sense and think *otherwise*. Al-Saji's argument is that race tends to be naturalised by essentialising the other and thus unseeing his or her difference ('relational-ity', 'plasticity, 'liveness' and, more generally, singularity). In a formula: I am unable to see my seeing, that is, the invisible field through which I see (cf. Brighenti 2010b). It is on this atrophying tendency of vision (*I cannot see*

otherwise), that the socio-historical structures of racism—and not only racism—find hold, proliferate and shape the embodied domain of the visible.
Machine vision threatens to promote an even more extensive and capillary
affective ankylosis, as the selective process of essentialising the other is
increasingly outsourced to algorithms and machine-to-machine communication, with the risk of freezing urban life within a choreography of pre-coded
behaviour that may easily become oppressive, and asymmetrically so. In this
sense, and contrary to police rhetoric, not only predictive analytics seems to
fall short of 'multiplying' the capacity to see, know and act of police,[37] but it
risks to indeed weaken such capacity.

Take for instance this analyst at Motorola, which provides the technological infrastructure of predictive policing to the New Orleans Police Department, as he explains to the *Wall Street Journal* how automated machine
vision functions:

> The camera will learn the normal motion activities in a scene over about a
> week or two weeks, and after that learning period it will just automatically
> create an event and flag you when something happens that's unusual for that
> scene . . . There is zero human input in this situation. You basically turn it on,
> the camera learns and does everything automatically.[38]

Precisely because it acts with no supervision, the system may end up flagging all sorts of behaviours: for instance, walking a dog at night or, more
troublingly, 'an African-American walking through a predominantly White
neighborhood with very little foot traffic', as the *WSJ* journalist cannot help
but notice. This may result in crystallising a rigid urban normativity—albeit
one that is paradoxically 'without norms', see note 19 above—which not
only reduces the possibility of unusual behaviour (since *unusual* or *unexpected*
increasingly tend to be equated with *suspicious*), but also tends to train 'users'
to be predictable (Chun 2021), while reinforcing class and racial biases.[39] Far
from innocent, this 'flagging' is also far from being innocuous since, as the
same journalist reminds, and innumerable events of police violence against
Black and Brown people showed all too well, 'every police encounter is potentially dangerous'.

This brings us for the last time to the question opening this chapter.
We can concede that systems like Blue CRUSH or the one developed by
Motorola could have flagged the 'Ferguson Market and Liquor' store at the
particular moment when Michael Brown was to be there—after all, they
would be working on data from an organisation that has long considered
liquor stores at night to be crime 'hot spots'. But, since we know that this

would not have reduced the possibility of the encounter—we have seen how the evidence of these systems to reduce the event of crime does not exist—what matters is whether an encounter mediated by an algorithm rather than an emergency call would have been different. It seems to us—and the *WSJ* video shows with striking banality—that this may even have increased the suspicion of the officer when stepping into an area defined by the software to be at high risk (see Benjamin 2019, 88–89).

Rather than tools to reduce future violence, it seems that predictive policing tools have the capacity to reshape it. Critique, then, should be able to take into account the ontogenetic, world-producing effects this apparatus has vis-à-vis the urban and its violence.[40] There is much more to predictive policing than the superficial debate about whether or not it works, or how to provide guarantees against its misuse. An infra-structural understanding of urban violence must take into account the violence that is produced and reproduced in everyday urban life through practices of extraction, translation, orientation. By threatening to freeze urban atmospheres in the sense just exposed, predictive policing does risk rigidifying and naturalising all sorts of discriminations, by literally 'engraining them' into the urban infrastructure, and thus engendering an infra-structural urban violence that is all more powerful insofar as increasingly invisible and automated. Likewise, another troubling result in the long run may be a systematic de-skilling of the police force (Tulumello and Iapaolo 2022, 460), as the outsourcing of the practice of observing, framing and assessing the environment to machine vision threatens to lessen the ability of 'figuring out' a situation, to remove the possibility to 'hesitate' (cf. Al-Saji 2014) before resorting to a certain course of action and to release from the necessity to build an intersubjective relation with a given community.[41]

Granted, we are far from willing to romanticise pre-digital policing, and in the previous chapters we exposed at length the historical entanglement between police and urban violence. It is evident, however, that excessive reliance to predictive analytics may turn out to be toxic in the long run: on the one hand, reliance on algorithmic prediction increases police's 'functional stupidity' (Alvesson and Spicer 2012); on the other, this very reliance, sold as unbiased insofar as supposedly bypassing the 'human' side of police-community interaction, threatens to remove the value this very relationship may play in challenging those biases in the first place.[42]

Admittedly, there is a serious epistemological problem when dealing with this issue. As Bellanova and colleagues put it, 'we know indeed how to study data collection. We know how to study algorithms. But we know very little about how to study those operations of translation that allow discourse, images, sounds, and data to be computed and made actionable' (2021, 142). This is why, they conclude,

> it is vital to attend to the multiplicity and ambiguity of algorithmic violence, as well as to the effects of seemingly innocent necessities like the fixation of the past into fact/data as necessary to fix the social for computational treatment, and thus to enable such computation to make the future actionable, something security can intervene in . . . Focusing on data infrastructures and their making in diverse security contexts can help resituating algorithms as part of complex and messy practices, and thus avoid disembodying them (which would end up cautioning the same frictionless discourse that promotes algorithmic governance). (idem, 144–145)

In other words, if the algorithm is being placed at the centre of the epistemology, and increasingly ontology, of infra-structural (urban) violence, then de-fetishising the algorithm is key to the urge to de-fetishise its very infrastructure, discourse and aesthetics[43]—an endeavour that has only marginally begun.[44]

In conclusion, an effort to provide a transformative critique of predictive policing must therefore go beyond providing simple 'evidence' that it does not work and that it produces violence in turn. Besides that, a transformative critique needs, on the one hand, to be aimed at the level of the very imaginary that underlines predictive policing and the smart city more generally: 'only by giving up the illusion that urban problems can be "solved" merely by means of technical and technological management we may find more just ways to draw paths to navigate this messy world of ours' (Tulumello and Iapaolo 2022, 462). On the other, the critique must engage the concrete working of algorithms, with the patchiness and messiness of their actual operation, and, crucially, with their potential to positively augment human action: 'the road to such positive pairings of humans and machines is littered with controversy and consternation' (Phillips and Pohl 2021, 18). And yet, it seems a road worth travelling.

Researching Urban Violence: Chicago Strikes Back?

As previously mentioned, the label predictive policing includes two types of programmes: those map-based, that is, focused on the time-space distribution of crimes—the most common typology, that of PredPol and Blue CRUSH; and those subject-centred, that is, focused on creating lists of individual subjects considered to be at risk of committing, or becoming victims of, violent crime. Beyond most widespread, the map-based programmes have also been the object of most critique in urban studies and critical geography—on which we have built to discuss the continuity of predictive policing with long-term approaches to crime mapping. In this last Researching Urban Violence section, we believe it is worth spending a few more words on the least common, less inquired, subject-centred typology, for the way it helps us reflect, first, on the relation with space (and the urban) and, second, on the medical reductionism of violence—thereby closing the circle with the reflections developed on the first Researching Urban Violence section (chapter 1).

At a superficial level, subject-based predictive policing may seem to be less central to our discussion because of its apparently a-spatialised, ultimately 'non-urban' nature. This is, however, as Carlo Gatti (2022b) recently argued, a quite problematic distinction. Rather than working on geographic data about crime, subject lists elaborate individual risk assessments based on any number of data-points. In the case of the Chicago Police Department's Strategic Subject List, the list of data-points includes the most 'obvious' ones—and especially past convictions or other contacts with the police and the judiciary, based on the idea that 'criminals' tend to be 'recidivist'—but also information that makes the 'list' become a 'network'. Not only does one's individual data count, but also those of one's acquaintances do: having been previously convicted adds to the individual risk score but also to the scores of that individual's acquaintances. The rationale behind this decision, which is also common in the algorithms of Facebook's advertising strategies and in credit scoring, is 'homophily, the principle that similarity breeds connection' (Chun 2021, 21). In other words, the idea that people with similar characters and that communicate often tend to do similar things: the 'birds of a feather, statistically speaking, do fly together' (O'Neil 2016, 102).

While we point the reader to the previous discussion for the problems in terms of discrimination and injustice, what we want to point out here is how space, beyond the surface, remains central to the working of the algorithm: on a first level, as an abstract, networked space where the relationships and trajectories of the observed individuals are traced; on a second level, as the urban space where said individuals live, since acquaintances tend to not only be more in contact, but also to reside in the same areas or neighbourhoods—particularly in highly segregated contexts, of which US cities are quintessential examples. These networks have a specifically urban nature: indeed, the Chicago subject list was inspired by the work of network scientist and sociologist Andrew Papachristos on social networks and homicide victimisation in two majority African American communities in the city (Chun 2021, 18; see Papachristos and Wildeman 2014). In North American cities, this spatialisation is also deeply racialised—as Wendy Chun (2021, 19) notes, race did not need to feature in the list of data-points because 'it was already factored in through residential segregation'. Through networks, and the spatialised/racialised urban nature of networks (at least in North American cities), the strategic list has fundamentally re-purposed one of the main lynchpins of the understanding of the city we have seen to be central to the reductionism of urban violence (see chapters 2 and 5), that is, the 'neighbourhood effect' of the Chicago School—that this list was developed in the very same city may be a coincidence, but a telling one.[45]

The specific understanding of the neighbourhood effect in the Chicago strategic list is summarised by Papachristos himself: 'if you hang around people who are getting shot, even if you're not actively doing anything, then you become exposed . . . It's just like sharing needles. It puts you at risk because of the behaviors of your friends and your associates' (interviewed in Gorner 2013). This is precisely the language that we already have seen at play in the medicalised discourse on violence promoted by Gary Slutkin and his peers (see chapter 1, Researching Urban Violence).[46] A discourse, we have seen, that not only reproduces many of the reductionisms of violence, but also depoliticises and ultimately, if indirectly, individualises the 'problem' of violence.

We have already discussed the problematics of the specific reductionism within the health metaphor. In conclusion, we would like to mention the way the use of this metaphor in the context of predictive policing has been part and parcel of the circulation of contagion models between public health and urban security, as recently discussed by Maximilian Heimstädt and colleagues (2020) in the context of the Covid-19 pandemic. While at a general level, the adoption of public health contagion models in predictive policing based on individual risk assessment has translated 'the health-based concept of infection-by-association . . . into the concept of guilt-by-association' (idem, 2), Heimstädt and colleagues move further, discussing how, during the pandemic, data infrastructure providers have offered tools developed in the context of predictive policing to help public agencies predict the spread of infection. Not only does this open up to the possibility that technologies of digital contact tracing apps may be used in policing in the future. But it is worth noticing the place where much of this circulation has happened. Chicago, home to the Strategic Subject List, has also been the birthplace for many influential ideas about urban life, particularly those of the Chicago School that have proven so central in shaping the understanding of violence globally. In this sense, the way health models work in the context of (predictive) policing can be seen as shaped by the circulation of ideas, like the neighbourhood effect or collective efficacy, that have centred conceptions of urban violence upon the specific association between place and behaviour.

Overcoming this essentialised relation, we believe, is a necessary step for understanding urban violence.

Notes

1. This is the Anaximander's fragment as translated by Friedrich Nietzsche in his early, uncompleted work *Die Philosophie im tragischen Zeitalter der Griechen* (1873).

2. Tommaso Venturini and his colleagues (2017) from Science PO's Médialab (founded by Bruno Latour) have defended that digital methods and big data analysis can break traditional quantitative/qualitative divides and foster a 'continuous' sociology (see Tulumello 2019, for a discussion).

3. In Virilio's words, 'the idea of logistics is not only about oil, about ammunitions and supplies but also about images. Troops must be fed with ammunitions and so on but also with information, with images, with visual intelligence. Without these elements troops cannot perform their duties properly. This is what is meant by the logistics of perception' (interviewed in Armitage 2000, 6).

4. More precisely, *cybernétique* was introduced by André-Marie Ampère in nineteenth-century French to designate 'the science of governing humans'.

5. A writing technique based on the cut-up of words, phrases and entire sentences, and the rearrangements of pieces.

6. Deleuze employs the notion of control to suggest that a different diagram of power emerges, in response to a novel problem: no longer that of disciplining bodies in enclosures (panopticism), or managing the life of a population (governmentality). For a discussion in this regard, see Pavoni (2018a, ch. 4, section 1.4).

7. On the difference between a 'philosophical' and a 'scientific' approach to problems, see Deleuze and Guattari (1994[1991]).

8. For Lynch, disorientation has always a very negative connotation: 'let the mishap of disorientation once occur, and the sense of anxiety and even terror that accompanies it reveals to us how closely it is linked to our sense of balance and well-being. The very word "lost" in our language means much more than simple geographical uncertainty; it carries overtones of utter disaster' (Lynch 1960, 4).

9. If truth be said, Richard Janikowski, creator of Memphis's Blue CRUSH (see below), told us in an interview (March 2016) that he believed 'forecasting is probably the best way to put it . . . I am not sure you can predict'—thereby stressing an almost exclusively probabilistic role for predictive policing. For Janikowski, by using real-time data, it would be possible to identify 'acute outbreaks' and distinguish them from chronic crime problems—hence distinguishing solutions between rapid intervention (for the former) and problem-oriented policing (for the latter). These considerations, also based on the distinction of typologies of crime as being more or less driven by rational choice, show a much more nuanced understanding of the potentialities and limits of predictive policing, but have fundamentally been lost in the rhetoric, implementation and commercialisation of available 'products', as we will exemplify in what follows.

10. This is the key to Deleuze's notion of control. As Nathan Moore puts it, commenting on Deleuze's *Postscript*, 'control seeks to control the very creation of propositions, striking pre-emptively in the attempt to determine what it will be possible to think and say' (2007b, 441).

11. See www.innovations.harvard.edu/compstat-crime-reduction-management -tool.

12. This is Abbott's definition of predictive analytics (2014, 3).

13. See chapter 3 for the emergence of this rationality in American neoliberalism and the critique by Foucault.

14. This approach is grounded on rational choice theories of crime, like routine activity (Brunet 2002) or opportunity (Felson and Clarke 1998), which explain crime as the result of the encounter of a rationally motivated criminal with a potential victim in a favourable time/space context.

15. Hot spot is an approach to policing—diffused especially in North America—based on the idea that few places at specific times concentrate significant amounts of crime and that intervening on those time-places is an effective way to reduce crime writ large. Heat maps are GIS representations of crime hot spots, usually using gradients of colours similar to those used by thermographic cameras.

16. POL is a method of surveillance based on the study of patterns of movement and on the identification of non-routine behaviours.

17. It is in this sense that predictive policing, which operates by 'looking'—mostly performed by machine vision—at the relation between data in a feature space, is significantly different from crime prediction based on statistical modelling (Aradau and Blanke 2017, 384). Of course, this does not mean one approach substitutes the other, and many and contextually specific are the intersections, which we do not have the space here to explore.

18. 'Unsupervised learning aims to find hidden structures in unlabelled raw data without giving any hint to the search algorithm. In this way, machine learning unveils hidden patterns, correlations, tendencies, and structures that would be otherwise unconceivable for human cognition' (Pasquinelli 2017, 288).

19. As Gregoire Chamayou explains, 'from a philosophical standpoint, one has to note that the notion of normal patterns or forms of life is not based here, unlike for instance in the discourse of transcendent morals, on any particular "must be" or normative imperative. These are, in a sense, *normativities without norm*. Their notion of the normal is strictly empirical: it is *learned* by the machine on the basis of an analysis of frequencies and repetitions in given sets of activities. It is then a discrepancy with such patterns of regularities—an *anomaly*, rather than an *abnormality*—that will trigger the red-orange alert on the analyst's screen' (2014; emphasis in original).

20. Our emphasis. Quoted from PredPol's website: www.predpol.com/testimonials/.

21. On this understanding of time, see for instance Agamben (1978).

22. The news was released by a local newspaper (*The Commercial Appeal* 2012; Maki 2012), which, however, never followed up on the issue—and never answered our requests of information.

23. Our emphasis. Quoted by Lum and Isaac (2016, 18) and originally found on PredPol website (available through Internet Archive's Wayback Machine: https://web.archive.org/web/20160713022328/https://www.predpol.com/about/).

24. Alikhademi and colleagues (2021) have argued that, though the paper concludes that PredPol 'did not lead to racially biased arrests when compared with the control method of allocation', its findings 'do not show that PredPol improves on any bias in the control method'.

25. Following the news coverage from *The Verge* (Winston 2018b), the City of New Orleans terminated the contract with Palantir (Winston 2018a), but maintained the cooperation with Motorola, which had been involved in the predictive policing program, having provided AI software with automated object detection (Stein 2017).

26. In the words of an activist from the Mid-South Peace & Justice Center (interviewed in Tulumello and Iapaolo 2022, 457; see also Garner 2019).

27. Lucy Parsons Labs, based in Chicago, focuses on the intersection between digital rights and 'on-the-streets issues' (see https://lucyparsonslabs.com/). The report, obtained through a Freedom of Information Act request is available at www.muckrock.com/foi/elgin-7770/foia-elgin-police-dept-predpol-documents-51858/#file-190432.

28. Our emphasis. Quoted in PredPol's website: www.predpol.com/testimonials/.

29. On the role of predictive policing in pushing toward the platformisation of police work in turn, see Egbert (2019).

30. See chapter 1 for a discussion of Easterling's argument on infrastructure space and, in particular, note 28 on 'dispositions'.

31. We will hint below at the importance to notice that the acceptance of predictive policing by police officers on the ground is not always so smooth.

32. As Kasy (2019) explains, machine learning is grounded on two basic concepts: *regularisation*, that is, the selection of relevant patterns and the discounting of irrelevant ones; and *tuning*, that is, the comparison of 'the predictions for the validation data to the actually observed outcomes'.

33. In this sense, one may argue that algorithms have an in-built normativity: insofar as they tend to crystallise, and thus provide, the most economic, cost-effective solution to a given problem, they seemingly embody that de-politicising solutionism—i.e., the tendency to solve, without questioning, problems—that characterise the smart city logics.

34. Something that is particularly relevant for crime and police data, as we explored earlier (see chapter 2, Researching Urban Violence).

35. Neural network, the basis of contemporary machine learning algorithm, has only recently become the forefront of artificial intelligence research and practice. In the type of artificial intelligence dominant throughout the 1970s and 1980s,

algorithms were understood as recipes, that is, static operational apparatuses, which were fed with a set of normative rules they were supposed to replicate. This is why AI mostly worked in closed settings—i.e., games such as chess—and proved unable to deal with the complexity of 'open' life. Conversely, today's machine learning algorithms are *left free* to roam over large bodies of data, applying multivariate linear regression computations to get progressively closer to an optimal result. The artificial intelligence paradigm devised by I.J. Good, Marvin Minski and others in the 1960s was mostly moulded upon a formalistic vision of human rationality. The neural network model changed the approach, reformulating the relation between the machine and the world, 'basing the performance of prediction on the world itself' and in this way 'renewing the adaptive promises of the *reflection machines* of cybernetics' (Cardon et al. 2018, 203; emphasis in original). *Recursivity* is the key property, what makes algorithms fully 'capable of integrating contingency into their operations' (Yuk Hui interviewed in Lovink 2019).

36. The world is rendered as a vector space—hence 'vectorisation'—supporting a topological system of pattern recognition based on statistical proximities (Topological Data Analysis).

37. See a promotional video by Motorola and the New Orleans Police Department: https://video.motorolasolutions.com/detail/video/5776112478001.

38. See www.youtube.com/watch?v=H_fyQCeBaeM.

39. Mirroring and deepening processes typical of community (self-)policing in racially segregated cities (see Tulumello and Falanga 2022, 150–151 and note 14).

40. As Scannell (2015) puts it, 'every time a body is stopped and frisked by the NYPD, the relationship that is enacted is not a one-to-one, but also a production and performance of data, virtualizing the dissolving and dangerous body of crime into a graspable and controllable horizon of the real. These spectral data bodies are not preempting the real; they are actively producing the real. Data is neither representational nor hauntological (Derrida 2000), it is ontogenetic'.

41. See Brighenti and Pavoni (2021a) for a more general application of this argument to urban life at large. On the notion of 'figuring out' and its depletion, we draw from AbdouMaliq Simone, who reflects on this aspect in the context of the practice of urban inhabitants in African and Southeast Asian cities such as Khartoum, Kinshasa or Jakarta. While much ethnographic work would be needed to assess this process in detail, we believe it is not preposterous to apply this discussion to police work, with respect to which the following does ring more than a bell: 'this proliferation of relationalities can be seen through the use of sophisticated number-crunching packages, where a larger volume of relationships is made for us, instead of us trying to figure how things are connected. This figuring-out of connections was one of the key skills and preoccupations of residents inhabiting popular districts' (Simone 2016, 149). On the toxic effects of the socio-technical infrastructure of algorithmic computation on the general ability to do, sense, think and live (*savoir-faire*, *savoir-penser*, *savoir-vivre*), we refer to the invaluable work of Bernard Stiegler.

42. We point the reader to decades of attempts at reducing bias through building policing-community relations. In extreme summary, with all the limits of approaches like community policing—which we have discussed at length (e.g., Tulumello and Falanga 2022)—it is hard to deny that policing approaches centred on the formation of relationships with citizens are associated with lower levels of police violence (Preito-Hodge and Tomaskovic-Devey 2021).

43. On the aesthetics, see Toscano (2019), Pavoni and Tomassoni (2022, 44–45).

44. One of the—elementary, indeed—components of this endeavour, coming back to the operations of predictive policing, is that of peeking beyond the curtains of police rhetoric about efficiency and effectiveness. In one of the very few ethnographies made inside police agencies that make use of predictive policing, Ajay Sandhu and Peter Fussey (2021) have shown how, off camera, police officers seem to be less enthusiastic about delegating decision making to the machine and, at the same time, quite sceptical of the potential therein—thereby being often reluctant to follow software's instructions.

45. It is also worth pointing to a specific, and deeply troubling, character of the Chicago subject list, which 'lump[s] together murderer and murder victim within the category of "strategic subjects"' (Chun 2021, 18).

46. No surprise that they are happy to discuss the similarities between their approaches, which they frame as consistent with the more general, 'holistic approach' to violence. (see for instance this 2017 interview: https://www.npr.org/2017/01/07/508722484/researchers-begin-to-look-at-gun-violence-as-public-health-issue). More surprising, perhaps, is that only six years earlier Papachristos (2011) was rather more critical with respect to Slutkin's model.

CHAPTER NINE

~

Cum cura

Nam tua res agitur, paries cum proximus ardet, et neglecta solent incendia sumere uires.[1]

For a book to be worthwhile, Deleuze once observed, at least three criteria should be met:

1) you think that the books on the same subject or on a neighbouring subject fall into a type of overall *error* (polemical function of the book); 2) you think that something essential has been *forgotten* in relation to the subject (inventive function); 3) you believe yourself capable of creating a new *concept* (creative function).[2]

This book was inspired by what we saw as a general limit in the literature, namely the 'redundant' and simplistic way in which 'urban violence' is often discussed and deployed. This is, we argue, no minor impasse. It lends urban violence to be employed and exploited as a rationale for oppressive security politics, and a tool for statistical reductionism whereby framing neighbourhoods, populations and whole cities through a discriminatory and colonialist gaze. Something 'essential' has been forgotten, we thought. On the one hand, the conceptual evolution of the notions of *urban* and *violence* in their profound genealogical intersection. On the other hand, the role played by security—as a desire, a sense, a practice, and the socio-historical configuration these take—as their overlooked blind spot. Urban violence, we argued, can only be understood, ontologically, epistemologically and ethically, once we take into account the third vertex of this complex triangle. By exploring at the same time the unfolding of security, violence and the urban, with reference to the imaginary, the process and the atmosphere through which they have unfolded in modern and contemporary times, we have therefore proposed an original theorisation of urban violence vis-à-vis the existential oscillation of urban life: its flourishing, or empowerment, and its depletion, or suffocation. We introduced, first, the concept of infra-structural violence to grasp the relation between the ontological fabric of co-existence and the role played by violence as a force of construction, maintenance or destruction. We subsequently introduced the concept of atmospheric violence to grasp the gaseous effects of the frictional 'encounter' between violent imaginaries and processes on the urban everyday, that is, the toxic by-product of these frictions, unequally affecting urban bodies as they are forced to flexibly cope with, and adapt, to this everyday turbulence.

What is left, in concluding this book, is to subject the notion of security to an equally creative effort. We have extensively argued that, while we share the *pars destruens* of many critiques of contemporary security, we do not believe security should be disposed together with its dirty bathwater. At the same time, we have cautioned against attempts to rescue security, from Giddens onwards, by reasserting its essential or universal value without addressing—that is, by taking for granted—its implicit ontology and anthropology. In other words, what is exactly the security that is desired and by whom? What is that security is meant to *secure*? Whereas in various instances of this book we have shown, both theoretically and empirically, the extent to which taking for granted 'ontological security' while *forgetting* its ontology is a pernicious *error*, what is left for us is to *create* a concept of security that be able to overcome these limits. This is the task of this concluding chapter.

Across this book, we showed that answering these kinds of questions without exploring the ontological, anthropological and epistemological presuppositions that feed them is pointless at best. At worst, it can be dangerous, as the reactionary degeneration of left-wing security politics in the last decades has shown all too well. Security, we believe, can neither be left to the Right, nor be uncritically endorsed, since this would turn it into nothing but a trojan horse doomed to bring the Left rightwards. Therefore, in this concluding chapter we set out to sketch the lineaments of a different understanding of security by not rethinking the actual concept but the 'plane of immanence', so to speak, out of which it is constructed.[3] This is done via three main moves, meant to reconstitute as many relations that, we saw, took a particular, historically and geographically situated, and therefore by no means necessary, configuration in the mainstream understanding of security: the relation between security and responsibility, beyond the structure of *delega-tion*; the relation between security and freedom, beyond the myth of *balance*; and the relation between security and care, beyond the logic of *sine-cura*.

Security/Freedom (Again)

Is security a *right of the Left*, as the Blairite rhetoric went, or is it a (poisoned) leftover of the Right? At a public talk in 2017, the then Italian minister of the interior, Marco Minniti, assertively claimed that 'security is a word that belongs to the Left', echoing the words expressed few days earlier by his party's secretary, Matteo Renzi, who had argued that 'security is a concept that does not belong to the right' (apud Schianchi 2017). If taken outside their context, both sentences have a point. Security may indeed be part of left-wing politics and, yes, security does not belong to the Right. Yet, recon-ceptualising security was not the concern of Minniti and Renzi. What they aimed to do, instead, was to simply take the concept of security *as it had been constructed* by the Right and use it within the domain of the Left. Of course, it would be easy to point out that the orientation of their Democratic Party (PD) is far from 'leftist'. This is not our concern here. This example is meant to show a very common misuse of the concept of security, one that assumes security to be a sort of neutral tool employed to address specific issues, most notably violence and the fear thereof. Needless to say, there are no innocent concepts, and we dedicated a whole chapter, the third, to describing the genealogical evolution of contemporary security as we know it. The extent to which the 'security' the PD had in mind is laden with a conservative con-ceptual toolbox could have been found already a decade earlier in a famous statement by the then secretary and founder of the party, Walter Veltroni, who had reclaimed the notion of *legalità* (legality) as neither belonging to the Left or the Right, but as a fundamental right of the citizens. That his successors at the leadership of the PD would plan to increase security by in-creasing both the number of violations—as we discussed in chapter 7—and the weight of the punishment was therefore not surprising. As they countless times reclaimed, security, for both Minniti and Renzi, as well as a vast array of party colleagues and mayors across Italy, was coessential with the so-called 'principle of legality'—i.e., with the absolute respect of the law.[4]

Admittedly, the use of the notion of 'the Left' in the last vignette could appear as grotesque. Its interest for us, however, does not lie in the all too easy way in which the positions expressed by PD representatives could be criticised and mocked.[5] Instead, it does lie in the way this expresses the fundamental configuration of contemporary security in its imaginary and

juridico-political institutionalisation, what we term the structure of delegation. Elsewhere we referred to the latter, geometrically, as the condition of
horizontal separation via vertical delegation that is increasingly pervasive
in the neoliberal logic of contemporary security: on the one hand, the responsibilisation of the individual for one's own security, that is, the framing
of security as an eminently individual and proprietary right; on the other
hand, the simultaneous de-responsibilisation of the same individual for what
concerns the security of—and the care for—the society at large, a task that
is instead delegated to the institution itself, that is, to its laws and police
(see on this Pavoni 2017b; Brighenti and Pavoni 2019). It is here that the
negative connotation of security as carelessness (see chapter 3) finds an institutional formalisation, what in the field of legal theory Scott Veitch (2007)
refers to as 'organised irresponsibility': since my responsibility only concerns
the compliance with the law—i.e., legality—this 'exonerates' or 'disburdens'
me from any other responsibility I have vis-à-vis the society beyond such a
compliance (Gehlen, 1988[1974]; Esposito 2009[1998]; 2011[2002]). Security, in this way, is framed simultaneously out of the respect of the law and a
relief from the burden of *caring for* the common: *sine cura*.

We saw already that this configuration, which systematically breaks up
the common into individual boxes by severing the relations composing the
social fabric for the sake of the chimera of absolute security, found its most
coherent and influential formulation in the theory of Thomas Hobbes. Albeit not always emphasised, this was, for Hobbes, an inevitable consequence
of his mechanicist understanding of freedom, in turn premised on an individualistic ontology and pessimistic anthropology. The story is well known.
Applying Galilean motion to political thought, Hobbes defines freedom as
'the absence of Opposition; (by Opposition, I mean externall Impediments
of motion;) . . . And according to this proper, and generally received meaning of the word, A FREE-MAN, is "he, that in those things, which by his
strength and wit he is able to do, is not hindred to doe what he has a will to"'
(2002[1651], ch. XXI). Freedom is a frictionless movement that bodies enjoy
the absence of relations. This atomised ontology legitimates an anthropology
of predation granted by nature:

> The RIGHT OF NATURE, which Writers commonly call Jus Naturale, is the
> Liberty each man hath, to use his own power, as he will himselfe, for the pres-
> ervation of his own Nature; that is to say, of his own Life; and consequently, of
> doing any thing, which in his own Judgement, and Reason, hee shall conceive
> to be the aptest means thereunto. (idem, ch. XIV)

Yet, 'judgement' and 'reason' are constantly overcome by desire. Hobbes breaks with the classical tradition of political philosophy, oriented around the definition of a model, that is, an ideal end to which individuals must conform and that, from Plato onwards, founded the authority of the wise. Contrary to that, Hobbes places the power of desire at the centre of his anthropology, thus revoking the privilege of reason: no one is born civil, rational or religious, and in the state of nature the war of all against all unavoidably erupts. We are free, yes, but utterly unable to control our passions. Hence the necessity to overcome this fearful condition through a pact: freedom must be revoked in the name of State security; only in the 'silence of the law' will the individual be truly free to do as he pleases and to enjoy the comforts of life.[6] In the state of nature, *nulla securitas, sed libertas unicuique plena et absoluta.* Freedom is inversely proportional to security: if the former becomes absolute, the latter disappears, and vice versa. A pessimistic anthropology, understanding humans as fundamentally egoistic, is coupled by an atomistic ontology assuming beings as pre-formed entities that pre-exist the relations in which they are involved.

Freedom, it follows, is to be understood in the inertial sense in which a river is 'free' to flow downhill, and free to overflow its riverbed and flood the surrounding valley if the banks are not high enough.[7] This is precisely what the Leviathan is meant to be: nothing but a geometric system of channels and dams, whereby the free-flowing and egotistic freedom of the individuals is suppressed within a static configuration: security.

The phantasy of the social contract, drawn via a supposedly 'consensual' pact, perfectly exemplifies the structure of delegation, in the same way as the phantasy of a state of nature made by individuals 'at war' with each other grounds the opposition between freedom and security that remains at the foundation of modern political science. The extent to which the structure of delegation reduces individual responsibility to the mere compliance with the law (leaving absolute freedom for what concerns action 'in the silence of law') is made explicit by Hobbes's negative definition of justice: 'when a Covenant is made, then to break it is Unjust: And the definition of INJUSTICE, is no other than The Not Performance Of Covenant. And whatsoever is not Unjust, is Just' (idem, ch. XXV).[8] In other words, the end is not the justice of the covenant, but security itself. This is precisely the meaning of Hobbes's absolute delegation: by entering the civil state, the individual overcomes the fear of violent death by sacrificing his freedom unconditionally to the great protector, that is, the State. As Mauro Camellone reminds us, 'the need for life (the fear of death) leads individuals to agree on their unconditional obedience to the sovereign and to make his will the only positive source of justice' (2018, 249; our translation). To be sure, an ideal model—absolute security—is implicitly proposed by Hobbes, yet one that does not have a morally normative form, but a purely legalistic one: security is coessential with the principle of legality, no less, no more.

The reason for yet another, brief incursion in the thought of Hobbes was to reassert the extent to which a certain understanding of freedom—in the form of what Crawford Macpherson would famously term 'possessive individualism' (1962)—fed by an atomised ontology and a pessimistic anthropology, shapes the juridico-political infrastructure of delegation that still articulates contemporary security politics around the 'myth' of balance we explored in chapter 3. The contract establishes the dominion of the Leviathan and instantiates a notion of security that is opposed to freedom, as if they were the two sides of the same scale: an increase in one implies a decrease in the other, and vice versa. The security sanctioned by the Leviathan, it follows, deprives the citizens from their 'right of nature' and therefore their freedom. When centre-left politicians argue that 'security is freedom', in this sense they are not really opposing the balance. Quite the contrary: they are trying to subsume the very concept of freedom within that of security, understood as the condition of being free *from* danger, *under* the law of the state. In other words, they still employ a notion of security that relies on three vectors (delegation, balance, carelessness) that, we believe, are constitutive of the 'moral' understanding of peace that, in his survey of the notion of peace through history and geography, Wolfgang Dietrich (2012) indicates as typical of Western modernity. The 'moral image' frames peace negatively, and statically, as absence of (psycho-physical) violence, binding this condition to an institutional apparatus that be able to provide it, while severing any connection between security and care—by severing the relation itself.[9]

These are the vectors that are required to be rethought, if a different concept of security is to be put forwards: the relation between security and responsibility (beyond *delegation*); security and freedom (beyond *balance*); and security and care (beyond *sine-cura*).[10]

Beyond Delegation

To the 'moral', Dietrich opposes what he terms an 'energetic' image of peace, of which he finds instances both in premodern Western thought and in various non-Western philosophies and cosmologies. In these accounts, peace is framed *dynamically* as a positive, material and relational practice that is not statically established from above by a transcendent sovereign, but is immanently, performatively and continuously enacted. Let us recall the rationale of Arnold Gehlen's negative anthropology of disburdening, as exposed by Esposito:

> To allow the community to withstand the entropic risk that threatens it, and with which it ultimately coincides, it must be sterilized of its own relational contents. It must be immunized from the *munus* that exposes it to contagion using that which, coming from within it, goes beyond it. To this end are ordered the forms—roles, rules, institutions—by which anthropology divides life from its common content. What remains in common is nothing but mutual separation. (2011[2002], 13)

To be together in separation: this is the logic of delegation feeding the 'moral image' of peace, in which the relation constituting the common ends up being sacrificed for the sake of security. Security, in this sense, literally dis-empowers the individuals, insofar as depriving them from their (relational) power to affect and be affected. From Hobbes to contemporary neoliberal ideology, the structure of delegation is crystallised at the juridical, political and socio-technical level. Take the neoliberal ethos of individual hyper-responsibilisation, where responsibility is confined to the realm of personal choice, consumption and lifestyle, while complemented by the systematic outsourcing of ethical, social and practical action to an ever-growing techno-juridical infrastructure of procedures, regulations, litigation, protocols and smart devices (Dean 1999; Hay 2006; Battistelli 2013; Lippert 2014; Low and Maguire 2019). As we noted in the last chapter, a certain socio-technical articulation of AI and machine learning technologies threatens to further expand and intensify this process, not only prompting novel addictions, with related psycho-social pathologies, and forms of 'social de-skilling' whose consequences are still to be explored; but also fracturing social, professional, and organised forms of imagination, action and solidarity (e.g. Alvesson and Spicer 2012; Morozov 2013; Bragazzi and Del Puente 2014; Lovink 2019b; Stiegler, Bernard 2019; Brighenti and Pavoni 2021a). Increasingly, as a result, the responsibility to act 'outside' of the pre-channelled field of indi-vidualised interaction can be—and indeed often is—outsourced, threatening both a practical and an ethical de-skilling, insofar as immunising anyone from the need to act and thus from the risk of being 'held responsible' (Pavoni 2018a). Infra-structural violence is palpable at this level, taking the form of a quintessential *debilitating* force, which is debilitating (i.e., *sad*, in Spinozist terms; see also Lovink 2019b) insofar as it *separates* us from what we can do, that is, from our common power to act (cf. Deleuze 1968).[11]

This logic can be seen as feeding the dominant imaginaries through which the contemporary city is branded. Smart, Green, Sustainable, Resilient, Safe, Healthy, Liveable and so forth. Different definitions sharing the same normative framework, which promises a comfortable and safe life in the city where decisions, worries and commitments are outsourced to scientific, technological, aesthetic and juridical devices: surveillance apparatuses, quality-of-life policing, endless litigation, comfortable urban design, big data and a plethora of smart phone apps relieving us from any need to care for talking, asking, interacting, interpreting, evaluating, reacting, committing and 'figuring out' (Simone 2016).[12] While we are here focusing on security, it is evident that such a discussion could be framed within the broader 'reign of carelessness' ushered in by the violence of neoliberalism, where care has been turned into self-care and the social infrastructure of care has been systematically disintegrated, leaving 'most of us less able to *provide* care as well as less likely to *receive* it' (The Care Collective 2020, 4; emphasis in original).

Rather than a space of care, the contemporary urban is better defined as a space of *curation*, where the possibility to live comfortably—i.e., away from stress, conflict and violence—is increasingly dependent on the politics of comfort and its greatly unequal unfolding. As we explored extensively in chapter 7, the comfort society appears as the aesthetic and affective expression of this infrastructure of delegation, one whose (socially and psycho-physically) 'weakening' effects on the urban fabric go directly against the originary meaning of the term, where the noun *fortis*, meaning 'strong', is propelled by the particle *cum*, here indicating an intensification but also, one may add—according to the other meaning of *cum*, that is, 'with'—a relation. If the original comfort was an empowering relation, the contemporary comfort often takes the form of a disempowering isolation, whose pernicious, de-skilling effects sociology, psychology and anthropology have widely explored.

Conversely, an 'energetic' notion assumes peace as a dynamic condition, which is achieved not against, but rather *through* the relational fabric of coexistence, which is in turn understood neither as an atomised picture of a society made of separated individuals, nor as an all-encompassing container into which individuals are subsumed.[13] It is exactly to overcome the false alternative between possessive individualism and social organicism,[14] that we introduced the notion of atmosphere, namely the emergent, engineered and excessive configuration through which the 'social' is articulated. In this respect, the challenge is to think security beyond the individual-society dichotomy, that is, security as the preservation—and therefore empowering—of what we referred to as (urban) vitality. What constitutes this relational ontology and vital materialism is not a substance, but rather a *power* to affect and be affected (see introduction). How to secure a power, rather than a substance, then?

This question has been accompanying, often implicitly, the whole of this book. Taking inspiration from Spinoza, and on the escort of the reflection on violence developed by Fanon, Nixon, Berlant, Povinelli and Puar among others, we introduced the notion of atmospheric (urban) violence by looking at the degree of toxicity and suffocation an atmosphere may hold vis-à-vis the bodies that compose and endure it, with disempowering or debilitating effects. This understanding was premised on the non-substantial definition of body Spinoza's modal ontology implies: a body, that is, not understood as a substance or an essence but as a power (*potentia*), an oscillation between an increase or a decrease of the capacity to affect and be affected. Understanding bodies as an oscillating power to affect and be affected does also mean understanding bodies as always already in relation, something the concept of atmosphere helped us clarify. As there is no life outside of the atmosphere, atmospheric violence is to be explored with respect to the actual conditions of life within an always turbulent, problematic and crowded configuration of coexistence. In the previous chapters we looked at the way the project, process and experience of the urban overlap in shaping our common infrastructure, by zooming in onto the forms of violence that slowly and surreptitiously impinge on the 'capacity' or 'capabilities' of bodies that are nonetheless tied to this very infrastructure.

As we discussed at length, the question of urban violence is never one of overcoming violence in the direction of an ideal society beyond violence, but rather one of reconfiguring the common with a view to increase and make flourish urban capabilities while avoiding their incapacitation. Such capabilities are nothing but the capacity of bodies to think, imagine, experience and live otherwise, that is, the capacity to express one's own power according to one's own *singular* constitution in a necessarily, ontologically common existence. In this regard, the political question is that of how to organise a multitude into a common configuration that maximises their collective power and their security. This is the question Spinoza explored in his political works. While this is obviously not the place to engage with its complexity, a brief incursion will be useful to pave the way to the concept of security we have in mind.

Freedom

Like Hobbes, in his two political works—*Tractatus Theologico-Politicus* (1670), and *Tractatus Politicus* (1677)—Spinoza resorts to the conceptual locus of the 'state of nature' in order to reflect on the transition to the 'civil state'. Like Hobbes, also Spinoza argues that there is a 'right of nature' that precedes the surfacing of the society proper. His notion, however, is radically different from both the English philosopher and the natural law tradition. According to the latter, natural rights are provided universally to any human being, who is in turn assumed as an abstract person (e.g., Esposito 2007). In Hobbes, who surely does not belong to this tradition, and for whom right and wrong are established by human law (positivism), the 'right of nature' is defined as, bluntly put, the absolute freedom to do as one pleases, that is equally and universally possessed by every human being. Spinoza's own conception radically departs from both abstractions, first, by decentring the human from the picture and second, by crafting a notion of right *as* power—*jus sive potentia*—that does not abstractly belong to an abstract person, but concretely adheres to a body and her power (Spinoza 2002[1670], ch. 16). It is a practical jurisprudence (cf. Deleuze 1988[1970]), in the sense of concerning the material and practical life of a body, rather than the abstract and universal right of a 'person'. Coherent with his ontology, the right of nature concerns power rather than substance. It is not a reactive means of protection, but rather an active means of empowerment, which however does not depend on a subject's free will to do as she pleases, but on a body's power to act according to her capacity. A birch tree can do very different things from a violin spider that, in turn, has very different powers with respect to a human being. Yet, all three have a natural right to express their own powers, that is, not to be separated from their power—dis-empowered or debilitated.

Spinoza's natural right is not concerned with the freedom an individual has to do what she *wants*, as per Hobbes, but rather with the freedom a body has to express what she *can*. The notion of freedom, it goes without saying, has a very different meaning for the two thinkers. Spinoza famously assumes freedom and necessity as synonymous (see 2002a[1677], p. 1, def. 7, pr. 17 and scholium). Accordingly, it makes no sense to say that I am free to do as I please, since the very presupposition of a 'free' will that I would autonomously exercise in isolation is, simply put, an illusion. There is no isolation. I am always taken in all sorts of relations and concatenations, always taken and acted upon by all sorts of desires, passions and imagination. As psychanalysis and neurology will extensively show centuries later, consciousness, the Cartesian *I think*, is always an *a posteriori* emergence, the shadow thrown by the action itself (cf. Agamben 2018[2017]). In the famous words of Nietzsche,

> For just as the popular mind separates the lightning from its flash and takes the latter for an action, for the operation of a subject called lightning, so popular morality also separates strength from expressions of strength, as if there were a neutral substratum behind the strong man, which was free to express strength or not to do so. But there is no such substratum; there is no 'being' behind doing, effecting, becoming; 'the doer' is merely a fiction added to the deed—the deed is everything. (1967[1887/1888], 1.13)

While the Hobbesian understanding of freedom does have little sense in this context, the very concept of freedom does not disappear. For Spinoza, instead, freedom is nothing but power, that is, the expression of one's own potential. I am free where I can express my own power and I experience this condition as joy. I am (violently) constrained, unfree, when I am separated from my own power, when I am debilitated; and I experience this condition as sadness. Of course, each one of us may have a rather different idea about her being free or unfree. Yet, as these neoliberal times show all too well, the apparent empowerment provided by the seemingly endless freedom of choice we are presented with is often accompanied by a gradual, *slow* depletion of our powers, as the reality of unequal opportunities, existential precariousness and psycho-physical depletion sets it—the work of Berlant (2011) and Nixon (2011), as we showed, have been particularly valuable in this sense. We may indeed believe we are free, but are we really? In his original and counterintuitive reflection, Spinoza argued that, for such a question to be answered, the presupposition of a constitutive separation between freedom and necessity must be revoked. It is necessity that posits freedom. What does it mean? Let us take a deep breath.

In order to live, I need to breathe. This is a necessity that comes with my constitution as an aerobic body. Therefore, I am at the freest when I am able to breathe the cleaner and most enlivening air, while I am at my most unfree when I am suffocating. In other words, my freedom coincides with the maximal expression of my own necessity (to breathe), according to my own constitution. I may convince myself to be free and yet, if I am enduring an atmosphere filled with stale, over-saturated, toxic or thin air, I am indeed depleted from my own power (to breathe) and therefore I am less free. Air, however, and therefore the composition of a given atmosphere, as we showed extensively (see chapter 6), is never innocent, or 'natural', but always engineered by all sorts of forces, structures and power relations. This is what the concept of atmospheric violence sought to address: how breathability, or the vitality of the atmosphere, is unequally distributed across lines of race, class, gender, as well as species.

The political question for Spinoza thus follows. For him it would make no sense to assume that in the state of nature there is absolute freedom and no security. In the state of nature, to be precise, there is neither freedom nor security, since my capacity to express my own power is constantly threatened by more powerful bodies and forces that may overwhelm me. Freedom, contrary to Hobbes, is never an individual right, or condition, but always depends on an immanent composition that is relational, material and historical. Spinoza is a realist thinker and certainly does not indulge in wishful thinking. He does not aim to overcome a realist depiction of human nature (i.e., to overcome the 'state of nature', understood as the way human beings are, into an abstract configuration, as liberal authors sought to do), but to affirm this realism and seek a way to organise it immanently (cf. Del Lucchese 2004). The political question that obsesses Spinoza, therefore, is that of organisation: how to structurally organise coexistence in a way able to maximise the possibility for each body to express her power within a society?[15] In other words, how to organise coexistence so as to maximise freedom *and* security, rather than assuming them as the two opposed sides of a scales? This means focusing on the actual and material conditions of existence, and the way they increase or decrease one's freedom *qua* capacity to breathe.

Relation

In Hobbes, we saw it, the State emerges by 'contract' as a security apparatus that is meant to disempower individuals by depriving them from their 'right of nature' and separating them into a compartmentalised configuration. Conversely, for Spinoza the State is a dynamic organisation that is meant to empower bodies, and where security—which he defines as the 'virtue of the State' (2002b[1677], 1.6)—is meant to maximise the power or vitality of the common, while minimising the toxic relations that unavoidably emerge out of the complexity of social life. This is why Spinoza gradually abandoned the language of the social contract, still present in his *Theological-Political Treatise*, in his later *Political Treatise*. 'The contract', argues Elizabeth Povinelli in another context, '*creates* the discursive situation in which parties can feel and act as if they were separate things' (interviewed in Lucchetti and Wielander, no date[2018]; our emphasis). The contract suppresses the relation, that is, the common, in advance by reducing it to an atomised political configuration. This is unthinkable and illogical from Spinoza's point of view. If we accept the ontological primacy of relation, then a society must correspond to a particular *organisation* of the relation and never to its suppression. Crucially, accepting the ontological primacy of relation also means to accept the inevitability of conflict, as precisely stated by Spinoza in the axiom of the fourth part of the *Ethics*: 'there is in Nature no individual thing that is not surpassed in strength and power by some other thing. Whatsoever thing there is, there is another more powerful by which the said thing can be destroyed'. While this apparently resonates with Hobbes, the crucial difference is that, according to Spinoza, for a political organisation to be sound—and therefore neither oppressive nor enslaving—conflict cannot be suppressed or neutralised. Guaranteeing the security of the political community (*multitudo*) is a necessary task to be achieved by conserving, rather than neutralising, its own power and therefore freedom.[16]

This does not mean that conflict is something positive we should aim for, as at times some in the domain of critical theory overenthusiastically argued. Conflict is an ambiguous element of the social, and it can be extremely tiring, debilitating, poisonous and lethal. Yet, it is an unavoidable facet of the relational composition of the social. Conflict, in other words, is to be understood as 'not a pathological but a physiological element of politics' (Del Lucchese 2004, 208, our translation). It must surely be managed by minimising its toxic effects, and yet it can never be altogether suppressed, since it is a constitutive expression of society's multiplicity and difference, and therefore the source of its vitality and power.[17] This is why Spinoza, who read Tacitus, stressed that 'peace is not the absence of war, it is a virtue, a state of mind, a disposition of benevolence, confidence, justice' (2002b[1677], 5.4). Security, accordingly, cannot unfold from a peace that is imposed from above, justified by a sovereign power that paternalistically promises to take care for the biological survival of the population (Del Lucchese 2004, 210). It must instead emerge as a 'virtue', a *force* fed by the immanent organisation of the multitude.

Granted, this does neither imply, nor are we advocating, to get rid of the structure of delegation, which is a fundamental logic for complex societies. More precisely, it means that delegation does not take the rigid form of an absolute and unconditional 'disburdening'. It is rather articulated in a configuration that is *conditional* on the very capacity of the government to maximise the freedom, and therefore the power, of the multitude that constitutes the political collective. If this relation between government and the multitude's power is severed, then the State will be *naturally* exposed to the resurfacing of conflict.[18]

Freedom is in this sense relational, dynamic and *energetic*. It is not a transcendent moral Good (as opposed to 'evil'), but an immanent, common good (as opposed to 'bad') (cf. Deleuze 1968; see introduction). Politics becomes a chemical matter of composition: the socio-political relation that must be held together and preserved in the same way as a bacterial culture is, by nourishing the fermenting multitude of micro-organisms and preserving its chemical composition without suffocating it. By leaving it free to act and therefore express its own power (*jus sive potentia*) within an environment that is still structured and 'controlled', albeit not in a repressive way (cf. Lorimer 2020). In this sense, let us clarify, the (field for) security we are thinking about does not get rid of institutions, be they the 'State' or any other form it may take in the future—rather, it is about making institutions capable of non-repressive structuration and control. Politics, as we argued, has to do with enhancing the breathability or vitality of the atmosphere. Since each body constantly breathes in and out—i.e., composes—this very atmosphere, it follows that breathability cannot be imposed from above but is an always situated, common effort, whose conditions are not defined in advance but are the result of a dynamic process that is never settled once and for all. 'In an energetically founded worldview and image of peace', writes Dietrich, 'there exist no ultimate values, but only dynamic relations . . . Energetic peace can thus neither be taught, nor exported, nor "produced" via objective conditions, but it can only be experienced and put into context' (2012, 30).

This has been all the more evident in the midst of the global Covid-19 pandemic, where the predicament of the Anthropocene suddenly became dramatically explicit: in the words of Michael Taussig (e.g., 2020, 74), we—humans and nonhumans alike—*are all cosmically implicated*, interconnected and interdependent. That the socio-biological atmosphere through which everyday life unfolds is material, permeable and fragile, increasingly saturated with particulates, fear, CO^2, hate, viruses, ressentiment, depression—and increasingly unbreathable—may seem a platitude. And yet, never before the first respiratory pandemic of the age of globalisation and digital interconnection had this been so immediately obvious at the planetary scale of experience. In this context, Achille Mbembe called for a 'universal right to breathe' as a way to recognise breathing 'beyond its purely biological aspect, and instead as that which we hold in-common' (2020). This suggestion, which we explored in chapter 6, perfectly chimes with the relation between notions of breathing, life and peace we find in various non-Western and pre-modern cosmologies.[19] The universal right to breathe—which is dynamic and relational, differently from the right to be comfortable—points to an energetic peace that does not produce the desert that Tacitus and climate scientists alike have prefigured, but rather unfolds in the common effort of making our common atmosphere breathable. 'Good governance', thus understood, has no moral bases but exquisitely 'physical' ones: it is not about guaranteeing the well-being of the population out of moral duty or paternalistic care, but as a matter of social 'statics', or tensegrity—that is, as a matter of keeping and maintaining the common infrastructure in place (Berlant 2016). Every politics is always already a biopolitics, in this sense. The question, thus, is whether a given biopolitics is actually maximising the 'life' of the multitude or, conversely, disempowering it—as we know all too well, a disempowerment that is always asymmetrical across lines of class, gender, race, ability and species. Here lies, in a sense, the difference between a negative and an affirmative biopolitics (cf. Esposito 2008[2004]).

It is in these terms, we believe, that an affirmative conception of security should be thought. Referring to the term *laafi bala*, which in Burkina Faso's Mooré language means 'peace' as well as, literally, 'fresh air', Dietrich thus asks

in what manner are societies which can perceive peace energetically, for example as fresh air, different from those which have substituted the ultimate explanation of peace with a construction of normative, moral precepts or proscriptions? (2012, 4)

A partial answer, then, may come from the effort of rescuing security from its entrapment into the logic of delegation, balance and carelessness for the common, by restoring its ontological relation with each body's power to think, imagine, sense and live collectively, by 'recognising and embracing our *interdependencies*' (The Care Collective 2020, 5; emphasis in original). This is the direction of rethinking the notion of *care* that has been lately developed by a host of radical, materialist feminist thinkers such as Donna Haraway, Maria Puig de la Bellacasa, Elizabeth Povinelli, Isabelle Stengers, Jean Tronto and many others. What they gesture towards, we argue, is the possibility to reconceptualise security *cum cura*.

Care

In a tensegritous architecture, each part has a material obligation to 'care' for the other parts in order to keep the infrastructure in place and therefore prevent collapse. In an atmosphere, each body is materially bound to the breathability of the air she contributes to compose, saturate and pollute, whether or not she is aware of that. In a relational ontology, the concept of care assumes a material dimension that is incompatible with the field of normative morality, individual empathy, selfless altruism, since it has to do with the pre-individual, infrastructural 'holding together' of the given assemblage.

Care, in this sense 'is a force distributed across a multiplicity of agencies and materials and supports of our worlds as a thick mesh of relational obligation' (de la Bellacasa 2017, 20). These obligations are not a matter of good will, empathy or solidarity—they are indeed *matter*, matters of care, that imply a necessary ethical and political involvement in the world's ongoing mattering, that is, in the actual unfolding of life.[20] Life requires effort, maintenance, repair. It is in this infrastructural work of conservation that care unfolds.[21] This means that there is no neutral position: we are always already *implicated* and *interdependent* in caring and uncaring relations, and therefore always already responsible for the conservation or degeneration of the human and non-human common. The extent to which ontology and ethics are in this way inextricable is perfectly clarified by Karen Barad, when she observes that:

> Ethics is an integral part of the diffraction (ongoing differentiating) patterns of worlding, not a superimposing of human values onto the ontology of the world (as if 'fact' and 'value' were radically other). The very nature of matter entails an exposure to the Other. Responsibility is not an obligation that the subject chooses but rather an incarnate relation that precedes the intentionality of consciousness. Responsibility is not a calculation to be performed. It is a relation always already integral to the world's ongoing intra-active becoming and not-becoming. (2010, 265)

This is not a question of 'free' choice, that is, not a normative *ought* from which one can opt out. In the explicit words of Povinelli, 'I am not obligated to someone, something, some mood or action. I find myself already bound to a formative outside in the moment of encountering that someone, something, some mood or action' (2018, 152). This is the kind of 'grounded normativity' that Povinelli finds in the traditional relation with land of the Indigenous First Nations' people she engages with, according to which 'people and land were in a relation of co-obligated bodily belonging', and that she sees to be dangerously compromised when such people embrace the contractual logic of sovereignty, which instead threatens to sever this relation by replacing it with contractual structures of delegation (idem, 158). As Dene thinker Glen Coulthard observes, 'the theory and practice of Indigenous anticolonialism, including Indigenous anticapitalism, is best understood as a struggle primarily inspired by and oriented *around the question of land*—a struggle not only for land in the material sense, but also deeply *informed* by what the land as system of reciprocal relations and obligations can teach us about living our lives in relation to one another and the natural world in nondominating and nonexploitative terms' (2014, 13; emphasis in original). In this sense, reclaiming land within a discourse of sovereignty—what we referred to as a contractual logic of delegation—risks producing 'a reorientation of Indigenous struggle' from such a grounded normativity 'to a struggle that is now increasingly *for* land, understood now as a material resource to be exploited in the capital accumulation process' (idem, 78; emphasis in original).[22]

This is an interesting position that questions the *severing* logic of delegation on the account that there are no individuals, societies and territories, but rather socio-natural atmospheres to which we are already bound and implicated, in a relation of interdependence and obligation, so that the ethical and political task is that of attending to, caring for and therefore *securing* this complex interweaving. There is a clear difference between a materialist understanding of care as a pre-individual socio-natural relation to which one is bound in the terms of a nonnormative necessity—i.e., an actually existent *condition*—and the abstract relation instituted by contract. Assuming our being in the world in the form of a 'co-obligated bodily belonging' is also a way to dismiss any pretence of innocence 'beyond violence'. *There is violence*, in the form of violent relations we are already entangled with, or a violent atmosphere we all breathe, at a greater or lesser extent, whether or not we are aware of that. For instance, it is the violence that the 'quality of life' of a class, a neighbourhood or a city indirectly perpetrates over that of another class, a neighbourhood or a city *in order* to maintain itself as such. This violent relation and its material responsibility are erased when the 'solution' to improve the quality of life of a given 'unliveable' city is understood as simply providing it with the standards and infrastructures of a liveable one. What is conveniently overlooked is the extent to which the latter's 'liveability' is premised on the former's 'un-liveability'.[23]

Care, we can see, is a material and immanent force that is already in place, in the form of those caring and uncaring relations that hold us together, albeit rarely recognised as such, beyond the altruism, solidarity, romantic good intentions, moral principles or normative ideals that one *ought to* follow. It is a necessary relation of interdependence, that is. As de la Bellacasa put it, inspired by Deleuze's Spinozism, 'the notion of "ethical obligation" shifts meaning, from ethical commitments arising out of moral principles—such as contracts or promises—to be embedded in vital material forces involved in the constraints of everyday continuation and maintenance of life' (de la Bellacasa 2017, 22). In this sense, and differently from the long tradition of so-called 'ethics of the other', matters of care do not actually concern my fellow human or non-human being, but are rather directed to the *relation* itself or, more to the point, to the excessive power of the relation, that is, its vitality. This is, after all, what the various micro-organisms composing each of us do, co-evolving as interdependent and interconnected by building alliances and resisting toxic forces of decomposition, that is, caring for each other *not* for the sake of each other, but for the sake of the preservation of the whole composition, or 'body', of which they are part. A preservation that, as vastly discussed, depends on the capacity of a body to variate and differentiate, that is, a capacity to take care for its own excessive potential (see introduction). This is precisely the definition of care provided by Joan Tronto, namely: 'everything that we do to maintain, continue and repair "our world" so that we can live in it as well as possible' (1993, 103)—a definition that, for obvious reasons, is increasingly central in the context of the Anthropocene. It is this notion of maintenance to be crucial here, since it shifts the attention from the moral *intention* to 'care about' to the actual *work* of 'caring for' (cf. de la Bellacasa 2017, 5). This work does not begin from 'liberal' freedom and abstract rights, but rather from the necessity and obligation that take place by engaging with the necessary constraints of co-existence: it is the building of mutual dependency in an interconnected world (cf. The Care Collective 2020).

A key reason for emancipating this understanding of care from preconstituted normative frameworks and their related understanding of 'good' is that practices of care may indeed disturb such understanding in the first place—e.g., the understanding of urban liveability, quality of life or happiness we take for granted as the unquestioned goals that supposedly orient policy 'solutions'. Rethinking problems and the violent ways in which they have been constructed via matters of care implies an effort aimed at conceiving novel sets of values, obligations, commitments. 'There are no solutions', writes Barad, 'there is only the ongoing practice of being open and alive to each meeting, each intra-action, so that we might use our ability to respond, our responsibility, to help awaken, to breathe life into ever new possibilities for living justly' (2007, x).

Not a normative injunction then, caring is the material obligation of bodies to maintain the breathability of their common, and therefore to break it open, and violently so if need be, when suffocation sets in. This is what many people did when invading the streets and risking their lives because they cared, because their Black lives *mattered*, because within the atmosphere of urban violence encompassing their cities they could no longer breathe.

Security

The question then is how to think a security—and the related institutions—that would not imply contractual delegation, security-freedom balance and individualistic carelessness, but would be grounded on a common, co-obligated responsibility or, as per Haraway's suggestion (2008; 2016), a *response-ability*—that is, acknowledging, and experimenting with, our being always already entangled in a complex and troubling common. Assuming co-implication removes any possibility of abstract 'disburdening' and challenges the 'organised irresponsibility' on which the contemporary security politics is premised. At the same time, it sanctions as untenable any balance between security and freedom, since a security that debilitates the common cannot but decrease freedom, and vice versa. As repeatedly stressed, however, this does not mean to simply re-burden the individual vs. the institution, or the society—a move, let us remind, that is structural to the neoliberal politics of security. Rather, we are gesturing towards a reconfiguration of the institutional structure of delegation beyond this artificial opposition, in turn sustained upon the security-freedom balance, whose mythical status we amply questioned.

Let us reflect one last time on the Covid-19 pandemic, since it did offer an aesthetic and affective possibility to experience and sense the condition of co-implication, all the way from uncontrolled deforestation and violence on animals, to the lethal effect one's own breathing may have. On the one hand, for the most part the 'emergency' that its various waves brought about have been dealt with through delegation, balance and carelessness. Consider again the Italian case (see chapter 3, Researching Urban Violence), where, during the first lockdown in 2020, the industrial sector kept pressing the government to keep a quite expansive definition of 'essential activities'—i.e., those activities which were not to be affected by the lockdown measures—which basically left most industrial activity untouched by the regulations. In this context, writer Wu Ming I (2021, 340) emphasised a telling contradiction: while, he argued, the health situation should have been addressed by 'staying home' (*restare a casa*)—i.e., not going to work and halting industrial activity—the Italian (and other) governmental and public discourses have rather been framed around the imperative of 'staying at home' (*restare in casa*). While a large part of the population—fundamentally, blue collar, care and gig workers—was obliged to go to work (thereby maintaining productivity), they were also prohibited to engage in non-dangerous outdoor activities (e.g., walking, fitness, socialisation), which could have increased psycho-physical well-being without hampering the security of the community. Albeit unthreatening from a scientific perspective, all sorts of activities, solo running included, were legally forbidden and socially stigmatised.[24] One should also remember that staying at home was not peaceful, demonstrated by the steep increase of gender and domestic violence recorded all around the world. And, again in the Italian case, 'irrational'[25] measures were also implemented after the first, chaotic months, for instance in the punitive imposition of a surreptitious vaccination mandate in 2021 (the so-called

Green Pass) even in contexts of very low risk and despite extremely high rates of vaccination in the country, in a context marked by naming and shaming campaigns against those who chose to not vaccinate (see Tulumello 2021b).[26] In this context, the responsibilisation of the individual—to stay home, to vaccinate oneself—was detached from the actual care for the common and instead tied to the strict observation of the rule—*legality*, again. Yes, in the mainstream rhetoric we were repeatedly told to comply with the rules 'for the common good'. Yet, this common was narrowly framed, as a sort of pre-existent substance we must abide to, rather than a relation that is continuously re-constructed through material caring and uncaring relations: an ongoing commoning, that is (cf. Linebaugh 2008; Hardt and Negri 2009; Harvey 2012).[27]

A similarly reductive, implicit understanding of the common is what often feeds models of community policing where, although a notion of co-responsibility is foregrounded, this is tied to a homogeneous and 'substantial' understanding of crime (as an exogenous, most often external, threat) and of the 'community' itself, supposedly formed by pre-existent and clearly defined individuals—all too often along lines of race, class, sexual orientation and so on. Notwithstanding the appearance, then, the consequence is often that of ushering in another form of 'organised irresponsibility' vis-à-vis the heterogenous, vital excess of the common. No surprise many forms of community policing often end up supporting exclusionary practices against marginal categories, non-human bodies included (see also note 12 above).

As Martin Kornberger and Christian Borch put it, 'the commons is not just something that is shared by pre-existing commoners; rather the commoners may be constituted in the creation of production of a commons' (2015, 9; see also Stavrides 2016; Pavoni 2021). During the pandemic, instead, a homogeneous understanding of the common led to often overlook the different degrees of exposition and vulnerability of the bodies that composed it, while a narrow construction of 'security' ignored the risks for the physical and mental health of the population that went beyond those tied to the virus itself. The society was presented as a homogeneous and flat 'substance', with respect to which the championing of a de-politicised notion of life as survival ended up systematically erasing inequalities and asymmetries and to which each one of us was to be passively subsumed.

On the other hand, the main challenge to this rhetoric—at least in the mainstream media representation and political debate—came from the symmetrically opposite standpoint, namely the libertarian individualist claim that everyone has the right to do *as one pleases* and therefore cannot be compelled to wear masks or take vaccines. While discursively opposed, these two positions implicitly converged in reasserting the same individual-society dichotomy, without acknowledging that the common, that is, the very relation constituting the social, is already held together by an infrastructure of care and violence that said dichotomy simply overlooks. The position of those who sought to avoid falling into one side or the other of the dichotomy pointed to the task of recomposing the common by retracing, repairing and reconstituting the caring relations that hold it together. This has been the case of various solidarity initiatives emerged during the pandemic, often autonomously, via spontaneism, grassroots organisation or local non-profit associations, which were rarely mentioned, let alone encouraged, by the mainstream discourse, which was overconcerned with reclaiming the strict observation of the rule.[28] The candid declarations of some politicians about the purely affective rationale of certain draconian measures such as the campaign against runners ('we knew it had no health meaning, but we wanted to send a message') is a clear case in point (cf. Wu Ming I 2021, ch. 21).

As we argued (chapter 3, Researching Urban Violence), repressive restrictions and libertarian defiance were the two sides of the same logic, showing once more that the rhetorical exaltation of an acritical and homogeneous understanding of 'society' (or 'nation') is the perfect complement to the libertarian exaltation of individual freedom: they form the two poles of the same immunitary paradigm and are the basis around which the myth of the freedom-security balance is articulated. Still entrapped within this dichotomy is also the tension Sheila Jasanoff (2020) underlined, in the US context, between, on the one hand, the use of law as an instrument of enforcement of medical directives, and, on the other, its use as a tool to counter them by reasserting the right to religious assembly or election. In this tension 'between human beings as biomedical subjects, more acted upon than acting, and as social and political subjects, more acting than acted upon' (idem, § 4), what has been copiously missing, at least from the public radar, have been understandings of 'health', 'life', 'security' and 'freedom' that do not depend on the society-individual dichotomy.

Following Haraway, de la Bellacasa advocates,

> a politics of care as an everyday practice that refuses moral orders that reduce it to innocent love or the securitization of those in need. Adequate care requires a form of knowledge and curiosity regarding the situated needs of an 'other'—human or not—that only becomes possible through being in relations that inevitably transform the entangled beings. (2017, 90)

A 'security politics of care', then, means assuming security itself as a practice of caring, maintenance and repairing that is not predetermined in advance (cf. Tulumello 2021a, 322-323), and does not preliminary assume the 'what' that is being secured but rather constructs it through the very process of securing-as-caring.[29] Security in this way is framed not as a problem of rights but as a right to problems, that is, a right to participate in the *creation of new problems* (Deleuze 2006[1986]), including the 'problem' of security, rather than narrowly reducing it onto the technocratic task of finding and securing solutions. This is after all the quintessential trouble with the pernicious forms of delegation we explored above: *the delegation of troubles*, that is, the pre-emptive (and post-political) neutralisation of problems.[30] In other words, the assumption that security is simply a matter of 'securing' something or someone, rather than a relation (of care) that must be enacted and maintained in the first place.

Rethinking security in this sense is at the same time a matter of, on the one hand, radical pluralism, and, on the other, speculation and experimentation. With the former, we refer here to a line of thinking that joins William Connolly's case (2005) for radical democracy and Bonnie Honig's agonistic feminism (1992; 2008[2006]), to which we draw the need for an ontological (re-)politicisation of security as 'the positive cultivation of inevitable dissonances and dislocations' (Howart 2008, 176 on Connolly's pluralism; cf. Tulumello 2021a).[31] With the latter, we refer to the need to relearn how to 'stay', experience and engage with the troubles, where 'trouble' takes a triple sense: a *problem*; a *turbulence* or perturbation, and therefore a conflictual condition; and a *turba*, that is, a disordered multitude of human and non-human entities—viruses included—which is increasingly critical for us to acknowledge, engage with and build alliances within, rather than senselessly suppress (Haraway 2016).

At this intersection we find the limit of a merely *critical* approach to security. In its debunking effort, it goes as far as removing those caring links that hold us together. This does not mean abandoning the critique of security, of course, but rather complement it with a different understanding of security as a material obligation each of us have for composing the common in which we are all already implicated. Again, this became particularly explicit in the pandemic context, during which common life (and care) could only exist by accepting risk and exposure—vulnerability, with Judith Butler (2003)—responsibility and obligations: the only alternative would have been a total erasure of common life amid a permanent lockdown—total, that is, for those who could afford to isolate themselves, leaving the exploited and marginalised to take the toll of the exposure that was necessary to keep the system going.

This was a particularly evident version of a broader problem that this book has tended towards: what remains beyond the dichotomy between an absolute security (an imaginary for all and an experience for those on the 'right' side of the epistemological fracture; cf. Feltran 2020) and an absolute liberty (in the name of a destructive individualism), and indeed the destruction of the common that they share? It remains the trouble of critique, that is, the need to embrace critique as (in)security (see Burgess 2019). Troubles, conflict and turbulence cannot be the negative counterpoint of care, they are rather the very dimension through which 'security as care' (*cum cura*, that is) must unfold, in the form of a critical stance that is critical vis-à-vis the present without being oriented by a normative presupposition, since it does attend to (care for) the protection and fostering collective life, while at the same time challenges the normative ideal of 'good life' that lies beneath.

Re-Defining Urban Violence

In defining the problem (see introduction), we suggested that the necessary effort at expanding violence beyond its reductionisms (cf. chapter 1) implies that urban violence cannot—and should not—be defined by delimiting a specific field of actions or a peculiar geography. We argued that only by re-defining the urban (chapter 2) and in relation to security (chapter 3) could urban violence become an analytically and strategically powerful concept. We dedicated, then, the core of the book to re-articulate the genealogical relations between security as an imaginary (chapter 4) and urbanisation as a process (chapter 5), proposing urban atmospheric violence (chapter 6) as an analytical lens through which urban violence can be precisely captured in its ontological, epistemological and ethical dimensions—its historical roots in capitalist urbanisation, its emergence in the urban experience, its appearance in relation to the imaginary of security. We could, then, move to explore what we consider important dimensions of the present urban/violence/security bundle, in the ideology of comfort, with its Italian declination as decorum (chapter 7), and in the imaginary of the smart/safe city, with its algorithmic actualisations through predictive policing (chapter 8). Finally, this last chapter was dedicated to the strategic endeavour of setting some coordinates for a security as care—that is, breaking out of the dichotomies (delegation/responsabilisation, security/freedom, repression/carelessness) that frame the mainstream logics of security, thereby offering a way forward for re-thinking security.

In closing, we are left with the question of whether, beyond redefining the ontological, epistemological and ethical frameworks through which urban violence is to be analytically conceptualised (and researched), is it possible to strategically re-define it in light of an understanding of security as care. Violence, we reflected, is a tricky concept, one that eschews attempts to make it 'observable' and thus amenable to categorisation. Urban violence, in this sense, can be understood as one of its possible characterisations, one emerged from the history of urbanisation, the atmospheres of urban experience and the imaginary of (urban) security, with respect to which it has always been mobilised, implicitly or explicitly, as a counterpoint. What happens, then, once we reframe such an imaginary?

Urban violence, we propose, needs to be clearly distinguished from trouble and conflict, from the messy problem of managing the urban common. Once this is done, urban violence can be strategically reconfigured as not the counterpoint to absolute security, but to security as *care*: be it physical or structural, institutional or insurgent, urban violence is the infra-structural force that debilitates the (collective) vitality of the urban, suffocating the excessive, 'surplus-value' of urban life that urban life itself continuously generates. As such, we believe, urban violence can be dealt with, without imposing further violence in turn.

Epilogue: In the Crowd

Eugene Thacker (2017, 363) proposes that the life that is the subject of biopolitics be understood not only according to the classical dichotomy of *zoe* and *bios*, 'bare' and 'qualified' life, but also gesturing towards what Aristotle calls *psukhe*, a notion that is usually translated as 'soul' but that, he argues, is better translated as 'a principle of life, a vital principle, the Life of the living', a sort of impersonal and relational 'vital breath'—the excessive dimension of a vitality that circulates, flows through and overflows the living. Relevant, in this sense, is Aristotle's description of the effect, or affection, that characterises the collective experience of tragedy, namely *catharsis*. What is at issue with catharsis is not simply the production of a certain emotion—*pathos*—but more precisely its *circulation* through the audience. A *pathological* collective experience, Thacker continues, 'catharsis is less an emotion and more an affect—it proceeds by a sort of logic of miasmatic contagion or swarming, passing from stage to amphitheatre, from actor to audience, and between one audience member and another' (idem, 367-368). No one perhaps described the ambiguous nature of this pathological *becoming-common* more vividly than Antonin Artaud, who famously equated the theatre with the plague itself, that is, as a contagion that produces 'collective abscesses' and, by cathartically releasing the vital potential of the common atmosphere, its breathability, 'unravels conflicts, liberates powers, releases potential' that are unpredictable and not necessarily desirable, since 'if these powers are dark, this is not the fault of the plague or theatre, but life' (2013[1978], 21).

It is such an intensive, excessive and in-becoming quality of life, we argued, to be implicitly at stake with contemporary security politics, namely the necessity to govern the multitude by systematically preventing the ambiguous excess from unfolding. Since Hobbes, this was the political question par excellence: how to turn a multitude into ordered people, how to separate the overflowing relationality of the common into an ordered set of atomised individuals—how to neutralise vitality of life, that is. One is reminded of Elias Canetti's reflections in *Crowds and Power*, where the crowd is presented as an 'organism' that emerges when the individuals (be)come together, overcoming their distances and the fear of being touched by others. If 'there is nothing that man fears more than the touch of the unknown' (Canetti 1962[1960], 15), the crowd paradoxically appears to Canetti as the radical overcoming of this fear, the destruction of the boundaries between individuals which is achieved by becoming-common:

> Only together can men free themselves from their burdens of distance; and this, precisely, is what happens in a crowd. During the discharge distinctions are thrown off and all feel equal. In that density, where there is scarcely any space between, and body presses against body, each man is as near the other as he is to himself; and an immense feeling of relief ensues. (idem, 18)

This 'immense feeling of relief' resonates with what Fanon writes in *The Wretched of the Earth* (1963[1961]), a book almost contemporaneous to *Crowds and Power*, which had been published, in German, only a year before Fanon's book and that, presumably, he did not know. For Fanon, the toxic atmosphere of colonialism was not challenged via an ideological *prise de conscience*, but also, and most importantly, by the material performance of the colonised bodies that crowded the streets and the squares of the colonial city in order to express their anger at the colonial regime. By doing so, they created a breach in the atmosphere of violence, allowing fresh air to seep through, reanimating the vital breath of their radical commonality, what the colonial power had systematically sought to suffocate. It is on the material and collective quality of this 'breaching' that Fanon reflects when asking 'how do we pass from the atmosphere of violence to violence in action? What makes the lid blow off?' (idem, 71). There is a difference, he notes, between the collective violence *of* the colonised and the colonial violence deployed *on* the colonised. The latter is a toxic atmosphere that suffocates their excessive vitality. The former is 'an attack to all boundaries' (cf. Canetti 1962[1960], 20), that is, the violence of a vital excess that overflows the individual bodies and their abstract—and violently enforced—separation, by triggering a becoming-common. A monstrous becoming indeed, that the colonial power fears the most.[32] As Fanon continues, 'the native who has the opportunity to return to the people during the struggle for freedom will discover the falseness of this theory', namely 'the idea of a society of individuals where each person shuts himself up in his own subjectivity, and whose only wealth is individual thought', which 'the colonialist bourgeoisie had hammered into the native's mind' (1963[1961], 47). Critical consciousness will not suffice to grasp the 'falseness' of this theory—it is by practically *returning to the people* that this awareness will occur instead, that is, by putting the bodies at risk in order to materially overcome the individual separations, letting the ontological 'truth' of a common becoming emerge.

This experience of becoming-common, which literally breaks open the unbreathable saturation of the colonial atmosphere, releases novel postcolonial subjectivities. It is a chemical process, a collective (trans)individuation, as Gilbert Simondon would say, a change of state in the molecular composition of the crowd. Within the crowd, what is common circulates and activates the single bodies, releasing relational subjectivities that did not exist before. This is why the crowd is never simply the sum of its parts. It is *more*, as it exceeds its internal partitions (physical, normative, cultural); and, at the same time, it is *less*, since it is transient, fragile, temporary, heading towards an inevitable disintegration.[33] Within the crowd, novel bonds are generated in the form of reciprocal relations and obligations, significantly re-articulating the meaning, and indeed the mattering, of care and security. In the rebellious crowd Fanon describes, there is no chance to delegate security and care to any transcendent apparatus. Each body is bound to care and provide security for the other bodies that constitute the crowd, and this is not done out of moral empathy or solidarity but, more precisely, because the very life of the crowd, its breathability, depends on the capacity of these immanent relations to hold: if they break up, the crowd will dissolve and the brutal colonial repression will set in.

In this collective body-become-multitude, the *conatus* is a vital principle of preservation that can only unfold *together* and *dynamically*, via a constant transformation. Like fire, the crowd 'always wants to grow' (Canetti 1962[1960], 81), in it there is an excessive vitality that cannot be suppressed without suppressing the crowd itself: if it stops growing, if it is no longer able to exceed itself, it is bound to collapse. This is the 'paradoxical conservatism' of the multitude, its need to constantly transform, that is, to become, in order to preserve itself.[34] As Bove writes, the relational dynamic of resistance and alliance that characterises the 'strategy of the *conatus*' (see introduction) is 'first of all a problem of space, a space to build, conquer, free but also a space to defend' (1996, 15; our translation), that is, to care for and secure. This is consistent with the rebellious crowd Fanon describes, where security and care are no longer distinguishable, nor can they be 'disburdened' to external authorities or apparatuses, but are wholly dependent on internal and imma-nent bounds of obligation and responsibility.

If the crowd attacks the colonial apparatus, this is not because it has become *careless* of the dangers but, more precisely, because it 'understands' that only by becoming common through mutual care is it possible to be actu-ally *secured* against those very dangers. This is precisely the type of security gestured in the transfeminist walks promoted in Italy by Non Una di Meno[35] and similar movements. Explicitly framed as *indecorose* (indecorous) in reac-tion to the type of security promoted by advocates of *decoro urbano* (Tulu-mello and Bertoni 2019), the walks are centred in the collective practice of bodies cross-cutting public space, placing vulnerability and care at the centre of urban politics (Castelli 2016; Tola 2019). The security of the crowd, for and beyond these movements, is immanently generated by the relation of co-obligation among its parts, not in the name of an abstract altruistic principle, but in the name of a common exposure to danger, a common fragility, which is not open to a pietistic politics of recognition but, rather, a co-responsible ethics of struggle. This is piercingly stated by Fanon when he notes that, after the revolt,

> the interests of one will be the interests of all, for in concrete fact *everyone* will be discovered by the troops, *everyone* will be massacred—or *everyone* will be saved. The motto 'look out for yourself', the atheist's method of salvation, is in this context forbidden. (1963[1961], 47; emphasis in translation)

The crowd co-breathes and conspires in the awareness that it is this com-mon breath that keeps each individual alive and that each individual has the obligation to care for. If such a care were to lack, then also the common would collapse. No one could find private relief in some comfort bubble: if the mass crowd is no longer able to become, everyone will be equally an-nihilated. In the crowd, in other words, there is security, and yet of a kind that is incompatible with the security structured via delegation, balance and carelessness that we have described so far. This security cannot be delegated to a transcendent authority, nor is it simply dependent on the (good) will of individuals. Rather it depends on what Elizabeth Povinelli (2011, 33) terms 'immanent obligation', that is, 'a form of relationality that one finds oneself drawn and finds oneself nurturing, or caring for in the midst of critical reflexivity'.[36] Once the 'illusion' of the pre-existent individual is removed, the coessentiality of security and freedom becomes apparent, in the form of a dynamic relation that must be sustained, maintained, and cared for: *cum cura*. This care, we repeat, is not a care for the other, but more precisely a *care for the crowd itself*, that is, a care for the relation and its vital and excessive capacity to overflow, to transform and to become. An *intensive care*, that is, able to simultaneously break open the consensual imaginary of 'social cohesion',[37] that, like the theatre Artaud envisaged, 'unravels conflicts, liberates powers, releases potential' (2013[1978], 21). It is here then that the original meaning of comfort as *cum fortis* is expressed: an 'immense feeling of relief' that is not a passive relation of relaxation, but a mutual strengthening, a common process of both empowering and immunisation—co-immunity.

Peter Sloterdijk has observed that 'all social organisations in history, from the primal hordes to the world empires, can, from a systemic perspective, be explained as structures of co-immunity', where 'immune advantages' have been distributed unequally, and violently so (2013[2009], 450). Logics of delegation, balance and carelessness have institutionally shaped security accordingly, with the troubling outcomes we have been describing in this book. The question this example allegorically gestures towards, however, is not one of spontaneism against organisation, horizontality against institution, anarchy against the law. It is, rather, a radical way to rethink security *with* freedom, responsibility and care. This requires decoupling the notion of justice from the structures of normativity and morality—the promise that a radical understanding of spatial justice pointed towards (see Philippopoulos-Mihalopoulos 2015; Pavoni 2018a). Not a search for a more just space or a city whose criteria are normatively defined in advance. Instead, the task is to *spatialise* justice, that is, making justice *breathable* by challenging the structures of living surreptitiously suffocating urban life. This is an effort that requires moving away from the liberal understanding of notions of freedom, security or right, not to jettison them, but rather reconfiguring them within a semantic of obligation: the obligation each of us has, differently, asymmetrically, and yet necessarily, to support, maintain and foster—that is, to care for—the common atmosphere through which we all, humans and nonhumans, breathe.[38] Such an effort, of course, cannot be simply left to altruism, spontaneism or solidarity. Creative ways to *institutionalise* it must be envisaged, and for this purpose, a speculative endeavour is also needed.

Notes

1. Horace, *Epistularum*. 'Tis your own safety that's at stake, when your neighbour's wall is in flames, and fires neglected are wont to gather strength' (Horace 1926, 375).

2. In a letter (dated 1986) to Arnaud Villani, apud Deleuze (2020[2015], 86; emphasis in the translation used).

3. The plane of immanence is to be understood as a given articulation of the parameters of thinking (a given image of thought) that are the condition of possibility for a concept to be created. A plane of immanence is not a-historical, nor simply discursive, it is rather socio-material or material-discursive, in the sense we referred to above (see chapter 1). 'The plane of immanence is not a concept that is or can be thought but rather the image of thought, the image thought gives itself of what it means to think, to make use of thought, to find one's bearing in thought' (Deleuze and Guattari 1994[1991], 37). Truly thinking, Deleuze explains, always entails engaging with the outside of a given plane of immanence, breaking open the existence image of thought, dismantling the ruling common sense. It follows that truly *rethinking* security implies redrawing a new plane of immanence by first of all dismantling the former one and the three main vectors, as we show below, through which it is articulated.

4. The recent use of *legalità* on the Italian left, for its part, has a quite specific history. On the one hand, it links to the violence of, and the 'war' against, the mafias in the 1980s and early 1990s, particularly the murders of high-profile police officers and magistrates by Cosa Nostra—the most spectacular of which were the two bombs that killed, in 1992, magistrates Giovanni Falcone, Francesca Morvillo and Paolo Borsellino together with several officers of their security detail. In the following years, the progressive civil society in Palermo and other Sicilian cities reacted, pushing significant political changes, with the concept of *legalità* at the centre of the political horizon—see the account by Leoluca Orlando (2001), mayor of Palermo in the 1990s and again in the 2010s. On the other hand, *legalità* was a central political argument used by national progressive movements during Silvio Berlusconi's political trajectory and three tenures as prime minister, during which several trials and controversial laws were considered by the Left to be '*ad personam*'—that is, aiming to protect Berlusconi from the judicial procedures. More recently, *legalità* has been one of the main rallying words for the 'populist' 5 Stars Movement.

5. Incidentally, it should be noted that problematic uses of the concepts of *sicurezza* and *libertà* have also long characterised Italian parties to the Left of the moderate, centre-left PD—the problem goes well beyond the gradual shift towards the right.

6. Domenico Fisichella observes that for Hobbes security is understood as 'not the mere preservation of life, but also all the satisfactions and comforts of life that each person will acquire in the course of his existence thanks to his legitimate industriousness and without damage and danger to the State' (2008, 69; our translation). It is

evident, however, that these 'satisfactions and comforts' are only provided insofar as the State—and therefore its violent infrastructure—are not compromised.

7. 'And so of all living creatures, whilst they are imprisoned, or restrained with walls or chains; and of the water whilst it is kept in by banks or vessels that otherwise would spread itself into a larger space; we use to say they are not at liberty to move in such manner as without those external impediments they would' (Hobbes 2002[1651], ch. XXI, par. 1).

8. As it is known, Hobbes (2002[1651], ch. XIV) goes as far as suggesting that even if extorted by force, a pact cannot be rescinded.

9. Recall Esposito's observation, already quoted in chapter 1: for Hobbes, 'if the relation between men is in itself destructive, the only route of escape from this unbearable state of affairs is the destruction of the relation itself' (Esposito 2009[1998], 27).

10. By excavating Hobbes once again we do not want to imply there is some sort of original structure of security that flows unchanged as of today. We are aware that genealogical work is more about 'discontinuities' than 'continuity and concealment', as Alberto Toscano (2011) puts it. The evolution of security we traced in chapter 3 exemplifies this complexity. Nonetheless, the role played by the three vectors referred above in articulating contemporary security politics is still apparent.

11. To be sure, this is not a deterministic reflection. Technology is never abstracted from its socio-political context, and therefore can never be analysed and assessed as such: both techno-optimism and techno-pessimism are marred by the same techno-determinism (cf. Bina et al. 2020). Gig economy workers are a remarkable instance, both of the pernicious effects of the techno-juridical infrastructure of delegation, and of the novel forms of resistance and struggle that surface through its cracks (e.g., *Into the Black Box* 2022). A compelling reflection in this sense is the one provided by Bernard Stiegler (2016[2015]), whose complex analysis diagnoses the ongoing atrophy of the collective capacity to elaborate common horizons that be alternative to the dominant ones, due to a pernicious convergence between automation and capitalism, as result of which the technical system takes direct control of the modalities through which the collective production of imaginaries unfold, via automatic storing (surveillance), automatic generation (algorithms) and automatic sharing (social media). Through this argument, which is far more sophisticated than these few lines would suggest, Stiegler updates to the digital age Walter Benjamin's reflection on the 'destruction of experience' (1963[1936]; see Benjamin and Osborne 1994), and provides a socio-technical explanation to the condition that Mark Fisher's formula (2009), after Fredrick Jameson, famously captured: *capitalist realism*, or the growing incapacity to imagine an alternative, what is today represented by the rise of the technocratic logic of *solutionism* (e.g., Morozov, 2013).

12. Part of this trend can also be seen in the progressive replacement, in Anglophone contexts, of traditional forms of community policing with 'community practices' characterised by the mediation of digital technology—for instance, the virtual communities of apps like Next Door (https://nextdoor.com/), to which police

forces are increasingly participating and contributing themselves. At the same time, the term community policing has historically been used to describe a large variety of practices, including aggressive forms of order maintenance (e.g., Goetz and Mitchell 2003), thereby representing in and of itself a form of delegation; and has most often been characterised by exclusionary forms of communitarianism—hardly practices centred on community discussion and 'figuring out'.

13. Cf. the argument on a dynamic and relational—against an absolute—understanding of security made in Tulumello (2021a, 332–333).

14. On this see Pavoni (2018a, ch. 1).

15. See for instance Nunes (2021) for a recent, compelling Spinozist attempt to develop a novel 'theory of political organisation'.

16. The 'infrastructural' holding together of society only takes place as long as the 'natural right' and thus the common good are maximised: the sovereign *potestas*, in this sense, must not suppress the *potentia* of the multitude, as instead occurred in Hobbes—it must increase it. See on this matter the famous answer Spinoza provided in a letter to Jelles, who had asked him what was the difference between him and Hobbes: 'with regard to political theory, the difference between Hobbes and my-self, which is the subject of your inquiry, consists in this, that I always preserve the natural right in its entirety, and I hold that the sovereign power in a State has right' (2002[1674], 891).

17. It is conflict, in the form of 'indignatio' and outright 'revolt', that Spinoza will indicate as the extrema ratio that the multitude will necessarily resort to, if the government will turn out to be toxic. In this sense there can be no freedom without security, since the condition of insecurity represses the body's capacity to live and breathe, making it less free. At the same time, as it was also the case for Machiavelli, there can be no security without freedom. As Spinoza shows well in chapter XX of the *Tractatus-Theologicus Politicus* (2002[1670]), oppressing freedom of expression ends up preparing the field for sedition, rebellion and the violent disintegration of the state. In this sense, conflict ends up 'protecting' the community from the risk of a tyrannical drift (for an analysis on the notion of *indignatio* in these terms, see Del Lucchese 2004).

18. As Spinoza writes in concluding the *Tractatus Theologico-Politicus*: 'finally, we have shown not only that this freedom can be granted without detriment to public peace, to piety, and to the right of the sovereign, but also that it must be granted if these are to be preserved' (2002[1670b], ch XX). Let us qualify that there is obviously no room here to adequately account for such an eminently political interpretation of Spinoza, which often draws from the influential interpretations of Gilles Deleuze and Louis Althusser, and that has been proposed by a series of authors usually referred to as neo-Spinozist, including Alexandre Matheron, Pierre Macherey, Antonio Negri, Laurent Bove, François Zourabichvili, Filippo del Lucchese and others.

19. E.g., the Chinese for peace, *he ping*, 'signifies the "calm breath in resonance with the divine breath in the whole world"'. This is evident in various terms from across the world, e.g., *pneuma, prana, Ruach, spirit, anima* [*anemos* (soul, as wind)],

lil, *qi*, *psukhe* (breeze, breath), *atman* (force of life, resonant with the German *Atem*, breath) or *brahman* (the general world-soul in which everything is connected), differently associated with life, energy and peace (see Dietrich 2012).

20. The premises of such a non-moral take on responsibility where already laid out in Spinoza. For instance, in the scholium to the 49th proposition of the second part of the *Ethics* (2002a[1677]), where he writes, about his own teaching, that 'this doctrine assists us in our social relations, in that it teaches us to hate no one, despise no one, ridicule no one, be angry with no one, envy no one. Then again, it teaches us that each should be content with what he has and should help his neighbor, not from womanish [sic] pity, or favor, or superstition, but from the guidance of reason as occasion and circumstance require'.

21. Cf. Peter Frase's reflections on care in his speculation on a post-capitalist, post-climate disaster world (2016, ch. 1 and 3).

22. See on this question, especially regarding indigenous relation with water, the work of Marisol de la Cadena (e.g., 2019).

23. Hence Povinelli's call (2018, 155) for sharing the toxicity, that is acknowledging our co-implication in planetary violence, prior to vow to provide help for those in need.

24. Granted, during the early months of the pandemic one preprint (Blocken et al. 2020)—to the best of our knowledge, never published—did suggest that outdoor running may have been a factor of contagion, causing some panic (see the reconstruction by Samuel 2020). And yet, 'irrational' closures of public spaces and outdoor sport facilities kept being mandated later in the pandemic and in other contexts (e.g., Tulumello 2021c).

25. We have discussed time and again the limits of a critique centred on the irrationality of security policies.

26. Granted, we are not defending any individual 'right' to decide whether to vaccinate or not (more on this below). And yet, we cannot but notice how the stigmatisation of 'No Vax', as they were called during those tense months, has reached, in Italy but also elsewhere, peaks of violence often disconnected from the health implications of the small minority of unvaccinated.

27. In this discussion, to be sure, we are strategically collating the ontological meaning of 'common' consistent with the relational ontology developed so far, and the more conventional meaning of 'commons'—a move that is more or less explicit in much of the recent literature on the subject (see for a brief recap Pavoni 2021).

28. See SOLIVID (www.solivid.org/), a collaborative project for mapping solidarity initiatives during the Covid-19 crisis. In Italy, see also the examples of services collected on magazine *Animazione Sociale* under the tag 'racconta il tuo servizio' ('tell us about your service') at www.animazionesociale.it/ (see also Aggiornamenti Sociali 2020; Minuchin and Maino 2022).

29. This is also implicit in arguments for conceptualising security as a historicised, sociopolitically and geographically determined relation (e.g., Bigo 2014, 199; Burke 2011, 110; Nunes 2012, 351; 2016).

30. Indeed, the incapacity to question 'the problem' of security seems to be at the core of the difficulty of (mainstream) literature on urban security and public safety to escape violence reductionism (Tulumello and Falanga 2015).

31. As discussed above and in chapter 6, this does not imply romanticising conflict, rather accepting its inevitability and building a security politics upon it.

32. It would be certainly interesting to explore this 'violence' through the lens of Benjamin's divine violence. Some interesting suggestions in this sense come from Hamacher (1994).

33. For a description of Canetti's crowd through the Deleuzoguattarian assemblage, see Brighenti (2010b).

34. We are referring to Zourabichvili's (2002) original interpretation of Spinoza's political thought, grounded on the formula: 'conservation *sive* transformation', according to which the preservation and survival of the multitude is premised on its constant transformation, not against but *through* conflict.

35. Italian chapter of the global feminist movement Ni Una Menos.

36. As she continues, 'this being "drawn to" or "repelled" is often initially a very fragile connection, a sense of an immanent connectivity. Choices are then made to enrich and intensify these connections. But even these choices need to be understood as retrospective—the subject choosing is herself continually deferred by the choice. In other words, she is and is beginning to be different in the vicinity of this choice . . . I might be able to describe why I am drawn to a particular space and I may try to nurture this obligation or to break away from it, but still I have very little that can be described as "choice" in the original orientation' (Povinelli 2011, 33).

37. As per the definition of public safety in the Italian Decree of the Ministry of Internal Affairs of 5 August 2008, art. 1, which we discussed in relation to *decoro/decorum* (see chapter 7).

38. This could be a way to materialise, in atmospheric and post-human sense, Simone Weil's observation: 'there exists an obligation towards every human being for the sole reason that he or she is a human being, without any other condition requiring to be fulfilled' (2002[1949]).

References

Aalbers, Manuel B. 2016. "Housing finance as harm." *Crime, Law and Social Change* 66 (2): 115–129.

Abbot, Carl. 2006. "The light on the horizon: Imagining the death of American cities." *Journal of Urban History*, 32 (2): 175–196.

Abbott, Dean. 2014. *Applied Predictive Analytics: Principles and Techniques for the Professional Data Analyst*. Chichester: John Wiley & Sons.

Adams, Ross E. 2014. "Natura Urbans, Natura Urbanata: Ecological urbanism, circulation, and the immunization of nature." *Environment and Planning D* 32 (1): 12–29.

Adams, Ross E. 2019. *Circulation & Urbanization*. London: Sage.

Adams, Ross E. 2020. "On breath: Epistemologies of breath and the urbanisation of the body." *We Like Blog*, December 9. www.platform-austria.org/en/blog/breathing-in-the-cloud.

Adams, Suzie, Paul Blokker, Natalie J. Doyle, John W. M. Krummel, and Jeremy C. A. Smith. 2015. "Social imaginaries in debate." *Social Imaginaries* 1 (1): 15–52.

Adey, Peter. 2014a. *Air. Nature and Culture*. London: Reaktion Books.

Adey, Peter. 2014b. "Security atmospheres or the crystallisation of worlds." *Environment and Planning D* 32 (5): 834–851.

Adey, Peter, Laure Brayer, Damien Masson, Patrick Murphy, Paul Simpson, and Nicolas Tixier. 2013. "'Pour votre tranquillité': Ambiance, atmosphere, and surveillance." *Geoforum* 49: 299–309.

Adorno, Theodor W. 1973[1966]. *Negative Dialectics*. New York: Continuum.

Adorno, Theodor W. and Max Horkheimer. 1997[1944]. *Dialectic of Enlightenment*. London: Verso.

Agamben, Giorgio. 1978. *Infanzia e storia. Distruzione dell'esperienza e origine della storia*. Turin: Einaudi.

Agamben, Giorgio. 1998[1995]. *Homo Sacer: Sovereign Power and Bare Life*. Stanford: Stanford University Press.

Agamben, Giorgio. 2001. "On security and terror." *Frankfurter Allgemeine Zeitung*, September 20: 45.

Agamben, Giorgio. 2005[2003]. *State of Exception*. Chicago: University of Chicago Press.

Agamben, Giorgio. 2011[2009]. *The Kingdom and the Glory: For a Theological Genealogy of Economy and Government*. Stanford: Stanford University Pres.

Agamben, Giorgio. 2015. *Stasis. La guerra civile come paradigma politico. Homo sacer, II*. Turin: Bollati Boringhieri.

Agamben, Giorgio. 2016[2014]. *The Uses of Bodies*. Stanford: Stanford University Press.

Agamben, Giorgio. 2018[2017]. *Karman: A Brief Treatise on Action, Guilt, and Gesture*. Stanford: Stanford University Press.

Aggiornamenti Sociali. 2020. "Distanziati ma vicini: la solidarietà ai tempi della COVID-19. Intervista a Tommaso Vitale." *Aggiornamenti Sociali*, May: 376–386.

Åhäll, Linda, and Thomas A. Gregory. 2013. "Security, emotions, affect." *Critical Studies on Security* 1 (1): 117–120.

Ahmed, Sara. 2004. *The Cultural Politics of Emotion*. Edinburgh: Edinburgh University Press.

Aijmer, Göran, and Jon Abbink, eds. 2000. *Meanings of Violence: A Cross Cultural Perspective*. New York: New York University Press.

Aksoy, Asu, and Kevin Robins. 1997. "Modernism and the millennium: Trial by space in Istanbul." *City* 2 (8): 21–36.

Alikhademi, Kiana, Emma Drobina, Diandra Prioleau, Brianna Richardson, Duncan Purves, and Juan E. Gilbert. 2021. "A review of predictive policing from the perspective of fairness." *Artificial Intelligence and Law*. https://doi.org/10.1007/s10506-021-09286-4.

Allen, John. 2006. "Ambient power: Berlin's Potsdamer Platz and the seductive logic of public spaces." *Urban Studies* 43 (2): 441–455.

Al-Saji, Alia. 2014. "Phenomenology of hesitation: Interrupting racializing habits of seeing." In *Living Alterities: Phenomenology, Embodiment, and Race*, edited by Emily Lee, 133–172. Albany: State University of New York Press.

Alvesson, Mats, and André Spicer. 2012. "A stupidity-based theory of organizations." *Journal of Management Studies* 49 (7): 1994–1220.

Amaral, Augusto J., and Andrey H. Andreolla. 2020. "Drogas, urbanismo militar e gentrificação: o caso da 'Cracolândia' paulistana." *Revista Direito e Práxis* 11 (4): 2162–2187.

Amin, Ash. 2007. "Re-thinking the urban social." *City* 11 (1): 100–114.

Amin, Samir. 1974[1970]. *Accumulation on a World Scale: A Critique of the Theory of Underdevelopment*. New York: Monthly Review Press.

Amoore, Louise. 2013. *The Politics of Possibility. Risk and Security beyond Probability.* Durham: Duke University Press.

Amoore, Louise. 2020. *Cloud Ethics: Algorithms and the Attributes of Ourselves and Others.* Durham: Duke University Press.

Anand, Nikhil, Akhil Gupta, and Hannah Appel, eds. 2018. *The Promise of Infrastructure.* Durham: Duke University Press.

Anderson, Ben. 2009. "Affective atmospheres." *Emotion, Space and Society* 2 (2): 77–81.

Anderson, Ben. 2010a. "Preemption, precaution, preparedness: Anticipatory action and future geographies." *Progress in Human Geography* 34 (6): 777–798.

Anderson, Ben. 2010b. "Security and the future: Anticipating the event of terror." *Geoforum* 41(2): 227–235.

Anderson, Ben. 2014. *Encountering Affect. Capacities, Apparatuses, Conditions.* Farnham: Ashgate.

Anderson, Ben. 2021. "Affect and critique: A politics of boredom." *Environment and Planning D* 39 (2): 197–217.

Anderson, Ben, and Colin McFarlane. 2011. "Assemblage and geography." *Area* 43 (2): 124–127.

Anderson, Benedict. 1983. *Imagined Communities: Reflections on the Origin and Spread of Nationalism.* London: Verso.

Anderson, Elijah. 1999. *Code of the Street. Decency, Violence, and the Moral Life or the Inner City.* New York: Norton & Company.

Anderson, Warwick. 2021. "The model crisis, or how to have critical promiscuity in the time of Covid-19." *Social Studies of Science* 51 (2): 167–188.

Andrews, Frank M. 1989. "The evolution of a movement." *Journal of Public Policy* 9 (4): 401–405.

Angelo, Hillary and Boris Vormann. 2018. "Long waves of urban reform. Putting the smart city in its place." *City* 22 (5–6): 782–800.

Angelo, Hillary, and David Wachsmuth. 2015. "Urbanizing urban political ecology: A critique of methodological cityism." *International Journal of Urban and Regional Research* 39 (1): 16–27.

Anttiroiko, Ari-Veikko. 2014. *The Political Economy of City Branding.* London: Routledge.

Aradau, Claudia, and Tobias Blanke. 2017. "Politics of prediction: Security and the time/space of governmentality in the age of big data." *European Journal of Social Theory* 20 (3): 373–391.

Aradau, Claudia, and Rens van Munster. 2012. "The time/space of preparedness: Anticipating the 'next terrorist attack'." *Space and Culture* 15 (2): 98–109.

Aranda, Julieta, Brian K. Wood, and Anton Vidokle. 2012. "Editorial—'Structural Violence'." *e-flux journal* 38. www.e-flux.com/journal/38/61195/editorial-structural-violence/.

Arboleda, Martin. 2016. "In the nature of the non-city: Expanded infrastructural networks and the political ecology of planetary urbanisation." *Antipode* 48 (2): 233–251.

Arboleda, Martin. 2020. *Planetary Mine. Territories of Extraction under Late Capitalism*. London: Verso.

Arends, Fredrik M. 2011. "From Homer to Hobbes and beyond—Aspects of 'security' in the European tradition." In *Globalization and Environmental Challenges. Reconceptualizing Security in the 21st Century*, edited by Hans G. Brauch, Úrsula O. Spring, Czeslaw Mesjasz, John Grin, Pál Dunay, Navnita C. Behera, Béchir Chourou, Patricia Kameri-Mbote, P. H. Liotta, 263–277. New York: Springer.

Arendt, Hannah. 1958. *The Human Condition*. Chicago: University of Chicago Press.

Armitage, Paul. 2000. "Ctheory interview with Paul Virilio. The Kosovo war took place in orbital space." *Ctheory*, October 18. https://journals.uvic.ca/index.php/ctheory/article/view/14599.

Arthaud, Antonin. 2013[1978]. *The Theatre and Its Double*. Richmond: Alma Classics.

Ascari, Paolo. 2020. *Corpi e recinti. Estetica ed economia politica del decoro*. Roma: Ombre Corte.

Aspholm, Roberto R. 2020. *Views from the Streets. The Transformation of Gangs and Violence on Chicago's South Side*. New York: Columbia University Press [ebook].

Atkinson, Rowland. 2020. *Alpha City. How London Was Captured by the Super-Rich*. London: Verso.

Atkinson, Rowland, and Gary Bridge, eds. 2005. *Gentrification in a Global Context: The New Urban Colonialism*. London: Routledge.

Atkinson, Rowland, and Gareth Millington. 2018. *Urban Criminology. The City, Disorder, Harm and Social Control*. London: Routledge.

Atkinson, Rowland, and Gareth Millington. 2020. "Urban criminology. Thinking beyond the paradox." *Criminological Encounters* 3 (1): 62–72.

Aureli, Pier V. 2011. *The Possibility of an Absolute Architecture*. Cambridge: MIT Press.

Aureli, Pier V. 2013. "Means to an end: The rise and fall of the architectural project of the city." In *The City as a Project*, edited by Pier V. Aureli, 14–38. Berlin: Ruby Press.

Austin, Jonathan L. 2016. "Torture and the material-semiotic networks of violence across borders." *International Political Sociology* 10 (1): 3–21

Austin, Jonathan L. 2017. "We have never been civilized: Torture and the materiality of world political binaries." *European Journal of International Relations* 23 (1): 49–73.

Austin, Jonathan L. 2021. "The poetry of moans and sighs: Designs for, and against, violence." *Frame: Journal of Literary Studies* 33 (2): 13–31.

Austin, Jonathan L. 2023. "The plasma of violence: Towards a preventive medicine for political evil." *Review of International Studies* 49 (1): 105–124.

Auyero, Javier. 2011. "Researching the urban margins: What can the United States learn from Latin America and vice versa?" *City & Community* 10 (4): 431–436.

Auyero, Javier, and Maria F. Berti. 2015. *In Harm's Way. The Dynamics of Urban Violence*. Princeton: Princeton University Press.

Auyero, Javier, Agustín B. de Lara, and Maria F. Berti. 2014. "Violence and the state at the urban margins." *Journal of Contemporary Ethnography* 43 (1): 94–116.

Bacon, Francis. 2004[1605]. *The Advancement of Learning*, edited by Henry Morley. Salt Lake City: Project Guthenberg.

Baldissone, Riccardo. "Does reconciliation need truth? On the legal production of the visibility of the past" *In See*, edited by Andrea Pavoni, Danilo Mandic, Caterina Nirta, and Andreas Philippopoulos-Mihalopoulos, 1–28. London: University of Westminster Press.

Baldwin, David. 1997. "The concept of security." *Review of International Studies* 23 (1): 5–26.

Balibar, Étienne. 2015[2010]. *Violence and Civility: On the limits of Political Philosophy*. New York: Columbia University Press.

Baliga, Sandeep, and Jeffrey C. Ely. 2016. "Torture and the commitment problem." *The Review of Economic Studies* 83 (4): 1406–1439.

Balzacq, Thierry, Sarah Léonard, and Jan Ruzicka. 2015. "'Securitization' revisited: theory and cases." *International Relations* 39 (4): 494–531.

Banfield, Edward C. 1958. *The Moral Basis of a Backward Society*. Glencoe: The Free Press.

Banfield, Edward C. 1974. *The Unheavenly City Revisited*. Boston: Little, Brown & Company.

Bannister, Jon, and Anthony O'Sullivan. 2020. "Towards a planetary urban criminology." *Criminological Encounters* 3 (1): 10–31.

Banuazizi, Ali, and Siamak Movahedi. 1975. "Interpersonal dynamics in a simulated prison: A methodological analysis." *American Psychologist* 30 (2): 152–160.

Barad, Karen. 2003. "Posthumanist performativity: Toward an understanding of how matter comes to matter." *Signs* 28 (3): 801–831.

Barad, Karen. 2007. *Meeting the Universe Halfway. Quantum Physics and the Entanglement of Quantum and Meaning*. Durham: Duke University Press.

Barad, Karen. 2010. "Quantum entanglements and hauntological relations of inheritance: Dis/continuities, spacetime enfoldings, and justice-to-come." *Derrida Today* 3 (2): 240–268.

Barbe, Frédéric. 2016. "La 'zone à défendre' de Notre-Dame-des-Landes ou l'habiter comme politique." *Norois* 238–239: 109–130.

Barkawi, Tarak, and Mark Laffey. 2006. "The postcolonial moment in security studies." *Review of International Studies* 32 (2): 329–352.

Barnett, Clive. 2011. "Geography and ethics: Justice unbound." *Progress in Human Geography* 35 (2): 246–255.

Barua, Maan, and Anindya Sinha. 2019. "Animating the urban: An ethological and geographical conversation." *Social & Cultural Geography* 20 (8): 1160–1180.

Basu, Gautam. 2014. "The strategic attributes of transnational smuggling: Logistics flexibility and operational stealth in the facilitation of illicit trade." *Journal of Transportation Security* 7 (2): 99–113.

Bataille, George. 2000[1976]. *The Limit of the Useful*. Cambridge: MIT Press.

Battistelli, Fabrizio. 2013. "Sicurezza urbana 'partecipata': privatizzata, statalizzata o pubblica?" *Quaderni di Sociologia* 63: 105–126.

Bauman, Zygmunt. 1982. *Memories of Class: The pre-history and after-life of class*. Abingdon: Routledge and Kegan Paul.

Baumann, Hanna, and Haim Yacobi. 2022. "Introduction: Infrastructural stigma and urban vulnerability." *Urban Studies* 59 (3): 475–489.

Beck, Charlie. 2009. "Predictive policing: What can we learn from Wal-Mart and Amazon about fighting crime in a recession?" *The Police Chief* LXXVI (11) [online].

Beck, Ulrich. 1992[1986]. *Risk Society: Towards a New Modernity*. London: Sage.

Beck, Ulrich. 2002. "The terrorist threat. World risk society revisited." *Theory, Culture and Society* 19 (4): 39–55.

Becker, Gary S. 1968. "Crime and punishment: An economic approach." *Journal of Political Economy* 76 (2): 169–217.

Becker, Gary S., Francois Ewald, and Bernard E. Harcourt. 2013. "Becker and Foucault on Crime and Punishment—A Conversation with Gary Becker, François Ewald, and Bernard Harcourt: The Second Session." *University of Chicago Public Law & Legal Theory Working Paper* 440. https://chicagounbound.uchicago.edu/public_law_and_legal_theory/410/.

Bell, Colleen. 2012. "War and the allegory of medical intervention: Why metaphors matter." *International Political Sociology* 6 (3): 325–328.

Bellanova, Rocco, Kristina Irion, Katja L. Jacobsen, Francesco Ragazzi, Rune Saugmann, and Lucy Suchman. 2021. "Toward a critique of algorithmic violence." *International Political Sociology* 15 (1): 121–150.

Benjamin, Andrew and Peter Osborne. 1994. *Walter Benjamin's Philosophy. Destruction and Experience*. London: Routledge.

Benjamin, Ruha. 2019. *Race after Technology: Abolitionist Tools for the New Jim Code*. Cambridge: Polity.

Benjamin, Walter. 1963[1936]. "The story-teller: Reflections on the works of Nicolai Leskov." *Chicago Review* 16 (1): 80–101.

Benjamin, Walter. 1996[1921]. "Critique of Violence." In *Walter Benjamin. Selected Writings, 1: 1913–1926*, edited by Michael W. Jennings, 236–252. Cambridge: Harvard University Press.

Benjamin, Walter. 2002[1982]. *The Arcades Project*. Cambridge: Harvard University Press.

Benjamin, Walter. 2005[1940]. "On the Concept of History." *Marxists.org*. /www.marxists.org/reference/archive/benjamin/1940/history.htm.

Bennett, Jane. 2010. *Vibrant Matter: A Political Ecology of Things*. Durham: Duke University Press.

Benveniste, Émile. 1971[1966]. *Problems in General Linguistics*. Coral Gables: University of Miami Press.

Berardi, Franco B. 2011. *After the Future*. Edinburgh: AK Press.

Berglund-Snodgrass, Lina. 2016. "Demanding certainty. A critical examination of Swedish spatial planning for safety." PhD diss., Blekinge Institute of Technology.

Berlant, Lauren. 2007. "Slow death (sovereignty, obesity, lateral agency)." *Critical Inquiry* 33 (4): 754–780.

Berlant, Laurent. 2011. *Cruel Optimism*. Durham: Duke University Press.

Berlant, Laurent. 2016. "The commons: Infrastructures for troubling times." *Environment and Planning D* 34 (3): 393–419.

Berlinski, Claire. 2009. "The dark figure of corruption." *Policy Review*, May 29. www.hoover.org/research/dark-figure-corruption.

Bernt, Matthias. 2018. "Gentrification between urban and rural." *Dialogues in Human Geography* 8 (1): 31–35.

Bettencourt, Luis M. A., José Lobo, Dirk Helbing, Christian Kühnert, and Geoffrey B. West. 2007. "Growth, innovation, scaling, and the pace of life in cities." *Proceedings of the National Academy of Science* 104 (17): 7301–7306.

Bettencourt, Luis M. A., and Geoffrey B. West. 2010. "A unified theory of urban living." *Nature* 467: 912–913.

Beverungen, Armin, and Florian Sprenger. 2017. "Computing the City: FCJ-212 Editorial." *The Fibreculture Journal* 29: 1–9.

Biehler, Dawn D. 2013. *Pests in the City. Flies, Bedbugs, Cockroaches, and Rats*. Seattle: University of Washington Press.

Bigo, Didier. 2014. "Afterword—Security: Encounters, misunderstandings and possible collaborations." In *The Anthropology of Security: Perspectives from the Frontline of Policing, Counter-Terrorism and Border Control*, edited by Mark Maguire, Catarina Frois, and Nils Zurawski, 189–205. London: Pluto.

Bille, Mikkel, Peter Bjerregaard, and Tim F. Sørensen. 2015. "Staging atmospheres: Materiality, culture, and the texture of the in-between." *Emotion, Space and Society* 14: 31–38.

Bina, Olivia, Andy Inch, and Lavínia Pereira. 2020. "Beyond techno-utopia and its discontents: On the role of utopianism and speculative fiction in shaping alternatives to the smart city imaginary." *Futures* 115: article 102475.

Birchall, C., Gary Hall, and Peter Woodbridge. 2010, "Deleuze's Postscript on the Societies of Control." *Liquid Theory TV project video*, January 28. http://www.youtube.com/watch_popup?v=GIus7lm_ZK0.

Bissel, David. 2008. "Comfortable bodies: sedentary affects." *Environment and Planning A* 40 (7): 1697–1712.

Bissel, David, Maria Hynes, and Scott Sharpe. 2012. "Unveiling seductions beyond societies of control: Affect, security, and humour in spaces of aeromobility." *Environment and Planning D* 30 (4): 694–710.

Blackstone, William. 1791[1765]. *Commentaries on the Laws of England. Book the Fourth. The Eleventh Edition*. London: Strahan and Woodfall.

Bloch, Ernst. 1986[1954–1959]. *The Principle of Hope*. Oxford: Basil Blackwell.

Bloch, Ernst. 2000[1923]. *The Spirit of Utopia*. Stanford: Stanford University Press.

Bloch, Stefano, and Dugan Meyer. 2019. "Implicit revanchism: Gang injunctions and the security politics of white liberalism." *Environment and Planning D* 37 (6): 1100–1118.

Blocken, Bert, Fabio Malizia, Thijs van Druenen, and Thierry Marchal. 2020. "Towards aerodynamically equivalent COVID19 1.5 m social distancing for walking and running." Preprint. www.urbanphysics.net/Social%20Distancing%20 v20_White_Paper.pdf.

Bloomberg, Ramon. 2019. "Dronological Power: Remote Control Occupation and the New Epistemo-Technologies of Sovereignty." PhD diss., Goldsmiths, University of London.

Boano, Camillo. 2021. "Beyond violence. Toward a politics of inhabitation." *Lo Squaderno* 59: 67–71.

Body-Gendrot, Sophie. 1995. "Urban violence: A quest for meaning." *Journal of Ethnic and Migration Studies* 21 (4): 525–536.

Boni, Stefano. 2014. *Homo comfort. Il superamento tecnologico della fatica e le sue conseguenze*. Milan: elèuthera.

Bonneuil, Christophe, and Jean-Baptiste Fressoz. 2013. *L'evènement Anthropocène. La terre, l'histoire et nous*. Paris: Le Seuil.

Bonta, Mark, and John Protevi. 2004. *Deleuze and Geophilosophy: A Guide and a Glossary*. Edinburgh: Edinburgh University Press.

Booth, Ken. 1994. "Security and self. Reflections of a fallen realist." *YCISS Occasional Paper* 26. http://hdl.handle.net/10315/1414.

Booth, Ken. 2005. "Introduction to Part 3." In *Critical Security Studies and World Politics*, edited by Ken Booth, 181–187. Boulder: Lynne Rienner.

Booth, Ken. 2007. *Theory of World Security*. Cambridge: Cambridge University Press.

Borch, Christian. 2005. "Urban imitations: Tarde's sociology revisited." *Theory, Culture and Society* 22 (3): 81–100.

Borch, Christian. 2008, "Foam architecture: Managing co-isolated associations." *Economy and Society* 37 (4): 548–571.

Borch, Christian. 2010. "Organizational atmospheres: Foam, affect and architecture." *Organization: The Critical Journal of Organization, Theory and Society* 17 (2): 223–241.

Borch, Christian. 2012. *The Politics of Crowds: An Alternative History of Sociology*. Cambridge: Cambridge University Press.

Borch, Christian. 2015. *Foucault, Crime and Power. Problematisations of Crime in the Twentieth Century*. Abingdon: Routledge.

Borch, Christian, and Martin Kornberger, eds. 2015. *Urban Commons. Rethinking the City*. London: Routledge.

Bottici, Chiara. 2014. *Imaginal Politics: Images beyond Imagination and the Imaginary*. New York: Columbia University Press.

Boullier, Dominique 2010. *La ville-événement. Foules et publics urbains.* Paris: Presses Universitaires de France.

Boullier, Dominique. 2011. "Méthodes de tri des foules et des publics dans le parc humain lors des *événements.*" *Lo Squaderno* 19: 9–14.

Bourdieu, Pierre. 1990[1980]. *The Logic of Practice.* Stanford: Stanford University Press.

Bourdieu, Pierre. 1991[1982/1983]. *Language and Symbolic Power.* Cambridge: Polity.

Bourgois, Philippe. 2001. "The power of violence in war and peace: Post-Cold War lessons from El Salvador." *Ethnography* 2 (1): 5–34

Bousquet, Antoine. 2018. *The Eye of War: Military Perception from the Telescope to the Drone.* Minneapolis: University of Minnesota Press.

Bove, Laurent. 1996. *La stratégie du conatus. Affirmation et resistance chez Spinoza.* Paris: VRIN.

Bowden, Sean. 2015. "Human and nonhuman agency in Deleuze." In *Deleuze and the Non/Human,* edited by Jon Roffe and Hannah Stark, 60–80. Basingtoke: Palgrave

Bowless. Nellie. 2020. "Abolish the police? Those who survived the chaos in Seattle aren't so sure." *New York Times,* August 7. www.nytimes.com/2020/08/07/us/defund-police-seattle-protests.html.

Boyle, Philip, and Kevin D. Haggerty. 2009. "Spectacular security: Mega-events and the security complex." *International Political Sociology* 3 (3): 257–274.

Bragazzi, Nicola L., and Giovanni Del Puente. 2014. "A proposal for including no-mophobia in the new DSM-V." *Psychology Research and Behavior Management* 7: 155–160.

Brantingham, Jeffrey P. 2013. "Prey Selection among Los Angeles Car Thieves." *Crime Science* 2 (3): 1–11.

Brantingham, Jeffrey P., Matthew Valasik, and George O. Mohler. 2018. "Does pre-dictive policing lead to biased arrests? Results from a randomized controlled trial." *Statistics and Public Policy* 5 (1): 1–6.

Bratton, Benjamin H. 2015. "Cloud megastructure and platform utopias." In *Entr'acte. Performing Publics, Pervasive Media, and Architecture,* edited by Jordan Geiger, 35–51. New York: Palgrave Macmillan.

Bratton, Benjamin H. 2021. "Agamben WTF, or how philosophy failed the pan-demic." *Verso,* July 28. www.versobooks.com/blogs/5125-agamben-wtf-or-how-philosophy-failed-the-pandemic.

Braverman, Irus. 2013. "Animal Mobilegalities: The regulation of animal movement in the American city." *Humanimalia* 5 (1): 104–135.

Brauch, Hans G., Úrsula O. Spring, Czeslaw Mesjasz, John Grin, Pál Dunay, Navnita C. Behera, Béchir Chourou, Patricia Kameri-Mbote, and P. H. Liotta, eds. 2011. *Globalization and Environmental Challenges. Reconceptualizing Security in the 21st Century.* Cham: Springer.

Braun, Bruce, Ben Anderson, Steve Hinchliffe, Christian Abrahamsson, Nicky Gregson, and Jane Bennett. 2011. "Book review forum: Vibrant Matter: A Politi-cal Ecology of Things." *Dialogues in Human Geography* 1 (3): 390–406.

Brennan, Theresa. 2004. *The Transmission of Affect*. Ithaca: Cornell University Press.

Brenner, Neil. 2004. *New State Spaces: Urban Governance and the Rescaling of State-hood*. Oxford: Oxford University Press.

Brenner, Neil. 2013. "Theses on urbanization." *Public Culture* 25 (1): 85–114.

Brenner, Neil, and Christian Schmid. 2013. "The 'Urban Age' in question." *International Journal of Urban and Regional Research* 38 (3): 731–755.

Brenner, Neil, and Christian Schmid. 2015. "Towards a new epistemology of the urban?" *City* 19 (2–3): 151–182.

Brenner, Neil, David J. Madden, and David Wachsmuth. 2011. "Assemblage urbanism and the challenges of critical urban theory." *City* 15 (2): 225–240.

Brighenti, Andrea M. 2010a. "Lines, barred lines. Movement, territory and the law." *International Journal of Law in Context* 6 (3): 217–227.

Brighenti, Andrea M. 2010b. *Visibility in Social Theory and Social Research*. Basingstoke: Palgrave Macmillan.

Brighenti, Andrea M. 2021. "Monster-measures and monstrous values. A short reflection on the foundations of individual-environmental theory." In *Monstrous Ontologies: Politics, Ethics, Materiality*, edited by Caterina Nirta, and Andrea Pavoni, 1–14. Wilmington: Vernon Press.

Brighenti, Andrea M., and Matthias Kärrholm. 2020. *Animated Lands: Studies in Territoriology*. Lincoln: University of Nebraska Press.

Brighenti, Andrea M., and Andrea Pavoni, eds. 2016. "Urban animals." *Lo Squaderno* 42.

Brighenti, Andrea M., and Andrea Pavoni. 2018. "Urban animals—domestic, stray, and wild: Notes from a bear repopulation project in the Alps." *Society & Animals* 26 (6): 576–597.

Brighenti, Andrea M., and Andrea Pavoni. 2019. "City of unpleasant feelings. Stress, comfort and animosity in urban life." *Social and Cultural Geography* 20 (2): 137–156.

Brighenti, Andrea M., and Andrea Pavoni. 2020. "Vertical vision and atmocultural navigation. Notes on emerging urban scopic regimes." *Visual Studies* 35 (5): 429–441.

Brighenti, Andrea M., and Andrea Pavoni. 2021a. "On urban trajectology: algorithmic mobilities and atmocultural navigation." *Distinktion: Journal of Social Theory*, online first. Doi: 10.1080/1600910X.2020.1861044.

Brighenti, Andrea M., and Andrea Pavoni. 2021b. "Situating urban animals—a theoretical framework." *Contemporary Social Science* 16 (1): 1–13.

Brown, Kevin J. 2020. "Punitive reform and the cultural life of punishment: Moving from the ASBO to its successors." *Punishment & Society* 22 (1): 90–107.

Brown, Lauren, and Jeff Rose. 2021. "Slow violence and homelessness. Activating public space and amplifying displacement." *Lo Squaderno* 59: 47–51.

Brunet, James R. 2002. "Discouragement of crime through civil remedies: An application of a reformulated routine activities theory." *Western Criminology Review* 4 (1): 68–79.

Bryant, Levy L. 2011. *The Democracy of Objects*. Ann Arbor: Open Humanities Press.

Buck-Morss, Susan. 1989. *The Dialectics of Seeing. Walter Benjamin and the Arcades Project*. Cambridge: MIT Press.

Buitrago-Sevilla, Álvaro. 2022. *Against the* Commons. *A Radical History of Urban Planning*. Minneapolis: University of Minnesota Press.

Bukowski, Wolf. 2019. *La buona educazione degli oppressi. Piccola storia del decoro*. Roma: Alegre.

Burgess, J. Peter. 2019. "The insecurity of critique." *Security Dialogue* 50 (1): 95–111.

Burke, Anthony. 2011. "Humanity after biopolitics." *Angelaki: Journal of the Theoretical Humanities* 16 (4): 101–114

Butler, Judith. 1990. *Gender Trouble: Feminism and the Subversion of Identity*. London: Routledge.

Butler, Judith. 2003. "Violence, mourning, politics." *Studies in Gender and Sexuality* 4 (1): 9–37.

Butler, Judith. 2004a. *Undoing Gender*. New York: Routledge.

Butler, Judith. 2004b. *Precarious Life: The Powers of Mourning and Violence*. London: Verso.

Butler, Judith. 2020. *The Force of Nonviolence*. London: Verso.

Cahill, Caitlin, and Rachel Pain. 2019. "Representing slow violence and resistance: On hiding and seeing." *ACME: An International Journal for Critical Geographies* 18 (5): 1054–1065.

Caimi, Mario. 2014. *Kant's B Deduction*. Newcastle upn Tyne: Cambridge Scholars.

Caldeira, Teresa. P. R. 2000. *Cidade de muros: Crime, segregação e cidadania em São Paulo*. São Paulo: Edusp.

Camellone, Mauro F. 2018. "Thomas Hobbes e la cristianità del Leviatano sulla duplice funzione della sovranità." *Etica & Politica* XX (2): 245–264.

Camp, Jordan T., and Christina Heatherton, eds. 2016. *Policing the Planet. Why the Policing Crisis Led to Black Lives Matter*. London: Verso.

Canetti, Elias. 1962[1960]. *Crowds and Power*. New York: Farar, Straus and Giroux.

Canguilhem, Georges. 1966. *Le normal et le pathologique*. Paris: Presses Universitaires de France.

Caprotti, Federico. 2008. "Internal colonisation, hegemony and coercion: Investigating migration to Southern Lazio, Italy, in the 1930s." *Geoforum* 39 (2): 942–957.

Cardon, Dominique, Jean-Philippe Cointet, and Antoine Mazières. 2018. "Neurons spike back. The invention of inductive machines and the artificial intelligence controversy." *Réseaux* 211 (5): 173–220.

Care Collective, The. 2020. *The Care Manifesto. The Politics of Interdependence*. London: Verso.

Carli, Renzo, and Rosa M. Paniccia. 2003. *L'analisi della domanda. teoria e tecnica dell'intervento in psicologia clinica*. Bologna: Il Mulino.

Carrabine, Eamonn. 2012. "Just images: Aesthetics, ethics and visual criminology." *British Journal of Criminology* 52 (3): 463–489.

Carrington, Kerry, Russell Hogg, and Máximo Sozzo. 2016. "Southern criminology." *The British Journal of Criminology* 56 (1): 1–20.

Carse, Ashley. 2014. *Beyond the Big Ditch: Politics, Ecology, and Infrastructure at the Panama Canal*. Cambridge: MIT Press.

Carter, Paul. 2002. *Repressed Spaces: The Poetics of Agoraphobia*. London: Reaktion Books.

Cassidy, Rebecca, and Molly Mullin, eds., 2007. *Where the Wild Things Are Now: Domestication Reconsidered*. Oxford: Berg.

Cassirer, Ernst. 1961[1946]. *The Myth of the State*. New Haven: Yale University Press.

Castelli, Federica. 2016. "Spazio pubblico appassionato. Corpi e protesta tra esposizione, vulnerabilità, relazioni." *Leussein* IX (1–2–3): 85–93.

Castoriadis, Cornelius. 1987[1975]. *The Imaginary Institution of Society*. Cambridge: MIT Press.

Castoriadis, Cornelius. 1997[1986]. "The discovery of the imagination." In *World in Fragments: Writings on Politics, Society, Psychoanalysis, and the Imagination*, edited by David A. Curtis, 246–272. Stanford: Stanford University Press.

Castriota, Rodrigo, and João Tonucci. 2018. "Extended urbanization in and from Brazil." *Environment and Planning D* 36 (3): 512–528.

Castro, Eduardo V. 2014[2009]. *Cannibal Metaphysics*. Minneapolis: University of Minnesota Press.

Castro, Eduardo V. 2019. "On models and examples: engineers and bricoleurs in the Anthropocene." *Current Anthropology* 60 (suppl. 20): S296–S308

Cavalletti, Andrea. 2005. *La città biopolitica. Mitologie della sicurezza*. Milan: Mondadori.

Cepelewicz, Jordana. 2021. "The hard lessons of modeling the Coronavirus pandemic." *Quanta Magazine*, January 28. www.quantamagazine.org/the-hard-lessons-of-modeling-the-coronavirus-pandemic-20210128/.

Cerdá, Idelfonso. 1867. *Teoría general de la urbanización y aplicación de sus principios y doctrinas a la reforma y ensanche de Barcelona*. Madrid: Imprensa Española.

Cerdá, Idelfonso. 2018[1867]. *General Theory of Urbanization. 1867*, edited by Vicente Guallart. Barcelona: Iaac and Actar.

Cervellati, Pier L., and Roberto Scannavini. 1973. *Bologna: Politica e metodologia nel restauro dei centri storici*. Bologna: Il Mulino.

Cesaire, Aimé. 2000[1958]. *Discourse on Colonialism*. New York: Monthly Review Press.

Chabert, Jean-Luc. 1999[1994]. "Introduction." In *A History of Algorithms. From the Pebble to the Microchip*, edited by Jean-Luc Chabert, 1–6. Berlin: Springer.

Chakrabarty, Dipesh. 2000. *Provincializing Europe: Post Colonial Thought and Historical Difference*. Princeton: Princeton University Press.

Chakrabarty, Dipesh. 2009. "The climate of history: Four theses." *Critical Inquiry* 35 (2): 197–222.

Chamayou, Grégoire. 2014. "Patterns of life: A very short history of schematic bodies." *The Funambulist*, December 4. https://thefunambulist.net/editorials/the-funambulist-papers-57-schematic-bodies-notes-on-a-patterns-genealogy-by-gregoire-chamayou.

Chesluk, Benjamin. 2004. "'Visible Signs of a City Out of Control': Community Policing in New York City." *Cultural Anthropology* 19 (2): 250–275.

Chiti, Mario P. 1998. "La nuova nozione di 'beni culturali' nel d.lg. 112/1998: prime note esegetiche." *Aedon* 1998 (1) [online].

Choat, Simon. 2018. "Science, agency and ontology: A historical-materialist response to new materialism." *Political Studies* 66 (4): 1027–1042.

Chwałczyk, Franciszek. 2020. "Around the Anthropocene in eighty names—Considering the Urbanocene proposition." *Sustainability* 12 (11): article 4458.

Chiaramonte, Xenia. 2019. *Governare il Conflitto. La Criminalizzazione del Movimento No TAV*. Milan: Meltemi.

Choy, Timothy, and Jerry Zee. 2015. "Condition—Suspension." *Cultural Anthropology* 30 (2): 210–223.

Chun, Wendy H.K. 2021. *Discriminating Data. Correlation, Neighbourhoods, and the New Politics of Recognition*. Cambridge: MIT Press.

Çinar, Alev, and Thomas Bender. 2007a. "Introduction. The city: Experience, imagination, and place." In *Urban Imaginaries. Locating the Modern City*, edited by Alev Çinar, and Thomas Bender, xi-xxvi. Minneapolis: University of Minnesota Press.

Çinar, Alev, and Thomas Bender, eds. 2007b. *Urban Imaginaries. Locating the Modern City*. Minneapolis: University of Minnesota Press.

Clark, Bruce. 2016. "Control and control societies in Deleuze and systems theory." Presented at *Control. The 10th meeting of the European Society for Literature, Science, and the Arts*, June 14–17. www.academia.edu/31640128/Control_and_Control_Societies_in_Deleuze_and_Systems_Theory.

Clarke, Ronald V. 1983. "Situational crime prevention: Its theoretical basis and practical scope." *Crime and Justice* 4: 225–256.

Clastres, Pierres. 2010[1980]. *Archaeology of Violence*. Cambridge: MIT Press.

Clear, Todd, and Eric Cadora. 2012[2001]. "Risk and community practice." In *Crime, Risk and Justice: The Politics of Crime Control in Liberal Democracies*, edited by Kevin Stenson, and Robert R. Sullivan, 51–67. Abingdon: Routledge.

Coccia, Emanuele. 2019[2017]. *The Life of Plants. A Metaphysics of Mixture*. Cambridge: Polity.

Cocola-Gant, Agustin. 2016. "Holiday rentals: The new gentrification battlefront." *Sociological Research Online* 21 (3) [online].

Coleman, Clive, and Jenny Moynihan. 1996. *Understanding Crime Data: Haunted by the Dark Figure*. Buckingham: Open University Press.

Coletta, Claudio, and Rob Kitchin. 2017. "Algorithmic governance: Regulating the 'heartbeat' of a city using the Internet of Things." *Big Data and Society* 4 (2): 1–16.

Commercial Appeal, The. 2012 "Troubling issues at MPD." *The Commercial Appeal*, January 29 [downloaded from NewsBank online resource].

Conceição, José A. 2008. *Segurança pública: Violência e direito constitucional*. São Paulo: Nelpa.

Connolly, Creighton. 2019. "Urban political ecology beyond methodologial cityism." *International Journal of Urban and Regional Research* 43 (1): 63–75.

Connolly, Creighton, Roger Keil, and S. Harris Ali. 2021. "Extended urbanisation and the spatialities of infectious disease: Demographic change, infrastructure and governance." *Urban Studies* 58 (2): 245–263.

Connolly, William E. 2005. *Pluralism*. Durham: Duke University Press.

Coole, Diana, and Samantha Frost. 2010. *New Materialisms: Ontology, Agency, and Politics*. Durham: Duke University Press.

Coomaraswamy, Ananda K. 1939. "Ornament." *Art Bulletin* 21 (4): 375–382.

Corboz, André. 1998. *Ordine sparso. Saggi sull'arte, il metodo, la città e il territorio. A cura di Paola Viganò*. Milan: FrancoAngeli.

Correia, David, and Tyler Wall. 2018. *Police. A Field Guide*. London: Verso.

Corso, Gregory, and Allen Ginsberg. 1992[1961]. "Interview with William S. Burroughs." *RealityStudio*. https://realitystudio.org/interviews/1961-interview-with-william-s-burroughs-by-gregory-corso-and-allen-ginsberg/.

Costa, Pietro. 1974. *Il progetto giuridico: ricerche sulla giurisprudenza del liberalismo classico. Vol. 1, Da Hobbes a Bentham*. Milan: Giuffrè.

Coulthard, Glen S. 2014. *Red Skin, White Masks: Rejecting the Colonial Politics of Recognition*. Minneapolis: University of Minnesota Press.

Courtheyn, Christopher. 2017. "Peace geographies: Expanding from modern-liberal peace to radical trans-relational peace." *Progress in Human Geography* 42 (5): 741–758.

Cowen, Deborah. 2014. *The Deadly Life of Logistics. Mapping Violence in Global Trade*. Minneapolis: Minnesota University Press.

Cox, Kathie. 2020. "'The gates of hell': the cruel optimism of national security in Secret City." *Journal of Media & Cultural Studies* 34 (1): 102–116.

Crang, Mike, and Stephen Graham. 2007. "Sentient cities. Ambient intelligence and the politics of urban space." *Information, Communication & Society* 10 (6): 789–817.

Crowe, Timothy D., and Lawrence J. Fennelly. 2013. *Crime Prevention Through Environmental Design*. Amsterdam: Butterworth-Heinemann.

Crowley, John E. 2001. *The Invention of Comfort. Sensibilities & Design in Early Modern Britain & Early America*. Baltimore: The Johns Hopkins University Press.

Cryle, Peter, and Elizabeth Stephens. 2017. *Normality. A Critical Genealogy*. Chicago: University of Chicago Press.

Cunha, Christina V. 2012. "A cidade para os civilizados: Significados da ordem pública em contextos de violência urbana." *DILEMAS: Revista de Estudos de Conflito e Controle Social* 5 (2): 211–232.

Cunningham, David. 2005. "The concept of metropolis: Philosophy and urban form." *Radical Philosophy* 133: 13–25.

Cunningham, David. 2008. "Spacing abstraction: Capitalism, law and the metropolis." *Griffith Law Review* 17 (2), 454–485.

Cuppini, Niccolò, and Valentina Antoniol. 2021. "Stasis in the planetary-city: Conflict and spatiality within the fading of western modernity." *Meta: Research in Hermeneutics, Phenomenology, and Practical Philosophy* XIII (2): 623–656.

Cuppini, Niccolò, and Mattia Frapporti. 2018. "Logistics genealogies. A dialogue with Stefano Harney." *Into the Black Box*, October 5. www.intotheblackbox.com/articoli/logistics-genealogies-a-dialogue-with-stefano-harney/

Dear, Michael J. 2000. *The Postmodern Urban Condition.* Oxford: Blackwell.

Curry, Michael R. 2000. "The power to be silent: Testimony, identity, and the place of place." *Historical Geography* 28 (1): 13–24.

Danaher, John, Michael J. Hogan, Chris Noone, Rónán Kennedy, Anthony Behan, Aisling De Paor, Heike Felzmann, Muki Haklay, Su-Ming Khoo, John Morison, Maria H. Murphy, Niall O'Brolchain, Burkhard Schafer, and Kalpana Shankar. 2017. "Algorithmic governance: Developing a research agenda through the power of collective intelligence." *Big Data and Society* 4 (2): 1–21.

Darwin, Charles. 1868. *The Variations of Animals and Plants under Domestication.* London: John Murrey.

Datta, Ayona. 2015. "New urban utopias of postcolonial India: 'Entrepreneurial urbanization' in Dholera smart city, Gujarat." *Dialogues in Human Geography* 5 (1): 3–22.

Datta, Ayona, and Nancy Odendaal. 2019. "Smart cities and the banality of power." *Environment and Planning D* 37 (3): 387–392.

Davies, Thom. 2019. "Slow violence and toxic geographies: 'Out of sight' to whom?" *Environment and Planning C*, online first. https://doi.org/10.1177/2399654419841063.

Davies, Thom, Arshad Isakjee, and Surindar Dhesi. 2017. "Violent inaction: The necropolitical experience of refugees in Europe." *Antipode* 49 (5): 1263–1284.

Dean. Mitchell. 1999. *Governmentality: Power and Rule in Modern Society.* London: Sage.

de Certeau, Michel. 1984[1980]. *The Practice of Everyday Life.* Berkeley: University of California Press.

De Genova, Nicholas. 2007. "The Production of culprits: From deportability to detainability in the aftermath of 'Homeland Security'." *Citizenship Studies* 11 (5): 421–448.

de Jouvenel, Bertrand. 1997[1957]. *Sovereignty: An Inquiry into the Political Good.* Indianapolis: Liberty Fund.

De Koster, Margo. 2020. "Negotiating Controls, Perils, and Pleasures in the Urban Night. Working-Class Youth in Early-Twentieth-Century Antwerp." *Criminological Encounters* 3 (1): 32–49.

de la Bellacasa, María P. 2017. *Matters of Care: Speculative Ethics in More than Human Worlds.* Minneapolis: University of Minnesota Press.

de la Cadena, Marisol. 2019. "Uncommoning nature: Stories from the Anthropo-not-seen." In *Anthropos and the Material*, edited by Penny Harvey, Christian Krohn-Hansen, and Knut G. Nustad, 35–58. Durham: Duke University Press.

DeLanda, Manuel. 2005. "Space: Extensive and intensive, actual and virtual." In *Deleuze and Space*, edited by Ian Buchanan, and Gregg Lambert, 80–88. Edinburgh: Edinburgh University Press.

DeLanda, Manuel. 2016. *Assemblage Theory*. Edinburgh: Edinburgh University Press.

de Leeuw, Sarah. 2016. "Tender grounds: Intimate visceral violence and British Columbia's colonial geographies." *Political Geography* 52: 14–23.

Deleuze, Gilles. 1968. *Spinoza et le Problème de l'Expression*. Paris: Éditions de Minuit.

Deleuze, Gilles. 1985[1967]. *Kant's Critical Philosophy: The Doctrine of the Faculties*. Minneapolis: University of Minnesota Press.

Deleuze, Gilles. 1988[1970]. *Spinoza, Practical Philosophy*. San Francisco: City Lights Books.

Deleuze, Gilles. 1990[1969]. *The Logic of Sense*. New York: Columbia University Press.

Deleuze 1991[1966]. *Bergsonism*. Cambridge: MIT Press.

Deleuze, Gilles. 1992[1990]. "Postscript on the Societies of Control." *October* 59: 3–7.

Deleuze, Gilles. 1993. *Critique et Clinique*. Paris: Éditions de Minuit.

Deleuze, Gilles. 1995[1990]. *Negotiations, 1972–1990*. New York: Columbia University Press.

Deleuze, Gilles. 2000[1964]. *Proust and Signs. The Complete Text*. Minneapolis: University of Minnesota Press.

Deleuze, Gilles. 2004[1955]. "Instincts and institutions." In *Desert Islands and Other Texts, 1953–1974*, edited by David Lapoujade, 19–21. Los Angeles: Semiotext(e).

Deleuze, Gilles. 2004[1968]. *Difference and Repetition*. London: Continuum.

Deleuze, Gilles. 2006. "Desire and pleasure." In *Two Regimes of Madness: Texts and Interviews 1975–1995*, edited by David Lapoujade, 122–134. New York: Semiotext(e).

Deleuze, Gilles. 2006[1986]. *Foucault*. London: Continuum.

Deleuze, Gilles. 2020[2015]. *Gilles Deleuze: Letters and Other Texts*, edited by David Lapoujade. South Pasadena: Semiotext(e).

Deleuze, Gilles, and Félix Guattari. 1977[1972]. *Anti-Oedipus. Capitalism and Schizophrenia*. Minneapolis: University of Minnesota Press.

Deleuze, Gilles, and Félix Guattari. 1994[1991]. *What Is Philosophy?* London: Verso.

Deleuze, Gilles, and Félix Guattari. 2004[1980]. *A Thousand Plateaus: Capitalism and Schizophrenia*. London: Continuum.

Deleuze, Gilles, and Claire Parnet. 1987[1977]. *Dialogues*. New York: Columbia University Press.

Del Lucchese, Filippo. 2004. *Tumulti e indignatio. Conflitto, diritto e moltitudine in Machiavelli e Spinoza*. Milan: Ghibli.

Derrida, Jacques. 1995. *Points…: Interviews, 1974–1994*. Stanford: Stanford University Press.

Derrida, Jacques. 2006[1993]. *Specters of Marx: The State of the Debt, the Work of Mourning and the New International*. London: Routledge.

Derrida, Jacques. 2009[2008]. *The Beast & the Sovereign. Volume 1*. Chicago: University of Chicago Press.

Descola, Philippe. 2013[2005]. *Beyond Nature and Culture*. Chicago: University of Chicago Press.

de Warren, Nicolas. 2006. "The apocalypse of hope: Political violence in the writings of Sartre and Fanon." *Graduate Faculty Philosophy Journal* 27 (1): 25–59.

Di Bella, Arturo. 2020. "Global urbanism and mega events planning in Rio de Janeiro amid crisis and austerity." *International Planning Studies* 25 (1): 23–37.

Dietrich, Wolfgang. 2012. *Interpretations of Peace in History and Culture*. Basingstoke: Palgrave Macmillan.

Dijkema, Claske. 2021. "What is urban about urban violence in France? Violence in marginalised neighbourhoods as body politics." *Lo Squaderno* 59: 17–20.

Dikeç, Mustafa. 2006. "Two Decades of French Urban Policy: From Social Development of Neighbourhoods to the Republican Penal State." *Antipode* 38 (1): 59–81.

Dillon, Michael. 1996. *Politics of Security: Towards a Political Philosophy of Continental Thought*. London: Routledge.

Dinale, Riccardo. 2014. "Nowcasting: How big data predict the present." Bachelor's dissertation, LUISS Guido Carli, Rome. http://tesi.eprints.luiss.it/12588/.

Dines, Nick. 2014. "L'eterno abietto: le classi popolari napoletane nelle rappresentazioni del Partito Comunista Italiano." *Itinerari di Ricerca Storica* 28 (2): 77–96.

Djukanovic, Slavisa, Gordon Harrison, and Dragan Randjelovic. 2015. "Predictive analytics in police work." In *Thematic Conference Proceedings of International Significance. Vol. 1 / International Scientific Conference "Archibald Reiss Days"*, edited by Dorde Kolarić, 101–108. Beograd: Kriminalističko-Policijska Akademija.

Dodd, James. 2009. *Violence and Phenomenology*. New York: Routledge.

Dodsworth, Francis. 2019. *The Security Society. History, Patriarchy, Protection*. London: Palgrave Macmillan.

Doel, Marcus. 1999. *Poststructuralist Geographies: The Diabolical Art of Spatial Science*. Lanham: Rowman & Littlefield.

Doherty, Jacob. 2019. Filthy flourishing. Para-sites, animal infrastructure, and the waste frontier in Kampala." *Current Anthropology* 60 (suppl. 20): S321-S332.

Dolphijn, Rick, and Iris van der Tuin. 2012. *New Materialism: Interviews & Cartographies*. Ann Arbor: Open Humanities Press.

Donald, Diana. 1999. "'Beastly Sights': The treatment of animals as a moral theme in representations of London c.1820–1850". Art History 22 (4): 514–544.

Dosi, Giovanni, and Andrea Roventini. 2016. "The irresistible fetish of utility theory: From 'pleasure and pain' to rationalising torture." Intereconomics 51 (5): 286–287.

Doucet, Jessica M., and Matther R. Lee. 2015. "Civic communities and urban violence." *Social Science Research* 52: 303–316.

Doyle, Aaron, Randy Lippert, and David Lyon, eds. 2012. *Eyes Everywhere. The Global Growth of Camera Surveillance*. London: Routledge.

Dubber, Markus D. 2005. *The Police Power: Patriarchy and the Foundations of American Government*. New York: Columbia University Press.

Dubber, Markus D., and Mariana Valverde. 2008. "Introduction: Policing the Rechtsstaat." In *Police and the Liberal State*, edited by Markus D. Dubber, and Mariana Valverde, 1–14. Stanford: Stanford University Press.

Duff, Koshka. 2018. "Feminism against crime control. On sexual subordination and state apologism." *Historical Materialism* 26 (2) [online].

Duff, Koshka, ed. 2021. *Abolishing the Police*. London: Dog Section Press.

Easterling, Keller. 2014. *Extrastatecraft: The Power of Infrastructure Space*. New York: Verso.

Egbert, Simone. 2019. "Predictive policing and the platformization of police work." *Surveillance & Society* 17 (1–2): 83–88.

EIU (The Economist Intelligence Unit). 2021. The Global Liveability Index 2021. How the Covid-19 pandemic affected liveability worldwide. Free summary report. www.eiu.com/n/campaigns/global-liveability-index-2021/.

Elden, Stuart. 2007. "Governmentality, calculation, territory." *Environment and Space D* 25 (3): 562–580.

Elias, Norbert. 2000[1939]. *The Civilizing Process: Sociogenetic and Psychogenetic Explorations*. Oxford: Blackwell.

Elliott-Cooper, Adam, Phil Hubbard, and Loretta Lees. 2020. "Moving beyond Marcuse: Gentrification, displacement and the violence of un-homing." *Progress in Human Geography* 44 (3): 492–509.

Enns, Charis, and Adam Sneyd. 2021. "More-than-human infrastructural violence and infrastructural justice: A case study of the Chad–Cameroon Pipeline Project." *Annals of the American Association of Geographers* 111 (2): 481–497.

Epstein, Dora. 1998. "Afraid/not: Psychoanalitical directions for an insurgent planning history." In *Making the Invisible Visible: A Multicultural Planning History*, edited by Leonie Sandercock, 209–226. Berkeley: University of California Press.

Espeland, Wendy, and Vincent Yung 2019. "Ethical dimensions of quantification." *Social Science Information* 58 (2): 238–260.

Esposito, Roberto. 2007. *Terza persona. Politica della vita e filosofia dell'impersonale*. Turin: Einaudi.

Esposito 2008[2004]. *Bíos: Biopolitics and Philosophy*. Minneapolis: University of Minnesota Press.

Esposito, Roberto. 2009[1998]. *Communitas. The Origin and Destiny of Community*. Stanford: Stanford University Press.

Esposito, Roberto. 2011[2002]. *Immunitas: The Protection and Negation of Life*. Cambridge: Polity.

Esposito, Roberto. 2012[2008]. *Terms of the Political: Community, Immunity, Biopolitics*. New York: Fordham University Press.

Evans, Brad. 2017. "Histories of violence: Affect, power, violence—the political is not personal." *Los Angeles Review of Books*, November 13. https://lareviewofbooks.org/article/histories-of-violence-affect-power-violence-the-political-is-not-personal/.

Fanon, Frantz. 1963[1961]. *The Wretched of the Earth*. New York: Grove Press.

Fanon, Frantz. 1965[1959]. *Studies in a Dying Colonialism*. New York: Monthly Review Press.

Fanon, Frantz. 1970[1952]. *Black Skin, White Masks*. London: Paladin.

Farías, Ignacio. 2010. "Introduction: decentring the object of urban studies." In *Urban Assemblages. How Actor-Network Theory Changes Urban Studies*, edited by Ignacio Farías, and Thomas Bender, 1–23. London: Routledge.

Farinelli, Franco. 2003. *Geografia. Un'introduzione ai modelli del mondo*. Milan: Einaudi.

Farinelli, Franco. 2016. *L'invenzione della Terra*. Palermo: Sellerio.

Farmer, Paul. 2004. "An anthropology of structural violence." *Current Anthropology* 45 (3): 305–325.

Fassin, Didier. 2011. "Coming back to life: An anthropological reassessment of biopolitics and governmentality." In *Governmentality: Current Issues and Future Challenges*, edited by Ulrich Bröckling, Susanne Krasmann, and Thomas Lemke, 185–200. London: Routledge.

Febvre, Lucien. 1930. "Civilisation: Evolution d'un mot et d'un groupe d'idées." In *La Civilisation, le mot et l'idée : première semaine internationale de synthèse (du 10 au 29 mai 1929)*. Paris: La Renaissance du livre.

Feigenbaum, Anna. 2015. "Riot control agents: The case for regulation." SUR 22 [online].

Feigenbaum, Anna. 2017. *Tear Gas: From the Battlefields of World War I to the Streets of Today*. London: Verso.

Felski, Rita. 2015. *The Limits of Critique*. Chicago: University of Chicago Press.

Felson, Marcus and Ronald V. Clarke. 1998. "Opportunity makes the thief. Practical theory for crime prevention." *Police Research Series Paper* 98. https://popcenter.asu.edu/sites/default/files/opportunity_makes_the_thief.pdf.

Feltran, Gabriel. 2014. "Crime e periferia." In *Crime, polícia e justiça no Brasil*, edited by Renato S. de Lima, José L. Ratton, and Rodrigo G. Azevedo, 299–307. São Paulo: Contexto Editora.

Feltran, Gabriel. 2020. *The Entangled City. Crime as Urban Fabric in São Paulo*. Manchester: Manchester University Press.

Feltran, Gabriel, ed. 2022. *Stolen Cars. A Journey through São Paulo's Urban Conflict*. Hoboken: Wiley.

Fenton III, Robert P. 2021. "Cacao capitalism and extended urbanization: On the contradictory origins of bounded urbanism in nineteenth-century coastal Ecuador." *International Journal of Urban and Regional Research* 45 (1): 5–20.

Ferguson, Adam. 1792. *Principles of Moral and Political Science. Vol. I*. Edinburgh: Strahan and Cadell.

Ferguson, Andrew G. 2012. "Predictive policing and reasonable suspicion." *Emory Law Journal* 62 (2): 259–325.

Ferguson, James. 2012. "Structures of responsibility." *Ethnography* 13 (4): 558–562.

Ferguson, Neil M., Daniel Laydon, Gemma Nedjati-Gilani et al. 2020. "Report 9: Impact of non-pharmaceutical interventions (NPIs) to reduce COVID-19 mortality and healthcare demand." MRC Centre for Global Infectious Disease Analysis, Imperial College London, March 16. www.imperial.ac.uk/mrc-global-infectious-disease-analysis/covid-19/report-9-impact-of-npis-on-covid-19/.

Ferrarin, Alfredo. 2021. "L'elemento immaginario e le significazioni sociali istituenti." In *Cornelius Castoriadis, L'Elemento Immaginario*, edited by Alfredo Ferrarin, 5–12. Pisa: Edizioni ETS.

Fields, Desiree, and Elora L. Raymond. 2021. "Racialized geographies of housing financialization." *Progress in Human Geography* 45 (6): 1625–1645.

Finelli, Roberto. 1987. *Astrazione e dialettica dal Romanticismo al Capitalismo: Saggio su Marx*. Rome: Bulzoni.

Fisher, Mark. 2009. *Capitalism Realism: Is There No Alternative?* Winchester: Zero Books.

Fisher, Mark. 2016. *Ghosts of My Life: Writings on Depression, Hauntology and Lost Futures*. Winchester: Zero Books.

Fisichella, Domenico. 2008. *Alla ricerca della sovranità: Sicurezza e libertà in Thomas Hobbes*. Rome: Carocci.

Fittered, J., T.A. Nelson, and F. Nathoo. 2015. "Predictive crime mapping." *Police Practice and Research* 16 (2): 121–135.

Florez, Marion, Guy Baudelle, and Magali Hardouin. 2022. "Notre-Dame-des-Landes or redefining the relationship to space through the territorial embeddedness of a struggle." *Antipode* 54 (3): 772–799.

Flory, Daniel D. 1995. "Fear of Imagination in Western Philosophy and Ethics." PhD diss., University of Minnesota.

Foucault, Michel. 1977[1975]. *Discipline and Punish: The Birth of the Prison*. New York: Vintage Books.

Foucault, Michel. 1980[1977]. "The confession of the flesh." In *Power/Knowledge. Selected Interviews and Other Writings 1972–1977. Michel Foucault*, edited by Colin Gordon, 194–228. New York: Pantheon Books.

Foucault, Michel. 1984[1982]. "Space Knowledge and Power." In *The Foucault Reader*, edited by Paul Rabinow, 239–256. New York: Pantheon Books.

Foucault, Michel. 1988. "The political technology of the individual." In *Technologies of the Self: A Seminar with Michel Foucault*, edited by Luther H. Martin, Huck Gutman, and Patrick H. Hutton, 145–162. Amherst: The University of Massachusetts Press.

Foucault, Michel. 1994[1966]. *The Order of Things: An Archaeology of the Human Sciences*. New York: Vintage Books.

Foucault, Michel. 1994[1976]. Two Lectures. In *Power/Knowledge. Selected Interviews and Other Writings 1972–1977. Michel Foucault*, edited by Colin Gordon, 78–108. New York: Pantheon Books.

Foucault, Michel. 1997[1984]. "The ethics of the concern for self as a practice of freedom." In *Essential Works of Foucault 1954–1984, Volume 1: Ethics, Subjectivity and Truth*, edited by Paul Rabinow, 281–302. New York: The New Press.

Foucault, Michel. 1998[1973]. *A verdade e as formas jurídicas*. Rio de Janeiro: NAU.

Foucault, Michel. 2003[1977]. *Society Must Be Defended: Lectures at the Collège de France (1975–1976)*. London: Allen Lane.

Foucault, Michel. 2007[2004]. *Security, Territory, Population. Lectures at the Collège de France 1977–1978*. New Yok: Palgrave Macmillan.

Foucault, Michel. 2010[1969]. *The Archeology of Knowledge and the Discourse on Language*. London: Vintage Books.

Foucault, Michel. 2010[2004]. *The Birth of Biopolitics. Lectures at the Collège de France 1978–1989*. New York: Palgrave Macmillan.

Frase, Peter. 2016. *Four Futures. Life after Capitalism*. London: Verso.

Fraser, Alistair, and John M. Hagedorn. 2018. "Gangs and a global sociological imagination." *Theoretical Criminology* 22 (1): 42–62.

Fregonese, Sara, and Suncana Laketa. 2022. "Urban atmospheres of terror." *Political Geography* 96: 102569.

French, Jennifer L. 2012. "Voices in the wilderness: Environment, colonialism, and coloniality in Latin American literature." *Review: Literature and Arts of the Americas* 45 (2): 157–166.

Galli, Carlo. 2001. *Spazi politici. L'età moderna e l'età globale*. Bologna: Il Mulino.

Galli, Carlo. 2011. "All'insegna del Leviatano. Potenza e destino del progetto politico moderno." Introduction to Hobbes, Thomas, *Leviatano*, V-L. Segrate: Rizzoli.

Galtung, Johan. 1969. "Violence, peace and peace research." *Journal of Peace Research* 6 (3): 167–191.

Galtung, Johan. 1990. "Cultural violence." *Journal of Peace Research* 27 (3): 291–305.

Gamble, Christopher N., Joshua S. Hanan, and Thomas Nail. 2019. "What is new materialism?" *Angelaki* 24 (6): 111–134.

Gandy, Matthew. 2017. "Urban atmospheres." *cultural geographies* 24 (3): 353–374.

Gardner, Benjamin. 2012. "Tourism and the politics of the global land grab in Tanzania: markets, appropriation and recognition." *The Journal of Peasant Studies* 30 (2): 377–402.

Gargiulo, Enrico. 2018. "Una filosofia della sicurezza e dell'ordine. Il governo dell'immigrazione secondo Marco Minniti." *Meridiana* 91: 151–173.

Garland, David. 1996. "The limits of the sovereign state. Strategies of crime control in contemporary society." *The British Journal of Criminology* 36 (4): 445 471.

Garland, David. 2001. *The Culture of Control. Crime and Social Order in Contemporary Society*. Oxford: Oxford University Press.

Garland, David. 2003. "The rise of risk." In *Risk and Morality*, edited by Richard V. Ericson, and Aaron Doyle, 48–86. Toronto: University of Toronto Press.

Garner, Betsie. 2018. "The distinctive south and the invisible north: Why urban ethnography needs regional sociology." *Sociology Compass* 12: e12589.

Garner, Paul. 2019. "Questions remain about the shooting of Brandon Webber." *Mid-South Peace and Justice Center*, January 7. Available at: https://midsouthpeace. org/2019/06/20/webber-statement/.

Gastaldi, Juan L. 2009. "La politique avant l'être. Deleuze, ontologie et politique." *Cités* 40: 59–73.

Gaston, Robert W. 2013, "How words control images: the rhetoric of decorum in counter reformation Italy." In *The Sensuous in the Counter-Reformation Church*, edited by Marcia B. Hall, and Tracy E. Cooper, 74–90. New York: Cambridge University Press.

Gatens, Moira, and Genevieve Lloyd. 1999. *Collective Imaginings: Spinoza, Past and Present*. Abingdon: Routledge.

Gatti, Carlo. 2022a. "Monitoring the monitors: a demystifying gaze at algorithmic prophecies in policing." *Justice, Power and Resistance* 5 (3): 227–248.

Gatti, Carlo. 2022b. "Policing the poor through space: The fil rouge from criminal cartography to geospatial predictive policing." *Oñati Socio-Legal Series* 12 (6): 1733–1758.

Gehlen, Arnold. 1988[1974]. *Man, His Nature and Place in the World*. New York: Columbia University Press.

Gentili, Dario, and Federica Giardini. 2020. "Selva e stato di natura: variazioni cin-estesiche per il contemporaneo." *Vesper* 3: 76–95.

Gerbaudo, Paolo. 2012. *Tweets and the Streets. Social Media and Contemporary Activism*. London: Pluto.

Ghertner, D. Asher. 2015. "Why gentrification theory fails in 'much of the world'." *City* 19 (4): 552–563.

Ghertner, D. Asher, Hydson McFann, and Daniel M. Goldstein, eds. 2020. *Futureproof. Security Aesthetics and the Management of Life*. Durham: Duke University Press.

Giannini, Chiara. 2017. "Sicurezza è libertà. Lavoro volontario per i migranti accolti." *ilGiornale.it*, March 30. Available at: https://www.ilgiornale.it/news/politica/sicurezza-libert-lavoro-volontario-i-migranti-accolti-1380570.html.

Giddens, Anthony. 1991. *Modernity and Self-Identity*. Stanford: Stanford University Press.

Gillespie, Tom, Kate Hardy, and Paul Watt. 2021. "Surplus to the city: Austerity urbanism, displacement and 'letting die'." *Environment and Planning A* 53 (7): 1713–1729.

Girard, René. 1972. *La violence et le sacré*. Paris: Bernard Grasset.

Glass, Michael R., Taylor B. Seybolt, and Phil Williams, eds. 2022. *Urban Violence, Resilience and Security. Governance Responses in the Global South*. Cheltenham: Edward Elgar.

Glover, William. 2008. *Making Lahore Modern. Constructing and Imagining a Colonial City*. Minneapolis: University of Minnesota Press.

Goetz, Barry, and Roger Mitchell. 2003. "Community Building and Reintegrative Approaches to Community Policing: The Case of Drug Control." *Social Justice* 30 (1): 222–247.

Goffey, Andrew. 2008. "Algorithm." In *Software Studies. A Lexicon*, edited by Matthew Fuller, 15–20. Cambridge: MIT Press.

Goffman, Erving. 1971. *Relations in Public. Microstudies of the Public Order*. New York: Basic Books.

Goldstein, Daniel M. 2010. "Toward a critical anthropology of security." *Current Anthropology* 51 (4): 487–517.

Goldstein, Kurt. 1995[1934]. *The Organism: A Holistic Approach to Biology Derived from the Pathological Data in Man*. New York: Zone Books.

Goonewardena, Kanishka. 2008. "Marxism and everyday life: On Henry Lefebvre, Guy Debord, and some others." In *Space, Difference, Everyday Life: Reading Henri Lefebvre*, edited by Kanishka Goonewardena, Stefan Kipfer, Richard Milgrom, and Christian Schmid, 117–133. New York: Routledge.

Gorner, Jeremy. 2013. "'Heat list' used to curb violence in Chicago." *South Bend Tribune*, August 26. https://eu.southbendtribune.com/story/news/2013/08/26/heat-list-used-to-curb-violence-in-chicago/46396375/.

Gould, Deborah. 2009. *Moving Politics: Emotion and ACT UP's Fight against AIDS*. Chicago: University of Chicago Press.

Graeber, David, and David Wengrow. 2021. *The Dawn of Everything: A New History of Humanity*. New York: Farrar, Straus and Giroux.

Graham, Stephen. 2010. *Cities Under Siege: The New Military Urbanism*. London: Verso.

Graham, Stephen. "Life support: the political ecology of urban air." *City* 19 (2–3): 192–215.

Grant, Evadné. 1991. "Last month's law reports." *De Rebus*, July: 464–468.

Graziani, Terra, Joel Montano, Ananya Roy and Pamela Stephens. 2022. "Property, personhood, and police: The making of race and space through nuisance law." *Antipode* 52 (2): 439–461.

Grosz, Elizabeth A. 1995. *Space, Time, and Perversion: Essays on the Politics of Bodies*. New York: Routledge.

Gruppo di esperti sull'ambiente urbano. 1996. Città Europee sostenibili. Relazione. Bruxelles, Marzo 1996. IT/11/96/01490100.P00.

Grusin, Richard. 2015. "Radical mediation." *Critical Inquiry* 42 (1): 142–148.

Guallart, Vicente. 2018. "Urbanization: The science of making cities." In *General Theory of Urbanization. 1867*, edited by Vicente Guallart, 11–33. Barcelona: Iaac and Actar.

Guattari, Félix. 2009[1973]. *Chaosophy. Texts and Interviews 1972–1977*. Edited by Sylvère Lotringer. Los Angeles: Semiotext(e).

Guernsey, Brenda. 2008. "Constructing the wilderness and clearing the landscape: A legacy of colonialism in Northern British Columbia." In *Landscapes of Clearance*.

Archaeological and Anthropological Perspectives, edited by Angèle Smith, and Amy Gazin-Schwartz, 112–124.Walnut Creek: Left Coast Press.

Gunder, Michael. 2003. "Passionate planning for the others' desire: An agonistic response to the dark side of planning." *Progress in Planning* 60 (3): 235–319.

Gusfield, Joseph R. 1981. *The Culture of Public Problems: Drinking-Driving and the Symbolic Order*. Chicago: University of Chicago Press.

Gutting, Gary. 1990. "Foucault's genealogical method." *Midwest Studies in Philosophy* 15 (1): 327–343.

Hacking, Ian. 2003. "Risk and dirt." In *Risk and Morality*, edited by Richard V. Ericson, and Aaron Doyle, 22–47. Toronto: University of Toronto Press.

Haila, Yrjö. 1997. "Wilderness' and the multiple layers of environmental thought." *Environment and History* 3 (2): 129–147.

Haiven, Max, and Alex Khasnabish. 2014. *The Radical Imagination: Social Movement Research in the Age of Austerity*. London: Zed Books.

Halpern, Orit. 2014. *Beautiful Data: A History of Vision and Reason since 1945*. Durham: Duke University Press.

Hamacher, Werner. 1994. "Affirmative, strike, Benjamin's 'critique of violence." In *Walter Benjamin's Philosophy: Destruction and Experience*, edited by Andrew Benjamin, and Peter Osborne, 110–138. London: Routledge.

Hamilton, John. 2013. *Security. Politics, Humanity, and the Philology of Care*. Princeton: Princeton University Press.

Han, Byung-Chul. 2018. *Topology of Violence*. Cambridge: MIT Press.

Handel, Ariel. 2021. "Urban violence. The dialectics of city-making and ruination in settler-colonial settings." *Lo Squaderno* 59: 21–24.

Haney, Craig, Curtis Banks, and Phillip G. Zimbardo. 1973. "Interpersonal dynamics in a simulated prison." *International Journal of Criminology & Penology* 1 (1): 69–97.

Hanhardt, John. 2013. "Vibrant matter: The art of Rafael Lozano-Hemmer." In *Rafael Lozano-Hemmer: Vicious Circular Breathing. Exhibition catalogue*, 19–26. Istanbul: Borusan Contemporary.

Harari, Yuval N. 2014[2011]. *Sapiens. A Brief History of Humankind*. Toronto: McClelland & Stewart.

Haraway, Donna. 2008. *When Species Meet*. Minneapolis: University of Minnesota Press.

Haraway, Donna. 2015. "Anthropocene, Capitalocene, Plantationocene, Chthulucene: Making Kin." *Environmental Humanities* 6 (1): 159–165.

Haraway, Donna. 2016. *Staying with the Trouble: Making Kin in the Chthulucene*. Durham: Duke University Press.

Haraway, Donna, Noboru Ishikawa, Scot F. Gilbert, Kenneth Olwig, Anna L. Tsing, and Nils Bubandt. 2016. "Anthropologists are talking—about the Anthropocene." *Ethnos* 81 (3): 535–564.

Harcourt, Bernard. 1998. "Reflecting on the Subject: A Critique of the Social Influence Conception of Deterrence, the Broken Windows Theory, and Order-Maintenance Policing New York Style." *Michigan Law Review* 97: 291–389.

Hardt, Michael, and Antonio Negri. 2009. *Commonwealth*. Cambridge: Belknap Press.

Hariman, Robert. 1992. "Decorum, power, and the courtly style." *Quarterly Journal of Speech* 78 (2): 149–172.

Harney, Stefano, and Fred Moten. 2013. *The Undercommons: Fugitive Planning & Black Study*. Wivenhoe: Minor Compositions.

Harpaz-Rotem, Ilan, Robert A. Murphy, Steven Berkowitz, Steven Marans, and Robert A. Rosenheck. 2007. "Clinical epidemiology of urban violence: Responding to children exposed to violence in ten communities." *Journal of Interpersonal Violence* 22 (11): 1479–1490.

Harper, David. 2013. "The affective atmosphere of surveillance." *Theory and Psychology* 23 (6): 716–731.

Harrington, Cameron. 2017. "Posthuman security and care in the Anthropocene." In *Reflections on the Posthuman in International Relations: The Anthropocene, Security and Ecology*, edited by Clara Eroukhmanoff and Matt Harker, 73–86. Bristol: E-International Relations.

Harvey, David. 1978. "The urban process under capitalism." *International Journal of Urban and Regional Research* 2 (1–4): 101–131.

Harvey, David. 1990. *The Condition of Postmodernity. An Inquiry into the Origins of Cultural Change*. Cambridge: Blackwell.

Harvey, David. 2003. *The New Imperialism*. Oxford: Oxford University Press.

Harvey, David. 2004. *Paris, Capital of Modernity*. New York: Routledge.

Harvey, David. 2012. *Rebel Cities: From the Right to the City to the Urban Revolution*. London: Verso.

Hay, James. 2006. "Designing homes to be the first line of defense." *Cultural Studies* 20 (4): 349–377.

Heath-Kelly, Charlotte. 2018. "Forgetting ISIS: enmity, drive and repetition in security discourse." *Critical Studies on Security* 6 (1): 85–99.

Heidegger, Martin. 1997[1929]. *Kant and the Problem of Metaphysics*. Bloomington: Indiana University Press.

Heidegger, Martin. 2006[1938–39]. *Mindfulness*. London: Continuum.

Heimstädt, Maximilian, Simon Egbert, and Elena Esposito. 2020. "A pandemic of prediction: On the circulation of contagion models between public health and public safety." *Sociologica* 14 (3): 1–24.

Heller-Roazen, Daniel. 2007. *The Inner Touch: Archaeology of a Sensation*. New York: Zone Books.

Hentschel, Christine. 2015. *Security in the Bubble: Navigating Crime in Urban South Africa*. Minneapolis: University of Minnesota Press.

Herbert, Steve. 1999. "The end of the territorially-sovereign state? The case of crime control in the United States." *Political Geography* 18 (2): 149–172.

Herrnstein, Richard J., and Charles Murray. *The Bell Curve. Intelligence and Class Structure in American Life*. New York: The Free Press.

Herzing, Rachel. 2016. "The magical life of broken windows." In *Policing the Planet: Why the Policing Crisis Led to Black Lives Matter*, edited by Jordan T. Camp, and Christina Heaterton, 267–278. London: Verso.

Heylighen, Francis, and Cliff Joslyn. 2003. "Cybernetics and second-order cybernetics." In *Encyclopedia of Physical Science and Technology, Eighteen-Volume Set, Third Edition*, edited by Robert A. Meyers, 155–169. Waltham: Academic Press.

Hickman, Leo. 2013. "How algorithms rule the world." *The Guardian*, July 1. www.theguardian.com/science/2013/jul/01/how-algorithms-rule-world-nsa.

Hildebrandt, Mireille, and Katja de Vries, eds. 2013. *Privacy, Due Process and the Computational Turn: The Philosophy of Law Meets the Philosophy of Technology*. Abingdon: Routledge.

Hill, Kashmir. 2020. "The secretive company that might end privacy as we know it." *The New York Times*, January 18. www.nytimes.com/2020/01/18/technology/clearview-privacy-facial-recognition.html.

Hinton, Elizabeth. 2016. *From the War on Poverty to the War on Crime: The Making of Mass Incarceration in America*. Cambridge: Harvard University Press.

Hollands, Robert G. 2008. "Will the real smart city please stand up? Intelligent, Progressive or Entrepreneurial?" *City* 12 (3): 303–320.

Hobbes, Thomas. 1841[1656]. "The Questions Concerning Liberty, Necessity, and Chance, Clearly Stated and Debated between Dr. Bramhall, Bishop of Derry, and Thomas Hobbes of Malmesbury." In *The English works of Thomas Hobbes of Malmesbury. Volume 5*, edited by William Wolesworth, London: John Bohn.

Hobbes, Thomas. 2002[1651]. *Leviathan*, produced by Edward White, and David Widger [ebook]. Salt Lake City: Project Guthenberg. www.gutenberg.org/files/3207/3207-h/3207-h.htm.

Holmberg, Tora. 2015. *Urban Animals. Crowding in Zoocities*. London: Routledge.

Holmes, Brian. 2008. *Unleashing the Collective Phantoms: Essays in Reverse Imagineering*. New York: Autonomedia.

Holston, James. 1998. "Spaces of insurgent citizenship." In *Making the Invisible Visible: A Multicultural Planning History*, edited by Leonie Sandercock, 37–56. Berkeley: University of California Press.

Holston, James. 2007. *Insurgent Citizenship: Disjunctions of Democracy and Modernity in Brazil*. Princeton: Princeton University Press.

Holtorf, Cornelious. 2015. "Averting loss aversion in cultural heritage." *International Journal of Heritage Studies* 21 (4): 405–421.

Honig, Bonnie. 1992. "Toward an agonistic feminism: Hannah Arendt and the politics of identity." In *Feminists Theorize the Political*, edited by Judith Butler, and Joan W. Scott, 215–235. New York: Routledge.

Honig, Bonnie. 2008[2006]. "Another cosmopolitanism? Law and politics in the new Europe." In *Seyla Benhabib: Another Cosmopolitanism*, edited by Robert Post, 102–127. Oxford: Oxford University Press.

Hönke, Jana, and Markus-Michael Müller. 2012. "Governing (in)security in a postcolonial world: Transnational entanglements and the worldliness of 'local' practice." *Security Dialogue* 43 (5): 383–401.

hooks, bell. 1991. *Yearning: Race, Gender, and Cultural Politics*. London: Turnaround.

Hope, Tim. 2018. "The social epidemiology of victimization: The paradox of prevention." In *Handbook of victims and victimology: 2nd edition*, edited by Sandra Walklate [ebook]. Routledge, London.

Hope, Tim. 2020. "Epistemic public criminology. The fallacies of evidence-based policing." In *Criminology and Democratic Politics*, edited by Tom Daems and Stefaan Pleysier [ebook]. London: Routledge.

Horace. 1926. *Satires. Epistles. The Art of Poetry*. Translated by H. Rushton Fairclough. Cambridge: Harvard University Press.

Howarth, David R. 2008. "Ethos, agonism and populism: William Connolly and the case for radical democracy." *British Journal of Politics and International Relations* 10 (2): 171–193.

Huertas, Julian. 2015. "'It's out of control and spreading': Graffiti as the supposed cause of urban crisis in 1970s–1980s New York City." *Bowdoin Journal of Art* I [online].

Huggan, Graham, and Helen Tiffin. 2015. *Postcolonial Ecocriticism. Literature, Animals, Environment*. London: Routledge.

Hughes, David M. 2005. "Third nature: Making space and time in the Great Limpopo Conservation Area." *Cultural Anthropology* 20 (2): 157–184.

Hui, Yuk. 2015. "Modulation after control." *New Formations* 84/85: 74–91.

Hui, Yuk. 2016. *On the Existence of Digital Objects*. Minneapolis: University of Minnesota Press.

Hulsman, Louk H. C. 1986. "Critical criminology and the concept of crime." *Contemporary Crises* 10 (1): 63–80.

Hunt, Priscilla, Jessica Saunders, and John S. Hollywood. 2014. *Evaluation of the Shreveport Predictive Policing Experiment*. Santa Monica: RAND Corporation.

Husak, Douglas. 2008. *Overcriminalization: The Limits of the Criminal Law*. Oxford: Oxford University Press.

Huysmans, Jeff. 2011. "What's in an act? On security speech acts and little security nothings." *Security Dialogue* 42 (4–5): 371–383.

Huyssen, Andreas. 2008. *Other Cities, Other Worlds: Urban Imaginaries in a Globalizing Age*. Durham: Duke University Press.

Hvistendahl, Mara. 2016. "Can 'predictive policing' prevent crime before it happens?" *Sciencemag*, September 28. www.sciencemag.org/news/2016/09/can-predictive-policing-prevent-crime-it-happens.

Iadicola, Peter, and Anson Shupe. 2003. *Violence, Inequality, and Human Freedom*. Lanham: Rowman & Littlefield Publishers.

ICHRP (International Council on Human Rights Policy). 2010. *Modes and Patterns of Social Control Implications for Human Rights Policy*. Geneva: ICHRP.

ICHRP. 2011. "Navigating the dataverse: Privacy, technology, human rights. Discussion Paper." International Council on Human Rights Policy, Geneva.

Ignatieff, Michael. 2003. *The Lesser Evil. Political Ethics in an Age of Terror*. Edinburgh: Edinburgh University Press.

Ilan, Jonathan. 2019. "Cultural Criminology: The Time is Now." *Critical Criminology* 27 (1): 5–20.

Ingold, Tim. 2010. "Footprints through the weather-world: Walking, breathing, knowing." *Journal of the Royal Anthropological Institute* 16 (S1): S121-S139.

Into the Black Box. 2022. "Nas lutas da circulação: reprodução, metabolismo e logística." In *A produção do mundo. Problemas logísticos e sítios críticos*, edited by Andrea Pavoni, and Franco Tomassoni, 93–112. Lisbon: Outro Modo.

Irigaray, Luce. 1999[1983]. *The Forgetting of Air in Martin Heidegger*. Austin: University of Texas Press.

Jacobs, Bruce A., and Richard Wight. 2010. "Bounded rationality, retaliation, and the spread of urban violence." *Journal of Interpersonal Violence* 25 (10): 1739–1766.

Jacobs, Jane. 1961. *The Death and Life of Great American Cities*. New York: Random House.

Jameson, Fredric. 2004. "The politics of utopia." *New Left Review* 25: 35–54.

Jameson, Fredric. 2013. *The Antinomies of Realism*. London: Verso.

Jamieson, Liz. 1998. "Understanding crime data: haunted by the dark figure [book review]." *Criminal Behaviour and Mental Health* 8 (3): 241–242.

Jasanoff, Sheila. 2015. "Future imperfect: Science, technology, and the imaginations of modernity." In *Dreamscapes of Modernity Sociotechnical Imaginaries and the Fabrication of Power*, edited by Sheila Jasanoff, and Sang-Hyun Kim, 1–33. Chicago: University of Chicago Press.

Jasanoff, Sheila. 2020. "Pathologies of liberty. Public health sovereignty and the political subject in the Covid-19 crisis." *Cahiers Droit, Sciences & Technologies* 11: 125–149

Jasanoff, Sheila, and Sang-Hyun Kim. 2009. "Containing the atom: sociotechnical imaginaries and nuclear power in the United States and South Korea." *Minerva* 47 (2): 119–146.

Jefferson, Brian J. 2016. "Broken windows policing and constructions of space and crime: Flatbush, Brooklyn." *Antipode* 48 (6): 1270–1291.

Jefferson, Brian J. 2018a. "Policing, data, and power-geometry: intersections of crime analytics and race during urban restructuring." *Urban Geography* 39 (8): 1247–1264.

Jefferson, Brian J. 2018b. "Predictable policing: Predictive crime mapping and geographies of policing and race." *Annals of the American Association of Geographer,* 108 (1): 1–16.

Jeffery, Clarence R. 1971. *Crime Prevention through Environmental Design*. Beverly Hills: Sage.

Jensen, Casper B., and Atsuro Morita. 2017. "Introduction: Infrastructures as Ontological Experiments." *Ethnos* 82 (4): 615–626.

Johnston, John. 1999. "Machinic vision." *Critical Inquiry* 6 (1): 27–48.

Kaal, Harm. 2011. "A conceptual history of livability. Dutch scientists, politicians, policy makers and citizens and the quest for a livable city. *City* 15 (5): 532–547.

Kalifa, Dominique. 2013. *Les bas-fonds: Histoire d'un imaginaire*. Paris: Seuil [ebook].

Kann, Mark E. 2008. "Limited Liberty, Durable Patriarchy." In Police and the Liberal State, edited by Markus D. Dubber, and Mariana Valverde, 74-91. Redwood City: Stanford University Press.

Kaplan, Ami. 2008/2009. "In the name of security." *Review of International American Studies* 3 (3) / 4 (1): 15–24.

Kasy, Maximilian. 2019. "The politics of machine learning, pt. I." *Phenomenal World*, June 27. www.phenomenalworld.org/analysis/politics-of-machine-learning/.

Kean, Hilda. 2011. "Traces and representations: Animal pasts in London's present." *The London Journal* 36 (1): 54–71

Keil, Roger. 2018. "Extended urbanization, 'disjunct fragments' and global suburbanisms." *Environment and Planning D* 36 (3): 494–511.

Kelling, George L., and William J. Bratton. 2015. "Why we need broken windows policing." *City Journal*, Winter. www.city-journal.org/html/why-we-need-broken-windows-policing-13696.html.

Kelling, George L., and James Q. Wilson. 1982. "Broken Windows: The police and neighborhood safety." *The Atlantic*, March. www.theatlantic.com/magazine/archive/1982/03/broken-windows/304465/.

Kern, Leslie. 2010. "Selling the 'scary city': Gendering freedom, fear and condominium development in the neoliberal city." *Social and Cultural Geography* 11 (3): 209–230.

Kertscher, Tom. 2017. "Is Donald Trump's executive order a 'Muslim ban'?" *Politifact*, February 3. www.politifact.com/article/2017/feb/03/donald-trumps-executive-order-muslim-ban/.

Kettner, Andrew. 2020. *The Smell of Slavery: Olfactory Racism and the Atlantic World*. Cambridge: Cambridge University Press.

Kilcullen, David. 2013. *Out of the Mountains: The Coming Age of the Urban Guerrilla*. London: Hurst & Company.

Kinnvall, Catarina, Ian Manners, and Jennifer Mitzen. 2018. "Introduction to 2018 special issue of European Security: 'ontological (in)security in the European Union'." *European Security* 27 (3): 249–265.

Kirmani, Nida. 2020. "Can fun be feminist? Gender, space and mobility in Lyari, Karachi." *South Asia: Journal of South Asian Studies* 43 (2): 319–331.

Kitchin, Rob. 2014. "Big Data, new epistemologies and paradigm shifts." *Big Data and Society* 1 (1): 1–12.

Kitchin, Rob, and Martin Dodge. 2011. *Code/Space: Software and Everyday Life*. Cambridge: MIT Press.

Koch, Regan, and Alan Latham. 2012. "Rethinking urban public space: accounts from a junction in West London." *Transactions of the Institute of British Geographers* 37 (4): 515–529.

Kopenawa, Albert B. 2023[2013]. *The Falling Sky: Words of a Yanomami Shaman*. Cambridge: Harvard University Press.

Kornberger, Martin, and Christian Borch. 2015. "Introduction: Urban commons." In *Urban Commons: Rethinking the City*, edited by Christian Borch, and Martin Kornberger, 1–21. Abingdon: Routledge.

Kosek, Jake. 2010. "Ecologies of empire: On the new uses of the honeybee." *Cultural Anthropology* 25 (4): 650–678.

Koselleck, Reinhart. 2006[1972]. "Crisis." *Journal of the History of Ideas* 67 (2): 357–400.

Kracauer, Sigfried. 1995[1963]. *The Mass Ornament: Weimar Essays*. Cambridge: Harvard University Press.

Laclau, Ernesto, and Chantal Mouffe. 1985. *Hegemony and Socialist Strategy: Towards a Radical Democratic Politics*. London: Verso.

Lambert, Léopold. 2010. "Architectures of joy. A Spinozist reading of Parent/Virilio and Arakawa/Gins' architecture." *The Funambulist*, December 18. https://thefunambulist.net/editorials/philosophy-architectures-of-joy-a-spinozist-reading-of-parentvirilio-and-arakawagins-architecture.

Landim, Leilah and Raíza Siqueira. 2013. *Trajetos de violência, da segurança pública e da sociedade civil na cidade do Rio de Janeiro*. Brasília: IPEA.

Laporte, Dominique. 2000[1978]. *History of Shit*. Cambridge: MIT Press.

Larkins, Erika R. 2015. *The Spectacular Favela. Violence in Modern Brazil*. Oakland: University of California Press.

Larsen, Signe. 2013. "Notes on the thought of Walter Benjamin: Critique of violence." *Critical Legal Thinking*, October 11. https://criticallegalthinking.com/2013/10/11/notes-thought-walter-benjamin-critique-violence/.

Latham, Alan. 1999. "The power of distraction: Distraction, tactility, and habit in the work of Walter Banjamin." *Environment and Planning D* 17 (4): 451–473.

Latour, Bruno. 1993[1991]. *We Have Never Been Modern*. Cambridge: Harvard University Press.

Latour, Bruno. 2005. *Reassembling the Social. An Introduction to Actor-Network-Theory*. Oxford: Oxford University Press.

Latour, Bruno, and Émilie Hermant. 1998. *Paris ville invisible*. Paris: Empecheurs de Penser en Rond.

Law, John. 2004. *After Method: Mess in Social Science Research*. London: Routledge.

Lawrence, Bruce B., and Aisha Karim. 2007a. "General introduction: Theorizing violence in the twenty-first century." In *On Violence: A Reader*, edited by Bruce B. Lawrence, and Aisha Karim, 1–16. Durham: Duke University Press.

Lawrence, Bruce B., and Aisha Karim, eds. 2007b. *On Violence: A Reader*. Durham: Duke University Press.

Lazarsfeld, Paul F., and Robert K. Merton. 1954. "Friendship as social process: A substantive and methodological analysis." In *Freedom and Control in Modern Society*, edited by Morroe Berger, Theodore Abel, Charles H. Page, 18–66. New York: Van Nostrand.

Le Corbusier 2003[1925]. "Una città contemporanea." In *Le Corbusier. Scritti*, edited by Rosa Tamborrino, 94–106. Turin: Einaudi.

Le Corbusier 2003[1935]. "Ma Cartesio è americano?" In *Le Corbusier. Scritti*, edited by Rosa Tamborrino, 252–262. Turin: Einaudi.

Lee, Matthew R. 2011. "Reconsidering culture and homicide." *Homicide Studies* 15 (4): 319–340.

Lees, Loretta, Hyun B. Shin, and Ernesto López-Morales, eds. 2015. *Global Gentrifications. Uneven Development and Displacement*. Bristol: Policy Press.

Lees, Loretta, Hyun B. Shin, and Ernesto López-Morales. 2016. *Planetary Gentrification*. Cambridge: Policy.

Lefebvre, Henri. 1974. *La Production de l'Espace*. Paris: Anthropos.

Lefebvre, Henri. 2003[1970]. *The Urban Revolution*. Minneapolis: University of Minnesota Press.

Lefebvre, Henri. 2014[1989]. "Dissolving city, planetary metamorphosis." *Environment and Planning D* 32 (2): 203–205.

Lefort, Claude. 1978. *Les Formes de l'Histoire*. Paris: Gallimard.

Lehman, Charles F. 2021. "Abolition Fantasyland. A new book distills the problem with the Left's anti-police imaginings." *City Journal*, September 3. www.city-journal.org/review-of-a-world-without-police-by-geo-maher.

Lennon, Kathleen, 2015. *Imagination and the Imaginary*. Abingdon: Routledge.

León, Luis A., and Jovanna Rosen. 2020. "Technology as ideology in urban governance." *Annals of the American Association of Geographers* 110 (2): 497–506.

Lepenies, Wolf. 1992[1969]. *Melancholy and Society*. Cambridge: Harvard University Press.

Leroi-Gourhan, André. 1993[1964]. *Gesture and Speech*. Cambridge: MIT Press.

Le Texier, Thibault. 2019. "Debunking the Stanford Prison Experiment." *American Psychologist* 74 (7): 823–839.

Leung, Gilbert. 2013. "Breach of the peace or violence and/of silence." In *Disobedience: Concept and Practice*, edited by Elena Loizidou, 37–47. Abingdon: Routledge.

Levine, E. S., Jessica Tisch, Anthony Tasso, and Michael Joy. 2017. "The New York City police department's domain awareness system." *Interfaces* 47 (1): 70–84.

Levitas, Ruth. 2013. *Utopia as Method: The Imaginary Reconstitution of Society*. Basingstoke: Palgrave.

Levy, Brian L., Nolan E. Phillips, and Robert J. Sampson. 2020. "Triple Disadvantage: Neighborhood Networks of Everyday Urban Mobility and Violence in U.S. Cities." *American Sociological Review* 85 (6): 925–956.

Li, Tania M. 2017. "After the land grab: Infrastructural violence and the 'Mafia System' in Indonesia's oil palm plantation zones." *Geoforum* 96: 328–337.

Lianos, Michalis. 2003. "Social control after Foucault." *Surveillance and Society* 1 (3): 412–430.

Lianos, Michalis, and Mary Douglas. 2000. "Dangerization and the end of deviance: The institutional environment." *The British Journal of Criminology* 40 (2): 261–278.

Lindner, Christoph, and Miriam Meissner, eds. 2019. *The Routledge Companion to Urban Imaginaries. 1st Edition.* London: Routledge.

Linebaugh, P. 2008. *The Magna Carta Manifesto: Liberties and Commons For All.* Berkeley: University of California Press.

Lippert, Randy K. 2014. "Neo-liberalism, police and the governance of little urban things." *Foucault Studies* 18: 49–65.

Lippman, Walter. 1937. *The Good Society.* Boston: Little, Brown, and Company.

Locke, John. 2003[1690]. *Second Treitise of Civil Government,* produced by Dave Gowan, and Chuck Greif. Salt Lake City: Project Guthenberg. www.gutenberg. org/files/7370/7370-h/7370-h.htm.

Lombroso, Cesare. 1878. *L'uomo delinquente in rapporto all'antropologia, giurisprudenza e alle discipline carcerarie.* Turin: Bocca.

Lópes-Morales, Ernesto. 2018. "A rural gentrification theory debate for the Global South?" *Dialogues in Human Geography* 8 (1): 47–50.

Lorimer, Jamie. 2020. *The Probiotic Planet: Using Life to Manage Life.* Minneapolis: University of Minnesota Press.

Lorimer, Jamie, Timothy Hodgetts, and Maan Barua. 2019. "Animals' atmospheres." *Progress in Human Geography,* 43 (1): 26–45.

Lourenço, Nelson. 2012. "Città, violenza urbana e sentimento di insicurezza." *Rivista di Criminologia, Vittimologia e Sicurezza* 6 (3): 131–148.

Lovink, Geert. 2019a. "Cybernetics for the twenty-first century: An Interview with philosopher Yuk Hui." *e-flux journal,* 102. www.e-flux.com/journal/102/282271/cybernetics-for-the-twenty-first-century-an-interview-with-philosopher-yuk-hui/.

Lovink, Geert. 2019b. *Sad by Design.* London: Pluto Press.

Low, Setha, and Mark Maguire, eds. 2018. *Spaces of Security: Ethnographies of Securityscapes, Surveillance, and Control.* New York: NYU Press.

Löwy, Michael. 1970. *O pensamento de Che Guevara.* São Paulo: Expressão Popular.

Loyd, Jenna M and Alison Mountz. 2018. *Boats, Borders and Bases: Race, the Cold War, and the Rise of Migration Detention in the United States.* Oakland: University of California Press.

Lucchetti, Matteo, and Judith Wielander, [2018]. "Indigenous, not homogenous. An interview with Elizabeth A. Povinelli." *Visible.* www.visibleproject.org/blog/text/indigenous-not-homogenous/.

Luhmann, Niklas. 2003[1980]. *Social Structure and Semantics.* Stanford: Stanford University Press.

Luke, Timothy. 2016. "Environmental governmentality." In *The Oxford Handbook of Environmental Political Theory,* edited by Teena Gabrielson, Cheryl Hall, John M. Meyer, and David Schlosberg, 460–474. Oxford: Oxford University Press.

Lum, Kristian and William Isaac. 2016. "To predict and serve?" *Significance* 13 (5): 14–19.

Lynch, Kevin. 1960. *The Image of the City.* Cambridge: MIT Press.

Macedo, Marta. 2021. "Agricultura, administración y violencia." *Sabers en Acció,* July 19. https://sabersenaccio.iec.cat/es/agricultura-administracion-y-violencia/.

Machado, Talita C., and Alecsandro J.P. Ratts. 2017. "As mulheres e a rua: Entre o medo e as apropriações feministas da Cidade de Goiânia, Goiás." *Revista Latino-Americana de Geografia e Gênero* 8 (1): 194–213.

Macpherson, Crawford B. 1962. *The Political Theory of Possessive Individualism: Hobbes to Locke*. London: Oxford University Press.

Madarie, Renushka, and Edwin W. Kruisbergen. 2020. "Traffickers in transit: Analysing the logistics and involvement mechanisms of organised crime at logistical nodes in the Netherlands: Empirical results of the Dutch Organised Crime Monitor." In *Understanding Recruitment to Organized Crime and Terrorism*, edited by David Weisburd, Ernesto U. Savona, Badi Hasisi, and Francesco Calderoni, 277–308. Cham: Springer.

Maguire, Mark. 2018. "Policing future crimes." In *Bodies as evidence. Security, knowledge, and power*, edited by Mark Maguire, Ursula Rao and Neil Zurawski, 137–158. Durham: Duke University Press.

Maguire, Mark, Ursula Rao, and Nils Zurawski, eds. 2018. *Bodies as Evidence. Security, Knowledge, and Power*. Durham: Duke University Press.

Maher, Geo. 2021. *A World Without Police. How Strong Communities Make Cops Obsolete*. London: Verso.

Maloutas, Thomas. 2018. "Travelling concepts and universal particularism: A reappraisal of gentrification's global reach." *European Urban and regional Studies* 25 (3): 250–265.

Maki, Amos. 2012. "Crimes lurk in Memphis Police Department memos." *The Commercial Appeal*, January 25. www.pressreader.com/usa/the-commercial-appeal/20120125/281492158200040.

Mandelbaum, Moran M. 2020. *The Nation/State Fantasy: A Psychoanalytical Genealogy of Nationalism*. Cham: Palgrave Macmillan.

Mansilla, José L. 2018. "No es turismofobia, es lucha de clases. Políticas urbanas, malestar social y turismo en un barrio de Barcelona." *Revista NODO* 23: 21–47.

Marsi, Federica. 2021. "NGOs condemn 'rescue gap' as 10 migrants die on boat off Libya." *Al Jazeera*, November 17. https://www.aljazeera.com/news/2021/11/17/ngos-decry-rescue-gap-as-10-bodies-found-on-boat-off-libya.

Martén, Ricardo, and Camillo Boano. 2022. "Checkpoint urbanism: Violent infrastructures and border stigmas in the Juárez border region." *Urban Studies* 59 (3): 526–547.

Marx, Karl, 1978[1856]. "Speech at the anniversary of the people's paper." In *The Marx-Engels Reader, second ed.*, edited by Rovert C. Tucker, 577–578. London: Norton.

Marx, Karl. 2008/2009[1844]. "On *The Jewish Question*." *Marxist.org*. /www.marxists.org/archive/marx/works/1844/jewish-question/.

Marzec, Robert P. 2007. *An Ecological and Postcolonial Study of Literature: From Daniel Defoe to Salman Rushdie*. Basingstocke: Palgrave.

Marzocca, Ruggiero. 2001. "L'assenza di una definizione legislativa di 'centro storico'." *Lexambiente*, November 30. https://lexambiente.it/materie/beni-culturali/171-dottrina171/1774-Beni%20culturali.%20Centri%20storici.html.

Massumi, Brian. 2005. "Fear (the spectrum said)." *positions: east asia cultures critique* 13 (1): 31–48.

Massumi, Brian. 2011. "Affect in the key of politics." *Identities: Journal for Politics, Gender and Culture* 8 (1), 37–44.

Massumi, Brian. 2015. *The Politics of Affect*. Cambridge: Polity.

Massumi, Brian. 2018. *99 Theses on the Revaluation of Value: A Postcapitalist Manifesto*. Minneapolis: University of Minnesota Press.

Mattern, Shannon. 2015. "Mission control: A history of the urban dashboard." *Places Journal*, March. https://placesjournal.org/article/mission-control-a-history-of-the-urban-dashboard/.

Mauloni, Lorenzo. 2021. "Legitimizing violence when the State is untrustworthy. Tales from Medellín." *Lo Squaderno* 59: 39–43.

Mawani, Renisa. 2019. "Atmospheric pressures: On race and affect." York University Department of Sociology Annual Lecture, February 26 [mimeo].

Maze, Jacob. 2018. "Towards and analytic of violence: Foucault, Arendt & power." *Foucault Studies* 25: 140–145.

Mbembe, Achille. 2003. "Necropolitics." *Public Culture* 15 (1): 11–40.

Mbembe, Achille. 2019. *Necropolitics*. Durham: Duke University Press.

Mbembe, Achille. 2020. "The universal right to breathe." *Critical Inquiry*, April 13. https://critinq.wordpress.com/2020/04/13/the-universal-right-to-breathe/.

Mbembe, Achille, and Janet Roitman. 1995. "Figures of the subject in times of crisis." *Public Culture* 7 (2): 323–352.

McArthur, Jenny, and Enora Robin. 2019. "Victims of their own (definition of) success: Urban discourse and expert knowledge production in the Liveable City." *Urban Studies* 56 (9): 1711–1728.

McCormack, Derek P. 2008. "Engineering affective atmospheres on the moving geographies of the 1897 Andrée expedition." *cultural geographies* 15 (4): 413–430.

McCormack, Derek P. 2012. "Geography and abstraction: Towards an affirmative critique." *Progress in Human Geography* 36 (6): 715–734.

McCormack, Derek P. 2018. *Atmospheric Things: On the Allure of Elemental Envelopment*. Durham: Duke University Press.

McCullough, Malcolm. 2013. *Ambient Commons: Attention in the Age of Embodied Information*. Cambridge: MIT Press.

McFarlace, Colin. 2011. "Assemblage and critical urbanism." *City* 15 (2): 204–224.

McFarlane, Colin. 2018. "Fragment urbanism: Politics on the margins of the city." *Environment and Planning D* 36 (6): 1007–1025.

McKim, Joel. 2009. "Of microperception and micropolitics. An interview with Brian Massumi, 15 August 2008." *INFLeXions. A Journal for Research Creation* 3 [online].

McLean, Heather. 2018. "In praise of chaotic research pathways: A feminist response to planetary urbanization. *Environment and Planning D* 36 (3): 547–555.

McNeill, Donald. 2015. "Global firms and smart technologies: IBM and the reduction of cities." *Transactions of the Institute of British Geographers* 40 (4): 562–574.

McNeur, Catherine. 2014. *Taming Manhattan. Environmental Battles in the Antebellum City*. Cambridge: Harvard University Press.

Meijer, Albert, and Martijn Wessels. 2019. "Predictive Policing: Review of benefits and drawbacks." *International Journal of Public Administration* 42 (12): 1031–1039.

Melhuish, Clare, Degen, Monica, and Gillian Rose. 2016. "'The real modernity that is here': Understanding the role of digital visualisations in the production of a new urban imaginary at Msheireb Downtown, Doha." *City & Society* 28 (2): 222–245.

Melossi, Dario. 2003. "'In a peaceful life'. Migration and the crime of modernity in Europe/Italy." *Punishment and Society* 5 (4): 371–397.

Mendieta, Eduardo. 2019. "Edge city. Reflections on the Urbanocene and the Plantatiocene." *Critical Philosophy of Race* 7 (1): 81–106.

Merrifield, Andy. 2000. "The dialectics of dystopia: Disorder and Zero Tolerance in the city." *International Journal of Urban and Regional Research* 24 (2): 473–489.

Meyer, Dugan. 2021. "Security symptoms." *cultural geographies* 28 (2): 271–284.

Mezzadra, Sandro. 2013. "Questione di sguardi. Du Bois e Fanon." In *Fanon postcoloniale. I dannati della terra oggi*, edited by Miguel Mellino, 189–205. Verona: ombre corte.

Mezzadra, Sandro, and Brett Neilson. 2019. *The Politics of Operations: Excavating Contemporary Capitalism*. Durham: Duke University Press.

Mialon, Hugo M., Sue H. Mialon, and Maxwell B. Stinchcombe. 2012. "Torture in counterterrorism: Agency incentives and slippery slopes." *Journal of Public Economics* 96 (1–2), 33–41.

Mignolo, Walter D. 2009. "Epistemic disobedience, independent thought and decolonial freedom." *Theory, Culture and Society* 26 (7–8): 159–181.

Mignolo, Walter D. 2017. "Racism and coloniality. The invention of 'HUMAN(ITY)' and the three pillars of the colonial matrix of power (racism, sexism, and nature)." In *The Routledge Companion to Philosophy of Race* edited by Paul C. Taylor, Linda Martín Alcoff, and Luvell Anderson, 461–474. New York: Routledge.

Milgram, Stanley. 1974. *Obedience to Authority; An Experimental View*. New York: Harper & Row.

Miller, Jon. 2015. *Spinoza and the Stoics*. Cambridge: Cambridge University Press.

Minuchin, Leandro, and Julieta Maino. 2022. "Counter-logistics and municipalism: Popular infrastructures during the pandemic in Rosario." *Urban Studies*, online first. Doi: 10.1177/0042098022111849.

Miraftab, Faranak. 2009. "Insurgent planning: Situating radical planning in the Global South." *Planning Theory* 8 (1): 32–50.

Misse, Michel. 2008. "Sobre a acumulação social da violência no Rio de Janeiro. *Civitas—Revista de Ciências Sociais* 8 (3): 371–385.

Misse, Michel, and Carolina C. Grillo. 2014. "Río De Janeiro. Sufrir la violencia, decir la paz." In *Ciudades en la encrucijada: violencia y poder criminal en Río de Ja-*

neiro, Medellín, Bogotá y Ciudad Juárez, edited by Ana M. Jaramillo, and Carlos M. Perea, 49–116. Medellín: Corporación Región.

Mitchener-Nissen, Timothy. 2014. "Failure to collectively assess surveillance-oriented security technologies will inevitably lead to an absolute surveillance society." *Surveillance and Society* 12 (1): 73–88.

Mohler, G. O., M. B. Short, Sean Malinowski, Mark Johnson, G. E. Tita, Andrea L. Bertozzi, and Jeffrey P. Brantingham. 2015. "Randomized controlled field trials of predictive policing." *Journal of the American Statistical Association* 512: 1399–1411.

Mol, Annemarie. 2008. "I eat an apple. On theorizing subjectivities." *Subjectivity* 22 (1): 28–37.

Moncada, Eduardo. 2013. "The politics of urban violence: Challenges to development in the Global South." *Studies in Comparative International Development* 48 (3): 217–239.

Mongoven, Ann. 2006. "The war on disease and the war on terror: A dangerous metaphorical nexus?" *Cambridge Quarterly of Healthcare Ethics*, 15 (4): 403–416.

Moore, Nathan. 2007a. "Icons of control: Deleuze, signs, law." *International Journal for the Semiotics of Law* 20 (1): 33–54.

Moore, Nathan. 2007b. "Nova law: William S. Burroughs and the logic of control." *Law and Literature* 19 (3): 435–470.

Moore, Jason. 2015. *Capitalism in the Web of Life: Ecology and the Accumulation of Capital*. London: Verso.

Morenoff, Jeffrey D., Robert J. Sampson, and Stephen W. Raudenbush. 2001. "Neighborhood inequality, collective efficacy, and the spatial dynamics of urban violence." *Criminology* 39 (3): 517–558.

Morin, Marie-Eve. 2009. "Cohabitating in the globalised world: Peter Sloterdijk's global foams and Bruno Latour's cosmopolitics." *Environment and Planning D* 27 (1): 58–72.

Morozov, Evgeny. 2013. *To Save Everything, Click Here: The Folly of Technological Solutionism*. New York: Public Affairs.

Moser, Caroline N. 2004. "Urban violence and insecurity: An introductory roadmap." *Environment and Urbanization* 16 (2): 3–16.

Moser, Caroline N. and Cathy McIlwaine. 2014. "Editorial: New frontiers in twenty-first century urban conflict and violence." *Environment and Urbanization* 26 (2): 331–344.

Moser, Caroline N., and Dennis Rodgers. 2012. "Understanding the tipping point of urban conflict: Global policy report." *Urban Tipping Point Project Working Paper 7*, University of Manchester.

Moses, Lyria B., and Janet Chan. 2018. "Algorithmic prediction in policing: assumptions, evaluation, and accountability." *Policing and Society* 28 (7): 806–822.

Mosselson, Aidan. 2019. "Everyday security: privatized policing, local legitimacy and atmospheres of control." *Urban Geography* 40 (1): 16–36.

Mouffe, Chantal. 1999. "Deliberative democracy or agonistic pluralism?" *Social Research* 66 (3): 745–758.

Mouffe, Chantal. 2000. *The Democratic Paradox*. London: Verso.

Muggah, Robert. 2012. *Researching the Urban Dilemma: Urbanization, Poverty and Violence*. Ottawa: International Development Research Center.

Muggah, Robert. 2014. "Deconstructing the fragile city." *Environment and Urbanization* 26 (2): 1–14.

Müller, Markus-Michael. 2012. "The rise of the penal state in Latin America." *Contemporary Justice Review* 15 (1): 57–76.

Mumford, Lewis. 1961. *The City in History: Its Origins, Its Transformations, and Its Prospects*. New York: Harcourt, Brace and World.

Munn, Nathan. 2018. "This predictive policing company compares its software to 'broken windows' policing." *Motherboard*, June 11. https://motherboard.vice.com/en_us/article/d3k5pv/predpol-predictive-policing-broken-windows-theory-chicago-lucy-parsons.

Murphy, Michelle. 2017. *The Economization of Life*. Durham: Duke University Press

Nancy, Jean-Luc. 1991. *The Inoperative Community*. Minneapolis: University of Minnesota Press.

Narayanan, Yamini. 2017. "Street dogs at the intersection of colonialism and informality: 'Subaltern animism' as a posthuman critique of Indian cities." *Environment and Planning D* 35 (3): 475–494.

Narayanan, Yamini. 2022. "The dangerous populist science of Yuval Noah Harari." *Current Affairs*, July 6. www.currentaffairs.org/2022/07/the-dangerous-populist-science-of-yuval-noah-harari.

Neal, Andrew W. 2019. *Security as Politics. Beyond the State of Exception*. Edinburgh: Edinburgh University Press.

Negarestani, Reza. 2015. "Where is the concept? (Localization, ramification, navigation)." In *When Site Lost the Plot*, edited by Robin Mackay, 225–251. Falmouth: Urbanomic.

Neocleous, Mark. 2000. "Against security." *Radical Philosophy* 100: 7–15.

Neocleous, Mark. 2003. *Imagining the State*. Maidenhead: Open University Press.

Neocleous, Mark. 2007. "Security, liberty and the myth of balance: Towards a critique of security politics." *Contemporary Political Theory* 6 (2): 131–149.

Neucleous, Mark. 2008. *Critique of Security*. Edinburgh: Edinburgh University Press.

Neocleous, Mark. 2019. "*Securitati perpetuae*. Death, fear and the history of insecurity." *Radical Philosophy* 2.06: 19–33.

Neocleous, Mark. 2021[2000]. *A Critical Theory of Police Power. The Fabrication of the Social Order*. London: Verso.

Newheiser, David. 2016. "Foucault, Gary Becker and the Critique of Neoliberalism." *Theory, Culture and Society* 33 (5): 3–21.

Newman, Oscar. 1972. *Defensible Space: Crime Prevention through Urban Design*. New York: Macmillan.

Niceforo, Alfredo, and Scipio Sighele. 1898. *La Mala Vita a Roma*. Turin: Roux Frassati & Co.

Nietzsche, Friedrich. 1967[1887/1888]. *On the Genealogy of Morals: Ecce Homo*. New York: Vintage Books.

Nietzsche, Friedrich. 1962[1873]. *Philosophy in the Tragic Age of the Greeks*. Washington: Regnery Publishing.

Nietzsche, Friedrich. 2001[1882–87]. *The Gay Science. With a Prelude in German Rhymes and an Appendix of Songs*. Cambridge: Cambridge University Press.

Nirta, Caterina. 2017. *Marginal Bodies, Trans Utopias*. London: Routledge.

Nieuwenhuis, Marijn. 2015. "Skunk water: Stench as a weapon of war." *Open Democracy*, December 17. https://www.opendemocracy.net/en/skunk-water-stench-as-weapon-of-war/ .

Nieuwenhuis, Marijn. 2016. "Breathing materiality: aerial violence at a time of atmospheric politics." *Critical Studies on Terrorism* 9 (3): 499–521.

Nieuwenhuis, Marijn. 2018. "Atmospheric governance: Gassing as law for the protection and killing of life." *Environment and Planning D* 36 (1): 78–95.

Nixon, Rob. 2011. *Slow Violence and the Environmentalism of the Poor*. Cambridge: Harvard University Press.

Noble, Safiya U. 2018. *Algorithms of Oppression: How Search Engines Reinforce Racism*. New York: NYU Press.

Norton, Richard J. 2003. "Feral cities." *Naval War College Review* LVI (4): 97–106.

Nugent, David, and Adeem Suhail. 2021. "Crisis, disorder and management: Smart cities and contemporary urban inequality." In *Urban Inequalities. Ethnographically Informed Reflections*, edited by Italo Pardo, and Giuliana B. Prato, 145–169. Cham: Palgrave Macmillan.

Nunes, João. 2012. "Reclaiming the political: Emancipation and critique in security studies." *Security Dialogue* 43 (4): 345–361.

Nunes, João. 2016. "Security, emancipation and the ethics of vulnerability." In *Ethical Security Studies: A New Research Agenda*, edited by Jonna Nyman, and Anthony Burke, 89–101. Abingdon: Routledge.

Nunes, Rodrigo. 2021. *Neither Vertical nor Horizontal: A Theory of Political Organization*. London: Verso.

Nuttall, Sarah, and Achille Mbembe. 2004. "A blasé attitude: A response to Michael Watts." *Public Culture* 17 (1): 193–202.

Nyman, Jonna. "Pragmatism, practice and the value of security." In *Ethical Security Studies: A New Research Agenda*, edited by Jonna Nyman, and Anthony Burke, 131–144. Abingdon: Routledge.

Nyman, Jonna. 2021. "The everyday life of security: Capturing space, practice, and affect." *International Political Sociology* 15 (3): 313–337.

O'Brien, Daniel T., Chelsea Farrell, and Brandon C. Welsh. 2019. "Looking Through Broken Windows: The Impact of Neighborhood Disorder on Aggression and Fear of Crime Is an Artifact of Research Design." *Annual Review of Criminology* 2: 53–71.

Ojeda, Diana. 2012. "Green pretexts: Ecotourism, neoliberal conservation and land grabbing in Tayrona National Natural Park, Colombia." *The Journal of Peasant Studies* 39 (2): 357–375.

Oksala, Johanna. 2012. *Foucault, Politics, and Violence.* Evanston: Northwestern University Press.

Olsson, Gunnar. 2007. *Abysmal a Critique of Cartographic Reason.* Chicago: University of Chicago Press.

O'Neil, Cathy. 2016. *Weapons of Math Destruction. How Big Data Increases Inequality and Threatens Democracy.* New York: Crown.

Orlando, Leoluca. 2001. *Fighting the Mafia and Renewing the Sicilian Culture.* New York: Encounter Books.

Osborne, Peter. 2004. "The reproach of abstraction." *Radical Philosophy* 127: 21–28.

Owens, Michael L. 2020. "The urban world is a world of police." *Journal of Race, Ethnicity and the City* 1 (1–2), 11–15.

Pain, Rachel. 2009. "Globalized fear? Towards an emotional geopolitics." *Progress in Human Geography* 33 (4): 466–486.

Pain, Rachel. 2014. "Gendered violence: rotating intimacy." *Area* 46 (4): 351–353.

Paone, Sonia, and Agostino Petrillo. 2019. "La violenza dei ricchi e l'intelligenza delle periferie." In *Il campo di battaglia urbano. Trasformazioni e conflitti dentro, contro e oltre la metropoli,* edited by Laboratorio Crash, 75–85. Rome: Red Str Press.

Papachristos, Andrew V. 2011. "Too big to fail: The science and politics of violence prevention." *Criminology & Public. Policy* 10 (4): 1053–1061.

Papachristos, Andrew V., and Christopher Wildeman. 2014. "Network exposure and homicide victimization in an African American Community." *American Journal of Public Health* 104 1: 143–150.

Parnaby, Patrick F. 2006. "Crime Prevention through Environmental Design: Discourses of risk, social control, and a neo-liberal context." *Canadian Journal of Criminology and Criminal Justice* 48 (1): 1–29.

Pasquale, Frank. 2015. *The Black Box Society. The Secret Algorithms that Control Money and Society.* Cambridge: Harvard University Press.

Pasquinelli, Matteo. 2014. "The labour of abstraction: Seven transitional theses on marxism and accelerationism." *Fillip* 19 (Spring). https://fillip.ca/content/the-labour-of-abstraction.

Pasquinelli, Matteo. 2015. "What an apparatus is not: On the archeology of the norm in Foucault, Canguilhem, and Goldstein." *Parrhesia* 22: 79–89.

Pasquinelli, Matteo. 2017. "Arcana mathematica imperii: The evolution of Western computational norms." In *Former West. Art and the Contemporary after 1989,* edited by Maria Hlavajova, and Simon Sheikh, 281–293. Cambridge: MIT Press.

Pasquinelli, Matteo. 2019. "Three thousand years of algorithmic rituals: The emergence of AI from the computation of space." *e-flux journal* 101. www.e-flux.com/journal/101/273221/three-thousand-years-of-algorithmic-rituals-the-emergence-of-ai-from-the-computation-of-space/.

Pasquinelli, Matteo, and Vladan Joler. 2021. "The Nooscope manifested: AI as instrument of knowledge extractivism." *AI & Society* 36 (4): 1263–1280.

Pavoni, Andrea. 2011. "Tuning the city: Johannesburg and the 2010 World Cup." *urbe. Revista Brasileira de Gestão Urbana* 3 (2): 191–209.

Pavoni, Andrea. 2017a. "Abstracting method. Taking legal abstractions seriously". In *Research Methods in Environmental Law: A Handbook*, edited by Andreas Philippopoulos-Mihalopoulos, and Victoria Brooks, 51–79. Cheltenham: Edward Elgar Publishing.

Pavoni, Andrea. 2017b. "Sharing conflict. Law, justice, and the street." In *Street-Level Sovereignty: The Intersection of Space and Law*, edited by Sarah Marusek, and John Brigham, 37–66. Lanham: Lexington.

Pavoni, Andrea. 2018a. *Controlling Urban Events: Law, Ethics and the Material*. Abingdon: Routledge.

Pavoni, Andrea. 2018b. "Introduction." In *See*, edited by Andrea Pavoni, Danilo Mandic, Caterina Nirta, and Andreas Philippopoulos-Mihalopoulos, 1–28. London: University of Westminster Press.

Pavoni, Andrea. 2020. "Profanating gastro-normativity: Exploring the nonhuman materiality of making and tasting wine in the natural wine movement." *Cultural Politics* 16 (3): 367–386.

Pavoni, Andrea. 2021. "Vandalizing the commons." In *Political Graffiti in Critical Times: The Aesthetic of Street Politics*, edited by Ricardo Campos, Yiannis Zaimakis, and Andrea Pavoni, 149–172. New York: Berghahn Books.

Pavoni, Andrea, and Andrea M. Brighenti. 2017. "Airspacing the city: Where technophysics meets atmoculture." *Azimuth* 10 (2): 91–103.

Pavoni, Andrea, and Franco Tomassoni. 2022. "Introdução", in *A produção do mundo. Problemas logísticos e sítios críticos*, edited by Andrea Pavoni, and Franco Tomassoni, 21–59. Lisboa: Outro Modo.

Pavoni, Andrea, and Simone Tulumello. 2020. "What is urban violence?" *Progress in Human Geography* 44 (1): 49–76.

Patel, Deepali M., Melissa A. Simon, and Rachel M. Taylor. 2013. "Introduction." In *Contagion of Violence. Workshop Summary*, edited by IOM (Institute of Medicine) and NRC (National Research Council), 94–111. Washington: The National Academies Press.

Peano, Irene, Marta Macedo, and Colette Le Petitcorps. 2023. "Introduction: Viewing plantations at the intersection of political ecologies and multiple space-times." In *Global Plantations in the Modern World. Sovereignties, Ecologies, Afterlives*, edited by Colette Le Petitcorps, Marta Macedo, and Irene Peano, 1–32. Cham: Palgrave.

Pearson, Keith A. 1999. *Germinal Life: The Difference and Repetition of Deleuze*. London: Routledge.

Pearson, Chris. 2021. *Dogopolis. How Dogs and Humans Made Modern New York, London, and Paris*. Chicago: University of Chicago Press.

Pease, Daniel E. 2004. "The extraterritoriality of the literature for our planet." *ESQ: A Journal of the American Renaissance* 50 (1–3): 177–221.

Penglase, Ben R. 2011. "Lost bullets: Fetishes of urban violence in Rio de Janeiro, Brazil." *Anthropological Quarterly* 84 (2): 411–438.

Penney, Terry L. 2014. "Dark figure of crime (problems of estimation)." In *The Encyclopedia of Criminology and Criminal Justice*, edited by Jay S. Albanese [ebook]. Hoboken: Wiley.

Perera, Suvendrini, and Joseph Pugliese. 1998. "Parks, mines and tidy towns: Enviropanopticism, 'post' colonialism, and the politics of heritage in Australia." *Postcolonial Studies: Culture, Politics, Economy* 1 (1): 69–100.

Perera, Suvendrini and Joseph Pugliese. 2011. "Introduction: Combat breathing: State violence and the body in question." *Somatechnics* 1 (1): 1–14.

Perry, Walt L., Brian McInnis, Carter C. Price, Susan C. Smith, and John S. Hollywood. 2013. *Predictive Policing. The Role of Crime Forecasting in Law Enforcement Operations*. Santa Monica: RAND.

Peršak, Nina, and Anna Di Ronco, eds. 2021. *Harm and Disorder in the Urban Space: Social Control, Sense and Sensibility*. Abingdon: Routledge.

Peršak, Nina, and Simone Tulumello. 2020. "Urban Criminology—Criminology of the Urban." *Criminological Encounters* 3 (1): 3–9.

Petti, Alessandro. 2007. *Arcipelaghi e enclave: Architettura dell'ordinamento spaziale contemporaneo*. Milan: Bruno Mondadori.

Peyrefitte, Magali. 2020. "Suburban verticalisation in London. Regeneration, intra-urban inequality, and social harm." *Criminological Encounters* 3 (1): 50–61.

Philippopoulos-Mihalopoulos, Andreas. 2013. "The normativity of animal atmosphere." In *Law and the Question of the Animal: A Critical Jurisprudence*, edited by Yoriko Otomo, and Ed Mussawir, 149–155. Abingdon: Routledge.

Philippopoulos-Mihalopoulos, 2015. *Spatial Justice: Body, Lawscape, Atmosphere*. London: Routledge.

Philippopoulos-Mihalopoulos, Andreas. 2016. "Withdrawing from atmosphere: An ontology of air partitioning and affective engineering." *Environment and Planning D* 34 (1): 150–167.

Philippopoulos-Mihalopoulos, Andreas, Danilo Mandic, Caterina Nirta, and Andrea Pavoni, eds. 2023. *Smell*. London: University of Westminster Press.

Phillips, Martin. 1993. "Rural gentrification and the processes of class colonisation." *Journal of Rural Studies* 9 (2): 123–140.

Phillips, Peter J., and Gabriela Pohl. 2021. "Algorithms, human decision-making and predictive policing." *SN Social Sciences* 1: #109.

Peirce, Charles S. 2019. "Guessing." *Hound and Horn* 2: 267–282.

Pinçon, Michel, and Monique Pinçon-Charlot. 2013. *La violence des riches. Chronique d'une immense case sociale*. Paris: La Découverte.

Pisanello, Carmen. 2017. *In nome del decoro. Dispositivi estetici e politiche securitarie*. Verona: Ombre Corte.

Pitch, Tamar. 2013. *Contro il decoro. L'uso politico della pubblica decenza*. Roma: Laterza.

Plato. 1967/1968. *Plato in Twelve Volumes, Vols. 10 & 11* translated by R.G. Bury. Cambridge: Harvard University Press. http://data.perseus.org/citations/urn:cts:greekLit:tlg0059.tlg034.perseus-eng1:6.778e.

Pløger, John. 2008. "Foucault's *dispositive* and the city." *Planning Theory* 7 (1): 51–70.

Plumwood, Val. 1993. *Feminism and the Mastery of Nature*. London: Routledge.

Poe, Ryan. 2021. "Richard Janikowski, 'father' of Memphis' Blue CRUSH model of policing, dies at 69." *The Commercial Appeal*, March 24. https://eu.commercialappeal.com/story/news/local/2021/03/24/richard-janikowski-father-memphis-blue-crush-model-policing-dies-age-69/6966107002/.

Postema, Gerald J. 2014. "The Soul of Justice: Bentham on Publicity, Law, and the Rule of Law." In *Bentham's Theory of Law and Public Opinion*, edited by Xiaobo Zhai and Michael Quinn, 40–62. Cambridge: Cambridge University Press.

Pottage, Alan. 1998. "Power as an art of contingency: Luhmann, Deleuze, Foucault." *Economy and Society* 27 (1): 1–27.

Povinelli, Elizabeth. A. 2011. *Economies of Abandonment. Social Belonging and Endurance in Late Liberalism*. Durham: Duke University Press.

Preito-Hodge, Kayla, and Donald Tomaskovic-Devey. 2021. "A tale of force: Examining policy proposals to address police violence." *Social Currents* 8 (5): 403–423.

Protevi John. 2009. *Political Affect: Connecting the Social and the Somatic*. Minneapolis: University of Minnesota Press.

Puar, Jasbir. 2017. *The Right to Maim: Debility, Capacity, Disability*. Durham: Duke University Press.

Pugliese, Joseph, and Susan Stryker 2009. "The somatechnics of race and whiteness." *Social Semiotics* 19 (1): 1–8.

Rae, Gavin, and Emma Ingala, eds. 2019. *The Meanings of Violence from Critical Theory to Biopolitics*. New York: Routledge.

Rahola, Federico. 2014. "Urban at large. Notes for an ethnography of urbanization and its frictious sites." *Etnografia e Ricerca Qualitativa* 7 (3): 379–400.

Ramsay, Peter. 2008. "The theory of vulnerable autonomy and the legitimacy of the civil preventative order." LSE Law, Society and Economy Working Papers 1/2008. https://papers.ssrn.com/sol3/papers.cfm?abstract_id=1091782.

Ranasinghe, Prashan. 2013. "Discourse, practice and the production of the polysemy of security." *Theoretical Criminology* 17 (1): 89–107.

Ranciere, Jacques. 1999[1995]. *Dis-agreement: Politics and Philosophy*. Minneapolis: University of Minnesota Press.

Rancière, Jacques. 2001. "Ten theses on politics." *Theory and Event* 5 (3) [online],

Rancière, Jacques. 2004[2000]. *The Politics of Aesthetics: The Distribution of the Sensible*. London: Bloomsbury.

Rapport, Nigel. 2000. "'Criminals by instinct'. On the 'tragedy' of social structure and the 'violence' of individual Creativity." In *Meanings of Violence. A Cross-Cultural Perspective*, edited by Jon Abbink, and Goran Aijmer, 39–54. London: Routledge.

Razack, Sherene H. 2011. "The space of difference in law: Inquests into aboriginal deaths in custody." *Somatechnics* 1 (1): 87–123.

Recasens, Amadeu, Carla Cardoso, Josefina Castro, and Gian G. Nobili. 2013. "Urban security in Southern Europe." *European Journal of Criminology* 10 (3): 368–382.

Reddy, Rajyashree N. 2018. "The urban under erasure: Towards a postcolonial critique of planetary urbanization." *Environment and Planning D* 36 (3): 529–539.

Rehmann, Jan, 2013. *Theories of Ideology: The Powers of Alienation and Subjection.* Leiden: Brill.

Reichel, Philip L. 1992. "The misplaced emphasis on urbanization in police development." *Policing and Society* 3 (1): 1–12.

Reinarz, Jonathan. 2014. *Past Scents: Historical Perspectives on Smell.* Chicago: University of Illinois Press.

Reiner, Robert. 2016. *Crime: The Mystery of the Common-sense Concept.* Cambridge: Polity.

Richardson, Rashida, ed. 2019. "Confronting Black Boxes: A Shadow Report of the New York City Automated Decision System Task Force." *AI Now Institute,* December 4. https://ainowinstitute.org/ads-shadowreport-2019.html.

Ricoeur, Paul. 1986. *Lectures on Ideology and Utopia.* New York: Columbia University Press.

Riemann, Malte. 2019. "Problematizing the medicalization of violence: a critical discourse analysis of the 'Cure Violence' initiative." *Critical Public Health* 29 (2): 146–155.

Rigakos, George S., and Richard W. Hadden. 2001. "Crime, capitalism and the 'risk society': Towards the same old modernity?" *Theoretical Criminology* 5 (1): 61–84.

Rigakos, George S., John L. McMullan, Joshua Johnson, and Gulden Ozcan. 2009. "Introduction: Towards a critical political economy of police." In *A General Police System: Political Economy and Security in the Age of the Enlightenment,* edited by George S. Rigakos, John L. McMullan, Joshua Johnson, and Gulden Ozcan, 1–32. Ottawa: Red Quill Books.

Roche, Gerald, James Leibold, and Ben Hillman. 2020. "Urbanizing Tibet: differential inclusion and colonial governance in the People's Republic of China." *Territory, Politics, Governance,* online first. Doi:10.1080/21622671.2020.1840427.

Rodgers, Dennis. 2004. "'Disembedding' the city: Crime, insecurity and spatial organization in Managua, Nicaragua." *Environment and Urbanization* 16 (2): 113–124.

Rodgers, Dennis. 2006. "The State as a Gang: Conceptualising the Governmentality of Violence in contemporary Nicaragua." *Critique of Anthropology* 26 (3): 315–330.

Rodgers, Dennis. 2016. "Critique of urban violence: Bismarckian transformations in contemporary Nicaragua." *Theory, Culture & Society* 33 (7–8): 85–109.

Rodgers, Dennis, and Bruce O'Neill. 2012. "Infrastructural violence: Introduction to the special issue." *Ethnography* 13 (4): 401–412.

Rodrigues, Thiago, Mariana Kalil, Roberto Zepeda, and Jonathan D. Rosen. 2017. "War zone Acapulco: Urban drug trafficking in the Americas." *Contexto Internacional* 39 (3): 609–631.

Rojas-Durazo, Ana Clarissa. 2016. "Medical violence against people of color and the medicalization of domestic violence." *Color of Violence: The Incite! Anthology,* edited by INCITE! Women of Color Against Violence, 179–189. Durham: Duke University Press.

Roitman, Janet. 2014. *Anti-Crisis*. Durham: Duke University Press.

Ronchi, Rocco, and Bernard Stiegler. *L'ingovernabile. Due lezioni sulla politica*. Genova: il melangolo.

Ros, Jerome. 2014. "From New York to Greece, we revolt 'cus we can't breathe." *Roar Magazine*, December 7. https://roarmag.org/essays/eric-garner-protests-we-cant-breathe/.

Rose, Geoffrey. 1985. "Sick individuals and sick populations." *International Journal of Epidemiology* 30 (3): 427–432.

Rose, Nikolas, and Peter Miller. 1992. "Political power beyond the state: Problematics of government." *The British Journal of Sociology* 43 (2): 173–205.

Rosin, Hanna. 2008. "American murder mystery." *The Atlantic*, July/August. www.theatlantic.com/magazine/archive/2008/07/americanmurdermystery/306872/.

Ross, Daniel. 2017. "Black country, white wilderness. Conservation, colonialism, and conflict in Tasmania." *The Journal for Undergraduate Ethnography* 7 (1): 1–24.

Rossi, Ugo. 2016. "The variegated economics and the potential politics of the smart city." *Territory, Politics, Governance* 4 (3): 337–353.

Rouse, Joseph. 2009. "Standpoint theories reconsidered." *Hypatia* 29 (4): 200–209.

Rouvroy, Antoinette. 2013. "The end(s) of critique: Data behaviourism versus due process." In *Privacy, Due Process and the Computational Turn. Philosopher of Law Meet Philosophers of Technology*, edited by Mireille Hildebrandt and Katja de Vries, 143–167. Abingdon: Routledge.

Roy, Ananya. 2016. "What is urban about critical urban theory?" *Urban Geography* 37 (6): 810–823.

Rubenhold, Hallie. 2019. *The Five: The Untold Lives of the Women Killed by Jack the Ripper*. New York: Doubleday.

Ruby, Andreas. 2001[1996]. "The time of the trajectory." In *Virilio Live*, edited by John Armitage, 58–65. London: Sage.

Ruda, Frank. 2011. *Hegel's Rabble: An Investigation into Hegel's Philosophy of Right*. London: Bloomsbury.

Ruddick, Sue. 2015. "Situating the Anthropocene: Planetary urbanization and the anthropological machine." *Urban Geography* 36(8): 1113–1130.

Rushing, Wanda. 2009. *Memphis and the Paradox of Place. Globalization and the American South*, Chapel Hill: University of North Carolina Press.

Saborio, Sebastian. 2013. "The Pacification of the favelas: Mega events, global competitiveness, and the neutralization of marginality." *Socialist Studies* 9 (2): 130–145.

Saborio, Sebastian. 2014/2015. "Le unità di polizia pacificatrice: Il controllo della violenza urbana a Rio de Janeiro." PhD diss., Università degli Studi di Urbino and Universidade Federal de Rio de Janeiro.

Saborio, Sebastian. 2019. "Violencia urbana: análisis crítico y limitaciones del concepto." *RevistArquis* 8 (1): 61–71.

Saldanha, Arun. 2006. "Reontologising race: The machinic geography of pheno-type." *Environment and Planning D* 24 (1): 9–24.

Salzani, Carlo. 2021. "The Limits of a paradigm: Agamben, the yellow star, and the Nazi analogy." *The Paris Institute for Critical Thinking*, September 2. https:// parisinstitute.org/the-limits-of-a-paradigm-agamben-the-yellow-star-and-the-nazi-analogy/.

Salzano, Edoardo. 1998. *Fondamenti di urbanistica. La storia e la norma*. Rome: Laterza.

Sampson, Robert J. 2011. *Great American City: Chicago and the Enduring Neighborhood Effect*, Chicago: Chicago University Press.

Samuel, Sigal. 2020. "Why you're unlikely to get the coronavirus from runners or cyclists." *Vox*, August 13. www.vox.com/future-perfect/2020/4/24/21233226/coronavirus-runners-cyclists-airborne-infectious-dose.

Sanchez, Magali R. 2006. "Insecurity and violence as a new power relation in Latin America." *The Annals of the American Academy of Political and Social Science* 606: 178–195.

Sandercock, Leonie. 2002. "Difference, fear, and habitus: A political economy of urban fear." *Urbanistica* 119: 8–19.

Sandercock, Leonie. 2003. *Cosmopolis II. Mongrel Cities in the 21st Century*. London: Continuum.

Sandhu, Ajay, and Peter Fussey. 2021. "The 'uberization of policing'? How police negotiate and operationalise predictive policing technology." *Policing and Society* 31 (1): 66–81.

Sarmento, João, and Denis Linehan. 2019. "The Colonial Hotel: Spacing violence at the Grande Hotel, Beira, Mozambique." *Environment and Planning D* 37 (2): 276–293.

Sartre, Jean-Paul. 1957[1933–34]. *The Transcendence of the Ego: An Existentialist Theory of Consciousness*. New York: Noonday Press.

Sassen, Saskia. 2014. *Expulsions: Brutality and Complexity in Global Economy*. Cambridge: Harvard University Press.

Satcher, David. 1995. "Violence as a public health issue." *Bulletin of the New York Academy of Medicine* 72 (1): 46–46.

Saunders, Jessica, Priscilla Hunt and John S. Hollywood. 2016. "Predictions put into practice: a quasi-experimental evaluation of Chicago's predictive policing pilot." *Journal of Experimental Criminology* 12 (3): 347–371.

Savage, Kevin, and Robert Muggah. 2012. "Urban violence and humanitarian action: Engaging the fragile city." *The Journal of Humanitarian Assistance*, January19. https://sites.tufts.edu/jha/archives/1524.

Saville, Gregory, and Gerard Cleveland. 2008. "Second-generation CPTED. The rise and fall of opportunity theory." *In 21st Century Security and CPTED. Designing for Critical Infrastructure Protection and Crime Prevention*, edited by Randall Atlas, 79–90. Boca Raton: CRC Press.

Sayad, Abdelmalek. 2004. *The Suffering of the Immigrant*. Cambridge: Polity.

Scandurra, Enzo, and Norman Krumholz. 1999. "Cities in revolt." *Plurimondi* 1: 7–18.

Scannell, Josh. 2015. "What can algorithms do?" *DIS Magazine*, February. http://dismagazine.com/discussion/72975/josh-scannell-what-can-an-algorithm-do/.

Scheper-Hughes, Nancy, and Philippe I. Bourgois. 2004a. "Introduction: Making sense of violence." In *Violence in War and Peace: An Anthology*, edited by Nancy Scheper-Hughes, and Philippe I. Bourgois, 1–27. Malden: Blackwell.

Scheper-Hughes, Nancy, and Philippe I. Bourgois, eds. 2004b. *Violence in War and Peace: An Anthology*. Malden: Blackwell.

Schianchi, Francesca. 2017. "'La sicurezza è di sinistra'. Minniti detta la linea al Pd." *La Stampa*, March 21. www.lastampa.it/politica/2017/03/21/news/la-sicurezza-e-di-sinistra-minniti-detta-la-linea-al-pd-1.34634602/.

Schivelbusch, Wolfgang. 2014[1977]. *The Railway Journey. The Industrialization of Time and Space in the Nineteenth Century, With a New Preface*. Oakland: University of California Press.

Schmidt, Bettina, and Ingo Schroeder, eds. 2001. *The Anthropology of Violence and Conflict*. London: Routledge.

Schmitt, Carl. 1986[1942]. *Terra e mare*. Milan: Giuffrè.

Schmitt, Carl. 2005[1922]. *Political Theology: Four Chapters on the Concept of Sovereignty*. Chicago: University of Chicago Press.

Schneider, Cathy L. 2014. *Police Power and Race Riots. Urban Unrest in Paris and New York*. Philadelphia: University of Pennsylvania Press.

Schwartz, David 1997. *Culture & Power. The Sociology of Pierre Bourdieu*. Chicago: University of Chicago Press.

Sclofsky, Sebastián. 2021. "Broken windows in the Rio de la Plata: Constructing the disorderly other." *Criminological Encounters* 4 (1): 31–49.

Scott, James C. (1990). *Domination and the Arts of Resistance: Hidden Transcripts*. New Haven: Yale University Press.

Seaver, Nick. 2017. "Algorithms as culture: Some tactics for the ethnography of algorithmic systems." *Big Data & Society* 4 (2).

Sennett, Richard. 1992[1970]. *The Uses of Disorder: Personal Identity & City Life*. New York: W. W. Norton & Company.

Sennett, Richard. 2018. *Building and Dwelling: Ethics for the City?* New York: Farrar, Straus and Giroux.

Serres, Michel. 1990. *The Natural Contract*. Ann Arbor: University of Michigan Press.

Serres, Michel. 1999. *Variations sur le corps*. Paris: Le Pommier.

Serres, Michel. 2020[2004]. *Branches: A Philosophy of Time, Event and Advent*. London: Bloomsbury Academic.

Shapiro, Aaron. 2017. "Reform predictive policing." *Nature* 541: 458–460.

Shapiro, Aaron. 2019. "Predictive Policing for Reform? Indeterminacy and Intervention in Big Data Policing." *Surveillance and Society* 17 (3–4): 456–472.

Shapiro, Bruce. 1997. "Zero Tolerance gospel." *Index on Censorship* 26 (4): 17–23.

Sharpe, Christina. 2016. *In the Wake: On Blackness and Being*. Durham: Duke University Press.

Shepherd, Laura J. 2008. *Gender, Violence and Security*. London: Zed.

Shepherd, Laura J. 2020. "The paradox of prevention in the Women, Peace and Security Agenda." *European Journal of International Security* 5 (3): 316–331.

Shields, Christopher. 2016. *Aristotle: De Anima*. Oxford: Oxford University Press.

Shildrick, Margrit (ed.. 1997. *Leaky Bodies and Boundaries: Feminism, Postmodernism and (Bio)ethics*. London: Routledge.

Shildrick, Margrit. 2015. "Living on; not getting better." *Feminist Review* 111 (1): 10–24.

Shishadeh, Edward S., and Nicole Flynn. 1996. "Segregation and crime: The effect of black social isolation on the rates of black urban violence." *Social Forces* 74 (4): 1325–1352.

Silva, Luiz A.M. 2004. "Sociabilidade violenta: por uma interpretação da criminalidade contemporânea no Brasil urbano." *Sociedade e Estado* 19 (1): 53–84.

Silva, Luiz A.M. 2008. *Vida sob cerco: Violência e rotina nas favelas do Rio de Janeiro*. Rio de Janeiro: Nova Fronteira.

Silva, Luiz A. M. 2010. "Violência urbana, segurança pública e favelas—O caso do Rio de Janeiro atual." *Caderno CRH* 23 (59): 283–300.

Silva, Luiz A. M. 2011. "Polícia e violência urbana em uma cidade brasileira." *Etnográfica* 15 (1): 67–82.

Silva, Moises L. 2014. "The violence of structural violence: Ethical commitments and an exceptional day in a Brazilian favela." *Built Environment* 40 (3): 314–325.

Simmel, Georg. 2002[1903]. "The metropolis and mental life." In *The Blackwell City Reader*, edited by Gary Bridge and Sophie Watson, 103–110. Malden: Wiley-Blackwell.

Simmons, Kristen. 2017. "Settler atmospherics." *Cultural Anthopology*, November 20. https://culanth.org/fieldsights/settler-atmospherics.

Simon, Jonathan. 2007. *Governing through Crime: How the War on Crime Transformed American Democracy and Created a Culture of Fear*. New York: Oxford University Press.

Simondon, Gilbert. 1992[1964]. "The genesis of the individual." In ZONE 6: *Incorporations*, edited by Jonathan Crary, and Sanford Kwinter, 297–319. New York: Zone.

Simone, AbdouMaliq. 2004. "People as infrastructure: Intersecting fragments in Johannesburg." *Public Culture* 16(3): 406–428.

Simone, AbdouMaliq. 2016. "City of potentialities: An introduction." *Theory, Culture and Society* 33 (7–8): 5–29.

Simone, AbdouMaliq, and Vanesa C. Broto. 2022. "Radical unknowability: an essay on solidarities and multiform urban life." *City*, online first. Doi: 10.1080/136048 13.2022.2124693.

Sites, William. 2012. "'We travel the spaceways': Urban utopianism and the imagined spaces of Black experimental music." *Urban Geography* 33 (4): 566–592.

Sitte, Camillo. 1986[1889]. "City planning according to artistic principles." In *The Birth of Modern City Planning. With the Translation of the 1989 Austrian Edition of*

His City Planning According to Artistic Principles, edited by George R. Collins, and Christiane C. Collins, 129–332. Mineola: Dover.

Sloterdijk, Peter. 2006. "The nomotop. On the emergence of law in the island of humanity." *Law & Literature* 18 (1): 1–14.

Sloterdijk, Peter. 2007[1998]. *Spheres. Volume I: Bubbles. Microspherology*. Los Angeles: Semiotext(e).

Sloterdijk, Peter. 2008[2007]. "Foam city: About urban spatial multitudes." *Urban Future Lab*, September 19. www.urbanfuturelab.org/foam-city-about-urban-spatial-multitudes/.

Sloterdijk, Peter. 2013[2005]. *The World Interior of Capitalism. For a Philosophical Theory of Globalization*. Malden: Polity.

Sloterdijk, Peter. 2013[2009]. *You Must Change Your Life*. Cambridge: Polity Press.

Sloterdijk, Sloterdijk. 2014[1999]. *Spheres. Volume II: Globes. Macrospherology*. Los Angeles: Semiotext(e).

Sloterdijk, Peter. 2016[2004]. *Spheres. Volume III: Foams. Plural Spherology*. Los Angeles: Semiotext(e).

Slutkin, Gary. 2011. "Gary Slutkin: rioting is a disease spread from person to person— the key is to stop the infection." *The Guardian*, August 14. www.theguardian.com/uk/2011/aug/14/rioting-disease-spread-from-person-to-person.

Slutkin, Gary. 2013. "Violence is a contagious disease." In *Contagion of Violence. Workshop Summary*, edited by IOM (Institute of Medicine) and NRC (National Research Council), 94–111. Washington: The National Academies Press.

Slutkin, Gary. 2020. "Why we need to treat violence like a contagious epidemic." *The Guardian*, January 13. https://www.theguardian.com/us-news/commentisfree/2020/jan/13/changing-violence-requires-the-same-shift-in-understanding-given-to-aids.

Smart, Ariane. 2001. "Déviance et barbarie. Nouvelles perceptions de la violence populaire à Paris au XIX e siècle." In *(Ab)normalities*, edited by Catherine Dousteyssier-Khoze, and Paul Scott, 65–76. Durham: Durham Modern Languages Series.

Smith, Jackson L., Vanessa, and Greg Miller. 2021. "Policing Gentrification. The Financial Geography of Law Enforcement Practices in Philadelphia." *ACME: An International Journal for Critical Geographies* 20 (6): 637–665.

Smith, Jeffery. 2010. "Memphis police leverage analytics to fight crime." *CivSource*, July 21. https://civsourceonline.com/2010/07/21/memphis-police-leverage-analytics-to-fight-crime/.

Smith, Neil. 1996. *The New Urban Frontier: Gentrification and the Revanchist City*. London: Routledge.

Sohn-Rethel, Alfred. 1978. *Intellectual and Manual Labour: A Critique of Epistemology*. London: Macmillan.

Solove, Daniel J. 2007. "'I've got nothing to hide' and other misunderstandings of privacy." *San Diego Law Review* 44 (4): 745–773.

Sorensen, Severin, John G. Hayes, and Randall Atlas. 2008. "Understanding CPTED and situational crime prevention." In *21st Century Security and CPTED. Designing for Critical Infrastructure Protection and Crime Prevention*, edited by Randall Atlas, 53–78. Boca Raton: CRC Press.

Spade, Dean. 2015. *Normal Life. Administrative Violence, Critical Trans Politics, and the Limits of Law*. Durham: Duke University Press.

Spencer, Douglas. 2011. "Architectural Deleuzism: Neoliberal Space, Control and the 'Univer-city'." *Radical Philosophy* 168 (9): 9–21.

Spinoza, Baruch. 2002[1670]. "Theological-political treatise." In *Spinoza. Complete Works*, edited by Michael L. Morgan, 383–583. Indianapolis: Hackett.

Spinoza. 2002[1674]. "Letter 50 to Jarig Jelles." In *Spinoza. Complete Works*, edited by Michael L. Morgan, 891–892. Indianapolis: Hackett.

Spinoza, Baruch. 2002a[1677]. "Ethics." In *Spinoza. Complete Works*, edited by Michael L. Morgan, 213–382. Indianapolis: Hackett.

Spinoza, Baruch. 2002b[1677]. "Political treatise." In *Spinoza. Complete Works*, edited by Michael L. Morgan, 676–754. Indianapolis: Hackett.

Spivak, Gayatri C. 1988. "Can the subaltern speak?" In *Marxism and the Interpretation of Culture*, edited by Cary Nelson, and Lawrence Grossberg, 271–313. Urbana-Champaign: University of Illinois Press.

Springer, Simon. 2009a. "Culture of violence or violent Orientalism? Neoliberalisation and imagining the 'savage other' in post-transitional Cambodia." *Transactions of the Institute of British Geographers* 34 (3): 305–319.

Springer, Simon. 2009b. "Neoliberalizing Violence: (Post)Marxian Political Economy, Poststructuralism and the Production of Space in 'Postconflict' Cambodia." PhD diss., University of British Columbia.

Springer, Simon. 2011. "Violence sits in places? Cultural practice, neoliberal rationalism, and virulent imaginative geographies." *Political Geography* 30 (2): 90–98.

Springer, Simon, and Philippe Le Billon. 2016. "Violence and space. An introduction to the geographies of violence." *Political Geography* 52: 1–3.

Srnicek, Nick. 2017. *Platform Capitalism*. Cambridge: Polity.

Stavrides, Stavros. 2016. *Common Space: The City as Commons*. London: Zed Books.

Steger, Manfred, and Paul James. 2013. "Levels of subjective globalization: Ideologies, imaginaries, ontologies." *Perspectives on Global Development and Technology* 12 (1–2): 17–40.

Stein, Michael I. 2017. "'Holy cow': the powerful software behind the city's surveillance system." *The Lens*, December 20. https://thelensnola.org/2018/12/20/holy-cow-the-powerful-software-behind-the-citys-surveillance-system/.

Steinberg, Philip. 2001. *The Social Construction of the Ocean*. Cambridge: Cambridge University Press.

Stewart, Kathleen. 2007. *Ordinary Affects*. Durham: Duke University Press.

Stewart, Kathleen. 2011, "Atmospheric attunements." *Environment and Planning D* 29 (3): 445–453.

Steyerl, Hito. 2011. "In free fall: A thought experiment on vertical perspective." *e-flux journal* 24 [online].

Stiegler, Bernard. 2016[2015]. *Automatic Society, Vol. 1: The Future of Work*. Cambridge: Polity.

Stiegler, Bernard. 2019. *The Age of Disruption: Technology and Madness in Computational Capitalism*. Cambridge: Polity.

Stiegler, Barbara. 2019. *Il faut s' adapter. Sur un nouvel impératif politique*. Paris: Gallimard.

Stigler, George J. 1970. "The Optimum Enforcement of Laws." *Journal of Political Economy* 78 (3): 526–536.

Stoneman, Ethan. 2011. "Appropriate indecorum rhetoric and aesthetics in the political theory of Jacques Ranciere." *Philosophy & Rhetoric* 44 (2): 129–149.

Stramignoni, Igor. 2004. "Francesco's devilish Venus: Notations on the matter of legal space." *California Western Law Review* 41 (1): 147–240.

Strauss, Claudia. 2006. "The imaginary." *Anthropological Theory* 6 (3): 322–344.

Stroud, Matt. 2014. "The minority report: Chicago's new police computer predicts crimes, but is it racist?" *The Verge*, February 19. www.theverge.com/2014/2/19/5419854/the-minority-report-this-computer-predicts-crime-but-is-it-racist.

Strüver, Anke, and Sybille Bauriedl, eds. 2022. *Platformization of Urban Life. Towards a Technocapitalist Transformation of European Cities*. Bielefeld: Transcript Verlag

Sutherland, Edwin, and Donald R. Cressey. 1978. *Criminology*. Philadelphia: Lippincott.

Sutzl, Wolfgang, and Geoff Cox, eds. 2009. *Creating Insecurity: Art and Culture in the Age of Security*. New Yordk: Autonomedia.

Tarde, Gabriel. 2012[1893]. *Monadology and Sociology*. Melbourne: re.press.

Taussig, Michael. 1987. *Shamanism, Colonialism, and the Wild Man: A Study in Terror and Healing*. Chicago: University of Chicago Press.

Taussig, Michael. 2020. *The Mastery of Non-mastery in the Age of Meltdown*. Chicago: University of Chicago Press.

Taylor, Charles. 2003. *Modern Social Imaginaries*. Durham: Duke University Press.

Tedeschi, Miriam. 2020. *Crime, Bodies and Space. Towards an Ethical Approach to Urban Policies in the Information Age*. London: Routledge.

ten Bos, René. 2009. "Towards an Amphibious Anthropology: Water and Peter Sloterdijk." *Environment and Planning D* 27 (1): 73–86

Thacker, Eugene. 2017. "Nekros; or, the poetics of biopolitics." In *Zombie Theory: A Reader*, edited by Sarah J. Lauro, 361–380. Minneapolis: University of Minnesota Press.

Thiranagama, Sharika, Tobias Kelly, and Carlos Forment. 2018. "Introduction: Whose civility?" *Anthropological Theory* 18 (2–3): 153–174.

Thompson, John. B. 1982. "Ideology and the social imaginary: An appraisal of Castoriadis and Lefort." *Theory and Society* 11 (5): 659–681.

Thoreau, Henry D. 1962[1854], *The Variorum Walden*. New York: Twayne Publishers.

Thörn, Catharina. 2011. "Soft policies of exclusion: Entrepreneurial strategies of ambience and control of public space in Gothenburg, Sweden." *Urban Geography* 32(7): 989–1008.

Thrift, Nigel. 2003. "An urban impasse?" *Theory, Culture & Society* 10 (2): 229–238.

Thrift, Nigel. 2008. *Non-Representational Theory. Space / Politics / Affect.* Abingdon: Routledge.

Tiqqun. 2010[2009]. *Introduction to Civil War.* Los Angeles: Semiotext(e).

Tola, Miriam. 2019. "La città dei corpi indecorosi: femminismi, spazi urbani e politiche securitarie in Italia." In *La libertà è una passeggiata. Donne e spazi urbani tra violenza strutturale e autodeterminazione*, edited by Chiara Belingardi, Federica Castelli, and Serena Olcuire, 109–117.

Tomba, Massimiliano. 2011. *Strati di tempo. Karl Marx materialista storico.* Milan: Jaka Books.

Tonry, Michael. 2011. "Less imprisonment is no doubt a good thing. More policing is not." *Criminology and Public Policy* 10 (1): 137–152.

Toscano, Alberto. 2004. "Factory, territory, metropolis, Empire." *Angelaki* 9 (2): 197–216.

Toscano, Alberto. 2008a. "The culture of abstraction." *Theory, Culture and Society* 25 (4): 57–75.

Toscano, Alberto, 2008b. "The open secret of real abstraction." *Rethinking Marxism* 20 (2): 273–287.

Toscano, Alberto. 2011. "Against speculation, or, a critique of the critique of critique: A remark on Quentin Meillassoux's After Finitude (After Colletti)." In *The Speculative Turn: Continental Materialism and Realism*, edited by in Levi R. Bryant, Nick Srnicek, and Graham Harman, 84–91. Melbourne: re.press.

Toscano, Alberto. 2019. "Logistics as will and representation." In *Aesthetics and Politics of Logistics. Marghera*, edited by Hamed Khosravi, Taneja K. Bacchin, and Filippo LaFleur, 31–38. Milan: Humboldt Books.

Townsend, Anthony. 2015. "Cities of data: Examining the new urban science." *Public Culture* 27 (2): 201–212.

Townsend, Marc. 2021. "Plymouth gunman ranted online that 'women are arrogant' days before rampage." *The Guardian*, August 14. www.theguardian.com/world/2021/aug/14/plymouth-gunman-ranted-online-that-women-are-arrogant-days-before-rampage.

Travers, Max. 2019. "The idea of a Southern Criminology." *International Journal of Comparative and Applied Criminal Justice* 34 (1): 1–12.

Tremblay, Jean-Thomas, Hsuan L. Hsu, and Aleesa Cohene. 2023. "Skunk: Olfactory violence and morbid speculation," in *Smell*, edited by Andreas Philippopoulos-Mihalopoulos, Danilo Mandic, Caterina Nirta, and Andrea Pavoni, in press. London: University of Westminster Press.

Trogisch, Lisa. 2022. Navigating fearscapes: women's coping strategies with(in) the conservation-conflict nexus in the Eastern Democratic Republic of the Congo." *Gender, Place and Culture*, online first. Doi: 10.1080/0966369X.2022.2035695.

Trogisch, Lisa, and Robert Fletcher. 202. "Fortress tourism: Exploring dynamics of tourism, security and peace around the Virunga transboundary conservation area." *Journal of Sustainable Tourism* 30 (2–3): 352–371.

Tsing, Anna L. 2005. *Friction: An Ethnography of Global Connection.* Princeton: Princeton University Press.

Tsing, Anna L. 2012. "On nonscalability: The living world is not amenable to precision-nested scales." *Common Knowledge* 18: 505–524.

Tsing, Anna L., Jennifer Deger, Alder K. Saxena, and Feifei Zhou, eds. 2020. *Feral Atlas. The More-than-Human Anthropocene.* Princeton: Princeton University Press.

Tucker, Patrick. 2015. "After Ferguson unrest, St. Louis Police bought stink weapons to launch at protesters." *Defense One,* August 11. www.defenseone.com/technology/2015/08/after-ferguson-unrest-st-louis-police-bought-stink-weapons-launch-protesters/119044/.

Tulumello, Simone. 2017a. *Fear, Space and Urban Planning. A Critical Perspective from Southern Europe.* Switzerland: Springer.

Tulumello, Simone. 2017b. "Toward a Critical Understanding of Urban Security within the Institutional Practice of Urban Planning: The Case of the Lisbon Metropolitan Area." *Journal of Planning Education and Research* 37 (4): 397–410.

Tulumello, Simone. 2018a. "Neoliberalisation of security, austerity and the 'end of public policy': Governing crime in Memphis (TN, USA) through predictive policing, community, grants and police 'mission creep'." *ACME: An International Journal for Critical Geographies* 17 (1): 171–200.

Tulumello, Simone. 2018b. "The multi-scalar nature of urban security and public safety: Crime prevention from local policy to policing in Lisbon (Portugal) and Memphis (the United States)." *Urban Affairs Review* 54 (6): 1134–1169.

Tulumello, Simone. 2019. "Generalization, epistemology and concrete: What can social sciences learn from the common sense of engineers." *Fennia. International Journal of Geography* 197 (1), 121–131.

Tulumello, Simone. 2021a. "Agonistic security: Transcending (de/re)constructive divides in critical security studies." *Security Dialogue* 52 (4): 325–342.

Tulumello, Simone. 2021b. "A proposito di Green Pass." *il Mulino. Rivista di Cultura e Politica,* October 26. www.rivistailmulino.it/a/a-proposito-di-green-pass-br-efficienza-proporzionalit-politica.

Tulumello, Simone. 2021c. "Intervention—The 'Outdoor' Paradox: Public Policies and Scientific Evidence during the Covid-19 Pandemic in Portugal." *Antipode Online,* February 22. https://antipodeonline.org/2021/02/22/the-outdoor-paradox/.

Tulumello, Simone, and Fabio Bertoni. 2019. "'Nessun decoro sui nostri corpi': sicurezza, produzione di margini e movimenti indecoros*." *Tracce Urbane* 5: 90–109.

Tulumello, Simone, and Roberto Falanga. 2015. "An exploratory study of uses of 'urban security' and 'urban safety' in international urban studies literature." *Dedalus—Revista Portuguesa de Literatura Comparada* 19: 55–85.

Tulumello, Simone, and Roberto Falanga. 2022. "Homeland as a multi-scalar community: (Dis)continuities in the US security/safety discourse and practice." *Environment and Planning C* 40 (1): 143–164.

Tulumello, Simone and Fabio Iapaolo. 2022. "Policing the future, disrupting urban policy today. Predictive policing, smart city, and urban policy in Memphis (TN)." *Urban Geography* 43 (3) 448–469.

Tyner, James A., and Joshua Inwood. 2014. "Violence as fetish: Geography, Marxism, and dialectics." *Progress in Human Geography* 38 (6): 771–784.

Tzaninis, Yannis, Tait Mandler, Maria Kaika, and Roger Keil. 2021. "Moving urban political ecology beyond the 'urbanization of nature'." *Progress in Human Geography* 45 (2): 229–252.

Urbinati, Nadia. 1998. "The Souths of Antonio Gramsci and the concept of hegemony." In *Italy's 'Southern Question': Orientalism in One Country*, edited by Jane Schneider, 135–156. Oxford: Berg.

Valayden, Diren. 2016. "Racial feralization: Targeting race in the 'age of planetary urbanization.'" *Theory, Culture & Society* 33 (7–8): 159–182.

Valencia, Sayak. 2018. *Gore Capitalism*. South Pasadena: Semiotext(e).

Valverde, Mariana. 2008. "Police, sovereignty, and law: Foucaultian reflections." In *Police and the Liberal State*, edited by Markus D. Dubber, and Mariana Valverde, 15–32. Stanford: Stanford University Press.

Valverde, Mariana. 2011. "Questions of security: A framework for research." *Theoretical Criminology* 15 (1): 3–22.

van den Berg, Marguerite, and Danielle Chevalier. 2020. "'A good city is like a good party'. But not everyone is invited." *Discover Society*, April 1. https://archive.discoversociety.org/2020/04/01/a-good-city-is-like-a-good-party-but-not-everyone-is-invited/.

van der Walt, Johan. 2007. "Johannesburg: A tale of two cases." In *Law and the City*, edited by Andreas Philippopoulos-Mihalopoulos, 221–236. London: Routledge.

van Dijk, Jan. 2009. *Approximating the Truth about Crime. Comparing Crime Data Based on General Population Surveys with Police Figures of Recorded Crimes*. Guyancourt: GERN-CNRS.

Vanolo, Alberto. 2017. *City Branding. The Ghostly Politics of Representation in Globalising Cities*. New York: Routledge.

Vázquez-Arroyo, Antonio I. 2008. "Universal history disavowed: on critical theory and postcolonialism." *Postcolonial Studies* 11 (4): 451–473.

Veitch, Scott. 2007. *Law and Irresponsibility. On the Legitimation of Human Suffering*. Abingdon: Routledge-Cavendish.

Venturini, Tommaso, Mathieu Jacomy, Axel Meunier, and Bruno Latour. 2017. "An unexpected journey: a few lessons from Sciences Po Médialab's experience." *Big Data and Society* 4 (2) 205395171772094.

Videtta, Cristina. 2019 "Il decoro urbano tra le ragioni di protezione del patrimonio storico-artistico e il perseguimento degli obiettivi di sicurezza urbana." *Rivista Giuridica di Urbanistica* 2019 (1): 39–66.

Vidler, Anthony. 1992. *The Architectural Uncanny. Essays in the Modern Unhomely.* Cambridge: MIT Press.

Vilalta, Carlos J., Robert Muggah, and Gustavo Fondevila. 2020. "Homicide as a function of city block layout: Mexico City as case study." *Global Crime* 21 (2): 111–129.

Villarreal, Ana. 2021. Reconceptualizing urban violence from the Global South. *City & Community* 20 (1): 48–58.

Villarreal, Luis P. 2004. "Are viruses alive?" *Scientific American* 291 (6): 100–105.

Vinciguerra, Lorenzo. 2012 . "Mark, image, sign: A semiotic approach to Spinoza." *European Journal of Philosophy* 20 (1): 130-144.

Virgolette. 2020. "Sala ha detto che la campagna 'Milano non si ferma' è stata un errore." *Il Post*, March 23. www.ilpost.it/2020/03/23/coronavirus-milano-non-si-ferma-sala/.

Virilio, Paul. 1989[1984]. *War and Cinema: The Logistics of Perception.* London: Verso.

Virno, Paolo. 2001[1992]. "The two masks of materialism." *Pli* 12: 167–173.

Virno, Paolo. 2004. *A Grammar of the Multitude. For an Analysis of Contemporary Forms of Life.* Los Angeles: Semiotext(e).

Vlahos, James. 2012. "The department of pre-crime." *Scientific American* 306 (1): 62–67.

von Uexküll, Jakob J. 2010[1934]. *A Foray into the Worlds of Animals and Humans: With a Theory of Meaning.* Minneapolis: University of Minnesota Press.

Wacquant, Loïc. 1999. *Les prisons de la misère.* Paris: Raisons d'Agir.

Wacquant, Loïc. 2002. "Scrutinizing the street: Poverty, morality, and the pitfalls of urban ethnography. Review symposium." *American Journal of Sociology* 107 (6): 1468–1532.

Wacquant, Löic. 2004. "Comment to Paul Farmer's An Anthropology of Structural Violence." *Current Anthropology* 45 (3): 322.

Wacquant, Loïc. 2008. "Ordering Insecurity. Social Polarization and the Punitive Upsurge." *Radical Philosophy Review* 11 (1): 1–19.

Wacquant, Loïc. 2022. *The Invention of the "Underclass": A Study in the Politics of Knowledge.* Cambridge: Polity.

Wæver, Ole. 2011. "Politics, security, theory." *Security Dialogue* 42 (4–5): 465–480.

Waldron, Jeremy J. 2006. "Safety and security." *Nebraska Law Review* 82 (2): 457–507.

Wall, Illan R. 2021. *Law and Disorder: Sovereignty, Protest, Atmosphere.* London: Routledge.

Wallas, Graham. 1914. *The Great Society: A Psychological Analysis.* New York: The Macmillan Company.

Watkins, Josh. 2015. "Spatial imaginaries research in geography: Synergies, tensions, and new directions." *Geography Compass* 9 (9): 508–522.

Watson, Sophie, and Katherine Gibson, eds. 1995. *Postmodern Cities and Spaces.* Oxford: Basil Blackwell.

Watts, Michael J. 1983. *Silent Violence: Food, Famine, and Peasantry in Northern Nigeria*. Berkeley: University of California Press.

Weber, Max. 1958[1905]. *The Protestant Ethic and the Spirit of Capitalism*. New York: Scribner.

Weheliye, Alexander G. 2014. *Habeas Viscus: Racializing Assemblages, Biopolitics, and Black Feminist Theories of the Human*. Durham: Duke University Press.

Weil, Simone. 2002[1949]. *The Need for Roots: Prelude to a Declaration of Duties toward Mankind*. London: Routledge.

Weizman, Eyal. 2007. *Hollow Land: Israel's Architecture of Occupation*. New York: Verso.

Weizman, Eyal. 2010. "Political plastic (Interview)." *Collapse, VI: Geo/Philosophy*, edited by Robin Mackay, 267–313. Falmouth: Urbanomic.

Werneck, Alexandre, Cesar P. Teixeira, and Vittorio G. Talone. 2020. "An outline of a pragmatic sociology of violence." *Sociologias* 54: 286–326.

White, James M. 2016. "Anticipatory logics of the smart city's global imaginary." *Urban Geography* 37 (4): 572–589.

Whitehead, Alfred N. 1978[1929]. *Process and Reality: An Essay in Cosmology*. New York: The Free Press.

Whitehead, Neil L. 2007a. "On the poetics of violence." In *Violence*, edited by Neil L. Whitehead, 55–77. Santa Fe: School of American Research Press.

Whitehead, Neil L. 2007b. "Violence and cultural order." *Dedalus* 136 (1): 40–50.

Wiener, Norbert. 1948. *Cybernetics: Or Control and Communication in the Animal and the Machine*. Cambridge: MIT Press.

Wiener, Norbert. 1950. *The Human Use of Human Beings: Cybernetics and Society*. Boston: Houghton Mifflin.

Winett, Liana B. 1998. "Constructing violence as a public health problem." *Public Health Reports* 113 (6): 498–507.

Wilkinson, Claire. 2007. "The Copenhagen School on tour in Kyrgyzstan: Is securitization theory useable outside Europe?" *Security Dialogue* 38 (1): 5–25.

Williams, Michael C. 2003. "Word, images, enemies: Securitization and international politics." *International Studies Quarterly* 47 (4): 511–531.

Williams, Phil. 2022. "Urban violence in the Global South: drug traffickers, gangs, and organized crime." In *Urban Violence, Resilience and Security. Governance Responses in the Global South*, edited by Michael R. Glass, Taylor B. Seybolt, and Phil Williams, 21–38. Cheltenham: Edward Elgar.

Williams, Raymond. 2007. "Keywords." In *On Violence: A Reader*, edited by Bruce B. Lawrence, and Aisha Karim, 181–182. Durham: Duke University Press.

Wilson, Japhy, and Manuel Bayón. 2016. "Black hole capitalism. Utopian dimensions of planetary urbanization." *City* 20 (3): 350–367.

Wilson, Peter J. 2007. "Agriculture or architecture? The beginnings of domestication." In *Where the Wild Things Are Now: Domestication Reconsidered*, edited by Rebecca Cassidy, and Molly Mullin, 101–122. Oxford: Berg.

Winston, Ali. 2018a. "New Orleans ends its Palantir predictive policing program." *The Verge*, March 15. www.theverge.com/2018/3/15/17126174/new-orleans-palantir-predictive-policing-program-end.

Winston, Ali. 2018b. "Palantir has secretly been using New Orleans to test its predictive policing technology." *The Verge*, February 27. www.theverge.com/2018/2/27/17054740/palantir-predictive-policing-tool-new-orleans-nopd.

Wirth, Louis. 1938. "Urbanism as a way of life." *American Journal of Sociology* 44 (1): 1–24.

Wu, Janguo, and Orie L. Loucks.1995. "From balance of nature to hierarchical patch dynamics: A paradigm shift in ecology." *The Quarterly Review of Biology* 70 (4): 439–466.

Wu Ming I. 2021. *La Q di Qomplotto. QAnon e dintorni. Come le fantasie di complotto difendono il sistema.* Rome: Alegre.

Yiftachel, Oren. 2009. "Theoretical notes on 'gray cities': The coming of urban apartheid?" *Planning Theory* 8 (1): 88–100.

Young, Alyson. 2019. "Arrested mobilities: Affective encounters and crime scenes in the city." *Law, Culture and the Humanities*, online first. Doi: 10.1177/1743872119889824.

Young, Iris M. 1990. *Justice and the Politics of Difference.* Princeton: Princeton University Press.

Yusoff, Kathryn. 2012. "Aesthetics of loss: biodiversity, banal violence and biotic subjects." *Transactions of the Institute of British Geographers* 37 (4): 578–592

Zaluar, Alba. 2004. "Urban violence and drug warfare in Brazil." In *Armed Actors. Organised Violence and State Failure in Latin America*, edited by Kees Koonings and Dirk Kruijt, 139–154. London: Zed Books.

Zedner, Lucia. 2009. *Security.* New York: Routledge.

Zeiderman, Austin, Sobia A. Kaker, Jonathan D. Silver, and Astrid Wood. 2015. "Uncertainty and urban life." *Public Culture* 27 (2): 281–304.

Zimbardo, Philip G. 1970. "A social-psychological analysis of vandalism: Making sense of senseless violence." ONR technical report: Z-05. December. Stanford University, Department of Psychology. https://apps.dtic.mil/sti/citations/AD0719405.

Zimbardo, Philip G. 2011. *The Lucifer Effect: Understanding How Good People Turn Evil.* New York: Random House.

Zimbardo, Philip G., and Chris Haney. 2020. "Continuing to acknowledge the power of dehumanizing environments: Comment on Haslam et al. (2019) and Le Texier (2019)." *American Psychologist* 75 (3): 400–402.

Žižek, Slavoj. 1994. "Introduction. The spectre of ideology." In *Mapping Ideology*, edited by Slavoj Žižek, 1–33. London: Verso.

Žižek, Slavoj. 1999. *The Ticklish Subject: The Absent Centre of Political Ontology.* London: Verso.

Žižek, Slavoj. 2008. *Violence*. New York: Picador.

Zourabichvili, Francois. 2012[1994]. "Deleuze: A philosophy of the event (1994/2004)." In *Deleuze: A Philosophy of the Event. Together with the Vocabulary of Deleuze*, edited by Gregg Lambert, and Daniel W. Smith, 33–136. Edinburgh: Edinburgh University Press.

Zourabichvili, Francois. 2012[2003]. "The vocabulary of Deleuze (2003)." In *Deleuze: A Philosophy of the Event. Together with the Vocabulary of Deleuze*, edited by Gregg Lambert, and Daniel W. Smith, 137–221. Edinburgh: Edinburgh University Press.

Index of Names and Places

~

About the Authors

Andrea Pavoni is assistant research professor at DINAMIA'CET-Iscte, Instituto Universitário de Lisboa, Portugal. His research explores the relation between materiality, normativity, and aesthetics in the urban. He is associate editor at Lo Squaderno, Explorations in Space and Society, and the author of *Controlling Urban Events: Law, Ethics and the Material* (2018).

Simone Tulumello is assistant research professor in geography at Instituto de Ciências Sociais, Universidade de Lisboa. With research interests at the border between human geography, critical urban studies and political economy, Simone is interested in the multi-scalar dimensions of urbanisation. He is deputy editor-in-chief of Análise Social and author of *Fear, Space and Urban Planning: A Critical Perspective from Southern Europe* (2017).

www.ingramcontent.com/pod-product-compliance
Lightning Source LLC
Chambersburg PA
CBHW032308280326
41932CB00009B/738